THE NEW INTERNATIONAL COMMENTARY
ON THE NEW TESTAMENT

GORDON D. FEE
General Editor

The Book of the
ACTS

Revised Edition

by

F. F. BRUCE

Emeritus Professor
University of Manchester

WILLIAM B. EERDMANS PUBLISHING COMPANY
GRAND RAPIDS, MICHIGAN

© 1988 Wm. B. Eerdmans Publishing Co.

2140 Oak Industrial Drive N.E., Grand Rapids, Michigan 49505 /

P.O. Box 163, Cambridge CB3 9PU U.K.

Printed in the United States of America

12 11 10 09   21 20 19 18

Library of Congress Cataloging-in-Publication Data

Bruce, F. F. (Frederick Fyvie), 1910-1990

The book of the Acts / by F. F. Bruce. — Rev. ed.

p.   cm.

(The New International Commentary on the New Testament)

Rev. ed. of: Commentary on the book of the Acts.

Bibliography: p.

Includes indexes.

ISBN 978-0-8028-2505-6

1. Bible. N.T. Acts — Commentaries.   I. Title.   II. Series.

BS2625.3.B74   1988

226'.6077 — dc19   88-6887

CIP

www.eerdmans.com

TO
ROBINA HOWLEY
In Memory of Cecil

CONTENTS

CONTENTS

CONTENTS

PREFACE

The first edition of this work contained a foreword from the General Editor of the series, the late Ned Bernard Stonehouse, in which he introduced the commentator to the readers, doing so in characteristically generous terms. After Dr. Stonehouse's untimely death in 1962, the commentator himself was invited to become General Editor, a responsibility which he still holds. For this revised edition it seems appropriate to replace the original Editor's Foreword and Author's Preface with a single preface.

When Dr. Stonehouse invited me to contribute the volume on Acts to this series, I was engaged on a commentary on the Greek text of that book, which was published in 1951. (That commentary has now received a comprehensive revision simultaneously with the present volume.) I accepted Dr. Stonehouse's invitation the more readily because the preparation of the work on the Greek text had suggested various trains of thought which could not be brought within its scope, and it seemed to me that an exposition of the English text would give an opportunity to develop them.

During the past thirty years and more some notable contributions have been made to the study of Luke's history as a whole, and of Acts in particular. In 1951 Martin Dibelius's collected *Studies in the Acts of the Apostles* appeared in German (the English translation followed five years later). A number of the papers reissued in that volume had been difficult of access when they were first published, owing to a breach in communication between Germany and the English-speaking countries. But it soon became clear that Dibelius's studies marked a new era in the interpretation of Acts; their influence is unmistakable in much of the work on Acts produced in the following years. Another influential writer was Hans Conzelmann, whose monograph *Die Mitte der Zeit* (published in 1954) was translated into English under the less precise title *The Theology of St. Luke*. Here it was argued that Luke was moved by the deferment of the once imminently expected parousia to replace the primitive Christian perspective with a new one in which the ministry of Jesus, crowned by his death and resurrection, was recognized no longer as the eschaton but as the middle age of history, preceded by the age of the law and the prophets (cf. Luke 16:16) and followed by the age of the church. Professor Conzelmann has also contrib-

uted the latest commentary on Acts (now available in English) to Lietzmann's Handbuch zum Neuen Testament.

Ernst Käsemann, in several papers, has maintained that Luke is the
first spokesman of "primitive catholicism" *(Frühkatholizismus),* with a perspective in which not the ministry of Jesus but the age of the church is the
center of time and the original and Pauline *theologia crucis* has been superseded by a *theologia gloriae.* Some criticisms of this assessment have been
made by C. K. Barrett in a number of articles which whet the reader's
appetite for the volume on Acts which he is preparing for the new International Critical Commentary series.

The noblest work on Acts produced thus far within the school which
draws its inspiration from Martin Dibelius is Ernst Haenchen's commentary,
first published in the Meyer series in 1966 and available since 1971 in a fine
English translation, *The Acts of the Apostles.* While his affinities are recognizably with Dibelius, Conzelmann, and Käsemann, Professor Haenchen
does not follow them uncritically; his concern is to expound Luke's composition—a composition marked by a creative freedom which makes the
historical narrative the vehicle of Luke's theology. This theology is not a
declension from true Paulinism; it is one of the variant forms of Gentile
Christian theology which grew up alongside and after the theology of Paul,
and in virtual independence of him.

But these writers have not monopolized recent literature on the subject: Luke-Acts remains, as W. C. van Unnik once put it, "a storm center in
contemporary scholarship." These words form the title of his introductory
essay in the symposium *Studies in Luke-Acts,* presented to Paul Schubert in
1966. The aptness of his words is demonstrated by the variety of perspectives which find expression in the eighteen other essays in this volume. From
outside the Schubert symposium this variety could be illustrated further by
the work of Johannes Munck, notably by his volume *Paul and the Salvation
of Mankind* (as it is entitled in its English translation). Munck waged a
courageous battle against prevalent trends and insisted that justice could be
done to the history and literature of the apostolic age only when the last
vestige of the influence of Ferdinand Christian Baur and his associates had
been removed. During those years, too (from 1950 to the present day), our
understanding of Acts has been enriched by a succession of positive and
valuable studies by Dom Jacques Dupont. More recently the record of Acts,
together with other areas of early Christianity, has been illuminated by the
learning and acumen of Martin Hengel.

A new and fresh approach to Acts is evidenced in a number of fine
commentaries on the book which have appeared in 1980 and the following
years—by I. Howard Marshall in English and by Jürgen Roloff, Gottfried
Schille, Gerhard Schneider, and Arnold Weiser in German. In this field

there is today an *embarras de richesse*—a contrast to the situation when the first edition of the present commentary was taking shape.

As in all the original volumes of the New International Commentary on the New Testament, the American Standard Version of 1901 served as the basis for the exposition in the first edition of this. It has now been replaced by an *ad hoc* translation of my own.

In the preface to the second edition of his *Römerbrief,* Karl Barth complains of the tendency of many biblical commentators to confine themselves to a form of textual interpretation which in his eyes was "no commentary at all, but merely the first step towards a commentary." As an example of a real commentary he cited Calvin on Romans: "how energetically Calvin, having first established what stands in the text, sets himself to rethink the whole material and to wrestle with it, till the walls which separate the sixteenth century from the first become transparent! Paul speaks, and the child of the sixteenth century hears."

No doubt, by Barth's criterion, my volume on the Greek text was but "the first step towards a commentary," devoted as it was to the linguistic, textual, and historical aspects of Acts. Be it so: those who do not take the first step will never take the second. It cannot be claimed, indeed, that even the present work has made the wall between the first and twentieth centuries transparent. In particular, I realize now as I did not in the 1950's that I have done much less than justice to Luke's distinctive theology. Instead of trying to remedy this deficiency at this time of day, I advise my readers to make it good by digesting I. Howard Marshall's *Luke: Historian and Theologian.* But I may be permitted still to indulge the hope, first expressed in 1954, that whatever I have heard in the course of this study, not only of the voice of Luke but of the word of God, may be caught by some of my readers in the late twentieth century.

F. F. BRUCE

PRINCIPAL ABBREVIATIONS

AASF	Annales Academiae Scientiarum Fennicae
AB	Anchor Bible
ad loc.	*ad locum* (at the place referred to)
AGG	*Abhandlungen der (königlichen) Gesellschaft der Wissenschaften zu Göttingen*
AJA	*American Journal of Archaeology*
AJP	*American Journal of Philology*
AJT	*American Journal of Theology*
AnBib	Analecta Biblica (Rome: Pontifical Biblical Institute)
ANRW	*Aufstieg und Niedergang der römischen Welt* (Berlin: de Gruyter)
Ant.	*Antiquities* (Josephus)
Ap.	*Against Apion* (Josephus)
AS	*Anatolian Studies*
ASNU	Acta Seminarii Neotestamentici Upsaliensis
ASTI	*Annual of the Swedish Theological Institute* (Leiden: Brill)
ASV	American Standard Version (1901)
ATANT	Abhandlungen zur Theologie des Alten und Neuen Testaments (Zürich: Zwingli Verlag)
BA	*Biblical Archaeologist*
BAGD	W. Bauer–W. F. Arndt–F. W. Gingrich–F. W. Danker, *Greek-English Lexicon of the New Testament and Early Christian Literature* (Chicago/Cambridge, 1957, ²1979)
BCH	*Bulletin de Correspondance Hellénique*
BDF	F. Blass–A. Debrunner–R. W. Funk, *Greek Grammar of the New Testament and Other Early Christian Literature* (Chicago, 1961)
Beginnings	*The Beginnings of Christianity*, ed. F. J. Foakes-Jackson and K. Lake (London: Macmillan, 1920-33)
BETL	Bibliotheca Ephemeridum Theologicarum Lovaniensium
BGBE	Beiträge zur Geschichte der biblischen Exegese
BGU	*Aegyptische Urkunden aus den Museen zu Berlin: Griechische Urkunden*, I-VIII (1895-1933)
Bib.	*Biblica*
BJ	*Jewish War* (Josephus)
BJRL	*Bulletin of the John Rylands (University) Library*, Manchester

BMI	*The Collection of Ancient Greek Inscriptions in the British Museum*
BNTC	Black's (Harper's) New Testament Commentaries
BRD	*The Bearing of Recent Discovery on the Trustworthiness of the New Testament* (W. M. Ramsay)
BZ	*Biblische Zeitschrift*
BZNW	Beihefte zur *Zeitschrift für die Alttestamentliche Wissenschaft*
CBCNEB	Cambridge Bible Commentary on the New English Bible
CBQ	*Catholic Biblical Quarterly*
CBSC	Cambridge Bible for Schools and Colleges
CD	Covenant of Damascus (= Zadokite Work)
CDA	*The Composition and Date of Acts* (C. C. Torrey)
CentB	Century Bible
CGT	Cambridge Greek Testament
Chron.	*Chronicon* (Eusebius)
CIG	*Corpus Inscriptionum Graecarum* (1828-77)
CIJ	*Corpus Inscriptionum Judaicarum*, ed. J.-B. Frey (1936)
CIL	*Corpus Inscriptionum Latinarum* (1863-1909)
ClarB	Clarendon Bible (Oxford)
Clem. Recog.	*Clementine Recognitions*
CNT	Commentaar op het Nieuwe Testament
CRINT	Compendia Rerum Iudaicarum ad Novum Testamentum
DCB	*Dictionary of Christian Biography*, ed. W. Smith
ÉB	Études Bibliques
EGT	*Expositor's Greek Testament*, ed. W. R. Nicoll
EKK	Evangelisch-katholischer Kommentar
ENT	Erläuterungen zum Neuen Testament
Ep(p).	*Epistle(s)*
EQ	*Evangelical Quarterly*
ERE	*Encyclopaedia of Religion and Ethics*, ed. J. Hastings
E.T.	English Translation
Exp.	*Expositor*, ed. W. R. Nicoll
ExT	*Expository Times*
FGNTK	Forschungen zur Geschichte des neutestamentlichen Kanons
FRLANT	Forschungen zur Religion und Literatur des Alten und Neuen Testaments
Geog.	*Geography*
GNC	Good News Commentary (Harper & Row)
GNS	Good News Studies (M. Glazier)
HDB	*Hastings' Dictionary of the Bible*, I-V
HE	*Ecclesiastical History* (Eusebius)
Hist.	*History*
Hist. Christ.	*Christian History* (Philip of Side)
HNT	Handbuch zum Neuen Testament, ed. H. Lietzmann
HSNT	Die Heilige Schrift des Neuen Testaments

HTR	*Harvard Theological Review*
HTS	Harvard Theological Studies
HUCA	*Hebrew Union College Annual*
HUL	Home University Library
IB	*Interpreter's Bible*
ibid.	*ibidem*, in the same place
IEJ	*Israel Exploration Journal*
IG	*Inscriptiones Graecae*, 1873-
IGRR	*Inscriptiones Graecae ad Res Romanas pertinentes*, ed. R. Cagnat, I-IV (1911-14)
ILS	*Inscriptiones Latinae Selectae*, ed. H. Dessau
Insch. Eph.	*Inschriften von Ephesos*, ed. H. Wankel, etc., I-VIII (Bonn: Habelt, 1979-84)
INT	*Introduction to the New Testament*
JAC	*Jahrbuch für Antikes und Christentum*
JAOS	*Journal of the American Oriental Society*
JBL	*Journal of Biblical Literature*
JEH	*Journal of Ecclesiastical History*
JHS	*Journal of Hellenic Studies*
JJS	*Journal of Jewish Studies*
JQR	*Jewish Quarterly Review*
JRS	*Journal of Roman Studies*
JSJ	*Journal for the Study of Judaism*
JSNT	*Journal for the Study of the New Testament*
JSOT Sup.	Supplement(s) to *Journal for the Study of the Old Testament*
JTC	*Journal for Theology and the Church*
JTS	*Journal of Theological Studies*
KEK	Kritisch-Exegetischer Kommentar (= Meyer Kommentar)
KJV	King James Version (1611)
KV	Korte Verklaring der heilige Schrift
LD	Lectio Divina
LXX	Septuagint (pre-Christian Greek version of OT)
MAMA	*Monumenta Asiae Minoris Antiqua*
MHT	J. H. Moulton–W. F. Howard–N. Turner, *Grammar of New Testament Greek*, I-IV (Edinburgh: T. & T. Clark, 1906-76)
MM	J. H. Moulton and G. Milligan, *The Vocabulary of the Greek Testament* (London: Hodder & Stoughton, 1930)
MNTC	Moffatt New Testament Commentary
MT	Masoretic Text (of Hebrew Bible)
NA[26]	E. and E. Nestle, K. Aland, etc., *Novum Testamentum Graece*, 26. neu bearbeitete Auflage (Stuttgart: Deutsche Bibelstiftung, 1979)
Nat. Hist.	*Natural History* (Pliny)
NCB	New Century Bible
NClarB	New Clarendon Bible

NEB	New English Bible
New Docs.	*New Documents illustrating Early Christianity*, ed. G. H. R. Horsley, I- (Macquarie University, 1981-)
NF	Neue Folge
NGG	*Nachrichten der (königlichen) Gesellschaft der Wissenschaften zu Göttingen*
NICNT	New International Commentary on the New Testament
NIGTC	New International Greek Testament Commentary
NIV	New International Version
NovT	*Novum Testamentum*
NovT Sup.	Supplement(s) to *Novum Testamentum*
n.s.	new series
NT	New Testament
NTD	Das Neue Testament Deutsch
NTL	New Testament Library
NTS	*New Testament Studies*
NTTS	New Testament Tools and Studies
ODCC	*Oxford Dictionary of the Christian Church*
OGIS	*Orientis Graeci Inscriptiones Selectae*, ed. W. Dittenberger
OT	Old Testament
Pan.	*Panarion* (Epiphanius)
Pap.Bibl.Nat.	Papyri of the *Bibliothèque Nationale* (Paris)
PEQ	*Palestine Exploration Quarterly*
P.Lond.	*Papyri of the British Museum (London)*
P.Mich.	*Michigan Papyri*
P.Oxy.	*Oxyrhynchus Papyri*
Ps.Sol.	*Psalms of Solomon*
Q	Qumran
1QS	"Rule *(Serek)* of the Community" from Qumran Cave 1
4QDt^q	Deuteronomy manuscript from Qumran Cave 4
4QEx^a	Exodus manuscript from Qumran Cave 4
QD	Quaestiones Disputatae
QDAP	*Quarterly of the Department of Antiquities of Palestine*
RAC	*Reallexikon für Antikes und Christentum*
RE	*Real-Enzyklopädie für die Altertumswissenschaft* (Pauly-Wissowa)
RÉG	*Revue des Études Grecques*
RNT	Regensburger Neues Testament
RSPT	*Revue des Sciences Philosophiques et Théologiques* (Paris)
RSR	*Revue des Sciences religieuses* (Strasbourg)
RSV	Revised Standard Version
RTR	*Reformed Theological Review*
SBLDS	Society for Biblical Literature Dissertation Series
SBT	Studies in Biblical Theology
Schürer	E. Schürer, *History of the Jewish People in the Age of Jesus Christ*, I-III (Edinburgh, 1973-87)

SEÅ	*Svensk Exegetisk Årsbok*
SEG	*Supplementum Epigraphicum Graecum*
SIG	*Sylloge Inscriptionum Graecarum*, ed. W. Dittenberger
SJLA	Studies in Judaism in Late Antiquity
SJT	*Scottish Journal of Theology*
SMB:SBO	Série Monographique "Benedictina": Section Biblico-Oecuménique
SNT	Schriften des Neuen Testaments
SNTSM	Society for New Testament Studies Monograph(s)
ST	*Studia Theologica*
SUNT	Studien zur Umwelt des Neuen Testaments
s.v.	*sub verbo, sub vocabulo* (under the word in question)
TAPA	*Transactions of the American Philological Association*
TB	Babylonian Talmud
TBC	Torch Biblical Commentaries
TDNT	*Theological Dictionary of the New Testament*, ed. G. Kittel and G. Friedrich, E.T. by G. W. Bromiley, I-X
Theod.	Theodotion (Greek translator of OT)
THKNT	Theologischer Hand-Kommentar zum Neuen Testament
TJ	Jerusalem (Palestinian) Talmud
TKNT	Theologischer Kommentar zum Neuen Testament
TNTC	Tyndale New Testament Commentaries
Tos.	Tosefta
TQ	*Theologische Quartalschrift*
TR	Textus Receptus ("Received Text"), 1633
TU	*Texte und Untersuchungen*
TynB	*Tyndale Bulletin*
TZ	*Theologische Zeitschrift*
VT	*Vetus Testamentum*
WC	Westminster Commentaries
WMANT	Wissenschaftliche Monographien zum Alten und Neuen Testament
WNT	Westminster New Testament
WTJ	*Westminster Theological Journal*
WUNT	Wissenschaftliche Untersuchungen zum Neuen Testament
ZKG	*Zeitschrift für Kirchengeschichte*
ZKNT	Zahn-Kommentar zum Neuen Testament
ZNW	*Zeitschrift für die neutestamentliche Wissenschaft*
ZTK	*Zeitschrift für Theologie und Kirche*
ZWT	*Zeitschrift für wissenschaftliche Theologie*

The Book of the
ACTS

INTRODUCTION

I. ACTS IN THE NEW TESTAMENT

The Acts of the Apostles is the name given since the second century A.D. to the second volume of a *History of Christian Origins* composed by a first-century Christian and dedicated to a certain Theophilus. The earlier volume of this *History* is also extant as one of the twenty-seven documents ultimately included in the New Testament canon: it is the work ordinarily known to us as *The Gospel according to Luke.*[1]

Originally, as we might expect, these two volumes circulated together as one complete and independent *History,* but not for long. Early in the second century the four "canonical" Gospels (as we call them) were gathered together into one collection and began to circulate as the fourfold Gospel. This meant that the earlier volume of our twofold *History* was detached from its sequel and attached to three works by other writers which covered more or less the same ground, relating the story of Jesus and ending with the witness to his resurrection. The second volume was thus left to pursue a career of its own, but an important and influential career, as it proved.

About the same time as the four Gospels were gathered together to form one collection, another collection of Christian documents was also being made—the collection of Paul's letters. These two collections—*The Gospel* and *The Apostle,* as they were called—make up the greater part of our New Testament. But there would be a hiatus between the two collections were it not for the second volume of the *History of Christian Origins,* the volume to which from now on we shall refer briefly as Acts. Acts played an indispensable part in relating the two collections to each other. As regards the Gospel collection, Acts forms its general sequel, as it was from the first the proper sequel to one of the four documents making up that collection (the third Gospel). As regards the Pauline collection, Acts provides a narrative

1. That these two documents were written by the same author is almost universally acknowledged. The only serious denial of identity of authorship in the twentieth century came from A. C. Clark, *The Acts of the Apostles* (Oxford, 1933), pp. 393-408; his arguments were scrutinized and effectively answered by W. L. Knox, *The Acts of the Apostles* (Cambridge, 1948), pp. 2-15, 100-109.

background against which several of its component letters can more readily be understood, and—more important still in the eyes of some Christians in the latter half of the second century—Acts provides cogent independent evidence for the validity of Paul's claim, made in his letters, to be a servant of Jesus Christ who labored "more abundantly" than any of the others.[2]

The importance of Acts was further underlined about the middle of the second century as a result of the dispute to which Marcion and his teaching gave rise. Marcion of Sinope was an exceptionally ardent devotee of Paul who nevertheless misunderstood him.[3] About A.D. 144 he promulgated at Rome what he held to be the true canon of divine scripture for the new age inaugurated by Christ. Christ, in Marcion's teaching, was the revealer of an entirely new religion, completely unrelated to anything that had preceded his coming (such as the faith of Israel documented in our Old Testament). God the Father, to whom Christ bore witness, had never been known on earth before: he was a superior being to the God of Israel, who created the material world and spoke through the prophets. Paul, according to Marcion, was the only apostle who faithfully preserved Christ's new religion in its purity, uncontaminated by Jewish influences. The Old Testament could have no place in the Christian canon. The Christian canon, as promulgated by Marcion, comprised two parts—one called *The Gospel* (a suitably edited recension of the third Gospel) and the other called *The Apostle* (a similarly edited recension of Paul's nine letters to churches and his letter to Philemon).

The publication of Marcion's canon was a challenge and a stimulus to the leaders of the Roman church and other churches which adhered to the "catholic" faith (as it came to be called). It did not compel them to *create* the canon of holy scripture which has been accepted, with minor variations, throughout the historic Christian church;[4] but it did compel them to *define* that canon with greater precision. For them, the writings of the new age did not supersede the Old Testament canon; they stood alongside it as its divinely ordained complement. For them, *The Gospel* comprised not one document only but four, and those four included the full text of the one which Marcion had published in a mutilated form. For them, *The Apostle* included not ten but thirteen Pauline letters, and not Pauline letters only but

---

2. 1 Cor. 15:10; cf. Rom. 15:17-20; 2 Cor. 11:23.

3. On Marcion see above all A. Harnack, *Marcion: Das Evangelium vom fremden Gott* (Leipzig, 1921, ²1924), supplemented by his *Neue Studien zu Marcion* (Leipzig, 1923); also E. C. Blackman, *Marcion and his Influence* (London, 1948).

4. Tertullian's statement that Valentinus, a Gnostic leader (*c.* A.D. 140), "seems to use the entire *instrumentum*," i.e., New Testament (*Prescription against heretics* 38.7), is borne out to a large extent by the evidence of early Valentinian treatises found among the Nag Hammadi papyri (cf. W. C. van Unnik, *Newly Discovered Gnostic Writings*, E.T. [London, 1960], pp. 58-68, and the caveat by H. von Campenhausen, *The Formation of the Christian Bible*, E.T. [London, 1972], p. 140, n. 171).

letters of other "apostolic men" as well. And, linking *The Gospel* and *The Apostle*, Acts was now seen to have greater importance than ever, for not only did it validate Paul's claims but it validated the authority of the original apostles—those whom Marcion had repudiated as false apostles and corruptors of the truth as it is in Jesus. The position of Acts as the keystone in the arch of the Christian canon was confirmed. A catholic work like Acts was a suitable pivot for a catholic canon; it could have no place in a sectarian canon like Marcion's.[5]

This significant aspect of Acts is reflected in the title *The Acts of the Apostles*, which it has been given from that time to this. So far as extant evidence goes, it first receives this title in the so-called Anti-Marcionite Prologue to the Third Gospel, late in the second century (the earliest extant document, also, to ascribe the authorship of the twofold work to Luke, the physician of Antioch).[6] The title *The Acts of the Apostles* may have been intended to point out its witness to the fact that Paul was not (as Marcion thought) the only faithful apostle of Christ. Even so, it makes an exaggerated impression: the only apostle (apart from Paul) of whom any extended account is given is Peter. (If the title be rendered simply *Acts of Apostles*, then the reference might be to Paul and Peter—although the author, who for the most part restricts the appellation "apostle" to members of the Twelve, does not give it to Paul in anything like the sense in which Paul claimed it for himself.)[7] Even more exaggerated is the form of the title given to the work in another document of around the same date, the Muratorian Canon; here it is called *The Acts of All the Apostles*,[8] although nothing is said about most of them after they co-opt Matthias to take the place of Judas at the end of the first chapter.

---

5. See A. Harnack, *The Origin of the New Testament*, E.T. (London, 1925), pp. 44-53, 63-68.

6. The consensus which held the so-called anti-Marcionite prologues to the Gospels to belong to one collection and to come from a date between Papias and Irenaeus (cf. D. de Bruyne, "Les plus anciens prologues latins des Évangiles," *Revue Bénédictine* 40 [1928], pp. 193-214; A. Harnack, "Die ältesten Evangelien-Prologe und die Bildung des Neuen Testaments," *Sitzungsbericht der Preussischen Akademie der Wissenschaften*, phil.-hist. Klasse [Berlin, 1928], Heft 24) has been vigorously challenged by J. Regul, *Die antimarcionitischen Evangelienprologe* (Freiburg, 1969). The position taken here is that the so-called anti-Marcionite prologue to Luke (extant in both Greek and Latin) does exhibit an anti-Marcionite tendency and probably dates from the last decades of the second century. The same designation Πράξεις Ἀποστόλων is given to Acts in the Greek text of the anti-Marcionite prologue to Luke as in Greek manuscripts of the NT.

7. In the two places where he gives it to Paul (Acts 14:4, 14), he couples Paul and Barnabas together as "the apostles" (see p. 271 below, n. 7).

8. This may be an anti-Marcionite exaggeration, or it may imply a criticism of the many uncanonical Acts which began to circulate in the second half of the second century (*Acts of Paul, Acts of Peter, Acts of John*, etc.); there is only one authoritative account of the acts of *all* the apostles, the compiler may mean, and that is Luke's Acts (*acta autem omnium apostolorum sub uno libro scripta sunt*).

II. ORIGIN AND PURPOSE OF ACTS

The important part played by Acts in the middle of the second century has suggested to some scholars that (in its final form at least) it was composed about that time in order to play that part. One scholar has argued, indeed, that Luke-Acts was composed as a catholic Gospel-and-Apostle corpus in order to meet the challenge posed by Marcion's sectarian Gospel-and-Apostle canon.[9] Against such views one consideration tells with special weight: the historical, geographical, and political situation presupposed by Acts, and for that matter by Luke-Acts as a whole, is unmistakably that of the first century and not of the second. This is specially true of Paul's invocation of his Roman citizenship and his appeal to Caesar.[10]

The purpose of Acts cannot be considered in isolation from the purpose of Luke's Gospel. The two parts, for all their stylistic differences,[11] make up an integral whole, with one coherent purpose. The author does not leave his readers to speculate what that purpose might be: he states it explicitly in the prologue to his Gospel, which should be read as a prologue to the twofold work. Here are his words (Luke 1:1-4):

> Inasmuch as many have undertaken to compile a narrative of the things which have been accomplished among us, just as they were delivered to us by those who from the beginning were eyewitnesses and ministers of the word, it seemed good to me also, having followed all things closely for some time past, to write an orderly account for you, most excellent Theophilus, that you may know the truth concerning the things of which you have been informed.[12]

He himself, it appears, could not claim to be an eyewitness of the earlier events recorded in his history, but he had access to the information which eyewitnesses could supply. He was not the first to draw up an account based on eyewitness information (he thinks, perhaps, of Mark's Gospel as a

9. J. Knox, *Marcion and the New Testament* (Chicago, 1942), pp. 119-39. A careful and detailed critique of this work was contributed by N. B. Stonehouse to *WTJ* 6 (1943-44), pp. 86-98. Another line of argument for the dating of Acts about the middle of the second century is followed by J. C. O'Neill in *The Theology of Acts in its Historical Setting* (London, 21970): its apologetic emphases place it alongside Justin Martyr, neither Justin nor Luke showing any knowledge of each other's works.

10. Cf. A. N. Sherwin-White, *Roman Society and Roman Law in the New Testament* (Oxford, 1963), pp. 144-62, 172-89.

11. The first volume conforms to the Gospel *genre*, which had been established by Mark; the second volume follows the precedent set by earlier Greek historians (see E. Plümacher, *Lukas als hellenistischer Schriftsteller* [Göttingen, 1972]).

12. See S. Brown, "The Role of the Prologues in Determining the Purpose of Luke-Acts," in *Perspectives on Luke-Acts*, ed. C. H. Talbert (Edinburgh, 1978), pp. 99-111; L. C. A. Alexander, "Luke's Preface in the Context of Greek Preface-Writing," *NovT* 28 (1986), pp. 48-74.

record earlier than his own), but he claims for his account that it rests on thorough and accurate research and that it is arranged in a proper sequence.[13]

When he says that he himself had "followed all things closely for some time past," he implies that he had taken part in some at least of the later events which he records.[14] It is difficult to avoid linking this implied claim with the incidence of the "we" sections in Acts—that is to say, sections (dealing largely with journeys by sea made by Paul and some of his friends) in which the narrative is cast in the first person plural ("we"/"us") instead of the usual third person plural ("they"/"them").[15] It is a reasonable inference that the narrator was one of Paul's companions for the periods covered by those sections. This inference (which is not universally drawn)[16] may have given rise at an early date to the tradition that the author of the twofold work was Luke the physician, mentioned as one of Paul's companions in Col. 4:14. On the other hand, the tradition and the internal evidence of the "we" sections may be independent of each other, and so mutually confirmatory. The tradition appears at the end of the second century in the so-called anti-Marcionite prologue to Luke and in the Muratorian Canon, and possibly at an even earlier date it found its way into one or two recensions of Acts. The original text does not reveal the author's name, but the Western text of 11:28, telling of an incident at Antioch on the Orontes, soon after the founding of the church there, has the form of a "we" section ("when we were gathered together"), implying that the narrator was an Antiochene (and thus confirming the tradition to this effect in the anti-Marcionite prologue),[17] while another early recension (just possibly the same one) introduces the name of Luke into the "we" narrative at 20:13.[18] Throughout this commentary the Lukan authorship of the twofold work is accepted, while it is recognized that some scholars find it impossible to believe that the author could have been personally acquainted with Paul.[19]

---

13. Contrast Papias's statement that Mark recorded the memoirs of Peter, "not however in order" (Eusebius, *HE* 3.39.15). Papias probably treated some other record as the standard against which he evaluated the order of events in Mark's Gospel.

14. For the sense of παρακολουθέω ἄνωθεν (Luke 1:3) see H. J. Cadbury, "Commentary on the Preface of Luke," *Beginnings* I.2, pp. 489-510, especially pp. 501-3.

15. The three "we" sections are Acts 16:10-17; 20:5-21:18; 27:1-28:16. See H. J. Cadbury, "'We' and 'I' Passages in Luke-Acts," *NTS* 3 (1956-57), pp. 128-32; M. Hengel, *Acts and the History of Earliest Christianity,* E.T. (London, 1979), pp. 66-67.

16. For quite a different perspective on the "we" of Acts see E. Haenchen, "'We' in Acts and the Itinerary," E.T. in *JTC* 1 (1965), pp. 65-99.

17. See pp. 229 (n. 33), 230.

18. See p. 385, n. 31.

19. Cf. C. K. Barrett, "Acts and the Pauline Corpus," *ExT* 88 (1976-77), p. 4, col. 2; he refers to his *New Testament Essays* (London, 1972), pp. 82-83, 98, 115.

Luke, then (as the author will be called from now on), announces that his purpose in writing was to give Theophilus (whoever he may have been) an accurate and orderly account of the origins of Christianity, about which Theophilus had some information already. He was anxious that Theophilus should be able to rely confidently on the account now being given him. The earlier part of the account (contained in what we know as the Third Gospel) is in essence a record of the apostolic witness to Jesus' ministry of word, deed, suffering, and triumph, amplified by material collected by Luke himself.[20] The second volume takes up the tale after the resurrection of Jesus and carries it forward for some thirty years; it traces the progress of the gospel along the road leading from Judaea *via* Antioch to Rome, and ends with the chief herald of the gospel proclaiming it at the heart of the empire with the full acquiescence of the imperial authorities.

But it is not only information that Luke aims to give Theophilus. At the time when he wrote, Christianity was, to use one of his own phrases, "everywhere spoken against" (28:22). There was a widespread suspicion that it was a subversive movement, a menace to imperial law and order. And indeed in the eyes of those who set some store by imperial law and order Christianity started off with a serious handicap. Its Founder had admittedly been condemned to death by a Roman governor on a charge of sedition. Thus Tacitus's estimate of its criminal character is based partly on the fact that it owed its inception to one Christ, who "was executed by sentence of the procurator Pontius Pilate when Tiberius was emperor."[21] And the movement thus inauspiciously inaugurated seemed to be attended by tumult and disorder wherever it spread, both in the Roman provinces and in Rome itself. Luke sets himself to deal with this handicap.

The crucifixion of Christ is presented in his Gospel as a gross miscarriage of justice. True, Pilate sentenced him to death, but he had already pronounced him not guilty of the charges brought against him, and passed the death sentence only under pressure and against his better judgment.[22] Herod Antipas, tetrarch of Galilee (where the greater part of Jesus' public ministry had been carried on), agreed that the charges brought against him need not be taken seriously.[23]

Similarly in Acts a variety of officials, Gentile and Jewish, show goodwill to Paul and other Christian missionaries, or at least admit that there is no basis for the accusations pressed against them by their opponents. In

---

20. Cf. three major commentaries: E. E. Ellis, *The Gospel of Luke*, NCB (Grand Rapids/London, [2]1974); I. H. Marshall, *The Gospel of Luke*, NIGTC (Grand Rapids/Exeter, 1978); J. A. Fitzmyer, *The Gospel according to Luke*, AB (Garden City, NY, 1981-85).

21. *Annals* 15.44.4.

22. Luke 23:4, 24.

23. Luke 23:15.

Cyprus the proconsul of the island-province is favorably impressed by Paul and Barnabas, and by their message and activity.[24] At Philippi, a Roman colony, the chief collegiate magistrates apologize to Paul and Silas for their illegal beating and imprisonment.[25] At Corinth the proconsul of Achaia, Gallio (member of an influential Roman family), decrees that the charges brought before him against Paul by the local Jewish leaders relate to internal disputes of Jewish religion, and declares him guiltless of any offense against Roman law.[26] At Ephesus the Asiarchs, leading citizens of the province of Asia, show themselves to be Paul's friends, and the chief executive officer of the city administration absolves him and his associates of anything in the nature of public sacrilege.[27] During Paul's last visit to Judaea the procurators Felix and Festus successively find no substance in the charges urged against him by the Sanhedrin, whether of attempted violation of the sanctity of the Jerusalem temple or of stirring up unrest throughout the empire.[28] The Jewish client king Agrippa II agrees with Festus that Paul had done nothing deserving either death or imprisonment, and that he could have been discharged on the spot had he not taken the decision out of the procurator's hands by appealing to have his case referred to the imperial tribunal in Rome.[29] And when he is taken to Rome to have his case heard, he occupies the time of waiting by preaching the gospel there for two years, under constant surveillance, without any attempt to hinder him.[30] If Christianity were such a lawless movement as was widely believed, Paul would certainly not have been allowed to propagate it by the praetorian guard in whose custody he was.

How then, it might be asked, was the advance of Christianity attended by so much strife and disorder? Luke arraigns the Jewish authorities in Judaea and the other provinces as bearing chief responsibility for this. It was the chief-priestly establishment in Jerusalem that prosecuted Jesus before Pilate and, a generation later, Paul before Felix and Festus; and most of the disturbances which broke out when the gospel was introduced to the Roman provinces were fomented by local Jewish communities, who refused to accept the saving message themselves and were annoyed when their Gentile neighbors believed it.[31]

Yet Luke is not anti-Jewish in principle. Christianity is, for him, no

24. Acts 13:7, 12.
25. Acts 16:37-39.
26. Acts 18:12-17.
27. Acts 19:31, 35-41.
28. Acts 24:22–25:25.
29. Acts 26:30-32.
30. Acts 28:30-31.
31. There are two occasions in Acts when an attack on Christian missionaries came from Gentiles, and on both the reason was a real or imagined threat to property interests—at Philippi (16:16-21) and Ephesus (19:23-27).

innovation but the proper fulfilment of Israel's religion. He is at pains to present Paul as a loyal and law-abiding Jew. This comes out particularly in the speeches made by Paul in his own defense in Jerusalem, Caesarea, and Rome.[32] As with the other speeches reported in Acts, Luke (in the best Thucydidean tradition) aims to give the general purport of what was actually said,[33] while at the same time he makes the speeches an integral part of his presentation and argument. In those apologetic speeches, then, Paul claims to believe everything in the law and the prophets and to have done nothing contrary to Israel's ancestral customs.[34] The one point at issue between him and his accusers is the resurrection faith: by this he means the faith that Jesus rose from the dead, but Jesus' resurrection is for him the confirmation of the Jews' national hope. Why then should they object to it?[35] Nothing is said in these speeches about Paul's law-free gospel which, according to his letters, was the principal stumbling block in the sight of his opponents, whether they were Jews or judaizing Christians.

It is necessary, then, to look for an appropriate life-setting for a work which strikes the apologetic note in just this way. One attractive suggestion points to the period A.D. 66 or shortly afterward, when the chief accusers of Paul, the Judaean authorities, had so completely discredited themselves in Roman eyes by the revolt against imperial rule.[36] True, Paul himself was dead by then, but the accusations against him, especially that of fomenting public disorder, continued to be brought against Christians in general, and his defense, which could have been seen as vindicated in the event, might be validly pleaded on their behalf. In those years it would have been quite effective to emphasize that, unlike the rebellious Jews, Christians were not disloyal to the empire—that, in fact, it was the rebellious Jews themselves who had always done their best to disown Christianity.

The argument that there is nothing in Acts—or even in Luke[37]—that

32. Acts 22:3-21; 23:6; 24:10-21; 25:8, 10-11; 26:2-23; 28:17-20. See F. Veltmann, "The Defense Speeches of Paul in Acts," in *Perspectives on Luke-Acts*, ed. C. H. Talbert, pp. 243-56.

33. Thucydides set a precedent for serious historians by his policy on the inclusion of speeches in his work (*History* 1.22.1). See M. I. Finley's remarks on his statement of policy in *Ancient History: Evidence and Models* (London, 1985), pp. 13-15.

34. Acts 24:12; 28:17. See below, p. 508 with n. 63.

35. Acts 23:6; 24:14-15; 26:6-8, 23; 28:20.

36. Cf. T. W. Manson, *Studies in the Gospels and Epistles* (Manchester, 1962), pp. 56, 62-67. For other considerations pointing to a date between 66 and 70 see C. S. C. Williams, "The Date of Luke-Acts," *ExT* 64 (1952-53), pp. 283-84; *The Acts of the Apostles*, BNTC (London/New York, 1957), pp. 13-15.

37. The Lukan form of the Olivet discourse, especially the replacement of the "abomination of desolation" (Mark 13:14) with "Jerusalem surrounded by armies" (Luke 21:20), has generally been regarded as evidence for a date after A.D. 70. But see C. H. Dodd, "The Fall of Jerusalem and the 'Abomination of Desolation'" (1974), in *More New Testament Studies* (Manchester, 1968), pp. 69-83. The date of Luke's form of the Olivet discourse would, however, be irrelevant for the dating of Acts if C. S. C. Williams were

presupposes the Jewish revolt and the resultant destruction of the temple and city of Jerusalem (A.D. 70) has been used in defense of a pre-70 dating for the twofold work—early in the twentieth century by Adolf Harnack[38] and over sixty years later by J. A. T. Robinson.[39] Indeed, it has been further argued, since there is no allusion to two earlier events—the Neronian persecution and the execution of Paul—that the composition of Luke-Acts should probably be dated not later than A.D. 65.[40] So far as the Neronian persecution is concerned, even Tacitus (no friend to Christians) admits that it was the action of one man's malignity rather than an expression of public policy,[41] and the official reprobation of Nero's memory and actions at his death could have been held to cover his persecution of the Christians of Rome. So Luke's recording of favorable judgments which had been passed on Christianity by other Roman authorities might have been intended to suggest that Nero's anti-Christian activity was an irresponsible and criminal attack by that now execrated ruler on a movement whose innocence had been amply attested by many worthier representatives of Roman power.

Again, whether Paul's execution was or was not an incident in the Neronian persecution, the fact that it is not mentioned in Acts is not a decisive argument for the dating of the book:[42] Luke's goal has been reached when he has brought Paul to Rome and left him preaching the gospel freely there.[43] Certainly, Paul's arrival in Rome, his gospel witness there for two years, the legal procedure involved in the bearing of his appeal to Caesar, must have brought Christianity to the notice of classes in Roman society on which it had until then made no impression. The interest that was now aroused in it did not die out, but maintained itself and increased, until under Domitian (A.D. 81-96) it had penetrated the highest ranks of all. At any time in this period a work which gave an intelligible history of the rise and

---

right in holding that the "former treatise" to which Acts is the sequel should be identified with "proto-Luke" (substantially, Q + L) ("The Date of Luke-Acts").

38. *The Date of the Acts and of the Synoptic Gospels*, E.T. (London, 1911), pp. 90-116. Cf. R. B. Rackham, *The Acts of the Apostles* (London, 1901), pp. l-lv.

39. *Redating the New Testament* (London, 1976), pp. 86-92.

40. Cf. R. B. Rackham, "The Acts of the Apostles. 2. A Plea for an Early Date," *JTS* 1 (1899-1900), pp. 76-87.

41. Tacitus, *Annals* 15.44.8.

42. The fact that the outcome of Paul's trial is not mentioned in Acts has been explained by the hypothesis of Luke's own death before he could finish his work (cf. J. de Zwaan, "Was the Book of Acts a Posthumous Edition?" *HTR* 17 [1924], pp. 95-153; H. Lietzmann, *The Founding of the Church Universal*, E.T. [London, 1950], p. 78). But Luke probably finished his work exactly as he intended to do.

43. It is absurd to say, as Ramsay did, "No one can accept the ending of *Acts* as the conclusion of a rationally conceived history" (*St. Paul the Traveller*, pp. 351-52), and precarious to argue, as he and some others (including T. Zahn, *INT*, E.T. III [Edinburgh, 1909], pp. 58-61) have done, that Luke must have planned a third volume to complete his *History*.

progress of Christianity, and at the same time gave a reasoned reply to popular calumnies against it, was sure of a reception among the intelligent reading public—or rather listening public[44]—of Rome, of whom Theophilus was probably a representative. Its positive defense was best expressed in the words of Paul, the Roman citizen, whose appeal to Caesar was made not only on his own behalf but on behalf of the Christian community and its faith.

It is difficult to fix the date of composition of Acts more precisely than at some point within the Flavian period (A.D. 69-96), possibly about the middle of the period. The arguments by which Sir William Ramsay, late in the nineteenth century, concluded that it was composed about A.D. 80 are precarious,[45] but nothing that has been discovered since then has pointed to a more probable dating. One consideration, admittedly subjective, is the perspective from which the work has been composed. The relations between Paul, Peter, and James of Jerusalem are presented in a way which would be more natural if all three of them had died and the author had been able to view their lasting achievements in a more satisfactory proportion than would have been so easily attained if they had still been alive. Certainly the impression he gives us of their relations is not the impression received from Paul's letters, and this is more intelligible if they had been dead for some years and their disagreements (in the eyes of a man like Luke, at any rate)[46] no longer seemed so important as they would have done at the time.[47]

Luke's narrative as it stands cannot have been intended to serve as evidence for the defense when Paul's appeal came up for hearing in the imperial court. A document drawn up for this purpose may have served as a source for Acts, but there is much in Acts (and *a fortiori* in Luke-Acts) that would have been quite irrelevant forensically, whether it be (on the one hand) the detailed account of Paul's voyage and shipwreck or (on the other hand) the pervasive emphasis on the dominant role of the Holy Spirit in the

---

44. It was customary at Rome for a company to gather together to listen to a new work being read by the author or by somebody else. Cf. also M. Dibelius: "On the book market, which, unlike other early Christian writings, these 'two volumes' obviously reached, they were probably known as 'Luke's Acts of Jesus' and 'Luke's Acts of the Apostles,'" Acts in particular being written not only for Christian communities "but also for cultured readers, whether Gentile or Christian" (*Studies,* pp. 103-4).

45. Ramsay, holding that "the fifteenth year of Tiberius Caesar" (Luke 3:1) was reckoned from A.D. 12, "when Tiberius was associated by Augustus in the Empire," and not from his accession year (A.D. 14), concluded that such an unusual method of reckoning could only have been followed when a similar situation obtained (or had very recently obtained)—namely, Titus's association with Vespasian in the imperial rule on July 1, A.D. 71, eight years before his accession as sole emperor (*St. Paul the Traveller,* pp. 386-87). But his interpretation of Luke 3:1 is improbable.

46. See pp. 301-2 below (on 15:38-39).

47. Cf. A. Ehrhardt, *The Acts of the Apostles: Ten Lectures* (Manchester, 1969), pp. 4, 50, 88-89, *et passim.*

expansion of the gospel. This emphasis constitutes one of Luke's leading theological motifs.[48] Another is his concept of salvation history:[49] the gospel, based as it is on the resurrection of Christ, is the culmination of a long preparatory process of divine revelation and overruling, traced as far back as Israel's exodus from Egypt (as in Paul's synagogue address at Pisidian Antioch)[50] or even farther, to the call of Abraham (as in Stephen's defense before the Sanhedrin).[51]

Would these emphases have been more relevant for the intelligent public that Luke had in view than they would have been for Paul's defense consel before Nero? To many members of that public they would have meant little, but Theophilus himself, and some others like him, may well have been converts, or near-converts, to the Christian faith. In any case, Luke wishes to make it clear that the progress of this faith was no mere product of human planning; it was directed by divine agency. In a way, this may have contributed to Luke's apologetic purpose, although it would not have been of much use as a plea in a Roman law-court.

Luke is, in fact, the pioneer among Christian apologists, especially in that form of apologetic which is addressed to the civil authorities to establish the law-abiding character of Christianity. But other forms of apologetic are represented in the course of his work, particularly in some of the speeches of Acts. Thus, Stephen's defense is the prototype of Christian apologetic over against the Jews, designed to demonstrate that Christianity and not Judaism is the true fulfilment of the word of God spoken through Moses and the prophets, and that the Jews' rejection of the gospel is consistent with their rejection of the divine message brought to them by earlier messengers. Paul's address to the Athenian court of the Areopagus is one of the earliest examples of Christian apologetic to pagans, designed to show that the true knowledge of God is given in the gospel and not in the idolatrous vanities of paganism.[52] His farewell address at Miletus to the elders of the Ephesian church is partly apologetic; he replies by implication to some criticisms voiced against him within the Christian community.[53] And his speech at Caesarea before the younger Agrippa is the crowning *apologia* for his own missionary career.[54]

---

48. The Christian community is Spirit-filled and Spirit-led, so much so that its voice is the voice of the Spirit (cf., e.g., 5:3; 15:28), and the whole evangelistic enterprise, from Jerusalem to Rome, is directed by the Spirit (cf., e.g., 16:6-10).

49. Cf. E. Lohse, "Lukas als Theologe der Heilsgeschichte," *Evangelische Theologie* 14 (1954-55), pp. 254-75; H. Flender, *St. Luke: Theologian of Redemptive History*, E.T. (London, 1967).

50. Acts 13:16-41.

51. Acts 7:2-53.

52. Acts 17:22-31.

53. Acts 20:18-35.

54. Acts 26:2-23.

III. PAUL IN ACTS

In a number of his letters Paul found it necessary to defend the reality of his divine call and commission against those who questioned it, and he appealed in support of his claim to the "signs of an apostle" which attended his ministry.[55] It was unnecessary for him to describe those signs in detail to people who had firsthand experience of them. But other readers of his letters might be uncertain of the validity of this appeal were it not for Luke's record of Paul's ministry. No one could read Acts and doubt that Paul was really commissioned by the risen Christ as a "chosen instrument"[56] in his hand for the widespread proclamation of the gospel.

The vindication of Paul's claim was not Luke's primary purpose in writing. Luke does, in passing, show that Paul's commission was as valid as Peter's, and that both men were equally faithful to their commission. But these secondary aspects of his work acquired special importance in the second century, in view of the Marcionites' tendency to claim Paul peculiarly for themselves, and also in view of tendencies in other quarters to play down Paul's record in the interests of Peter's or James's.[57] Tertullian, for example, points out the inconsistency of those sectarians (the Marcionites in particular, no doubt) who rejected the testimony of Acts but appealed so confidently to the unique authority of Paul. "You must show us first of all who this Paul was," he says to them. "What was he before he became an apostle? How did he become an apostle?"[58] Paul in his letters gives his own answer to such questions, but for independent corroboration one would naturally appeal to Acts, when once that work had been published. But this the Marcionites could not do: Acts did vindicate the claims made by and for Paul, indeed, but since it simultaneously vindicated claims made by and for Peter, its testimony was unacceptable. Acts shows that Peter and the rest of the Twelve were true and faithful apostles of Jesus Christ (which the Marcionites denied) at the same time as it shows how Paul's missionary achievement was not only as great as theirs, but greater. One feature of Acts which will be observed in the course of our exposition is the series of parallels drawn between Peter's missionary activity and Paul's,[59] although neither of the two is made the standard of comparison by which the other is assessed.

55. 2 Cor. 12:12; cf. C. K. Barrett, *The Signs of an Apostle* (London, 1970).
56. Acts 9:15.
57. Tendencies which later found literary expression in the *Clementine Homilies* and *Clementine Recognitions* (3rd or 4th century A.D.).
58. *Prescription against heretics* 23. In the preceding section (22) Tertullian had said of Acts, "Those who do not accept this volume of scripture can have nothing to do with the Holy Spirit, for they cannot know if the Holy Spirit has yet been sent to the disciples, neither can they claim to be the church, since they cannot show when this body was established or where it was cradled."
59. See below, p. 364, n. 14, for some details of these parallels.

In recording the greatness of Paul's achievement Acts may have had happy consequences beyond Luke's immediate intention. A comparison of Paul's farewell speech at Miletus with the evidence of the Pastoral Epistles suggests that, after Paul left his Aegean mission field, his influence there, and especially in the province of Asia, declined, and that his opponents won at least a temporary victory in the churches.[60] Insofar as those opponents inculcated judaizing tendencies, however, their victory was very temporary. Before long, Paul's name and reputation were firmly reestablished and venerated in the areas which he had evangelized (even if his teaching was not understood or applied as consistently as he might have wished). Two reasons may be found for this vindication of Paul's memory. One was the dispersal of the church in Jerusalem shortly before the fall of that city in A.D. 70. Another, and more important, reason was probably the publication of Acts and its circulation among the Aegean churches—a more extended public than that to which Luke first addressed his *History*. The appearance of Acts must have brought about a revival of interest in Paul; it may even, as Edgar J. Goodspeed suggested, have done something to stimulate the collection of his writings into a literary corpus which circulated among the churches.[61] It is a noteworthy point (and one which has been interpreted variously) that the author of Acts betrays no knowledge of the letters of Paul;[62] whatever else this indicates, it means almost certainly that Acts was written before the letters began to be generally known as units in a collection.[63]

Paul no doubt is Luke's hero. And this fact goes far to explain the differences between the impression which Luke gives of Paul's personality and that which we receive from Paul's own letters. For Paul was certainly no hero in his own eyes. In Acts, from the time when Paul sets out from Antioch

---

60. Compare 20:29-30 with 2 Tim. 1:15.

61. E. J. Goodspeed, *INT* (Chicago, 1937), pp. 210-17.

62. This has been contested, especially by M. S. Enslin, according to whom Luke not only knew the authentic Pauline letters but used them as his main historical and literary source, reconstructing Paul's activities with their help on the principle that what *should* have been *must* have been and actually *was* (*Reapproaching Paul* [Philadelphia, 1962], p. 27; cf. his "'Luke' and 'Paul,'" *JAOS* 58 [1938], pp. 81-91; "Once Again: Luke and Paul," *ZNW* 61 [1970], pp. 253-71; "Luke, the Literary Physician," in D. E. Aune [ed.], *Studies in New Testament and Early Christian Literature: Essays in Honor of Allen P. Wikgren* = *NovT* Sup. 33 [Leiden, 1972], pp. 135-43).

63. If the Pauline letters did not supply Luke with a source, what sources did he use? The question is more difficult to answer for Acts (none of its sources having been preserved independently) than for the Third Gospel (where one or two of the sources are still available for separate inspection). Apart from the "we" narrative, he probably used another (third-personal) itinerary (especially for Barnabas and Paul's Anatolian journey of 13:13–14:26, and perhaps for Paul's journey of 18:22-23), one or more Jerusalem sources for the early history of the mother-church, a Hellenistic (Antiochene?) source (6:8–8:40; 11:19-26), and a collection of *Acts of Peter* (9:32–11:18; 12:1-17). It is not always easy to decide which putative sources were written and which were oral. See J. Dupont, *The Sources of Acts*, E.T. (London, 1964).

for extended missionary work, he dominates the situation. He is always sure of himself; he always triumphs. In his letters, Paul is too often the victim of conflicting emotions—"fightings without and fears within" (2 Cor. 7:5). He confesses that he has neither the self-assurance nor the self-assertiveness of the intruders who have stirred up trouble for him among his converts in Corinth: where those others exploit his converts, he refuses to claim his rights as their spiritual father, and some of them despise him for his weakness.[64] The Paul of the letters is a many-sided character. At times, to be sure, he can assert his authority,[65] and this is the side of him that Luke chiefly depicts.[66] But even if there are aspects of the real Paul at which we might scarcely guess if we did not have his letters, the picture of him that Luke gives is ineffaceable. And in giving us this picture, limited though it may be, Luke has made a great—indeed, a unique—contribution to the record of early Christian expansion. His narrative, in fact, is a sourcebook of the highest value for the history of civilization.[67]

It may, or it may not, be a good thing that over so much of the world today Christianity is looked on as a European religion. But how does it come about that a faith which arose in Asia should have become integrated into European rather than Asian civilization? The answer surely is that, in the providence of God, its leading herald and missionary in the three decades following its inception was a Roman citizen, who saw how the strategic centers and communications of the Roman Empire could be turned to the service of Christ's kingdom, and planted the Christian faith in those centers and along those lines of communication. "In little more than ten years St. Paul established the Church in four provinces of the Empire, Galatia, Macedonia, Achaia and Asia. Before A.D. 47 there were no Churches in these provinces; in A.D. 57 St. Paul could speak as if his work there was done, and could plan extensive tours into the far West without anxiety lest the Churches which he had founded might perish in his absence for want of his guidance and support."[68]

And Luke is the historian of this enterprise—one of the most far-reaching in world history. He shows plainly how it was carried out. "Generally speaking, Paul's activity was based on certain centres, from which he

---

64. 2 Cor. 10:1–12:13.

65. Cf. 1 Cor. 4:18-21; 5:3-5; 2 Cor. 13:1-4.

66. J. Jervell points out that Paul the charismatic man of power, to whom Acts bears clear testimony, is but one of the many aspects of Paul which he presents in his letters ("Der unbekannte Paulus," in *Die paulinische Literatur und Theologie*, ed. S. Pedersen [Aarhus/Göttingen, 1980]).

67. With Luke as a Greek historian there is none to compare between Polybius (fl. 146 B.C.) and Eusebius (fl. A.D. 325); see A. Ehrhardt, "The Construction and Purpose of the Acts of the Apostles," *The Framework of the New Testament Stories* (Manchester, 1964), p. 64.

68. R. Allen, *Missionary Methods: St. Paul's or Ours?* (London, 1927), p. 3.

undertook his longer and shorter journeys, and which in the course of years were transferred from one province to another."[69] The first of those centers was Damascus, from which (according to Paul's own account in Galatians) he penetrated Nabataean Arabia. He would have made his next center Jerusalem, had he not (according to Luke's account) been divinely directed not to settle there. He went back therefore to his native Tarsus, which provided a convenient base for the evangelization of the united province of Syria and Cilicia (for which Paul himself, again in Galatians, is our authority). Then, for shorter or longer periods, his successive centers were Antioch on the Orontes, Corinth, Ephesus, and Rome.[70] Something of his achievements as he worked in one after another of those centers, and preached the gospel along the roads leading from one to another, may be gathered from his letters. But it is Luke that we have to thank for the coherent record of Paul's activity.[71] Without his record, we should be incalculably poorer. Even with it, there is much about Paul's career that remains obscure to us; there would be much more if we had no book of Acts.

IV. SELECT BIBLIOGRAPHY

A. EDITIONS AND COMMENTARIES (ACTS)

Alexander, J. A., *A Commentary on the Acts of the Apostles* ([1857] London: Banner of Truth, 1965)

Alford, H., "The Acts of the Apostles," *The Greek Testament*, II (London: Rivingtons/Cambridge: Deighton Bell, [6]1871), pp. 1-310

Andrews, H. T., *The Acts of the Apostles*, WNT (London: Melrose, 1908)

Bartlet, J. V., *The Acts*, CentB (Edinburgh: Jack, 1902)

Bauernfeind, O., *Die Apostelgeschichte*, THKNT 5 (Leipzig: Deichert, 1939)

Bengel, J. A., *Gnomon Novi Testamenti* ([1742] London/Edinburgh: Williams & Norgate, [3]1862), pp. 388-489 ("Annotationes ad Acta Apostolorum")

Beyer, H. W., *Die Apostelgeschichte*, HNT 7 (Tübingen: Mohr, 1938)

Blass, F., *Acta Apostolorum sive Lucae ad Theophilum liber alter: editio philologica* (Göttingen: Vandenhoeck & Ruprecht, 1895)

Blass, F., *Acta Apostolorum sive Lucae ad Theophilum liber alter: secundum formam quae videtur Romanam* (Leipzig: Teubner, 1896)

Blunt, A. W. F., *The Acts of the Apostles*, ClarB (Oxford: Clarendon Press, 1923)

Browne, L. E., *The Acts of the Apostles*, Indian Church Commentaries (London: SPCK, 1925)

69. M. Dibelius, *Paul* (ed. W. G. Kümmel), E.T. (London, 1953), p. 69.

70. See D. T. Rowlingson, "The Geographical Orientation of Paul's Missionary Interests," *JBL* 69 (1950), pp. 341-44.

71. For attempts to present a coherent record of Paul's activity without the aid of Acts see J. Knox, *Chapters in a Life of Paul* (New York, 1950); G. Lüdemann, *Paul, Apostle to the Gentiles: Studies in Chronology*, E.T. (London, 1984).

Bruce, F. F., *The Acts of the Apostles: The Greek Text with Introduction and Commentary* (Grand Rapids: Eerdmans/Leicester: Inter-Varsity Press, ³1989)

Burnside, W. F., *The Acts of the Apostles*, CGT (Cambridge: University Press, 1916)

Camerlynck, A., and van der Heeren, A., *Commentarius in Acta Apostolorum* (Bruges: Beyaert, ⁷1923)

Clark, A. C., *The Acts of the Apostles: A Critical Edition* (Oxford: Clarendon Press, 1933)

Conzelmann, H., *Die Apostelgeschichte*, HNT 7 (Tübingen: Mohr, 1963, ²1972); E.T., *Acts*, Hermeneia (Philadelphia: Fortress, 1987)

Delebecque, E., *Les Actes des Apôtres: texte traduit et annoté* (Paris: Les Belles Lettres, 1982)

Dupont, J., *Les Actes des Apôtres*, Bible de Jérusalem (Paris: du Cerf, ²1954)

Findlay, J. A., *The Acts of the Apostles* (London: SCM, ²1936)

Foakes-Jackson, F. J., *The Acts of the Apostles*, MNTC (London: Hodder & Stoughton, 1931)

Furneaux, W. M., *The Acts of the Apostles: A Commentary for English Readers* (Oxford: Clarendon, 1912)

Grosheide, F. W., *De Handelingen der Apostelen*, I, II, CNT 5 (Amsterdam: van Bottenburg, 1942, 1948)

Grosheide, F. W., *De Handelingen der Apostelen*, KV (Kampen: Kok, 1950)

Hackett, H. B., *A Commentary on the Acts of the Apostles* (Philadelphia: American Baptist Publication Society, 1882)

Haenchen, E., *The Acts of the Apostles*, E.T. from KEK 5, ¹⁴1965 (Oxford: Blackwell, 1971)

Hanson, R. P. C., *The Acts of the Apostles*, NClarB (Oxford: Clarendon, 1967)

Hilgenfeld, A., *Acta Apostolorum graece et latine secundum antiquissimos testes* (Berlin: Reimer, 1899)

Holtzmann, H. J., *Die Apostelgeschichte*, Hand-Kommentar zum Neuen Testament I.2 (Tübingen: Mohr, ³1901)

Jacquier, E., *Les Actes des Apôtres*, ÉB (Paris: Lecoffre, ²1926)

Kelly, W., *An Exposition of the Acts of the Apostles* (London: Hammond, ³1952)

Knopf, R., *Die Apostelgeschichte*, SNT III (Göttingen: Vandenhoeck & Ruprecht, ³1917)

Knowling, R. J., "The Acts of the Apostles," *Expositor's Greek Testament*, ed. W. R. Nicoll, II (London: Hodder & Stoughton, 1900), pp. 1-554 (repr. Grand Rapids: Eerdmans, 1951)

Krodel, G.A., *Acts*, Augsburg Comm. (Minneapolis: Augsburg, 1986)

Lake, K., and Cadbury, H. J., *The Acts of the Apostles: English Translation and Commentary* = *Beginnings* I.4 (London: Macmillan, 1933)

Loisy, A., *Les Actes des Apôtres* (Paris: É. Nourry, 1920)

Lumby, J. R., *The Acts of the Apostles*, CBSC (Cambridge: University Press, 1882)

MacGregor, G. H. C., "The Acts of the Apostles," *IB* IX (New York/Nashville: Abingdon-Cokesbury, 1954), pp. 3-352.

Marshall, I. H., *The Acts of the Apostles*, TNTC (Leicester: Inter-Varsity Press/Grand Rapids: Eerdmans, 1980)

Meyer, H. A. W., *Critical and Exegetical Handbook to the Acts of the Apostles*, I, II, E.T. from KEK 3, ⁴1870 (Edinburgh: T. & T. Clark, 1877)

Munck, J., *The Acts of the Apostles*, AB 31 (Garden City, NY: Doubleday, 1967)

Neil, W., *The Acts of the Apostles*, NCB (London: Oliphants, 1973)

Packer, J. W., *The Acts of the Apostles*, CBCNEB (Cambridge: University Press, 1966)

Page, T. E., *The Acts of the Apostles: The Greek Text . . . with Explanatory Notes* (London: Macmillan, 1886)

Pesch, R., *Die Apostelgeschichte*, I, II, EKK (Neukirchen/Vluyn: Neukirchener, 1986)

Preuschen, E., *Die Apostelgeschichte*, HNT 4.1 (Tübingen: Mohr, 1913)

Rackham, R. B., *The Acts of the Apostles*, WC (London: Methuen, 1901)

Rendall, F., *The Acts of the Apostles in Greek and English with Notes* (London/ New York: Macmillan, 1897)

Roloff, J., *Die Apostelgeschichte*, NTD 5 (Göttingen: Vandenhoeck & Ruprecht, 1981)

Ropes, J. H., *The Text of Acts = Beginnings* I.3 (London: Macmillan, 1926)

Schille, G., *Die Apostelgeschichte des Lukas*, THKNT 5 (Berlin: Evangelische Verlagsanstalt, 1983)

Schlatter, A., *Die Apostelgeschichte*, ENT 4 (Stuttgart: Calwer Verlag, 1948)

Schneider, G., *Die Apostelgeschichte*, I, II, TKNT 5 (Freiburg/Basel/Wien: Herder, 1980, 1982)

Stählin, G., *Die Apostelgeschichte*, NTD 5 (Göttingen: Vandenhoeck & Ruprecht, 1962)

Steinmann, A., *Die Apostelgeschichte übersetzt und erklärt*, HSNT (Bonn: Hanstein, ⁴1934)

Strack, H. L., and Billerbeck, P., *Kommentar zum Neuen Testament aus Talmud und Midrasch*, II (Munich: Beck, ²1956), pp. 588-773

Walker, T., *The Acts of the Apostles* ([1910] Chicago: Moody Press, 1965)

Weiser, A., *Die Apostelgeschichte*, I, II, Ökumenischer Taschenbuch-Kommentar zum Neuen Testament 5.1, 2 (Gütersloh: Mohn/Würzburg: Echter Verlag, 1980, 1985)

Weiss, B., *Die Apostelgeschichte: Textkritische Untersuchungen und Textherstellung = TU* 9.3/4 (Leipzig: Hinrichs, 1893)

Wendt, H. H., *Die Apostelgeschichte*, KEK 3 (Göttingen: Vandenhoeck & Ruprecht, ⁹1913)

Wikenhauser, A., *Die Apostelgeschichte übersetzt und erklärt*, RNT 5 (Regensburg: Pustet, ³1956)

Williams, C. S. C., *The Acts of the Apostles*, BNTC (London: A. & C. Black/ New York: Harper, 1957)

Williams, D. J., *Acts*, GNC (San Francisco: Harper & Row, 1985)

Williams, R. R., *The Acts of the Apostles*, TBC (London: SCM, 1953)

Wilson, J. M., *The Acts of the Apostles: Translated from the Codex Bezae, with* an *Introduction on its Lucan Origin and Importance* (London: Rivingtons, 1877)

Zahn, T., *Die Apostelgeschichte des Lucas*, I, II, ZKNT (Leipzig: Deichert, ³1922, ³·⁴1927)

Zahn, T., *Die Urausgabe der Apostelgeschichte des Lukas*, FGNTK 9 (Leipzig: Deichert, 1916)

de Zwaan, J., *De Handelingen der Apostelen*, Het Nieuwe Testament (Groningen: Wolters, ²1932)

B. OTHER BOOKS

Abrahams, I., *Studies in Pharisaism and the Gospels*, I, II (Cambridge: University Press, 1917)

Barker, C. J., *The Acts of the Apostles: A Study in Interpretation* (London: Epworth, 1969)

Barrett, C. K., *Freedom and Obligation* (London: SPCK, 1985)

Barrett, C. K., *Luke the Historian in Recent Study* (London: Epworth, 1961)

Barrett, C. K., *New Testament Essays* (London: SPCK, 1972)

Barrett, C. K., *The Signs of an Apostle* (London: Epworth, 1971)

Baur, F. C., *The Church History of the First Three Centuries*, E.T., I, II (London/Edinburgh: Williams & Norgate, 1878, 1879)

Baur, F. C., *Paul: His Life and Works*, E.T., I, II (London/Edinburgh: Williams & Norgate, 1875, 1876)

Bernard, T. D., *The Progress of Doctrine in the New Testament* ([1864] London: Macmillan, ⁵1900)

Bishop, E. F. F., *Apostles of Palestine* (London: Lutterworth, 1958)

Black, M., *An Aramaic Approach to the Gospels and Acts* (Oxford: Clarendon Press, ³1967)

Blass, F., *Philology of the Gospels* (London: Macmillan, 1898)

Bornhäuser, K., *Studien zur Apostelgeschichte* (Gütersloh: Bertelsmann, 1924)

Brown, R. E., and Meier, J. P., *Antioch and Rome* (London: Chapman, 1983)

Brown, S., *The Origins of Christianity* (Oxford/New York: Oxford University Press, 1984)

Burchard, C., *Der dreizehnte Zeuge*, FRLANT 103 (Göttingen: Vandenhoeck & Ruprecht, 1970)

Burkitt, F. C., *Christian Beginnings* (London: University of London Press, 1924)

Cadbury, H. J., *The Book of Acts in History* (New York: Harper/London: A. & C. Black, 1955)

Cadbury, H. J., *The Making of Luke-Acts* ([1927] Naperville, IL: Allenson/London: SPCK, 1958)

Cadbury, H. J., *The Style and Literary Method of Luke*, 1. *The Diction of Luke and Acts*, HTS 6 (Cambridge, MA: Harvard University Press, 1920)

von Campenhausen, H., *Tradition and Life in the Church*, E.T. (London: Collins, 1968)

Cassidy, R. J., and Scharper, P. J., *Political Issues in Luke-Acts* (Maryknoll, NY: Orbis, 1983)

Chase, F. H., *The Credibility of the Book of the Acts of the Apostles* (London: Macmillan, 1902)

Clemen, C., *Die Apostelgeschichte im Lichte der neueren text-, quellen- und historisch-kritischen Forschungen* (Giessen: Töpelmann, 1905)

Conzelmann, H., *History of Primitive Christianity*, E.T. (London: Darton, Longman & Todd, 1973)

Conzelmann, H., *The Theology of St. Luke*, E.T. (New York: Harper/London: Faber, 1960)

Cullmann, O., *Christ and Time*, E.T. (London: SCM, 1951)

Cullmann, O., *The Early Church*, E.T. (London: SCM, 1956)

Cullmann, O., *Peter: Disciple–Apostle–Martyr*, E.T. (London: SCM, 1953)

Cullmann, O., *Salvation in History*, E.T., NTL (London: SCM, 1965)

Davies, W. D., *Jewish and Pauline Studies* (London: SPCK, 1984)

Davies, W. D., *Paul and Rabbinic Judaism* (London: SPCK, 1948, ²1958)

Deissmann, (G.) A., *Bible Studies*, E.T. (Edinburgh: T. & T. Clark, ²1903)

Deissmann, A., *Light from the Ancient East*, E.T. (London: Hodder & Stoughton, ²1927)

Deissmann, A., *Paul: A Study in Social and Religious History*, E.T. (London: Hodder & Stoughton, ²1926)

Dibelius, M., *Paul* (ed. W. G. Kümmel), E.T. (London: Longmans, 1953)

Dibelius, M., *Studies in the Acts of the Apostles*, E.T. (London: SCM, 1956)

Dietrich, W., *Das Petrusbild der lukanischen Schriften* (Stuttgart: Kohlhammer, 1972)

Dodd, C. H., *The Apostolic Preaching and its Developments* (London: Hodder & Stoughton, 1936, 1944)

Duncan, G. S., *St. Paul's Ephesian Ministry* (London: Hodder & Stoughton, 1929)

Dunn, J. D. G., *Baptism in the Holy Spirit*, SBT 2.15 (London: SCM, 1973)

Dunn, J. D. G., *Jesus and the Spirit*, NTL (London: SCM, 1975)

Dunn, J. D. G., *Unity and Diversity in the New Testament* (London: SCM, 1977)

Dupont, J., *Études sur les Actes des Apôtres*, LD 45 (Paris: du Cerf, 1967)

Dupont, J., *Nouvelles Études sur les Actes des Apôtres*, LD 118 (Paris: du Cerf, 1984)

Dupont, J., *The Sources of Acts*, E.T. (London: Darton, Longman & Todd, 1964)

Easton, B. S., *The Purpose of Acts* (1936) in *Early Christianity: The Purpose of Acts and Other Papers* (Greenwich, CT: Seabury, 1954)

Ehrhardt, A., *The Acts of the Apostles: Ten Lectures* (Manchester: University Press, 1969)

Ehrhardt, A., *The Framework of the New Testament Stories* (Manchester: University Press, 1964)

Ellis, E. E., *The Gospel of Luke*, NCB (Grand Rapids: Eerdmans/London: Oliphants, ²1974)

Epp, E. J., *The Theological Tendency of Codex Bezae in Acts*, SNTSM 3 (Cambridge: University Press, 1966)

Féret, H.-M., *Pierre et Paul à Antioche et à Jérusalem* (Paris: du Cerf, 1955)

Field, F., *Notes on the Translation of the New Testament* (Cambridge: University Press, 1899)

Filson, F. V., *Three Crucial Decades* (London: Epworth, 1964)

Finkelstein, L., *The Pharisees*, I, II (New York: Jewish Publication Society of America, 1938)

Fitzmyer, J. A., *The Gospel according to Luke*, I, II, AB (Garden City, NY: Doubleday, 1981, 1985)

Flender, H., *St. Luke: Theologian of Redemptive History*, E.T. (London: SPCK/Philadelphia: Fortress, 1967)

Foakes-Jackson, F. J., and Lake, K. (eds.), *The Beginnings of Christianity*, Part I, vols. 1-5 (London: Macmillan, 1920-33)

Foakes-Jackson, F. J., *The Life of St. Paul* (London: Jonathan Cape, 1927)

Foakes-Jackson, F. J., *Peter: Prince of Apostles* (London: Hodder & Stoughton, 1927)

Gasque, W. W., *A History of the Criticism of the Acts of the Apostles*, BGBE 17 (Tübingen: Mohr, 1975)

Gasque, W. W., and Martin, R. P. (eds.), *Apostolic History and the Gospel* (Exeter: Paternoster/Grand Rapids: Eerdmans, 1970)

Goguel, M., *La naissance du christianisme* (Paris: Payot, 1946)

Goguel, M., *L'église primitive* (Paris: Payot, 1947)

Goulder, M. D., *Type and History in Acts* (London: SPCK, 1964)

Harnack, A., *The Acts of the Apostles*, E.T. (London: Williams and Norgate, 1909)

Harnack, A., *Date of the Acts and of the Synoptic Gospels*, E.T. (London: Williams & Norgate, 1911)

Harnack, A., *Luke the Physician*, E.T. (London: Williams & Norgate, 1907)

Harnack, A., *Mission and Expansion of Christianity*, E.T., I, II (London: Williams & Norgate, ²1908)

Hengel, M., *Acts and the History of Earliest Christianity*, E.T. (London: SCM, 1979)

Hengel, M., *Between Jesus and Paul*, E.T. (London: SCM, 1983)

Hobart, W. K., *The Medical Language of St. Luke* (Dublin: Hodges, Figgis/London: Longmans, Green, 1882)

Hock, R. F., *The Social Context of Paul's Ministry: Tentmaking and Discipleship* (Philadelphia: Fortress, 1980)

Holtz, T., *Untersuchungen über die alttestamentlichen Zitate bei Lukas = TU* 104 (Berlin: Akademie-Verlag, 1968)

Hort, F. J. A., *The Christian Ecclesia* (London: Macmillan, 1897)

Hort, F. J. A., *Judaistic Christianity* (London: Macmillan, 1894)

Hull, J. H. E., *The Holy Spirit in the Acts of the Apostles* (London: Lutterworth, 1967)

Hunter, A. M., *Paul and his Predecessors* (London: SCM, ²1961)

Jervell, J., *Luke and the People of God* (Minneapolis: Augsburg, 1972)

Jervell, J., *The Unknown Paul* (Minneapolis: Augsburg, 1984)

Jewett, R., *Dating Paul's Life/A Chronology of Paul's Life* (London: SCM/Philadelphia: Fortress, 1979)

Jones, A. H. M., *Cities of the Eastern Roman Provinces* (Oxford: Clarendon Press, 1937)

Jones, A. H. M., *The Herods of Judaea* (Oxford: Clarendon Press, 1938)

Jones, A. H. M., *Studies in Roman Government and Law* (Oxford: Blackwell, 1960)

Judge, E. A., *The Social Pattern of Christian Groups in the First Century* (London: Tyndale Press, 1960)

Juel, D., *Luke-Acts* (London: SCM, 1984)

Keck, L. E., and Martyn, J. L. (eds.), *Studies in Luke-Acts* (Nashville/New York: Abingdon, 1966)

Kennedy, G. A., *The Art of Rhetoric in the Roman World* (Princeton: University Press, 1972)

Kenyon, F. G., *The Western Text in the Gospels and Acts* (London: British Academy, 1939)

Kertelge, K. (ed.), *Paulus in den neutestamentlichen Spätschriften*, QD 89 (Freiburg: Herder, 1981)

Klausner, J., *From Jesus to Paul*, E.T. (London: Allen & Unwin, 1944)

Klostermann, A., *Probleme im Aposteltexte* (Gotha: Perthes, 1883)

Knox, J., *Chapters in a Life of Paul* (New York/Nashville: Abingdon-Cokesbury, 1950)

Knox, J., *Marcion and the New Testament* (Chicago: University of Chicago Press, 1942)

Knox, W. L., *The Acts of the Apostles* (Cambridge: University Press, 1948)

Knox, W. L., *Some Hellenistic Elements in Primitive Christianity* (London: British Academy/Oxford University Press, 1944)

Knox, W. L., *St. Paul and the Church of the Gentiles* (Cambridge: University Press, 1939)

Knox, W. L., *St. Paul and the Church of Jerusalem* (Cambridge: University Press, 1925)

Kremer, J. (ed.), *Les Actes des Apôtres: Traditions, rédaction, théologie*, BETL 48 (Gembloux: Duculot/Leuven: University Press, 1979)

Krenkel, M., *Beiträge zur Aufhellung der Geschichte und der Briefe des Apostels Paulus* (Braunschweig: Schwetschke, 1890)

Krenkel, M., *Josephus und Lucas* (Leipzig: Haessel, 1894)

Lake, K., *The Earlier Epistles of St. Paul* (London: Rivingtons, 1911)

Lampe, G. W. H., *The Seal of the Spirit* (London: Longmans, Green, 1951)

Lampe, G. W. H., *St. Luke and the Church of Jerusalem* (London: Athlone Press, 1969)

Lekebusch, E., *Die Composition und Entstehung der Apostelgeschichte* (Gotha: Perthes, 1854)

Lietzmann, H., *The Beginnings of the Christian Church*, E.T. (London: Lutterworth, ²1949)

Lightfoot, J. B., *Biblical Essays* (London: Macmillan, 1893)

Lightfoot, J. B., *Dissertations on the Apostolic Age* (London: Macmillan, 1892)

Lohmeyer, E., *Galiläa und Jerusalem*, FRLANT 52 (Göttingen: Vandenhoeck & Ruprecht, 1936)

Löning, K., *Die Saulustradition in der Apostelgeschichte* (Münster: Aschendorff, 1973)

Loyd, P., *The Holy Spirit in the Acts* (London: Mowbray, 1952)

Lüdemann, G., *Paul: Apostle to the Gentiles*, I. *Studies in Chronology*, E.T. (London: SCM, 1984)

Lüdemann, G., *Paulus der Heidenapostel*, II. *Antipaulinismus im frühen Christentum*, FRLANT 130 (Göttingen: Vandenhoeck & Ruprecht, 1983)

McLachlan, H., *St. Luke: the Man and his Work* (Manchester: University Press, 1920)

Maddox, R., *The Purpose of Luke-Acts* (Edinburgh: T. & T. Clark, 1982)

Manson, T. W., *Studies in the Gospels and Epistles* (Manchester: University Press, 1962)

Marshall, I. H., *The Gospel of Luke*, NIGTC (Grand Rapids: Eerdmans/Exeter: Paternoster, 1979)

Marshall, I. H., *Luke: Historian and Theologian* (Exeter: Paternoster, 1970)

Mattill, A. J., and Mattill, M. B., *A Classified Bibliography of Literature on the Acts of the Apostles*, NTTS 7 (Leiden: Brill, 1966)

Meyer, E., *Ursprung und Anfänge des Christentums*, I-III (Stuttgart/Berlin: Cotta, 1921-23)

Momigliano, A., *Claudius: The Emperor and his Achievement*, E.T. (Cambridge: Heffer, ²1961)

Morgenthaler, R., *Die lukanische Geschichtsschreibung als Zeugnis: Gestalt und Gehalt der Kunst des Lukas*, I, II, ATANT 14, 15 (Zürich: Zwingli Verlag, 1948)

Morton, A. Q., and MacGregor, G. H. C., *The Structure of Luke and Acts* (London: Hodder & Stoughton, 1964)

Munck, J., *Paul and the Salvation of Mankind*, E.T. (London: SCM, 1959)

Nock, A. D., *Early Gentile Christianity and its Hellenistic Background*, Harper Torchbooks (New York: Harper, 1964)

Nock, A. D., *St. Paul*, HUL (London: Lutterworth, 1938)

Norden, E., *Agnostos Theos: Untersuchungen zur Formengeschichte religiöser Rede* (Leipzig/Berlin: Teubner, 1913, ²1929)

Ogg, G., *The Chronology of the Life of Paul* (London: Epworth, 1968)

O'Neill, J. C., *The Theology of Acts in its Historical Setting* (London: SPCK, ²1970)

O'Toole, R. F., *The Christological Climax of Paul's Defense*, AnBib 78 (Rome: Biblical Institute Press, 1978)

Overbeck, F., Introduction to W. M. L. de Wette, *Kurze Erklärung der Apostelgeschichte, 4te Auflage, bearbeitet und stark erweitert von Frz. Overbeck* (Leipzig: Hirzel, 1870); E.T. of the Introduction appears as preface to E. Zeller, *The Contents and Origin of the Acts of the Apostles*, E.T. (London/Edinburgh: Williams & Norgate, 1875)

Paley, W., *Horae Paulinae* (London: J. Davis, 1790, etc.)

Pallis, A., *Notes on St. Luke and the Acts* (London: H. Milford, 1928)

Pierson, A. T., *The Acts of the Holy Spirit* (London: Morgan & Scott, ²1913)

Plümacher, E., *Lukas als hellenistischer Schriftsteller: Studien zur Apostelgeschichte*, SUNT 9 (Göttingen: Vandenhoeck & Ruprecht, 1972)

Ramsay, W. M., *The Bearing of Recent Discovery on the Trustworthiness of the New Testament* (London: Hodder & Stoughton, 1915)

Ramsay, W. M., *The Church in the Roman Empire to A.D. 170* (London: Hodder & Stoughton, [4]1895)

Ramsay, W. M., *The Cities and Bishoprics of Phrygia*, I, II (Oxford: Clarendon Press, 1895, 1897)

Ramsay, W. M., *The Cities of St. Paul* (London: Hodder & Stoughton, 1907)

Ramsay, W. M., *Historical Geography of Asia Minor* (London: John Murray, 1890; repr. Amsterdam: A. M. Hakkert, 1962)

Ramsay, W. M., *Luke the Physician and Other Studies in the History of Religion* (London: Hodder & Stoughton, 1908)

Ramsay, W. M., *Pauline and Other Studies* (London: Hodder & Stoughton, 1906)

Ramsay, W. M., *Pictures of the Apostolic Church: Its Life and Teaching* (London: Hodder & Stoughton, 1910)

Ramsay, W. M., *St. Paul the Traveller and the Roman Citizen* (London: Hodder & Stoughton, 1895, [14]1920)

Ramsay, W. M., *The Teaching of Paul in Terms of the Present Day* (London: Hodder & Stoughton, [2]1914)

Reicke, B., *Glaube und Leben der Urgemeinde*, ATANT 32 (Zürich: Zwingli Verlag, 1957)

Reitzenstein, R., *Die hellenistischen Wundererzählungen* (Leipzig: Teubner, 1906)

Robinson, J. A. T., *Redating the New Testament* (London: SCM, 1976)

Robinson, J. A. T., *Twelve New Testament Studies*, SBT 34 (London: SCM, 1962)

Ropes, J. H., *The Apostolic Age in the Light of Modern Criticism* (New York: Scribner/London: Hodder & Stoughton, 1906)

Safrai, S., and Stern, M. (eds.), *The Jewish People in the First Century*, I, II, CRINT 1 (Assen: Van Gorcum, 1974, 1976)

Sahlin, H., *Der Messias und das Gottesvolk*, ASNU 12 (Uppsala: Almquist & Wiksells, 1945)

Sanders, E. P., *Paul and Palestinian Judaism* (Philadelphia: Fortress/London: SCM, 1977)

Sanders, E. P., *Paul, the Law and the Jewish People* (Philadelphia: Fortress, 1983)

Sanders, J. T., *The Jews in Luke-Acts* (London: SCM, 1987)

Schneckenburger, M., *Über den Zweck der Apostelgeschichte* (Bern: Fisher, 1841)

Schoeps, H.-J., *Aus frühchristlicher Zeit* (Tübingen: Mohr, 1950)

Schoeps, H.-J., *Paul: The Theology of the Apostle in the Light of Jewish Religious History*, E.T. (London: Lutterworth, 1961)

Schoeps, H.-J., *Theologie und Geschichte des Judenchristentums* (Tübingen: Mohr, 1949)

Schürer, E., *The History of the Jewish People in the Age of Jesus Christ*, revised English edition, I-III (Edinburgh: T. & T. Clark, 1973-86)

Schütz, R., *Apostel und Jünger* (Giessen: Töpelmann, 1921)

Sherwin-White, A. N., *Roman Society and Roman Law in the New Testament* (Oxford: Clarendon Press, 1963)

Simon, M., *St. Stephen and the Hellenists in the Primitive Church* (New York/ London: Longmans, Green, 1958)

Simon, M., *Verus Israel* (Paris: Boccard, 1948, ²1964), E.T. (Oxford: Oxford University Press, 1986)

Smallwood, E. M., *The Jews under Roman Rule*, SJLA 20 (Leiden: Brill, 1976)

Smith, J., *The Voyage and Shipwreck of St. Paul* (London: Longmans, Green, 1848, ⁴1880)

Spitta, F., *Die Apostelgeschichte: ihre Quellen und derer geschichtlicher Wert* (Halle: Waisenhaus, 1891)

Still, J. I., *St. Paul on Trial* (London: SCM, 1923)

Stonehouse, N. B., *Paul before the Areopagus and Other New Testament Studies* (London: Tyndale Press/Grand Rapids: Eerdmans, 1957)

Stonehouse, N. B., *The Witness of Luke to Christ* (Grand Rapids: Eerdmans, 1951)

Suhl, A., *Paulus und seine Briefe: Ein Beitrag zur paulinischen Chronologie* (Gütersloh: Mohn, 1975)

Talbert, C. H., *Literary Patterns, Theological Themes and the Genre of Luke-Acts* (Missoula, MT: Scholars Press, 1974)

Talbert, C. H. (ed.), *Perspectives on Luke-Acts* (Edinburgh: T. & T. Clark, 1978)

Torrey, C. C., *The Composition and Date of Acts*, HTS 1 (Cambridge, MA: Harvard University Press, 1916)

Torrey, C. C., *Documents of the Primitive Church* (New York: Harper, 1941)

Trocmé, É., *Le "livre des Actes" et l'Histoire* (Paris: Presses Universitaires de France, 1957)

van Unnik, W. C., *Tarsus or Jerusalem: The City of Paul's Youth*, E.T. (London: Epworth, 1962)

Waszink, J. H., van Unnik, W. C., and de Beus, C. (eds.), *Het oudste Christendom en die antieke Cultuur*, I, II (Haarlem: Willink & Zoon, 1951)

Weiss, J., *Earliest Christianity* (1917), I, II, E.T., Harper Torchbooks (New York: Harper, 1959)

Weiss, J., *Über die Absicht und den literarischen Charakter der Apostelgeschichte* (Göttingen: Vandenhoeck & Ruprecht, 1897)

Wellhausen, J., *Kritische Analyse der Apostelgeschichte*, AGG NF 15 (1914) (Berlin: Weidemann, 1914)

Wellhausen, J., *Noten zur Apostelgeschichte*, NGG, phil.-hist. Kl. (1907), pp. 1-21

Wikenhauser, A., *Die Apostelgeschichte und ihr Geschichtswert* (Münster: Aschendorff, 1921)

Wilckens, U., *Die Missionsreden der Apostelgeschichte*, WMANT 5.2 (Neukirchen/Vluyn: Neukirchener Verlag, ²1963)

Wilcox, M., *The Semitisms of Acts* (Oxford: Clarendon Press, 1965)

Willi, H., *Am Urquell: Die urchristliche Gemeinde in Jerusalem* (Basel: Gaiser, 1945)

Williams, C. S. C., *Alterations to the Text of the Synoptic Gospels and Acts* (Oxford: Blackwell, 1951)

Wilson, J. M., *The Origin and Aim of the Acts of the Apostles . . . with an Appendix on Codex Bezae* (London: Macmillan, 1912)

Wilson, S. G., *The Gentiles and the Gentile Mission in Luke-Acts,* SNTSM 23 (Cambridge: University Press, 1973)

Wilson, S. G. *Luke and the Law,* SNTSM 50 (Cambridge: University Press, 1983)

Yoder, J. D., *Concordance to the Distinctive Greek Text of Codex Bezae,* NTTS 2 (Leiden: Brill, 1961)

Zeller, E., *The Contents and Origin of the Acts of the Apostles, Critically Investigated,* I, II, E.T. (London/Edinburgh: Williams & Norgate, 1875, 1876) (See also Overbeck, above.)

Text, Exposition, and Notes

ACTS 1

I. THE BIRTH OF THE CHURCH (1:1–5:42)

A. THE FORTY DAYS AND AFTER (1:1-26)

The first chapter of Acts provides a brief introduction to the narrative of the Pentecostal outpouring of the Spirit and its sequel. It deals with two topics: the risen Lord's conversations with his disciples on the eve of his ascension, and the co-opting of Matthias to fill the vacancy in the apostolate caused by the treachery and death of Judas Iscariot.

1. Prologue (1:1-3)

1 *The first volume which I wrote,[1] Theophilus, was concerned with all that Jesus began to do and teach*
2 *until the day he was taken up, after he had given his commandment through the Holy Spirit to the apostles whom he had chosen.[2]*
3 *It was to them that he presented himself alive after his passion by many compelling tokens: he appeared to them over a period of forty days and spoke to them about the kingdom of God.*

1-2 Theophilus, to whom the second volume of Luke's history is here dedicated, is similarly addressed at the beginning of the first volume, where

---

1. The "I" of "I wrote" (ἐποιησάμην) is identical with the "me" of "it seemed good to me" (ἔδοξε κἀμοί) in Luke 1:3, and is most probably included in the "we" of the "we" narratives of Acts (cf. p.7). See H. J. Cadbury, "'We' and 'I' Passages in Luke-Acts," *NTS* 3 (1956-57), pp. 128-32.
2. The original Western text of v. 2 probably ran: "until the day in which he by the Holy Spirit gave his commandment to the apostles whom he had chosen, and bade them preach the gospel." The omission of "he was taken up" (Gk. ἀνελήμφθη) is noteworthy, because the corresponding words in Luke 24:51, "and was carried up into heaven" (Gk. καὶ ἀνεφέρετο εἰς τὸν οὐρανόν), are missing from the Western text (they are among those phrases at the end of Luke which Westcott and Hort bracketed as "Western non-interpolations").

he receives the title "most excellent" (Luke 1:3). There has been much indecisive speculation about him. Some have even suggested that he was no particular individual, but that the name Theophilus—which means "dear to God"—is used here to designate the "Christian reader." The use of the honorific title "most excellent" makes this improbable. We cannot be sure, however, whether the title "most excellent" is bestowed on Theophilus in a technical sense, indicating his rank, or is given him by way of courtesy.[3] Nor is much to be gained by pondering the omission of the title in Acts, as when it is suggested that Theophilus had become a Christian since he received the "first volume" and therefore would no longer expect worldly titles of rank or honor from a fellow-Christian.

Another suggestion is that the name Theophilus masks the identity of some well-known person, such as Titus Flavius Clemens, cousin of the Emperor Domitian.[4] Even this is unlikely: Theophilus was a perfectly ordinary personal name, attested from the third century B.C. onward. Despite the evident apologetic motive in Luke's history, it is equally unlikely that Theophilus was the advocate briefed for Paul's defense at the hearing of his appeal to Caesar.[5] It is quite probable that Theophilus was a representative member of the intelligent middle-class public at Rome whom Luke wished to win over to a less prejudiced and more favorable opinion of Christianity than that which was current among them. This much is certain from the prologue to Luke's first volume (which serves also as a prologue to the twofold work): that Theophilus had already learned something about the rise and progress of Christianity, and Luke's aim was to put him in possession of more accurate information than he already had.[6]

Such dedications were common form in contemporary literary cir-

---

3. Gk. κράτιστος might designate a member of the Roman equestrian order (representing Lat. *egregius*) or it might be a courtesy title (corresponding to Lat. *optimus*). Cf. the later occurrences of the word in Acts, where it is a courtesy title given to the Roman governors of Judaea—Felix (23:26; 24:3) and Festus (26:25).

4. Cf. B. H. Streeter, *The Four Gospels* (London, 1924), pp. 534-39.

5. Cf. C. A. Heumann, "Dissertatio de Theophilo, cui Lucas historiam sacram inscripsit," *Bibliotheca Historico-Philologico-Theologica,* Cl. 4 (Amsterdam, 1721), pp. 483-505; M. V. Aberle, "Exegetische Studien. 1. Ueber den Zweck der Apostelgeschichte," *TQ* 37 (1955), pp. 173-236; D. Plooij, "The Work of St. Luke: A Historical Apology for Pauline Preaching before the Roman Court," *Exp.* 8,8 (1914), pp. 511-23; "Again: The Work of St. Luke," *Exp.* 8,13 (1917), pp. 108-24; J. I. Still, *St. Paul on Trial* (London, 1923), pp. 84-98. More generally, G. S. Duncan suggests that Luke's narrative was "designed to supply information which it was hoped might reach those who would decide the apostle's fate at Rome" (*St. Paul's Ephesian Ministry* [London, 1929], p. 97).

6. On the significance of Luke 1:1-4 cf. H. J. Cadbury, "Commentary on the Preface of Luke," *Beginnings* II, pp. 489-510; N. B. Stonehouse, *The Witness of Luke to Christ* (London, 1951), pp. 24-45; I. H. Marshall, *The Gospel of Luke* (Grand Rapids/ Exeter, 1978), pp. 39-44; L. C. A. Alexander, "Luke's Preface in the Context of Greek Preface-Writing," *NovT* 28 (1986), pp. 48-74. See p. 6 above.

cles. For example, Josephus dedicated his *Jewish Antiquities*, his *Autobiography*, and his two volumes *Against Apion* to a patron named Epaphroditus. At the beginning of the first volume *Against Apion*, he addresses him as "Epaphroditus, most excellent of men";[7] and he introduces the second volume of the same work with the words: "By means of the former volume, my most honored Epaphroditus,[8] I have demonstrated our antiquity." These opening words are remarkably similar to those of Luke's second volume.

Luke begins with a brief reference to his former[9] volume as an account of "all that Jesus began to do and teach until the day he was taken up"—or, if we follow the Western text, "until the day when, by the Holy Spirit, he commissioned the apostles whom he had chosen, and charged them to proclaim the gospel." This exactly summarizes the scope of the Gospel of Luke from 4:1 onward: the commissioning of the apostles is recorded in Luke 24:44-49. The implication of Luke's words is that his second volume will be an account of what Jesus *continued*[10] to do and teach after his ascension—no longer in visible presence on earth but by his Spirit in his followers. The expression "to do and teach" well sums up the twofold subject matter of all the canonical Gospels: they all record *The Work and Words of Jesus* (to quote the title of one presentation of their subject matter).[11]

It was "through the Holy Spirit" that Jesus gave his parting charge to his apostles. Almost invariably[12] Luke restricts the designation "apostles" to the twelve men whom Jesus chose at an early stage in his ministry (Luke 6:13-16), except that Judas Iscariot was replaced by Matthias (as we are told later in this chapter). His charge to them made them the chief heralds of the good news which he had brought. The extension of the good news in the power of the Spirit is the theme of Acts. At his baptism Jesus had been "anointed" with the Holy Spirit and power (10:38), and more recently, in

7. κράτιστε ἀνδρῶν Ἐπαφρόδιτε (*Ap.* 1.1).

8. τιμιώτατέ μοι Ἐπαφρόδιτε (*Ap.* 2.1).

9. The word "former" in v. 1 renders Gk. πρῶτος, which literally means "first." W. M. Ramsay presses the classical force of πρῶτος here and concludes that Luke contemplated a work of three volumes (*St. Paul the Traveller and the Roman Citizen* [London, 141920], pp. 27-28, 309). Cf. T. Zahn, *Die Apostelgeschichte des Lucas*, I (Leipzig/Erlangen, 31922), pp. 16-18. More recently some scholars have envisaged the Pastoral Epistles as constituting the third part of Luke's work; cf. S. G. Wilson, *Luke and the Pastoral Epistles* (London, 1979); J. D. Quinn, "The Last Volume of Luke: The Relation of Luke-Acts to the Pastoral Epistles," in *Perspectives on Luke-Acts*, ed. C. H. Talbert (Edinburgh, 1978), pp. 62-75. But in Hellenistic Greek πρότερος, the word which strictly means the "former" of two, was largely displaced by πρῶτος. Luke never uses πρότερος, and it occurs very rarely in the vernacular papyri.

10. This implies that the verb "began" in v. 1 carries a certain emphasis and is not to be regarded merely as a semitizing auxiliary.

11. A. M. Hunter, *The Work and Words of Jesus* (London, 1950, 21973).

12. For an exception see 14:4, 14, with comments.

Paul's words, he had been "designated Son of God in power, according to the Spirit of holiness, by his resurrection from the dead" (Rom. 1:4). In the Johannine account of the commission laid on his disciples by the risen Christ, he indicated the power by which they were to carry out their commission when he "breathed into them" and said, "Receive the Holy Spirit" (John 20:22).[13] Luke makes it plain that it is by the power of that same Spirit that all the apostolic acts which he goes on to narrate were performed, so much so that some have suggested, as a theologically more appropriate title for his second volume, *The Acts of the Holy Spirit*.[14]

3 Over a period of forty days between his resurrection and ascension Jesus appeared at intervals to his apostles and other followers in a manner which could leave no doubt in their minds that he was really alive again, risen from the dead. The most primitive and comprehensive list of these appearances is that given by Paul in 1 Cor. 15:5-7, although the Gospel narratives indicate that even Paul's list is not exhaustive. In both parts of Luke's work the resurrection appearances are confined to Jerusalem and its neighborhood.[15]

What did Jesus teach them during those days? Many Gnostic schools which flourished in the second century and later claimed that he gave them certain esoteric teaching, not recorded in the canonical literature of the catholic church, of which they themselves were now the custodians and interpreters. Within the frontiers of Christian orthodoxy there was one line of tradition which represented him as giving the apostles instructions about church order.[16] But Luke declares that he continued to instruct them on the

13. Gk. ἐνεφύσησεν, the same verb as is used in Gen. 2:7 LXX of the Creator's breathing into Adam's nostrils the breath of life (cf. also Ezek. 37:9). The relation of the insufflation (as the act of Christ in John 20:22 is called) to the outpouring of the Spirit recorded in Acts 2:1-4 is an interesting critical and theological question. It is a relevant point that Luke appears generally to think of the Spirit as coming with external manifestations of power, whereas the incident recorded by John is marked by none of the visible and audible phenomena experienced on the day of Pentecost. "What John records is no mere anticipation of Pentecost but a real impartation of the Spirit for the purpose specified. The Pentecostal outpouring of the Spirit was more public, and involved the birth of the Spirit-indwelt community, the church of the new age" (F. F. Bruce, *The Gospel of John* [Grand Rapids/Basingstoke, 1983], p. 397).

14. Cf. J. A. Bengel, *Gnomon Novi Testamenti* ([Tübingen, 1742] London, ³1862), p. 389 on Acts 1:1 (the acts of the Holy Spirit rather than of the apostles, as the former volume contains the acts of Jesus Christ); A. T. Pierson, *The Acts of the Holy Spirit* (London, ²1913).

15. See H. von Campenhausen, *Tradition and Life in the Church*, E.T. (London, 1968), pp. 42-89; also S. H. Hooke, *The Resurrection of Jesus* (London, 1967); R. H. Fuller, *The Formation of the Resurrection Narratives* (London, 1971); J. W. Wenham, *Easter Enigma* (Exeter, 1984).

16. The full title of the early second-century manual called the *Didachē*—"The Teaching of the Lord through the Twelve Apostles to the Gentiles"—bears some such implication. The fourth-century Syriac manual, *The Testament of our Lord*, claims explicitly to convey Jesus' own directions on church order given to the apostles before his

same subjects as had formed the burden of his teaching before his passion—things relating to the kingdom of God.

From the earliest times in Israel, God was acknowledged as king (cf. Ex. 15:18). His kingship is universal (Ps. 103:19), but is manifested most clearly where men and women recognize it in practice by doing his will. In Old Testament times his kingship was specially manifested on earth in the nation of Israel: to this nation he made known his will and he called it into covenant relationship with himself (cf. Ps. 147:20). When human kings arose over Israel, they were regarded as vicegerents of the divine King, representing his sovereignty on earth. With the fall of the monarchy and the end of national independence, there arose a new conception of the kingdom of God as destined to be revealed on earth in its fullness at a later date (cf. Dan. 2:44; 7:13-14). It is in the light of this later conception that we should understand the New Testament teaching about the kingdom of God. Jesus inaugurates the kingdom: it "drew near" with the inception of his public ministry (cf. Mark 1:14-15) and was released in power by his death and exaltation (cf. Mark 9:1). The things relating to the kingdom of God which form the theme of his postresurrection teaching at the beginning of Acts are identical with "the things relating to the Lord Jesus Christ" which form the theme of Paul's teaching in Rome at the end of the book (28:31). When they told the story of Jesus, the apostles proclaimed the good news of the kingdom of God—the same good news as Jesus himself had announced earlier, but now given effective fulfilment by the saving events of his passion and triumph. It may reasonably be concluded that the teaching about the kingdom of God given to the apostles during the forty days was calculated to make plain to them the bearing of these saving events on the message of the kingdom.

Luke supplies one sample of this teaching toward the end of his Gospel, where he shows the risen Lord opening his disciples' minds to understand the scriptures: "Thus it is written, that the Christ should suffer and on the third day rise from the dead, and that repentance and forgiveness of sins should be preached in his name to all nations, beginning from Jerusalem" (Luke 24:45-47). "The kingdom of God is conceived as coming in the events of the life, death and resurrection of Jesus, and to proclaim these facts, in their proper setting, is to preach the Gospel of the Kingdom of God."[17] These words of C. H. Dodd may be adopted with one qualification:

---

ascension. The Coptic work called *Pistis Sophia,* a product of Valentinian Gnosticism, claims to record revelations made by Jesus to his disciples eleven years after his resurrection, not over a period of merely forty days.

17. C. H. Dodd, *The Apostolic Preaching and its Developments* (London, 1936), pp. 46-47. Dodd believed that the teaching of Jesus and the primitive apostolic preaching presented a completely "realized" eschatology; cf. also his *The Parables of the Kingdom* (London, 1935); *The Coming of Christ* (Cambridge, 1952).

when the apostles proclaimed the good news, they did not stop short at the resurrection and exaltation of Christ, but went on to speak of one further event which would consummate the saving series. Peter told the household of Cornelius how Christ had charged his apostles "to preach to the people and testify that he is the one ordained by God as judge of the living and the dead" (10:42). Paul told the Areopagites at Athens that God "has set a day on which he is going to judge the world in righteousness, by a man whom he has appointed, and of this he has provided a pledge to all, by raising him from the dead" (17:31). This judgment of the world coincides, in the apostolic preaching, with the parousia of Christ, the final and perfect manifestation of the divine kingdom, when every knee will bow at his name and every tongue confess him as Lord (Phil. 2:10-11), when God's will shall be done on earth as it is in heaven (Matt. 6:10). At Christ's first coming the age to come invaded this present age; at his coming in glory the age to come will have altogether superseded this present age.[18] Between the two comings the two ages overlap; the people of Christ live temporally in this present age while spiritually they belong to the heavenly kingdom and enjoy by anticipation the life of the age to come. Biblical eschatology is largely, but not completely, "realized"; there remains a future element, to become actual at the parousia. A balanced account of the New Testament presentation of the kingdom of God requires that due regard be paid to this future element as well as to those which have been realized.[19]

2. The Apostles' Commission (1:4-8)

4 *While he was eating with them[20] he commanded them not to leave Jerusalem but wait for what the Father had promised. "About this," he said, "you have heard me speak.*
5 *For John indeed baptized with water, but you will be baptized with the Holy Spirit in a few days' time."*

---

18. O. Cullmann suggests that the Second Advent bears a relation to "the Christ-event at the mid-point" of history comparable to that which the Victory Day celebrations bear to the decisive battle in a war (*Christ and Time,* E.T. [London, 1951], pp. 139-43).
19. On this subject see *(inter alia)* R. Otto, *The Kingdom of God and the Son of Man,* E.T. (London, 1943); G. Vos, *The Kingdom and the Church* (Grand Rapids, [2]1951); H. N. Ridderbos, *The Coming of the Kingdom,* E.T. (Philadelphia, 1962); R. Schnackenburg, *God's Rule and Kingdom,* E.T. (Edinburgh/London, 1963); G. Lundström, *The Kingdom of God in the Teaching of Jesus,* E.T. (Edinburgh, 1963); N. Perrin, *The Kingdom of God in the Teaching of Jesus* (London, 1963); G. E. Ladd, *The Presence of the Future* (Grand Rapids, 1974); J. Gray, *The Biblical Doctrine of the Reign of God* (Edinburgh, 1979); B. D. Chilton (ed.), *The Kingdom of God in the Teaching of Jesus* (London, 1985); G. R. Beasley-Murray, *Jesus and the Kingdom of God* (Grand Rapids/Exeter, 1986).
20. Gk. συναλιζόμενος, literally "eating salt (ἅλς) with" (this sense is borne out by the Latin, Syriac, and Bohairic Coptic versions). Less probably it is a popular spelling of συναυλιζόμενος, "lodging with."

6 *When they had come together, then, they put this question to him: "Is this the time, Lord, when you are about to restore the kingdom to Israel?"*

7 *"It is not for you,"* he replied, *"to learn[21] about times or seasons which the Father has reserved under his own control.[22]*

8 *But you will receive power when the Holy Spirit has come on you, and you will be my witnesses in Jerusalem, and in all Judaea and Samaria, and to the end of the earth."*

4 That the risen Christ ate in the presence of his disciples when he appeared to them is stated explicitly in Luke 24:42-43 (cf. Acts 10:41). Plainly his resurrection body had no need of material food and drink for its sustenance. But Luke may imply that he took food in the company of his disciples, not for any personal need of his own, but in order to convince them that he was really present with them and that they were seeing no phantom. There may also be a hint that what he shared with them was a eucharistic meal, a token that the new age had dawned, comparable to his self-disclosure at Emmaus "in the breaking of the bread" (Luke 24:30-31, 35).[23]

In the course of these resurrection appearances, Jesus instructed the apostles not to leave Jerusalem until the Father fulfilled his promise to them and they were "clothed with power from on high" (to quote from the parallel narrative of Luke 24:49). He had already told them, he reminded them, of this promised gift. If we ask when and where he had told them of it, the Fourth Evangelist will give us an answer: it was on the night of his betrayal, in the upper room in Jerusalem, after they had celebrated the Last Supper together, before they left the house to cross the Kidron valley and spend the remaining hours on the slope of Olivet. Certainly we have no account of a previous reference by Jesus to the promised Spirit which fits the present allusion so well as the five well-known passages in John 14–16. And it is particularly noteworthy "that the emphasis of these five passages is precisely that which underlies the conception of the Spirit in Acts 1–15."[24]

21. The original Western reading was probably "no one can learn" (οὐδεὶς δύναται γνῶναι); cf. T. Zahn, *Die Urausgabe der Apostelgeschichte* (Leipzig, 1916), p. 241.

22. Or "which the Father has fixed by his own authority" (cf. 17:26 for a similar idea).

23. See I. H. Marshall, *The Gospel of Luke*, pp. 898, 903; *Last Supper and Lord's Supper* (Exeter, 1980), pp. 124-26.

24. W. F. Lofthouse, "The Holy Spirit in the Acts and the Fourth Gospel," *ExT* 52 (1940-41), p. 336. The five passages are John 14:15-17, 26; 15:26-27; 16:7-10, 12-15 (see W. F. Howard, *The Fourth Gospel in Recent Criticism and Interpretation* [London, ⁴1955], pp. 226-27; *Christianity according to St. John* [London, 1943], pp. 71-80). As for Lukan antecedents, in addition to John's prophecy in Luke 3:16 there is Jesus' promise in Luke 11:13.

5 This promise, moreover, was foreshadowed by the ministry of John the Baptist.[25] To those who came to receive the baptism of repentance at his hands John had said, "I baptize you with water, but he who is mightier than I . . . will baptize you with the Holy Spirit"[26] (Luke 3:16 par. Mark 1:8). The time was now drawing very near, said Jesus, when these words of John would be fulfilled: "you will be baptized with the Holy Spirit in a few days' time." According to Old Testament prophecy, the days of fulfilment would be marked by a widespread outpouring of the Spirit of God,[27] and John's baptism in water not only prepared his repentant hearers for the coming judgment but also pointed them on to that spiritual baptism of which the prophets had spoken.

6 These matters had been the subject of conversation between the risen Lord and his disciples from time to time during the forty days. The formula of transition at the beginning of verse 6[28] suggests that Luke now moves on to the last conversation of all, belonging to the risen Lord's appearance to them immediately before his ascension.

The apostles evidently maintained their interest in the hope of seeing the kingdom of God realized in the restoration of Israel's national independence. They had at an earlier date been captivated by the thought that in such a restored order they themselves would have positions of authority (cf. Mark 10:35-45; Luke 22:24-27). So now, hearing their Master speak of the coming gift of the Spirit, the sign of the new age, they asked if this was to be the occasion for restoring Israel's sovereignty.

7 Jesus' answer did not take the form of a direct "No." He told them that the epochs of the fulfilment of the divine purpose[29] were matters which lay within the Father's sole jurisdiction. Similarly, he had assured them on a former occasion that not even the Son knew the day or hour of his parousia; this knowledge was reserved to the Father alone (Mark 13:32). Whatever purposes of his own God might have for the nation of Israel, these were not to be the concern of the messengers of Christ. The kingdom of God

25. John is never called "the Baptist" or "the Baptizer" in Acts (cf. 1:22; 10:37; 11:16; 13:24-25; 18:25; 19:3-4).

26. Luke 3:16 adds "and with fire" (so also Matt. 3:11), producing what has commonly been regarded as a conflation of the Markan "with the Holy Spirit" with the Q reading "with fire." For the idea of fire cf. 2:3. Justin Martyr records a tradition that, when Jesus was baptized, "a fire was kindled in Jordan" (*Dialogue with Trypho* 88.3).

27. Cf. Joel 2:28-32, quoted in Acts 2:17-21.

28. οἱ μὲν οὖν . . . (Luke uses μὲν οὖν with resumptive force: "So then").

29. If there is a distinction between "times" (χρόνοι) and "seasons" (καιροί), the "times" would denote the interval before the consummation of the kingdom of God, the "seasons" the critical events accompanying its establishment. But probably here, "as in other cases of paronomasia, the combination has become stereotyped and the original distinction between the words forgotten" (Lake-Cadbury, *Beginnings* I.4, p. 8). Cf. 1 Thess. 5:1; Tit. 1:2-3. See J. Barr, *Biblical Words for Time*, SBT 33 (London, 1962).

which they were commissioned to proclaim was the good news of God's grace in Christ. Their present question appears to have been the last flicker of their former burning expectation of an imminent theocracy with themselves as its chief executives. From now on they devoted themselves to the proclamation and service of God's spiritual kingdom, which men and women enter by repentance and faith, and in which chief honor belongs to those who most faithfully follow their Lord in the path of obedience, service, and suffering.

8 Instead of the political power which had once been the object of their ambitions, a power far greater and nobler would be theirs. When the Holy Spirit came upon them, Jesus assured them, they would be vested with heavenly power—that power by which, in the event, their mighty works were accomplished and their preaching made effective. As Jesus had been anointed at his baptism with the Holy Spirit and power, so his followers were now to be similarly anointed and enabled to carry on his work.[30] This work would be a work of witness-bearing—a theme which is prominent in the apostolic preaching throughout Acts.[31] An Old Testament prophet had called the people of Israel to be God's witnesses in the world (Isa. 43:10; 44:8); the task which Israel had not fulfilled was taken on by Jesus, the perfect Servant of the Lord, and shared by him with his disciples. The close relation between God's call to Israel, "you are my witnesses," and the risen Lord's commission to his apostles, "you will be my witnesses," can be appreciated the more if we consider the implications of Paul's quotation of Isa. 49:6 in Acts 13:47.[32] There the heralds of the gospel are spoken of as a light for the Gentiles, bearing God's salvation "to the end of the earth"; here "the end of the earth" and nothing short of that is to be the limit of the apostolic witness.

In Acts we do not find an apostolic succession in the ecclesiastical sense, nor a succession of orthodox tradition, but "a succession of witness to Christ, an apostolic testimony *in* Jerusalem to the self-styled leaders of Israel until they finally reject it, and an apostolic testimony *from* Jerusalem to Rome and the Gentile world of Luke's own day."[33]

It has often been pointed out that the geographical terms of verse 8 provide a sort of "Index of Contents" for Acts. "You will be my witnesses" might be regarded as announcing the theme of the book; "in Jerusalem"

30. The apostles had already (it appears) received John's baptism; the promised baptism with the Holy Spirit would complete for them, in their measure, the anointing with the Holy Spirit and power which Jesus himself experienced on the occasion of his baptism in the Jordan (cf. 10:38). He had been anointed then as God's chosen Servant; they were soon to be anointed to share the Servant's ministry, carrying God's salvation throughout the world.

31. Cf. 1:22; 2:32; 3:15; 5:32; 10:39, 41; 13:31, etc.

32. See pp. 266-67.

33. G. W. H. Lampe, *St. Luke and the Church of Jerusalem* (London, 1969), p. 27.

covers the first seven chapters, "in all Judaea and Samaria" covers 8:1 to 11:18, and the remainder of the book traces the progress of the gospel outside the frontiers of the Holy Land until at last it reaches Rome.[34]

3. The Ascension (1:9-11)

9 *Having said this he was taken up, while they looked on, and a cloud received him out of their sight.*

10 *As he went, they remained gazing into heaven, when suddenly two men in white clothing stood beside them.*

11 *"Men of Galilee," they said, "why do you stand looking into heaven? This Jesus, who has been taken up from you into heaven, will come in the same way as you have seen him going into heaven."*

9 When the Lord had made their commission sufficiently plain to them, he disappeared from their sight, and no further resurrection appearances were granted to them, of the kind which they had experienced on several occasions during the past forty days.

It is Luke's mention of this period of forty days that is responsible for the arrangement in the Christian calendar by which Ascension Day falls on the fortieth day after Easter. In the apostolic witness Jesus' resurrection and ascension seem to form one continuous movement, and both together constitute his exaltation. But his exaltation was not postponed to the fortieth day after his triumph over death. The ascension here recorded was not the first occasion when he vanished from his companions' sight after his resurrection. He did so after he made himself known in the breaking of the bread to the two with whom he walked to Emmaus (Luke 24:31). Nor are we intended to suppose that the intervals between his resurrection appearances during the forty days were passed by him in some intermediate, earth-bound state. The resurrection appearances, in which he accommodated himself to the disciples' temporal condition of life, even going so far as to eat with them, were visitations from that eternal order to which his "body of glory" now belonged. What happened on the fortieth day was that this series of visitations came to an end with a scene which impressed on the disciples their Master's heavenly glory.

This was not the first occasion on which some of them at least had had his heavenly glory brought home to them in a similar way. The words "a cloud received him out of their sight" are reminiscent of those with which the Gospel incident of the transfiguration comes to an end: "a cloud came and overshadowed them; . . . and a voice came out of the cloud, saying, 'This is

---

34. It has been suggested that "the end of the earth" here is a direct reference to Rome, as in *Ps. Sol.* 8:16, where Pompey is sent by God against the disobedient people of Jerusalem "from the end of the earth" (ἀπ' ἐσχάτου τῆς γῆς), i.e., from Rome. But the sense of the phrase need not be so limited in the present context.

my Son, my Chosen; listen to him!' And when the voice had spoken, Jesus was found alone" (Luke 9:34-36).[35] They are reminiscent, too, of Jesus' own language about the parousia of the Son of Man—"coming in clouds with great power and glory" (Mark 13:26); "coming with the clouds of heaven" (Mark 14:62).[36] The transfiguration, the ascension (as here described), and the parousia are three successive manifestations of Jesus' divine glory.[37] The cloud in each case is to be understood as the cloud which envelops the glory of God (the *shekhinah*)—that cloud which, resting above the Mosaic tabernacle and filling Solomon's temple, was the visible token to Israel that the divine glory had taken up residence there (Ex. 40:34; 1 Kings 8:10-11). So, in the last moment that the apostles saw their Lord with outward vision, they were granted "a theophany: Jesus is enveloped in the cloud of the divine presence."[38]

10 There is no need to be alarmed by suggestions that the ascension story is bound up with a pre-Copernican conception of the universe, and that the former is therefore as obsolete as the latter. Anyone leaving the earth's surface appears to spectators to be ascending, and so, when the cloud enveloped their Lord, his disciples stood "gazing into heaven" as he disappeared. Some of them, perhaps, remembering a previous experience, expected that the cloud would dissolve and Jesus be left with them, as on the Mount of Transfiguration. Instead, they suddenly became aware of two white-robed men standing by. Luke intends his readers to understand these men to be angelic messengers, like the two men who appeared to the women at the empty tomb of Jesus "in dazzling apparel" (Luke 24:4).[39] In both instances the fact that there were two suggests that they are viewed as witnesses, two being the minimum number for credible witness-bearing (Deut. 19:15). On the former occasion the two men bore witness to Jesus' resurrection; here they bear witness to his forthcoming parousia.

11 They need not stand gazing skyward, said the heavenly visi-

---

35. See G. H. Boobyer, *St. Mark and the Transfiguration Story* (Edinburgh, 1942); H. Riesenfeld, *Jésus transfiguré* (Uppsala, 1947); A. M. Ramsey, *The Glory of God and the Transfiguration of Christ* (London, 1949).

36. See N. B. Stonehouse, *The Witness of Matthew and Mark to Christ* (Grand Rapids, ²1958), pp. 238-43; J. A. T. Robinson, *Jesus and His Coming* (London, 1975), pp. 43-58.

37. Cf. Rev. 1:7.

38. A. M. Ramsey, "What was the Ascension?", *Studiorum Novi Testamenti Societas, Bulletin* 2 (Oxford, 1951), p. 49. See also J. Denney, *HDB* I (Edinburgh, 1898), pp. 161-62 (*s.v.* "Ascension"); J. H. Bernard, *ERE* II (Edinburgh, 1909), pp. 151-57 (*s.v.* "Assumption and Ascension"); P. Benoit, "The Ascension" (1949), E.T. in *Jesus and the Gospel*, I (New York, 1973), pp. 209-53; B. M. Metzger, "The Ascension of Jesus Christ," in *Historical and Literary Studies* (Leiden/Grand Rapids, 1968), pp. 77-87.

39. Cf. Mark 16:5 par. Matt. 28:3; John 20:12. Jesus' own garments when he was transfigured became "dazzling white" (Luke 9:29), "glistening, intensely white" (Mark 9:3).

tants. "This Jesus" would return in the same manner as he went. From Luke's perspective, this promise would indeed be fulfilled, but not immediately. The disciples had seen Jesus go in power and glory; in power and glory he would come back. But an interval would elapse between his exaltation and his parousia, and in that interval the presence of the Spirit would keep his people in living union with their risen, glorified, and returning Lord.[40]

Christ is ascended, but his abiding presence and energy fill the whole book of Acts, and the whole succeeding story of his people on earth. His exaltation "at God's right hand"[41] means that he is the more effectually present with his people on earth "always, to the close of the age" (Matt. 28:20). As it is put in Eph. 4:10, he "ascended far above all the heavens, that he might fill all things."

4. In the Upper Room (1:12-14)

12 *Then they returned to Jerusalem from Mount Olivet,[42] which is near Jerusalem, a sabbath day's journey distant.*

13 *When they entered (the city), they went up to the upper room where they were staying. There were Peter, John, James, and Andrew; Philip and Thomas, Bartholomew and Matthew; James the son of Alphaeus, Simon the Zealot, and Judas the son of James.*

14 *All of these together were giving themselves continually to prayer, along with some women, including Mary the mother of Jesus, and his brothers.*

12 The apostles' immediate duty was plain: it was to wait in Jerusalem until the heavenly power came on them. So they returned to the city. The place where their Master was taken from their sight, Luke tells us, was the Mount of Olives, to the east of Jerusalem, "a sabbath day's journey distant." This was a distance of 2,000 cubits or around one kilometer, ingeniously reckoned by interpreting Ex. 16:29 ("let no one go out of his place on the seventh day") in the light of Num. 35:5 (where the Levites' pasturelands are defined by a radius of 2,000 cubits from any one of the six "cities of refuge").[43] According to Luke 24:50, Jesus "led them out as far as Bethany"; but it is not certain that the same occasion is referred to there as here.

---

40. This aspect of the Spirit's ministry is developed more especially by Paul, according to whom the Spirit is also the "seal," "firstfruits," or "guarantee" (Gk. ἀρ-ραβών) of believers' coming heritage of glory (Rom. 8:23; 2 Cor. 1:22; 5:5; Eph. 1:14; 4:30).

41. On this expression see 2:33-35, with comments.

42. Gk. ἐλαιών, "oliveyard."

43. Cf. Mishnah, *Sôṭāh* 5.3. The general regulations for sabbath observances and the sabbath limits are contained in the Mishnah tractates *Shabbāṭ* and *ʿĒrûḇîn*.

Bethany lies on the eastern slopes of Olivet, about fifteen stadia (two and a half kilometers) from Jerusalem (cf. John 11:18).

13 Back in Jerusalem, the apostles went to the place where their company was lodging in the city—the "upper room." It is possible (although naturally it cannot be proved) that this was the room where Jesus had kept the passover meal with them on the eve of his execution; it may also have been the room where he appeared to some of them on Easter Day (cf. Luke 24:33, 36; John 20:19, 26).[44] It is an attractive speculation that the house which contained this upper room was the house of Mary, mother of John Mark (cf. 12:12),[45] but this is even less demonstrable.

Luke now gives a list of the apostles,[46] identical with that given earlier in Luke 6:14-16, save for a few variations in the order of names and, of course, the deletion of Judas Iscariot. The lists of the Twelve in Mark 3:16-19 and Matt. 10:2-4 differ from Luke's lists mainly by putting Thaddaeus where he has "Judas the son of James." Otherwise, while the lists vary considerably in order, the same apostles are named together in each of the three groups into which the Twelve are divided by all three writers; and Peter, Philip, and James the son of Alphaeus always come first, fifth, and ninth respectively. There is no sufficient reason for supposing that James the son of Alphaeus was a blood relative of Jesus, or that the name Alphaeus should be identified with Clopas (John 19:25).[47]

Simon the Zealot, as he is called here and in Luke 6:15, is called "Simon the Cananaean" in Mark 3:18 (followed by Matt. 10:4). "Cananaean" represents the Hebrew or Aramaic word corresponding to "Zealot" (from Gk. *zēlōtēs*). The word might denote Simon's zealous temperament, but Mark's retention of the untranslated Semitic word suggests that it is used as a technical term, denoting a member of the party of the Zealots.[48] The Zealots

---

44. So T. Zahn, *Die Apostelgeschichte des Lucas*, p. 44; he argues that the definite article τό before ὑπερῷον would certainly have indicated one special upper room to early Christian readers.

45. Cf. T. Zahn, *Die Apostelgeschichte des Lucas*, pp. 387-90.

46. See the discussion of "The Twelve and the Apostles" in V. Taylor, *The Gospel according to St. Mark* (London, 1952), pp. 619-27; also K. H. Rengstorf, *TDNT* 1, pp. 407-47 (*s.v.* ἀπόστολος); A. Fridrichsen, *The Apostle and his Message* (Uppsala, 1947); C. K. Barrett, *The Signs of an Apostle* (London, 1970); R. Schnackenburg, "Apostles before and during Paul's Time," in *Apostolic History and the Gospel*, ed. W. W. Gasque and R. P. Martin (Grand Rapids/Exeter, 1970), pp. 287-303; J. H. Schütz, *Paul and the Anatomy of Apostolic Authority*, SNTSM 26 (Cambridge, 1975).

47. Alphaeus is Aram. *ḥalpai*. There is no means of knowing if this Alphaeus was the father of Levi the tax-collector (Mark 2:14). Clopas is said by Hegesippus to have been the brother of Joseph the carpenter and father of Simeon, who succeeded James the Just as leader of the Jerusalem church (cf. Eusebius, *HE* 3.11).

48. Gk. ζηλωτής, Heb. *qannāʾi*, Aram. *qanʾanāʾ*. The Zealots were the spiritual heirs of the Hasmonaean insurgents of the second century B.C., who rose in response to the call of Mattathias: "Whoever is zealous (ζηλῶν) for the law and supports the covenant, let him come out with me!" (1 Macc. 2:27). Mattathias in turn acted in the spirit of Elijah,

constituted the militant wing of the Jewish independence movement in the first century A.D.; it was they who took the lead in the revolt against Rome in A.D. 66. Although the name "Zealots" (or its Semitic counterpart) is not explicitly attested for them before A.D. 66,[49] Josephus dates their rise from the earlier revolt of A.D. 6, when Judas the Galilaean refused to acknowledge the Roman Emperor's right to receive tribute from Judaea,[50] and describes their political doctrine as a "fourth philosophy" among the Jews (in addition to the "philosophies" of the Pharisees, Sadducees, and Essenes).[51]

Judas the son of James may reasonably be identified with "Judas not Iscariot" of John 14:22.[52]

Of the apostles here listed, only Peter, James, and John are mentioned again in Acts (or in any other New Testament document apart from the Gospels).

14   These eleven apostles had in their company the women who had gone up to Jerusalem from Galilee with Jesus and his followers (cf. Luke 8:2-3; 23:55), and in particular Mary the mother of Jesus. It is worth noting that the latest occasion on which Mary figures in New Testament history— or in any other narrative which can be regarded as in any sense historical— finds her joining in worship with Jesus' disciples after his ascension.

With these women Jesus' brothers are also mentioned. It has been warmly debated whether these were his uterine brothers or more remote relatives.[53] The burden of proof lies on those who would understand the term in another than its usual sense. Jesus' brothers did not believe in him during his ministry (cf. John 7:5), but after his resurrection they figure prominently

---

who was "very zealous ($\zeta\eta\lambda\tilde{\omega}\nu$ $\dot{\epsilon}\zeta\dot{\eta}\lambda\omega\kappa\alpha$) for Yahweh, the God of hosts" (1 Kings 19:10), and earlier still of Phinehas, who "was zealous ($\dot{\epsilon}\zeta\dot{\eta}\lambda\omega\sigma\epsilon\nu$) for his God" (Num. 25:13). Cf. 21:20.

49. Josephus, *BJ* 2.651; 4.160-61, etc. It is similarly in the context of the Jewish War that the *qannā'îm* first appear in rabbinical sources (e.g., `Abôt de-Rabbi Nathan 6.8).

50. See 5:37 (with comment).

51. Josephus, *Ant.* 18.9, 23. See M. Hengel, *The Zealots*, E.T. (Edinburgh, 1988).

52. Called "Judas Thomas" (Judas the Twin) in the Curetonian Syriac version. We have no means of identifying his father James.

53. In the fourth century Epiphanius (*Panarion* 78) argued that these brothers were sons of Joseph by a former wife. He was not the first to hold this view, but others, such as Tertullian (*Against Marcion* 4.19; *On the Flesh of Christ* 7) had understood them to be uterine brothers, sons of Joseph and Mary. This latter view was championed about A.D. 380 by Helvidius, a Roman Christian (as part of his campaign against the prevalent teaching that virginity was a superior way of life to matrimony). In reply to him Jerome wrote a treatise *(Against Helvidius: On the Perpetual Virginity of the Blessed Mary)*, in which he propounded a new view, that the Lord's "brothers" were his first cousins, sons of Alphaeus by "Mary of Clopas" (whom he inferred, probably wrongly, from John 19:25 to be the Virgin's sister). The perpetual virginity of Joseph as well as Mary was thus safeguarded. Of the sons of Mary of Clopas two are named in Mark 15:40 as James the less and Joses, James the less ($\dot{\delta}$ $\mu\iota\varkappa\varrho\dot{\delta}\varsigma$) being so called probably to distinguish him from James the Just, soon to become leader of the church of Jerusalem (cf. Gal. 1:19).

among his followers. Their change in attitude may have resulted from his resurrection appearance to James (1 Cor. 15:7), who in due course occupied a position of undisputed leadership in the Jerusalem church (cf. 12:17; 15:13-21; 21:18). Three other brothers of Jesus are mentioned by name— Joses, Judas, and Simon (Mark 6:3).[54] Since the brothers of Jesus receive separate mention here from the apostles, it is evident that the James and Judas who are included in the third quaternion of the apostolic list are not identical with the James and Judas named as two of the brothers of Jesus.[55] "The brothers of the Lord" continued to form a distinct group in the church well into the apostolic age (1 Cor. 9:5).[56] Here, at the inception of the church's life, they are recorded as faithfully observing the seasons of united prayer with the other members of this considerable company of believers in Jesus.[57]

5. A Replacement for Judas Iscariot (1:15-26)

15 *During these days Peter stood up among the brothers (who numbered about 120 all told).*

16 *"Brothers," he said, "there must be[58] a fulfilment of the scripture which the Holy Spirit spoke in advance through the mouth of David, concerning Judas, who acted as guide to those who arrested Jesus.*

17 *He was numbered among us, and received his share in this ministry."*

18 *[This man acquired a field with his unrighteous gain, and falling headlong there[59] he was ruptured, and all his entrails were spilt out.*

54. In the parallel Matt. 13:55 "Joseph" appears in place of Mark's "Joses." In both places the sisters of Jesus are also mentioned, but not named.

55. The brothers James and Judas may be intended in Jude 1, "Jude (Judas), a servant of Jesus Christ and brother of James."

56. See J. B. Lightfoot, "The Brethren of the Lord," *St. Paul's Epistle to the Galatians* (London, 1865), pp. 252-91; J. B. Mayor, *The Epistle of St. James* (London, 21897), pp. v-xxxvi; T. Zahn, "Brüder und Vettern Jesu," *Forschungen zur Geschichte des neutestamentlichen Kanons*, VI (Leipzig, 1900), pp. 225-363; J. Chapman, "The Brethren of the Lord," *JTS* 7 (1905-6), pp. 412-33; R. E. Brown and others, *Mary in the New Testament* (London, 1978), pp. 65-72, 270-78.

57. This was the original company of Jesus' witnesses, including "those who had gone up with him from Galilee to Jerusalem" (13:31). The article τῇ before προσευχῇ ("prayer") may indicate the appointed service of prayer. See P. T. O'Brien, "Prayer in Luke-Acts," *TynB* 24 (1973), pp. 111-27; A. A. Trites, "The Prayer-Motif in Luke-Acts," in *Perspectives on Luke-Acts*, ed. C. H. Talbert, pp. 215-42. G. W. H. Lampe points out that, as Jesus prays before the descent of the Spirit on him (Luke 3:21), so the apostles and their companions pray before the descent of the Spirit on *them;* this, he says, illustrates Luke's "repeated doctrine that the grand object of prayer is the gift of the Spirit" (*The Seal of the Spirit* [London, 1951], p. 44).

58. Reading δεῖ ("it is necessary") with the Western text rather than ἔδει ("it was necessary").

59. Gk. πρηνὴς γενόμενος. This has sometimes been translated "swelling up" (cf. RSV mg.), as though πρηνής were cognate with πρήθω or πίμπρημι (cf. 28:6). The

19 *This became known to all the inhabitants of Jerusalem; in consequence, that field came to be called in their speech Hakel-dama, that is, "the field of blood."]*

20 *"It is written in the book of Psalms," Peter went on:*

'Let his residence become desolate;
let it be without inhabitant,'

and

'Let someone else take over his responsibility.'

21 *Now then, of the men who accompanied us all the time that the Lord Jesus went out and in at our head,[60]*

22 *right on from John's baptism until the day he was taken up from us, one must become a witness to his resurrection along with us."*

23 *So they put forward[61] two: Joseph called Barsabbas,[62] whose surname was Justus, and Matthias.*

24 *Then they prayed, "O Lord, thou who knowest the hearts of all, show which one of these two thou hast chosen*

25 *to take the place in this ministry and apostleship from which Judas defected, to go to his own place."*

26 *Then they cast lots between them, and the lot fell on Matthias, so he was reckoned along with the eleven[63] apostles.*

15 The number of those followers of Jesus who were together in Jerusalem was 120 or thereabout.[64] In addition, there were more followers of his elsewhere, especially in Galilee. According to 1 Cor. 15:6, there was one occasion when he appeared in resurrection to more than five hundred of his followers; this is probably to be regarded as a Galilaean appearance. The presence and influence of so many followers of Jesus in Galilee should not

---

Old Syriac version seems to have taken it thus, to judge from secondary versions based on it and from a comment by Ephrem. In Wisd. 4:19 πρηνεῖς is rendered *inflatos* in the Latin Vulgate. A tradition that Judas did actually swell up to monstrous proportions was preserved by Papias (see J. B. Lightfoot, *The Apostolic Fathers* [London, 1891], pp. 523-24, 534-35). See F. H. Chase, "On ΠΡΗΝΗΣ ΓΕΝΟΜΕΝΟΣ in Acts I 18," *JTS* 13 (1912), pp. 278-85, 415.

60. Gk. ἐφ' ἡμᾶς ("among us" is inadequate as a translation).

61. The Western text reads "he put forward" (ἔστησεν instead of ἔστησαν), as though Peter took the initiative in nominating them.

62. The Western text reads "Barnabas," by confusion with the Joseph of 4:36.

63. The Western text reads "twelve" (the clause would then have to be rendered "he was numbered among the twelve apostles"). Augustine conflates the two readings: "he was counted twelfth with the eleven apostles" (this is accepted by Zahn as the original text; cf. his *Urausgabe der Apostelgeschichte des Lucas*, pp. 29, 244).

64. Luke regularly qualifies his numerical data with the particle ὡς or ὡσεί ("about").

be forgotten, even if Luke is concerned to trace the expansion of the gospel along the road which begins at Jerusalem and leads to Rome.[65]

The whole company of 120[66] is here referred to as the "brothers"—a wider use of that word than in verse 14 (where it denotes Jesus' relatives). Among them Peter takes the leading place, as to a large extent he did during the period covered by the Gospel narrative. His denial of Jesus in the courtyard of the high priest might well have discredited him irretrievably in his colleagues' eyes, but the risen Lord's personal appearance to him and recommissioning of him rehabilitated him and ensured for him a position of leadership never to be forfeited.[67]

16-17 On this occasion Peter takes the lead in filling the vacancy among the apostles caused by the treachery and death of Judas Iscariot. With one exception, where the term "apostles" bears a somewhat different sense,[68] Luke restricts the use of this term to the Twelve. The total of twelve was significant: it corresponded to the number of the tribes of Israel, and may have marked the apostles out as leaders of the new Israel.[69]

Both the defection of Judas and the necessity of replacing him are viewed here as subjects of Old Testament prophecy. The use of messianic "testimonies" from the Old Testament—texts which had found their fulfilment in the story of Jesus and its sequel and therefore had great evidential value in witnessing to Jews—was a prominent feature of primitive Christian testimony and apologetic.[70] It has been held that collections of such "testimonies" were compiled and circulated at an early date for ready reference, their nucleus being provided by Jesus' own instruction to his disciples on the fulfilment of Old Testament prophecy (cf. Luke 24:25-27, 32, 44-47). Even before the time of Jesus some of the material in the Psalter (especially in the

---

65. R. Schütz, *Apostel und Jünger* (Giessen, 1921), argued for a stream of Gentile Christianity flowing north from Galilee. Whatever may be said in favor of such a hypothesis, it cannot be established on Schütz's premises, which are bound up with an unacceptable analysis of Acts as derived from a Judaean "apostles" source and a Galilaean "disciples" source. On the possibility of an independent development of Galilaean Christianity in the apostolic age see also E. Lohmeyer, *Galiläa und Jerusalem* (Göttingen, 1936); W. Marxsen, *Mark the Evangelist*, E.T. (Nashville, 1969); for a caveat see G. B. Caird, *The Apostolic Age* (London, 1955), pp. 87-99.

66. It is difficult to be sure if any design underlies the fact that this number is ten times the apostolic total.

67. See G. W. H. Lampe, "St. Peter's Denial," *BJRL* 55 (1972-73), pp. 346-68.

68. See 14:4, 14, with comments (pp. 271, 276).

69. Cf. Luke 22:30 par. Matt. 19:28.

70. See J. R. Harris, *Testimonies*, I, II (Cambridge, 1916, 1920); B. P. W. S. Hunt, *Primitive Gospel Sources* (London, 1951); C. H. Dodd, *According to the Scriptures* (London, 1952); R. V. G. Tasker, *The Old Testament in the New Testament* (London, ²1954); B. Lindars, *New Testament Apologetic* (London, 1961); A. T. Hanson, *The Living Utterances of God* (London, 1983).

"royal psalms") was interpreted in a messianic sense.[71] For those who believed that Jesus was the Messiah of David's line, this meant that many of the experiences of the psalmist (David) were understood as prophetically applicable to Jesus (cf. 2:25-31, 34-36). Moreover, in the light of Jesus' passion, many of the afflictions endured by a righteous sufferer in the Psalms were also interpreted of him. It followed that what was said of the enemies of the Lord's anointed or of the righteous sufferer would be interpreted of the enemies of Jesus (cf. 4:25-28). Among his enemies Judas was unenviably prominent, and it was not difficult to find Old Testament texts which pointed to him. In John 13:18 Jesus, announcing the presence of a traitor in the company in the upper room, quotes Ps. 41:9 ("he who ate my bread has turned against me"), and in praying for his disciples in John 17:12 he says, "none of them is lost but the son of perdition, that the scripture might be fulfilled." Matthew brings together a text from Zechariah with one from Jeremiah to provide a composite "testimony" of the price which Judas received for his betrayal and the field which was bought with it (Matt. 27:9-10).[72] So Peter here adduces further "testimonies" from the Psalter. Their real author, he affirms, is the Holy Spirit, who spoke through the prophet; David, being a prophet, was but a spokesman or mouthpiece of the Spirit (cf. 2:30; 4:25).

18-19 Before Luke reproduces the actual texts from the Psalter which Peter cited to establish his point, he inserts a parenthesis in order that his readers may understand the background of Peter's remarks. Peter did not need to tell his hearers in the upper room what had happened to Judas, nor can the words of verse 19, "that field came to be called in *their* speech Hakeldama," be part of Peter's direct speech. But when Luke visited Jerusalem in A.D. 57, he was probably told the story of Judas's death, and he inserts it here. Judas, he was told, bought a field with his ill-gotten gain. But he did not live to enjoy the fruits of his shameful act, for he fell and sustained a fatal rupture.[73] The field was accordingly called by an Aramaic name meaning "the field of blood."[74]

---

71. The words addressed to the Lord's anointed in Ps. 2:9 are referred to the coming Davidic Messiah in *Ps. Sol.* 17:26 (mid-first century B.C.).

72. Cf. F. F. Bruce, *This is That: The New Testament Development of Some Old Testament Themes* (Exeter/Grand Rapids, 1968), pp. 108-10.

73. The Latin Vulgate harmonizes this account with that of Matt. 27:5 by saying that "having hanged himself he burst open *(crepuit)*."

74. Aram. *ḥāqal dᵉmāʾ* (the final letter of Ἀκελδαμάχ is a visual, not phonetic, transcription of final *aleph*, as in Σιράχ for *Sîrāʾ*). According to Matt. 27:7, it was the potter's field, and was used thereafter to bury aliens in. Matthew further says that it was the chief priests who bought it with the money which Judas threw back at them; E. Jacquier (*Les Actes des Apôtres* [Paris, 1926], p. 34) and others have suggested that they bought it in Judas's name.

20 After this parenthesis, Luke continues with his report of Peter's speech, and quotes the two texts from the Psalter to which Peter appealed. The former, from Ps. 69:25, is a prayer that the dwelling place of the psalmist's enemies may be deserted; the latter, from Ps. 109:8, prays that a certain enemy may die before his time and be replaced in his responsible position by someone else. Here, then, is warrant for the appointment of a successor to Judas.

21-22 The essential qualifications of an acceptable successor to Judas are then set forth: he must have been an associate of the Lord and his apostles from the time of John the Baptist's activity to the day of the Lord's ascension; he must in particular be a witness to the resurrection, as the other apostles were. It is noteworthy in the first place that the period indicated is the period covered in the primitive apostolic preaching, the *kerygma* (cf. 10:37; 13:24-25). In the second place, the statement that the apostles had been in Jesus' company since the days when John was baptizing agrees with the evidence of the Fourth Gospel, according to which nearly half of the Twelve began to follow Jesus in the days immediately following his baptism by John (John 1:35-51). The call of the apostles recorded in the Synoptic Gospels took place after John's imprisonment (Mark 1:14-20).

23 The disciples' choice fell on two of their number who possessed the necessary qualifications. Joseph's additional name Barsabbas ("son of the sabbath") may have been given to him because he was born on the sabbath day.[75] Like many other Jews at that time, he bore a Gentile name as well as his Jewish one: the Latin cognomen Justus bore a superficial similarity to Joseph and may further have been regarded as a rendering of the Hebrew epithet *ṣaddîq* ("righteous").[76] According to Eusebius and the later writer Philip of Side, Papias reported on the authority of Philip's daughters (cf. 21:9) that this Joseph, when challenged by unbelievers, drank snake venom in the Lord's name and suffered no harm.[77] As for Matthias, he is said by Eusebius to have been one of the seventy disciples of Luke 10:1.[78] Perhaps he was, but Eusebius (or his source) may only be guessing. Later tradition represents Matthias as a missionary to the Ethiopians.

24-26 The disciples did not cast lots haphazardly: they first selected the two men whom they judged worthiest to fill the vacancy. It may

75. Aram. *Bar-šabbā*'; a less probable derivation is from *Bar-Sābā*' ("son of the elder"). Another bearer of the patronymic Βαρσαββᾶς is mentioned in 15:22.

76. Cf. "Jesus called Justus" in Col. 4:11. Other bearers of Jewish and Gentile names are John/Mark (12:12) and Saul/Paul (13:9).

77. Eusebius, *HE* 3.39.8; Philip, *Hist. Christ.* The drinking of poison without harmful consequences is mentioned as a "sign" in the longer Markan appendix (Mark 16:18).

78. Eusebius, *HE* 1.12.3.

well be that there was nothing to choose between Joseph and Matthias; in that case the casting of lots, which had very respectable precedent in Hebrew sacred history, was a reasonable way of deciding on one of the two, especially since they besought God to overrule the lot, in the spirit of Prov. 16:33:

"The lot is cast into the lap,
     but the decision is wholly from the LORD."[79]

There is, to be sure, no New Testament example of this procedure after the descent of the Spirit on the day of Pentecost; this may or may not be significant.

The prayer is couched in dignified language, with liturgical echoes.[80] The question whether the "Lord" to whom it is addressed is God the Father or the Lord Jesus is probably settled by the fact that the same verb is used in verse 24 ("thou hast chosen") as in verse 2 ("the apostles whom he [Jesus] had chosen").[81] The same Lord who had chosen the apostles at the beginning of his ministry would choose this replacement for Judas.

The reference to Judas's going "to his own place" is no doubt euphemistic, but the reticence with which they alluded to his fate might be marked and emulated. The circumstances of his death gave them little ground for optimism in this regard, but they would not take it on themselves to say what "his own place" was.[82]

The lots, then, were cast; Matthias was indicated as the man to be co-opted in Judas's place. The number of the apostles was restored to twelve. It was Judas's defection and not the mere fact of his death that created the vacancy; no steps were taken to appoint a successor to James the son of Zebedee when he died by the executioner's sword some years later.[83] Unlike Judas, James was faithful unto death, and might hope to reign with Christ in resurrection, if not (as he had once expected) in this present life.[84]

It has sometimes been suggested that the apostles were wrong in co-opting Matthias to complete their number, that they should have waited

---

79. One may compare the procedure by which magistrates were elected in ancient Athens under Solon's constitution—by κλήρωσις ἐκ προκρίτων, i.e., casting lots among candidates previously selected on more rational grounds.

80. Note in particular the invocation "O Lord, thou who knowest the hearts of all" (σὺ κύριε, καρδιογνῶστα πάντων); the same epithet occurs in 15:8.

81. Gk. ἐκλέγομαι.

82. Cf. Ignatius, *To the Magnesians* 5:1, "each is to go to his own place" (which could conceivably be an echo of the present passage). Ignatius refers to both bad and good. Polycarp (*To the Philippians* 9:2) and Clement of Rome (*To the Corinthians* 5:4) use similar language of the appointed place of glory.

83. Acts 12:2.

84. Mark 10:35-37.

until, in God's good time, Paul was ready to fill the vacancy.[85] This is a complete mistake, and betrays a failure to appreciate the special character of Paul's apostleship. Paul did not possess the qualifications set out in verses 21 and 22. He himself would certainly have dismissed as preposterous the idea that he was rightfully the twelfth apostle, on the same footing as Peter and the rest of the eleven.

85. Cf. R. Stier, *The Words of the Apostles*, E.T. (Edinburgh, 1869), pp. 12-15; G. Campbell Morgan, *The Acts of the Apostles* (New York, 1924), pp. 19-20.

ACTS 2

B. THE DAY OF PENTECOST (2:1-47)

1. The Descent of the Spirit (2:1-4)

1 When[1] the day of Pentecost arrived, they were all together in the same place.
2 Suddenly from heaven came a sound of a strong, rushing wind, and it filled all the house where they were sitting.
3 Then there appeared tongues as of fire, distributed among them so that one settled on each of them,
4 and they were all filled with the Holy Spirit and began to speak in other tongues, as the Spirit granted them utterance.

1 The day of Pentecost was so called because it fell on the fiftieth day[2] after the presentation of the first sheaf to be reaped of the barley harvest, that is, the fiftieth day from the first Sunday after Passover (*pentēkostos* being the Greek word for "fiftieth").[3] Among Hebrew- and Aramaic-speaking Jews it was known as "the feast of weeks"[4] (Ex. 34:22a; Deut. 16:10) and also as

---

1. The Western text amplifies: "And it came to pass in those days. . . ."
2. The feminine form of the ordinal, ἡ πεντηκοστή (*sc.* ἡμέρα or ἑορτή), is first found as a name for this festival in Tob. 2:1 and 2 Macc. 12:32. On the significance of Pentecost in Acts see G. Kretschmar, "Himmelfahrt und Pfingsten," *ZKG* 66 (1954-55), pp. 209-53; J. D. G. Dunn, *Jesus and the Spirit* (London, 1975), pp. 135-56; I. H. Marshall, "The Significance of Pentecost," *SJT* 30 (1977), pp. 347-69; A. T. Lincoln, "Theology and History in the Interpretation of Luke's Pentecost," *ExT* 96 (1984-85), pp. 204-9.
3. The Sadducean party in the first century A.D. interpreted the sabbath in the phrase "the morrow after the sabbath" (Lev. 23:15) as the weekly sabbath. While the temple stood, the Sadducean interpretation would be normative for the public celebration of the festival. Christian tradition accordingly has fixed the anniversary of the descent of the Spirit on a Sunday (the "fifty days" of Lev. 23:15 being reckoned inclusively). The Pharisees, however, took the "sabbath" of Lev. 23:15 to be the festival day of unleavened bread (on which, according to Lev. 23:7, no servile work was to be done); in this case Pentecost would always fall on the same day of the month (Siwan 6), but not on the same day of the week. The Pharisees could appeal to Josh. 5:11 ("the morrow after the Passover"), read in the light of Lev. 23:10-14. Cf. Mishnah Menāḥôt 10.3; Tos. Menāḥôt 10.23.528; TB Menāḥôt 65a; see also L. Finkelstein, *The Pharisees* (Philadelphia, 1946), pp. 115-18.
4. Heb. šābū'ôt, by which name the day is commonly designated among Jews.

49

"the day of the firstfruits" (Num. 28:26; cf. Ex. 23:16a) because on that day "the firstfruits of wheat harvest" (Ex. 34:22a) were presented to God. At a later date it was reckoned to be the anniversary of the giving of the law on Sinai[5]—a not unreasonable deduction from Ex. 19:1, according to which the Israelites arrived in "the wilderness of Sinai" on the third new moon after their departure from Egypt (i.e., at the beginning of Siwan, about forty-four days after the first Passover).

The "place" where the disciples were on this occasion, the "house" of verse 2, is not more precisely specified; it may have been the upper room of 1:13, but there is no means of knowing.

2   On the morning of the day of Pentecost, then, the place where the disciples were sitting together was suddenly filled with what seemed like a great gale of wind from heaven.[6] It is perhaps pointless to ask explicit questions about this wind, for there is no likelihood of their being satisfactorily answered. Was it only the disciples who heard it, or was it audible to others? There is no way of knowing. What is certain is that the wind was held to symbolize the Spirit of God. When Ezekiel, by divine command, prophesied to the wind and called it to blow on the dead bodies in the valley of his vision, it was the breath of God that breathed into them and filled them with new life (Ezek. 37:9-14). And, probably with an allusion to Ezekiel's vision, Jesus said to Nicodemus, "The wind blows where it pleases, and you hear the sound of it, but you do not know whence it comes or whither it goes; so it is with every one who is born of the Spirit" (John 3:8). Whatever else may be said about the disciples' experience, this at least is clear: the Spirit of God came on them in power.

3   John the Baptist had foretold how the Coming One would carry out a baptism with wind and fire (Luke 3:16-17). In the disciples' Pentecostal experience, then, fire had a part to play as well as wind: the manifestation of the Spirit's advent was visible as well as audible. What appeared to be tongues of fire were seen, one of which lighted on each of them. Again, it is difficult to translate this experience into terms which will convey its true significance. As in the burning bush, fire denotes the divine presence (Ex. 3:2-5). Perhaps no one has expressed the spiritual meaning of the "pure celestial fire" which came down at Pentecost so well as Charles Wesley in his hymn "O Thou Who Camest from Above."[7]

5. This reckoning perhaps originated in sectarian Judaism; cf. Jub. 1:1 with 6:17. It is first attested in rabbinical Judaism by Jose ben Ḥalafta, c. A.D. 150 (Seder 'Ôlām R. 5), and then by Eleazar ben Pedath, c. A.D. 270 (TB Pᵉsāḥîm 68b). See B. Noack, "The Day of Pentecost in Jubilees, Qumran, and Acts," ASTI 1 (1962), pp. 73-95.

6. Ephrem the Syrian (4th cent. A.D.) says that the house was filled with fragrance; this may be a reminiscence of Isa. 6:4.

7. This hymn (Methodist Hymn Book 386) is in origin a meditation on Lev. 6:13 ("The fire shall ever be burning upon the altar; it shall never go out"), but the invocation of

It is uncertain how far the "tongues as of fire" are intended to symbol-ize the "other tongues" in which the disciples proceeded to speak. F. H. Chase suggests that, "at the moment when the illuminating Spirit was poured upon the Church, the sunlight of a new day smote upon the Apostles," and he goes on to ask, "was it unnatural that Christians should see a deeper meaning in the sun's rays streaming through the colonnades and the arches of the Temple and resting upon the Apostles, and connecting the sight with the wonders of Apostolic utterance which ensued, should play upon a not un-common use of the word 'tongue' and speak of 'tongues like as of fire' resting on the Apostles?"[8]

This implies that the "house where they were sitting" was the temple, but the fact of their "sitting" there seems to rule this out. Certainly the temple courts would be suitable for the gathering of the large crowds who heard Peter's words (vv. 14-41), and if the disciples were in a private house when the Spirit first took possession of them (which is more probable),[9] they must have left it for the streets, or else their outburst of inspired utterance would not have made the impression it did. If they came into the streets still speaking with tongues, the crowds would certainly have gathered at the sound, and it may be supposed that they followed the disciples to the temple area, where Peter turned and addressed them. This involves reading more into the narrative than Luke actually records, but any attempt to envisage what actually happened involves that.[10]

4 However the sensible phenomena are to be understood, the disci-ples' inward experience is plainly stated: "they were all filled with the Holy Spirit." The spiritual baptism foretold by John and promised afresh by the Lord was now an accomplished fact. Being filled with the Spirit was an experience to be repeated on several occasions (cf. 4:8, 31), but the baptism in the Spirit which the believing community now experienced was an event which took place once for all.[11]

In Old Testament times when men or women were possessed by the

---

one who came from heaven to earth "the pure celestial fire to impart" is reminiscent also of the Prometheus theme.

8. F. H. Chase, *The Credibility of the Book of the Acts of the Apostles* (London, 1902), p. 35.

9. The word "house" (οἶχος) is used of the temple as well as of a private house (cf. 7:47; Mark 11:17; John 2:16; Isa. 6:4 and LXX *passim*). According to Luke 24:53 the disciples, after Jesus' departure, "were continually in the temple"; but the wording in Acts 2:2 suggests an ordinary house rather than the temple.

10. An argument for a setting in the temple is adduced by R. A. Cole (*The New Temple* [London, 1950], p. 38, n. 18); he points out that if the coming of the Spirit was manifested in the temple precincts there is a link with Ezek. 47:1-2, where the life-giving stream issues from beneath the threshold of the temple (a passage perhaps underlying John 7:38).

11. See comment on v. 38 below (p. 69).

Spirit of God, they prophesied. So it was with Eldad and Medad when the Spirit rested on them in the camp of Israel (Num. 11:26), and so it was with many another. So now the descent of the Spirit on the disciples was attended by prophetic speech, but prophetic speech of a peculiar kind—utterance in "other tongues."

Speaking with tongues, or glossolalia (as it is commonly called), is not an unparalleled phenomenon. Not only are the speakers' words partially or completely beyond their conscious control, but they are uttered in languages of which they have no command in normal circumstances. Within the New Testament there is ample attestation of another form of glossolalia—it was a "spiritual gift" highly valued in the Corinthian church. Paul acknowledges that the Corinthian glossolalia is a genuine gift of the Holy Spirit, but deprecates the undue importance which some members of the church of Corinth attach to it (1 Cor. 12:10, 28-30; 14:2-19). As cultivated in the church of Corinth, glossolalia was uttered in a speech which no hearer could understand until someone present received the correlative spiritual gift of interpretation. But in Jerusalem on the day of Pentecost the words spoken by the disciples in their divine ecstasy were immediately recognized by the visitors from many lands who heard them. Possibly "what happened on that occasion was that the multitude of pilgrims heard the Christians praising God in ecstatic utterances; and were amazed to observe that many of the words which they uttered were not Jewish or Greek words at all, but belonged to the local languages of Egypt, Asia Minor and Italy."[12]

The mere fact of glossolalia or any other ecstatic utterance is no evidence of the presence of the Holy Spirit. In apostolic times it was necessary to provide criteria for deciding whether such utterances were of God or not, just as it had been necessary in Old Testament times.[13] Paul laid down, as a simple but infallible test, the witness which such an utterance bears to Jesus: "no one can say 'Jesus is Lord' except by the Holy Spirit" (1 Cor. 12:3). A few decades later John takes account of a tendency in his own

12. P. Loyd, *The Holy Spirit in the Acts* (London, 1952), p. 32. Cf. also R. B. Rackham, *The Acts of the Apostles* (London, 1901), pp. 15-16: "Every new beginning in thought or life is inevitably accompanied by disturbance. There is the struggle with the old, and the re-adjustment to the new, environment. So the coming of the Spirit is followed by irregular and abnormal phenomena. Like Jordan, the full and plenteous flood of the Spirit 'overflows all its banks' (Josh. 3:15). At first the old worn-out vessels of humanity cannot contain it; and there is a flood of strange and novel spiritual experiences. But when it has worn for itself a deep channel in the church, when the laws of the new spiritual life are learnt and understood, then some of the irregular phenomena disappear, others become normal, and what was thought to be miraculous is found to be a natural endowment of the Christian life."

13. Cf. Deut. 18:22 (if a man's predictions fail to come true, he is a false prophet); 13:1-5 (even if his predictions do come true, but he seduces his hearers from their allegiance to the true God, he is a false prophet). See also the more pedestrian tests applied to prophets in the *Didachē* (11:1–12:5).

environment by insisting on a more explicit test: "every spirit which confesses that Jesus Christ has come in the flesh is of God" (1 John 4:2). The matter is more important than the manner; the medium is not the message. On the present occasion the content of the ecstatic utterances was "the mighty deeds of God" (v. 11), and the range of the languages in which these were proclaimed suggests that Luke thought of the coming of the Spirit more particularly as a preparation for the worldwide proclamation of the gospel. The church of Christ still speaks in many tongues, and if her speech is not now normally of the supernatural order that marked the day of Pentecost, the message is the same—the mighty deeds of God.[14]

2. The Crowd's Amazement (2:5-13)

5 *There were residing in Jerusalem Jews,[15] devout men from every nation under heaven.*

6 *When this sound was heard, the crowd came together and was confounded, because each individual heard them speaking in his own speech.*

7 *They were astounded and amazed: "Are not all these people who are speaking Galilaeans?" they asked.*

8 *"How then does each of us hear (their words) in our own speech, in which we were born?*

9 *Parthians, Medes, Elamites, and the inhabitants of Mesopotamia, Judaea, Cappadocia, Pontus and Asia,*

10 *Phrygia and Pamphylia, Egypt and the districts of Libya around Cyrene, visitors from Rome,*

11 *both Jews and proselytes, Cretans and Arabs, we hear them telling in our own tongues the mighty deeds of God."*

12 *They were all astounded and perplexed, saying one to another, "What does this mean?"*

13 *Others said in ridicule, "They are full of new wine."*

5-8 The Jews who were resident in Jerusalem on this occasion were to a large extent pilgrims from various lands of the dispersion who had come to the holy city to celebrate the festival of Pentecost. Even if the word "Jews" is an addition to the original text, it is Jews or proselytes who are indicated by

---

14. On glossolalia see K. Lake, *The Earlier Epistles of Paul* (London, 1911), pp. 241-52; A. L. Drummond, *Edward Irving and his Circle* (London, 1937), pp. 236-70, 278-97, and bibliography, p. 300; J. G. Davies, "Pentecost and Glossolalia," *JTS* n.s. 3 (1952), pp. 228-31; J. P. M. Sweet, "A Sign for Unbelievers: Paul's Attitude to Glossolalia," *NTS* 13 (1966-67), pp. 240-57; K. Haacker, "Das Pfingstwunder als exegetisches Problem," in *Verborum Veritas*, ed. O. Böcher and K. Haacker (Wuppertal, 1970), pp. 125-31; W. J. Samarin, *Tongues of Men and Angels* (New York, 1972); A. J. M. Wedderburn, "Romans 8:26—Towards a Theology of Glossolalia," *SJT* 28 (1975), pp. 369-77; W. E. Mills, *Speaking in Tongues* (Grand Rapids, 1986).

15. Ἰουδαῖοι *om.* ℵ* (see p. 55).

the phrase "devout men."[16] Only at the Jerusalem temple could they attend the special sacrificial services prescribed for that "holy convocation" and take part in them (Num. 28:26-31). Many of the visitors were astonished as they heard the loud praises of God uttered by the disciples in inspired language (this, rather than the noise of a rushing wind, is what is meant by the "sound" of v. 6),[17] because they recognized the indigenous languages and dialects of their native lands. The visitors from the lands to the east knew Aramaic, and those from the lands to the west knew Greek, but neither Aramaic nor Greek was a strange tongue to the disciples. The Galilaean accent was easily recognized, as Peter knew to his cost on an earlier occasion;[18] but these Galilaeans appeared for the moment to share among them a command of most of the tongues spoken throughout the known world.

When the law was given at Sinai, according to later rabbinic tradition, "the ten commandments were promulgated with a single voice, yet it says, 'All the people perceived the *voices*' (Ex. 20:18); this shows that when the voice went forth it was divided into seven voices and then went into seventy tongues, and every people received the law in its own language."[19] Late as this form of the tradition is, it was already accepted in some Jewish circles that Pentecost marked the anniversary of the giving of the law,[20] and there may be an implied parallel between that event and what was now happening in the statement that people "from every nation under heaven" heard the praises of God, "each individual . . . in his own speech." Such an implied parallel was discerned and expressed by John Keble in his Whitsuntide hymn, "When God of Old Came Down from Heaven."[21]

---

16. Gk. ἄνδρες εὐλαβεῖς (for εὐλαβής cf. 8:2; 22:12; Luke 2:25).

17. Gk. τῆς φωνῆς ταύτης (the word translated "sound" in v. 2 is ἦχος).

18. See Mark 14:70 par. Matt. 26:73 and Luke 22:59. Galilaean speech was distinguished by its confusion or loss of laryngeals and aspirates; cf. A. Neubauer, "The Dialects of Palestine in the Time of Christ," in *Studia Biblica*, I (Oxford, 1885), p. 51; G. Dalman, *Grammatik des jüdisch-palästinischen Aramäisch* (Leipzig, 1894), pp. 33-40, 42-51; F. Rosenthal, *Die aramäistische Forschung* (Leiden, 1939), p. 108 n.; E. Y. Kutscher, *Studies in Galilaean Aramaic* (Bar-Ilan University Press, Israel, 1976).

19. Midrash *Tanḥuma* 26c; cf. R. Yoḥanan (d. A.D. 279) in TB *Shabbāṭ* 88b. The true sense of the words quoted from Ex. 20:18 is "all the people perceived the thunderings" (RSV). The "seventy tongues" correspond to the seventy nations enumerated in Gen. 10:2-31. With this total rabbinical exegesis linked Deut. 32:8 MT, "the Most High . . . fixed the bounds of the peoples according to the number of the children of Israel"—the "children of Israel" being the seventy "persons of the house of Jacob, that came into Egypt" (Gen. 46:27 MT). Cf. Philo, *Decalogue* 36. See n. 24 below.

20. See p. 50, n. 5.

21. J. Keble, *The Christian Year* (London, 1872), No. 47. The stanza "The fires, that rushed on Sinai down
  In sudden torrents dread,
 Now gently light, a glorious crown,
  On every sainted head"

The people who heard the sounds on this occasion, however, were not Gentiles but Jews and proselytes; the evangelization of Gentiles was a revolutionary development, recorded with a fanfare of trumpets, at a later stage in the narrative of Acts.[22] Yet those "devout"[23] visitors are apparently considered by Luke to be representatives of the various lands from which they had come, and of the local dialects of those lands.

9-11   There follows an impressive roll call of the nations so represented. Such geographical lists appear elsewhere in ancient literature, notably in the *Rudiments* of Paulus Alexandrinus, a fourth-century astrological treatise, where the nations of the world are apportioned among the twelve signs of the zodiac.[24] But the resemblance between the list of nations in Paulus and the much earlier list here presented by Luke has been exaggerated. Luke's list is relevant to its context and has some features of special interest.[25]

Parthia, Media,[26] Elam (Elymais), and Mesopotamia lay east of the Euphrates; the Jews in those parts spoke Aramaic. These were the lands of the earliest dispersion, to which exiles from the ten northern tribes of Israel had been deported by the Assyrians in the eighth and seventh centuries B.C. They did not lose their identity as completely as has been traditionally

---

is reminiscent not only of the "tongues as of fire" of Acts 2:3 but also of Virgil's description of the lambent flame, betokening the favor of heaven, which played around the head of Iulus, son of Aeneas, at the fall of Troy (*Aeneid* 2.681-86).

22. See 10:1–11:18; 11:19-26; 15:7-11.

23. See p. 54, n. 16. The word is not one of those used to denote "God-fearing" Gentiles (cf. 10:2, p. 203, n. 7).

24. S. Weinstock, "The Geographical Catalogue in Acts 2:9-11," *JRS* 38 (1948), pp. 43-46, reports on a marginal note found in an offprint of F. Cumont, "La plus ancienne géographie astrologique," *Klio* 9 (1909), pp. 263-73 (an article on the division of the countries of the earth among the signs of the zodiac). The marginal note, in F. C. Burkitt's hand, tabulated the catalogue of nations in Acts 2:9-11 alongside Paul of Alexandria's list. Weinstock concludes that Burkitt must have regarded astrological geography as the key to the understanding of Luke's catalogue, and that Luke consequently, "however strange his list is, meant in fact to say 'the whole world' . . . all nations who live under the twelve signs of the zodiac received the gift to understand their preaching immediately." Cf. J. A. Brinkman, "The Literary Background of the 'Catalogue of the Nations' (Acts 2:9-11)," *CBQ* 25 (1963), pp. 418-27. In view of the reference to Deut. 32:8 in n. 19 above it is not irrelevant to recall that the Hebrew fragment 4QDt𐤒 with LXX renders the closing part of that verse, "he fixed the boundaries of the nations according to the number of the sons of God" (i.e., the angels)—a reading which has sometimes been interpreted (or misinterpreted) astrologically.

25. If there were a literary relationship between Luke and Paulus, we should have to assume an earlier source for Paulus. See B. M. Metzger, "Ancient Astrological Geography and Acts 2:9-11," *New Testament Studies: Philological, Versional and Patristic*, NTTS 8 (Leiden, 1980), pp. 46-56.

26. In 1 Enoch 56:5 "Parthians and Medes" play a leading part in the last Gentile war against Israel.

supposed. Their numbers were later augmented by the Judaean deportations in Nebuchadrezzar's time. In spite of Persian royal decrees authorizing their return, many of the descendants of those exiles preferred to remain where they were, and their settlements were increased by further immigration, so that the total Jewish population of those eastern territories amounted probably to several tens, if not hundreds, of thousands. Artaxerxes III of Persia planted a settlement of Jewish captives in Hyrcania on the Caspian Sea (c. 353 B.C.).[27] Josephus has much to say about Jewish settlements in Mesopotamia and adjacent regions;[28] it was for their benefit that he produced the first draft of his *History of the Jewish War* in Aramaic.[29]

The reference to "Judaea" has frequently been regarded as a scribal error, partly for grammatical reasons[30] and partly because it is unlikely that special mention would be made of Judaeans as residing in Jerusalem.[31] Many emendations have been suggested, but in view of the vastly preponderant textual evidence for "Judaea" it is best to agree with B. M. Metzger that "probably the least unsatisfactory solution to an admittedly difficult problem is to accept the reading attested by the overwhelming weight of witnesses."[32] If "Judaea" could be understood here in its widest possible sense, it might denote the extent of the land from the Egyptian frontier to the Euphrates, controlled directly or indirectly by the Judaean kings David and Solomon. This would explain the absence of Syria from the list.[33]

As for those living in Cappadocia, Pontus and Asia, Phrygia and Pamphylia, there is ample evidence of the large Jewish communities in those areas of Asia Minor. The central chapters of Acts (13–20) afford abundant proof of this; Philo declares that "the Jews are exceedingly numerous in each

27. Jerome, *Chronicle* (on Olympiad 105); Syncellus, *History,* ed. G. Dindorf, 1.486.

28. Josephus, *Ant.* 11.133; 15.14; 18.310-79.

29. Josephus, *BJ* 1.3, 6.

30. The absence of the article before Ἰουδαίαν is a difficulty (since the word is properly an adjective): "anarthrous Ἰουδαίαν . . . is certainly corrupt" (BDF §261, n. 4). But Ἰουδαίαν τε καὶ Καππαδοκίαν may come under the regimen of τήν before the preceding Μεσοποταμίαν.

31. As Bede pointed out in the eighth century.

32. B. M. Metzger, "Ancient Astrological Geography and Acts 2:9-11," *New Testament Studies,* p. 56.

33. Jerome actually read Syria here. Other emendations offered have been Armenia (Tertullian and Augustine), India (Chrysostom and, much later, R. Bentley), Galatia (M. Dibelius), Ionia (W. L. Knox), Iberia (J. M. Ross, *ExT* 96 [1984-85], p. 217), and Gordyaea, i.e., Kurdistan (F. C. Burkitt, *Encyclopaedia Biblica,* col. 4992). This last emendation has the support of a few Arabic MSS of the NT: Bodleian Canon. Or. 129 (Acts and the Epistles in Arabic) opens the list with *Akrād* (plural of *Kurdi*)—a reading supported by the Old Cairo MS 99 and by an early eighteenth-century Aleppo MS of the NT in Arabic (in the library of the Maronite bishop), chiefly translated from the Peshitta, but not entirely, since its text of the present list agrees with that of the Bodleian MS already mentioned (E. F. F. Bishop, "Professor Burkitt and the Geographical Catalogue," *JRS* 42 [1952], pp. 84-85).

city of Asia and Syria."[34] Jewish presence is attested in Lydia as early as the sixth century B.C. (the Sepharad of Obad. 20 is Sardis, the Lydian capital). Antiochus III brought 2,000 Jewish families from Babylonia and planted them as military settlers in Lydia and Phrygia (c. 213 B.C.).[35] From the north coast of Asia Minor some Jews crossed the Black Sea; Jewish inscriptions have been found in the Crimea.

Those visitors who came from Egypt and "the districts of Libya around Cyrene" belonged to another very populous sector of the Jewish dispersion. Jews had lived continuously in Egypt since the early years of the sixth century B.C., and were always receiving fresh accessions, especially after Alexander's conquest of Egypt and the founding of Alexandria in 331 B.C. According to Philo, himself an Alexandrian Jew, two out of the five wards which made up the city of Alexandria were Jewish in population;[36] he estimated that in A.D. 38 there were about a million Jews in Egypt[37] (if his total be divided by ten, it might be nearer the mark). Jews of Cyrenaica are mentioned elsewhere in Acts (6:9; 11:20; 13:1), and Simon of Cyrene figures in the passion narrative (Mark 15:21 par. Luke 23:26). Ptolemy I of Egypt (323-283 B.C.) is said to have settled a number of Jews in Cyrenaica to ensure its loyalty.[38]

The "visitors from Rome, both Jews and proselytes" form the only contingent from the European mainland included in Luke's list. Visitors from Greece may have been present as well, but they are not specifically mentioned.[39] Luke is interested in Rome because it is the goal toward which his narrative is moving. It is at least a possibility that the Roman church, whose origins are so obscure, may go back to some of those "visitors from Rome" who heard the gospel in Jerusalem that day and carried it home when they returned. "By the autumn following the Crucifixion it is quite as possible that Jesus was honoured in the Jewish community at Rome as that He was at Damascus."[40]

There was a Jewish colony in Rome in the second century B.C., and it was augmented by the Jews who were brought there from Judaea to grace Pompey's triumph in 61 B.C. and were later set free. By the beginning of the Christian era, it is estimated, there were between 40,000 and 60,000 Jews

---

34. Philo, *Embassy to Gaius* 245 (cf. 15:21, where Syria and Asia Minor are chiefly in view).

35. Josephus, *Ant.* 12.149; cf. F.F. Bruce, *Colossians–Philemon–Ephesians*, NICNT (Grand Rapids, 1984), pp. 8-13.

36. Philo, *Flaccus* 55.

37. Philo, *Flaccus* 43.

38. Josephus, *Against Apion* 2.44.

39. This is an argument against the Burkitt-Weinstock thesis (p. 55, n. 24); Paul of Alexandria's list places "Greece and Ionia" (under the sign of the Virgin) between Asia (under the Lion) and Libya and Cyrene (under the Scales).

40. F. J. Foakes-Jackson, *Peter, Prince of Apostles* (London, 1927), p. 195.

resident in Rome.[41] Our knowledge of them is derived not only from contemporary literary sources but also from the study of six Jewish catacombs.[42] No Jewish synagogue from the imperial period has yet been excavated in Rome, but the names of eleven are known from inscriptions.[43] It was probably the spread of Christian teaching in some of these synagogues that led to the rioting of A.D. 49, the occasion of "Claudius's edict that all Jews should leave Rome" (18:2).[44]

Nowhere was Jewish proselytizing activity carried on more energetically than in Rome, and it is not surprising that the Roman contingent included proselytes as well as Jews by birth.[45] A proselyte was a Gentile by birth who was converted to Judaism. Such a person undertook to keep the Jewish law in its entirety and was admitted to membership of the chosen people by a threefold rite: (1) circumcision (for male proselytes), (2) a purificatory self-baptism in the presence of witnesses,[46] and (3) the offering of a sacrifice (while the Jerusalem temple stood).[47] Because of the circumcision requirement, full proselytization seems to have been more common among women than among men. Many men were content with that looser attachment to Judaism conventionally indicated by the term "God-fearers."[48]

The catalogue is concluded with the reference to Cretans[49] and Arabs. The "Arabs" probably lived in the Nabataean kingdom, east of Syria and Judaea, which stretched from the Red Sea to the Euphrates, with its capital at Petra. It was at this time at the height of its power under Aretas IV (9 B.C.–A.D. 40).[50] This monarch's relations with Judaea may be illustrated

---

41. H. J. Leon, *The Jews of Ancient Rome* (Philadelphia, 1960), pp. 135-36; Schürer III, pp. 73-81.

42. H. J. Leon, *The Jews of Ancient Rome*, pp. 46-66.

43. H. J. Leon, *The Jews of Ancient Rome*, pp. 135-66; Schürer III, pp. 95-98.

44. See p. 347 with n. 9.

45. At the beginning of the second century A.D. Juvenal still has occasion to satirize the proselytizing activity of Jews in Rome (*Satire* 14.96-106).

46. See H. H. Rowley, "Jewish Proselyte Baptism and the Baptism of John" (1940) in *From Moses to Qumran* (London, 1963), pp. 211-35; T. F. Torrance, "Proselyte Baptism," *NTS* 1 (1954-55), pp. 150-54; T. M. Taylor, "The Beginnings of Jewish Proselyte Baptism," *NTS* 2 (1955-56), pp. 193-98; K. Pusey, "Jewish Proselyte Baptism," *ExT* 95 (1983-84), pp. 141-45.

47. According to G. W. H. Lampe, *The Seal of the Spirit* (London, 1951), p. 83, this sacrifice "was not indispensable, and it was in any case probably a merely ideal or theoretical regulation, since there is no real evidence that this complex of ceremonies dates back to the days of the Temple." See also Schürer III, pp. 173-74.

48. See p. 203, n. 7.

49. For Jews in Crete cf. Tit. 1:10-14; Josephus, *BJ* 2.103; *Ant.* 17.327. Josephus's second wife was a Cretan Jewess (*Life* 427).

50. He is mentioned in 2 Cor. 11:32 (cf. p. 192 below, on 9:23-25).

by the fact that a daughter of his was the first wife of the tetrarch Herod Antipas—the wife whom Antipas divorced in order to marry Herodias.[51]

All these visitors, then, heard the ecstatic exclamations of the apostles and their companions. The Jewish authorities appear to have sanctioned the use of any language in the reciting of certain religious formularies—the *Shema* ("Hear, O Israel . . . ," Deut. 6:4), the "Eighteen Benedictions," and the blessing invoked over meals.[52] The praises of God in various tongues were thus heard frequently in Jerusalem during the great festivals, when so many pilgrims of the dispersion were present in the city. Now, to their surprise, these pilgrims heard the praises of God in all the tongues of the dispersion being uttered by Galilaeans of all people! The event was nothing less than a reversal of the curse of Babel.[53]

12-13 The public amazement and perplexity spread. One kind of ecstasy is superficially much like another, and even Paul, who himself had the gift of glossolalia,[54] had to warn the Corinthian Christians that a stranger entering one of their meetings when they were all "speaking with tongues" would certainly conclude that they were mad (1 Cor. 14:23).[55] So on this occasion some in the crowd dismissed the strange event with a jibe: "They are full of new wine"—that is, sweet wine[56] (for, although the vintage of the current year was still some months off, there were ways and means of keeping wine sweet all the year round).[57]

3. Peter's Proclamation (2:14-36)

a. "This is that" (2:14-21)

14 *Then Peter, standing up with the eleven, raised his voice and addressed them. "Men of Judaea," he said, "and all you who are resident in Jerusalem, let this be known to you; pay attention to my words.*

---

51. Josephus, *Ant.* 18.109-15 (cf. p. 99 below, on 4:27).

52. Mishnah *Sôṭāh* 7.1; cf. Schürer II, pp. 22 (n. 78), 454-63.

53. "The account of Pentecost is dependent upon the account of Babel" (J. G. Davies, "Pentecost and Glossolalia," pp. 228-29).

54. 1 Cor. 14:18.

55. Cf. the contrast in Eph. 5:18 between being "drunk with wine" and being "filled with the Spirit."

56. Gk. γλεῦκος. Cf. Elihu in Job 32:19a LXX, speaking by constraint of the spirit within: "My belly is like a tightly tied wineskin fermenting with new ('sweet') wine" (γλεύκους ζέων).

57. "If you wish to keep new wine sweet the whole year round," says the Roman writer Cato, "put new wine in a jar, cover the stopper with pitch, submerge it in a pool of water, take it out after the thirtieth day; you will have sweet wine all the year round" (*On Agriculture* 120).

15 *These men are not drunk, as you suppose; it is only the third hour of the day.*

16 *No; this is what was said through the prophet Joel:*[58]

17 *'It shall be in the last days, says God,*
I will pour out some of my spirit on all the human race:
Your sons and your daughters will prophesy,
your young men will see visions,
your old men will dream dreams.

18 *Yes; on my servants, male and female, in those days*
I will pour out some of my spirit, and they will prophesy.[59]

19 *I will give wonders in heaven above,*
and signs on earth below,
blood and fire and smoky mist;[60]

20 *the sun will be turned into darkness*
and the moon into blood,
before the great and notable day of the Lord comes;

21 *and every one who invokes the Lord's name will be saved.'*

14-15 The ecstatic utterances had achieved a useful purpose in attracting a large crowd around the disciples. Now Peter stood up, supported by his eleven fellow-apostles, and he began to address those who had gathered around. Whatever account may be given of the geography of verses 1-4, it is difficult to think of a more appropriate or probable setting for Peter's address than the outer court of the temple.

There is no suggestion that Peter now spoke in a tongue unknown to himself, although the verb "addressed" may imply divine inspiration.[61] Before he proclaims the apostolic message, based on the resurrection of the crucified Jesus, he gives an explanation of the phenomena that had drawn the wondering multitude together.

He starts with a brief rebuttal of the charge of drunkenness. If the charge itself was made in jest, there is good humor in Peter's dismissal of it; it is too early in the morning, he says, for them to have had an opportunity to drink to excess.

16 Then comes a statement of tremendous import: "This is what was said through the prophet Joel." Joel, like other Old Testament prophets,

58. Cod. D and some other Western authorities omit "Joel."
59. The Western text omits "and they will prophesy" (probably by harmonization with the OT text).
60. The Western text omits "blood and fire and smoky mist."
61. The Greek verb is ἀποφθέγγομαι, used already of Spirit-inspired "utterance" in v. 4. (In LXX it is used of prophesying in 1 Chron. 25:1, of soothsaying in Mic. 5:12.)

had spoken of what was going to take place in the "last days." Peter's quotation of his prophecy means that these days, the days of the fulfilment of God's purpose, have arrived. In another place Peter tells how the prophets who foretold the coming manifestation of God's grace "searched and inquired about this salvation; they inquired what person or time was indicated by the Spirit of Christ within them when predicting the sufferings of Christ and the subsequent glories" (1 Pet. 1:10-11). But now that Christ has been "made manifest at the end of the times" (1 Pet. 1:20), his followers have no further need to search and inquire (as the prophets themselves did) what person or time the prophetic Spirit pointed to, for they *know:* the person is Jesus; the time is now. The "last days" began with Christ's appearance on earth and will be consummated by his reappearance; they are the days during which the age to come overlaps the present age. Hence the assurance with which Peter could quote the prophet's words and declare "This is it."

17-18   The quotation comes from Joel 2:28-32. Joel announces the coming of the day of the Lord, the day when he will act in righteousness and mercy. Joel says that the events of that day will come "hereafter";[62] Luke, matching the prediction to the fulfilment, uses the more precise phrase "in the last days."[63] For Luke the sign of the age to come is the presence of the Spirit. The context of Joel's prophecy contains a call to repentance in hope of divine forgiveness (Joel 2:12-14)—a call which is echoed by Peter later on (v. 38). But the prominent feature of the words which Peter quotes is the prediction of the outpouring of God's Spirit on the whole human race— literally, "on all flesh." Luke sees in these words an adumbration of the worldwide Gentile mission, even if Peter could not have realized their full import when he quoted them on the day of Pentecost. Certainly the outpouring of the Spirit on 120 Jews could not in itself fulfil the prediction of such outpouring "on all flesh"; but it was the beginning of the fulfilment. Joel's words may have harked back to Moses' exclamation: "Would that all the LORD's people were prophets, that the LORD would put his spirit upon them!" (Num. 11:29). The effect of the Spirit's outpouring is the gift of prophecy, exercised in visions and dreams and by word of mouth.

19-21   The wonders and signs to be revealed in the world of nature may have more relevance in their immediate setting than is sometimes realized. "It is remarkable," says B. J. Hubbard, how Peter's quotation from

---

62. LXX μετὰ ταῦτα (cf. 15:16 below), translating Heb. *'aḥărê kēn*. For "in the last days" introducing an oracle cf. Isa. 2:2 par. Mic. 4:1. There are other variations from the OT text in this citation: in the OT "your young men will see visions" follows and does not precede "your old men will dream dreams"; the clause "and they will prophesy" (v. 18) is absent from the OT, as also are the words "above," "signs," and "below" (v. 19).

63. Similar phraseology is used by other NT writers to denote the new age inaugurated by the Christ-event: "the ends of the ages" (1 Cor. 10:11), "these last days" (Heb. 1:2), "the consummation of the ages" (Heb. 9:26), "the last times" (1 Pet. 1:20), "the last hour" (1 John 2:18).

Joel "alludes to so many of the phenomena (including dreams and visions) which characterize the Lukan version of Christian origins."[64] More particularly, little more than seven weeks earlier the people of Jerusalem had indeed seen the darkening of the sun, during the early afternoon of Good Friday; and later in that same afternoon the paschal full moon may well have risen blood-red in the sky in consequence of that preternatural gloom.[65] These phenomena are now interpreted as harbingers of the advent of the day of the Lord[66]— a day of judgment, to be sure, but more immediately the day of God's salvation to all who invoked his name.[67]

b. The resurrection of Jesus proclaimed (2:22-28)

22 *"Men of Israel, listen to this. I speak of Jesus of Nazareth, a man attested to you by God by mighty works and wonders and signs which God did among you[68] through him, as you yourselves know.*

23 *He was delivered up to you in accordance with God's appointed counsel and foreknowledge; you took him[69] and by the agency of lawless men you nailed him up[70] and killed him.*

24 *But God raised him up, loosing the pangs of death, because it was not possible for death to hold him fast.*

25 *David says with regard to him,
'I saw the Lord before me always,
        because he is at my right hand, that I may not be moved;*

26 *therefore my heart has rejoiced
        and my tongue has exulted,
        and my flesh moreover will rest in hope*

27 *because you will not abandon my soul to Hades,
        nor let your holy one see corruption.*

28 *You have made known to me the ways of life;
        with your presence you will make me full of joy.'*

---

64. B. J. Hubbard, "The Role of Commissioning Accounts in Acts," in *Perspectives on Luke-Acts*, ed. C. H. Talbert (Edinburgh, 1978), p. 198.

65. It could not have been a solar eclipse, because the moon was full at Passovertide. On the meaning of Luke 23:44-45, "the sun's light failed" (τοῦ ἡλίου ἐκλιπόντος), see G. R. Driver, "Two Problems in the New Testament," *JTS* n.s. 16 (1965), pp. 331-37 (he attributes the darkness on Good Friday to a *ḥamsin* wind). Cf. C. J. Humphreys and W. G. Waddington, "Dating the Crucifixion," *Nature* 306 (1983), pp. 743-46 (they explain the blood-red appearance of the moon by a lunar eclipse on April 3, A.D. 33).

66. The adjective "notable" (LXX ἐπιφανής) presupposes Heb. *nir'eh* in place of MT *nôrā'* ("terrible").

67. Cf. the description of the great day of wrath in Rev. 6:12, based on this same oracle of Joel.

68. The Western text reads "us" (ἡμᾶς) instead of "you" (ὑμᾶς).

69. "You took him" reflects the participle λαβόντες, read in א² D E Ψ and the majority of cursives (but omitted from most critical editions).

70. Gk. προσπήγνυμι and not the more usual σταυρόω (lit. "fasten to a stake").

22 Peter now takes up his main theme: the proclamation of Jesus as Lord and Messiah. The early apostolic preaching[71] regularly comprises four elements (not always in the same order): (1) the announcement that the age of fulfilment has arrived; (2) an account of the ministry, death, and triumph of Jesus; (3) citation of Old Testament scriptures whose fulfilment in these events proves Jesus to be the one to whom they pointed forward; (4) a call to repentance. These four elements are present in Peter's proclamation here. He has already announced that the age of fulfilment has come (v. 16); now he summarizes the story of Jesus.

The "mighty works and wonders and signs" which God accomplished through Jesus of Nazareth[72] among the "men of Israel" needed no elaboration; they were fresh in the minds of all. That these acts were indeed performed by divine power had been generally acknowledged except by those who saw that such an acknowledgment would involve unwelcome theological implications.[73] The miracles of Jesus were not mere "wonders"; they were "mighty works," evidences of the power of God operating among the people, and "signs" of the kingdom of God—"the powers of the age to come," in the language of Heb. 6:5. "If it is by the finger of God that I cast out demons," said Jesus on one occasion, "then the kingdom of God has come upon you" (Luke 11:20). And the generality of those who saw his mighty works agreed: "God has visited his people" (Luke 7:16).[74]

23 Yet this Jesus had been put to death by crucifixion. While the judge who sentenced him to this form of death and the soldiers who carried out the execution were Romans, "lawless men" in the sense of being outside the range of the law of Israel,[75] yet it was the Jewish authorities, more

---

71. Often called the *kerygma* (κήρυγμα, from κηρύσσω, "proclaim as a herald," κῆρυξ).

72. Or "Jesus the Nazoraean" ('Ιησοῦν τὸν Ναζωραῖον, v. 22). In spite of a variety of other explanations of the title Ναζωραῖος as used of Jesus, it seems clear that the NT writers took it to be synonymous with Ναζαρηνός, "belonging to Nazareth." There is no difference in sense between "Jesus the Nazoraean" here and "Jesus from Nazareth" in 10:38 below. Gk. Ναζωραῖος is equivalent to Heb. *noṣrî* (with vowel metathesis). See M. Black, *An Aramaic Approach to the Gospels and Acts* (Oxford, ³1967), pp. 197-200. For the plural Ναζωραῖοι used of the followers of Jesus (24:5) see p. 440, n. 15.

73. See Luke 11:15 for the charge that he exorcised demons by the power of Beelzebul.

74. Cf. D. S. Cairns, *The Faith that Rebels* (London, 1929); A. Richardson, *The Miracle Stories of the Gospels* (London, 1941); C. Brown, *Miracles and the Critical Mind* (Grand Rapids, 1984), pp. 293-325. The Greek word for "miracles" (τέρατα) is never used in the NT except in conjunction with the word for "signs" (σημεῖα). Here a third word, "mighty works" (δυνάμεις), is added to make the significance of these miracles even plainer. Cf. Heb. 2:4.

75. Gk. ἄνομοι, in the sense which it bears, e.g., in 1 Cor. 9:21, where the ἄνομοι are Gentiles, as opposed to those ὑπὸ νόμον (Jews). As for the more general

particularly the chief priests, who handed him over to the Romans. Such an action was not unparalleled: another Jesus, the son of one Ananias, was handed over to the Roman governor for appropriate treatment in A.D. 62 by the Jerusalem magistrates when they found themselves unable to handle him.[76] Peter's words are here addressed to the people of Jerusalem, not to the Jewish visitors who were present in the city for Pentecost.

Nevertheless, the action of those who took part, directly or indirectly, in putting Jesus to death was overruled by "God's appointed counsel and foreknowledge." God himself is said by Paul not to have spared his own Son but to have "given him up for us all" (Rom. 8:32). It was the divine purpose, revealed through the prophets, that the Messiah should suffer (cf. 3:18, etc.). This carries with it no diminution of the guilt of those who handed him over to death or carried the sentence out; but it does point the way to the removal of their guilt and the assurance of pardon. Peter, however, says nothing about this until his hearers are truly convicted of their sin.

24 The sentence passed on Jesus by an earthly court and executed by Roman soldiers has been reversed, Peter asserts, by a higher court. They put him to death, but God raised him up and "loosed the pangs of death."[77] It was not possible that the chosen one of God should remain in the grip of death; "the abyss can no more hold the Redeemer than a pregnant woman can hold the child in her body."[78] If his suffering and death were ordained by the determinate counsel of God, so were his resurrection and glory.

25-28 Now comes an Old Testament "testimony" confirming Peter's claim. The quotation is from the Greek version of Ps. 16:8-11.[79] From early days the Christian church maintained that the exaltation of Jesus took place in fulfilment of God's promise to David (cf. 13:34, with its quotation

---

sense of the word (cf. KJV "wicked"), it is relevant that the Romans are sometimes referred to in Jewish literature as *hārᵉšāʿîm*, "the wicked" (the Roman Empire is *malᵉkût hārᵉšāʿîm*, "the kingdom of the wicked"); cf. Mark 14:41, "the Son of man is betrayed into the hands of sinners" (ἁμαρτωλοί).

76. Josephus, *BJ* 6.303; cf. G. Vermes, *Jesus and the World of Judaism* (London, 1983), pp. viii-ix.

77. Gk. λύσας τὰς ὠδῖνας τοῦ θανάτου. The Hebrew phrases *ḥeḇlê māwet*, "the cords of death" (Pss. 18:4; 116:3) and *ḥeḇlê šᵉʾōl*, "the cords of Sheol" (Ps. 18:5), are rendered ὠδῖνες θανάτου and ὠδῖνες ᾅδου respectively in LXX, possibly because of the similarity between Heb. *ḥeḇel* ("cord") and *ḥēḇel* ("birthpang"). But one need not see here an allusion to the *ḥeḇlô šel māšîaḥ*, "the birthpangs of Messiah" (i.e., the troubles ushering in the messianic age; cf. Mark 13:8). Polycarp (*Ep.* 1:2) may echo this passage of Acts when he speaks of Jesus as the one "whom God raised up, having loosed the pangs of Hades" (τὰς ὠδῖνας τοῦ ᾅδου).

78. G. Bertram, *TDNT* 9, p. 673 (*s.v.* ὠδίν).

79. LXX has "I beheld" (προορώμην) for MT "I have set" (*šiwwîtî*) and "my tongue" (ἡ γλῶσσά μου) for MT "my glory" (*kᵉḇōdî*); it renders *lāḇeṭaḥ* ("in safety," "securely") by ἐπ᾽ ἐλπίδι ("in hope") and *šaḥat* ("pit") by διαφθορά ("destruction," "corruption").

from Isa. 55:3). In the Hebrew and Greek texts alike Ps. 16 is assigned to David. But the words now quoted from it (Peter's argument runs) cannot refer to David, for his soul did go to the abode of the dead; his body did undergo decomposition. No one would claim that David had been rescued from the grave; his tomb—and not an empty tomb—was still a well-known landmark (v. 29). The words, "you will not abandon my soul to Hades, nor let your holy one see corruption," refer therefore to the Messiah of David's line, "great David's greater Son," whom David himself prefigured and in whose name he spoke those words by the Spirit of prophecy. (That the messianic interpretation of the words persisted in Jewish tradition is indicated by the gloss on Ps. 16:9 in a much later *midrash:* "my glory rejoices over the Lord Messiah, who will rise from me," that is, from David.[80]) These prophetic words, Peter goes on to argue, have been fulfilled in Jesus of Nazareth and in no one else; Jesus of Nazareth is therefore the expected Messiah.

c. Jesus: Lord and Messiah (2:29-36)

29 *"My brothers, I can speak to you openly about the patriarch David. He died and was buried, and his tomb is with us to this day.*

30 *But he was a prophet, and knew that God had sworn an oath to him that one of his descendants would sit on his throne,[81]*

31 *so by foresight he spoke of the resurrection of the Christ, saying that he was not abandoned to Hades nor did his flesh undergo corruption.*

32 *This Jesus has been raised up by God; of this we are all witnesses.*

33 *So, having been exalted by the right hand of God, and having received from his Father the promise of the Holy Spirit, he has poured out this,[82] as you both see and hear.*

34 *It was not David who ascended into heaven; rather, David himself says,*

'The Lord said to my lord,
Sit at my right hand,

35 *until I make your enemies a footstool for your feet.'*

36 *Let the whole house of Israel therefore know for certain that God has made him—this Jesus, whom you crucified—both Lord and Christ."*

29 It was a matter of public knowledge in and around Jerusalem that

---

80. *Midrash Tehillim* on Ps. 16:9.

81. The KJV expansion, "that of the fruit of his loins, according to the flesh [cf. Rom. 1:3; 9:5], he would raise up Christ to sit on his throne," goes back through the Byzantine recension to a Western reading.

82. Some Western authorities add "gift" after "this" (τοῦτο τὸ δῶρον); though not part of the original text, the addition indicates the true meaning.

David—the "patriarch,"[83] as Peter calls him (because he was the founder of a dynasty)—died and was buried and had never been raised from the tomb where he lay to the south of the city, near Siloam. His tomb is mentioned in Neh. 3:16 (the site having been remembered from preexilic times). It was entered and robbed by John Hyrcanus during the siege of Jerusalem in 135/4 B.C.; over a century later Herod, having been halted (by divine action, it was believed) in an attempt to follow Hyrcanus's example, made amends for his impiety by building a monument of white marble at the entrance to the tomb.[84] Like David, Jesus had died and been buried, but even if his tomb could be pointed out, there was no need to do so because, unlike David, he was risen; he was no longer there.

30-32 Before he died, however, David received a solemn promise from God, as Ps. 132:11 declares:

> "The LORD swore to David a sure oath
> from which he will not turn back:
> 'One of the sons of your body
> I will set on your throne.' "[85]

It was with regard to that descendant of whom the promise spoke that David, as an inspired prophet, uttered words betokening deliverance from the grave and resurrection from the dead. And in asserting that Jesus of Nazareth had been so delivered and raised up by God, Peter and his colleagues were making a claim which they could confirm by their personal ocular testimony: "of this we are all witnesses."

In Jesus' own teaching no emphasis is laid on his Davidic descent, but his identity and authority were early interpreted in terms of a "Son of David" christology. The expectation of the Davidic Messiah burned brightly in the hearts of pious Jews in the first century B.C., including those of the circle into which Jesus was born.[86] Paul does not develop a "Son of David" christology, but he takes Jesus' Davidic descent for granted as something which was widely known and confessed in the primitive church (cf. Rom. 1:3; 15:12).

33 But where was Jesus now, if he had been raised from the dead? He was enthroned on high, exalted by God's right hand.[87] He had received from his Father the promised gift of the Holy Spirit, and had now poured out that Spirit on his followers; all Peter's hearers had just witnessed the external tokens of this outpouring. The triumph of Jesus was attested by the witness

83. Gk. πατριάρχης denotes the founder or ancestor of a family; it is used in 7:8-9 below of the twelve sons of Jacob and in Heb. 7:4 of Abraham.

84. Josephus, *BJ* 1.61; *Ant.* 7.393; 13.249; 16.179-83.

85. There is another allusion to this psalm in 7:46-47 below.

86. *Ps. Sol.* 17:23-51; Luke 1:32-33, 69.

87. Instrumental dative (τῇ δεξιᾷ); cf. 5:31, also Ps. 118:16 (LXX 117:16), δεξιὰ κυρίου ὕψωσέν με ("the Lord's right hand has exalted me").

of his disciples and the witness of Old Testament prophecy, as it was also to be attested by his own enduring activity (3:6; 4:10, etc.) and by the witness of the Holy Spirit (5:32).

He who had earlier received the Spirit for the public discharge of his own earthly ministry had now received that same Spirit to impart to his representatives, in order that they might continue, and indeed share in, the ministry which he had begun. His present impartation of the Spirit to them, attended as it was by sensible signs, was a further open vindication of the claim that he was the exalted Messiah.

34-35   The claim is now clinched by another proof from scripture, this time from Ps. 110:1.[88] The belief that this too was a Davidic psalm, and that the "lord" to whom the invitation, "Sit at my right hand," was addressed by God was the Messiah, is attested in the Gospel incident of Mark 12:35-37. Peter's argument is similar to that already based on Ps. 16:10. The invitation to sit at God's right hand was not addressed to David: David did not ascend personally to heaven to share the throne of God. The invitation was addressed to the son of David, and has found its fulfilment in Jesus. He has been exalted not only *by* God's right hand (as has been stated in v. 33) but to take his place *at* God's right hand, the position of supremacy over the universe. Thus the words were vindicated with which he had shocked the Jewish court of inquiry less than two months previously: "from now on the Son of man shall be seated at the right hand of the power of God" (Luke 22:69). This exaltation of Jesus, in accordance with Ps. 110:1, is an integral part of the primitive apostolic message, as it remains an integral part of the historic Christian creeds.

36   The good news has been proclaimed: the witness of the apostles and the testimony of prophecy have combined to give assurance of the truth of the proclamation.[89] The attested facts point to ône conclusion: God has

---

88. Cf. the use made of Ps. 110:1 in Rom. 8:34; 1 Cor. 15:25; Col. 3:1; Heb. 1:3, 13, etc. (and of Ps. 110:4 in Heb. 5:6, etc.). The oracle here quoted may have had its original life-setting in the enthronement ceremony for a Davidic king; it provides the foundation for the credal assertion that Christ is seated at the right hand of God. See D. M. Hay, *Glory at the Right Hand: Psalm 110 in Early Christianity* (Nashville/New York, 1973); M. Gourgues, *À la droite de Dieu: Résurrection de Jésus et actualisation du Psaume 110,1,* EB (Paris, 1978).

89. The "whole house of Israel" is called on to take cognizance of the exaltation of the crucified Jesus. For this phrase cf. Ezek. 37:11; it appears in the *Qaddish,* an Aramaic prayer in the Jewish liturgy:

"Magnified and sanctified be his great name
In the world which he created according to his will;
May he establish his kingdom in your life and in your days,
And in the life of *the whole house of Israel,*
Speedily and at a near time.
And say ye, Amen."

THE BOOK OF THE ACTS

made the crucified Jesus both Lord and Messiah.[90] The contrast is pointed between the treatment which Jesus received from his earthly judges and that which he has received from God. When he claimed to be "the Messiah, the Son of the Blessed" (Mark 14:61), his claim was rejected as false and judged to be worthy of death. But God has vindicated his claim as true, and brought him back from death, exalting him to the highest place that heaven affords. His messiahship, acclaimed at his baptism, was confirmed by his resurrection; by it he was "designated Son of God in power" (Rom. 1:4). But he has been exalted not only as Messiah and Son of God, but as Lord. The first apostolic sermon concludes with the first apostolic creed: "Jesus is Lord" (cf. Rom. 10:9; 1 Cor. 12:3; Phil. 2:11)—"Lord" not only as bearer of a courtesy title but as bearer of "the name which is above every name" (Phil. 2:9). To a Jew there was only one name "above every name"—the ineffable name of the God of Israel, frequently represented in synagogue reading and in the Greek Bible by the designation "Lord."[91] That the early Christians meant to give Jesus the title "Lord" in this highest sense of all is indicated by their not hesitating on occasion to apply to him passages of Old Testament scripture referring to Yahweh.[92] Indeed, in this very context it may well be that the promise of Joel 2:32, "all who call on Yahweh's name shall be delivered," is viewed as being fulfilled in those members of Peter's audience who repentantly invoke Jesus as Lord.

4. Call to Repentance (2:37-40)

37 When they heard this, they were conscience-stricken and said to Peter and the other apostles,[93] "What are we to do, brothers?"
38 "Repent," said Peter to them, "and let each of you be baptized in the

90. Gk. κύριον . . . καὶ Χριστόν. Cf. the conjunction of the two titles, Χριστὸς κύριος ("the Anointed Lord" or "the Lord Messiah") in Luke 2:11 (also in Ps. Sol. 17:36).

91. The name whose consonantal skeleton is YHWH came to be regarded among Jews as so sacred that it might not be pronounced (except, it is said, by the high priest on the annual day of atonement, as long as the temple stood). MT supplies the consonantal skeleton YHWH with the vowel points of whatever word is to be substituted for it in public reading—usually ʾăḏōnāi, "Lord." In Christian MSS of LXX YHWH is regularly represented by κύριος (most often without the definite article). In Ps. 110:1 (LXX 109:1), quoted in v. 34 (εἶπεν [ὁ] κύριος τῷ κυρίῳ μου), the first κύριος represents YHWH, the second represents ʾăḏōn, a common noun meaning "lord." When Peter says that God has made Jesus "Lord," he gives that title a fullness of meaning far beyond that of a mere courtesy title. Cf. V. Taylor, The Names of Jesus (London, 1953), pp. 38-51; W. Kramer, Christ, Lord, Son of God, E.T., SBT 50 (London, 1966), pp. 65-107, 151-82, 215-22; F. Hahn, The Titles of Jesus in Christology, E.T. (London, 1969), pp. 68-135.

92. Consider, e.g., the application of Isa. 45:23 in Phil. 2:10 ("that at the name of Jesus every knee should bow"), and of Isa. 8:13 in 1 Pet. 3:15 ("sanctify in your hearts Christ as Lord").

93. Various Western authorities omit "other" before "apostles" and frame the following question thus: "What are we to do then, brothers? Show us."

name of Jesus Christ[94] for the forgiveness of your sins, and you will receive the gift of the Holy Spirit.

39 *For the promise is for you and your children,[95] even for all who are far away—all, in fact, whom the Lord our God may call."*

40 *He warned them with many further words, appealing to them, "Save yourselves from this perverse generation."*

37 Peter's preaching proved effective, not only persuading his hearers' minds but convicting their consciences. If Jesus of Nazareth was indeed their appointed Messiah, then no guilt could be greater than the guilt of treating him as he had been treated. If they had refused him in whom all their hope of salvation rested, what hope of salvation was left to them now? Well might they cry out in anguish of heart, "What are we to do, brothers?"

38 The reply was unspeakably reassuring. Incredible as it must appear, Peter told them that there was hope even now. Let them repent of their sin and turn to God; let them submit to baptism in the name of Jesus, confessed as Messiah. Then not only would they receive forgiveness of sins, but they would receive also the gift of the Holy Spirit—the gift which had been bestowed on the apostles themselves only a few hours before.

Since John the Baptist distinguished his own baptism in water—a "baptism of repentance for the forgiveness of sins" (Mark 1:4 par. Luke 3:3)—from the baptism in the Spirit to be administered by the Coming One, it might have been expected that, when the disciples experienced the outpouring of the Spirit from the day of Pentecost onward, they would discontinue water baptism as having been superseded by something better. In fact they did not: they continued to baptize converts in water "for the forgiveness of sins," but this baptism was now part of a more comprehensive initiation which took its character especially from the receiving of the Spirit.

Repentance was plainly called for: a complete change of heart, a spiritual about-face, was essential if those who had failed to recognize their God-sent deliverer in Jesus were nevertheless to enjoy the deliverance which he had come to procure for them and was now offering them from his place of exaltation. The call to repentance had been sounded by John and Jesus (and by Jesus' disciples in his name) in the years preceding the crucifixion,[96] and it remained an essential element in the proclamation of the apostolic message.[97]

As in John's preaching, a call to baptism is conjoined with the call to repentance. Apparently the command to be baptized occasioned no surprise. The practice of baptism was tolerably familiar to Peter's hearers, who (like

94. The Western text inserts "the Lord" before "Jesus Christ."
95. The Western text reads "for us and for our children."
96. Mark 1:4, 15; Luke 5:32; 13:3, 5.
97. Cf. 3:19; 8:22; 17:30; 20:21; 26:20. On Paul's usage see p. 389, n. 45.

John's hearers before them) were required to receive baptism in water as the outward and visible sign of their repentance. But there are now two new features in the rite of water baptism: it is administered "in the name of Jesus Christ" and it is associated with "the gift of the Holy Spirit." These new features emphasize, in G. W. H. Lampe's words, that Christian baptism "is still an eschatological rite, for it looks forward to the final redemption which is still to come at the Lord's return in glory; but, considered in relation to John's baptism, it represents a realization and fulfilment of Israel's hope."[98]

It is administered "in the name of Jesus Christ"—not only by his authority but also, probably, in the sense that his name was invoked or confessed by the person being baptized (cf. 22:16). In addition, the person who administered the baptism appears to have named the name of Jesus over converts as they were being baptized (cf. 15:17). And it is associated with "the gift of the Holy Spirit." Baptism in the Spirit is an inward work; baptism in water now becomes its external token. Baptism in water is thus given a richer significance than it formerly had, thanks to the saving work of Christ and the reception of the Spirit. The baptism of the Spirit which it was our Lord's prerogative to bestow was, strictly speaking, something that took place once for all on the day of Pentecost when he poured out the promised gift on his disciples and thus constituted them the people of God in the new age; baptism in water continued to be the visible sign by which those who believed the gospel, repented of their sins, and acknowledged Jesus as Lord were publicly incorporated into the Spirit-baptized fellowship of the new people of God.[99]

It would indeed be a mistake to link the words "for the forgiveness of sins" with the command "be baptized" to the exclusion of the prior command to repent. It is against the whole genius of biblical religion to suppose that the outward rite could have any value except insofar as it was accompanied by the work of grace within. In a similar passage in the next chapter (3:19) the blotting out of the people's sins is a direct consequence of their repenting and turning to God; nothing is said about baptism, although it is no doubt implied (the idea of an unbaptized believer does not seem to be entertained in the New Testament). So here the reception of the Spirit is conditional not on baptism in itself but on baptism in Jesus' name as the expression of repentance.[100]

98. G. W. H. Lampe, *The Seal of the Spirit,* p. 33.

99. This aspect is more prominent in Paul (cf. 1 Cor. 12:13) than in Luke (who nevertheless implies it by effectively dating the life of the Christian church from the Pentecostal descent of the Spirit). The vital unity of the people of God under the new covenant with the people of God in earlier days is not denied; the new beginning to which OT believers had looked forward was now an accomplished fact in the experience of those who received the gift of the Spirit.

100. On baptism see H. G. Marsh, *The Origin and Significance of New Testament Baptism* (Manchester, 1941); W. F. Flemington, *The New Testament Doctrine of*

The gift of the Spirit is to be distinguished from the *gifts* of the Spirit. The gift of the Spirit is the Spirit himself, bestowed by the exalted Lord under the Father's authority; the gifts of the Spirit are those spiritual faculties which the Spirit imparts, as he "apportions to each one individually as he wills" (1 Cor. 12:11). It is true, as has frequently been pointed out, that Luke thinks of the receiving of the Spirit in particular relation to the impressive manifestations which commonly accompanied it in the apostolic age,[101] but the gift which is promised in verse 38 to those who repent and are baptized is the Spirit himself. This gift may comprehend a variety of *gifts* of the Spirit, but first and foremost "the saving benefits of Christ's work as applied to the believer by the Spirit."[102] The relation between these saving benefits and the work of Christ by which they are made available is not explicitly set out by Luke in the present context, but it is implicit here and is stated more expressly elsewhere in his record.

There is no suggestion here that believers' reception of the Spirit was conditional on their having apostolic hands laid on them. To be sure, in such a brief summary various details would inevitably be left out; but if Luke held that the laying on of apostolic hands was an indispensable prerequisite for the receiving of the Spirit (as some have precariously inferred from 8:16), it is remarkable that he has nothing to say about it in this Pentecostal narrative.[103]

39 The promise of the gospel was extended not only to those present on that occasion, not only to the contemporary generation but to their descendants as well,[104] not only to the people of Jerusalem but to those of distant lands (and, as appears later in Luke's narrative, not only to Jews but to Gentiles also). Peter's words echo two prophetic passages—Isa. 57:19 ("Peace, peace to the far and to the near, says the LORD") and Joel 2:32, where the words quoted in verses 17-21 above are continued thus: "for in Mount Zion and in Jerusalem there shall be those who escape, as the LORD has said, and among the survivors shall be those whom the LORD calls."

Baptism (London, 1948); O. Cullmann, *Baptism in the New Testament*, E.T. (London, 1950); G. W. H. Lampe, *The Seal of the Spirit;* G. R. Beasley-Murray, *Baptism in the New Testament* (London, 1962); K. Barth, *Church Dogmatics*, E.T., 4/4 (Edinburgh, 1969); J. K. Howard, *New Testament Baptism* (London, 1970); J. D. G. Dunn, *Baptism in the Holy Spirit* (London, 1970).

101. Cf. Lampe, *The Seal of the Spirit*, pp. 47-48.

102. N. B. Stonehouse, "Repentance, Baptism and the Gift of the Spirit," in *Paul Before the Areopagus and Other New Testament Studies* (Grand Rapids, 1957), p. 85.

103. Cf. Lampe, *The Seal of the Spirit*, pp. 64-67, with the literature to which he refers. Note his answer to the view that "be baptized" in v. 38 is used by synecdoche to cover the whole initiatory rite, including the imposition of apostolic hands: "there is absolutely no evidence to support it, so far as the New Testament is concerned" (p. 68). Cf. pp. 168-70 below (on 8:16).

104. Cf. the promises to Noah (Gen. 9:9), Abraham (Gen. 13:15; 17:7-8; Gal. 3:16), and David (Pss. 18:50; 89:34-37; 132:11-12).

Those who call on the name of the Lord are those whom the Lord himself has called—and called effectually.

40 In such terms, then, Peter bore his reasoned witness to the gospel facts and to the promise of salvation.[105] The generation to which his hearers belonged had been upbraided by Jesus as a "faithless and perverse generation" and as an "evil generation" because of its unbelieving response to him and his message (Luke 9:41; 11:29). But there was a way of deliverance from the judgment which such faithlessness must inevitably incur. The deliverance of which Joel had spoken was to be enjoyed by a remnant of the whole people; so now Peter urged his hearers to make sure, by a repentant calling on the Lord, that they belonged to this remnant and saved themselves from that perverse generation. The new community is viewed, in fact, as the believing remnant of the old Israel and the nucleus of the new.

5. The First Christian Church (2:41-47)

41 *Those then who accepted his message were baptized: that day about three thousand persons were added to them.*

42 *They adhered to the apostles' teaching[106] and fellowship, the breaking of bread, and the prayers.*

43 *A sense of awe fell on every person, and many wonders and signs were done through the apostles.[107]*

44 *All the believers were together in fellowship[108] and they held everything in common:*

45 *they sold their property, real and personal, and distributed the proceeds[109] to all according to the need of each one.*

46 *They met together constantly in the temple day by day and, breaking bread at home, they shared their food with exultation and generosity of heart,*

47 *praising God and enjoying favor with all the people.[110] And the Lord added to their fellowship[111] day by day those who received salvation.*

---

105. See E. Lövestam, "Der Rettungsappell in Ag 2,40," *ASTI* 12 (1983), pp. 84-92.

106. The Western text adds "in Jerusalem."

107. P^{74} ℵ A C and some other authorities add: "in Jerusalem, and great fear was upon all."

108. The Greek phrase ἐπὶ τὸ αὐτό, translated "together in fellowship" in v. 44 and "to their fellowship" in v. 47 (cf. 1:15), seems to have acquired a semitechnical sense, "in church fellowship" (see MHT II, p. 473). These believers may have constituted a kind of synagogue within the wider Jewish community—the "synagogue of the Nazarenes."

109. The Western text reads: "And as many as had property, real or personal, sold it, and distributed it daily. . . ."

110. For "all the people" the Western text reads "all the world" (for the idiom cf. Fr. *tout le monde*).

111. Gk. ἐπὶ τὸ αὐτό ("together"). The Western text adds "to the church."

41 Those of Peter's hearers, accordingly, who believed his message were baptized, some three thousand in all. Through the apostolic witness Jesus thus acquired more followers in one day than in the whole of his public ministry. No wonder that, according to the Fourth Evangelist, he told his disciples that, as a result of his returning to the Father, they would perform greater works than they had ever seen him do (John 14:12).

42 Luke presents in this paragraph an ideal picture of this new community, rejoicing in the forgiveness of sins and the gift of the Spirit. The community, the apostolic fellowship, was constituted on the basis of the apostolic teaching. This teaching was authoritative because it was the teaching of the Lord communicated through the apostles in the power of the Spirit. For believers of later generations the New Testament scriptures form the written deposit of the apostolic teaching. The apostolic succession is recognized most clearly in those churches which adhere most steadfastly to the apostolic teaching.

The apostolic fellowship found expression in a number of practical ways, of which two are mentioned in verse 42—the breaking of bread and prayers. The "breaking of bread" probably denotes more than the regular taking of food together: the regular observance of what came to be called the Lord's Supper seems to be in view. While this observance appears to have formed part of an ordinary meal, the emphasis on the inaugural action of breaking the bread, "a circumstance wholly trivial in itself," says Rudolf Otto, suggests that this was "the significant element of the celebration. . . . But it could only be significant when it was a 'signum', viz. of Christ's being broken in death."[112] As for the prayers in which they participated, the primary reference is no doubt to their own appointed seasons for united prayer, although we know that the apostles also attended the Jewish prayer services in the temple (cf. 3:1). The community's prayers would follow Jewish models, but their content would be enriched because of the Christ-event.[113]

43 The conviction of sin that followed Peter's preaching was no momentary panic, but filled the people with a lasting sense of awe. God was at work among them; they were witnessing the dawn of the new age. This impression was intensified by the wonders and signs performed through the apostles. The words of Joel which Peter had quoted at the outset of his address declared that the "great and notable day" would be heralded by "wonders in heaven above" and "signs on earth below." Among those signs on earth must be reckoned the works of mercy and power which God

112. R. Otto, *The Kingdom of God and the Son of Man*, E.T. (London, 1943), p. 315.

113. On the wider implications of v. 42 see P. H. Menoud, *La vie de l'église naissante* (Neuchâtel/Paris, 1952).

accomplished through Jesus, in token of the advent of his kingdom (v. 22). And just as the miracles of Jesus when he was on earth were "signs" of the kingdom of God, those performed through his apostles partook of the same character (cf. 3:6).

44-45 In addition to the expressions of fellowship mentioned in verse 42, the members of the new community, living together thus and experiencing a deep sense of their unity in the Spirit, gave up all thought of private property and "held everything in common." Jesus and his apostles had shared a common purse, and the pooling of property was practised by at least one of the more rigorous parties among the Jews. The idea, therefore, was not entirely new. Those of the believers, then, who had landed property, as well as those whose belongings were of a more portable character, began to sell their assets and share out the proceeds among the members of their community, according to individual need.[114] This pooling of property could be maintained voluntarily only when their sense of spiritual unity was exceptionally active. As soon as the flame began to burn a little lower, the attempt to maintain the communal life was beset with serious difficulties.

46-47 So, in the weeks that followed the first Christian Pentecost, the believers met regularly in the temple precincts for public worship and public witness, while they took their fellowship meals in one another's homes and "broke the bread" in accordance with their Master's precedent. The part of the temple precincts where they seem to have gathered habitually was Solomon's colonnade, running along the east side of the outer court (cf. 3:11; 5:12). Their community was probably organized along the lines of the voluntary type of organization called a *ḥăḇûrāh,* a central feature of which was the common meal. The common meal could not conveniently be eaten in the temple precincts, so they ate "by households" (as the Greek phrase may be translated).[115] Within the community there was a spirit of rejoicing and generosity;[116] outside it, they enjoyed great popular goodwill. The praises of God were constantly on their tongues, and their numbers were constantly increased as he added more and more believers to the faithful

---

114. It is unnecessary to restrict this action to those Jews who had come to Jerusalem from their homes in the dispersion and bought burial plots in the Holy Land so as to enjoy certain advantages on the resurrection day, as suggested by K. Bornhäuser, *Studien zur Apostelgeschichte* (Gütersloh, 1934). Further details of this community of goods are given in 4:32-35. Similar wording to Luke's (εἶχον ἅπαντα κοινά) is used by Iamblichus of the Pythagoreans: κοινὰ γὰρ πᾶσι πάντα (*Life of Pythagoras* 30.168). For the Qumran community of goods see on 4:32-35 (p. 100 with n. 54).

115. Gk. κατ᾽ οἶκον, for which the sense "by households" is attested in papyri. Cf. 20:20 below, κατ᾽ οἴκους.

116. Gk. ἀφελότης καρδίας may be rendered "generosity of heart"; cf. ἁπλότης (τῆς) καρδίας in much the same sense in Eph. 6:5; Col. 3:22.

remnant.[117] It is the Lord's prerogative to add new members to his own community; it is the joyful prerogative of existing members to welcome to their fellowship those whom he has accepted.

117. In view of the force of σῴζω in vv. 21 and 40 one might almost translate τοὺς σῳζομένους here as "the remnant."

ACTS 3

C. AN ACT OF HEALING AND ITS CONSEQUENCES (3:1–4:31)

1. A Cripple Cured (3:1-10)

1 *One day Peter and John were going up to the temple[1] at the time of prayer (the ninth hour),*
2 *when a man, lame from his birth,[2] was being carried there. They used to set him down every day at the "Beautiful Gate" of the temple (as it is called), to seek alms from those who were going into the temple.*
3 *When he saw Peter and John about to enter the temple, he asked for alms.*
4 *Peter (with John beside him) fixed his eyes on him and said, "Look at us."*
5 *He paid attention to them, expecting to receive something from them.*
6 *Then Peter said, "I have no silver or gold, but I am giving you what I have: in the name of Jesus Christ of Nazareth, [get up and][3] walk!"*
7 *Then he took hold of him by the right hand and raised him up. Immediately[4] his feet and ankles were strengthened,*
8 *and at a bound he stood up and began to walk,[5] and went into the temple with them, walking and leaping, and as he did so he praised God.*
9 *All the people saw him walking and (heard him) praising God,*
10 *and they recognized him as the man who sat (begging) for alms at the Beautiful Gate of the temple, and were filled with surprise and amazement at what had happened to him.*

1-3 After the events of Pentecost, we have been told, "many wonders and signs were done through the apostles" (2:43). Luke now gives a fuller

---

1. After "temple" there is a Western addition: "for the evening (oblation)."
2. Lit., "lame from his mother's womb."
3. The words "get up and" are omitted by ℵ B D cop^{sah} (the agreement of B and D is particularly impressive; ἔγειρε καί may have been added under the influence of Luke 5:23 par.).
4. The Western text inserts "he stood up and" (ἐστάθη καί).
5. The Western text adds "rejoicing and exulting."

account of one of these, selecting one which was attended by exceptional publicity.

The apostles continued to live as observant Jews, attending the set services of worship in the Jerusalem temple. The two principal daily services accompanied the offering of the morning and evening sacrifices. One afternoon, as two of the apostles, Peter and John,[6] went up the steps leading from the outer court to the inner courts,[7] in order to be present in the Court of Israel for the service of prayer which accompanied the evening sacrifice (about 3 p.m.),[8] they were arrested by the sight of a cripple who lay begging at the "Beautiful Gate." This may be identical with the Nicanor Gate, as it is called in the Mishnah,[9] leading into the Court of the Women; the name here given to it may be more readily understood if it is further identified with the gate of Corinthian bronze described by Josephus, of such exquisite workmanship that it "far exceeded in value those gates that were plated with silver and set in gold."[10]

4-6   Fixing his eyes on the cripple, Peter attracted his attention. When he looked up expectantly, he received something more valuable than the most generous gift he had ever received from a charitable passer-by. The command to walk, given by Peter "in the name of Jesus Christ of Nazareth," was accompanied by the power to walk, imparted by that same name.

According to Cornelius a Lapide, Thomas Aquinas once called on

6. Presumably John the son of Zebedee, who appears as Peter's companion on two occasions in Acts (3:1–4:23 and 8:14-25); in both narratives he is but a lay figure alongside Peter. (It is doubtless the same John who is mentioned as one of the three "pillars" of the mother church in Gal. 2:9.)

7. The outer court of the temple as rebuilt and extended by Herod did not form part of the sacred precincts in the strictest sense: it was open to Gentiles, and therefore sometimes called the Court of the Gentiles (see p. 409, n. 46). From this court one might ascend steps to pass through the barrier which separated it from the inner courts. Notices in Greek and Latin were fixed to this barrier, warning Gentiles not to penetrate farther, on pain of death (see p. 409, nn. 47-49, on 21:28-29). The Beautiful Gate was probably one of the gates leading through the barrier. The first of the inner courts, containing the treasury (cf. Mark 12:41-44), was called the Court of the Women because Jewish women might enter thus far, but no farther. Jewish laymen might proceed farther, into the Court of Israel. Beyond this was the Court of the Priests (containing, among other things, the altar of burnt offering); at the west end of this inmost court stood the sanctuary building (the ναός), with its two compartments, the holy place and the holy of holies.

8. For the evening oblation see Ex. 29:39-42. Josephus says that public sacrifices were offered in the temple "twice daily, in the early morning and about the ninth hour" (*Ant.* 14.65). A service of public prayer accompanied these two sacrifices and there was a further prayer service at sunset. The "continual burnt offering," comprising the morning and evening sacrifices, is the subject of the Mishnaic treatise *Tāmîd*. See Schürer II, pp. 299-307.

9. Mishnah, *Middôt* 2.3. See E. Stauffer, "Das Tor des Nikanor," *ZNW* 44 (1952-53), pp. 44-66.

10. Josephus, *BJ* 5.201. (Josephus, *BJ* 5.184-247, and the Mishnaic tractate *Middôt* are our principal sources of information about the temple before its destruction in A.D. 70.)

Pope Innocent II when the latter was counting out a large sum of money. "You see, Thomas," said the Pope, "the church can no longer say, 'Silver and gold have I none.'" "True, holy father," was the reply; "neither can she now say, 'Rise and walk.'" The moral of this tale may be pondered by any Christian body that enjoys a fair degree of temporal prosperity.

7-8 Suiting his action to his word, Peter held out his hand and, taking the cripple's right hand, raised him to his feet. At that very moment, this man who had never been able to stand, let alone walk, became aware of a strange new strength in his legs and feet: instead of collapsing beneath him, they actually supported him.[11] First he practised standing, and when he found he could do that, he put one foot forward and tried to walk; when he found he could do that as well, ordinary walking seemed too humdrum a means of progress. His exultation must find more vigorous expression, so, leaping in the air and bounding along, discovering all that his new limbs were now capable of doing, he accompanied the two apostles into the inner precincts.[12] Nor was it with his limbs alone that he rejoiced in God's goodness to him; the temple courts echoed his shouts of joyful praise.

9-10 Naturally such indecorous behavior collected a curious crowd. The people recognized the man as the lame beggar who was such a familiar sight at the Beautiful Gate. They knew that there had been nothing fraudulent about his lameness, for he had been born lame; naturally, then, they were astonished at what they saw. It was marvelous enough, to be sure, but it was more than a marvel; it was a sign. The two apostles had not cured the man by any power or skill of their own; it was when they invoked the name and authority of Jesus Christ of Nazareth that he sprang up and found his feet for the first time in his life. Plainly, then, the power by which Jesus had healed such people during his public ministry was still present and active, exercised no longer directly but through his disciples.

But, as Peter and John went on to point out, that power was not confined to bodily healing. On a memorable occasion in Capernaum, Jesus had cured a paralyzed man by commanding him to rise and walk, in very similar terms to those which Peter used now; and his word which enabled the paralytic to walk was designed to supply public confirmation of his authority

11. "That which the physician observes during the months of the ordinary *gradual* cure of a lame man is here compressed into a moment" (A. Harnack, *Luke the Physician*, E.T. [London, 1907], p. 191). See also W. K. Hobart, *The Medical Language of St. Luke* (Dublin, 1882), pp. 34-37 (but Hobart's lexical data must be carefully checked).

12. In other words, "into the temple" (εἰς τὸ ἱερόν) in the sense in which this expression occurs in vv. 1, 2, and 3. The ἱερόν comprises the whole temple area, including the outer court; the ναός is the holy house itself (ναός is not used of the Jerusalem sanctuary in Acts, but is so used several times in the four Gospels, as in Luke 1:9, 21-22; 23:45).

to forgive sins as well as to heal the sick (Mark 2:10-11).[13] So, too, his disciples not only healed the sick in his name but also received from him "power and commandment . . . to declare and pronounce to his people, being penitent, the absolution and remission of their sins."[14] Again, on the present occasion, the very conduct of the former cripple was itself a token, to those who had eyes to see, of the advent of the new age.[15] Of the new age it had been said long before, "then shall the lame man leap like a hart" (Isa. 35:6). What Jesus' personal mighty works had signified was corroborated by this mighty work performed through his disciples: he was indeed Lord and Messiah.

2. Peter's Address in Solomon's Colonnade (3:11-26)

a. The power of Jesus' name (3:11-16)

11 *While the man was holding on to Peter and John, all the people, filled with amazement, ran together toward them in Solomon's Colonnade (as it is called).[16]*

12 *Seeing this, Peter addressed the people: "Men of Israel," he said, "why are you surprised at this, or why do you fix your eyes on us, as though we had made this man walk by some power or piety[17] of our own?*

13 *'The God of Abraham, Isaac, and Jacob,[18] the God of our fathers,' has glorified his Servant Jesus,[19] whom you handed over and repudiated in the presence of Pilate,[20] when he had decided to release him.*

14 *Yes, you repudiated[21] the Holy and Righteous One, you asked for a man who was a murderer to be released as a favor to you,*

13. Par. Matt. 9:6; Luke 5:24 (see p. 76, n. 3). Cf. John 5:8 (in the healing of the disabled man at the pool of Bethesda).

14. From the General Absolution in the Anglican *Book of Common Prayer*.

15. Compare the terms in which Jesus reassures John the Baptist that he was indeed the Coming One to whom John had pointed forward (Luke 7:18-23 par. Matt. 11:2-6); "the lame walk" was one of the signs which John's messengers were to report to him.

16. There is a Western expansion of this verse: "And as Peter and John came out, he came out with them, holding on to them; and the others, filled with amazement, took up their position in Solomon's Colonnade (as it is called)."

17. Chrysostom and several of the versions (Old Latin, Syriac, and Armenian) read "authority" (ἐξουσίᾳ) for "piety" (εὐσεβείᾳ). The Latin version of Irenaeus omits "or piety."

18. The Western text here (and in 7:32) repeats "the God of" before "Isaac" and "Jacob" (in conformity with Ex. 3:6).

19. After "Jesus" the Western text adds "Christ."

20. After "Pilate" the Western text reads "who judged him, when he was willing to release him."

21. There is a Western reading "oppressed" (ἐβαρύνατε) instead of "repudiated" (ἠρνήσασθε), possibly through transposition of consonants in an Aramaic original

15 *and you procured the death of the author of life. But God raised him from the dead; of this we are witnesses.*

16 *It is by faith in his name that he has strengthened this man,[22] whom you see and know; yes, it is the faith that comes through his name[23] that has given him this full health in the sight of you all.*

11   When the service of prayer and worship was over, Peter and John, together with the man who had been cured of his lameness, came out from the inner area of the temple to the outer court, probably going back through the Beautiful Gate, and made their way to the east side of the outer court, along which Solomon's Colonnade ran. The tradition tracing this colonnade or portico back to Solomon himself was certainly unfounded; the temple platform did not extend so far to the east in Solomon's day. The crowd of wondering spectators thronged them, and when they reached Solomon's Colonnade, Peter had a large audience, ready to listen to anything he might say. If the true significance of the healing miracle escaped many of the crowd (as no doubt it did), Peter had an excellent opportunity of bringing it home to them; and the man himself, who stuck fast by his two benefactors, provided visible confirmation of Peter's words.

12   Do not imagine, said Peter, addressing the multitude, that it was by any special power or piety of our own that we made this man walk. Do not stare at us, as though there were anything wonderful about us; and do not be so surprised at what has happened to this man: this is God's doing.

13   "The God of Abraham, Isaac, and Jacob, the God of our fathers," said Peter (using time-honored liturgical language, which goes back to the theophany at the burning bush),[24] "has glorified his Servant Jesus." In order to explain how the cripple had been cured, Peter found it necessary to relate the act of God which had so recently been accomplished in their midst. The cripple had been cured because Jesus had been glorified. From his place of exaltation Jesus had endowed his disciples with power to act in his name, and to perform mighty works such as he himself had performed in the days of his bodily presence among them.

(see M. Wilcox, *The Semitisms of Acts* [Oxford, 1965], pp. 139-41), but more probably representing a not very successful effort to improve the style by avoiding the repetition of ἠρνήσασθε in two consecutive clauses.

22. Lit., "his name, by faith in his name, has healed this man"; C. C. Torrey shows the way to a simplification of this construction by suggesting that, in an Aramaic stage of the transmission, *taqqîp šāmēh*, "he has made whole," was changed to *taqqēp šᵉmēh*, "his name has strengthened" (*Composition and Date of Acts* [Cambridge, Mass., 1916], pp. 14-16).

23. Taking the genitive pronoun αὐτοῦ in ἡ πίστις ἡ δι' αὐτοῦ to be neuter (referring to "his name") rather than masculine ("through him").

24. Where God introduced himself to Moses as "the God of Abraham, the God of Isaac, and the God of Jacob . . . the God of your fathers" (Ex. 3:6, 15). The Eighteen

In speaking of the exaltation of Jesus, following his humiliation and death, Peter uses language taken from the portrayal of the obedient and suffering Servant of the Lord in Isa. 52:13–53:12, a portrayal which begins with the words: "Behold, my servant . . . shall be exalted and lifted up, and shall be very high."[25] The voice from heaven which came to Jesus at his baptism addressed him in the language of Isa. 42:1, where the Servant makes his first appearance: "Behold my servant, whom I uphold, my chosen, in whom my soul delights."[26] The figure of this Servant has exercised a profound influence on New Testament thought and language.[27]

Like the prophet, Peter began by speaking of the Servant's being glorified by God, and then went back to tell of his sufferings. He does not exonerate his Jerusalem audience from a share in the responsibility for Jesus' death; this is in line with Luke's passion narrative, according to which "the people" concurred with "the chief priests and the rulers" in demanding the release of Barabbas and the crucifixion of Jesus (Luke 23:13-25). God has glorified his Servant, Peter tells him, but when he was in your power you handed him over to be executed by the Romans; when the Roman governor was disposed to discharge him, you spoke against him.[28]

14-15 You repudiated the Holy and Righteous One, said Peter (using a twofold designation which is rooted in Old Testament language).[29] You refused to acknowledge him as your divinely appointed King and

---

Benedictions (see p. 59 with n. 52) open with the invocation: "Blessed art thou, O Lord our God and God of our fathers, God of Abraham, God of Isaac, and God of Jacob. . . ."

25. LXX δοξασθήσεται ("shall be glorified"), whence ἐδόξασεν ("has glorified") in this passage. In the (later) Targum of Jonathan on the Prophets, "my servant" in Isa. 52:13 (as in Isa. 42:1) is explained by the additional word "Messiah". On Peter's use of the Servant concept here see O. Cullmann, *Peter: Disciple–Apostle–Martyr*, E.T. (London, 1953), pp. 66-68.

26. Mark 1:11 par. Luke 3:22, where words from Isa. 42:1 are preceded by "You are my Son" from Ps. 2:7 (cf. 13:33 below, pp. 259-60 with nn. 79-82). The identification of the Servant with the Davidic Messiah is implied.

27. Cf. 8:32-35 below (pp. 175-77 with nn. 66-70). See V. Taylor, *Jesus and his Sacrifice* (London, 1937), pp. 39-48; W. Zimmerli and J. Jeremias, *TDNT* 5, pp. 654-717 (*s.v.* παῖς θεοῦ), published separately as *The Servant of God*, E.T., SBT 20 (London, 1957); also, by way of a caveat, M. D. Hooker, *Jesus and the Servant* (London, 1959).

28. See further references to Pilate in 4:27 (where his hostility to Jesus is asserted); 13:28.

29. The title "the holy one" (ἅγιος, not ὅσιος as in 2:27) is paralleled in the NT in Mark 1:24; Luke 4:34; 1 John 2:20; Rev. 3:7. In the first of these passages "it is probable . . . that the demoniac uses ὁ ἅγιος τοῦ θεοῦ with Messianic significance, as expressing a sense of the presence of a supernatural person" (V. Taylor, *The Gospel according to St. Mark* [London, 1952], p. 174). Similar titles are given in the OT to Aaron the priest (Ps. 106:16) and Elisha the prophet (2 Kings 4:9); in both these places (as elsewhere) Heb. *qādôš* is rendered ἅγιος in LXX (where ὅσιος appears in LXX it regularly corresponds to Heb. *ḥāsîd*). The title "the righteous one" (δίκαιος) is paralleled in the NT in Acts 7:52; 22:14; Jas. 5:6; 1 John 2:1. For OT insistence on the righteousness of the Lord's Anointed see 2 Sam. 23:3; Isa. 32:1; Zech. 9:9 (cf. also "my righteous Servant" in Isa. 53:11).

Savior, and when Pilate offered to release him, you asked for a condemned murderer to be released instead. (The role of Pilate here conforms to the fuller presentation in Luke 23:1-25.) Yes, Peter continued, you asked that a murderer's life should be spared, but killed the very Author of life[30]—an amazing paradox! This is what *you* did, but *God* restored him to life again, and we are here to bear witness to the fact of his resurrection. Again it is clear how the apostolic preaching in Acts loves to emphasize the contrast between men's treatment of Jesus and God's.

16 It is through his name—the name of the once humbled and now glorified Servant of God—that this man has been cured, said Peter; and it is by faith in that same name that he has appropriated the blessing and strength which he now exhibits. The completeness of his cure was plain for all to see; Peter impressed on them that the power which had wrought the cure resided in Jesus' name, and that the man had availed himself of this power by the exercise of faith. There was no merely magical efficacy in the words which Peter pronounced when, in Jesus' name, he commanded the cripple to walk; the cripple would have known no benefit had he not responded in faith to what Peter said. But once this response of faith was made, the power of the risen Christ filled his body with health and strength. Here is a further principle which gives the healing miracles of Acts the same evangelical quality as those recorded in the Gospels.

b. Call to repentance (3:17-21)

17 *"Now then, my brothers, I know[31] that you acted[32] in ignorance, and so did your rulers.*

18 *But in this way God has fulfilled what he announced in advance by the mouth of all the prophets—namely, that the Messiah was to suffer.*

19 *Repent, therefore, and turn (to God), so that your sins may be wiped out,*

20 *in order that seasons of refreshment may come from the presence of*

Messiah is called "the righteous one" in 1 Enoch 38:2 (cf. 1 Enoch 46:3; 53:6; *Ps. Sol.* 17:35); the plural style, "righteous and holy ones," is used of the messianic people in 1 Enoch 38:5; 48:1, 7; 51:2. See V. Taylor, *The Names of Jesus* (London, 1953), pp. 80-83.

30. Gk. τὸν . . . ἀρχηγὸν τῆς ζωῆς. The word ἀρχηγός is used four times of Christ in the NT. Here and in Heb. 2:10 it denotes him as the source of life or salvation (since "life" and "salvation" are both represented by one Aramaic word, *ḥayyê*, the phrase used here is practically synonymous with τὸν ἀρχηγὸν τῆς σωτηρίας in Heb. 2:10; cf. A. F. J. Klijn, "The Term 'Life' in Syriac Theology," *SJT* 5 [1952], pp. 390-97. In 5:31 below ἀρχηγός is used rather in the sense of "prince" or "leader"; in Heb. 12:2 it is applied to Christ as the "pioneer" or "exemplar" of faith (τὸν τῆς πίστεως ἀρχηγόν).

31. The Western text has "we know" (ἐπιστάμεθα) for "I know" (οἶδα).

32. The Western text, more explicitly, reads "you did an evil thing" (ἐπράξατε πονηρόν).

the Lord, that he may send him who has been designated as your
Messiah—namely, Jesus.
21 *He must be received into heaven until the time for establishing all*
that God has spoken by the mouth of his holy prophets since ages
past.33

17-18   Peter conceded that the treatment meted out by the people of Jerusalem to their Messiah was the result of ignorance.34 They did not realize
that Jesus of Nazareth was their divinely sent Savior. Even their rulers did
not realize this, in spite of his own plain words. It is natural to recall Jesus'
saying from the cross, "they know not what they do" (Luke 23:34), though
that is more often taken as a reference to the Roman executioners.35 It may
be thought that Peter's words were surprisingly lenient to people like
Caiaphas and the other chief priests, whose determination to have Jesus put
to death is underscored in all the Gospels. Nevertheless, here is the proclamation of a divine amnesty, offering a free pardon to all who took part in
Jesus' death, if only they acknowledge their error, confess their sin, and turn
to God in repentance. For all those things that happened to Jesus in his
suffering and death happened in fulfilment of the words of the prophets, who
foretold that the Messiah must suffer.36 True, they did not foretell in so
many words that it was the Messiah who was to suffer: they spoke of the
obedient Servant of God as suffering for the sins of others. But Jesus himself
accepted and fulfilled his messianic mission in the terms of the prophetic
account of the Servant and other righteous sufferers,37 and the apostles'
interpretation followed his own. The Servant's sufferings were endured in
order that through them salvation might be brought to many. God had
foretold this through his servants the prophets; Peter and his hearers had seen
the prophetic oracles fulfilled and the salvation of God brought near in these
last days.

19   All they had to do to avail themselves of this salvation was to
change their former attitude to Jesus and bring it into line with God's

33. The Western text omits "since ages past" (ἀπ' αἰῶνος), for which cf. Luke
1:70.

34. It is assumed, perhaps for dramatic effect, that the Jerusalemites addressed
by Peter are identical with "the people" of Luke 23:15 who sided with Jesus' prosecutors,
in contrast to the weeping women of Luke 23:27 or the many spectators who returned from
the crucifixion beating their breasts (Luke 23:48).

35. On the text and meaning of Luke 23:34a see I. H. Marshall, *The Gospel of
Luke,* pp. 867-68. Cf. p. 160, n. 132.

36. The phrase παθεῖν τὸν Χριστὸν αὐτοῦ is a characteristic Lucanism; cf.
17:3; 26:23; Luke 24:46.

37. The experiences of a righteous sufferer in the Psalter are woven into the NT
passion narratives and elsewhere; see Luke 23:35, echoing Ps. 22:7; 23:36, echoing Ps.
69:21 (also Rom. 15:3, citing Ps. 69:9); cf. the pierced one of Zech. 12:10 (John 19:37;
Rev. 1:7).

attitude. God had clearly declared his verdict by raising him from the dead. Let them therefore repent, let them repudiate with abhorrence their acquiescence in the murder of their true Messiah, let them turn back in heart to God, and the salvation and blessing procured by their Messiah's death would be theirs. Their sins would be blotted out, even that sin of sins which they had unwittingly committed in consenting to the death of the Author of life. Here is the heart of the gospel of grace.

Not only would their sins be blotted out; those times of refreshment and joy which the prophets had described as features of the new age would be sent to them by God.[38]

20-21 The dawn of those times of refreshment and joy was linked, in the expectation of many, with the coming of Messiah. Messiah indeed had come, but had been ignored and repudiated by the majority of those to whom he came. But would he come again? This is implied in Peter's words. When he speaks to his hearers of Jesus as the one "who has been designated as your Messiah," he does not mean that Jesus at present is only Messiah-designate, that his investment awaits his coming advent in glory. This indeed has been suggested by those who regard verses 19-21 as embodying "the most primitive Christology of all."[39] But there is nothing in the word translated "designated" to imply designation as opposed to full investment: the two other New Testament occurrences of the word, both in Acts (22:14; 26:16), relate to Paul's appointment as a herald of the gospel. It is applied to Jesus here in much the same sense as the words translated "appointed" in 2:22 and "ordained" in 10:42.[40] It is by his resurrection that Jesus has already been "designated" or appointed Messiah, in the sense of Paul's statement (perhaps echoing a primitive confession of faith) in Rom. 1:4 that he has been "designated Son of God in power . . . by his resurrection from the dead."

Thus invested with messianic dignity (says Peter), Jesus has been received into the divine presence, and will remain there until the consummation of all that the prophets, from earliest days, have foretold. But the word meaning "consummation" or "establishment" may also, in appropriate contexts, bear the sense "restoration" or "restitution."[41] If a reference to the

38. The Greek word rendered "refreshing" is ἀνάψυξις, "respite" (cf. Ex. 8:15, the only LXX occurrence of the word). Repentance would bring the people of Jerusalem a respite from the judgment foretold by Jesus, as it brought the Ninevites a respite from the destruction announced by Jonah. Possibly more than a respite is intended here, if "the 'times of refreshing' are the definitive age of salvation" (E. Schweizer, *TDNT* 9, pp. 664-65, *s.v.* ἀνάψυξις).

39. See J. A. T. Robinson, "The Most Primitive Christology of All?" in *Twelve New Testament Studies*, SBT 34 (London, 1962), pp. 139-53.

40. The word used here is προκεχειρισμένος (perfect participle passive of προχειρίζομαι), that in 2:22 is ἀποδεδειγμένος (from ἀποδείκνυμι), that in 10:42 is ὡρισμένος (from ὁρίζω, the aorist participle of which is used in Rom. 1:4).

41. Gk. ἀποκατάστασις. Cf. the corresponding verb ἀποκαθιστάνω in 1:6, of

"restoration of all things" were to be recognized here, we should be reminded of Jesus' words in Mark 9:12a, "Elijah does come first to restore[42] all things" (not found in Luke's account of the transfiguration).[43] It has indeed been held that Luke, in these words of Peter, transfers to the expected advent of Jesus language originally applied to the ministry of the returning Elijah.[44] Quite apart from that, if the meaning "restoration" (well attested for this word) were the only one possible here, one could adduce Paul's picture of a renovated creation coinciding with the investiture of the sons and daughters of God (Rom. 8:18-23). But the meaning "establishment" or "fulfilment" is equally well attested, and makes good sense in the present context, in reference to the fulfilment of all Old Testament prophecy, culminating in the establishment of God's order on earth. If Jesus must remain in heaven until this consummation, this is in line with Paul's exposition of Ps. 110:1: Christ must reign (at the right hand of God) until all hostile powers are overthrown.[45]

The people of Jerusalem (perhaps as representatives of "the whole house of Israel")[46] are called on to reverse the verdict of Passover Eve and to accord Jesus united allegiance as Messiah. While many did respond to this call in the earliest days of the church, they remained a minority; it is idle to speculate what might have happened if they had formed the majority. As it is, one of Luke's motifs in Acts is the progressive rejection of the gospel by Jews, *pari passu* (from 11:18 on) with its progressive acceptance by Gentiles. But, in the general context of Acts, Peter's words mean this: the gospel blessings destined to flow from Jesus' death and resurrection must spread throughout the world; then, and not till then, will he return from the right hand of power.

c. Witness of the prophets (3:22-26)

22 *"Moses said,[47] 'The Lord your God will raise up from you, from*

---

the restoring of the kingdom to Israel. The restoration here seems to be identical with the regeneration (παλιγγενεσία) of Matt. 19:28.

42. Gk. ἀποκαθιστάνει.

43. But see Luke 1:17, where John, endowed with "the spirit and power of Elijah," will "turn the hearts of the fathers to the children"—a detail quoted from the prophecy of the returning Elijah in Mal. 4:5-6 (to which Mark 9:12a also refers).

44. See O. Bauernfeind, *Die Apostelgeschichte* (Leipzig, 1939), pp. 66-68; "Tradition und Komposition in dem Apokatastasisspruch Apostelgeschichte 3, 20 f." in *Abraham unser Vater . . . Festschrift für Otto Michel*, ed. O. Betz, M. Hengel, and P. Schmidt (Leiden, 1963), pp. 13-23.

45. 1 Cor. 15:24-28. While Ps. 110:1 is frequently quoted with reference to Christ throughout the NT, only in 1 Cor. 15:24-28 is an interpretation offered of the "enemies" that are to be made his footstool.

46. See 2:36.

47. The Western text adds "to your fathers."

> *among your brothers, a prophet like me; you must listen to him, according to all that he says to you.*
> 23 *Every person who does not listen to that prophet will be destroyed from among the people.'*
> 24 *Yes, and all the prophets—all who spoke, from Samuel and his successors onward—also announced these days.*
> 25 *You are the descendants of the prophets and (heirs) of the covenant which God made with your fathers when he said to Abraham, 'And in your posterity all the families of the earth will be blessed.'*
> 26 *God, having raised up his Servant, sent him to you first, by way of turning each one of you from your wicked acts."*

22-23 Did all the prophets, from earliest days, indeed speak of this time in which Peter and his hearers were now living? Yes, even Moses, first and greatest of Israel's prophets, looked forward to the day of Christ. There follow words from Deut. 18:15-19 in which Moses warns the Israelites that, when they wish to ascertain the divine will, they must not have recourse to magic arts for this purpose, after the manner of the Canaanites. When the Lord has a communication to make to them, says Moses, he will "raise up for you a prophet like me from among you, from your brethren—him you shall heed— . . . and whoever will not give heed to my words which he shall speak in my name, I myself will require it of him" (Deut. 18:15, 19).[48] The primary reference of these words of Moses is to the institution of prophets in Israel, as a way appointed by God for making his will known to his people. But well before apostolic times this prophecy was interpreted as pointing to one particular prophet, a second Moses, who would exercise the prophet's full mediatorial function as Moses had done.[49] Among the Samaritans,[50] as later among the Ebionites,[51] the Messiah was envisaged in terms of this prophet like Moses, and we have clear evidence in the Fourth Gospel particularly of contemporaries of Jesus who found this form of expectation realized in him.[52] From the earliest days of the apostolic preaching, it appears,

48. The concluding part of this quotation reproduced in our present text bears a greater resemblance to Lev. 23:29 (anyone who does not observe the day of atonement "shall be cut off from his people") than to Deut. 18:19. See n. 53 below.

49. See the Qumran application of this prophecy in 4Q *Testimonia* 5-7; also 1QS 9.11 ("until the coming of a prophet and the anointed ones of Aaron and Israel"). Cf. F. F. Bruce, *Biblical Exegesis in the Qumran Texts* (Grand Rapids/London, 1960), pp. 46-50.

50. See J. Macdonald, *The Theology of the Samaritans* (London, 1964), pp. 359-65. The Coming One of Samaritan expectation was later called the "Restorer" *(Taheb)*. Cf. John 4:19, 25, 29.

51. See H.-J. Schoeps, *Theologie und Geschichte des Judenchristentums* (Tübingen, 1949), pp. 87-98.

52. See John 6:14 and 7:40, where Jesus, as the supplier of bread from heaven and the water of life, is hailed as "the prophet" (the second Moses); cf. John 1:21b, 25, where John denies that he himself is "the prophet." In the transfiguration narrative the

this text from Deuteronomy was invoked as a Mosaic prediction of Jesus, and it was regularly included in the "testimony" compilations which circulated in the church.[53]

In Peter's speech on the day of Pentecost the person and work of Jesus are expounded in terms of a "Son of David" christology.[54] In his present speech at least two, and possibly three, christologies are presented side by side: a "Servant" christology, possibly an "Elijah" christology, and certainly a "prophet" christology. It must not be supposed that these christologies were originally kept separate, each developed independently by one group or school of thought within the primitive church. They have been interwoven throughout the course of Christian history, and such evidence as is available indicates that it was so from the beginning. It has indeed been argued cogently by Martin Hengel that the crucial phase of christological development must be located within the first five years after the death and resurrection of Christ.[55] The various christologies were all integrated by the overriding acknowledgment of Jesus as Lord in a sense implying universal sovereignty.

24 The prophetic testimony to Christ which Moses began was carried on by Samuel and all the later prophets. Samuel may be specially mentioned as the next named prophet after Moses. It would be difficult to find a recorded prophecy of Samuel which could be applied to Jesus so explicitly as the words of Moses just quoted; but Samuel was the prophet who anointed David as king and spoke of the establishment of his kingdom,[56] and the promises made to David found their ultimate fulfilment in Jesus (cf. 13:34). And all the words of the prophets similarly found their ultimate fulfilment in him (cf. 10:43).

25-26 Those Israelites who stood listening to Peter were "sons of the prophets"—not in the Old Testament sense which denoted the professional prophetic guilds, but in the sense that they were heirs of the promises made by God through the prophets, promises which had found their fulfilment before their very eyes. So, too, they were "sons of the covenant" made by God with Abraham, and that in a special sense, for they had lived to see

command from the cloud enveloping the divine presence, "listen to him" (Mark 9:7), echoes Deut. 18:15, and identifies Jesus with the expected prophet.

53. Cf. the use made of Deut. 18:15 in Stephen's speech (7:37); see C. H. H. Scobie, "The Origins and Development of Samaritan Christianity," *NTS* 19 (1972-73), pp. 390-414. In the form in which it appears in our present text, conflated with Lev. 23:29 (see n. 48 above), the quotation recurs in *Clem. Recog.* 1.36 (this may suggest dependence on a testimony collection). See also C. H. Dodd, *According to the Scriptures* (London, 1952), pp. 53-57.

54. See p. 66 above.

55. M. Hengel, *Between Jesus and Paul*, E.T. (London, 1983), pp. 30-47.

56. See 1 Sam. 13:14; 15:28; 16:13; 28:17.

the day when that covenant was realized in Christ: "in your posterity all the families of the earth will be blessed."[57] For Christ was the descendant of Abraham through whom this blessing was secured, and while the blessing was for "all the families of the earth," the first opportunity of enjoying it was naturally extended to Abraham's own family.[58] It was among them that God had raised up his Servant Jesus—raised him up to be their leader and deliverer, just as centuries before he had raised up his servant Moses. (This, rather than Jesus' resurrection from the dead, is probably in view here.)[59] Jesus, as Abraham's promised descendant, had come to them to bestow God's best blessing on them, turning them away from their sin. They had not paid heed to him at first when God sent him; let them pay heed now, when God in his pardoning grace was giving them a second opportunity; otherwise they would forfeit the covenanted blessing.

57. This quotation conflates the LXX rendering of Gen. 12:3 ("in you all the families of the earth will be blessed") and of Gen. 22:18 ("in your posterity all the nations of the earth will be blessed"). Luke probably looks forward to the Gentile mission (cf. Paul's use of the same promise in Gal. 3:8-9, 16-29).

58. With "to you first" cf. 13:46 as well as Paul's statement of the principle "to the Jew first" (Rom. 1:16; 2:9-10).

59. Cf. also 5:30; 13:33. Here the verb is ἀνίστημι, as in v. 22 and 13:33 (in 5:30 it is ἐγείρω).

ACTS 4

3. Arrest of Peter and John (4:1-4)

1 *While they were speaking[1] to the people, the [chief] priests,[2] the captain of the temple, and the Sadducees came upon them.*
2 *They were annoyed because they were teaching the people and proclaiming, in the case of Jesus, resurrection from the dead.[3]*
3 *They arrested them and locked them up until the following day (for it was now evening).*
4 *But many of those who heard the word believed, and the number of the men grew to about five thousand.*

1 Such a crowd gathered around Peter and John while they addressed the people thus in Solomon's Colonnade that the temple authorities intervened. The "captain of the temple,"[4] the commander of the temple police, was responsible for maintaining order in the temple courts, and he may have had misgivings lest the obstruction caused by so large a crowd might lead to a riot.

2 But some of the other authorities had strong religious objections to the content of the apostles' preaching, in particular to the announcement that Jesus had been raised from the dead. It is noteworthy that the Sadducees[5]—

1. The Western text adds "these words."

2. The great majority of witnesses read "priests" (ἱερεῖς); "chief priests" (ἀρχιερεῖς) is the reading of B and C. In any case, the chief priests are meant.

3. Cod. D reverses the construction, reading ". . . announced Jesus in the resurrection of the dead."

4. The captain (στρατηγός) of the temple is referred to in rabbinical literature as the *sāgān*, or sometimes as *'îš har habbayit* ("the man of the temple mount"). He belonged to one of the chief-priestly families, and in the temple he ranked next to the high priest. The temple guard which he commanded was a picked body of Levites. Cf. 5:24, 26.

5. The name "Sadducees" is most probably derived from the personal name Zadok, but from which Zadok is not known. An association with the priestly family of Zadok is unlikely, because they first appear in history after the removal of the Zadokites from the high-priesthood, and as supporters of the high-priestly dynasty of the Hasmonaeans. All the high priests from the reign of Herod to the outbreak of the war against Rome in A.D. 66 belonged to their party. As the continued enjoyment of the high-priestly prerogatives and indeed the political existence of the Jews as a nation depended on Roman goodwill during those years, the Sadducees collaborated as far as possible with the

the party to which the chief-priestly families[6] belonged—are specially mentioned in this regard. They objected on principle to the doctrine of resurrection in itself, considering it to be a Pharisaic innovation, and they were greatly annoyed because the two apostles, by their insistence on the fact of Jesus' resurrection, were so publicly and cogently maintaining that doctrine.

3-4 It was now evening (an hour or two at least must have gone by since the afternoon prayers for which Peter and John had gone up to the temple in the first instance), and there was no time to hold an inquiry into the apostles' conduct before sundown. They were therefore locked up for the night. But the temple authorities could not undo the harm (as they considered it) that Peter and John had done; the healing of the cripple and the preaching which followed it had the effect of adding a large number to the three thousand who believed on the day of Pentecost. The number of men alone,[7] says Luke, now totaled some five thousand.

4. Peter and John before the Sanhedrin (4:5-12)

5 *The next day there came together in Jerusalem their rulers, elders, and scribes,*

6 *with Annas the high priest and Caiaphas, John[8] and Alexander, and all who belonged to the high-priestly family.*

7 *They set Peter and John in the midst and proceeded to inquire: "By what authority or in what name have you[9] done this?"*

8 *Then Peter, filled with the Holy Spirit, said to them, "Rulers of the people and elders!*

9 *If we are being questioned today regarding a good deed done to a cripple, by what means he has been healed,*

10 *let all of you, and all the people of Israel, take knowledge that this man is standing here before you all in perfect health through the*

Roman authorities, and opposed religious or nationalist aspirations which might incur their wrath.

There is no surviving evidence from the Sadducees themselves about their theology. What is recorded deals mainly with the points on which they differed from the Pharisees (see p. 114, n. 51, on 5:34). They rejected the "oral law" or "tradition of the elders" which the Pharisees maintained, holding that the written law should be preserved and applied without modification. Perhaps it was for this reason that they were reputed to be more severe in judgment than the Pharisees. They dismissed as innovations the Pharisaic belief in angelic and demonic hierarchies, together with the hope of bodily resurrection (see 23:8). See Josephus, *BJ* 2.164-66; *Ant.* 13.171, 298; 18.16-17; also Schürer II, pp. 404-14.

6. The chief priests included the high priest and the principal temple officers (J. Jeremias, *Jerusalem in the Time of Jesus,* E.T. [London, 1969], pp. 160-81), together with ex-high priests and members of the leading priestly families from which the high priest was regularly drawn at this period (see Schürer II, pp. 232-36).

7. Men as distinct from women and children: ἀνδρῶν, not ἀνθρώπων (cf. Matt. 14:21).

8. For "John" the Western text reads "Jonathan" (cf. n. 16 below).

9. Emphatic ὑμεῖς, "people like you."

name of Jesus Christ of Nazareth,[10] whom you crucified but whom God raised from the dead.

11 He is 'the stone which was rejected by the builders' —by you— 'but has been made top stone of the pediment.'

12 And there is no saving health[11] in anyone else, for indeed no other name under heaven has been given to human beings, by which we must be saved."

5-6 The next morning the Sanhedrin[12] met (probably in a building immediately to the west of the temple precincts[13]), and the chief-priestly, Sadducean, element in its membership was especially well represented. Annas, the senior ex-high priest,[14] was there, and so was his son-in-law Caiaphas,[15] the

10. Some Western witnesses add "and through no other" (cf. v. 12).

11. The phrase "saving health" is used here to render σωτηρία, indicating that the word covers both bodily and spiritual healing. (Cf. Ps. 67:2, KJV.)

12. The Sanhedrin (a Hebrew and Aramaic loanword from Gk. συνέδριον, the word translated "court" in v. 15 below) was the senate and supreme court of the Jewish nation. In the NT it is also called the πρεσβυτέριον, "body of elders" (22:5; Luke 22:66) and γερουσία, "senate" (5:21); Josephus also refers to it as the βουλή, "council" (BJ 2.331, 336; Ant. 20.11). The Mishnah calls it the Sanhedrin, the great Sanhedrin, the Sanhedrin of the seventy-one, the great law-court. It comprised the high priest, who presided over it by virtue of his office, and seventy other members. It first appears in history in the Hellenistic period (c. 200 B.C.) as the body which regulated the internal affairs of the nation (Josephus, Ant. 12.142); it maintained this role until the revolt of A.D. 66. (It should not be confused with the later Sanhedrin of scholars which regulated the religious law of Israel after the war of A.D. 66-73, under Yohanan ben Zakkai as its first president.) The Sanhedrin at this time included a majority of members from the Sadducean party, supporting the chief-priestly interests, and a powerful minority from the Pharisaic party, to which most of the scribes or professional exponents of the law of Moses belonged. The body is frequently referred to in the NT by some or all of its component groups; so here in v. 5, "their rulers, elders, and scribes" (cf. 5:23, "the chief priests and elders").

13. The council-chamber, according to Josephus (BJ 2.344; 5.144; 6.354), was situated at the eastern end of a bridge across the Tyropoeon valley (the bridge now represented by Wilson's Arch). At the western end of the bridge lay the open-air gathering place called the Xystus, "the polished (floor)." The Mishnaic name for the council-chamber, liškat haggāzît, means presumably not (as traditionally rendered) "the hall of hewn stones" but "the hall beside (or over against) the Xystus." See Schürer II, pp. 223-25; G. H. Dalman, Jerusalem und sein Gelände (Gütersloh, 1930), pp. 193-94; J. Simons, Jerusalem in the Old Testament (Leiden, 1952), pp. 252-53.

14. Annas or Ananus (Heb. Ḥānān), son of Sethi, was appointed to the high-priesthood by P. Sulpicius Quirinius, legate of Syria, in A.D. 6, and held the office for nine years. Even after his deposition he continued to exercise great influence: five of his sons, one son-in-law (Caiaphas), and one grandson became high priest for shorter or longer periods during the following half-century. His personal authority is reflected in the part he plays in the trial narrative of the Fourth Gospel (John 18:13-24). He is called "the high priest" here in the sense of ex-high priest (or, as we might say, high priest emeritus). In Luke 3:2 he is coupled with Caiaphas (reigning high priest at the time) in a chronological note: "in the high-priesthood of Annas and Caiaphas" (ἐπὶ ἀρχιερέως Ἄννα καὶ Καϊάφα).

15. Caiaphas was the surname of Joseph (Josephus, Ant. 18.35, 95), son-in-law

reigning high priest, who was president of the Sanhedrin by virtue of his office. Not many weeks had passed since these two men had taken a part in the arrest and condemnation of Jesus. If they hoped that they had got rid of him, their hope was short-lived; it looked now as if they were going to have as much trouble on his account as they had had before his death. With them were several of their kinsmen, two of whom are mentioned by name, although one of these cannot be identified with certainty, and the other cannot be identified at all.[16]

7 When the members of the court had taken their seats, Peter and John were fetched from the lock-up and set before them. They were then asked, presumably by the president, by what authority men like them[17] had presumed to act as they had done. Perhaps the Sanhedrin met on this occasion more as a court of inquiry than in a more formal capacity, but the presence of so many senior members indicates the seriousness with which they viewed the situation.

8-10 For such an occasion as this the apostles had already received instructions from their Master: "Settle it therefore in your minds, not to meditate beforehand how to answer; for I will give you a mouth and wisdom, which none of your adversaries will be able to withstand or contradict" (Luke 21:14-15). They now proved the truth of this assurance. In words inspired by the Holy Spirit,[18] Peter made his reply. If he and John were being examined with regard to an act of healing performed on a cripple, if the court wished to know the cause of the man's cure, then let them know, and let all the nation know, that the deed had been done in the name of Jesus of Nazareth, the Messiah. The former cripple was present in court with them: either he had been locked up with them overnight, as being partly responsible for the commotion in Solomon's Colonnade, or else he had been summoned as a witness. "This man stands here in your presence completely healed," said Peter, "by the name of Jesus the Messiah, Jesus of Nazareth, whom you sent to his death, but whom God raised from the dead." Of the responsibility of the men whom Peter was now addressing there could be no

---

to Annas according to John 18:13. He was appointed high priest by Valerius Gratus, prefect of Judaea, in A.D. 18 and held the office for the remarkably long term of eighteen years, which included the ten years of Pilate's administration. He was deposed at last by L. Vitellius (who as legate of Syria visited Judaea at the time of Pilate's recall in A.D. 36) and replaced by Jonathan, son of Annas.

16. If the Western reading "Jonathan" (instead of "John") be followed in v. 6, the reference might be to Jonathan, son of Annas, who eventually succeeded Caiaphas in the high-priesthood. No Alexander of the high-priestly family is otherwise known.

17. There is an implication of scorn in the emphatic "you" (ὑμεῖς) of v. 7, coming as it does at the end of the sentence.

18. Gk. πλησθεὶς πνεύματος ἁγίου, "filled with (the) Holy Spirit." A distinction should be made between this use of the aorist participle passive, denoting a special moment of inspiration, and the use of the adjective πλήρης ("full") to denote the abiding character of a Spirit-filled person (like Stephen in 6:5).

doubt; it was they who had handed Jesus over to Pilate, Caiaphas bearing the chief responsibility. (It is to Caiaphas that reference is probably made in Jesus' words to Pilate in John 19:11, "he who delivered me to you has the greater sin.") As before, there is a pointed contrast between men's treatment of Jesus and God's treatment of him.

11 The apostles are technically on the defensive, but actually they have gone over to the attack. Peter proceeds to preach the gospel to his judges, and he bases his argument on a well-known Old Testament text. "The stone which the builders rejected has become the head of the corner" (Ps. 118:22) is one of the earliest messianic testimonies. It was so used (by implication) by Jesus himself, as the conclusion of the parable of the vine-yard (Mark 12:10-11).[19] In the original Old Testament context the rejected stone is perhaps Israel, despised by the nations but chosen by God for the accomplishment of his purpose. But, as so often in the New Testament, God's purpose for Israel finds its fulfilment in the single-handed work of Christ.

Both here and in later Christian use of this "testimony," the "builders"[20] are interpreted as the rulers of the Jewish nation, who failed to acknowledge Jesus as the divinely sent deliverer; but the Stone which they disregarded has now received from God the place of highest distinction: Jesus now sits enthroned at God's right hand.

12 And from the once rejected but now glorified Jesus, and from him alone, comes true saving health. The deliverance of the cripple from a

---

19. In the parallel passage Luke 20:17-18 the rejected stone is linked with the stumbling stone of Isa. 8:14-15 against which "many . . . shall fall and be broken" and with the great stone in Nebuchadnezzar's dream which struck the image so that the wind carried its dust away like chaff (Dan. 2:35). In 1 Pet. 2:6 the rejected stone is further linked with the "precious cornerstone of a sure foundation" laid in Zion (Isa. 28:16), which is also interpreted of Christ by Paul in Rom. 9:33 and possibly in Eph. 2:20. The interdependent christological exegesis of these "stone" texts has been held to be strong evidence of a primitive collection of OT "testimonies." In later Christian literature other OT stones are brought into the interpretation, e.g., Jacob's stone at Bethel (Gen. 28:11) and the stone which supported Moses during the battle with Amalek at Rephidim (Ex. 17:12); cf. Cyprian, *Testimonies* 2:16. See J. A. Robinson, *The Epistle to the Ephesians* (London, 1904), pp. 163-64; J. R. Harris, *Testimonies*, I (Cambridge, 1916), pp. 30-31; E. G. Selwyn, *The First Epistle of Peter* (London, 1946), pp. 268-77; B. P. W. Stather Hunt, *Primitive Gospel Sources* (London, 1951), pp. 126-29; C. H. Dodd, *According to the Scriptures* (London, 1952), pp. 35-36, 69, 99-100; S. H. Hooke, *The Siege Perilous* (London, 1955), pp. 235-49; F. F. Bruce, "The Corner Stone," *ExT* 84 (1972-73), pp. 231-35. The "head of the corner" is equivalent to the "top stone of the pediment."

20. "Builders" appears in rabbinical literature as a figure of speech for teachers of the law. In the Qumran texts "the builders of the wall" are leaders of a religious community, whether of the true one (as in CD 4.12, applying Mic. 7:11) or a false one (as in CD 4.19, with reference to the rickety wall of Ezek. 13:10-16). In the present context, when once the rejected stone had been identified as Jesus, the "builders" who rejected it were bound to be interpreted as the Jewish authorities. Ps. 118:22 thus became "one of the sheet-anchors of early Christian teaching" (E. G. Selwyn, *First Peter*, p. 269).

bodily affliction might serve as a parable of deliverance from the guilt of sin and from judgment to come.[21] If the rulers persisted in their repudiation of Jesus, which had already involved them in blood-guiltiness, no deliverance from its consequences could be hoped for from any other quarter or by the power of any other name. The name of Jesus, by which the cripple had been empowered to spring to his feet and walk, was the name with which Israel's salvation (and, as was to appear later, the salvation of the world) was inextricably bound up. The course of duty and wisdom for the rulers was therefore clear; if they refused it and persisted in their present attitude, they would bring destruction on their nation as well as on themselves.

The founders of the great world-religions are not to be disparaged by followers of the Christian way. But of none of them can it be said that there is no saving health in anyone else; to one alone belongs the title: the Savior of the world.

5. Debate in the Sanhedrin (4:13-17)

13 *As they saw Peter and John's freedom of speech and realized that they were uneducated laymen, they were surprised, and recognized them as having been with Jesus.*

14 *And, as they saw the man who had been healed standing with them, they had no reply to make.[22]*

15 *So they ordered them to leave[23] the court, and conferred with one another.*

16 *"What shall we do to these men?" they said. "It is a matter of public knowledge[24] among all the residents in Jerusalem that a notable sign has been performed through them; we cannot deny it.*

17 *But to prevent this[25] from spreading more widely among the people, let us warn them, under severe penalties,[26] to speak no more to anyone in this name."*

13-14 Peter and John were obviously unversed in the formal learning of the rabbinical schools,[27] yet they spoke with a freedom and forthrightness

---

21. For the twofold sense of salvation (σωτηρία) cf. 14:9.

22. Lit., "They could say nothing against it"; the Western text has the amplified reading: "they could do or say nothing against it."

23. The Western text reads "to be led off" (ἀπαχθῆναι) for "to leave" (ἀπελθεῖν).

24. Cod. D has the comparative φανερώτερον (in the elative sense, "very clear," "all too clear") for the positive φανερόν.

25. Several Western authorities read "these matters" (τὰ ῥήματα ταῦτα).

26. Lit., "let us threaten them" (ἀπειλησώμεθα). The Byzantine text makes the threat more emphatic by adding ἀπειλῇ before ἀπειλησώμεθα (lit., "let us threaten with threatening"), whence KJV "let us straitly threaten them."

27. This is the force in the present context of ἀγράμματοι . . . καὶ ἰδιῶται. In papyri the former word appears with the sense "illiterate"; here it means rather "unedu-

that impressed their judges.[28] How could untrained laymen like these so ably sustain a theological disputation with members of the supreme court? The answer was not far to seek: the judges took cognizance of the fact[29] that they had been companions of Jesus. He too had sat at the feet of no eminent rabbi, yet he taught with an authority which they could well remember. People expressed the same surprise about him: "How is it that this man has learning,[30] when he has never studied?" (John 7:15). None could match him in his sure handling of the scriptures, his unerring ability to go back to first principles for the confirming of his own teaching and the discomfiture of his opponents. And plainly he had imparted something of that same gift to his disciples. Not only so, but he had supported his teaching with the mighty works which he performed; now Peter and John were doing the same. That the cripple had been cured was evident; he stood before them as a witness to the fact. Peter and John claimed that the cure had been effected by the power of Jesus' name; their judges were in no position to deny the claim.

15-17   Peter and John were accordingly sent outside the council-chamber while the court conferred.[31] It was difficult to know what action to take. They had broken no law in curing the cripple; besides, their action in doing so had made them popular heroes, and it would be impolitic to penalize them. On the other hand, it would be equally impolitic to set them at liberty to go on teaching and healing in the name of Jesus; the authorities would then be confronted once more with the problem which they had thought to be solved by Jesus' condemnation and execution, and that in a more intractable form than previously. The action on which they decided was a confession of their weakness: they would dismiss the two men, but threaten them with serious consequences if they did the like again.

---

cated" in respect of rabbinical training. As for ἰδιώτης, which means "private person" in ordinary Greek, it is interesting to note that it appears as a loanword in postbiblical Hebrew and Aramaic *(heḏyôṭ)* with the meaning "commoner," "layman," "unskilled." Here it implies that Peter and John, far from being professional exponents of scripture, were laymen—ʿammê hāʾareṣ ("people of the land") in the rabbinical sense of that phrase, denoting the rank and file of the Jewish population who could not be expected to know or practise the details of the oral law (cf. John 7:49). The wonder was that they showed such mastery of biblical argument.

28. The judges took note of their παρρησία, "freedom of speech" (cf. vv. 29, 31). "This freedom manifests itself . . . mainly in the clear witness about Jesus, who had been rejected by this very same council and yet was the exclusive Saviour" (W. C. van Unnik, "The Christian's Freedom of Speech in the New Testament," *BJRL* 44 [1961-62], p. 478).

29. Gk. ἐπεγίνωσκον—they directed special attention to this fact as an important piece of relevant evidence. If the compound ἐπιγινώσκω is to be distinguished from the simple γινώσκω, it may be by a certain decisive quality.

30. Gk. γράμματα οἶδεν, "knows letters" (cf. ἀγράμματοι here).

31. It is idle to inquire into the narrator's source of information about the conversation that took place when the apostles were sent out of the room. Its general drift could be readily inferred from what the judges said when Peter and John were brought back.

It is particularly striking that neither on this nor on any subsequent occasion did the authorities take any serious action to disprove the apostles' central affirmation—the resurrection of Jesus.[32] Had it seemed possible to refute them on this point, how eagerly would the opportunity have been seized! Had their refutation on this point been achieved, how quickly and completely the new movement would have collapsed! It is plain that the apostles spoke of a bodily resurrection when they said that Jesus had been raised from the dead; it is equally plain that the authorities understood them in this sense. The body of Jesus had vanished so completely that all the resources at their command could not produce it. The disappearance of his body, to be sure, was far from proving his resurrection, but the production of his body would have effectively disproved it. Now the apostles' claim that Jesus was alive had received public confirmation by the miracle of healing performed in his name. It was, for the Sanhedrin, a disturbing situation.

6. The Apostles Dismissed with a Caution (4:18-22)

18 *So they called them in and charged them absolutely not to speak or teach any more in Jesus' name.*
19 *Then Peter and John answered them, "Judge for yourselves if it is right in God's sight to listen to you rather than to God.*
20 *As for us, we cannot give up speaking of what we have seen and heard."*
21 *Then they threatened them further and released them: they could find no way of punishing them, because everyone was glorifying God for what had happened.*
22 *The man on whom this sign of healing had been performed was more than forty years old.*

18-20 They recalled Peter and John, and acquainted them with their decision. A complete ban was imposed on any further public mention of the name of Jesus. If they thought that any heed would be paid to this ban, they were quickly disillusioned. Peter and John had probably never heard of Socrates, and had certainly never read Plato's *Apology*, but they gave the same kind of answer as Socrates gave when he was offered his release on condition that he give up the pursuit and discussion of truth and wisdom: "I shall obey God rather than you."[33] It is, of course, the sort of answer that any person of principle will give when offered freedom at the price of abandoning the path that conscience dictates. But what weighed most of all with the

---

32. The action reported in Matt. 28:13 (which incidentally confirms that the tomb was found empty) can scarcely be called serious; had a more convincing refutation of the apostles' claim been possible, it would have been preferred.

33. Plato, *Apology of Socrates* 29D (for Socrates "the god" might be a more appropriate rendering of τῷ θεῷ than "God"). Cf. 5:29 below.

apostles was their personal commitment to the risen Lord to be his witnesses. If the point were put to those judges in the abstract, whether a divine commandment or a human regulation should be obeyed in the event of a clash between the two, they would affirm without hesitation that the divine commandment must be obeyed at all costs. Right, said Peter and John, "we cannot stop telling what we have seen and heard."[34]

21-22 Despite this open defiance, the court did nothing but repeat the threat of severe penalties. The popular enthusiasm was too great for them to do anything more. Luke points out here, by way of explaining the extent of the public amazement, that the cripple who had been cured was over forty years old: he had reached an age at which such cures, especially for a congenital defect, simply do not occur.[35] Peter and John were discharged.

"This," says a twentieth-century Jewish historian, "was the first mistake which the Jewish leaders made with regard to the new sect. And this mistake was fatal. There was probably no need to arrest the Nazarenes, thus calling attention to them and making them 'martyrs'. But once arrested, they should not have been freed so quickly. The arrest and release increased the number of believers; for these events showed on the one hand that the new sect was a power which the authorities feared enough to persecute, and on the other hand they proved that there was no danger in being a disciple of Jesus (he, of course, being the one who had saved them from the hand of their persecutors!)."[36]

7. Peter and John Rejoin Their Friends (4:23-31)

23 *When they had been released, Peter and John rejoined their companions and reported all that the chief priests and elders had said to them.*

24 *When they heard it, they raised their voices together[37] to God and said,*
"Sovereign Lord, who hast made heaven and earth and sea and all that is in them,

25 *who by the Holy Spirit hast spoken through thy servant David, our father:[38]*

---

34. Gk. οὐ δυνάμεθα . . . μὴ λαλεῖν.

35. Compare the man at the pool of Bethesda, whose infirmity had lasted for thirty-eight years (John 5:5); only it is not said to have been congenital.

36. J. Klausner, *From Jesus to Paul*, E.T. (London, 1944), pp. 282-83.

37. Gk. ὁμοθυμαδόν ("with one accord"), as in 1:14.

38. The Greek is very awkward here: Westcott and Hort speak of "the extreme difficulty of text, which doubtless contains a primitive error." The only way to construe it as it stands (ὁ τοῦ πατρὸς ἡμῶν διὰ πνεύματος ἁγίου στόματος Δαυὶδ παιδός σου εἰπών) is to take David as the "mouth" (i.e., mouthpiece) of the Holy Spirit: "who didst say through thy servant David our father, the mouthpiece of the Holy Spirit." The Western text reads: "who through the Holy Spirit didst speak through the mouth of David, thy servant." C. C. Torrey envisages an underlying text which might be rendered: "as our

> 'Why did the Gentiles rage,
> and the peoples make vain plans?
> 26 The kings of the earth set themselves in array,
> and the rulers were gathered together,
> against the Lord and against his anointed one' —
> 27 for in truth, in this city, there were gathered together against thy holy Servant Jesus, whom thou didst anoint, Herod and Pontius Pilate, with the Gentiles and peoples of Israel,
> 28 to do all that thy hand and counsel had foreordained to take place.
> 29 And now, O Lord, look on their threats, and empower thy servants to declare thy word with all freedom of speech,
> 30 while thou stretchest forth thy hand for healing and for the performance of signs and wonders through the name of thy holy Servant Jesus."
> 31 When they had prayed, the place where they were gathered together was shaken, and they were all filled with the Holy Spirit and continued to declare the word of God with freedom of speech.[39]

23-24 The two apostles, on their release, returned to the place where their fellow-apostles and other believers were, and when they told them of their experience before the Sanhedrin, the whole company resorted to prayer. They addressed God as Sovereign Lord,[40] the Creator of all, in time-honored liturgical language derived from Hebrew scripture.[41]

25-28 Then they quoted the opening words of the second Psalm, and found proof of their divine origin in the fulfilment which had so recently taken place in their own experience.

This psalm, with its explicit reference to Yahweh's anointed one (Messiah), had been interpreted of the coming deliverer of David's line at least as early as the middle of the first century B.C.;[42] the words "You are my Son" (Ps. 2:7), addressed to Jesus at his baptism by the heavenly voice, actually hailed him as that Messiah. In conformity with this understanding is the interpretation which the apostles now place on the opening verses of the psalm. The "Gentiles" raged against Jesus in the person of the Romans who

---

father David, thy servant, said by the mouth of the Holy Spirit" (*Composition and Date of Acts* [Cambridge, Mass., 1916], pp. 16-18). H. W. Moule (*ExT* 51 [1939-40], p. 396) suggested that the writer put down a first draft and then made corrections, and that a copyist, misunderstanding the signs for deletion or addition, combined words which were intended to be alternatives.

39. The Western text adds "to everyone who was willing to believe."

40. Gk. δέσποτα, vocative of δεσπότης (cf. Luke 2:29; Rev. 6:10).

41. Cf. Ex. 20:11; Neh. 9:6; Ps. 146:6; Isa. 42:5; also Wisd. 13:3, 4, 9 (and cf. 14:15; 17:24 below).

42. See *Ps. Sol.* 17:26, where Ps. 2:9 is applied to the expected son of David, the "anointed lord" (cf. p. 68, n. 90 above).

sentenced him to the cross and carried out the sentence; the "peoples" who plotted against him are (despite the plural) the Jews, or rather their rulers; the "kings" who set themselves in array are represented by Herod Antipas, tetrarch of Galilee and Peraea, while the "rulers" are represented by Pontius Pilate.[43] The reference to Herod harks back to the account in Luke 23:7-12, where Pilate, learning that Jesus is a Galilaean, performs a diplomatic courtesy by referring him to Herod. Luke is the only one of the four evangelists who gives Herod a role in the passion narrative.[44]

The prophetic language of the psalm showed that Pilate, Herod, and the others, in uniting against Jesus, were simply carrying out "God's appointed counsel and foreknowledge" (as it was called in 2:23), "that the Messiah was to suffer" (3:18).[45] In these words of the apostles there is an explicit identification of God's "holy Servant Jesus" with the royal Son of God addressed in Ps. 2:7. Jesus, God's obedient servant, is the one whom God "anointed" or made Messiah—at his baptism.[46]

29-30   The Sanhedrin might threaten, but the threats called not for intimidation and silence but for increased boldness of speech. The apostles therefore prayed that they themselves might have courage to proclaim their message without fear or favor,[47] and that God would place the seal of his public approbation on their witness by granting further mighty works of healing and similar signs and wonders through the same name which had cured the lame man—the name of his "holy Servant Jesus."[48]

---

43. See p. 81, n. 28 above.

44. For the improbable view that Luke's introduction of Herod was created out of Christian exegesis of Ps. 2:1-2 see M. Dibelius, "Herodes und Pilatus," *ZNW* 16 (1915), pp. 113-26; G. Lüdemann, *Paul: Apostle to the Gentiles*, E.T. (London, 1984), pp. 12-13, 36-37 (with n. 41).

45. Tertullian (*On the Resurrection of the Flesh* 20) gives a slightly different interpretation: "In the person of Pilate the nations (*gentes*) raged, and in the person of Israel the peoples (*populi*, plural) planned vain things; the kings of the earth stood up in Herod, and in Annas and Caiaphas the rulers were gathered together." The unusual application to Israel of the plural λαοί is due to the use of the singular λαός in reference to Israel as God's people over against ἔθνη, "Gentiles"; in Ps. 2:1 the Heb. plural *leʼummîm*, LXX λαοί, stands in synonymous parallelism with *gôyim*, LXX ἔθνη, not in opposition to it.

46. With "whom thou didst anoint" (ἔχρισας) cf. 10:38, "God anointed (ἔχρισεν) Jesus of Nazareth"; from the verb χρίω comes the form χριστός, "anointed one," "messiah."

47. They call themselves God's "slaves" (δοῦλοι), perhaps deliberately using a humbler term than that applied to Jesus as God's servant (παῖς).

48. Phrases like "through thy holy Servant Jesus" retained liturgical currency in the church for some generations; cf. *Did.* 9:2 ("through Jesus thy Servant"); 1 Clem. 59:3 ("through Jesus Christ thy beloved Servant"); *Mart. Pol.* 14.3 ("through . . . Jesus Christ thy dear Servant"); Hippolytus, *Apostolic Tradition* 4.4 ("through thy beloved Servant Jesus Christ"), etc.

31 The assurance of divine favor and help came even as they prayed. The place shook as with an earthquake—whether there was an objective shaking or this was the way in which God's presence and power were manifested to their consciousness cannot be said—and the Holy Spirit filled them all and sent them forth to proclaim the good news with renewed confidence. The description here is reminiscent of the description of what happened on the day of Pentecost, both in the external signs of the Spirit's advent and in the prayerful attitude of the disciples at his coming;[49] but while this was a fresh filling of the Spirit, it could not be called a fresh baptism.[50] If the narrative of 3:1–4:31 is based on a different source from that of 2:1-41, the filling of the Spirit here is not a duplicate of that in 2:4, when for the first time "they were all filled with the Holy Spirit"; in the present narrative Peter has already been "filled with the Holy Spirit" for his effective defense before the court (4:8).

D. ALL THINGS IN COMMON (4:32–5:11)

1. Community of Goods (4:32-35)

32 *Now the multitude of believers had one heart and soul,[51] and none of them claimed any of his property as his own: they held everything in common.*

33 *The apostles, with great power, bore witness to the resurrection of the Lord Jesus,[52] and much grace rested on them all.*

34 *No one was in need among them, for all who were owners of land or houses sold them and brought the price received from the sale*

35 *and placed it at the apostles' feet. Distribution was then made to each person according to individual need.*

32-35 The summary contained in these verses is similar to that in 2:43-47, but serves a different purpose in the narrative. The earlier summary concluded the account of the day of Pentecost; this summary introduces the contrasted episodes of Barnabas and Ananias.

The Spirit-filled community[53] exhibited a remarkable unanimity which expressed itself even in the attitude to private property. Whereas the institution of a communal purse was explicitly regulated in writing at Qumran,[54] the action taken by these early disciples of Jesus was intended to

49. See p. 42, n. 57 (on 1:14).
50. See the exposition of 2:38 (pp. 69-71).
51. The Western text adds "and there was no division among them."
52. Cod. D adds "Christ"; ℵ and A read "Jesus Christ the Lord."
53. The word πλῆθος, rendered "multitude" in v. 32, acquired the special sense of a civic community (in Athens) and of a religious community (among Jews and Christians). In LXX it twice renders Heb. *qāhāl* (Ex. 12:6; 2 Chron. 31:18), more usually rendered ἐκκλησία (cf. 5:11 below with n. 23 on p. 108). Cf. 6:2, 5; 15:12, 30.
54. Cf. 1QS 1.12; 5.2; 6.17-25.

be voluntary. Members regarded their private estates as being at the community's disposal; those who owned houses or lands sold these in order that they might be more conveniently available to the community in the form of money. The richer members thus made provision for the poorer, and for a time no one had any need to complain of hunger or want. (But later on, when funds ran out and especially after the country was hard hit by the famine mentioned in 11:28, the Jerusalem church became dependent on the generosity of fellow-believers in other places.) The apostles, as the community leaders, received the free-will offerings that were brought, but they apparently delegated the details of distribution to others, for they themselves had to devote their time and energy to their public testimony to the risen Christ. As they did so, the power of God, shown in mighty works, attended their preaching, in answer to their prayer (v. 30). And they continued to enjoy the experience of God's grace and the favor of the Jerusalem populace.[55]

2. The Generosity of Barnabas (4:36-37)

36 *There was one Joseph, whom the apostles surnamed Barnabas, meaning "son of encouragement." He was a Levite; his family belonged to Cyprus.*

37 *He had a field which he sold, and he brought the money and placed it at the apostles' feet.*

36-37 The exact etymology of Joseph's additional name Barnabas is a matter of debate,[56] but in all that we know of him he proved himself to be a true encourager. He was a Cypriot Jew, but he had relatives in Jerusalem[57] and a piece of land as well. The Pentateuchal regulations prohibiting priests and Levites from holding landed property seem to have become a dead letter by this time.[58] The piece of land[59] which he possessed may not have been large; whatever it was, he sold it and gave the purchase-price to the apostles for the benefit of the community.

55. The "grace" which rested on them all (v. 33) may include divine and human favor, together with a responsive spirit of gratitude (Gk. χάρις covers all these nuances).

56. It is explained as υἱὸς παρακλήσεως, variously translated "son of consolation" (KJV), "son of exhortation" (ASV) or, better than either of these, "son of encouragement" (RSV), this use of "son" to indicate a man's character being a familiar Semitic idiom. "Barnabas" might be the adaptation of a form like Palmyrene Bar-Nebo (cf. G. A. Deissmann, *Bible Studies*, E.T. [Edinburgh, ²1909], p. 188); another suggestion is that it represents Aram. *bar nᵉwāḥā'* (lit., "son of soothing"); cf. A. Klostermann, *Probleme im Aposteltexte* (Gotha, 1883), pp. 8-14. See T. Zahn, *Die Apostelgeschichte des Lucas*, pp. 183-88; S. P. Brock, "ΒΑΡΝΑΒΑΣ: ΥΙΟΣ ΠΑΡΑΚΛΗΣΕΩΣ," *JTS* N.S. 25 (1974), pp. 93-98.

57. See 12:12 below together with Col. 4:10.

58. For the prohibitions see Num. 18:20, 24; Deut. 10:9; 18:1-2; but members of priestly families like Jeremiah (Jer. 32:6-15) and Josephus (*Life* 422) held landed property.

59. The word used here is ἀγρός, which appears nowhere else in Acts; elsewhere in Acts a piece of land is a χωρίον (cf. v. 34; 1:18; 5:3, 8) or κτῆμα (2:45; 5:1).

ACTS 5

3. Deceit and Death of Ananias (5:1-6)

1 But[1] a man named Ananias, with his wife Sapphira, sold a piece of property[2]

2 and, with his wife's complicity, kept back some of the money received; then he brought the other part and placed it at the apostles' feet.

3 "Ananias," said Peter, "why did Satan fill[3] your heart, making you deceive the Holy Spirit and keep back some of the money received for the land?

4 While the land remained, did it not remain in your possession? And when it was sold, was the money not still under your control? Why did you conceive this thing[4] in your heart? You have lied to God, not to human beings."

5 Hearing these words, Ananias[5] fell down and died, and great fear came on all who heard about it.

6 The young men got up, wrapped him in a winding-sheet, carried him out, and buried him.

The story of Ananias is to the book of Acts what the story of Achan is to the book of Joshua. In both narratives an act of deceit interrupts the victorious progress of the people of God. It may be that the author of Acts himself wished to point this comparison: when he says that Ananias "kept back" part of the price (v. 2), he uses the same Greek word as is used in the Greek version of Josh. 7:1 where it is said that the Israelites (represented by Achan)

1. The Greek conjunction δέ need not have adversative force, but here it probably is adversative, in contrast to Barnabas (4:36-37).

2. Gk. κτῆμα (cf. 2:45, τὰ κτήματα), referring here to landed property, large or small, as is clear from the use of χωρίον ("piece of land") in v. 3.

3. Gk. ἐπλήρωσεν. By accidental omission of λ Cod. ℵ reads ἐπήρωσεν (which by itself would have the inappropriate meaning "maimed"); in P⁷⁴ etc. this appears emended to ἐπείρασεν ("tempted"); hence Vulgate temptauit.

4. The Western text reads "to do this (the) wicked thing" ([τοῦτο] ποιῆσαι τὸ πονηρὸν [πρᾶγμα]).

5. Before "fell down" the Western text inserts "immediately" (cf. v. 10).

"broke faith" by retaining for private use property that had been devoted to God.[6]

The incident of Ananias and Sapphira is felt by many readers to present a stumbling block partly ethical and partly intellectual. The intellectual difficulty is not so great as is sometimes supposed. We know almost nothing of the private beliefs of Ananias and his wife, but at a certain stage of religious awareness sudden death is a familiar sequel to the realization that one has unwittingly infringed a taboo. (It does not necessarily follow that Ananias's death must be accounted for in this way, but it shows how little substance there is in the idea that the story is essentially improbable.) As for the ensuing death of Sapphira, if it is thought that this "adds such improbability as lies in a coincidence,"[7] it must be remembered that she sustained the additional shock of learning of her husband's sudden death.

It is pointless to argue that the double death was not quite so sudden as the narrative suggests, as is done, for example, by Joseph Klausner. When the couple's deceit was detected, he says, "Peter became angry at them and rebuked them; and when they died shortly thereafter, of course their death was attributed to this rebuke by the chief and first apostle."[8] Even more improbable is the suggestion of P. H. Menoud, that Ananias and Sapphira were the first members of the believing community to die, and that their natural death came as such a shock to the others (who thought that Christ by his resurrection had abolished physical death for his people) that they felt obliged to explain it by the supposition that some previously undetected sin had found them out.[9]

A much more serious matter is the impression which the narrative gives of the personality of Peter, who had so recently experienced the forgiving and restoring grace of God after his denial of Christ in the high priest's palace. It is absurd to try to make him directly responsible for the death of the couple, but his language to them, and especially to Sapphira, has seemed to many readers to reflect the spirit of Elijah calling down fire from heaven on the soldiers who came to arrest him, or Elisha pronouncing sentence of perpetual leprosy on Gehazi, rather than the spirit of his Master. "It could not of course," says one commentator, "be laid as a charge against St. Peter that after his stern rebuke of Ananias the offender fell down dead suddenly, though one would have expected St. Peter in future to be more

6. The verb is νοσφίζομαι (translated "pilfer" in Tit. 2:10); with ἐνοσφίσατο ἀπὸ τῆς τιμῆς here cf. ἐνοσφίσατο ἀπὸ τοῦ ἀναθέματος in Josh. 7:1 LXX.

7. A. W. F. Blunt, *The Acts of the Apostles* (Oxford, 1923), p. 153.

8. J. Klausner, *From Jesus to Paul*, E.T. (London, 1944), p. 289.

9. P. H. Menoud, "La mort d'Ananias et de Saphira (Actes 5,1-11)," *Aux Sources de la Tradition Chrétienne: Mélanges offerts à M. Maurice Goguel* (Paris/ Neuchâtel, 1950), pp. 146-54.

careful in rebuking the sinful members of the congregation. But the story goes on to relate that Ananias was buried without word being said to his wife, although she must have been in the neighbourhood. When she came into the house three hours later, St. Peter instead of telling her of the dreadful fall of her husband so as to give her a chance of repentance cross-examined her in such a way that the sin in her heart was brought to light as a downright lie; and then he told her that her husband was dead and she would die too. . . . Try how we may, we cannot imagine Christ acting towards sinners as St. Peter is here represented as doing."[10]

It is no part of a commentator's work to pass moral judgment on Peter; it would be necessary, in any case, to know much more than is stated in the narrative. Sapphira, for aught that is known to the contrary, may have suggested the deceit to her husband. It is not Peter's character or even Ananias and Sapphira's deserts in which Luke is primarily interested. What he is concerned to emphasize is the reality of the Holy Spirit's indwelling presence in the church, together with the solemn practical implications of that fact. So early was it necessary to emphasize the lesson later formulated by Paul: "Do you not know that you are God's temple and that God's Spirit dwells in you? If anyone destroys God's temple, God will destroy him. For God's temple is holy, and that temple you are" (1 Cor. 3:16-17).[11]

The incident shows, too, that even in the earliest days the church was not a society of perfect people. Luke's picture of the primitive community is no doubt idealized, but it is not over-idealized. Lest his readers should overestimate the unity and sanctity of the first believers, he has recorded this incident which not only illustrates his honest realism but is intended also to serve as a warning to others.

1-2 Two members of the community, Ananias and his wife Sapphira,[12] like many other members, sold a piece of land which they possessed. They retained part of the price for their private use, as they had every right to do, and Ananias brought the rest to the apostles to be used for the benefit of the community, but he represented this balance as being the total purchase price that they had received.

3 Peter, perceiving the truth of the situation, broke out on Ananias in words calculated to convey to the wretched man the enormity of his sin.

10. L. E. Browne, *The Acts of the Apostles* (London, 1925), pp. 83-84.

11. H. A. W. Meyer's emphasis on the principle of church discipline is important for the assessment of the incident in its context (*The Acts of the Apostles*, E.T., I [Edinburgh, 1877], p. 142). See also O. Cullmann, *Peter: Disciple–Apostle–Martyr*, E.T. (London, 1953), p. 34.

12. Ananias is the OT Hananiah (*ḥānanyāhû*, "Yahweh has graciously granted"). Sapphira represents Aram. *šappîrā'*, "beautiful." J. Klausner (*From Jesus to Paul*, pp. 289-90) suggests that this may be the Sapphira whose name appears in Aramaic (or Hebrew) and Greek on an ossuary found in Jerusalem in 1923. The most that can be said in support of such an identification is that it cannot be disproved.

Sharp practice in the ordinary commerce of life was as common then as now, but a higher standard of probity must prevail among the followers of Christ. Ananias, in the effort to gain a reputation for greater generosity than he had actually earned, tried to deceive the believing community, but in trying to deceive the community he was really trying to deceive the Holy Spirit, whose life-giving power had created the community and maintained it in being. So real was the apostles' appreciation of the presence and authority of the Spirit in their midst. There may indeed be the further implication that Ananias and Sapphira had vowed to give the whole proceeds of the sale to God, but then changed their mind and handed over only part. A lie told to Peter as a private man might have been relatively venial, but this—whether Ananias knew it or not—was a lie told to God,[13] something prompted by none other than the great adversary of God and humanity.[14]

4 No compulsion had been laid on Ananias to sell his property: the virtue of such an act as Barnabas's lay in its spontaneous generosity. The community of goods in the primitive Jerusalem church was quite voluntary. The piece of land belonged to Ananias; he could keep it or sell it as he pleased, and when he had sold it the money he got for it was his to use as he chose.[15] The voluntariness of the whole procedure forms a contrast to much that has claimed this early Christian practice as a precedent. But the voluntariness of the whole procedure made Ananias's action the more gratuitous. If it is no part of a commentator's business to pass moral judgments on Peter, the temptation must equally be resisted to pass them on Ananias. The desire to gain a higher reputation than is one's due for generosity or some other virtue is not so uncommon that anyone can afford to adopt a self-righteous attitude toward Ananias. In a situation where those who followed Bar-

---

13. The Holy Spirit in the church is God himself present with his people (cf. 1 Cor. 14:25).

14. Gk. Σατανᾶς is a loanword from Aramaic; the corresponding Heb. *śāṭān* ("adversary") occurs as a common noun in the OT, sometimes to denote the chief prosecutor in the heavenly court (cf. 1 Chron. 21:1; Job 1:6–2:7; Zech. 3:1-2). Together with the transliteration Σατανᾶς the NT also uses the translation ὁ διάβολος, as in 10:38; 13:10 below (see p. 214, n. 58; p. 249, n. 26).

15. B. J. Capper, "The Interpretation of Acts 5.4," *JSNT* 19 (1983), pp. 117-31, points out that in the Qumran regulations a postulant for membership in the community handed over his property provisionally to the treasurer, but it was not merged with the assets of the community until he had completed his period of probation and was admitted to full membership (1QS 6.18-23). He suggests that Ananias similarly made a provisional transference of his money to the church, but he was expected to transfer it all, even if only provisionally; until then, it remained under his control in the sense that he could receive it back if he were not in due course admitted to full membership. But there is no evidence that such a provisional catechumenate was practised at this early stage in the church's life. The contrast may also be drawn between the penalty prescribed for deceiving the community in the matter of property—one year's exclusion from the fellowship meal and deprivation of one quarter of one's food ration (1QS 6.24-25)—and the consequences of Ananias and Sapphira's deceit.

nabas's example received high commendation within the group, the social pressure on others to do the same, or rather to appear to do the same, must have been considerable.

5 As Peter spoke, Ananias's sin came home to him, and he fell down dead. It was an evident act of judgment—the judgment that begins first at the house of God—and it is no wonder that all who heard about it were filled with fear. But it may have been an act of mercy as well, if the incident be considered in the light of Paul's words about another offender against the believing community: "deliver this man to Satan for the destruction of the flesh, that his spirit may be saved in the day of the Lord Jesus" (1 Cor. 5:5).[16] Some expositors have cited as a parallel to Ananias's sudden death the story of the Archbishop of York who fell dead with fright when King Edward I of England darted an angry look at him.[17] But it is no real parallel: nothing in Peter's personality stopped Ananias's heart from beating, but rather the sudden realization of the sacrilege that he had committed.

6 Immediately his dead body was carried out and buried by "the young men"—probably the younger members of the community rather than professional buriers. Burial in that climate followed quickly after death; what was required in the way of medical certification is uncertain. Apparently Sapphira was not told of her husband's death; there is no way of knowing if any attempt was made to communicate with her. The telescoping of such proceedings enhances the dramatic effect of the narrative, the first act of which is now to be followed by the second.

4. Death of Sapphira (5:7-11)

7 *There was a lapse of about three hours; then his wife came in. She did not know what had happened.*

8 *Peter said[18] to her, "Tell me, did you sell the land for so much?" "Yes," said she, "for so much."*

9 *Then Peter answered her, "What made you agree together to tempt the Spirit of the Lord? See, the feet of those who have buried your husband are at the door; they will carry you out too."*

10 *Immediately she fell down at his feet and died.[19] The young men*

16. It is not agreed whether this "destruction of the flesh" meant the death of the erring member of the Corinthian church or some severe bodily affliction (cf. 2 Cor. 12:7; Job 2:4-7). For the belief that Christians might die prematurely for serious sin see 1 Cor. 11:30; Jas. 5:20; 1 John 5:16-17.

17. F. J. Foakes-Jackson, *The Acts of the Apostles,* MNTC (London, 1931), p. 42.

18. Lit., "Peter answered (ἀπεκρίθη) her"; but she had not spoken. Here, as in some other places in the NT and LXX, ἀποκρίνομαι means simply "address."

19. Gk. ἐξέψυξεν (as in v. 5 above); it is used again in 12:23 of the death of Herod Agrippa I, and nowhere else in the NT. In LXX ἐκψύχω is used of the death of Sisera in Judg. 4:21 (recension A) and in Ezek. 21:12 (MT 7) of the "fainting" of everyone who hears of the destruction of Jerusalem.

came in, found her dead, carried her out,[20] *and buried her with her husband.*

11 *Great fear fell on the whole church and on all who heard of this.*

7-10   The death of Ananias may have come as a shock to Peter, but the following three hours gave him time to consider the tragedy and to recognize in it the divine judgment for an attempt to deceive the church, and to deceive the Spirit in the church. When Sapphira came in, he asked her plainly if she and her husband had sold the land for the sum which had actually been handed over. She had thus an opportunity to tell the truth, but when she brazened it out and repeated her husband's falsehood, Peter had no doubt that she would share her husband's fate, and he told her so bluntly. At this stage Peter had not had much experience in pastoral ministry; otherwise he would probably have broken the news of Ananias's death to her before he questioned her, and the result might have been happier. As it was, both husband and wife had been detected in a deliberately conceived plan to see how far they could go in presuming on the forbearance of the Spirit of God (which is what is meant by "tempting" him); and they had gone too far.[21] The conviction of complicity in this guilt, together with the rough-and-ready announcement of her husband's death, proved too much for Sapphira: she in her turn fell down dead and was carried out and buried.

11   There is no point in asking if Ananias and Sapphira were genuine believers or not, because there is no means of answering such a question. On the one hand, they did not behave as if they were genuine believers; on the other hand, it cannot be said for certain that they were not, unless one is prepared to say that no one who commits an act of deliberate deceit can be a genuine believer. The fear which fell on the whole community suggests that many a member of it (like many an Israelite when Achan was exposed) had reason to tremble and think, "There, but for the grace of God, go I." The best answer to questions of this kind is provided by the twofold inscription on the divinely laid foundation stone: "The Lord knows those who are his" and "Let everyone who names the name of the Lord depart from iniquity" (2 Tim. 2:19).

In verse 11 the word "church" (Gk. *ekklēsia*) occurs for the first time in the authentic text of Acts.[22] The Greek word has both a Gentile and a Jewish background. In its Gentile sense it denotes chiefly the citizen-assembly of a Greek city (cf. Acts 19:32, 39, 41), but it is its Jewish usage that

20. Cod. D and the Syriac Peshitta (probably preserving a Western reading) have "wrapped her round and carried her out" (cf. v. 6).

21. For the idea cf. Ex. 17:2, "Why do you put the LORD to the proof?" and Deut. 6:16, "You shall not put the LORD your God to the test" (quoted by our Lord in his wilderness temptation, Matt. 4:7 par. Luke 4:12).

22. See p. 72, n. 111, for its occurrence in the Western text of 2:47.

underlies its use to denote the community of believers in Jesus. In the Septuagint it is one of the words used to denote the people of Israel in their religious character as Yahweh's "assembly." It is a pity that in so many English versions of the New Testament it is rendered by a term ("church") which is absent from the English Old Testament. Readers of the Greek Bible could draw their own conclusions from the use of *ekklēsia* in Old and New Testament alike. So could readers of William Tyndale's English translation when they came on the word "congregacion" in both Testaments.[23]

E. THE APOSTLES BEFORE THE SANHEDRIN (5:12-42)

1. Signs and Wonders (5:12-16)

12 *Many signs and wonders were performed through the apostles among the people. They all met together in Solomon's Colonnade,*
13 *and none of the others[24] dared to join them; but the people held them in high esteem.[25]*

23. In Deuteronomy and the following OT books, except Jeremiah and Ezekiel, ἐκκλησία is the regular LXX rendering of Heb. *qāhāl*, "assembly"; in the first four books of the OT, as in Jeremiah and Ezekiel, *qāhāl* is regularly represented in LXX by συναγωγή, which is also used throughout LXX as the rendering of *ʿēḏāh*, "congregation." The Aramaic equivalent of *ʿēḏāh*, and occasionally of *qāhāl*, was *keništā'*, which may lie behind the dominical sayings of Matt. 16:18 and 18:17 and was possibly the term by which the group of Jesus' disciples was known in Jerusalem (the *keništā'* of the Nazarenes). In due course ἐκκλησία came to be specialized for Christian meetings and συναγωγή for Jewish meetings. The Christian ἐκκλησία was both new and old—new, because of its relation and witness to Jesus as Lord and to the epoch-making events of his death and exaltation and the sending of the Spirit; old, as the continuation of the "congregation of the LORD" which had formerly been confined within the limits of one nation but now, having died and risen with Christ, was to be open to all believers without distinction. See F. J. A. Hort, *The Christian Ecclesia* (London, 1897); K. L. Schmidt, *TDNT* 3, pp. 501-36 (*s.v.* ἐκκλησία); G. Johnston, *The Doctrine of the Church in the New Testament* (Cambridge, 1943); O. Cullmann, *The Early Church*, E.T. (London, 1956); E. Schweizer, *Church Order in the New Testament*, E.T. (London, 1961); H. Küng, *The Structures of the Church*, E.T. (London, 1965).

24. Because of a difficulty in reconciling v. 13a with v. 14a, attempts have been made to emend "of the others" (τῶν . . . λοιπῶν) or "join" (κολλᾶσθαι) or both. A. Hilgenfeld emended λοιπῶν to Λευιτῶν ("Levites"). A. Pallis adopted this emendation and also emended κολλᾶσθαι αὐτοῖς to κωλῦσαι αὐτούς ("prevent"): "And of the Levites none dared to prevent them" (from holding meetings in the temple precincts). F. Blass suggested that κολλᾶσθαι αὐτοῖς might be translated "meddle with them"; unfortunately no convincing evidence can be produced for the use of κολλᾶσθαι in this sense. M. Dibelius emended τῶν δὲ λοιπῶν ("but of the others") to τῶν ἀρχόντων ("of the rulers"). C. C. Torrey's attempts to solve the problem by reference to an Aramaic substratum are unconvincing (*Composition and Date of Acts* [Cambridge, Mass., 1916], pp. 31-32; *Documents of the Primitive Church* [New York, 1941], p. 96); besides, it is unlikely that a summarizing paragraph like 5:12-16 should have an Aramaic source. No emendation is necessary; see the exposition above.

25. *P45* omits "but the people held them in high esteem."

14 *More and more believed in the Lord and were added to their number,
multitudes of both men and women,*

15 *so that people even carried their sick folk into the open squares²⁶ and
laid them on couches and pallets, in order that even Peter's shadow
might fall on some of them as he came that way.²⁷*

16 *A multitude also came from the towns round about Jerusalem, bringing sick and demon-possessed people, and they were all healed.*

12-16 This paragraph is a further summary such as has been seen already
in 2:43-47 and 4:32-35. It provides a transition to the incident recorded in
verses 17-42.

One may wonder how the statement that "none of the others dared to
join" the disciples can be squared with the report of "more and more" being
added to their fellowship; the point seems to be that the death of Ananias and
Sapphira scared off all but the totally committed. Again we are told of the
"signs and wonders" performed through the agency of the apostles; the
general atmosphere is like that of the earlier days of our Lord's Galilaean
ministry (Mark 1:32-34 par. Luke 4:40-41). Peter's shadow was as
efficacious as a medium of healing power as the fringe of his Master's cloak
had been (Mark 6:56). No wonder that the common people sounded the
apostles' praises and that the number of believers increased. Even from
outlying towns and villages of Judaea people streamed into the capital with
their sick folk in hope of profiting from the apostles' healing ministry.
Peter's reputation evidently stood specially high in this regard.

2. The Apostles Imprisoned and Released (5:17-21a)

17 *Now the high priest and all his colleagues, the party of the Sadducees
as it then was, took action. They were filled with indignation,*

18 *so they arrested the apostles and put them in official custody.²⁸*

19 *But the angel of the Lord opened the prison doors by night and
brought them out.*

20 *"Go," he said, "stand in the temple and tell the people all the words
of this life."*

21a *On hearing that, they went into the temple at dawn and proceeded to
teach.*

17-18 It has been held that this incident is a duplicate of the account of
Peter and John's arrest and examination before the Sanhedrin given in the

---

26. Gk. εἰς τὰς πλατείας, lit., "into the broadways." The very similar passage
in Mark 6:56 (not paralleled in Luke) has ἐν ταῖς ἀγοραῖς ("in the marketplaces").

27. The Western text adds "for they were set free from every sickness which each
one of them had."

28. The Western text adds "and each one went to his own home" (cf. John 7:53).

preceding chapter (4:1-22), derived from a parallel source. Whether this is so or not, Luke clearly presents this incident as a sequel to the earlier one. This time all the apostles are involved, not two only, and instead of being merely dismissed with a caution they are punished for disobeying the court order imposed at the previous hearing. Peter and John gave notice that they would disregard that order (which forbade them to speak or teach any more in Jesus' name). They and their colleagues continued their preaching activity, together with a healing ministry which reproduced on a wider scale the miraculous cure which had led to their first appearance before the Sanhedrin. Now the temple authorities, at the instance of the chief-priestly group (who belonged, as we have been told already, to the party of the Sadducees), arrested the whole band of apostles—presumably while they were preaching in Solomon's Colonnade—and had them locked up overnight. The next day it was proposed to take more drastic steps with them than had been taken on the previous occasion.

19-21a But when the next day dawned, and a meeting of the Sanhedrin was convened to deal with the apostles, the apostles could not be found. The prison doors were locked, the members of the temple police force who were guarding them were at their posts, but the prisoners had gone. In classical literature we can trace a special "form" in which it was customary to describe unaccountable escapes from prison,[29] and elements of this "form" have been detected here; but such form criticism has but little to say about the historicity of the matter which is being narrated.

Luke ascribes the apostles' escape to divine agency. It was "the angel of the Lord" (or "an angel of the Lord"), he says, that opened the prison doors by night and freed them. The idiom is drawn from the Old Testament, where "the angel of the Lord" is an extension of the divine personality— Yahweh himself in his manifestation to human beings. Even if this is scarcely the sense in which Luke uses the expression, he does mean that the hand of God was at work in the apostles' release.[30] He does not say whether the agent was a supernatural being or a human messenger of God;[31] he gives no such details as he gives later of Peter's escape when he was held prisoner by Herod Agrippa (12:6-10). But whoever the "messenger" may have been on this occasion, he had a voice, for when he brought the apostles out of prison, he told them to resume proclaiming in the temple court "all the words of this life"—an apt term for the message of salvation.[32]

---

29. Cf. 12:6-10 (pp. 236-38 with nn. 15-21); 16:25-26 (p. 316 with n. 67). See R. Reitzenstein, *Die hellenistischen Wundererzählungen* (Leipzig, 1906), pp. 120-22.

30. Cf. 7:30 below (p. 140 with n. 50); also 27:23 (p. 488 with n. 70).

31. Gk. ἄγγελος, like Heb. *mal'āk,* means simply "messenger," but the words are most commonly used in the OT and NT of the spiritual messengers of God.

32. See p. 82, n. 30 (on 3:15) for the close relation between ζωή and σωτηρία.

3. The Apostles Brought before the Sanhedrin (5:21b-26)

21b The high priest and his colleagues arrived and[33] called the
Sanhedrin together—the whole senate of the people of Israel—and
sent to the prison for the apostles to be brought.

22 When the officers arrived there,[34] they did not find them in the
prison, so they came back and made their report:

23 "We found the prison most securely locked, and the guards standing
at the doors, but when we opened them, we found no one inside."

24 When the captain of the temple and the chief priests heard this, they
were greatly perplexed about the matter, wondering what it would
come to.

25 Then someone arrived and reported to them, "See, the men whom
you imprisoned are standing in the temple and teaching the people."

26 Then the captain of the temple went off with the officers and brought
them, using no force, for they were afraid that the people might stone
them.

21b-24   When the Sanhedrin met early in the morning, its leaders were
naturally perturbed to learn that the prisoners were not to be found. The
captain of the temple and his officers were even more perturbed, for they
were responsible for the prisoners' safekeeping.

25   However, if the prisoners had escaped, they had not gone far
away. While the Sanhedrin was in session, a messenger came in to tell the
authorities that the apostles were standing in the temple court again, teaching
the people as before. The authorities drew the disquieting conclusion that the
apostles had even more support than they had imagined: they had sympathizers, it appeared, in the ranks of the temple police, if not indeed among
some members of the Sanhedrin itself. How otherwise could they have been
so unobtrusively released from prison? Where was all this going to end?

26   The captain of the temple, hearing that the apostles were still
within his jurisdiction, went with his lieutenants[35] and persuaded them to
accompany him to the meeting of the court. No force was used, but no
resistance was offered. Had the apostles been minded to stand their ground,
they could have relied on the support of the crowd that was listening to them
and the temple officials would have been faced with an awkward situation;
thanks to the apostles' restraint, there was no breach of the peace.

The present expression is almost identical with "the word of this salvation" in 13:26 (in the
Syriac Peshitta the same word ḥaye, "life," translates σωτηρία as translates ζωή here).

33. The Western text adds "having risen early."

34. The Western text adds "having opened the prison."

35. Gk. ὑπηρέται, used similarly of the temple police in John 7:32, 45, 46;
18:3, 12.

4. The High Priest's Charge and the Apostles' Reply (5:27-32)

27 *When they brought them, they set them before the Sanhedrin. Then the high priest[36] questioned them:*

28 *"Did we not charge you strictly not to go on teaching in this name? But see, you have filled Jerusalem with your teaching, and you want to make us responsible for this man's blood."*

29 *Then Peter and the (other) apostles said in reply, "We must obey God rather than human beings.[37]*

30 *The God of our fathers raised up Jesus, but you put him to death, hanging him on a gibbet.*

31 *It is he whom God has exalted with his right hand as a prince and savior, to give to Israel repentance and forgiveness of sins.*

32 *We are witnesses of these things, and so is the Holy Spirit, whom God has given to those who obey him."*

27-28 When the apostles were brought in and stood before the Sanhedrin, the high priest, as president of the court, reminded them of the previous warning, and expostulated with them for the way in which they had ignored it, continuing to teach in the temple precincts and throughout the city. It appeared, he said, that they were endeavoring to place the responsibility for Jesus' death on him and his colleagues on the court. Perhaps the allusion to Jesus as "this man" is an early example of the curious reluctance in Jewish tradition to pronounce the name Jesus.[38] (One might, of course, refer to a curious Christian reluctance to pronounce his name, although for a different reason.)

29-31 The words "Peter and the apostles" no doubt imply that Peter made reply on behalf of the whole group, as he had done when addressing the crowd on the day of Pentecost (2:14). Their present reply is simply a repetition of the apostolic proclamation, emphasizing once more the contrast between what the rulers of the people did to Jesus and what God did to him. "The God of our fathers raised up Jesus" (v. 30) refers probably to the inauguration of Jesus' ministry: as God had once raised up David to be their king (13:22),[39] so he had more recently raised up Jesus to be their Messiah (cf. 3:26). The rulers, however, had compassed his death. It was the Romans who crucified him, indeed, but the chief-priestly authorities were responsible for handing him over to them. The manner of this death was the one on which the sacred law of Israel pronounced a curse: "a hanged man is ac-

36. Cod. D has ἱερεύς ("priest") for ἀρχιερεύς ("high priest"). The African Latin codex h (which exhibits a Western text) has *praetor*, which probably represents a Greek reading στρατηγός (i.e., captain of the temple).

37. The Western text paraphrases v. 29 more graphically: "But Peter said to him, 'Who should be obeyed? God, or human beings?' And he said, 'God.' And Peter said to him, 'The God of our fathers. . . .'"

38. Cf. J. Jocz, *The Jewish People and Jesus Christ* (London, 1949), p. 111.

39. The verb here and in 13:22 is ἐγείρω.

cursed by God" (Deut. 21:23).[40] His enemies, in other words, had inflicted the utmost disgrace on him. But God's mighty power[41] exalted him; God bestowed the utmost honor on him, investing him with the authority of Prince[42] and Savior, to bless his people with the grace of repentance and the gift of forgiveness. With such a proclamation entrusted to them, the apostles could do no other than insist, as they had done before, that they must obey God rather than any earthly court.[43] The authority of the Sanhedrin was great, but greater still was the authority of him who had commissioned them to make the good news known.

32 For they were not only heralds of the good news, but witnesses as well, and not simply witnesses on their own initiative, but witnesses under the direction of the divine witness, the Holy Spirit, imparted by God to all who obey him. In these words we mark again the primitive community's awareness of being indwelt and possessed by the Spirit to such a degree that they were his organ of expression. We also mark a noteworthy agreement with one of the paraclete passages in the Fourth Gospel: "when the Counselor comes," said Jesus to the disciples in the upper room, "whom I shall send to you from the Father, he will bear witness to me; and you also are witnesses, because you have been with me from the beginning" (John 15:26-27).[44]

5. The Court's Decision (5:33-40)

33 *Hearing this, they were enraged and were minded to put them to death.*
34 *But one of the Pharisees stood up in the Sanhedrin, Gamaliel by name. He was a doctor of the law, honored by all the people. He directed that the men should be put outside for a little,*
35 *and he said to his colleagues,[45] "Men of Israel, beware of what you plan to do about these men.*

40. The phrase κρεμάσαντες ἐπὶ ξύλου occurs again at 10:39; the cross of Jesus is similarly called a gibbet (ξύλον, "wood") in 13:29; 1 Pet. 2:24. This use of ξύλον goes back through LXX to Heb. *'ēṣ,* which denotes both a tree and the stake or pole on which bodies of executed criminals were hung (as in Deut. 21:22-23). For Paul's account of the paradox that the mediator of unique divine blessing should nevertheless have died under the divine curse see Gal. 3:10-14. See M. Wilcox, "'Upon the Tree'—Deut. 21:22-23 in the New Testament," *JBL* 96 (1977), pp. 85-99; J. A. Fitzmyer, "Crucifixion in Ancient Palestine, Qumran Literature, and the New Testament," *CBQ* 40 (1978), pp. 493-513. Another penal form of ξύλον ("stocks") appears in 16:24.

41. Lit., his right hand, as in 2:33.

42. Gk. ἀρχηγός, as in 3:15 (see p. 82, n. 30).

43. Peter's reply in v. 29 is more succinct than the parallel in 4:19, and even closer to the Socratic parallel quoted *ad loc.* (cf. p. 96, n. 33).

44. See W. F. Lofthouse, "The Holy Spirit in the Acts and the Fourth Gospel," *ExT* 52 (1940-41), pp. 334-36.

45. Lit., "he said to them" (Cod. D expands "them" to "the rulers and those who sat with them").

36 *Some time ago Theudas rose up, claiming to be somebody,[46] and about four hundred men went over to his side. But he was killed,[47] and all those who were persuaded by him were dispersed and came to nothing.*

37 *After him Judas the Galilaean rose up at the time of the enrollment, and led away a host after him. He too was destroyed, and all[48] those who were persuaded by him were scattered.*

38 *And now I tell you: do not interfere with these men; leave them alone.[49] If this idea or activity of theirs is of merely human origin, it will be overthrown;*

39 *but if it comes from God, you will not be able to overthrow them.[50] You may even be found to be fighting against God." They were persuaded by him*

40 *and, calling the apostles in, they flogged them and charged them not to go on speaking in Jesus' name. Then they dismissed them.*

33 The Sadducean leaders of the Sanhedrin were so enraged at this defiance of their orders that they considered sentencing the apostles to death (by stoning, presumably). But they could take no such action without the support of the Pharisaic members of the court.[51] The Pharisees were in the minority, but they commanded much more public respect than did the Sadducees, so much so that the Sadducean members of the court found it impolitic to oppose the Pharisees' demands.[52] This was particularly important in a case like the present, in which the defendants enjoyed the people's goodwill.

34 There was present at this meeting of the Sanhedrin a Pharisaic leader of quite exceptional eminence, Gamaliel the Elder, the greatest teacher of the day. According to later tradition he was a disciple of Hillel, whom he succeeded as head of his school. But those earlier traditions which reflect some direct memory of Gamaliel and his teaching do not associate him with

46. The Western text has "somebody great" (probably from 8:9).

47. Cod. D reads "was destroyed through his own act" (κατελύθη αὐτὸς δι' αὐτοῦ for ἀνῃρέθη).

48. P[45] and D omit "all."

49. D adds "not defiling your hands."

50. The Western text adds "neither you nor kings nor tyrants. Refrain therefore from these men."

51. The word "Pharisees" (Φαρισαῖοι) is rather clearly derived from Aram. pᵉrîšayyāʾ, Heb. pᵉrûšîm, "separated ones." This name may have indicated both their general tendency to keep aloof from contact with those who were careless about ceremonial purity and in particular their withdrawal from association with the Hasmonaeans during the rule of John Hyrcanus I (134-104 B.C.). They were the spiritual heirs of the ḥᵃsîdîm (the Hasidaeans, Ἀσιδαῖοι, of 1 Macc. 2:42; 7:13; 2 Macc. 14:6), the pious members of the community who in Hellenistic times gave themselves to the study, exposition, and practice of the written and oral law and opposed the popular hellenizing tendencies. When Antiochus IV tried to abolish the Jewish religion, the

the school of Hillel; they speak rather of others as belonging to the school of Gamaliel, as though he founded a school of his own.[53] According to Acts 22:3, Paul of Tarsus was one of his pupils. He was remembered in later generations as the embodiment of pure Pharisaism. "When Rabban Gamaliel the Elder died," it was said, "the glory of the Torah ceased, and purity and 'separateness' died."[54] He now rose up in court and directed that the apostles should be taken out of the council-chamber in order that he might speak his mind freely to his colleagues.

35-36 Gamaliel warned the others not to do anything rash. His advice consisted of "sound Pharisaic teaching; God is over all, and needs no help from men for the fulfilment of His purposes; all men must do is to obey, and leave the issue to Him."[55] Similar sentiments to Gamaliel's were expressed in the dictum of a second-century rabbi, Yohanan the sandal-maker: "Every assembly which is in the name of heaven will finally be established, but that which is not in the name of heaven will finally not be established."[56]

ḥᵃsîdîm supported the Hasmonaeans, the leaders of armed resistance to him, but withdrew their support when the Hasmonaeans went on to establish political as well as military supremacy for themselves and assumed the high-priesthood. The Pharisees were in opposition to the ruling party from the time of John Hyrcanus to the accession of Queen Salome Alexandra (76-67 B.C.); under her they occupied a position of great influence. In the first century A.D. they were reckoned to be some 6,000 strong, organized in closely knit "companies" or "associations" (Heb. *ḥᵃbûrôt*). They had great religious influence among the people; most of the scribes (cf. 4:5; 6:12; 23:9), the public expositors of the law, belonged to their party. Their two chief schools in NT times were those of Hillel and Shammai, leading rabbis who flourished in the later part of Herod's reign. After the fall of Jerusalem and the end of the temple order in A.D. 70 it was the Pharisees, and more particularly the heirs of the school of Hillel, who proved best able to survive the disaster and preserve the continuity of national life. For some of their distinctive beliefs see 23:6-8 (pp. 428-30, nn. 21-23). See L. Finkelstein, *The Pharisees* (Philadelphia, 1946); A. Finkel, *The Pharisees and the Teacher of Nazareth* (Leiden, 1946); J. Neusner, *The Rabbinical Traditions about the Pharisees before 70*, I-III (Leiden, 1971); J. Bowker, *Jesus and the Pharisees* (Cambridge, 1973); E. Rivkin, *A Hidden Revolution* (Nashville, 1978); Schürer II, pp. 388-403. We have contemporary accounts of the Pharisees from Josephus, who claims to have been one of them (*BJ* 2.162-63; *Ant.* 18.12-15).

52. Josephus, *Ant.* 18.17.

53. J. Neusner, *The Rabbinical Traditions about the Pharisees before 70*, I, pp. 341-76.

54. Mishnah, *Sôṭāh* 9.15. *Rabbān* ("our teacher") was an Aramaic term applied as an honorific title to certain distinguished teachers, marking them off from those who received the more ordinary title *rabbi* ("my teacher"). The word translated "separateness" (or "abstinence") is *pᵉrîšût*, from the same root as the word "Pharisees"; it denotes the sum total of Pharisaic virtues. Gamaliel (who tends to be confused in tradition with the later Gamaliel II, *c*. A.D. 100) is credited with introducing certain reforms in the regulations for divorce and remarriage, "as a precaution for the general good" (Mishnah, *Giṭṭin* 4.2-3; *Yᵉḇāmôt* 16.7).

55. J. A. Findlay, *The Acts of the Apostles* (London, 1936), p. 85.

56. *Pirqê 'Aḇôt* 4.14.

Gamaliel makes this point, and illustrates it by reminding his hearers of other movements within their lifetime which for a time enjoyed considerable support but were finally not established, because (evidently) they were not "in the name of heaven."

First, he reminded them of an insurgent named Theudas, who made large claims for himself and secured a following of four hundred men, but he achieved nothing but his own destruction and the dispersal of his followers. We have no other information about this Theudas, but since he is said to have flourished before the rising of Judas the Galilaean (A.D. 6), he may have been one of the many insurgent leaders who arose in Palestine after the death of Herod the Great (4 B.C.).[57]

37 Next, he reminded them of Judas the Galilaean. When Judaea was reduced to the status of a Roman province in A.D. 6, after the deposition of Archelaus, a census was held under the direction of the legate of Syria, P. Sulpicius Quirinius, to determine the amount of tribute to be paid by the new province to the imperial exchequer.[58] Judas, a man from Gamala in Gaulanitis (Golan), inaugurated a religious and nationalist revolt, contending that it was high treason against God, Israel's one true king, for his people

---

57. According to Josephus (*Ant.* 20.97-98) a magician named Theudas led a large company to the Jordan, promising that at his word of command the river would be divided, so that they might cross it dryshod. The procurator Cuspius Fadus (*c.* A.D. 44-46) sent a body of horsemen against them; they dispersed the multitude and brought the head of Theudas to Jerusalem. This event, however, must have taken place several years after the incident now being described by Luke. Even so, Luke's Theudas has been identified with Josephus's Theudas by some who find Luke guilty of a double blunder: *(a)* making Gamaliel refer to a rising which took place well after his present speech purports to have been delivered (for the situation of Acts 5 antedates by some years that of Acts 12, during Herod Agrippa's reign over Judaea, A.D. 41-44, and Josephus's Theudas arose shortly after Herod Agrippa's death); *(b)* making an event of A.D. 44 take place before the rising under Judas of Galilee, which is firmly dated in A.D. 6/7. The double blunder is accounted for by the supposition that Luke misread Josephus, who goes on, after his account of the magician Theudas, to mention the *sons* of Judas (M. Krenkel, *Josephus und Lucas* [Leipzig, 1894], pp. 162-74). But the arguments for Luke's knowledge of the *Antiquities* of Josephus are unconvincing, and involve us in the conclusion that Luke misread Josephus every time he drew on him. "Either Luke had not read Josephus, or else he forgot all he had read" (E. Schürer, "Lucas und Josephus," *ZWT* 19 [1876], p. 582).

58. Josephus, *Ant.* 17.355. The Judaean census was evidently made part of a wider census carried out by Quirinius throughout his province of Syria-Cilicia (which he governed A.D. 6-7). Apparently officers under his command were charged with supervising the census in various parts of the province: the funerary inscription of one Q. Aemilius Secundus (*CIL* 3.6687, the "lapis Venetus") tells how he supervised it in Apamea on the Orontes, and in Judaea it was probably supervised by Coponius, whom Augustus sent to Judaea as its first prefect (*BJ* 2.117). On the relation of this census to that of Luke 2:2, also associated with the name of Quirinius as governor of Syria, see I. H. Marshall, *The Gospel of Luke* (Grand Rapids/Exeter, 1978), pp. 96-104.

in his land to pay tribute to a pagan ruler.[59] The revolt was crushed by Rome, but the spirit which animated it lived on, and emboldened the party of the Zealots to take the lead in the Jewish revolt of A.D. 66.[60] Judas's movement proved not to be so ineffective as Gamaliel supposed it was.

38-39 Therefore, said Gamaliel, take no hostile action against these men. If their movement is not of God, it will come to nothing in any case; on the other hand, if after all it should prove to be of God, you would not wish to be found fighting against him.[61] There is much common sense in this position, for certain kinds of men—and movements—can safely be relied on to hang themselves if given enough rope; but Gamaliel's temporizing policy is not always the wisest one to follow, whether in religious or in political life. His pupil Paul of Tarsus was of a very different mind.

40 However, Gamaliel's advice prevailed on this occasion. It probably represented the viewpoint of the Pharisees as a whole. The court was content to inflict the minor penalty of flogging on the apostles—whether with the full tale of "forty stripes save one" or something more lenient is not said[62]—for disobeying its previous order, which was now reimposed: they must speak no more in the name of Jesus.

6. The Apostles Continue Their Public Witness (5:41-42)

> 41 *They, for their part, left the Sanhedrin with joy, because they had been counted worthy to suffer disgrace for the Name.*
>
> 42 *And every day, in the temple and in household groups,[63] they continued without ceasing to teach and to tell the good news of the Messiah, Jesus.*

41-42 The apostles paid no more attention to the repeated ban on speaking in Jesus' name than they had done the first time. Both in the temple court and in various homes they continued to bear witness to Jesus, the Messiah of Israel. As for the flogging they had received, this did not dishearten them; on the contrary, they found cause for joy in the thought that God had counted

---

59. See Josephus, *BJ* 2.118, 433; 7.253; *Ant.* 18.4-10, 23-25; 20.102.

60. See pp. 40-41, with nn. 48-51 (on 1:13).

61. Cf. Nicodemus's plea to Pilate on Jesus' behalf in the apocryphal *Acts of Pilate* 5:1, "Let him alone and do not contrive any evil against him: if the signs he performs are of God, they will stand; but if they are of men, they will come to nothing." (In Nicodemus's argument, which is no doubt modelled on Gamaliel's argument here, the works of the Egyptian magicians Jannes and Jambres serve the purpose which the risings of Theudas and Judas serve in Gamaliel's argument.)

62. The limit of forty stripes was fixed in Deut. 25:3; lest it should inadvertently be exceeded the limit was fixed in practice at thirty-nine (cf. 2 Cor. 11:24). Details for the infliction of the stripes are laid down in Mishnah, *Makkôt* 3.10-14.

63. Gk. κατ' οἶκον, as in 2:46 (cf. κατ' οἴκους, 20:20).

them worthy to endure this humiliation for the sake of Jesus' name.[64] It was insignificant indeed when compared with the disgrace and anguish that Jesus had endured; but, as far as it went, it was a participation in his suffering, such as he had warned them to expect.[65]

64. The text (v. 41) has simply "for the Name" (ὑπὲρ τοῦ ὀνόματος). To Christians there was one name above all others, the name of Jesus. This absolute use of τὸ ὄνομα recurs in 3 John 7 and here and there in the Apostolic Fathers.

65. Cf. Matt. 10:17-22; Mark 13:9-13; Luke 12:11-12; 21:12-19; John 15:18-25; 16:2-3.

ACTS 6

II. PERSECUTION AND EXPANSION (6:1–9:31)

A. STEPHEN (6:1–8:1A)

1. The Appointing of the Seven (6:1-6)

1 *At this time,¹ as the disciples² were increasing in number, a complaint was voiced by the Hellenists against the Hebrews, because their widows were being overlooked at the daily distribution.³*

2 *Then the Twelve called the whole body of the disciples to them and said, "It is not desirable that we should leave (the ministry of) the word of God and serve at tables.*

3 *So, brothers, look out seven men from your own number,⁴ men of good repute, full of the Spirit and wisdom, whom we may put in charge of this business.*

4 *We ourselves will continue in prayer and in the ministry of the word."*

5 *What they said was approved by the whole company, so they chose Stephen, a man full of faith and the Holy Spirit, Philip, Prochorus, Nicanor, Timon, Parmenas, and Nicolaus, a proselyte from Antioch.*

6 *They brought these men before the apostles, who prayed and laid their hands on them.*

The time has now come to record a new and momentous advance in the life of the new community. This advance involved the large-scale evangeliza-

---

1. Lit., "in these days" (ἐν . . . ταῖς ἡμέραις ταύταις), a formula marking the beginning of a new division of the work and here also the use of a new (Hellenistic) source, which went on to record the launching of the Gentile mission in Syrian Antioch (11:19-26).

2. This is the first occurrence in Acts of the word "disciples" (μαθηταί) as a designation for the followers of Jesus; it is used frequently in Luke and the other Gospels for those who accompanied him during his ministry.

3. The Western text adds "because it was being administered by Hebrews" (ἐν τῇ διακονίᾳ τῶν Ἐβραίων).

4. The Western reading is fuller: "What is it then, brothers? look out seven men from among yourselves. . . ."

tion of Gentiles. It was the Hellenists in the church who took the lead in this enterprise, and as they have not been mentioned in the record thus far, Luke introduces his account of it by saying something about them and their leaders.

1 The church of Jerusalem, we are now told, comprised both "Hebrews" and "Hellenists." The main distinction between the two groups was probably linguistic: the Hellenists were Jews whose habitual language was Greek and who attended Greek-speaking synagogues; the Hebrews spoke Aramaic (or Mishnaic Hebrew) and attended synagogues where the service was conducted in Hebrew. Many of the Hellenists had affinities with the lands of the Jewish dispersion around the Mediterranean shores, whereas the Hebrews were Palestinian Jews; there were doubtless several minor social and cultural differences between the two groups.[5] In the Jewish world as a whole there were tensions between them, and some of these tensions endured between members of the two groups who had joined the "disciples"[6]—as the followers of Jesus are here called for the first time in Acts.

It was over a practical issue, and not over a matter of theological importance, that disagreement became acute. As daily allocations were made to poorer members of the community from the common fund to which the wealthier members had contributed their property, complaints began to arise that one group was being favored at the expense of the other. Widows naturally formed a considerable proportion of the poorer members of the church, and the Hellenistic widows were said to be at a disadvantage in comparison with the Hebrew widows, perhaps because the distribution of charity was in the hands of the "Hebrews."

2-4 The apostles—or "the Twelve," as they are called here[7]— wisely determined to put the trouble right at once. It was not their primary business to supervise the financial arrangements of the community or to take an active part in the "daylie handreachinge" (as Coverdale's English version of 1535 calls it).[8] They therefore called the community together and bade them select seven men to be responsible for administering the charitable allocation. These seven should be men of honorable reputation, so that their

---

5. On the term "Hellenists" (Ἑλληνισταί) see H. J. Cadbury, "The Hellenists," in *Beginnings* I.5 (London, 1933), pp. 59-74; C. F. D. Moule, "Once More, Who Were the Hellenists?" *ExT* 70 (1958-59), pp. 100-102; M. Hengel, *Between Jesus and Paul,* E.T. (London, 1983), pp. 1-29; also H. Windisch, *TDNT* 2, pp. 511-12 (*s.v.* Ἕλλην); BAGD, *s.v.* Ἑλληνιστής.

6. We find this tension in the early Hellenistic period (cf. 1 Macc. 1:11-15), and it persisted into the Roman period; see M. Hengel, *Judaism and Hellenism,* E.T. (London, 1974); *Jews, Greeks and Barbarians,* E.T. (London, 1980); I. H. Marshall, "Palestinian and Hellenistic Christianity," *NTS* 19 (1972-73), pp. 271-87.

7. This term is used for the apostles here only in Acts (cf. "the Eleven" in 1:26; 2:14, where one of the Twelve receives special mention and the rest are referred to collectively), although it is quite common in Mark and Luke (cf. 1 Cor. 15:5).

8. A literal anglicization of Luther's *in der täglichen Handreichung.*

probity might command complete confidence; they should be wise men, competent in administration and also qualified to deal wisely with a situation in which such delicate human susceptibilities had to be considered; above all, they must be men of God, filled with his Spirit. These might be regarded as ideal requirements for all church appointments. If such men could be found, to take charge of the distribution and see that no further cause for justified complaint arose, the apostles would be free to devote their undistracted attention to directing the church's regular worship and to preaching the gospel.

5   The apostolic suggestion met with approval, and seven men were selected. All seven appear to have been Hellenists (this conclusion does not rest merely on the fact that they all have Greek names); indeed, they were probably the recognized leaders of the Hellenists in the church. Stephen heads the list: he is more particularly described as "a man full of faith and the Holy Spirit"—a description whose relevance and significance appear very clearly as the story proceeds. Philip also plays an important part in the subsequent narrative of Acts.[9] About the other five Luke has nothing further to say. Prochorus is represented in later tradition as being an attendant of John the evangelist, as bishop of Nicomedia, and as martyred at Antioch.[10] About Nicolaus, the last-named of the seven, two interesting facts are mentioned: he was not even a Jew by birth, but a proselyte (a convert to Judaism from paganism), and he belonged to Antioch—Antioch on the Orontes. That the only one of the seven to have his place of origin named should belong to Antioch may be a token of Luke's special interest in that city (to which, according to tradition, he himself belonged).[11] As early as the time of Irenaeus (c. A.D. 180), and possibly earlier, this Nicolaus was held to be the founder of the party of the Nicolaitans, who receive unfavorable mention in Rev. 2:6, 15.[12] The Nicolaitans certainly derived their name from some Nicolaus—whether from this Nicolaus or another must remain uncertain.

9. See 8:5-40; 21:8-9. On the possibility that he was one of Luke's informants for part of his narrative see p. 400 with n. 10.

10. Under his name there has come down to us an apocryphal fifth-century work called the *Acts of John*, an orthodox work, not to be confused with the second-century Gnostic composition with the same title.

11. J. Smith points out as a parallel that, out of eight accounts of Napoleon's Russian campaign (three by Frenchmen, three by Englishmen, and two by Scots), only the two Scots mention that the Russian general Barclay de Tolly was of Scots extraction (*The Voyage and Shipwreck of St. Paul* [London, ⁴1880], p. 4). See pp. 229-30, nn. 33, 40 (on 11:28).

12. Irenaeus, *Against Heresies* 1.23.1; cf. 3.11.7. Victorinus of Pettau (c. A.D. 300), in the earliest Latin commentary on the Apocalypse, has a note on Rev. 2:6: "Before that time factious and pestilential men had made for themselves a heresy in the name of the deacon Nicolaus, teaching that meat offered to idols could be exorcized, so that it might be eaten, and that one who had committed fornication might receive absolution on the eighth day." Victorinus is more circumstantial in his account than Irenaeus, and does not make Nicolaus personally responsible for Nicolaitanism; he may have drawn his information on

6 It was the community as a whole that selected these seven men and presented them to the apostles for their approbation; it was the apostles who installed them in office. This they did by laying their hands on them, after prayer. The imposition of hands is mentioned in a variety of contexts in the Old Testament for the bestowal of a blessing (cf. Gen. 48:13-20), for expressing identification, as when the sacrificer laid his hands on the head of the sacrificial victim (Lev. 1:4; 3:2; 4:4; 16:21, etc.), for commissioning a successor (cf. Num. 27:23), and so forth. According to the Mishnah, members of the Sanhedrin were admitted by the imposition of hands.[13] In the present instance the imposition of apostolic hands formally associated the Twelve with the appointment of the Seven to discharge their special duty. It did not, of course, impart the gift of the Spirit; the Seven were already "full of the Spirit" (v. 3).

The Seven have conventionally been called "deacons"; in a number of Christian traditions this designation has come to be used in a restricted sense of those who are responsible for the financial affairs of the church. While the Greek noun *diakonos,* from which "deacon" is derived, is not used in this passage,[14] the related noun *diakonia* is used (as is also the verb *diakoneō,* "serve," in v. 2);[15] but *diakonia* is used impartially of the daily "distribution" (v. 1) and the "ministry" of preaching (v. 4).[16] With reference to their present function, it might be better to describe the Seven as "almoners"; and where *diakonos* appears elsewhere in the Greek New Testament to denote an order of service in the church distinct from that of the "bishop" *(episkopos)* or "elder" *(presbyteros),*[17] it might be better to render it by the more general term "minister" (cf. Phil. 1:1; 1 Tim. 3:8-13).

While the Seven were appointed to service as almoners, it is plain that their activity was by no means confined to this. Stephen and Philip, at any rate, were well equipped for public leadership in general and for the particular forms of service in which Luke describes them as engaging— Stephen for the defense of the gospel and Philip for the work of evangelism.

---

this matter (as on much else) from Papias. The Nicolaitans evidently encouraged Christians to ignore the terms of the apostolic decree of 15:29 below (see pp. 299-300).

13. Mishnah, *Sanhedrin* 4.4. The ceremony was called s*mîkāh* in Hebrew. Cf. 8:17; 9:12, 17; 19:6 below, with accompanying exposition and notes.

14. The NT uses *diakonos* in a wide variety of senses, e.g., of domestic servants, of civil magistrates as servants of God, of Christian preachers and teachers as servants of Christ, and even of Christ himself, as a "servant to the circumcised" (Rom. 15:8).

15. Gk. διαϰονεῖν τραπέζαις, "to serve at tables," where the "tables" may have been used either for handing out food or (more probably) for distributing the money to buy food.

16. Gk. τῇ διαϰονίᾳ τῇ ϰαθημερινῇ . . . τῇ διαϰονίᾳ τοῦ λόγου.

17. For πρεσβύτερος and ἐπίσϰοπος see 20:17, 28 below, with exposition and notes.

2. Progress Report (6:7)

> 7 *The word of God advanced and the number of the disciples in Jerusalem increased greatly; moreover, a large company of the priests[18] were rendering obedience to the faith.[19]*

7 At this point Luke interrupts his narrative with a brief report of progress. Six such reports appear at intervals throughout Acts and serve to punctuate the history.[20] But here, immediately before the account of Stephen's activity, there is special relevance in Luke's emphasis on the church's increase in numbers and popularity. In particular, the fact that so many priests were joining the community meant that the ties which attached many of the believers to the temple order would be strengthened. It is not suggested that these priests relinquished their priestly office; the logic of such a step would not be generally appreciated at this stage.[21] The ordinary priests were socially and in other ways far removed from the wealthy chief-priestly families from which the main opposition to the gospel came. Many of the ordinary priests were no doubt men holy and humble of heart, like Zechariah, father of John the Baptist,[22] men who would readily be persuaded of the truth of the gospel. But it was not good that the new movement should be too closely attached to the old order, and there is "tremendous tension" in the juxtaposition of the reference to these priests and the account of Stephen's insistence that the temple order was now superseded.[23]

---

18. There is a variant reading "Jews" for "priests" in Cod. ℵ and a few cursives; there is also a Western variant "in the temple" (ἐν τῷ ἱερῷ for τῶν ἱερέων).

19. This objective use of "faith" (that which is to be believed, i.e., the gospel) is commoner in the Pastoral Letters (cf. 1 Tim. 1:19; 4:6; 6:10) than elsewhere in the NT. If the article were not present (ὑπήκουον τῇ πίστει), one might render "were obedient by faith" (cf. "obedience of faith" in Rom. 1:5; 16:26, i.e., the obedience which consists in faith).

20. Cf. 9:31; 12:24; 16:5; 19:20; 28:31. C. H. Turner ("Chronology of the New Testament," *HDB* I, pp. 421-23) points out that Acts is thus cut into six "panels" covering on an average five years each.

21. K. Bornhäuser interpreted the Letter to the Hebrews on the improbable theory that it was addressed to these believing priests (*Empfänger und Verfasser des Briefes an die Hebräer* [Gütersloh, 1932]). C. Spicq, who took a similar line in *L'épître aux Hébreux*, I (Paris, 1952), pp. 218, 226-31, later argued that these priests were "Esseno-Christians," former members of the Qumran community ("L'épître aux Hébreux: Apollos, Jean-Baptiste, les Hellénistes et Qumran," *Revue de Qumran* 1 [1958-59], pp. 365-90).

22. Luke 1:5-6.

23. A. Cole, *The New Temple* (London, 1950), p. 33.

3. Stephen's Activity Arouses Opposition (6:8-10)

8 *Stephen, who was full of grace and power, performed great wonders and signs among the people.*[24]

9 *Then some members of the Synagogue of the Freedmen (as it was called)—both Cyrenaeans and Alexandrians and men from Cilicia and Asia—rose up and engaged in debate with Stephen,*

10 *but they were unable to resist*[25] *the wisdom and spirit with which he spoke.*

8 Did Stephen perform "great wonders and signs" before the apostles' hands were laid on him? Since at that time he was already "full of faith and the Holy Spirit" (v. 5), it is reasonable to conclude that this fullness was accompanied by the "grace and power" which enabled him to perform them. It has been argued, however, that it is through the imposition of apostolic hands that "the Seven evidently receive (or rather, Stephen and Philip evidently receive) what Luke regards as the distinctive mode of the Spirit's activity in the missionary enterprise—the Spirit of God which confirms the word of God with signs and wonders."[26] But it was to authorize Stephen and his colleagues to discharge one special responsibility that the apostles laid their hands on them. At any rate, the "great wonders and signs" (which most probably included acts of healing) would naturally bring Stephen into favor "among the people," as they brought the apostles (5:12-13). But another aspect of Stephen's activity provoked fierce hostility.

9-10 Stephen expounded his distinctive teaching about the implications of the gospel in one of the synagogues[27] of Jerusalem which was frequented by Jews from several lands of the dispersion, the "Synagogue of the Freedmen," comprising worshipers from Cyrene, Alexandria, Cilicia, and Asia.[28] There were several synagogues in Jerusalem, some of them (like

24. For "grace" the Byzantine text reads "faith" (in conformity with v. 5). After "among the people" there is a Western addition: "by the name of the Lord (Jesus Christ)."

25. After "withstand" the Western text continues: ". . . the wisdom which was in him and the Holy Spirit by whom he spoke, for they were confuted before him with all freedom of speech. Being unable, therefore, to face up (ἀντοφθαλμεῖν) to the truth, they suborned men."

26. G. W. H. Lampe, *The Seal of the Spirit* (London, 1951), p. 74.

27. The synagogue was instituted, perhaps as early as the Babylonian exile, for the reading and exposition of the sacred scriptures. Especially in the lands of the dispersion, it served as the general community center for the Jews in any locality. In a large city there might be several Jewish synagogues, although the tradition that there were 480 in Jerusalem before its destruction (TJ *Megillah* 73d) may be taken with a grain of salt. See Schürer II, pp. 423-54.

28. It is most probable that only one synagogue is in view here, although some have seen a reference to two, three, four, or even five synagogues in the text. The emendation of "Libertines" to "Libyans" (so Beza, Tischendorf, M. Dibelius) is tempting in the vicinity of "Cyrenaeans" and "Alexandrians"; but the temptation should be resisted. A *libertinus* (the Latin term here taken over as a loanword into Greek) was either the

this one) attended by Hellenistic Jews. The mention of Cilicia raises the possibility that this was the synagogue attended by Saul, otherwise called Paul, whose native Tarsus was the principal city of Cilicia. (On the other hand, "a Hebrew born of Hebrews," as he calls himself in Phil. 3:5, might have preferred to attend a synagogue where the service was conducted in Hebrew.) One Hellenistic synagogue in Jerusalem from the period preceding A.D. 70 is known from a Greek inscription set up by its founder Theodotus and discovered on Ophel in 1913/14.[29] It has been held that this was the very synagogue to which Luke refers here:[30] the identification, in the nature of the case, is incapable of proof. Freedmen were former slaves (or the children of former slaves) who had been emancipated by their owners; if their owners were Roman citizens, their freedmen were enrolled as members of their family. Many Jews who were taken captive to Rome at the time of Pompey's conquest of Judaea (63 B.C.) were subsequently emancipated and thenceforth had the status of freedmen.

Stephen's teaching aroused keen opposition, and a full-dress debate was probably arranged. The exact subject of the debate is not stated; the messiahship of Jesus was no doubt the central issue, but Stephen expounded the implications of this messiahship more radically than his fellow-believers had hitherto done, with reference to the abiding validity of the law of Moses and especially of the temple order. The nature of his arguments may be inferred from the charges brought against him (vv. 13-14) and from his reply (7:2-53). The strength of his case was such that his opponents in the debate found themselves worsted. They accepted his premises (for like him they acknowledged the authority of Old Testament scripture), but they could not accept his conclusions, so scandalous and revolutionary did they appear.

4. Stephen Accused before the Sanhedrin (6:11-15)

11 *Then they put up men who said, "We have heard him speaking blasphemous words against Moses and against God."*
12 *They stirred up all the people, the elders and the scribes, and setting upon him they seized him and brought him before the Sanhedrin.*
13 *There they set up false witnesses, who said, "This man never ceases speaking out against the holy place and the law;*
14 *we have heard him say that this Jesus of Nazareth will destroy this place and change the customs which Moses handed down to us."*

---

manumitted slave of a Roman citizen (a *libertus*) or the son of one. See A. M. Duff, *Freedmen in the Early Roman Empire* (Oxford, 21957).

29. *CIJ* 1404; cf. A. Deissmann, *Light from the Ancient East*, E.T. (London, 21927), pp. 439-41.

30. Cf. L. H. Vincent, "Découverte de la Synagogue des Affranchis à Jérusalem," *RB* 30 (1921), pp. 247-77.

15 *All who sat in the Sanhedrin fixed their eyes on him and saw his face: it was like the face of an angel.*[31]

11 Unable to silence Stephen in open debate, his opponents adopted another course. Informers were put up to represent his arguments in the most damaging light. They are called "false witnesses" because, although their reports had a basis of truth, anyone who testifies against a spokesman of God is *ipso facto* a false witness. Stephen's arguments constituted an attack on Moses, they said, because they implied the abrogation of Moses' law; they constituted an attack on God because they threatened to undermine the temple order, the foundation of national worship, with which (it was believed) the glory of God was bound up.

According to the later formulation of rabbinical law, blasphemy involved the profane use of the ineffable name of Israel's God[32]—and any utterance of that name apart from the high priest's pronouncing of it on the day of atonement was a profane use. But, as the narrative of our Lord's appearance before the Sanhedrin indicates, blasphemy was interpreted in a wider sense in the early decades of the first century A.D. (cf. Mark 14:61-64). Stephen is later reported as making a claim for Jesus quite similar to that which Jesus himself had made before the Sanhedrin (7:56), but at this stage the charge of blasphemy against God was evidently based on the allegation that he had used language about the temple similar to the language which Jesus was unsuccessfully accused of using about it.

12 The charge brought against Stephen was all the deadlier because it was one which would infuriate the people of Jerusalem. Any threat, real or imagined, to the temple was not only an offense to their religious feelings; it was also a threat to their livelihood. The economic life of the city and its residents depended on the temple. The chief-priestly party knew that they need have no fear of popular disapproval this time in prosecuting a leading member of the Nazarene community; on the contrary, the people would support and indeed demand the severest sanctions of the law against this man. Stephen was accordingly arrested and put on his trial before the Sanhedrin.

13-14 The witnesses gave their evidence. Stephen's teaching, they said, threatened both the temple ("the holy place") and the law,[33] for he maintained persistently that Jesus of Nazareth would destroy the temple and change the customs handed down from Moses' time.

As with the "false witnesses" who brought similar testimony against Jesus before the Sanhedrin, their charges were not baseless fabrications.

---

31. The Western text adds: "standing in their midst."
32. "The blasphemer is not guilty until he have expressly uttered the Name" (Mishnah, *Sanhedrin* 7.5).
33. Compare the charge brought against Paul in 21:28 below.

Jesus had indeed said something about destroying the temple, and Stephen had evidently repeated his words. What Stephen meant (as appears in the sequel) was that the coming of Christ implied the end of the temple order. Jesus foretold the destruction of the material temple—"not one stone will be left standing on another," he said; "all will be thrown down" (Mark 13:2)—but the charge brought against him at his trial was not based on this prediction. As the charge was worded, he had said, "I will destroy this temple that is made with hands, and in three days I will build another, not made with hands" (Mark 14:58); on this the witnesses seem to have agreed, although in other details their testimony involved such discrepancies that it had to be disallowed. That Jesus had indeed said something of the kind was apparently a matter of general knowledge in Jerusalem; it was recalled in mockery when he was exposed to public derision on the cross (Mark 15:29-30). But we search the Synoptic Gospels in vain for any information about the setting in which he uttered those words, or words like them. John, however, says that when he was challenged to justify his action in cleansing the temple, he said, "Destroy this temple, and in three days I will raise it up" (John 2:19). John explains these words as a reference to the raising up of "the temple of his body" on the third day (John 2:21). He does not report Jesus as using the terms "made with hands" and "not made with hands," but the way in which those terms entered into the Christian vocabulary from an early date suggests strongly that they do indeed owe their origin to Jesus.[34]

It is noteworthy that Luke, in his narrative of the trial of Jesus, does not reproduce the incident of the false witnesses. This is not the only place where Luke omits a theme in the ministry of Jesus, featuring in the other Synoptic Gospels, in order to deal with it in a new context in the life of the early church.[35] Here we have an instance of this tendency in his treatment of the theme of the destruction of the temple by Jesus.

Whatever form of words Stephen used which gave rise to the accusation that he said Jesus would destroy the temple, he certainly grasped and expounded the inner meaning of Jesus' own words. The apostles and many of the rank and file of the Jerusalem church might continue to attend the temple services and to be respected as devout and observant Jews; Stephen held that the gospel meant the end of the sacrificial cultus and all the ceremonial law. As he and his fellow-Hellenists saw the situation, those things were the outward and visible sign of Jewish particularism, and could not be reconciled with the wider scope of the salvation accomplished by Jesus. Jesus himself had said that with his message of the kingdom "some-

34. Cf. 7:48. See C. F. D. Moule, "Sanctuary and Sacrifice in the Church of the New Testament," *JTS* n.s. 1 (1950), pp. 29-41; M. Simon, "St. Stephen and the Jerusalem Temple," *JEH* 2 (1951), pp. 133-37; R. J. McKelvey, *The New Temple* (Oxford, 1969), pp. 67-72, 77-80, 86-87.
35. Cf. 5:15 (p. 109, n. 26).

thing greater than the temple" had come (Matt. 12:6). The inauguration of the new order meant the supersession of the temple order by a new edifice not made with hands, that spiritual house of living stones described in 1 Pet. 2:4-10 where spiritual sacrifices, acceptable to God, are offered up through Jesus Christ by a holy priesthood.

15 When the attempt was made to convict Jesus on a charge of threatening the security or sanctity of the temple, it may have been because the profanation of the temple was an offense which the Roman administration expressly reserved to the jurisdiction of the Jewish authorities. Had he been convicted on that charge, they could have dealt with him at their own discretion, without reference to the prefect. The attempt failed against Jesus, but there was every prospect that a prosecution of Stephen on those grounds would be successful. It was unnecessary to elaborate the charge of speaking against the law, when the evidence for his speaking against the temple was so unambiguous. But while his accusers pressed their charge against him, Stephen stood before the Sanhedrin with face aglow, as one who stood consciously in the presence of God.[36] This was "not the mild, gentle look that is often seen in paintings of angels; not the fierce look of an avenging angel, but a look that told of inspiration within, clear eyes burning with the inner light."[37] Luke does not say explicitly at this stage that Stephen was filled with the Holy Spirit as he faced his judges,[38] although he says so of Peter when he made his defense before the same court a little earlier (4:8); he has no need to do so here, since his whole narrative implies it.

36. With the description of Stephen's face being "like the face of an angel" compare the pen-picture of Paul in the second-century *Acts of Paul* 3 (see p. 271 with n. 8): "full of grace, for at times he looked like a man, and at times he had the face of an angel."

37. L. E. Browne, *The Acts of the Apostles* (London, 1925), p. 111. Perhaps Professor Browne indulges his imagination somewhat when he goes on: "We can hardly doubt that it was Saul who remembered that look, a look which burnt into his soul until he too was turned to accept Jesus as his master and learnt in his own life to experience the presence of the Holy Spirit."

38. Stephen is explicitly said to have been "full of the Holy Spirit" when, having finished his defense, he saw the Son of Man at the right hand of God (7:55). See also v. 5 above.

ACTS 7

5. The High Priest's Question (7:1)

> 1 *The high priest said,¹ "Is this so?"*

1 The high priest was probably still Caiaphas, as at the trial of Jesus; he remained in office until A.D. 36.² As president of the Sanhedrin by virtue of his office, he was chief judge in Israel. It was necessary in Jewish court procedure that the accused person should know what the charges against him were, and have an opportunity of replying to them.³

6. Stephen's Reply (7:2-53)

a. The patriarchal age (7:2-8)

> 2 *Then Stephen said, "Brothers and fathers, listen. The God of glory appeared to Abraham our father when he was in Mesopotamia, before he took up residence in Harran,*
> 3 *and said to him, 'Leave your country and your kinsfolk, and come into the land that I will show you.'*
> 4 *Then he left the land of the Chaldaeans and took up residence in Harran. After his father's death, God made him migrate into this land in which you now reside.⁴*
> 5 *He gave him no inheritance in it, not even as much as his foot could cover, but he promised to give it as a possession to him and to his posterity after him, although as yet he was childless.*
> 6 *'Your posterity,' God told him, 'will be resident aliens in a foreign land; they will enslave them and ill-treat them for four hundred years.*
> 7 *But I will bring judgment on the nation by which they are enslaved,' said God, 'and after that they will come out, and worship me in this place.'*
> 8 *He gave him, moreover, the covenant of circumcision, and so, when*

---

1. The Western text adds "to Stephen."
2. See pp. 91-92, n. 15 (on 4:6).
3. Cf. the reference to Roman procedure in 25:16.
4. The Western text adds "and your fathers before you."

Isaac was born to Abraham he circumcised him on the eighth day, and Isaac did so in turn to Jacob, and Jacob to the twelve patriarchs.

This speech is commonly called Stephen's defense, or apology, but it is obviously not a speech for the defense in the forensic sense of the term.[5] Such a speech as this was by no means calculated to secure an acquittal before the Sanhedrin. It is rather a defense of pure Christianity as God's appointed way of worship; Stephen here shows himself to be the precursor of the later Christian apologists, especially those who defended Christianity against Judaism. The charges brought against Stephen by the witnesses for the prosecution may have been framed tendentiously; Stephen sets forth here in some detail the arguments of which those charges were travesties.

A major theme of the speech is its insistence that the presence of God is not restricted to any one land or to any material building. God revealed himself to Abraham long before Abraham settled in the holy land; he was with Joseph in Egypt; he gave his law to the people of Israel through Moses when they were wanderers in a wilderness. The people of God similarly should not be restricted to any one locality; a movable tent such as they had in the wilderness and in the earlier years of their settlement in Canaan was a more fitting shrine for the divine presence in their midst than the fixed structure of stone that King Solomon built. The period that Israel spent as a pilgrim people—"the church in the wilderness"—is viewed as setting forth the divine order; in this respect (as in some others) Stephen echoes the teaching of the great Old Testament prophets—though even in the wilderness Israel fell short of the divine ideal.

Another theme of the speech becomes a regular feature of later anti-Judaic apologetic—the insistence that the Jewish people's refusal to acknowledge Jesus as Messiah was all of a piece with their attitude to God's messengers from the beginning of their national history. Joseph's brothers hated him, although he was God's predestined deliverer for them; Moses, another divinely ordained deliverer, was repudiated by his people more than once. The prophets too were persecuted and killed by those to whom they

5. On Stephen's speech see B. W. Bacon, "Stephen's Speech: Its Argument and Doctrinal Relationship," in *Biblical and Semitic Studies* (Yale Bicentennial Publications, 1901), pp. 213-76; M. Jones, "The Significance of St. Stephen in the History of the Primitive Christian Church," *Exp.* 8, 13 (1917), pp. 161-78; W. Mundle, "Die Stephanusrede Apg.7: Eine Märtyrapologie," *ZNW* 20 (1921), pp. 133-47; F. J. Foakes-Jackson, "Stephen's Speech in Acts," *JBL* 49 (1930), pp. 283-86; A. Fridrichsen, "Zur Stephanusrede," *Le Monde Oriental* 25 (1931), pp. 44-52; A. F. J. Klijn, "Stephen's Speech—Acts VII.2-53," *NTS* 4 (1957-58), pp. 25-31; M. Simon, *St. Stephen and the Hellenists in the Primitive Church* (London, 1958), pp. 39-97; L. W. Barnard, "Saint Stephen and Early Alexandrian Christianity," *NTS* 7 (1960-61), pp. 31-45; J. Bihler, *Die Stephanusgeschichte im Zusammenhang der Apostelgeschichte* (Munich, 1963); T. Holtz, "Die Stephanusrede Act 7," in *Untersuchungen über die alttestamentlichen Zitate bei Lukas* = *TU* 104 (Berlin, 1968), pp. 85-127; J. Kilgallen, *The Stephen Speech: A Literary-Redactional Study of Acts 7:2-53* = AnBib 67 (Rome, 1976).

brought the word of God, and at last the one to whom the prophets bore witness in advance had been handed over to death by those to whom his saving message was first proclaimed.

It has been argued that Stephen's speech is marked by emphases which are characteristically Samaritan.[6] But the Samaritans did not dispute the *principle* of a temple, as Stephen did: they differed from the Jews on the question of its proper location—on Mount Gerizim or in Jerusalem (cf. John 4:20). Stephen's insistence that "the Most High does not dwell in houses made with hands" (v. 48) would have been as applicable to the Samaritan temple on Gerizim while it stood as it was to the temple in Jerusalem.

The attempt has also been made to relate Stephen's viewpoint to that of the Ebionites, those judaizing Christians who for some centuries maintained their distinctness from catholic Christianity.[7] They shared to some extent Stephen's negative attitude to the temple order and sacrificial ritual, and looked on Jesus as the Deuteronomic "prophet like Moses" (cf. v. 37). But the Ebionite attitude was the result of reflection on the theological implications of the destruction of the temple in A.D. 70, whereas Stephen appreciated the logic of the situation nearly forty years before that.[8]

The Ebionites were far from sympathizing with the Gentile world mission which was logically implied in Stephen's argument and which was inaugurated by his death. The Christians who embarked on this world mission were Hellenists like Stephen, and in his speech we may recognize the first manifesto of Hellenistic Christianity. Stephen and his fellow-Hellenists, as has already been pointed out, were more farsighted than their "Hebrew" brethren in appreciating the breach with the temple order implied in the teaching and work of Jesus. But it looks as if they were also more

---

6. See A. Spiro, "Stephen's Samaritan Background," Appendix V in J. Munck, *The Acts of the Apostles*, AB (Garden City, NY, 1967), pp. 285-300; M. H. Scharlemann, *Stephen: A Singular Saint* = AnBib 34 (Rome, 1968); C. H. H. Scobie, "The Origins and Development of Samaritan Christianity," *NTS* 19 (1972-73), pp. 390-414.

7. Cf. H.-J. Schoeps, *Theologie und Geschichte des Judenchristentums* (Tübingen, 1949), pp. 440-47. Schoeps pays special attention to similarities between the presentation of Stephen in Acts and that of James the Just in the pseudo-Clementine literature (which he finds to preserve much Ebionite material). The parallels between these two presentations are sufficiently striking to constitute an interesting problem in literary and historical criticism. But the solution of the problem is not that propounded by Schoeps, who concludes that Stephen, "far from being a historical character, is an *ersatz* figure brought forward by Luke for tendentious reasons, in order to unload on to him doctrines which the author found it inconvenient to acknowledge as his own" (p. 441). For a critique of Schoeps on this point see M. Simon, "Saint Stephen and the Jerusalem Temple," *JEH* 2 (1951), pp. 127-42; he concludes that, on the contrary, Stephen is the original and the pseudo-Clementine James the tendentious creation (p. 140).

8. Even the Qumran community and (it appears) the Essenes in general did not disapprove of the temple ritual in principle: they abstained from participation in it because it was controlled by an illegitimate hierarchy which "conveyed pollution to the sanctuary" (CD 4.18).

farsighted in appreciating the supranational and universal scope of the gospel. The opening words of Stephen's defense imply that the people of God must be on the march, must pull up their tent stakes as Abraham did, leaving national particularism and ancestral ritual, and go out where God may lead. This note indeed anticipated the call in Heb. 13:13 to abandon traditional Judaism for Jesus' sake and "go forth to him outside the camp." In a number of respects Stephen blazes a trail later followed by the writer to the Hebrews, although Stephen is in some ways the more radical of the two: in Hebrews the levitical ritual is treated as "a shadow of the good things to come" (Heb. 10:1), whereas Stephen maintains that the sacrificial system was a perversion from the wilderness period onward (vv. 41-43).[9]

There were doubtless different nuances of emphasis within Hellenistic Christianity. Luke himself does not share Stephen's wholly negative estimate of the temple: until a late point in his record he mentions it with respect, from the angelic annunciation to Zechariah in the holy place (Luke 1:8-22) to Paul's vision of Christ within the sacred precincts (Acts 22:17). Not until Paul's ejection from the temple during his last visit to Jerusalem (21:30) is its doom sealed.[10]

It is uncertain if Stephen's view of the temple order as a deviation from the authentic tradition of Israel's worship reflects a particular tendency within Hellenistic Judaism.[11] No doubt many Jews of the dispersion felt less

9. See especially W. Manson, *The Epistle to the Hebrews* (London, 1951), pp. 25-46 (the chapter entitled "Stephen and the World-Mission of Christianity"); on p. 36 he enumerates eight important features of Stephen's speech which recur in Hebrews, and suggests accordingly that Stephen's outlook may provide a starting point from which to seek an understanding of that epistle. M. Simon, on the other hand, contrasts Stephen's approach with that of Hebrews, particularly with regard to the temple. "To Stephen, the Temple means, from the very beginning, a falling away from the authentic tradition of Israel, as God inspired and directed it. . . . the view most commonly held later on was, I think, that which is expressed in *Hebrews:* the Temple and its cult was, together with the whole ritual Law, 'a shadow of good things to come'. It is indeed imperfect, but by no means bad and perverse. For these things are, as *Hebrews* again puts it, 'figures of the true'. Stephen's view is almost unparalleled in early Christian ecclesiastical thought" ("Saint Stephen and the Jerusalem Temple," pp. 127-28). It should be borne in mind that the writer to the Hebrews uses the tabernacle, not the temple, as "a parable for the present time" (Heb. 9:9).

10. See p. 410 with n. 51.

11. M. Simon ("Saint Stephen and the Jerusalem Temple," pp. 132-37) adduces some evidence, including the carefully chosen wording of LXX in significant passages, suggesting that a section of the Jewish dispersion "may well have directed against the Temple in Jerusalem, its ritual and its sacrifices, the same criticism which some Greek philosophers used to utter against the traditional pagan religion, its temples and ritual" (see below on 17:14-15, pp. 336-37 with nn. 64-67). Certainly in their proselytizing propaganda Jews of the dispersion would tend to emphasize the moral and spiritual character of their religion and soft-pedal its ritual requirements. See Schürer III, pp. 138-40; also J. Klausner, *From Jesus to Paul,* E.T. (London, 1944), pp. 123-205. But the hostility which Stephen's thesis provoked in *Hellenistic* circles in Jerusalem suggests that

attached to temple and sacrifice than did their fellow-Jews nearer home, but even Philo of Alexandria regarded the temple with veneration and went on pilgrimage to Jerusalem to offer prayers and sacrifices there.[12] Stephen's view, in any case, was controlled by his understanding of the difference that Christ had made.

2-3   Stephen has his reply ready. It takes the form of a historical retrospect—a form well established in Jewish tradition. "The protestation of faith is, in the Old Testament, often associated with a recital of the divine intervention in the life of Israel. 'God in history' was the underlying basis of Rabbinic optimism. The declaration at the bringing of the first-fruits (Deut. 26:5-10) is paralleled by Psalms 78 and 107. . . . Stephen's address in Acts 7 is thus in the true form. It is in the *sequel* that he differs from Hebrew models."[13]

Stephen's historical survey reviews the history of the nation from the call of Abraham to the building of Solomon's temple. His outline of the patriarchal age (vv. 2-8) and of Israel in Egypt (vv. 9-19) provides an introduction to his central themes; his account of Moses' early days (vv. 20-29), the call of Moses (vv. 30-34), and the wilderness wanderings (vv. 35-43) provides an indirect answer to the charge of speaking against Moses and a more direct answer to the charge of speaking against God; his contrast between the wilderness tent and the Jerusalem temple (vv. 44-50) replies particularly to the charge of speaking against the temple.

Beginning with the patriarchal age, then, he reminds his hearers that it was in Mesopotamia,[14] far from the promised land, that God first revealed himself to Abraham. One might well ask what could have persuaded Abraham to uproot himself as he did from the land of his birth and set out on a journey whose goal he did not know in advance. By all the prudential canons of ordinary life, it was a mad adventure; but as related in the biblical narrative it was an act of true wisdom. It was the God of glory[15] who appeared to him and summoned him to embark on the path of faith, and the

---

opposition on grounds of principle to the temple and its ritual was not generally acceptable in Hellenistic Judaism.

12. Cf. Philo, *On Providence* 2.64.

13. I. Abrahams, *Studies in Pharisaism and the Gospels*, II (Cambridge, 1924), p. 18. To the OT passages adduced by Abrahams might be added Pss. 105; 106; 135; 136; Neh. 9:6-37; cf. also Paul's synagogue address at Pisidian Antioch (13:16-41 below).

14. Mesopotamia represents the fuller Greek expression Συρία Μεσοποταμία ("Syria between the rivers"), referring to that part of North Syria lying between the Euphrates and the Orontes. Ancient Mesopotamia did not normally include the southern area of modern 'Iraq, in which lay the Babylonian city of Ur ("Ur of the Chaldees"), near the mouth of the Euphrates, which Abraham left to go to Harran. But here Mesopotamia is plainly synonymous with "the land of the Chaldaeans" (v. 4).

15. For the title cf. Ps. 29 (LXX 28):3 (and similar expressions in Eph. 1:17; 1 Cor. 2:8).

use of that title implies that God manifested himself to Abraham in glory so compelling that Abraham had no option but to obey. Those who are obedient to the heavenly vision, Stephen seems to suggest, will always live loose to any particular earthly spot, will always be ready to get out and go wherever God may guide.

A glance at any edition of the New Testament, Greek or English, in which Old Testament quotations or allusions are set in distinctive type, will show how far the very language of the Old Testament enters into the texture of Stephen's speech. (It is quoted regularly in the LXX form.) But the speech is no mere catena of quotations, studiously put together; the Old Testament wording is reproduced with a spontaneity which suggests that the author has the narrative at his fingertips and is able to use it with a striking freshness and freedom.[16] Here, in verse 3, he quotes from Gen. 12:1 the words spoken by God to Abraham in Harran after the death of his father Terah, but gives them a setting before Abraham's departure for Harran on the first stage of his journey. When it is stated in Gen. 15:7 and Neh. 9:7 that God brought Abraham from Ur of the Chaldees, it is probably implied that Abraham received a divine communication there as well as later, when he had settled in Harran. Philo and Josephus concur.[17]

4-5 Abraham accordingly left "the land of the Chaldaeans"[18]—a term which is plainly synonymous here with "Mesopotamia" (v. 2)[19]—and settled in Harran, in the upper Euphrates valley, at the intersection of important caravan trade routes, known to have been a flourishing city early in the second millennium B.C.[20] There he stayed until his father died; then, under divine direction, he continued his migration and arrived in Canaan.[21] But

---

16. Thus, in vv. 6-7, the words spoken to Abraham in Gen. 15:13-14 are rounded off with the clause "and they will worship me in this place" (i.e., in Canaan), which is an echo of the words addressed to Moses in Ex. 3:12: "you shall serve (worship) God on this mountain" (i.e., Sinai/Horeb). With this telescoping of distinct Pentateuchal texts may be compared the telescoping of distinct incidents in v. 16 (see p. 137 below with n. 35).

17. Cf. Philo, *On Abraham* 71; Josephus, *Ant.* 1.154.

18. In LXX "Ur of the Chaldees" (Heb. *'ûr kaśdîm*) is regularly rendered by "the land [Gk. χώρα, not γῆ as here] of the Chaldaeans." Gk. Χαλδαῖοι denotes both the *Ḥaldu* of Urartu (Armenia) and the *Kaldu* (Heb. *kaśdîm*, "Chaldaeans," "Chaldees") of southern Babylonia.

19. Josephus similarly, in his preamble to the story of Abraham, speaks of "the Chaldaeans and the other Mesopotamians" (*Ant.* 1.157).

20. See S. Lloyd and W. C. Brice, "Harran," *AS* 1 (1951), pp. 77-111. In Greek and Roman times it was known as Carrhae. Its name is not identical with that of Abraham's brother Haran (Gen. 11:27-31), which in Hebrew is spelled with initial *hē*, not *ḥēṭ*.

21. The chronological data of Gen. 11:26, 32; 12:4 would suggest that Terah's death took place sixty years after Abraham's departure from Ḥarran. J. Ussher and other chronologers of an earlier day harmonized the present statement of Stephen with the evidence of Genesis by the improbable expedient of supposing that Terah was seventy years old when his oldest son (Haran) was born, and that Abraham was not born until Terah was 130. That Abraham did not leave Ḥarran until his father was dead is asserted

even then Abraham was given no part of the land in actual possession: for the rest of his life he lived as a resident alien there. It was a promised land indeed to him—promised to him and his posterity before he had any children—but to him and his immediate posterity it remained no more than a *promised* land. Abraham had no tangible object in which to trust: he believed the bare word of God, and acted upon it.

6-7 Not only did Abraham receive no portion of the land as a present possession; his faith was further tested by the revelation that his descendants would leave that land for one that was not their own, and that they would suffer oppression and servitude there for several generations.[22] Yet their exile would not be permanent: in due course God would give them deliverance from their oppressors and bring them back to worship him in the land of Canaan.[23]

8 One sign was given to Abraham, the sign of circumcision, as the outward token of the covenant which God made with him.[24] Abraham's acceptance of this visible token for himself and his descendants was a further expression of his faith in God. And "thus, while there was still no holy place, all the essential conditions for the religion of Israel were fulfilled."[25] When Isaac was born, Abraham circumcised him on the eighth day after his birth,[26] and the sign of the covenant was transmitted from generation to generation, from Isaac to Jacob, and from Jacob to his twelve sons, the ancestors of the twelve tribes of Israel.[27]

---

also by Philo (*On the Migration of Abraham* 177), and is implied by the Samaritan Pentateuch, which in Gen. 11:32 gives Terah's age at death as 145, not 205 (MT, LXX). It would follow that Abraham, who left Harran at the age of 75 (Gen. 12:4), did so as soon his father had died. It would be unwarranted to see here evidence of Samaritan influence on Stephen's speech: apart from its recognizably sectarian variants, the Samaritan Pentateuch is basically a popular Palestinian text. Possibly Stephen (or Luke) and Philo relied on a Greek version (no longer extant) which agreed with the Samaritan reading of Gen. 11:32. P. E. Kahle says with greater assurance that "not a single MS. of the Christian 'Septuagint' has preserved in Gen. 11:32 a reading which Philo and Luke read in their Greek Tora in the first Christian century" (*The Cairo Geniza* [London, 1947], p. 144).

22. The figure of 400 years for the oppression of the Israelites is taken from Gen. 15:13. According to Ex. 12:40 (MT) their sojourning in Egypt lasted 430 years, for which 400 might be taken as a round number. But rabbinical exegesis reckoned the 400 years as running from the birth of Isaac to the Exodus. Cf. Paul in Gal. 3:17, where the giving of the law (in the third month after the Exodus) is dated 430 years after the promise to Abraham (Gen. 12:3, 7; 13:15, etc.). This accords with the Samaritan and LXX expansion of Ex. 12:40, which includes in the 430 years the Israelites' sojourning in Canaan as well as in Egypt. The period spent in Egypt would then be considerably shorter; cf. Gen. 15:16, "in the fourth generation they shall come back here."

23. Cf. p. 134, n. 16.

24. Cf. Gen. 17:9-14, 23-27.

25. K. Lake and H. J. Cadbury, *Beginnings* I.4, p. 72.

26. Gen. 21:4.

27. Circumcision, at puberty (cf. Gen. 17:25), if not in infancy, was practised by most of the nations with which Israel had dealings in patriarchal times, but only for Israel

b. Israel in Egypt (7:9-19)

9 *"The patriarchs, moved by jealousy, sold Joseph into Egypt; but God was with him,*

10 *and delivered him out of all his afflictions, and gave him favor and wisdom in the presence of Pharaoh, king of Egypt. Pharaoh appointed him governor over Egypt and over all his house.*

11 *Then a famine and great distress came upon the whole of Egypt and Canaan, and our forefathers could find no food.*

12 *Hearing that there was grain in Egypt, Jacob sent our forefathers there a first time.*

13 *On their second visit Joseph was made known to his brothers, and Joseph's kinship was disclosed to Pharaoh.*

14 *Then Joseph sent and called for his father Jacob and all his family, amounting in all to seventy-five persons.*

15 *So Jacob went down into Egypt[28] and died there, as also did our forefathers,*

16 *and they were brought back to Shechem and laid in the tomb which Abraham had bought for a price in silver from the sons of Hamor in Shechem.[29]*

17 *When the time was approaching for the (fulfilment of the) promise which God had made[30] to Abraham, the people increased and multiplied in Egypt,*

18 *until there arose over Egypt another king, who did not know[31] Joseph.*

19 *This king plotted against our people; he ill-treated our forefathers, making them expose their newborn infants so that they should not be brought up alive.*

9-10 As early as the patriarchal age, there was opposition to the purpose of God in calling Abraham and guiding the fortunes of his posterity. The sons of Jacob sold their brother Joseph into slavery in Egypt. But God was continuously superintending the accomplishment of that one increasing purpose which he inaugurated when he called the father of the faithful out of Mesopotamia, and which was to find its consummation in the coming of

---

had it this special covenant significance. The term "patriarchs" (Gk. πατριάρχαι), here used of the sons of Jacob as tribal ancestors, is so used of them in 4 Macc. 16:25 and in the title of the Greek version of *The Testaments of the Twelve Patriarchs.* Cf. p. 66, n. 83 (on 2:29).

28. Cod. B omits "into Egypt."

29. The Western and Byzantine texts read "of Shechem" (τοῦ Συχέμ), whence KJV "*the father* of Shechem."

30. Gk. ὡμολόγησεν. P45 and the Western text read ἐπηγγείλατο ("promised"); 81 and the Byzantine text read ὤμοσεν ("swore").

31. The Western text reads "did not remember" (οὐκ ἐμνήσθη).

Christ. He so ordered the fortunes of Joseph in Egypt that he rose to high authority in that land as grand vizier to Pharaoh.[32]

11-16 This worked out to the advantage of Joseph's family, for when famine arose in Canaan the sons of Jacob went to buy food in Egypt, where Joseph's foresight and authority had prepared large stores of grain. On the second occasion when they went to Egypt to buy food, Joseph (whom they had not recognized on their former visit)[33] revealed his identity to them, and they were forced to acknowledge him as their deliverer. (There may be a suggestion here that a greater than Joseph, who also was not recognized by his people when he came to them the first time, will be acknowledged by them as their divinely appointed deliverer when they see him the second time.) The result of the brothers' recognition of Joseph and their reconciliation to him was that Jacob and all his family went down to Egypt—seventy-five persons in all, says Stephen, following the Greek text.[34] There Jacob died; there, too, his sons also died in due course. But they were buried not in Egypt but in the land which God had promised to their descendants as their inheritance.[35] The presence of their tombs in the land of promise, where the tombs of Abraham and Isaac were already, was a token that, even if they died down in Egypt, they died in faith.[36]

17-19 Their children and grandchildren, however, stayed in Egypt

---

32. Stephen's language here reflects that of Ps. 105 (LXX 104):16-23 as well as that of Gen. 37–45.

33. W. M. Ramsay argues that "the first time" (πρῶτον) in v. 12 must mean the first of three, the third time being the occasion when the whole family of Jacob went down (*BRD*, p. 254n.). But the classical force of Gk. πρῶτος cannot be pressed in this way in Hellenistic times (cf. p. 30, n. 9, on 1:1). Here "the first time" (or "the former occasion") is simply correlative to "the second occasion" (ἐν τῷ δευτέρῳ).

34. Gen. 46:27; Ex. 1:5; Deut. 10:22 MT say seventy persons (including Jacob, and Joseph with his two sons). In Ex. 1:5 the fragmentary Hebrew MS 4QExᵃ says seventy-five persons; so also do Gen. 46:17; Ex. 1:5 LXX, omitting Jacob and Joseph, but giving Joseph nine sons instead of the two of MT (Gen. 46:27). Josephus (*Ant.* 2.176; 6.89) accepts the figure of seventy; Philo (*On the Migration of Abraham* 199-201) reconciles the discrepant readings allegorically: the number five, symbolizing the senses, has been omitted from the smaller number, signifying the transition from recalcitrant Jacob to Israel, the man with the vision of God (as though from Heb. *'îš rō'eh 'ēl*, "man seeing God").

35. Jacob was buried at Hebron, in the cave of Machpelah, which Abraham had bought from Ephron the Hittite for 400 silver shekels (Gen. 23:16; 49:29-32; 50:13). Joseph was buried at Shechem, in the piece of ground which Jacob had bought for 100 pieces of money (if that is the meaning of *qᵉśîṭāh*, NEB "sheep") from the sons of Hamor (Josh. 24:32). According to Josephus (*Ant.* 2.199), the other sons of Jacob were buried at Hebron. The two separate purchases of land are telescoped here. It is unlikely that the suppression of Hebron in favor of Shechem is a sign of Samaritan influence; the burial of Abraham, Isaac, and Jacob at Hebron is as clearly recorded in the Samaritan Bible as in MT.

36. Cf. Heb. 11:13.

and multiplied there, until the appointed time came for God to redeem his promise to the patriarchs and give their descendants possession of the land of Canaan. The instrument in God's hand for bringing about their departure from Egypt was a new king (presumably one of the early kings of the Nineteenth Dynasty)[37] who tried to restrict the increasing number of Israelites by forced labor and compulsory infanticide. But for his policy they might have found Egypt so comfortable that they would never have thought of leaving it.

c. Moses' early days (7:20-29)

20 *"It was at this time that Moses was born—an exceedingly beautiful[38] child. He was brought up for three months in his father's house.*

21 *Then he was exposed, but Pharaoh's daughter adopted him and brought him up as her son.*

22 *So Moses was educated in all the wisdom of the Egyptians; he was powerful in his words and deeds.*

23 *When he was nearly forty years old, he conceived the idea of visiting his brothers, the people of Israel.*

24 *When he saw one of them being unjustly treated, he went to his defense and avenged the injury inflicted on him by giving the Egyptian a mortal blow.[39]*

25 *He thought his brothers understood that God was giving them deliverance through him, but they did not.*

26 *The next day he accosted them when they were engaged in a fight and tried to reconcile them peacefully. 'Men,' he said, 'you are brothers.[40] Why should you harm each other?'*

27 *But the man who was attacking the other pushed him away: 'Who,' he asked, 'made you ruler and judge over us?*

28 *Do you want to kill me, as you killed the Egyptian yesterday?'*

29 *When he heard this, Moses fled. He lived as an alien in the land of Midian; there two sons were born to him.*

20-22 The edict that every male child born to the Israelites was to be exposed at birth, or thrown into the Nile, was defied by Moses' parents.

---

37. It is evident from the early chapters of Exodus that the Egyptian court was not far distant from the place of the Hebrews' settlement in Egypt; this suits Dynasty XIX rather than XVIII. The reference to the building of "Raamses" in Ex. 1:11 evidently points to Pi-Ramessē (near modern Qantir), the East Delta residence of Rameses II (c. 1290-1224 B.C.), the greatest king of Dynasty XIX.

38. Gk. ἀστεῖος τῷ θεῷ, "beautiful to God" ("divinely beautiful"). Such expressions occur elsewhere with elative force; cf. Jon. 3:3, where Nineveh is a city "great to God" (LXX πόλις μεγάλη τῷ θεῷ). Moses is described as ἀστεῖος in Ex. 2:2 (LXX for Heb. *ṭôḇ*, "good") and Heb. 11:23.

39. The Western text adds "of his race" after "being unjustly treated" and "and buried him in the sand" after "giving the Egyptian a mortal blow" (following Ex. 2:12).

40. The Western text reads "What are you doing, brothers?"

They kept him for three months before exposing him, and when at last they did expose him, they did so in such a way that he was quickly rescued.[41] A daughter of the king found him, was attracted by him, and brought him up as her son, in a style befitting a royal prince.[42] Thus Moses received the best education that the Egyptian court could provide, and distinguished himself in speech and action.[43] Stephen expresses himself with more moderation than other Jewish Hellenists, who represent Moses as the father of science and culture and as the founder of Egyptian civilization.[44]

23-28 That an Egyptian king should try to frustrate the divine purpose was intelligible, but some of the chosen people themselves tried unintentionally to hinder it. If Pharaoh was God's instrument in weaning the Israelites from their attachment to Egypt, Moses was his agent in leading them out. Moses had begun to be aware of this, but his fellow-Israelites were slow to recognize him as their deliverer. This was shown on the occasion when he presented himself to them as their champion, after he was fully grown,[45] but his intervention on their behalf was not appreciated. The writer to the Hebrews tells how at this time he made the great renunciation, refusing to be known any more as the son of a royal princess and casting in his lot by preference with the downtrodden people of God (Heb. 11:24-26). Here again a pattern of behavior is traced which was to find its complete and final

41. Cf. Ex. 2:1-10.

42. It is a vain task to try to identify this princess with any named daughter of an Egyptian king. The Hellenistic Jewish writer Artabanus, in his work *Concerning the Jews* (quoted by Eusebius, *Preparation for the Gospel* 9.27), calls her Merris, a name quite similar to that of a daughter of Rameses II by his Hittite wife—but this daughter of Rameses was probably a generation or more younger than Moses.

43. That he was mighty in words might seem to conflict with Moses' disclaimer of eloquence in Ex. 4:10, but that disclaimer should not be taken too seriously; later in the Pentateuchal narrative Moses is a forceful and persuasive speaker. The statement that he was mighty in deeds is illustrated by the legend preserved by Josephus (*Ant.* 2.238-53) of his leading an Egyptian campaign against the Ethiopians—a legend perhaps originating in an attempt to explain his marrying a Cushite wife (Num. 12:1, where LXX calls her an Ethiopian).

44. Artabanus (*loc. cit.*) says that the Egyptians owed all their civilization to Moses, whom he identifies with the Egyptian Hermes (Thoth). An earlier Hellenistic Jew, Eupolemus, describes Moses as the inventor of alphabetic writing (*On the Kings in Judaea*, quoted by Eusebius, *Preparation* 9.26). According to Philo (*Life of Moses* 1.20-24), Moses was proficient in geometry, arithmetic, poetry, music, philosophy, astrology, and all branches of learning. Josephus (*Ant.* 2.229-30) describes him as unique in wisdom, stature, and beauty. After all this, Stephen's language appears almost as an understatement! See also J. G. Gager, *Moses in Greco-Roman Paganism* (Nashville/New York, 1972).

45. "When Moses had grown up," says Ex. 2:11 (LXX μέγας γενόμενος, quoted in Heb. 11:24), but Stephen gives his age at the time as forty. This is paralleled in rabbinical tradition, where his life of 120 years (Deut. 34:7) is divided into three equal parts, the first ending at this point and the second at his return from Midian to Egypt (cf. Ex. 7:7).

expression when Jesus appeared among his people as the Savior provided by God.

29 Moses had exposed himself to grave peril by his attempt to champion his oppressed people. His action in killing an Egyptian bully was more widely known than he wished. His royal upbringing would not protect him if Pharaoh suspected that he planned to lead a slave revolt. Moses had to leave Egypt in haste, and find refuge in northwest Arabia.[46] There he in turn, like his patriarchal ancestors, became "a sojourner in a foreign land" (Ex. 2:22)—a fact which he acknowledged when he called his firstborn son Gershom ("a sojourner there").[47]

d. The call of Moses (7:30-34)

30 *"When forty years had elapsed, an angel appeared to him in the wilderness of Mount Sinai, in the flame of a burning bush.*

31 *When Moses saw it, he was amazed at the sight. As he was approaching it to look at it, the voice of the Lord came to him:*[48]

32 *'I am the God of your fathers, the God of Abraham, Isaac, and Jacob.'*[49] *Moses trembled and did not dare to look.*

33 *Then the Lord said to him, 'Take off your sandals from your feet; the place where you are standing is holy ground.*

34 *I have indeed seen the ill-treatment of my people in Egypt, I have heard their groaning, and I have come down to deliver them. Come now, let me send you to Egypt.'*

30-34 Moses' exile was part of the divine plan: it was there in northwest Arabia, "in the wilderness of Mount Sinai," that an angel of God appeared to him in the burning bush and the voice of God addressed him.[50] The God who revealed himself to Abraham in Mesopotamia and gave Joseph the assurance of his presence in Egypt now communicated with Moses by vision and voice in Midian, far from the frontiers of the holy land. That spot of Gentile territory was "holy ground" for the sole reason that God manifested himself

46. Midian is probably the region east of Aqaba.

47. The second son, Eliezer, is mentioned in Ex. 18:3-4.

48. The Western text reads "the Lord spoke to him, saying."

49. The Western text follows the OT (Ex. 3:6) by repeating "the God of" before "Isaac" and "Jacob." Cf. 3:13 (pp. 79-80, nn. 18, 24).

50. Cf. Ex. 3:1-4:17. The "mountain of God" is referred to there as Horeb; the identity of Horeb and Sinai is indicated by a comparison of Ex. 3:12 and Deut. 1:6, etc., with Ex. 19:11-25. The traditional identification of the biblical Mount Sinai with Jebel Musa in the Sinai Peninsula does not appear to antedate the *Pilgrimage of Egeria* (A.D. 385-88). The "angel" seen by Moses (v. 30) was the special *mal'ak Yahweh* (Ex. 3:2), i.e., Yahweh himself in his manifestation to human beings. In Ex. 3 he is variously called "the angel of Yahweh" (v. 2), "God" (v. 4), and "Yahweh" (v. 7); so in Stephen's narrative the angel speaks with the voice of the Lord (v. 31), claims to be God (v. 32), and is called "the Lord" (v. 33). Cf. vv. 35, 38, and 53 below (and nn. 56, 58, and 99).

to Moses there.[51] No place on earth possesses an innate sanctity of its own. In its Christian application this principle is expressed excellently in William Cowper's lines:

> "Jesus, where'er thy people meet,
> There they behold thy mercy-seat;
> Where'er they seek thee, thou art found,
> And every place is hallowed ground."

But it found expression much earlier in Israel's covenant law: "in every place," said Yahweh, "where I cause my name to be remembered, I will come to you and bless you" (Ex. 20:24).

The message which Moses received from God at that holy place was one of faithfulness to his promise. God had not forgotten his covenant with the patriarchs: he remained the God of Abraham, Isaac, and Jacob. Nor was he heedless of the distress of their descendants in Egypt: he was on the point of intervening for their deliverance, and in this deliverance Moses was to be his agent. "Come now, let me send you to Egypt."

e. The wilderness wanderings (7:35-43)

35 *"This man Moses, whom they repudiated with the words, 'Who made you our ruler and judge?'[52]—this is the man whom God has sent as their ruler and deliverer, with the power of the angel who appeared to him in the bush.*

36 *This is the man who brought them out, after performing wonders and signs in the land of Egypt and at the Red Sea, as also for forty years in the wilderness.*

37 *This is that Moses who said to the people of Israel, 'God will raise you up a prophet like me from among your brothers.'[53]*

38 *This is he who was in the assembly in the wilderness with the angel that spoke to him on Mount Sinai and with our forefathers; it is he who received living oracles to give to us.*

39 *But our fathers refused to obey him: they rejected him and turned back to Egypt in their hearts.*

40 *'Make us gods to go before us,' they said to Aaron; 'as for this man Moses, who brought us out of Egypt, we do not know what has happened to him.'*

41 *In those days, moreover, they made the calf, offered a sacrifice to the idol, and exulted in what their own hands had made.*

---

51. The removal of the shoes was a mark of reverence in the divine presence, as it was a mark of respect to one's host when paying a visit.

52. Some Alexandrian authorities (ℵ C 81) and the Western text add "over us" from v. 27.

53. The Western text, following the OT (Deut. 18:15), adds "you are to listen to him."

42 *So God turned (from them): he abandoned them to the worship of the
host of heaven. So it is written in the book of the prophets:*

*'Did you bring sacrifices and offerings to me,
Those forty years in the wilderness, O house of Israel?*

43 *No: you took up the tent of Moloch
and the star of your god Raiphan,
the images which you made for your worship.
I will remove you beyond Babylon.'*[54]

35-36 The very man whom his people had refused was the man chosen by
God to be their ruler and redeemer. They had rejected him the first time (as
Joseph's brothers had repudiated Joseph), but the second time he came to
them they had no option but to accept him (as Joseph's brothers recognized
him on the second occasion). The implied parallel with the recent refusal of
Jesus is too plain to require elaboration. All the authority of the divine
messenger whom he had seen at the burning bush lay behind Moses when he
went back to Egypt to lead his people out, and lead them out he did, amid
tokens of his heavenly commission that none could gainsay—"wonders and
signs[55] in the land of Egypt and at the Red Sea," not to speak of those which
marked the following years of wandering in the wilderness.[56]

37 Was Moses in all this a forerunner of Jesus, as Stephen appeared to claim? Moses' own words supply a sufficient answer—and here
Stephen quotes the promise about the prophet like Moses from Deut. 18:15
which Peter has already quoted in the temple court (3:22).

38 There in the wilderness Moses was the people's leader; there
they were constituted Yahweh's assembly;[57] there they had the "angel of the

54. For "beyond Babylon" the Western reading is "to the parts of Babylon"; this
was probably calculated to agree better with "beyond Damascus" in Amos 5:27.

55. So Jesus was divinely accredited to his contemporaries by "mighty works and
wonders and signs" which God performed through him among them (2:22).

56. The Exodus narrative well illustrates the two principal vehicles of special
revelation employed by God in OT times—mighty works and prophetic communication.
The mighty works attending the Exodus would not have been understood by the Israelites
had not Moses, as the prophet or spokesman of God, interpreted their significance to
them. But the mighty works were not caused by Moses or his words; they were plainly
beyond human control. The mighty works and the prophetic words supported each other,
and through both together God made himself known to his people. Cf. H. H. Rowley,
From Moses to Qumran (London, 1963), pp. 3-31.

57. In Deut. 18:16, immediately after Moses' reminder of the divine promise to
raise up a prophet like himself, he mentions the request which the people had made to God
"at Horeb, on the day of the assembly" (Heb. *qāhāl*, LXX ἐκκλησία), that they might not
hear his voice again speaking to them directly. As Moses was with the ἐκκλησία then,
Christ is with his ἐκκλησία now, and it is still a pilgrim ἐκκλησία, "the assembly in the
wilderness." See p. 108, n. 23 (on 5:11).

presence"[58] in their midst; there they received through Moses the living oracles of God.[59] What more could the people of God want?—and it was all theirs in the wilderness, far from the promised land and the holy city.

39-41 Even so, they were not content: they disobeyed Moses and repudiated his leadership, although he was God's spokesman and vicegerent among them. Was Stephen charged with speaking "blasphemous words against Moses"—with propagating doctrines which threatened the abiding validity of "the customs which Moses handed down to us"? Such a charge came well from the descendants of those who had refused Moses' authority in his very lifetime, from people whose attitude to the greater prophet than Moses had shown them to be such worthy children of their forefathers! Why, those Israelites in the wilderness, for all their sacred privileges, longed to go back to Egypt, from which Moses had led them out.[60] The invisible presence of God was not enough for them: they craved some form of divinity that they could see. When Moses was absent, receiving the "oracles" from God on Mount Sinai, they persuaded Aaron to manufacture "gods to go before us."[61] Thus they showed how much they cared for the pure, aniconic worship of their fathers' God. The long history of Israel's lapsing into idolatry, which called forth the remonstrance of one prophet after another and at last brought them into exile, had its beginnings in the wilderness, when they paid sacrificial homage to the golden calf and held high festival in honor of their own handiwork.[62]

42-43 The course of their idolatry, as traced throughout the Old Testament, from the wilderness wanderings to the Babylonian exile, Stephen finds summed up in the words of Amos 5:25-27. The full-blown worship of the "host of heaven," the planetary powers, to which Jerusalem gave itself over in the later years of the monarchy, under Assyrian influence, was the fruition of that earlier idolatry in the wilderness.[63] It was more than its fruition, in fact; it was the divinely ordained judgment for that rebellious attitude. God turned and "abandoned them to the worship of the host of

58. The "angel of the presence" of God (lit., "the messenger of his face," Heb. *mal'ak pānāw*) is the angel who makes his presence real to human beings—in other words, the angel of Yahweh (see n. 50 above). No mention is made of this angel in the Exodus narrative of the giving of the law; compare, however, "the angel of God" in Ex. 14:19; also Ex. 33:14, "my presence [Heb. *pānai*, 'my face,' but LXX αὐτός, 'I myself'] will go with you." See also Isa. 63:9, with reference to the Exodus and its sequel, "the angel of his presence saved them" (LXX "he himself saved them"). See also p. 153, n. 99 below.

59. Gk. λόγια ζῶντα (cf. Rom. 3:2; Heb. 4:12; 1 Pet. 1:23).

60. Cf. Num. 14:3-4.

61. Cf. Ex. 32:1-6.

62. Cf. Ps. 115 (LXX 114):4 and 135 (LXX 134):15, where the idols of the nations are described as "silver and gold, the work of men's hands."

63. For the "host of heaven" see Deut. 4:19; 17:3; 2 Kings (LXX 4 Kms.) 21:3, 5; 23:4-5; Jer. 8:2; 19:13; Zeph. 1:5. Cf. p. 145, n. 71 below.

heaven." These are terrible words, but the principle that men and women are given up to the due consequences of their own settled choice is well established in scripture and experience.[64] While Stephen asserts the principle here in relation to the Jewish nation, Paul asserts it in relation to the Gentile world in Rom. 1:24, 26, 28.

The Masoretic text of the words quoted from Amos differs considerably from the form reproduced here (the LXX rendering, with some variations). In the original wording and context Amos, prophesying on the eve of the Assyrian invasions which brought the northern kingdom of Israel to an end, warns the Israelites that they will be deported "beyond Damascus" and that they will carry with them into exile the very tokens of that idolatry— "Sakkuth your king and Kaiwan your star-god"—for which Yahweh is about to bring this judgment on them.[65] Both forms of the text begin with the question: "Did you bring me sacrifices and offerings during the forty years in the wilderness, O house of Israel?" And in both forms of the text the implied answer is "No."

It must be determined how the implied answer "No" was understood first by Amos and then by Stephen.

As for Amos's intention, it has commonly been believed that he implied that Israel's worship in the wilderness was entirely nonsacrificial. But this interpretation fails to bring out the main emphasis of his words. His question probably meant: "Was it mere sacrifices and offerings, sacrifices and offerings that were an end in themselves and not the expression of your loyalty of spirit, that you offered in the wilderness days?" The expected answer will then be: "No: we offered something more than that; we brought true heart-worship and righteousness."[66] Amos, like Jeremiah, looks back on the wilderness experience as Israel's honeymoon period, when Yahweh's will was her delight.[67]

Stephen, however, following the LXX, understands the implied "No" to mean: "No: we offered sacrifices and offerings indeed, but to other gods, not to the God of Israel."[68] He has just emphasized the unfaithfulness of Israel in worshiping the golden calf, and infers from that episode that the

---

64. Cf. Ezek. 20:25-26.

65. A comparable judgment is pronounced on Babylonia in Isa. 46:1-2.

66. For this interpretation of the words of Amos see H. H. Rowley, *From Moses to Qumran*, pp. 72-75; *The Unity of the Bible* (London, 1953), pp. 30-43. He cites D. B. Macdonald as propounding the same view in "Old Testament Notes: (2) Amos 5:25," *JBL* 18 (1899), pp. 214-15. Cf. Isa. 1:10-17; Jer. 7:21-23; Hos. 6:6; Mic. 6:6-8.

67. Cf. Jer. 2:2-3; also Hos. 2:14-15. Contrast Ezek. 20:13.

68. H.-J. Schoeps (*Theologie und Geschichte*, pp. 221-33, 238, 442-43) relates Stephen's implied denial that Israel offered sacrifices to Yahweh in the wilderness to the Ebionites' view that the sacrificial legislation was a spurious interpolation in the Mosaic law; one of the tasks of the Messiah, the prophet like Moses (cf. v. 37), when he came, would be (they believed) to remove those accretions and restore the law to its original

idolatry which the prophets later condemned had its origins in the wilderness. Even then the people had been rebellious in heart; even then they had gone astray after foreign divinities, taking up "the tent of Moloch" and "the star of your god Raiphan"—Raiphan being a designation of the planet Saturn.

Stephen certainly does not mean that the Mosaic tabernacle had actually become the "tent of Moloch" because of Israel's perversion of the pure order of worship:[69] the Mosaic tabernacle is spoken of with high respect in the next sentence, as the symbol of God's abiding faithfulness. Moloch and Raiphan are members of the "host of heaven";[70] Stephen means that the worship of the planetary powers, for which the nation lost its liberty and suffered deportation, was the climax of that idolatrous process which began in the wilderness. In principle at least the worship of those powers had its inception in the wilderness: it was to them that sacrifices and offerings were brought even at that early date.[71] Stephen does not mention the apostasy of Baal-peor, when Israel "ate the sacrifices of the dead" (Ps. 106 [LXX 105]:28), but that would have reinforced his argument.

Amos, foretelling the Assyrian exile of the northern kingdom, de-

---

purity. Even from the text of the Pentateuch as it stands it would be possible to infer that, while the sacrificial legislation was given through Moses in the wilderness, it was not to be carried into effect until after the settlement in Canaan (cf. Deut. 5:31b and more particularly Num. 15:2b)—but this would be irrelevant to Stephen's argument.

69. Cf. M. Simon ("St. Stephen and the Jerusalem Temple," p. 138): "Sacrifices, even if offered to Jahveh, a temple, even if built in Jerusalem, remain what they were in the beginning—works of idolatry. They proceed in all cases from mere human initiative and vanity: they have never been approved or sanctified by God. They are not only a consequence, accepted by God to prevent the worship of the golden calf: they are on a level with the golden calf." This deduction from Stephen's words is like the deduction commonly drawn from the great prophets' attack on contemporary sacrificial practice, that they were opposed to the principle of sacrifice and not merely to its misuse. The deduction in both cases may not reckon adequately with the tendency of prophetic diction to say "not this, but that" where we would say "not only this, but also that" or "not so much this as that." Stephen certainly speaks in the tradition of the great prophets.

70. "The tabernacle of Moloch" would represent Heb. *sukkat mōlek̠*, a revocalization of *sikkût malk̠ᵉk̠em*, "Sakkut your king," where *sikkût* is Akkadian *sakkut*, a name of the planet Saturn, equipped with the vowel points of Heb. *šiqqûṣ*, "abomination." (Similarly Moloch, better Molech, is probably Heb. *melek̠*, "king," used as a divine title, equipped with the vowel points of *bōšet̠*, "shame"—although Otto Eissfeldt, *Molk als Opferbegriff im Punischen und Hebräischen und das Ende des Gottes Moloch* [Halle, 1935], explained the form from Phoenician *molk*, a term for human sacrifice attested in Carthaginian inscriptions.) Raiphan (variously spelled Rephan, Remphan, Rompha, etc.) seems to be a form of *repa*, an Egyptian name of Saturn, used by the LXX translators to replace Kaiwan, an Assyrian name for the same planet (MT *kiyyûn*, cf. KJV Chiun, involves again the use of the vowel points of *šiqqûṣ*).

71. It was more particularly under the influence of Assyria in the eighth century B.C. that the worship of the planetary divinities became so popular in Israel, but the evidence of Canaanite place names shows that they were worshiped as early as the period of the Tell el-Amarna correspondence (c. 1370 B.C.).

scribed the place of their captivity as "beyond Damascus"; the LXX rendering concurs with the Masoretic text. But the same disloyalty to the God of their fathers brought a similar judgment on the southern kingdom more than a century later, in the Babylonian exile, and Stephen accordingly replaces "beyond Damascus" with "beyond Babylon" (perhaps as being more relevant in a Jerusalem setting). The idols which they had made for worship could give them no help in that terrible day.

f. Tabernacle and temple (7:44-50)

44 *"Our forefathers had the tent of testimony in the wilderness, as Moses was directed, by the one who spoke to him, to make it according to the model he had seen.*

45 *Our forefathers who succeeded them brought it in with Joshua when they dispossessed the nations which God drove out before them,[72] (and so it remained) until the days of David.[73]*

46 *David found favor in God's sight and sought to provide a tabernacle for the God[74] of Jacob.*

47 *But it was Solomon who built a house for him.*

48 *The Most High, however, does not dwell in houses made with hands. So the prophet says:*

49 *'Heaven is my throne;*
  Earth is a footstool for my feet.
What house will you build for me?' says the Lord,
  'Or what will be my resting-place?

50 *Was it not my hand that made all these things?'[75]*

44 But had the people of Israel no sanctuary in the wilderness, no reminder

---

72. Lit., "before our fathers."

73. It is not clear whether "until the days of David" marks the end of the process of dispossession or the end of the peregrination of the "tent of testimony"; in view of what follows, the latter is more probable.

74. For "God" (θεῷ), the reading of ℵc A C E Ψ byz lat syr cop etc., there is a very strongly attested variant "house" (οἴκῳ), read by P74 ℵ* B D H 049 pc copsa.cod. A powerful argument in favor of "house" is that it was more likely to be assimilated in transmission to "God," the LXX reading of Ps. 131 (MT 132):5, than *vice versa*. Hort and Ropes, agreeing that θεῷ may have been an emendation of οἴκῳ, suggest that οἴκῳ itself may have been a primitive corruption of κυρίῳ ("Lord"), written κ͞ω (in LXX τόπον τῷ κυρίῳ appears in parallelism with σκήνωμα τῷ θεῷ Ἰακώβ. The difficulty in accepting οἴκῳ is that "to provide a tabernacle for the *house* of Jacob" is an unnatural idea in the context, where the emphasis lies on the impossibility of making a dwelling place for *God*. Moreover, αὐτῷ in the next sentence must mean "for God"; it cannot have "the house of Jacob" as its antecedent. In support of οἴκῳ, see Lake-Cadbury, *Beginnings* I.4, p. 81; Schoeps, *Theologie und Geschichte*, p. 238; F. C. Synge, "Studies in Texts: Acts 7:46," *Theology* 55 (1952), pp. 25-26; for a defense of θεῷ see M. Simon, "Saint Stephen and the Jerusalem Temple," p. 128.

75. Isa. 66:1-2.

of the presence of God in their midst, that they should so unaccountably and so quickly forget him and lapse into idolatry? Yes indeed, says Stephen; they had the "tent of the testimony"—the "Trysting tent," to use James Moffatt's rendering. It was called the tent of the testimony because it housed the tables of the law, known comprehensively as "the testimony." The ark in which these tables were placed was accordingly called the "ark of the testimony"; the tent, which served as a shrine for the ark, was correspondingly called (among other things) the tent of the testimony.[76] It was no ordinary tent: it was made by the direct command of God, and constructed in every detail according to the model that Moses had been shown on the holy mount.[77] The writer to the Hebrews lays special emphasis on this model, identifying it with the heavenly sanctuary, "set up not by man but by the Lord" (Heb. 8:2). But, whereas the writer to the Hebrews draws attention to the sacrifices offered in association with the wilderness sanctuary and to their typological significance, Stephen is significantly silent about them; the only wilderness sacrifices which he mentions are those offered to idols.

Stephen has just countered the charge of blasphemy against Moses with a *vos quoque;* now he proceeds to counter the charge of blasphemy against God—that is, against his dwelling place—in the same way. The forefathers of his accusers and judges had rebelled against Moses; they paid similar disregard to the shrine which bore witness that God was continually dwelling among them as they moved from place to place.

45 When the Israelites at last entered the land of Canaan under Joshua's[78] leadership, they took the tent of the testimony with them, together with the sacred ark which it enshrined. The tent remained with them, in one place or another, through the period of their dispossession of the Canaanites and their settlement in the land, down to the time of David. "In its mobile character—so we may here fill out the interstices of the argument— the tent was a type or figure of God's never-ceasing, never-halted appointments for His people's salvation."[79]

46 Toward the end of the period of the judges, the ark was captured by the Philistines. When they found themselves compelled to restore it, Samuel wisely relegated it to a place of obscurity. When King David established his new capital at Jerusalem, he enhanced its sacral character by

76. LXX uses ἡ σκηνὴ τοῦ μαρτυρίου to render not only Heb. *miškan ʿēḏût*, as in Ex. 38:21 (LXX 37:19), etc., but also Heb. *ʾōhel môʿēḏ*, "tent of meeting," as in Ex. 27:21, etc. (It is the latter expression that Moffatt renders "Trysting tent.")

77. Ex. 25:9, 40; 26:30; 27:8. Cf. the elaboration of this theme in Heb. 8:5; 9:23-24.

78. Gk. Ἰησοῦς, whence KJV "Jesus" (as in Heb. 4:8). There may be a tacit suggestion that it is not by accident that the leader who brought them into the earthly land of promise bore the same name as the one under whose leadership the people of God were to inherit better promises.

79. W. Manson, *The Epistle to the Hebrews*, pp. 33-34.

bringing the ark out of its place of relegation at Kiriath-jearim and installing it in a tent-shrine which he had erected for it on Mount Zion.[80] His doing so is commemorated in Ps. 132:2-5, where it is related

"how he swore to Yahweh,
    and vowed to the Mighty One of Jacob:
'I will not enter my house
    or get into my bed;
I will not give sleep to my eyes
    or slumber to my eyelids,
till I find a place for Yahweh,
    a dwelling-place for the Mighty One of Jacob.'"[81]

But when he had put down his enemies inside and outside the land, David longed to provide a nobler dwelling place for the ark (the token of God's presence with his people) than this tent-shrine. The contrast between his own palace, panelled in cedar-wood, and the curtained tent within which the ark abode, weighed on his mind. He confided in the prophet Nathan, and Nathan's first reaction was to commend the king and bid him act on his inclination and build a palace for the ark of God. But Nathan soon ascertained the mind of God more clearly, and went back to David with the message that God desired no house of cedar from him; instead, he would himself establish David's house—his dynasty—in perpetuity.

Nathan went on to tell David that his son and successor would build a house for the "name" of God. But Stephen evidently did not consider that the building of Solomon's temple was the fulfilment of this promise. It is plain that many early Christians interpreted the accompanying promise, that this son of David would have his throne established forever, as fulfilled in Christ.

"He will be great, and will be called the Son of the Most High;
and the Lord God will give to him the throne of his father David,
and he will reign over the house of Jacob forever;
and of his kingdom there will be no end" (Luke 1:32-33).

It was in Christ too, they believed, that the promise of a new house, built for the name of God, was truly fulfilled. It was directly after his entry into Jerusalem, when he was hailed as the son of David, that Jesus went into the temple area and ejected from the Court of the Gentiles the trespassers whose activity there prevented it from fulfilling its proper purpose. "Is it not written," he asked, "'My house shall be called a house of prayer for all the

80. Cf. 1 Sam. (LXX 1 Kms.) 4:1b–7:2; 2 Sam. (LXX 2 Kms.) 6:1–7:29.
81. According to M. Simon ("Saint Stephen and the Jerusalem Temple," p. 129), the "place" (Gk. τόπος) in this quotation is Jerusalem; the "dwelling place" (Gk. σκήνωμα, "tabernacle," "bivouac") is the tent-shrine which David erected for the ark on Zion (cf. 2 Sam. [LXX 2 Kms.] 6:17; 1 Chron. 15:1), by contrast with the "house" (Gk. οἶκος) which Solomon built (v. 47; cf. 2 Sam. [LXX 2 Kms.] 7:6 with 1 Chron. 17:5).

nations'?" (Mark 11:17).[82] In these words is an adumbration of that new temple in which those who were formerly "strangers and sojourners" are now made "fellow-citizens with the saints" and "built into" a living sanctuary which is a fit "dwelling place of God in the Spirit" (Eph. 2:19-22). The work of building began with Jesus' resurrection: it was of "the temple of his body" that he spoke when he undertook to raise up a new temple in three days (John 2:20-21). If some such intention is rightly traced in Stephen's language here, it underlines the relevance of this speech as a theological introduction to Luke's narrative of the Gentile mission.

47 By contrast with the "tabernacle" or bivouac[83] that David erected for God, the house[84] that Solomon his son built was a structure of stone, immobile, fixed to one spot. The brevity with which Solomon's building is introduced and dismissed, and the contrast implied with David's intention, which was not to be realized until the advent of a greater than Solomon, expresses plain disapproval. Yet perhaps it is not so much Solomon's action that Stephen deprecates—Solomon himself confessed that no temple made with hands could house the God of heaven: "Behold, heaven and the highest heaven cannot contain thee; how much less this house which I have built!" (1 Kings 8:27).[85] It was rather the state of mind to which the temple gave rise—a state of mind which could not have been engendered by the mobile tabernacle—that Stephen reprobated, as Jeremiah had done in his day.

48 The gods of the heathen might be accommodated in material shrines, but not God Most High. This was taught by the higher paganism, as well as by Jews and Christians.[86] The contrast between what is "made with

82. Was it our Lord's implied concern for those Gentiles who desired to draw as near as they could to worship the true God that led to the Greeks' request for an interview with him during Holy Week in Jerusalem (John 12:21)? It is noteworthy that he went on immediately to speak of his imminent "glorifying"—his being "lifted up" in a twofold sense—as the condition for his drawing to himself not Jewish believers only but all without distinction. It is noteworthy, too, that while the description of the temple as "a house of prayer for all the nations" is taken directly from Isa. 56:7, it also echoes a passage in Solomon's prayer of dedication where provision is made for the foreigner to "pray toward this house" (1 Kings [LXX 3 Kms.] 8:41-43).

83. Gk. σκήνωμα, as in Ps. 132 (LXX 131):5 (cf. n. 81 above).

84. Cf. 1 Kings (LXX 3 Kms.) 6:2, "the house (Gk. οἶκος, translating Heb. *bayit*) which King Solomon built for Yahweh."

85. It should also be observed that in the whole of Solomon's dedicatory prayer (1 Kings [LXX 3 Kms.] 8:23-53) nothing is said of the use of the temple for sacrifices; its prime function is to be a house of prayer. Cf. the view ascribed to Trypho the Jew in Justin's *Dialogue* (117.2), that Mal. 1:10-12 means that "God did not accept the sacrifices of those who dwelt then in Jerusalem, and were called Israelites; but declares his pleasure with the prayers of the dispersed members of that nation, and calls their prayers sacrifices."

86. It was constantly emphasized in Jewish, and later also in Christian, propaganda against paganism (cf. 17:24-25); for the higher paganism see the quotation from Euripides below, p. 336, n. 65. Cf. also *Sibylline Oracles* 4.8-11: "He has not for his habitation a stone set up as a temple, deaf and dumb, a bane and woe to mortals, but one

hands" and what is "not made with hands" is a prominent feature in the primitive catechesis of the New Testament and early Christian apologetic.[87] Where the temple is concerned, the contrast appears to go back to our Lord himself. Although the evidence given at his trial, to the effect that he said, "I will destroy this temple that is made with hands, and in three days I will build another, not made with hands" (Mark 14:58), is described as "false witness," it is not likely to have been false on this point.[88]

49-50 To emphasize the full agreement of his case with the prophetic revelation, Stephen quotes the opening words of Isa. 66—words which clearly anticipate his own argument, whether their primary reference was to the building of the second temple or to some other occasion.[89] There the prophet goes on to say in Yahweh's name, almost immediately after the passage quoted by Stephen: "But this is the man to whom I will look, he that is humble and contrite in spirit, and trembles at my word" (Isa. 66:2b). This well described the character of the people of God, who constitute his true temple (cf. Isa. 57:15). But to those who imagine that they can localize the presence of God, the scornful answer comes: "What is the place of my rest?" Do they think they can make God "stay put"—imprison him in a beautiful ornamented cage?[90] "The Temple was not intended . . . to become a *perma-*

---

which may not be seen from earth or measured by mortal eyes, since it was not fashioned by mortal hand." (Some later lines of this poem, 25-30, may be compared with Trypho's words quoted in n. 85 above: "Happy among human beings shall they be on earth who . . . turn away their eyes from every temple and all altars, vain structures of stones that cannot hear, defiled with the blood of living things and sacrifices of four-footed beasts, and look to the great glory of the one God.")

87. Cf. the disparaging reference in 19:26 below to "gods made with hands." By contrast, the compound adjective "not made with hands" (Gk. ἀχειροποίητος), used in Mark 14:58 of the new temple, is used in 2 Cor. 5:1 of the resurrection body, in Col. 2:11 of spiritual circumcision, as against "the so-called circumcision in the flesh, performed by human hand" (Eph. 2:11).

88. Cf. M. Simon, "Saint Stephen and the Jerusalem ⸏emple," pp. 133-37; C. F. D. Moule, "Sanctuary and Sacrifice in the Church of the New Testament," *JTS* n.s. 1 (1950), pp. 29-41.

89. The occasion is almost certainly the building of Zerubbabel's temple, although attempts have been made at times (e.g., by T. K. Cheyne and B. Duhm) to relate the oracle to a Samaritan temple on Gerizim. T. C. G. Thornton ("Stephen's Use of Isaiah LXVI," *JTS* n.s. 25 [1974], pp. 432-34) cites an Aramaic midrash in which Isaiah makes Isa. 66:1-2 (together with 1 Kings 8:27) the basis of a prediction of Nebuchadrezzar's destruction of Solomon's temple, and thus incurs the murderous rage of King Manasseh.

90. This is the gravamen of Stephen's argument. In many respects the tabernacle and the temple were comparable. Both were copies of divinely given patterns: the wilderness tabernacle was made according to the archetype shown to Moses on Sinai, and Solomon's temple, according to the Chronicler, was constructed according to a plan which David "made clear by the writing from the hand of Yahweh concerning it" (1 Chron. 28:19). Both, according to the canonical OT writings, were associated with sacrificial ritual, although Stephen is silent about this (it would, however, be unwise to draw positive conclusions from his silence). See M. Simon, *Verus Israel* (Paris, 1948),

nent institution, halting the advance of the divine plan for the people of God."[91]

Stephen's argument is thus concluded; all that remains is to drive it home to the conscience of his audience. He has answered the charges brought forward by the prosecution. As for the charge of subverting the Mosaic tradition, it is not he but the nation, and preeminently its leaders, that should plead guilty to this: their guilt is amply attested by their own sacred scriptures, back to Moses' own lifetime. As for the charge of blaspheming God by announcing the supersession of the temple by "this Jesus of Nazareth," he makes no attempt to deny it but justifies his position by the claim that it is the position occupied by the patriarchs and prophets, whereas the position of his opponents involves a point-blank denial of the consistent witness of the scriptures. "Stephen's speech thus resolves itself into a great defence of the doctrine of the Church Invisible, based on a broad survey of the history of the people of God."[92]

g. Personal application (7:51-53)

51 *"You obstinate people, disobedient in heart and hearing alike, you always oppose the Holy Spirit. Your forefathers did so, and so do you.*

52 *Which of the prophets did your forefathers not persecute? They killed those who announced in advance the advent[93] of the Righteous One; you have now betrayed and murdered him—*

53 *you, who received the law by the agency of angels, but have not kept it."*

51 Having defended his position thus, Stephen now applies the moral to his hearers in true prophetic vein. The suddenness of his invective has taken some of his commentators by surprise, as it perhaps took some of his hearers; and it is suggested that his immediately preceding words must have occasioned an angry outburst in the court, to which he now responds. But it is unnecessary to think of any interruption at this point. There was really nothing to add after his quotation of Isa. 66:1-2; that clinched his case. The words that follow sum up in pointed and personal terms the indictment which he has been building up throughout his speech.

That the nation was obstinate, "stiffnecked," was a complaint as old

---

pp. 111-17. The point on which Stephen concentrates is the main point which distinguished the two structures: the tabernacle was mobile, the temple was stationary.

91. W. Manson, *The Epistle to the Hebrews*, p. 34.

92. A. Cole, *The New Temple* (London, 1950), p. 38.

93. Gk. ἔλευσις. G. D. Kilpatrick has argued that this word may have been in use as a technical term of Hellenistic Judaism, designating the messianic advent ("Acts VII 52 ΕΛΕΥΣΙΣ," *JTS* 46 [1945], pp. 136-45). It occurs nowhere else in the Greek Bible.

as the wilderness wanderings—a complaint made by God himself (Ex. 33:5). The description of them as disobedient—"uncircumcised in heart and ears"—meant that, while they were circumcised in the literal sense, in accordance with the Abrahamic institution, their unresponsiveness and resistance to God's revelation were such as might have been expected from Gentiles to whom he had not made known his will (cf. Lev. 26:41; Deut. 10:16; Jer. 4:4; 6:10; 9:26; Ezek. 44:7). Moses and the prophets had described earlier generations in these terms; they were equally true, said Stephen, of the contemporary generation.

52 Many of the prophets of God in Old Testament times suffered persecution and sometimes death itself for their faithfulness to the divine commission. There is ample evidence of this in the canonical books, and Jewish tradition elaborated the theme,[94] describing, for example, the martyrdom of Isaiah by sawing asunder in the reign of Manasseh[95] and of Jeremiah by stoning at the hands of the people who had forced him to go down to Egypt with them.[96] Much of that opposition to the prophets was due to their attack on Israel's perverted notions of the true worship of God—an attack exemplified in the prophetic texts quoted in Stephen's speech. Stephen placed himself in the prophetic succession by attacking Israel's record on this very point; it is therefore especially relevant that Israel's traditional hostility to the prophets should be mentioned here.

But did not the Jews of later days reprobate their ancestors' behavior toward the prophets? Yes indeed. "If we had lived in the days of our fathers," they said, "we would not have taken part with them in shedding the blood of the prophets" (Matt. 23:30). They paid tribute to the prophets' memory and built monuments in their honor. But Stephen insists that they are still true sons of their ancestors, maintaining the same hostility to God's messengers:[97] if those ancestors killed those who foretold the advent of the Righteous One,[98] they themselves—and here Stephen's indictment is directed particularly to his chief-priestly judges—had carried that hostility to its logical conclusion by handing the Righteous One himself over to violent death.

53 By rejecting the Messiah, they had filled up the measure of their fathers. The fathers had all along resisted the plan of God, the very purpose for which he had made them a nation and called them into covenant relationship with himself; their descendants had now repudiated the one in whom the

---

94. See T. Schermann (ed.), *Prophetarum Vitae Fabulosae* (Leipzig, 1907); C. C. Torrey (ed.), *Lives of the Prophets* (Philadelphia, 1946); H.-J. Schoeps, "Die jüdischen Prophetenmorde," in *Aus frühchristlicher Zeit* (Tübingen, 1950), pp. 126-43.

95. See *Ascension of Isaiah* 5:1-14; TB Yᵉbāmôṯ 49b; *Sanhedrin* 103b; Justin, *Dialogue* 120.5; Tertullian, *On Patience* 14.

96. See Tertullian, *Remedy against Scorpions* 8; Jerome, *Against Jovinian* 2.37.

97. Cf. the argument in Matt. 23:29-37; 1 Thess. 2:15-16.

98. For this designation of Christ cf. 3:14 (p. 81, n. 29); 22:14.

divine plan and purpose were to be consummated. In the earliest days of the nation, it disobeyed the law of God, although it had received that law by angelic mediation.[99] And now in these last days, when God has spoken through no angel but through the Righteous One *par excellence*, Stephen's hearers had with even greater decisiveness rejected *him*.

7. The Stoning of Stephen (7:54–8:1a)

a. Stephen's final witness (7:54-56)

54 *Hearing this, they were filled with rage and ground their teeth at him.*

55 *But he, being full of the Holy Spirit, looked up into heaven and saw the glory of God, and Jesus[100] standing at God's right hand.*

56 *"Look!" he said, "I see heaven opened, and the Son of Man standing at God's right hand."*

54 To the earlier part of Stephen's speech his judges had perhaps listened with considerable interest, wondering where his outline of patriarchal times would lead him. But as he continued, the drift of his argument became clearer, and they heard him with increasing anger and horror.[101] And when he flung the charge of blasphemy, persistent opposition to God and his ways, back on themselves, their vexation and rage could no longer be restrained.[102]

---

99. The angels through whose mediation the law is said to have been instituted are mentioned elsewhere in the NT. In Gal. 3:19 the angelic administration of the law is adduced by Paul to show its inferiority to the promise which God made to Abraham without any mediation. In Heb. 2:2 it is argued that if even the law, "spoken through angels," imposed inexorable penalties on those who infringed it, much more inexorable must be the penalty for disregarding God's final revelation, communicated not through angels but in his Son, "as much superior to angels as the name he has obtained is more excellent than theirs" (Heb. 1:4). In Deut. 33:2 LXX God is said to have been attended by angels at his theophany on Sinai (ἐκ δεξιῶν αὐτοῦ ἄγγελοι μετ᾽ αὐτοῦ), and this is echoed in several later Jewish texts, but angelic attendance (cf. Ps. 68 [LXX 67]:17) need not imply angelic mediation. There is a possible parallel to Stephen's statement about angelic mediation in Josephus (*Ant*. 15.136), where Herod says that the Jewish doctrines and laws have been learned from God through angels (δι᾽ ἀγγέλων), but there the reference may be to human messengers, prophets. Yet Stephen (Luke), Paul, and the writer to the Hebrews all seem to treat the angelic mediation of the law as a familiar and accepted idea. Stephen's point is that the impiety of those who, having received the law, disregarded it was the more heinous because it was communicated through beings as high and holy as angels. See F. F. Bruce, *The Epistle to the Galatians*, NIGTC [Grand Rapids/Exeter, 1982], pp. 176-78).

100. The Western text reads "the Lord Jesus."

101. To call the speech "a tedious sketch of the history of Israel" (G. B. Shaw, *Androcles and the Lion* [London, 1928], p. lxxxv) betrays surprising insensitivity to its revolutionary tendency.

102. "They were cut to the quick" (Gk. διεπρίοντο). For the same verb cf. 5:33.

55-56 While his hearers gave vent to their annoyance, Stephen remained calm, fully controlled as before by the Spirit of God, when suddenly, as he kept his gaze fixed upward, a vision of the glory of God met his inward eye. Much more real to him in that moment than the angry gestures and cries of those around him was the presence of Jesus at God's right hand. "Look!" he exclaimed. "I see the heavens parted and the Son of Man standing at God's right hand."[103]

Not many years before, another prisoner had stood at the bar before the same court, charged with almost the same offenses as Stephen. But when the hostile evidence broke down, the high priest adjured the prisoner to tell the court plainly if he was indeed the Messiah, the Son of God. Had he said "Yes" and no more, it is not clear that he could have been convicted of a capital offense. "Messiah" was not his chosen self-designation, but if the question was put to him like that, he could not say "No." He went on, however, to reframe his answer in words of his own choosing: "you will see the Son of Man sitting at the right hand of the Almighty, and coming with the clouds of heaven" (Mark 14:62).[104] No more was required: Jesus was found guilty of blasphemy and judged to be worthy of death. Now Stephen in the same place was making the same claim on Jesus' behalf as Jesus had made for himself: he was claiming, in fact, that those words of Jesus, far from being false and blasphemous, were words of sober truth which had received their vindication and fulfilment from God. Unless the judges were prepared to admit that their former decision was tragically mistaken, they had no option but to find Stephen guilty of blasphemy as well.

This is the only New Testament occurrence of the phrase "the Son of Man" outside the Gospels.[105] Apart from this instance, it is found only on the lips of Jesus. It has its Old Testament roots in Dan. 7:13-14, where a human figure ("one like a son of man," in the literal rendering of the Aramaic) is seen coming to the enthroned Ancient of Days "with the clouds of heaven" to receive universal dominion from him. The un-Greek idiom "the Son of Man" (more literally "the son of the man") means "the 'one like a son of man'" who is to receive world dominion, but since it was not in

---

For the grinding of teeth as a gesture of rage cf. Job 16:9; Ps. 35 [LXX 34]:16). Elsewhere it is used of the fruitless anguish of despair; cf. Luke 13:28 (βρυγμὸς ὀδόντων, from βρύχω, the verb used here).

103. Similarly James the Just, according to Hegesippus, said to his judges, "Why do you ask me about the Son of Man? He sits at the right hand of the Almighty in heaven, and he will come on the clouds of heaven" (Eusebius, *HE* 2.23.13).

104. On the interrelation of the three Synoptic accounts of these words see I. H. Marshall, *The Gospel of Luke*, NIGTC (Grand Rapids/Exeter, 1978), pp. 849-51.

105. The expression in Rev. 1:13 and 14:4 is not the title ὁ υἱὸς τοῦ ἀνθρώπου but ὅμοιον υἱὸν ἀνθρώπου ("one like a son of man," i.e., a human figure, as in Dan. 7:13).

current use as a technical term, Jesus could and did employ it freely of himself and fill it with whatever meaning he chose. The background in Dan. 7:13-27 links the "one like a son of man" closely with "the saints of the Most High," whom the New Testament identifies with Jesus' disciples and their converts.[106]

Jesus' reply to the high priest's question combines Daniel's description of the "one like a son of man" coming with the clouds of heaven and the oracle of Ps. 110:1 in which the king of Israel is invited by Yahweh to sit at his right hand. This oracle underlies the description of Stephen's present vision. But Stephen sees the Son of Man not sitting but standing at God's right hand. Is there any significance in this change of verb?

Some commentators have thought not; C. H. Dodd, for example, remarks that the verb to stand "has commonly the sense 'to be situated', without any necessary implication of an upright attitude."[107] But in allusions to the oracle of Ps. 110:1 the participle "sitting" is so constant that this exception calls for an explanation. Various explanations have been offered. "He had not yet taken definitely his seat," says William Kelly, "but was still giving the Jews a final opportunity. Would they reject the testimony to Him gone on high indeed, but as a sign waiting if peradventure they might repent and He might be sent to bring in the times of refreshing here below?"[108] But from Luke's point of view this was no "final opportunity" for the Jews; they continue to receive further opportunities to the very end of his narrative.[109]

---

106. The literature on the "Son of Man" question is voluminous. See (among other discussions) C. Colpe, *TDNT* 8, pp. 400-477 (*s.v.* ὁ υἱὸς τοῦ ἀνθρώπου); T. W. Manson, "The Son of Man in Daniel, Enoch and the Gospels," in *Studies in the Gospels and Epistles* (Manchester, 1962), pp. 123-45; H. E. Tödt, *The Son of Man in the Synoptic Tradition*, E.T. (London, 1966); F. H. Borsch, *The Son of Man in Myth and History* (London, 1967); M. D. Hooker, *The Son of Man in Mark* (London, 1967); C. F. D. Moule, "Neglected Features in the Problem of 'the Son of Man,'" in *Neues Testament und Geschichte*, ed. J. Gnilka (Freiburg, 1974), pp. 413-28; R. Pesch and R. Schnackenburg (eds.), *Jesus und der Menschensohn* (Freiburg, 1975); M. Casey, *Son of Man* (London, 1979); A. J. B. Higgins, *The Son of Man in the Teaching of Jesus* (Cambridge, 1980); J. Coppens, *Le Fils de l'Homme Néotestamentaire* (Leuven, 1981) and *Le Fils de l'Homme Vétéro- et Intertestamentaire* (Leuven, 1983); B. Lindars, *Jesus: Son of Man* (London/Grand Rapids, 1983); S. Kim, *"The 'Son of Man'" as the Son of God*, WUNT 30 (Tübingen, 1983); G. Vermes, "The Present State of the 'Son of Man' Debate," in *Jesus and the World of Judaism* (London, 1983), pp. 89-99.

107. C. H. Dodd, *According to the Scriptures* (London, 1952), p. 35n.; cf. G. H. Dalman, *The Words of Jesus*, E.T. (Edinburgh, 1902), p. 311.

108. W. Kelly, *An Exposition of the Acts of the Apostles* (London, ³1952), pp. 102-3; cf. J. N. Darby: "He does not sit as it were till Israel has formally rejected the testimony, when the cry of Stephen reached His ear. He took His place, sitting down until His enemies are made His footstool, after their refusal to hear the Holy Ghost's testimony. Stephen being received to Christ in heaven, Israel as Israel must wait outside" (*Collected Writings* 28, p. 283).

109. Therefore E. W. Bullinger saw the dispensational transition not here but at

More plausibly, Jesus has been pictured as rising up from the throne of God to greet his proto-martyr; J. A. Bengel, who takes this view, quotes to the same effect from the sixth-century Christian poet Arator.[110] Others have understood Stephen to foresee the glory of Christ's advent: "Christ rises in preparation for his Parousia," says Huw Pari Owen.[111] A refinement of this interpretation is proposed by C. K. Barrett: Jesus is indeed standing because "he is about to come," but Luke believed that "the death of each Christian would be marked by what we may term a private and personal *parousia* of the Son of man."[112]

Most probably Stephen's words should be taken closely along with Jesus' promise: "everyone who acknowledges me before men, the Son of Man also will acknowledge before the angels of God" (Luke 12:8; in Matt. 10:33 "the Son of Man" is replaced by "I"). That is to say, Jesus stands up as witness or advocate in Stephen's defense. Stephen appeals from the adverse judgment of the earthly court, and "in the heavenly court . . . this member of the Son of Man community is already being vindicated by the head of that community—*the* Son of Man *par excellence*" (C. F. D. Moule).[113] If, at the moment when he was about to begin testifying before the Sanhedrin, Stephen had some foreview of this beatific vision, no wonder his face shone like an angel's (6:15).

Did Stephen's vision of the Son of Man involve an appreciation of his exercising world dominion? According to William Manson, *"Stephen grasped and asserted the more-than-Jewish-Messianic sense in which the office and significance of Jesus in religious history were to be understood. . . . Whereas the Jewish nationalists were holding to the permanence of their* national historical privilege, and even the 'Hebrew' Christians gathered round the Apostles were, with all their new Messianic faith, idealising the sacred institutions of the past, 'continuing stedfastly in the temple', 'going up to the temple at the hour of prayer' which was also the hour of the sacrificial service, sheltering under the eaves of the Holy Place, Stephen saw that the Messiah was on the throne of the universe."[114]

28:28; see *The Companion Bible* (London, 1909-21), Appendix 181 ("The Dispensational Position of the Book of the 'Acts'").

110. *Gnomon Novi Testamenti*, p. 420: "*stantem:* quasi obvium Stephano" (Bengel).

111. H. P. Owen, "Stephen's Vision in Acts VII 55-56," *NTS* 1 (1954-55), p. 225.

112. C. K. Barrett, "Stephen and the Son of Man," in *Apophoreta: Festschrift für Ernst Haenchen*, BZNW 30 (Berlin, 1964), pp. 32-38.

113. C. F. D. Moule, "From Defendant to Judge—and Deliverer" (1953), in *The Phenomenon of the New Testament*, SBT 2.1 (London, 1967), pp. 90-91.

114. W. Manson, *The Epistle to the Hebrews*, pp. 31-32. Since the Son of Man had now received unlimited world dominion, he goes on, the call to the people of God was now to march forward under the direction of the once rejected Jesus, "to whom the throne of the world and Lordship of the Age to Come belonged" (p. 32).

This may be a just assessment of Stephen's thought, but nothing like certainty on this is attainable. Manson's interpretation is part of his case for seeing Stephen as the antecursor of the writer to the Hebrews. What may be said with some confidence is that Luke treats the ministry of Stephen as an introduction to the Gentile mission, in which Christ's claim to world dominion began to be vindicated. The vindication of his sovereign claim by the Gentile mission appears again as the theme of James's speech at the Council of Jerusalem (15:14-18).

In short, the presence of the Son of Man at God's right hand meant that for his people a way of access to God had been opened up more immediate and heart-satisfying than the temple could provide. It meant that the hour of fulfilment had struck, and that the age of particularism had come to an end. The sovereignty of the Son of Man was to embrace all nations and races without distinction: under his sway there is no place for an institution which gives religious privileges to one group in preference to others.

b. Death of Stephen (7:57-60)

57 *But with a loud shout they stopped their ears and rushed on him as one man.*[115]
58 *Then they hustled him outside the city and proceeded to stone him. The witnesses laid down their clothes at the feet of a young man called Saul.*
59 *So they stoned Stephen, while he called on (the Lord): "Lord Jesus, receive my spirit," he said.*
60 *Then, falling on his knees, he cried aloud, "Lord, do not hold this sin against them." So saying, he fell asleep.*

57-58 Commentators differ about what happened next. Many who heard Stephen describe his vision must have felt that this was unabashed contempt of the Shekhinah.[116] Did the crowd of bystanders take the law into their own hands and lynch him? Joseph Klausner thought that Stephen's stoning was the work of "some fanatical persons . . . who decided the case for themselves. They saw in Stephen a 'blasphemer' worthy of stoning, although according to the Talmudic rule 'the blasphemer is not culpable unless he pronounces the Name itself'—which Stephen had not done. The fanatics did not trouble themselves about the judicial rule; they took Stephen outside the city and stoned him." It may be true, as Klausner goes on to say, that "in the

115. One Western authority (the African Latin codex h) makes the populace the subject of this sentence.
116. Rabbis of a later date debated whether or not the *shekhinah* (the divine presence) rested on the second temple as it did on Solomon's (1 Chron. 5:13-14; 7:1-2). But their debates (cf. TB Z⁽e⁾ḇāḥîm 118b; *Yômā'* 9b) were mainly exercises in theorizing; while the second temple stood, it was venerated as the habitation of God (cf. Matt. 23:21, "he who swears by the temple, swears by it and by him who dwells therein").

opinion of the Pharisees there was in his words no actual blasphemy, but only an offense requiring the forty stripes lacking one." But that does not justify the conclusion that "the Sanhedrin could not see fit to impose the death sentence on him." He conceded that Stephen "may have been deserving of that according to the rules of the Sadducees";[117] and in the trial of Stephen, as in the examination of Jesus, it was the Sadducean chief priests who played the leading part. We must beware of supposing that trials before the Sanhedrin in the early decades of the first century A.D. were invariably conducted in the atmosphere of severe impartiality and judicial calm prescribed in the idealized Mishnaic account.[118]

The reference to the witnesses suggests strongly that Stephen's stoning was carried out as a legal execution, as the penalty for blasphemy. The restriction of blasphemy to the actual pronouncing of the ineffable name was a later rabbinical refinement;[119] there is no reason to think that the Saducean authorities limited the offense in any such way. For Stephen to suggest that the crucified Jesus stood in a position of authority at the right hand of God must have ranked as blasphemy in the thinking of those who knew that a crucified man died under the divine curse.

As for the witnesses, it was their duty to play the chief part in such an execution—a duty prescribed in the written Torah. "The hand of the witnesses shall be first against him to put him to death, and afterward the hand of all the people" (Deut. 17:7; cf. Lev. 24:14; Deut. 13:9-10). In order to throw the first stones the witnesses would naturally divest themselves of their outer garments, as they are here said to have done.

The young man called Saul, who guarded the clothes of the chief executioners, will play an increasingly important part in the record of Acts, as a leading champion of the cause which he was now opposing. Saul was his family name as an Israelite; he is better known in history by his Roman cognomen Paullus (Paul). It may be regarded as an undesigned coincidence that while Luke alone informs us that his Jewish name was Saul, he himself claims to have belonged to the tribe of Benjamin.[120] His parents thus gave

---

117. J. Klausner, *From Jesus to Paul*, E.T. (London, 1944), p. 232.

118. See the Mishnaic tractate *Sanhedrin*. On the relation of Sanhedrin procedure to the trial of Jesus see J. Blinzler, *The Trial of Jesus*, E.T. (Cork, 1959); P. Winter, *On the Trial of Jesus* (Berlin, 1961); E. Bammel (ed.), *The Trial of Jesus*, SBT 2.13 (London, 1970); D. R. Catchpole, *The Trial of Jesus* (Leiden, 1971); W. Grundmann, "The decision of the Supreme Court to put Jesus to death (John 11:47-57) in its context: tradition and redaction in the Gospel of John," and K. Schubert, "Biblical criticism criticised: with reference to the Markan report of Jesus's examination before the Sanhedrin," in E. Bammel and C. F. D. Moule (eds.), *Jesus and the Politics of His Day* (Cambridge, 1984), pp. 295-318, 385-402.

119. Mishnah, *Sanhedrin* 7.5.

120. Rom. 11:1; Phil. 3:5.

him the name of the most illustrious member of that tribe in the nation's history—the name of Israel's first king, Saul.[121]

If the stoning of Stephen was a legal execution, how could it be carried out on the spot, without that authorization of the Roman governor which was required by provincial law? It is not an adequate answer to suggest that it may have taken place in the interregnum after Pilate's removal from his office in A.D. 36/37. For one thing, there was no interregnum (Lucius Vitellius, legate of Syria, saw to that);[122] for another thing, even if there had been an interregnum, the exercise of capital jurisdiction by the Jewish court would still have been a usurpation of Roman prerogative, as was shown when James the Just was executed in A.D. 62, in the interval between Festus's death and his successor's arrival.[123] The charge which was found proved against Stephen—speaking against the temple—probably belonged to the category of offenses against the temple for which the Roman administration, as an exceptional concession, allowed the Jewish authorities to carry out the death sentence without reference to the governor.[124]

59   The ancient law directing the witnesses to take the lead in the act of stoning was amplified in later times and is recorded thus in the Mishnah (late second century A.D.):

> "When the trial is finished, the man convicted is brought out to be stoned. . . . When ten cubits from the place of stoning they say to him, 'Confess;[125] for it is the custom of all about to be put to death to make confession, and every one who confesses has a share in the age to come.' . . . Four cubits from the place of stoning the criminal is stripped.[126] . . . The drop from the place of stoning was twice the height of a man. One of the witnesses pushes the criminal from behind, so that he falls face downward. He is then turned over on his back. If he dies from this fall, that is sufficient.[127] If not, the second witness takes the stone and drops

---

121. Cf. 13:21.
122. Josephus, *Ant.* 18.89.
123. Josephus, *Ant.* 20.200-203.
124. See on 21:28 (p. 409, nn. 47-49).
125. Cf. the case of Achan (Josh. 7:19).
126. For this reason F. C. Conybeare suggested that "their garments" (v. 58) should be emended to "his (Stephen's) garments" ("The Stoning of St. Stephen," *Exp.* 8, 6 [1913], pp. 466-70). But the text as it stands is confirmed by 22:20.
127. The account of the death of James the Just (see p. 154, n. 103) follows these Mishnaic prescriptions: "Then they seized him and threw him down and began to stone him, since he did not die from his fall" (Eusebius, *HE* 2.23.16). Cf. *Clem. Recog.* 1.70, where Simon Magus (a disguise for Paul?) stirs up a tumult against James and throws him down headlong from the top of a flight of steps in the temple precincts. Schoeps (*Theologie und Geschichte*, pp. 381-456) may be right in tracing this and much else in the pseudo-Clementine literature back to an Ebionite *Acts of the Apostles*, composed as a counterblast to the canonical Acts (cf. p. 131, n. 7).

it on his heart. If this causes death, that is sufficient; if not, he is stoned by all the congregation of Israel."[128]

In the Mishnah this (or any other) form of execution is treated as an unwelcome necessity, to be avoided if the slightest legal loophole can be found; Luke does not give the impression that Stephen's executioners stoned him reluctantly as a disagreeable but unavoidable duty.

Nor did Stephen make confession to his judges or executioners. Instead, as he was being stoned he committed himself to his advocate on high with the words: "Lord Jesus, receive my spirit." These words are reminiscent of Jesus' final utterance from the cross in Luke's passion narrative: "Father, into thy hands I commit my spirit!" (Luke 23:46).[129] There is this striking difference: whereas Jesus committed his spirit to God, Stephen committed his to Jesus—eloquent evidence for the rapid emergence of a high christology in the church.[130]

60 There was yet another of our Lord's words from the cross echoed by Stephen. For, on his knees among the flying stones, he made his last appeal to the heavenly court—not this time for his own vindication but for mercy toward his executioners. Before he was finally battered into silence and death, he was heard to cry aloud, "Lord, do not hold this sin against them" (the "Lord" being again, presumably, the Lord Jesus).[131]

There is an Old Testament story of another messenger of God who for his faithfulness was stoned to death, not (like Stephen) outside the city but in the temple court itself, "between the altar and the sanctuary," as our Lord said (Luke 11:51)—Zechariah the son of Jehoiada, priest and prophet. But as Zechariah was about to breathe his last, he prayed, "May Yahweh see and avenge!" (2 Chron. 24:22). The martyr-deaths were similar; the dying prayers were widely different. Stephen had learned his lesson in the school of him who, when he was being fixed to the cross, prayed, "Father, forgive them, for they know not what they do" (Luke 23:34).[132] Having prayed thus, says Luke, Stephen "fell asleep"—an unexpectedly peaceful description for so brutal a death, but one which fits the spirit in which Stephen accepted his martyrdom.

128. Mishnah, *Sanhedrin* 6.1-4.

129. A prayer from Ps. 31 (LXX 30):5, prefaced by the vocative "Father."

130. For the early emergence of a high christology in the church see M. Hengel, *Between Jesus and Paul*, E.T. (London, 1983), pp. 30-47.

131. "The martyr with his dying words begs the heavenly court for mercy towards those against whom he is vindicated" (C. F. D. Moule, *The Phenomenon of the New Testament*, SBT 2.1, p. 91). Hegesippus represents James as praying, while he was being stoned, "I beseech thee, Lord God and Father, forgive them; for they know not what they do" (Eusebius, *HE* 2.23.16). See further p. 83 with n. 35.

132. For the textual problem presented by these words of Jesus see commentaries on Luke *ad loc.*; cf. also J. R. Harris, *Side-lights on New Testament Research* (London, 1908), pp. 96-103; B. H. Streeter, *The Four Gospels* (London, ²1930), pp. 138-39.

ACTS 8

c. Saul's agreement (8:1a)

1a *Saul fully approved of his execution.*

1a Saul, a native of the Cilician city of Tarsus, as we learn later (9:11), may have attended the synagogue in Jerusalem where Stephen engaged in disputation with the spokesmen for the old order (6:9). He too was exceptionally farsighted, and realized as clearly as Stephen did the fundamental incompatibility between the old order and the new. The temporizing policy of his master Gamaliel[1] (5:34-39) was not for him: he saw that no compromise was logically possible, and if the old order was to be preserved, the new faith must be stamped out. Hence he expressed his agreement with Stephen's death sentence as publicly as possible by guarding the executioners' clothes[2]—an action which he did not readily forget (cf. 22:20). It has been suggested further that he acted as *praeco* or herald, charged with proclaiming that the convicted person was about to be executed for the specified offense.[3]

The refusal to compromise in the issue between Judaism and Christianity which determined his present attitude continued to determine his policy in later days when, as preacher of the gospel and teacher of the church, he built up the work which at first he had endeavored to destroy.

---

1. See 22:3.

2. Even here there is a parallel between the narratives of Stephen and James. The Ebionite *Acts of the Apostles* postulated by H.- J. Schoeps (see p. 159, n. 127) described how Paul "both planned and mounted a murderous attack on the leader of the church, James the Lord's brother, and set on foot a bloody pogrom against the Jewish Christians. This account of past events," Schoeps surmises (*Theologie und Geschichte*, p. 448), "perhaps comes nearer the truth than the report [of Acts 7:58-8:3]." But the Ebionite portrayal of James is much more likely to be based on the Lukan Stephen than *vice versa* (see p. 131, n. 7).

3. F. C. Conybeare, "The Stoning of St. Stephen," *Exp.* 8,6 (1913), pp. 468-69. The statement that Saul "approved" (ἦν συνευδοκῶν) of Stephen's execution need not imply his membership in the Sanhedrin; see on 22:20, where the expression occurs again (p. 419).

B. PHILIP (8:1B-40)

1. Persecution and Dispersion (8:1b-3)

1b *That day a great persecution[4] broke out against the church in Jerusalem, and they were all dispersed among the regions of Judaea and Samaria, except the apostles.[5]*

2 *Stephen's body was taken up and buried by pious men, who made loud lamentation over him.*

3 *But Saul proceeded to ravage the church: he entered their houses one by one, dragged away men and women, and handed them over for imprisonment.*

1b-2 The law prescribed the duty of burying the bodies of executed persons, but discouraged public lamentation for them.[6] Stephen, at any rate, received the last tribute due to him from devout[7] men who evidently disapproved of his condemnation and execution.

His death, however, was the signal for an immediate campaign of repression against the Jerusalem church. If we read the present paragraph in its wider context, we may conclude that it was the Hellenists in the church (the group in which Stephen had been a leader) who formed the main target of attack, and that it was they for the most part who were compelled to leave Jerusalem.[8] Some of them, indeed, may have been convinced that, by its rejection of Stephen's testimony, the city had incurred irrevocable doom; it was the path of wisdom, therefore, to abandon it.[9] From this time onward the Jerusalem church appears to have been a predominantly "Hebrew" body.[10]

The twelve apostles remained in Jerusalem, partly no doubt because they conceived it to be their duty to stay at their post,[11] and partly, one may gather, because the popular resentment was directed not so much at them as

---

4. Gk. διωγμός. The Western text adds "and tribulation" (καὶ θλῖψις), the term employed in 11:19.

5. The Western text adds "who remained in Jerusalem" (which is in any case implied).

6. Mishnah, *Sanhedrin* 6.6.

7. Gk. εὐλαβεῖς, used regularly in the NT of devout Jews (see pp. 53-55, nn. 16, 23 [on 2:5]); here probably Jewish followers of Jesus are meant.

8. Cf. 11:19-20.

9. See M. Hengel, *Acts and the History of Earliest Christianity*, E.T. (London, 1979), pp. 74-75. The mention of Mnason in 21:16 (more than twenty years later) shows that not all Hellenistic believers abandoned Jerusalem.

10. That is, until its dispersal *c*. A.D. 66, and even more so in exile after that. After the Emperor Hadrian refounded Jerusalem in A.D. 135 as the Roman colony of Aelia Capitolina, the church of Jerusalem was a completely Gentile-Christian community, having no continuity with the first-century Jewish-Christian church of Jerusalem.

11. Luke may have seen a theological fitness in their remaining in Jerusalem, as the leaders of the latter-day people of God; cf. G. W. H. Lampe, *St. Luke and the Church of Jerusalem* (London, 1969), p. 21.

at the leaders of the Hellenists in the church. The persecution and dispersion, however, brought about a beginning of the fulfilment of the risen Lord's commission to his disciples: "you will be my witnesses in Jerusalem, and in all Judaea and Samaria . . ." (1:8). "The churches of God in Christ Jesus which are in Judaea" (to borrow Paul's language in 1 Thess. 2:14)[12] traced their inception as separate communities from this time of persecution.

3 The prime agent in the repressive campaign was Saul of Tarsus, who now carried into more effective action the attitude to the new movement which he had displayed at the stoning of Stephen. Armed with the necessary authority from the chief-priestly leaders of the Sanhedrin,[13] he harried[14] the church, arresting its members in their own homes and sending them off to prison. A zealot for the ancestral traditions of his nation,[15] he saw that the new faith menaced those traditions. Drastic action was called for: these people, he thought, were not merely misguided enthusiasts whose sincere embracing of error called for patient enlightenment; they were deliberate impostors, proclaiming that God had raised from the tomb to be Lord and Messiah a man whose manner of death was sufficient to show that the divine curse rested on him.[16]

2. Philip in Samaria (8:4-8)

4 *Those, then, who were dispersed went about spreading the good news.*

5 *Philip went down to a[17] city of Samaria and began to preach Christ to them.*

6 *The crowds paid attention as one man to what Philip was saying as they listened to him and saw the signs which he performed.*

7 *For unclean spirits, with a loud noise, came out of many who were possessed,[18] and many paralyzed and lame people were cured.*

8 *There was great joy in that city.*

4 As the old Israel had its dispersion among the Gentiles, so must the new people of God be dispersed.[19] The words of an apocalyptic writer later in the

---

12. See on 9:31 (p. 196).

13. Cf. 9:1-2; 26:10.

14. Gk. ἐλυμαίνετο, a verb which, according to Lake-Cadbury (*ad loc.*), refers especially to the ravaging of a body by a wild beast. Paul himself says that he "tried to destroy" the church (Gal. 1:13), using a military term (πορθέω) which denotes the storming of a besieged city (cf. Acts 9:21).

15. Cf. Gal. 1:14.

16. Cf. Gal. 3:13, and see on 5:30 above (pp. 112-13 with n. 40).

17. Gk. εἰς πόλιν τῆς Σαμαρείας, read by C D E Ψ byz. The article τήν is added before πόλιν by P74 A B 1175 *pc* (ℵ has the aberrant reading εἰς τὴν πόλιν τῆς Καισαρείας). See p. 165.

18. Lit., "many of those who had unclean spirits came out. . . ."

19. Cf. the epistolary superscriptions in Jas. 1:1 ("To the twelve tribes in the dispersion") and 1 Pet. 1:1 ("To the exiles of the dispersion").

first century A.D. have been adduced as a parallel to Luke's narrative here: "I will scatter this people [the Jews of Judaea after A.D. 70] among the Gentiles, that they may do the Gentiles good" (2 Bar. 1:4).[20] On the present occasion, the dispersed believers did the utmost good to the people among whom they went, by telling them the good news of the deliverance accomplished by Christ. Not only did they do this in Palestine, but some of them carried the message much farther afield, according to a later passage of Acts which begins with the same wording as this (11:19-26).

5 For the present, however, the interest of the narrative is concentrated on Philip, another Hellenistic leader who, like Stephen, was one of the seven almoners appointed to manage the daily administration of the communal fund. Driven from his work in Jerusalem, Philip went north to Samaria and preached the gospel there.

Between the populations of Judaea and Samaria there was a longstanding cleavage, going back to the isolation of Judah from the other tribes of Israel in the settlement period (cf. Deut. 33:7). This cleavage found notable expression in the disruption of the Hebrew monarchy after Solomon's death (c. 930 B.C.). In spite of attempts to effect a reconciliation in postexilic times,[21] the cleavage was widened when the Samaritans were refused a share in the rebuilding of the Jerusalem temple and erected a rival temple on their sacred hill Gerizim.[22] The temple on Gerizim was destroyed by the Hasmonaean ruler John Hyrcanus I (134-104 B.C.) when he conquered Samaria and added it to his own realm.[23] With the Roman conquest of Palestine in 63 B.C., the Samaritans were liberated from Judaean domination, but the New Testament and the writings of Josephus bear ample witness to the unfriendly relations which persisted between the two groups.

It was thus a bold movement on Philip's part to preach the gospel to the Samaritans. The Samaritans did, however, share with the Jews the hope of a coming deliverer whom they envisaged in terms of the prophet like Moses of Deut. 18:15-19;[24] at a later time, if not at this stage, they described him as the Taheb or "restorer."[25] Philip would be able to build on this hope when he "began to preach Christ to them": Jesus, it appears, was already

20. This work, the Syriac *Apocalypse of Baruch*, belongs to the last quarter of the first century.

21. And even in preexilic times, under Hezekiah (2 Chron. 30:1-11) and Josiah (2 Kings 23:21-23).

22. Josephus, *Ant.* 11.310, 322-24, 346.

23. Josephus, *Ant.* 13.256. Even after the destruction of their temple, the Samaritans continued to worship on Mount Gerizim (as indeed they still do); cf. John 4:20, where the woman of Sychar says to our Lord, "Our fathers worshiped on this mountain."

24. See on 3:22-23; 7:37.

25. See J. Macdonald, *The Theology of the Samaritans* (London, 1964), pp. 362-71. It was probably to the Taheb (by whatever name she called him) that the woman of Sychar referred in John 4:25—"when he comes, he will show us all things."

identified by his followers in Jerusalem, both "Hebrews" and "Hellenists," as the promised prophet like Moses.

It is uncertain which city of Samaria was evangelized by Philip. The ancient city called Samaria had been refounded by Herod the Great and renamed Sebaste, in honor of the Roman emperor,[26] but it was a Hellenistic city, and the impression given by our narrative is that the people to whom Philip preached were genuine Samaritans. Another suggestion is that it was Gitta, which (according to Justin Martyr) was the home town of Simon Magus.[27] Most probably we are intended to think of a place in the neighborhood of Shechem. According to the Fourth Gospel, both John the Baptist and Jesus had been active for a period in this area (John 3:23; 4:4-42); their activity could have provided a foundation on which Philip built.[28]

6-8 Whichever city it was, Philip's ministry was marked by works of exorcism and healing so striking that great numbers believed his message and were filled with rejoicing. As usual in the record of Acts, the beneficiaries of the works of healing were paralytics and lame people. As in the ministry of Jesus himself and of his apostles, so in the ministry of Philip these works of mercy and power were visible "signs" confirming the message that he proclaimed.

3. Simon Magus Believes and Is Baptized (8:9-13)

9 *Now at that time there was in the city a man named Simon, practising magic and striking amazement into the Samaritan nation with his claim to be someone great.*

10 *They all paid heed to him, great and small: "This man," they said, "is the power of God which is called great."*

11 *They paid him the more heed because he had struck amazement into them for a long time with his magic arts.*

12 *But when they believed Philip as he preached the good news of the*

---

26. Gk. Σεβαστός (cf. 25:21) was used as the equivalent of Lat. *Augustus*.

27. Justin, *First Apology* 26.2 (Gitta is commonly identified with modern Jett, *c.* 11 miles southeast of Caesarea). Justin himself was a native of Samaria, having been born *c.* A.D. 100 at Flavia Neapolis (modern Nablus, about a mile west of ancient Shechem), founded as a colony by Vespasian in A.D. 72.

28. Cf. J. A. T. Robinson, "The 'Others' of John 4:38," in *Twelve New Testament Studies*, SBT 34 (London, 1962), pp. 61-66, in which it is argued that the "others" who labored there were John the Baptist and his companions, into whose "labors" the disciples of Jesus now entered. This is in part a reply to O. Cullmann, "Samaria and the Origins of the Christian Mission," E.T. in *The Early Church* (London, 1956), pp. 183-92, where it is argued that the "others" were Philip and his helpers, into whose labors the apostles Peter and John subsequently entered (cf. vv. 14-17 below). On Philip's Samaritan mission see also C. H. H. Scobie, "The Origins and Development of Samaritan Christianity," *NTS* 19 (1972-73), pp. 390-414; R. J. Coggins, "The Samaritans and Acts," *NTS* 28 (1981-82), pp. 423-34; M. Hengel, *Between Jesus and Paul*, E.T. (London, 1983), pp. 121-26.

kingdom of God and the name of Jesus Christ, they were baptized,
both men and women.

13 *Even Simon himself believed and was baptized, and adhered to*
Philip, and as he saw signs and great works of power being per-
formed, he was amazed.

9-11 Simon Magus plays an extraordinary role in early Christian literature. The word "magus" originally denoted a member of the Median priestly
tribe,[29] but it came to be used in an extended sense of a practitioner of
various kinds of sorcery and even quackery, like Elymas, the sorcerer of
Paphos in Cyprus, whom we meet later in the narrative of Acts (13:6-11).
The "magi" or "wise men" from the east (Matt. 2:1), who saw the rising star
of the newborn king of the Jews, were evidently astrologers. This Simon is
depicted in postapostolic writings as the father of all Gnostic heresies.[30]
Justin Martyr tells how he secured a following of devotees not only in
Samaria but in Rome, to which he went in the time of Claudius.[31] In the
apocryphal *Acts of Peter* (4-32) he is said to have corrupted the Christians in
Rome by his false teaching and made the authorities ill-disposed toward
them, but to have been worsted at last in a magical contest with Peter. But it
is in the pseudo-Clementine *Recognitions* and *Homilies* that the Simon
legend is most curiously elaborated: in them he not only appears as the
untiring adversary of Peter but seems, to some extent at least, to serve as a
camouflage for Paul, reflecting anti-Pauline sentiments among some of the
Ebionites and similar Jewish-Christian groups.[32] It has been thought by
some scholars that the heresiarch Simon, founder of the Gnostic sect of the

29. See J. H. Moulton, *Early Zoroastrianism* (London, 1913), pp. 182-253.

30. Irenaeus (*Against Heresies* 1.16) avers that Simon was the source of Gnosticism—of "the knowledge which is falsely so called" (τῆς ψευδωνύμου γνώσεως), he
says, quoting 1 Tim. 6:20, and that the sect of the Simonians was derived from him. He
further tells how Simon had as his consort a woman named Helena, whom he had
redeemed from slavery at Tyre, and whom he declared to be the current incarnation of
Ἔννοια (the thought or conception of the divine mind), from which the angelic powers
and the material universe had proceeded. Hippolytus (*Refutation of All Heresies* 6.2-15)
gives a fuller account of Simon's alleged system, based on a Gnostic work entitled *The
Great Disclosure* (ἡ μεγάλη ἀπόφασις), and relates how he allowed himself to be buried
alive in Rome, promising to rise on the third day—but the promise was not fulfilled.

31. At Rome, according to Justin (*First Apology* 26.2), Simon was honored with
a statue dedicated "To Simon the holy god"; but either Justin or the Simonians themselves
may have been misled by an inscription beginning SEMONI SANCO DEO, "To the god
Semo Sancus," in honor of an ancient Sabine divinity who safeguarded oaths (cf. *CIL*
6.567), which they misread as SIMONI SANCTO DEO. Tertullian (*Apology* 13.9) also
connects the statue and inscription with Simon Magus.

32. Cf. F. J. Foakes-Jackson, *Peter: Prince of Apostles* (London, 1927), pp.
165-82; H.-J. Schoeps, *Theologie und Geschichte des Judenchristentums*, pp. 127-35;
"Simon Magus in der Haggada?" in *Aus frühchristlicher Zeit* (Tübingen, 1950), pp.
239-54.

Simonians,[33] was originally a different person from the Simon of Acts, but that they became confused in later tradition.[34] More probably they were the same person: Luke knows more about Simon than he records; in this account he relates only what he judged relevant to his purpose.

At any rate, the Samaritan Simon impressed his fellow-countrymen greatly with the exercise of his magic powers, so much so that they accepted his own account of himself and regarded him as the grand vizier of the supreme God, the channel both of divine power and of divine revelation.[35]

12-13   But Simon Magus himself was impressed by the actions and words of Philip. Like the magicians of Egypt in the presence of Moses, he recognized that the messenger of the true God had access to a source of power that oustripped his own. The proclamation heralded by such an envoy must be accepted with respect, and Simon "believed." The nature of his belief must remain uncertain. No doubt it was sincere as far as it went, but it was superficial and inadequate. Jesus himself, we are told in John 2:23-24, attached little value to the faith that rests on miracles alone. Yet, when the others who believed Philip's announcement of the "good news of the king-dom of God and the name of Jesus Christ"[36] were baptized, Simon came to receive baptism too, and remained in Philip's company. No question seems to have been raised about the propriety of baptizing Samaritans: even if Samaritans were excluded from the scope of the original mission of the Twelve, they were indubitably "lost sheep of the house of Israel" (Matt. 10:5-6). The adhesion of Simon and his followers to Philip and his converts

33. By the middle of the third century only a handful of the Simonians survived (Origen, *Against Celsus* 1.57).

34. Cf. G. Salmon, "Simon Magus," *DCB* 4 (London, 1887), pp. 681-88; also *ODCC*, *s.v.* "Simon Magus."

35. Many real or imagined parallels to "the power of God which is called great" (ἡ δύναμις τοῦ θεοῦ ἡ καλουμένη μεγάλη) have been adduced. Particularly apposite is the Lydian inscription cited by W. M. Ramsay (*BRD*, p. 117; cf. *New Docs.* 3 [1978], §7): εἷς θεὸς ἐν οὐρανοῖς Μὴν οὐράνιος μεγάλη δύναμις τοῦ ἀθανάτου θεοῦ ("one God in heaven, heavenly Mēn, great power of the immortal God"). A feminine counterpart to this acclamation is supplied by a Samaritan inscription in honor of Korē (cf. D. Flusser, "The Great Goddess of Samaria," *IEJ* 25 [1975], pp. 13-20, pl. 2; *New Docs.* 1 [1976], § 68): εἷς θεὸς ὁ πάντων δεσπότης μεγάλη Κόρη ἡ ἀνείκητος ("one God, the ruler of all, great Korē [Maiden] the unconquered"). On Simon Magus see also R. P. Casey, "Simon Magus," in *Beginnings* I.5, pp. 151-63; A. Ehrhardt, *The Framework of the New Testament Stories* (Manchester, 1964), pp. 161-64; M. Smith, "The Account of Simon Magus in Acts 8," *H. A. Wolfson Jubilee Volume*, II (Jerusalem, 1965), pp. 735-49; K. Beyschlag, "Zur Simon-Magus-Frage," *ZTK* 68 (1971), pp. 395-426; *Simon Magus und die christliche Gnosis*, WUNT 16 (Tübingen, 1974); J. W. Drane, "Simon the Samaritan and the Lucan Concept of Salvation History," *EQ* 47 (1975), pp. 131-37; C. K. Barrett, "Light on the Holy Spirit from Simon Magus (Acts 8, 4-25)," in *Les Actes des Apôtres: Traditions, Rédaction, Théologie*, ed. J. Kremer, BETL 48 (Leuven, 1979), pp. 281-95.

36. Cf. 1:3 (exposition and notes on pp. 31-33).

might have given a peculiar color to Samaritan Christianity, but it was not destined to last long.

4. Peter and John Visit Samaria (8:14-17)

14 *When the apostles in Jerusalem heard that Samaria had received the word of God, they sent Peter and John to them.*

15 *When Peter and John came down, they prayed for the converts, asking that they might receive the Holy Spirit.*

16 *As yet he had not fallen on any of them; they had only been baptized into the name of the Lord Jesus.*

17 *Then Peter and John laid their hands on them, and they received the Holy Spirit.*

14 News of Philip's evangelistic enterprise in Samaria was brought to Jerusalem, and the apostles sent two of their number to Samaria to inspect this work. In the earlier years of the Christian mission, the Jerusalem apostles seem to have regarded it as their duty to exercise a general supervision over the progress of the gospel wherever it might be carried (cf. 11:22). Peter and John, the two leaders of the apostolate, carried out this mission. This is the last occasion on which John plays any part by name in the narrative of Acts; here, as before, his role is a silent one alongside Peter's. John, with his brother James, had once suggested that fire should be called down from heaven on a Samaritan community for its inhospitable behavior to their Master (Luke 9:52-55). It was with a different attitude that he now set out for Samaria with Peter. The earlier ban on the apostles' entering any city of the Samaritans (Matt. 10:5) had been rescinded by the unlimited commission of witness laid on them by the risen Christ, in which Samaria was one of the areas explicitly mentioned (Acts 1:8).

Philip now disappears from the Samaritan scene. It has been held that the account of Peter and John's visit was originally an alternative to the account of Philip's mission;[37] but Philip's mission is presupposed as a background to the events of Peter and John's visit.

15-17 The sequel to the apostles' arrival has been the subject of much theological debate. Unlike the Jerusalem converts on the day of Pentecost, the Samaritan converts, although baptized by Philip "into the name of the Lord Jesus,"[38] had not at the same time received the gift of the Holy

---

37. J. Behm, *Die Handauflegung im Urchristentum* (Leipzig, 1911), pp. 24-36, envisages two sources in Acts 8:1-25, in the former of which the Samaritans are evangelized by Philip, in the latter by Peter and John; v. 14 being the editorial link between the two.

38. This expression (εἰς τὸ ὄνομα τοῦ κυρίου ᾿Ιησοῦ), repeated in 19:5, differs somewhat from ἐν τῷ ὀνόματι ᾿Ιησοῦ Χριστοῦ in 2:38; 10:48 (see p. 70 with n. 98). The phrase εἰς τὸ ὄνομα is common in a commercial context, where some

Spirit. But when Peter and John came to their city, they prayed for them, asking God to grant them the Holy Spirit, and then, when they laid their hands on the converts, the Holy Spirit came on them. It is clearly implied that their reception of the Spirit was marked by external manifestations such as had marked his descent on the earliest disciples at Pentecost.[39]

Many ancient and modern commentators have inferred that what Peter and John did was to perform the rite of confirmation; some have inferred further that confirmation can be administered only by an apostle or someone in the succession of the apostolic ministry (i.e., in episcopal orders). But it is straining the sense of the present narrative to extract this meaning from it. If confirmation by an apostle were necessary for the reception of the Spirit,[40] one might have expected this to be stated more explicitly in one or more of the relevant New Testament passages. But no such thing is hinted at, even in passages where it would certainly be introduced if there were any substance in it. It is not suggested by Paul when he speaks in 2 Cor. 1:21-22 of Christians' being anointed, sealed, and given the Spirit in their hearts as a guarantee; he does not include the power of thus imparting the Spirit among the spiritual gifts listed in 1 Cor. 12:4-11, and when he thanks God that he did not baptize more than a handful of his Corinthian converts (1 Cor. 1:14-16) the whole force of his argument would disappear if we had to suppose that, even so, he confirmed them all. In other places in Acts, too, there is no hint that apostolic hands were laid on converts before they received the Spirit. Nothing is said about this being done to the Pentecostal believers at Jerusalem (2:38-42) or, later, to the household of Cornelius at Caesarea (10:44-48). The only near parallel to the present occasion is the exceptional case of the Ephesian disciples in 19:1-7. In general, it seems to be assumed throughout the New Testament that those who believe and are baptized have also the Spirit of God.

---

property is transferred or paid "into the name" of someone. So the person baptized "into the name of the Lord Jesus" bears public witness to having passed into the ownership of Jesus, now acknowledged as Lord. The trinitarian εἰς τὸ ὄνομα formula of Matt. 28:19 (cf. *Didachē* 7.1) was appropriate for "disciples of all the nations," turning from paganism to serve the living God, whereas Jews and Samaritans, who already worshiped the one true God, were required only to confess Jesus as Lord (cf. G. F. Moore, *Judaism*, I [Cambridge, Mass., 1927], pp. 188-89).

39. Cf. N. B. Stonehouse, "The Gift of the Holy Spirit," *WTJ* 13 (1950-51), pp. 10-11: "one must recognize the peculiar appropriateness in a volume largely concerned with the external course of early Christian history of centering attention upon the extraordinary miraculous power of the Spirit in the accomplishment of the divine plan for the people of God."

40. See for this point of view A. J. Mason, *The Relation of Confirmation to Baptism* (London, 1891); G. Dix, *Confirmation or the Laying On of Hands?* (London, 1936); *The Theology of Confirmation in Relation to Baptism* (London, 1946); N. Adler, *Taufe und Handauflegung* (Münster, 1951); and, for a masterly critique of it, G. W. H. Lampe, *The Seal of the Spirit* (London, 1951).

In the present instance, some special evidence may have been necessary to assure the Samaritans, so accustomed to being despised as outsiders by the people of Jerusalem, that they were fully incorporated into the new community of the people of God. It was one thing for them to be baptized by a free-lance evangelist like Philip, but not until they had been acknowledged and welcomed by the leaders of the Jerusalem church did they experience the signs which confirmed and attested their membership in the Spirit-possessed society. "The imposition of hands is then," in the words of G. W. H. Lampe, "primarily a token of fellowship and solidarity; it is only secondarily an effective symbol of the gift of the Spirit; it becomes such a symbol solely in virtue of being a sign of incorporation into the Church of the Spirit."[41]

Luke presents the Samaritan mission as the first important advance in the Christian mission. The record of a Samaritan "Pentecost" implies that a new nucleus of the expanding community has been established, so that the gospel could now "radiate outwards from this new centre of the Spirit's mission."[42] Moreover, "the new Israel of the Church of Jesus Christ had succeeded in bringing the whole kingdom of David under the sway of his Son's sceptre, something the Jews had tried, with much less success, by force of arms during the last five hundred years."[43]

5. Peter and Simon Magus (8:18-24)

18 *When Simon saw that the Spirit[44] was given through the laying on of the apostles' hands, he offered them money.*

19 *"Give me also this authority," he said, "so that anyone on whom I lay my hands may receive the Holy Spirit."*

20 *But Peter said to him, "Perdition take you and your silver together, for thinking that the gift of God could be obtained with money.*

21 *You have no part or share in this matter, for your heart is not upright before God.*

22 *So repent of this wickedness of yours, and pray to the Lord that the thought of your heart may be forgiven.*

23 *I see that you are still full of gall and wormwood, still wearing the fetters of unrighteousness."*

24 *Simon replied, "Do you please pray to the Lord for me, so that none of the things you have said may come on me."[45]*

---

41. Lampe, *The Seal of the Spirit*, p. 70.

42. Lampe, *The Seal of the Spirit*, p. 72.

43. A. Ehrhardt, *The Acts of the Apostles* (Manchester, 1969), p. 47.

44. For "Spirit" (πνεῦμα), the reading of ℵ B cop^sa, the amplified expression "the Holy Spirit" (τὸ πνεῦμα τὸ ἅγιον) appears in P45.74 A C D E Ψ byz lat syr cop^bo.

45. The Western text adds (awkwardly, at the end of the sentence), "who never stopped weeping copiously."

18-19 Whether the external signs which accompanied the reception of the Spirit on this occasion were identical with the Pentecostal signs or not, they were at any rate of so impressive a nature that Simon Magus craved the power to reproduce them at will. Now he felt he was getting near the heart of these mysteries; the latest phenomena were obviously associated with the imposition of hands. If only they could be associated with the imposition of *his* hands, what an access of authority and prestige would be his! So, regarding Peter and John as extraordinarily gifted practitioners of religious magic, he offered to buy from them a share in their secret power. It is this act of Simon that has given the term "simony" to our religious vocabulary.

20-23 Simon was quite unprepared for the stern words which his simple-minded request evoked. On an earlier occasion Peter and John were unable to give silver or gold (3:6); now they refused to accept any, and were shocked that it should have been offered to them. Simon's idea that God's free gift could be bought and sold showed that he had no appreciation at all of the inward character of the gospel or the operation of the Spirit. "Perdition take your silver," said Peter, "as it will take you too unless you repent and seek forgiveness for your wicked thought." Simon had believed Philip's message and been baptized, but he still manifested the signs of his old unregenerate nature. The poisonous root of superstitious self-seeking had not been eradicated from his heart; his soul was still held fast in the "fetters of unrighteousness."[46] It was doubtful, in Peter's eyes, if Simon had experienced the grace of God in any real sense. Simon interpreted all that he saw and heard in terms of his own standards, but the gospel belonged to a completely new dimension, to which he remained a stranger. In this realm he clearly had "neither part nor share."

Luke's account of this confrontation between Peter and Simon provides the archetype for accounts of later confrontations between the two. Philip might have been content with Simon's attachment to his converts, but the more stringent requirements of apostolic orthodoxy could find no room for Simon and his followers in the believing community. Those who care to speculate on the might-have-beens of history may consider what the outcome would have been if Simon and his followers had been incorporated in the church at this early stage, and decide whether it would have been a good thing or a bad thing for the progress of Christianity.[47] Arnold Ehrhardt felt

---

46. On the other hand, Peter may mean that Simon is heading for a bitter end: "I can see that you are doomed to taste the bitter fruit and wear the fetters of sin" (NEB). The construction (the verb "to be" followed by εἰς) denotes destination in papyri, and has been so used in v. 20 (lit., "may your silver be for perdition," εἴη εἰς ἀπώλειαν). Peter's language has an OT flavor; cf. Deut. 29:18 (echoed in Heb. 12:15) and Isa. 58:6, noting particularly ἐν χολῇ καὶ πικρίᾳ in LXX of the former text and σύνδεσμον ἀδικίας in LXX of the latter.

47. If Simon had remained within the church, there might have been more

that "the Church lost a man here, who might have been saved; St Peter trampled down the new plantation of St Philip."[48] Others will judge the situation differently.[49]

24 Simon was terror-stricken. That he should have incurred the displeasure of men who apparently had so much power at their command was an awful thought; the Western text which tells us that he kept on weeping all the time Peter was speaking may be true enough to the facts, if Simon was the emotionally unstable type of medium who is not unknown in our own day, although the picture does not agree so well with the Simon Magus of later tradition. Peter had told him to pray for forgiveness, but to Simon's way of thinking the prayers of such wielders of power as Peter and John would be more prevalent than his own, so he begged them to pray for him. Arnold Ehrhardt commends Simon for the "unexpected humility expressed in his beautiful reply" to Peter's denunciation; he confesses, indeed, "to a feeling that Simon comes out much better from this encounter with the apostles than the tempestuous St Peter, who gives him no word of consolation."[50]

Canonical literature bids farewell to Simon with this entreaty on his lips that by the apostles' intercession he may escape the judgment pronounced on his crooked heart.[51] Later records of his activity give the impression that either they did not intercede for him or else their intercession was ineffective. Even so, Simon and his followers continued to be known as Christians, as Justin Martyr admits[52]—a tribute, perhaps, to what Simon learned during the short time he spent in the company of Philip.

6. The Apostles Return to Jerusalem (8:25)

> 25 So, when they had borne their witness and spoken the word of the Lord, they made their way back to Jerusalem, and as they went they preached the gospel in many villages of the Samaritans.

25 Luke brings his account of the apostolic visitation to an end with a

plausibility in M. D. Goulder's diagnosis of Samaritan Gnosticism as one of "the two roots of Christian myth" in *The Myth of God Incarnate*, ed. J. Hick (London, 1977), pp. 64-86.

48. A. Ehrhardt, *The Acts of the Apostles*, p. 47.

49. Luke himself, for all his sympathy with Philip's Hellenistic mission, seems to approve of Peter's stern reproof of Simon. In his eyes Simon embodies the Hellenistic concept of the θεῖος ἀνήρ, the divinely possessed or divinely illuminated man—the only such person in Acts 8, "and Luke does not approve of him" (C. K. Barrett, "Theologia Crucis—in Acts," in *Theologia Crucis—Signum Crucis, Festschrift für E. Dinkler* [Tübingen, 1979], p. 80). See p. 209, n. 33.

50. A. Ehrhardt, *The Acts of the Apostles*, p. 46.

51. "Your heart is not straight (εὐθεῖα)," Peter tells him in v. 21 (similarly Ps. 77 [MT 78]:37, LXX).

52. Justin, *First Apology* 26.6.

"generalizing summary" before he resumes the story of Philip. After what Peter and John had seen of the work of God in Philip's temporary mission field, they had no hesitation in evangelizing other Samaritan communities as they took the southward road to Jerusalem.

7. Philip and the Ethiopian (8:26-40)

26 Now the angel of the Lord spoke to Philip. "Rise up," he said, "and make your way southward[53] by the road that goes down from Jerusalem to Gaza." (This is a desert road.)

27 So he rose up and set out on his way. There he came on a man of Ethiopia, a powerful official of Kandakē, queen of the Ethiopians, a chamberlain who was in charge of all her treasury. He had gone to Jerusalem to worship,

28 and on his return journey he was sitting in his chariot, reading the prophet Isaiah.

29 The Spirit said to Philip, "Go up to this chariot and join it."

30 So Philip ran up to him and heard him reading Isaiah the prophet. "Do you understand what you are reading?" he asked.

31 "How could I," said the man, "unless someone guides me?" And he invited Philip to get up and sit with him.

32 The passage of scripture which he was reading was this:

"Like a sheep he was led off to slaughter,
and like a lamb dumb before its shearer,
    so he does not open his mouth.

33 As he was humiliated his rights were taken away:
as for his progeny, who will declare it?
    because his life is taken away from the earth."

34 Then the chamberlain spoke up. "Tell me, please," he said to Philip: "who is the person about whom the prophet says this? Himself, or someone else?"

35 Then Philip began to speak: beginning at this scripture he told him the good news about Jesus.

36 As they journeyed along the road, they came to some water. "Look," said the chamberlain, "here is water.[54] What prevents me from being baptized?"[55]

38 He gave orders for the chariot to halt, and both of them, Philip and

---

53. Gk. κατὰ μεσημβρίαν. In LXX μεσημβρία regularly means "noon" (cf. περὶ μεσημβρίαν, 22:6 below), except in Dan. 8:4, 9 where it means "south" (Theodotion renders νότος). But here "southward" is the more natural sense (but see W. C. van Unnik, "Der Befehl an Philippus," ZNW 47 [1956], pp. 181-91).

54. P45 omits ἰδοὺ ὕδωρ.

55. Here the Western text adds: "And he said to him, 'If you believe with all your

the chamberlain, went down into the water, and Philip baptized him.

39 *When they came up out of the water, the Spirit of the Lord snatched Philip away,*[56] *and the chamberlain did not see him again; for he continued joyfully on his way.*

40 *As for Philip, he turned up at Azotus.*[57] *Then, passing through city after city, he preached the gospel in them all until he came to Caesarea.*

26   The story of Philip is now resumed. This part of it is told in a style which is in some respects reminiscent of the Old Testament narratives of Elijah.[58] While here, as in 5:19, the Greek phrase rendered "the angel of the Lord" is that used in LXX for the supernatural messenger who manifested the divine presence to human beings,[59] Luke's statement that "the angel of the Lord spoke to Philip, 'Rise up . . .'" is probably a vivid way of denoting Philip's divine guidance. In the following narrative it is difficult to see any real distinction between "the angel of the Lord" and "the Spirit of the Lord," although the Western text introduces a distinction in verse 39.

However that may be, Philip received a divine command to go south to join the Jerusalem-Gaza road—probably the road which ran by way of Beth-govrin, Ptolemy's Betogabris (refounded later as Eleutheropolis by Septimius Severus). The word "desert" might refer either to Gaza or to the road. The older city of Gaza was destroyed by the Hasmonaean king Alexander Jannaeus in 96 B.C.; a new city was built nearer the Mediterranean by Gabinius in 57 B.C., the old city, as Strabo says, "remaining desert."[60] On the other hand, it was important that Philip should know which road to take; had he taken another road, he would have missed the Ethiopian. Gaza figures in the Old Testament as one of the five cities of the Philistines.

27-28   Along the desert road to Gaza Philip came on a traveling chariot or covered wagon making its way southward; in it was seated the treasurer of the kingdom of Ethiopia (Nubia), who had made a pilgrimage to Jerusalem and was now returning home. The kingdom of Ethiopia lay on the Nile, south of the first cataract (at Aswan); its two chief cities were Meroe

---

heart, you may.' He said in answer, 'I believe that Jesus Christ is the Son of God.'" Although this addition is not found in the Byzantine text, it was incorporated by Erasmus in his printed editions; he thought it had been omitted through scribal carelessness. It is printed as v. 37 in KJV, but is properly omitted from the text of *The Greek New Testament according to the Majority Text*, ed. Z. C. Hodges and A. L. Farstad (Nashville, 1982), where it is mentioned in the apparatus as included in the Received Text.

56. The Western text reads "the Spirit of the Lord fell on the eunuch, and the angel of the Lord snatched Philip away."

57. Gk. εὑρέθη εἰς Ἄζωτον. With this use of the passive of εὑρίσκω cf. Fr. *se trouver*.

58. Cf. 1 Kings 18:12; 2 Kings 1:3; 2:16.

59. Cf. p. 140, n. 50; p. 143, n. 58 (on 7:35, 38).

60. Strabo, *Geography* 16.2.30 (μένουσα ἔρημος).

and Napata. The king of Ethiopia was venerated as the child of the sun and regarded as too sacred a personage to discharge the secular functions of royalty; these were performed on his behalf by the queen-mother, who bore the dynastic title Kandakē.[61]

The Ethiopian treasurer was probably a Gentile worshiper of the God of Israel. He is referred to by a term which may have the more general sense of "chamberlain" or the stricter sense of "eunuch."[62] Eunuchs were commonly employed as court officials in the Near East from antiquity until quite recent times. The law of Israel excluded eunuchs from religious privileges enjoyed by other members of the community (Deut. 23:1); the removal of this ban is foreshadowed in Isa. 56:3-5. At any rate, like the Greeks mentioned in John 12:20,[63] this man had visited Jerusalem as a worshiper, probably at the time of one of the great pilgrimage festivals, and was now beguiling his homeward journey by studying a scroll of the book of Isaiah in the Greek version.

29-31   The divine monitor (called the Spirit this time) instructed Philip to approach the chariot, and as he did so, he heard the Ethiopian reading aloud from his copy of Isaiah. Reading in antiquity was almost invariably done aloud.[64] Why this should be so will be apparent to anyone who tries to read a copy of an ancient manuscript: the words need to be spelled out, and this is done more easily aloud than in silence. In addition, beginners regularly read aloud; it requires considerable experience (not to say sophistication) to read silently, though this stage is reached more quickly with modern print than with ancient handwriting.

The actual passage of the prophecy which the Ethiopian was reading aloud gave Philip his cue immediately: "Do you understand what you are reading?"[65] he asked. The man frankly acknowledged that he did not—that he could not without a guide or interpreter. As Philip appeared to know what he was talking about, the reader invited him to come up into the chariot and sit beside him. He certainly could have found no more reliable guide to the meaning of what he read than the man who had thus strangely accosted him.

32-33   For the passage which he was reading was the great prophecy of the suffering Servant of the Lord which had found its fulfilment so recently

---

61. According to Bion of Soli (*Aethiopica* 1), "the Ethiopians do not reveal the fathers of their kings, but hand down a tradition that they are sons of the sun. They call the mother of each king Kandakē." See also Strabo, *Geography* 17.1.54; Pliny, *Natural History* 6.186; Dio Cassius, *History* 54.5.4.

62. Gk. εὐνοῦχος. Cf. Plutarch, *Demetrius* 25.5: "kings . . . were generally accustomed to have eunuchs as guardians of the treasury."

63. Cf. p. 149 with n. 82 (on 7:46).

64. In his *Confessions* (6.3) Augustine records as something worthy of note that Ambrose of Milan read silently.

65. There is word-play here (ἀρά γε γινώσκεις ἃ ἀναγινώσκεις), reproduced in the Latin Vulgate, *intellegis quae legis*?

in the sacrifice and death of Jesus of Nazareth. The prophet himself, as he gave utterance to these words, might well have wondered and "inquired what person or time was indicated by the Spirit of Christ within" him when thus "predicting the suffering of Christ and the subsequent glory" (1 Pet. 1:11), for it must have been almost impossible to understand how his words could be fulfilled until Jesus came and fulfilled them. Jesus himself appears to have spoken of his death in terms of this prophecy (Isa. 52:13–53:12)— for example, when he said that "the Son of man . . . came not to be served but to serve, and to give his life as a ransom for many" (Mark 10:45).[66] The words addressed to him by the heavenly voice at his baptism (Mark 1:11) implied that the royal Messiah, acclaimed by God as his Son in Ps. 2:7, was to fulfil his destiny in the mission mapped out for the Servant of the Lord introduced in Isa. 42:1. It was natural to link the oracle opening with "Behold my Servant" in Isa. 42:1 with that opening with similar words in Isa. 52:13. There is no evidence that anyone before the time of Jesus had identified the Isaianic Servant with the Davidic Messiah, but he seems to have identified them in his own person and by his own act. When he insisted that it was *written* concerning the Son of Man[67] that he should "suffer many things and be treated with contempt" (Mark 9:12), it is difficult to think of a more suitable scripture as the basis of such words than Isa. 52:13–53:12.

The section which Luke actually quotes (Isa. 53:7-8 LXX) does not indeed include any of the explicit statements of *vicarious* suffering found elsewhere in this "fourth Servant song." One may ask if, as often in the New Testament, the quotation of a few clauses from a "testimony" passage carries the whole context with it by implication:[68] this question could be answered with greater assurance here if some details were given of Philip's application of "this scripture." Luke certainly knows more of the context than is reproduced here: he cites Isa. 52:13 in Acts 3:13 and Isa. 53:12 in Luke 22:37. But if we pay attention only to the clauses that Luke reproduces, it would be difficult to deduce from them anything but a theology of suffering.

34-35 The Ethiopian's question, "who is the person about whom the prophet says this? Himself, or someone else?" often serves nowadays as the text for an academic essay or examination question, so numerous are the answers that have been offered.[69] But Philip found no difficulty, nor did he

66. These words are commonly supposed to echo the sense of Isa. 53:10, where the Servant's life is appointed as a guilt-offering (LXX περὶ ἁμαρτίας); see, on the other hand, M. D. Hooker, *Jesus and the Servant* (London, 1956), pp. 74-79 *et passim;* C. K. Barrett, "The Background of Mark 10:45," in *New Testament Essays: Studies in Memory of T. W. Manson,* ed. A. J. B. Higgins (Manchester, 1959), pp. 1-18.

67. On the relevance of the designation "the Son of Man" in this setting see M. Black, "Servant of the Lord and Son of Man," *SJT* 6 (1953), pp. 1-11. (See pp. 154-55 with nn. 104, 106, on 7:56.)

68. See C. H. Dodd, *According to the Scriptures* (London, 1952), pp. 88-94.

69. See C. R. North, *The Suffering Servant in Deutero-Isaiah* (Oxford, 1948),

hesitate between alternative answers. The prophet himself might not have known, but Philip knew, because the prophecy had come true in his day, and so, "beginning at this scripture, he told him the good news about Jesus." At a time when not one line of any New Testament document had been written, what scripture could any evangelist have used more fittingly as a starting point for presenting the story of Jesus to one who did not know him? It was Jesus, and no other, who offered up his life as a sacrifice for sin, and justified many by bearing their iniquities, exactly as had been written of the obedient Servant. As the historic fact of Jesus' undeserved suffering and death is certain, equally certain is it that through his suffering and death men and women of all nations have experienced forgiveness and redemption, just as the prophet foretold.[70]

36-38 Philip's persuasive exposition of the Servant's passion found its way home to the Ethiopian's heart. Did Philip also tell him, as Peter had told his Jerusalem audience on the day of Pentecost, that the appropriate response to such good news was repentance and baptism for the remission of sins and the reception of the Holy Spirit? We do not know. At any rate, as they journeyed on, they came to some running water—whether the Wadi el-Hesi northeast of Gaza, which is traditionally pointed out as the place, has been rightly or wrongly identified with it is totally uncertain. "See, here is water!" said the Ethiopian. "What is to prevent my being baptized?"[71] There

---

pp. 6-116, for a summary of the answers offered from pre-Christian times to the 1940s, and H. H. Rowley, *The Servant of the Lord and Other Essays on the Old Testament* (Oxford, ²1965), pp. 3-93, for a survey of answers given since 1921, when S. Mowinckel propounded the view that the prophet did say those things about himself.

70. On the interpretation of the Isaianic Servant Songs, especially the fourth, see also W. Zimmerli and J. Jeremias, *TDNT* 5, pp. 654-717 (*s.v.* παῖς θεοῦ); S. R. Driver and A. Neubauer, *The Fifty-Third Chapter of Isaiah according to the Jewish Interpreters* (Oxford, 1877); G. H. Dalman, *Der leidende und der sterbende Messias der Synagoge im ersten nachchristlichen Jahrtausend* (Berlin, 1888), and *Jesaja 53, das Prophetenwort vom Sühnleiden des Heilsmittlers mit besonderer Berücksichtigung der synagogalen Literatur* (Berlin, ²1914); J. J. Brierre-Narbonne, *Le Messie souffrant dans la littérature rabbinique* (Paris, 1940); H. W. Wolff, *Jesaja 53 im Urchristentum* (Berlin, 1950); H. W. Robinson, "The Cross of the Servant," in *The Cross in the Old Testament* (London, 1955), pp. 55-114; E. Lohmeyer, *Gottesknecht und Davidssohn*, FRLANT NF 43 (Göttingen, ²1953); A. Bentzen, *King and Messiah*, E.T. (London, 1955); E. Lohse, *Märtyrer und Gottesknecht*, FRLANT 64 (Göttingen, 1955); V. de Leeuw, *De Ebed Jahweh-Profetieën: Historisch-kritisch Onderzoek naar hun Ontstaan en hun Betekenis* (Assen, 1956); E. Fascher, *Jesaja 53 in christlicher und jüdischer Sicht* (Berlin, 1958); D. J. A. Clines, *I, He, We and They*, JSOT Sup. 1 (Sheffield, 1976); R. N. Whybray, *Thanksgiving for a Liberated Prophet*, JSOT Sup. 4 (Sheffield, 1978).

71. Gk. τί κωλύει με βαπτισθῆναι; From the use of the verb κωλύω here and in 10:47 (there on the lips of the preacher, not the convert), it has been inferred that it featured in a primitive baptismal formula (cf. also Mark 10:14 and parallels); this is doubtful. See O. Cullmann, *Baptism in the New Testament*, E.T., SBT 1 (London, 1950), pp. 71-80.

was nothing to prevent it, so the chariot was halted, they both went down into the water, and Philip baptized him.

This is the account in the original text. But at quite an early date (probably in the second century) an editor felt that this was not adequate. Philip must surely have satisfied himself of the genuineness of the Ethiopian's faith. (No doubt Philip was well satisfied, but there are some minds which cannot be content to leave such things to be inferred.) So some words were added in which Philip tests the man's faith, and he responds with a formal confession: "I believe that Jesus Christ is the Son of God."[72] The added words of the Western text reflect early Christian practice, to which the Ethiopian is made to conform.[73]

39 The divine purpose in sending Philip to the Gaza road was accomplished; he was now sped northward by the Spirit on another mission. The Western text, however, makes the *angel* of the Lord snatch Philip away, while the *Spirit* of the Lord falls on the Ethiopian.[74] The purpose of this textual alteration may be partly to bring in the angel of the Lord at the end of the episode, since he was active at the beginning of it; but the much more important effect of the longer reading is to make it clear that the Ethiopian's baptism was followed by the gift of the Spirit. Even with the shorter reading it is a reasonable inference that he did receive the Spirit,[75] although it would be an impermissible inference in the thinking of those who believe that the Spirit is bestowed only through the imposition of apostolic hands.[76] When the Ethiopian disappears from our view, continuing joyfully on his way, it need not be doubted that the joy which filled his heart was that "joy in the Holy Spirit" of which Paul speaks in Rom. 14:17.[77]

What became of him we cannot tell. According to Irenaeus, he became a missionary among his own people,[78] which we should naturally expect—although Irenaeus probably had no more specific information on the matter than we ourselves have. But with the record of his conversion Luke has begun to touch on the evangelization of Gentiles—a subject specially dear to his heart. The Ethiopians were regarded by the Greeks and their

---

72. See p. 173, n. 55.

73. See p. 418 (on 22:16); also O. Cullmann, *The Earliest Christian Confessions,* E.T. (London, 1949), pp. 19-20.

74. See p. 174, n. 56. For the action of the Spirit in snatching Philip away cf. the experiences of Elijah (p. 174, n. 58 above) and Ezekiel (Ezek. 3:14; 8:3).

75. Cf. G. W. H. Lampe, *The Seal of the Spirit,* pp. 43n., 65, 67.

76. See p. 169, n. 40.

77. Cf. Gal. 5:22, where "joy" figures next to "love" in "the fruit of the Spirit."

78. Irenaeus, *Against Heresies* 3.12.10. We have no record of the Ethiopic (Nubian) church earlier than the fourth century. See B. M. Metzger, "The Christianization of Nubia and the Old Nubian Version of the New Testament," in *Historical and Literary Studies,* NTTS 8 (Leiden, 1968), pp. 111-22.

neighbors, from Homer's time onward, as living on the edge of the world.[79] In Luke's day interest in them had been quickened by a Roman expedition of A.D. 61-63 which explored the Nile as far up as Meroe and beyond.[80] So soon after the risen Lord's commission to his disciples had their witness reached "the end of the earth" (1:8).

40 Philip next appeared at Azotus, the old Philistine city of Ashdod, some twenty miles north of Gaza. From there he headed north along the coastal road, preaching the gospel in all the cities through which he passed,[81] until at last he reached Caesarea.[82] There he seems to have settled down—at least, it is there that we find him when he makes his next appearance in the narrative, twenty years later (21:8). By that time he had become a family man, with four daughters, each one a prophetess—worthy children of such a father.[83]

79. Homer, *Odyssey* 1.23 (where the Ethiopians are called ἔσχατοι ἀνδρῶν, "the last of men").

80. Cf. Strabo, *Geography* 17.1.54; Pliny, *Natural History* 6.35.

81. Including probably Lydda and Joppa, soon afterward visited by Peter (9:32-43).

82. Caesarea was built by Herod the Great on the site of a Phoenician foundation, Strato's Tower, between Joppa and Dora. It was equipped with a splendid artificial harbor, so that it became the chief port in Herod's kingdom. He called the new city (completed in 13 B.C.) Caesarea in honor of Caesar Augustus. After A.D. 6 it became the residence of the Roman governors of Judaea, who established their official headquarters in Herod's praetorium (cf. 23:35). Vespasian was proclaimed emperor there in A.D. 69. After the Jewish war it remained the seat of government of the legate of the imperial province of Judaea, with a new status as a Roman colony *(Colonia Flavia Augusta Caesariensis)* and exemption from taxation. See Josephus, *BJ* 1.408-15; 3.409-13; *Ant.* 15.331-41; 16.136-41. Much of the Herodian and Roman city was extensively excavated from 1959 onward. See L. I. Levine, *Caesarea under Roman Rule,* SJLA 7 (Leiden, 1975).

83. See pp. 399-401 with nn. 8-10.

ACTS 9

C. CONVERSION OF SAUL OF TARSUS (9:1-31)

1. Saul's Expedition to Damascus (9:1-2)

1 As for Saul, he continued to breathe out murderous threats against
the Lord's disciples. He went to the high priest

2 and asked him for letters to the synagogues of Damascus, so that, if
he found any followers of The Way there, men or women, he might
bring them in chains to Jerusalem.

1 The narrative now returns to Saul of Tarsus and his campaign of repression against the believers in Jerusalem, which received passing mention in 8:3. He was not content with driving them from Jerusalem; they must be pursued and rooted out wherever they fled, not only within the frontiers of the land of Israel[1] but beyond them as well. "In the excess of my fury against them," as he was later to tell the younger Agrippa, "I pursued them even to foreign cities" (26:11). The great paragons of religious zeal in Israel's history—Phinehas,[2] Elijah,[3] and Mattathias[4] (father of the Maccabees)— were prepared to go to extremes of violence against the enemies of God, and they were the exemplars on whom Saul modeled himself in his zeal against the church.

2 When the Jewish state won its independence under the Hasmonaean dynasty of ruling priests (142 B.C.), the Romans, who patronized the new state for reasons of their own, required neighboring states to grant it the privileges of a sovereign state, including the right of extradition. A letter delivered at that time by a Roman ambassador to Ptolemy VIII of Egypt concludes with the demand: "If any pestilent men have fled to you from their own country [Judaea], hand them over to Simon the high priest, so that he may punish them according to their law" (1 Macc. 15:21). In 47 B.C. Julius Caesar confirmed those rights and privileges anew to the Jewish nation (although Judaea was no longer a sovereign state), and more particularly to

---

1. The land of Israel at this time consisted in the main of the Roman province of Judaea (which included Samaria) and Herod Antipas's tetrarchy of Galilee and Peraea.
2. Num. 25:7-13; Ps. 106:30-31.
3. 1 Kings 18:40; 19:10, 14.
4. 1 Macc. 2:23-28.

180

the high-priesthood.[5] Luke's narrative implies that the right of extradition continued to be enjoyed by the high priest under the provincial administration set up in A.D. 6. The followers of The Way whom Saul was authorized to bring back from Damascus were refugees from Jerusalem, not native Damascene disciples. The charge against them may have been complicity in Stephen's offense against the temple.

"The Way" is a designation for the new movement used several times in Acts (19:9, 23; 22:4; 24:14, 22; cf. also 16:17; 18:25-26). It was evidently a term used by the early followers of Jesus to denote their movement as the way of life or the way of salvation. Similar words are used in a religious sense elsewhere; a specially close parallel is the use of the Hebrew word for "way" in the Zadokite Work and other documents of the Qumran community to denote the membership and life-style of that community.[6]

The history of Damascus goes back to remote antiquity. It was a city in the days of Abraham, and at the time of the Israelite monarchy it was the capital of the most important Aramaean kingdom. Later it was the seat of administration of an Assyrian province. In Hellenistic times it was completely replanned, on the Hippodamian grid-system. From 64 B.C. on it belonged to the Roman province of Syria, but had a measure of municipal autonomy in the loose federation of cities called the Decapolis. There was a very large Jewish population in the city,[7] so it is not surprising that there were several synagogues, each exercising disciplinary supervision over its members.

2. The Light and Voice from Heaven (9:3-7)

3 As he went on his way he was approaching Damascus when suddenly a light from heaven flashed round about him.

---

5. Josephus, *Ant.* 14.192-95; see S. Safrai and M. Stern (ed.), *The Jewish People in the First Century,* I (Assen, 1974), p. 456.

6. CD 1.13; 2.6; 1QS 9.17-18; 10.20-21; see E. Repo, *Der "Weg" als Selbstbezeichnung des Urchristentums,* AASF B 132.2 (Helsinki, 1964). The Zadokite Work, discovered toward the end of the nineteenth century in two mutilated manuscripts in the ancient synagogue of Fostat (Old Cairo), and first published in *Fragments of a Zadokite Work,* ed: S. Schechter, I (Cambridge, 1910), revealed the presence in Damascus of a Jewish group (now known to have been closely related to, if not identical with, the Qumran community) bound together by covenant as a new and purified Israel, devoted to the Zadokite priesthood and a distinctive form of the messianic hope. See L. Ginzberg, *An Unknown Jewish Sect* (New York, 1976); P. R. Davies, *The Damascus Covenant,* JSOT Sup. 25 (Sheffield, 1983); also G. Vermes, *The Dead Sea Scrolls in English* (Harmondsworth, ²1975), pp. 95-117. If the "Damascus" of this document is to be understood literally, it may be asked what relation the covenanters of Damascus bore to the local disciples of Jesus, but it is probably impossible to answer the question with anything like certainty.

7. According to Josephus, *BJ* 2.561, the outbreak of the Judaean revolt in A.D. 66 was marked by the massacre of 10,500 Damascene Jews; in *BJ* 7.368, their number has risen to 18,000.

4 *He fell to the ground, and heard a voice saying to him, "Saul, Saul, why are you persecuting me?"*[8]

5 *"Who are you, my lord?" he asked. The other said,[9] "I am Jesus,[10] the one you are persecuting.*[11]

6 *But get up and go into the city, and you will be told what you must do."*

7 *The men who were traveling with him stood speechless; they heard the voice but did not see anyone.*[12]

3-6 Armed with the high priest's commission, Saul set out for Damascus, and had almost reached it when the momentous event took place. About midday[13] a light which outshone the sun flashed round him, and as he lay on the ground to which he had fallen, a voice sounded in his ears, addressing him in Aramaic:[14] "Saul! Saul! why are you persecuting me?"[15]

The voice which he heard, as far as literary parallels are concerned, may be recognized as the phenomenon known to the rabbis as *baṯ qôl*, "the daughter of the voice [of God]," the heavenly echo. In the latter days, they believed, when there were no more prophets to hear the direct voice of God, the echo of his voice might still occasionally be heard by some. The solemn repetition of the name of the person addressed is common in divine allocutions.[16] Saul probably discerned a divine quality about the voice as it spoke to him; hence "Who are you, my lord?" may be a better rendering of his

8. The Western addition, "It is hard for you to kick against the goads," is in two Greek MSS and some Latin and Syriac witnesses transferred here from v. 5 (see n. 11 below) in order to harmonize with 26:14.

9. The Byzantine text reads "The Lord said."

10. A few authorities, mainly Western in character, add "the Nazarene" from 22:8.

11. There is a Western addition here (drawn in part from 22:10 and 26:14): "it is hard for you to kick against the goads. And he, trembling and astonished, said, 'Lord, what will you have me to do?' And the Lord said to him" (the conjunction "but" at the beginning of v. 6 is consequently omitted). This addition occurs in no extant Greek MS, but is found in some Old Latin and Vulgate codices, and also in part as an asterisked reading in the Harclean Syriac. Erasmus, considering that the words had been accidentally lost from the Greek text, translated them back into the Greek NT; they thus formed part of the "Received Text" and so of KJV.

12. There is a Western addition, preserved only in the Old Latin codex h: "when he spoke. But he said to them, 'Raise me up from the earth'" (the opening words of v. 8 run accordingly: "And when they had raised him up . . .").

13. So 22:6; 26:13.

14. "In the Hebrew speech," says Paul in 26:14 (see p. 466, n. 24). Except in the Apocalypse, the "Hebrew" language in the NT regularly means Aramaic. G. H. Dalman reconstructs the Aramaic wording as *šāʾûl šāʾûl mā ʾatt rāḏᵉp̄innî* (*Jesus-Jeshua*, E.T. [London, 1929], p. 18). Was Aramaic spoken because it was Jesus' mother tongue or because it was Saul's mother tongue?

15. As Augustine put it, "it was the head in heaven crying out on behalf of the members that were still on earth" (*Sermon* 279.1).

16. Cf. Dalman, *Jesus-Jeshua*, p. 18.

response than "Who are you, sir?" But he was not prepared for the reply to his question: the one who spoke to him was Jesus, once crucified but now the heavenly Lord—the one whom he was zealously persecuting in the person of his followers.

Any attempt to explain Saul's Damascus-road experience in medical terms must reckon with its revolutionary and long-term effects. The extraordinary enhancement of illumination experienced by epileptics, as described (for example) by Dostoyevsky,[17] is a very different matter from a total conversion such as Saul underwent—a conversion of will, intellect, and emotion, which dictated the abiding purpose and direction of his subsequent life and activity. That the illumination was inward as well as external appears from his own language about the transition from unbelief to faith— "seeing the light of the gospel of the glory of Christ, who is the image of God. . . . For it is the God who said, 'Let light shine out of darkness,' who has shone in our hearts to give the light of the knowledge of the glory of God in the face of Christ" (2 Cor. 4:4, 6).

That Saul actually saw the risen Christ in addition to hearing his voice is not expressly stated in the conversion narrative itself, but is confirmed below in the words of Ananias (v. 17) and Barnabas (v. 27).[18] His own references to his conversion imply incidentally that he heard the voice of Christ but emphasize above all that he saw him as the risen and glorified one.[19] There are affinities between his conversion experience and Ezekiel's inaugural vision, in which the prophet saw the "likeness" of the heavenly throne and above it "a likeness as it were of a human form" (Ezek. 1:26);[20] but for Saul the one who bore a human form identified himself as a historical person: "I am Jesus." Few of Saul's distinctive insights into the significance of the gospel cannot be traced back to the Damascus-road event, or to the outworking of that event in his life and thought.[21]

As truly as Jesus the crucified one had appeared "alive after his passion" to Peter, James, and others on the first Christian Easter morning and the days that followed, so truly now, "as to one untimely born," did he appear to Saul (1 Cor. 15:5-8). His fellow-travelers (according to 22:9) saw the light that flashed so suddenly around them, but for them it was not accompanied by that blinding illumination within which wrought the revolution in the persecuting zealot, and diverted his zeal to the propagation of the faith which up to that moment he had endeavored to destroy.

17. See F. Dostoyevsky, *The Idiot*, E.T. (London, 1913), pp. 224-25; also the discussion in J. Klausner, *From Jesus to Paul*, E.T. (London, 1944), pp. 326-30.
18. Cf. 22:14; 26:16.
19. Cf. 1 Cor. 9:1; 15:8; Gal. 1:16.
20. Cf. C. Rowland, "The Influence of the First Chapter of Ezekiel on Jewish and Early Christian Literature" (diss. Cambridge, 1974); *The Open Heaven* (London, 1982), pp. 84-85, 95-96, *et passim*.
21. Cf. S. Kim, *The Origin of Paul's Gospel* (Tübingen/Grand Rapids, ²1984).

Saul's own account of his experience is not only adequate to the sequel: it is in character with it too. The more one studies it, the more one is driven to agree with the eighteenth-century statesman George Lyttelton, that "the conversion and apostleship of St. Paul alone, duly considered, was of itself a demonstration sufficient to prove Christianity to be a divine revelation."[22]

A striking modern parallel to the narrative is Sundar Singh's story of his own conversion after a period of bitter hostility to the gospel. Praying in his room in the early morning of December 18, 1904, he saw a great light. "Then as I prayed and looked into the light, I saw the form of the Lord Jesus Christ. It had such an appearance of glory and love. If it had been some Hindu incarnation I would have prostrated myself before it. But it was the Lord Jesus Christ whom I had been insulting a few days before. I felt that a vision like this could not come out of my own imagination. I heard a voice saying in Hindustani, 'How long will you persecute me? I have come to save you; you were praying to know the right way. Why do you not take it?' The thought then came to me, 'Jesus Christ is not dead but living and it must be He Himself.' So I fell at His feet and got this wonderful Peace which I could not get anywhere else. This is the joy I was wishing to get. When I got up, the vision had all disappeared, but although the vision disappeared the Peace and Joy have remained with me ever since."[23] Several circumstances make it difficult to set down this experience as a dream or as the effect of self-hypnotism; it is also interesting to be told that, to the best of his remembrance, "at that time he did not know the story of St. Paul's conversion; though, of course, on a point of that kind the human memory cannot be implicitly relied on"[24] (and even if he did not know the story at the time of his conversion, he knew it by the time he related his conversion in the words just quoted, and it may have influenced the wording of his narrative). Here too we cannot properly evaluate the Sadhu's account of his experience without taking into consideration the remarkable life which was its sequel and the exceptional signs that attended his ministry.[25]

7 The statement that Saul's fellow-travelers "stood speechless; they heard the voice, but did not see anyone," has sometimes been thought to conflict with his own statement, "we had all fallen to the ground" (26:14), and still more with his statement that the men who were with him "did not hear the voice of the one who was speaking to me" (22:9). The first discrep-

---

22. G. Lyttelton, *Observations on the Conversion and Apostleship of St. Paul* (London, 1747), paragraph 1, "a treatise," wrote Samuel Johnson, "to which infidelity has never been able to fabricate a specious answer" (*Lives of the Most Eminent English Poets* [London, 1779-81]).

23. B. H. Streeter and A. J. Appasamy, *The Sadhu* (London, 1921), pp. 6-8. It is of interest that the voice addressed him in Hindustani and not in English.

24. Streeter and Appasamy, *The Sadhu*, p. 8.

25. See pp. 236-37 below (on 12:10-11).

ancy is immaterial: presumably the others were able to get up while Saul remained lying on the ground. As for the other discrepancy, Chrysostom's explanation that the voice heard by the fellow-travelers was Saul's voice talking to the risen Lord[26] runs up against the difficulty that "the voice" in verse 7 is most naturally taken as referring back to the "voice" of verse 4. The more usual explanation is that, while the others heard a sound (like the crowd in John 12:29 which "said that it had thundered" when Jesus' prayer was answered by a heavenly voice), they did not distinguish an articulate voice.[27]

It is not made clear whether Saul's companions happened to be traveling in the same caravan, or had actually set out with him to attend him on his mission.[28] Since he was commissioned to bring the refugees in chains to Jerusalem, he would naturally have required the help of others (perhaps members of the temple police) to round them up and take them back.

3. Saul Enters Damascus (9:8-9)

8 *Saul got up from the ground, but when his eyes were opened he saw nothing; so they led him by the hand and brought him into Damascus.*

9 *He remained without sight for three days, and neither ate nor drank.*

8-9 At last Saul was able to rise from the ground, and when he did so, he was unable to see, "blinded by excess of light." His companions therefore took him by the hand and led him through the gate of Damascus to the place where, presumably, arrangements had been made for him to stay. There he stayed for three days, taking neither food nor drink. (There is no need to regard his abstinence as an early instance of fasting before baptism;[29] it was probably the result of shock.)

4. Ananias Sent to Saul (9:10-16)

10 *In Damascus there was a disciple named Ananias. To him the Lord said in a vision, "Ananias!" "Here I am, Lord," he replied.*

11 *The Lord said to him, "Get up and go to the street called Straight, and ask at the house of Judas for a man of Tarsus, named Saul. For, I tell you, he is praying*

26. Chrysostom, *Homilies on Acts* 47.

27. So J. H. Moulton, MHT I, p. 66. But his appeal to "an old and well-known distinction between the acc. and the gen. with ἀκούω" (contrast τὴν δὲ φωνὴν οὐκ ἤκουσαν in 22:9 with ἀκούοντες μὲν τῆς φωνῆς here) is not supported by Lukan usage; see R. G. Bratcher, "ἀκούω in Acts ix.7 and xxii.9," *ExT* 71 (1959-60), p. 243.

28. They are called his συνοδεύοντες, "those who were in the caravan with him" (cf. συνοδία, Luke 2:44).

29. The practice of fasting before Christian baptism is first attested in *Didachē* 7.4 and then in Justin, *First Apology* 61.2.

12 *and has seen [in a vision]³⁰ a man called Ananias coming in and placing his hands on him, so that he may recover his sight."*

13 *But Ananias answered, "Lord, I have heard about this man from many people—about all the harm he has done to your saints in Jerusalem.*

14 *And here he has authority from the chief priests to throw into chains all who call on your name."*

15 *"Be on your way," said the Lord to him; "this man is a chosen instrument for me, to bear my name before Gentiles and kings and Israelites.*

16 *I am going to show him all that he must suffer for the sake of my name."*

10-12 Toward the end of these three days, Saul, as he was praying, received a further vision, in which a man named Ananias came to him and laid his hands on him, with the result that his sight was restored. This Ananias turned out to be a real person, a man of Damascus who was a disciple of Jesus, although he was evidently not one of the fugitives from the persecution in Jerusalem.³¹ It appears that the gospel had already made its way independently to Damascus—possibly from its northern base in Galilee. Ananias knew, however, about the persecution in Jerusalem which had dispersed so many of the believers in that city, and he knew of the leading part that Saul had played in it. He knew, too, that Saul had come to Damascus with authority to arrest believers from Jerusalem who had fled there for refuge.³²

We may judge of Ananias's astonishment, then, when he in his turn received directions from the risen Christ³³ in a vision to go to the place where Saul was staying and lay his hands on him for the restoration of his sight. The "street called Straight," where Saul's host lived, is still one of the chief thoroughfares of Damascus, the *Darb al-Mustaqim*. The traditional location of the house of Judas is near its western end.

13-14 "Lord," said Ananias, as he received these instructions, "I have heard about this man from many people." He had not had any personal experience of Saul's harrying of the disciples, but those who could speak from firsthand knowledge had told him of Saul's activity, and the news of his coming to Damascus to prosecute his grim work there had reached the city before Saul himself arrived. When Ananias, in his reply to the Lord, spoke

30. The phrase "in a vision" (ἐν ὁράματι) is added in B and C, with the Byzantine text. Even if it is not part of the original text, it is exegetically true.

31. This may be inferred from the fuller account of Ananias and his character in 22:12.

32. The use of ἐκεῖσε rather than ἐκεῖ in τοὺς ἐκεῖσε ὄντας (22:5) implies that Saul went to Damascus to arrest those who had fled *thither*, not those who were regularly resident *there* (who would in any case not have been covered by his letters of extradition).

33. That "the Lord" in v. 10 is the risen Christ is evident from v. 17.

of "all who call on your name," he referred to the followers of Jesus, those who confessed him as Lord.[34] The background of the expression is to be found in Joel 2:32, "everyone who invokes the Lord's name will be saved," quoted by Peter on the day of Pentecost (Acts 2:21).

15 But Ananias's protest was overruled: the risen Lord had his eye on the man of Tarsus and had a great work for him to perform. In spite of his recent record as a persecutor, Saul was a chosen instrument[35] in the Lord's hand, a messenger who would spread the good news in Jesus' name more widely than anyone else. The Gentiles and their rulers, not only the people of Israel, would hear the proclamation of salvation from his lips. While Paul says that the revelation of God's Son which he received on the Damascus road was given in order that he might "proclaim him among the Gentiles" (Gal. 1:16), Luke consistently includes Jews among the beneficiaries of his ministry, in recognition of the fact that he did preach to Jews, as he was shortly to do in the synagogues of Damascus (v. 20), and numbered Jewish believers among his converts.

16 Moreover, Ananias was assured that, if Saul himself had inflicted suffering on those who believed in Jesus, he in his turn would have much suffering to endure for the sake of Jesus' name.[36]

5. Ananias Visits Saul (9:17-19a)

17 Ananias went off, entered the house, and placed his hands on him. "Brother Saul," he said, "the Lord—that is, Jesus, who appeared to you on the road by which you came—has sent me so that you may recover your sight and be filled with the Holy Spirit."
18 Immediately a scaly substance fell away from his eyes; he recovered his sight,[37] got up, and was baptized.
19a Then he took food and his strength was restored.

17 Ananias obediently made his way to the street called Straight, and entered the house of Judas. There, without delay, he fulfilled his commission, laying his hands on the blind man and addressing him in terms of brotherly friendship. The form of the name "Saul" in the original text at this

---

34. "All who call on your name" are the same as those called "your saints" in v. 13. "Saints" (ἅγιοι) is a common designation of Christians in the NT, especially in the Pauline letters; it denotes them as the people of God or Christ, set apart for him and his service.

35. For Paul's own sense of his election for special service see Rom. 1:1, 5; Gal. 1:15-16; Eph. 3:7-13.

36. On "suffering for the name" cf. 5:41; 21:13. Paul's own commentary on these words may be found in 2 Cor. 11:23-27. In the kingdom of Christ suffering for his sake is a token of his favor and an earnest of his reward (cf. 14:22; Matt. 5:11-12; Rom. 8:17; Phil. 1:29-30; 2 Thess. 1:5-8; 2 Tim. 2:12).

37. Several witnesses (C² E L 614 *pm* lat^p syr^hcl) add "immediately" (παραχρῆμα).

point—the same form as was used by the heavenly voice which Saul heard on the way[38]—suggests that Ananias spoke in Aramaic.

In his later speech to the Jerusalem populace from the top of the steps connecting the temple precincts with the Antonia fortress (22:14-16) Paul gives a fuller account of what Ananias said to him; in his speech before Agrippa (26:16-18) he includes Ananias's communication in what was said to him during the heavenly vision. In the present narrative, too, it is plain that the Damascus-road vision and the message of Ananias were mutually confirmatory; by this twofold communication Saul received his commission from the Lord.

In writing to the Galatians Paul is at pains to deny, in the most unqualified terms, that he received his apostolic commission from any mortal man, or through any mortal man: he received it, he asserts, immediately from the Christ who was revealed to him as God's Son (Gal. 1:1, 11-20). How does this square with the part ascribed to Ananias in Acts?

In the first place, Paul in Galatians is answering the charge that he was dependent, for such missionary authority as he might possess, on the apostles in Jerusalem. The part played by Ananias could not have affected the argument one way or the other. A private disciple like Ananias could not in any case have had the power to commission him. In the second place, Ananias for this special purpose occupied such an exalted status that his words to Saul were the words of the risen Christ. Having been sent by the risen Christ to lay his hands on Saul, he was on this particular occasion his agent and indeed his mouthpiece—Luke would not have called him an apostle but the designation would not be inappropriate.[39] Whether he is called an apostle or not, he was certainly a duly authorized prophet. It was as the spokesman of Christ that he went to Saul; he had nothing to say beyond the words that the Lord put in his mouth. Ananias uttered the words, but as he did so, it was Christ himself who commissioned Saul to be his ambassador. Ananias laid his hands on Saul, but it was the power of Christ that in the same moment enlightened his eyes and filled him with the Holy Spirit. That Saul should have received the filling of the Spirit through the imposition of the hands of such an obscure disciple as Ananias shows clearly that Luke did not reckon the imposition of *apostolic* hands to be necessary for this (in his understanding of the term "apostolic").[40] Such filling was the indispensable qualification for the prophetic ministry mapped out for Saul in

---

38. The form Σαούλ is used in the vocative by the Lord (v. 4 par. 22:7 and 26:14) and by Ananias (here and in 22:13); it is used in the accusative of King Saul in 13:21. Otherwise in Acts the hellenized form Σαῦλος is used.

39. Cf. G. W. H. Lampe, *The Seal of the Spirit* (London, 1951), p. 72: "Ananias . . . is, for the purpose of meeting Paul, a duly commissioned Apostle."

40. For Luke's understanding of the terms "apostle" and "apostolic" see p. 30 (on 1:2).

the Lord's words of verse 15—a ministry comparable to that to which Jeremiah was called in his day (Jer. 1:5). Henceforth Saul discharged this ministry as one endowed with heavenly power (cf. v. 22).

The commissioning of Saul, and the part played in it by Ananias, must ever remain a stumbling block in the path of those whose conception of the apostolic ministry is too tightly bound to one particular line of transmission or form of ordination. If the risen Lord commissioned such an illustrious servant in so "irregular" a way, may he not have done so again, and may he not yet do so again, when the occasion requires it?

So Ananias enters and leaves the narrative, and we know nothing more of him. But as Saul's first friend after his conversion, the first follower of Jesus to greet him as a brother, as well as the one who faithfully bore the Lord's commission to him, Ananias has an honored place in sacred history, and a special claim on the gratitude of all who in one way or another have entered into the blessing that stems from the life and work of the apostle to the Gentiles.

18-19a   When Ananias had executed his commission and laid his hands on Saul, a flaky substance fell away from Saul's eyes.[41] He was able to see again; he rose up and was baptized forthwith in the name of Jesus (receiving his baptism at the hands of Ananias, we should naturally suppose);[42] he ate food for the first time in three days and a return of bodily strength accompanied the influx of new spiritual power.

6. Saul Preaches in Damascus (9:19b-22)

19b *He stayed for some days[43] with the disciples in Damascus,*

20 *and without delay he began to preach Jesus in the synagogues, saying, "He is[44] the Son of God."*

21 *All who heard him were amazed. "Is not this the man," they asked, "who has devastated in Jerusalem those who call on this name? Has he not come here for the very purpose of taking them in chains to the chief priests?"*

22 *But Saul's power went on increasing[45] and he confounded the Jews who were resident in Damascus as he proved that this Jesus was the Messiah.[46]*

---

41. Cf. Tob. 3:17 ("to scale away the white films from Tobit's eyes"); 11:13 ("the white films scaled away from the corners of his eyes").

42. See p. 418 with n. 22 (on 22:16). Saul's baptism may, like that of Cornelius and his household in 10:44-48, have followed his reception of the Spirit; this cannot be determined with certainty from the narrative.

43. Gk. ἡμέρας τινάς, for which P[45] reads ἡμέρας ἱκανάς, "many days" (cf. vv. 23, 43).

44. Some Western authorities insert "the Christ."

45. Some Western authorities read "was the more strengthened in the word."

46. There is a Western addition: "in whom God was well pleased."

19b-20 According to the autobiographical outline supplied by Paul in Gal. 1:15-17, he did not confer with any human being after receiving his "revelation of Jesus Christ" but went away to Arabia (the Nabataean kingdom, which lay on the eastern frontier of Syria and stretched south to the Red Sea). This need not exclude a short period of such witness in Damascus as is described here—either before he set out for Arabia (which seems more probable) or after his return to Damascus ("without delay" in v. 20 need not be pressed overmuch, especially since Luke has nothing at all to say of the visit to Arabia).

It is more significant than might be supposed at first glance that the only occurrence of the title "Son of God" in Acts should be in this report of Saul's early preaching.[47] It was as the Son of God that Christ was revealed to him on the Damascus road (Gal. 1:16; cf. 2 Cor. 1:19; Rom. 1:4).

This title, or its equivalent, is used in the Old Testament (1) of the people of Israel (Ex. 4:22; Hos. 11:1), (2) of the anointed king of Israel (2 Sam. 7:14; Ps. 89:26-27), and therefore (3) of the ideal king of the future, the Messiah of David's line (see especially Ps. 2:7 as quoted below in 13:33; cf. also above, 2:25-26). For the messianic use of the title in the pseudepigrapha cf. 1 Enoch 105:2; 4 Ezra 7:28-29; 13:32, 37, 52; 14:9. That our Lord's contemporaries believed the Messiah to be in some special sense the son of God is rendered probable by the wording of the high priest's question to him at his trial: "Are you the Messiah, the Son of the Blessed One?" (Mark 14:61 par. Matt. 26:63; Luke 22:67, 70). As applied to our Lord, then, the title "Son of God" marks him out as the true representative of the Israel of God and as God's anointed king; but it is no merely official title. As he himself understood the heavenly voice which said to him at his baptism, "You are my Son" (Mark 1:11 par. Luke 3:22), it expressed his unique relationship and fellowship with the Father.[48] A. E. Harvey finds three aspects of sonship implicit in the ascription of the title to Jesus: his perfect obedience to God, his being the ultimate revealer of God, and his being the authorized agent of God.[49] The proclamation of Jesus as the Son of God represents an advance on the way in which his messiahship has been proclaimed thus far in Acts.

---

47. Cf. the quotation of Ps. 2:7 in Acts 13:33 (again on Paul's lips). Indeed, "the most interesting and most distinctively Pauline use of υἱός in Rom. 8 and Gal. 4, goes much deeper than mere messianism." But even in Acts 9:20 something "deeper than mere messianism" may be implied: Luke is not necessarily representing Paul here "on one of the shallower of Paul's own levels of thinking" (C. F. D. Moule, "The Christology of Acts," in *Studies in Luke-Acts,* ed. L. E. Keck and J. L. Martyn [Nashville, 1966], p. 174).

48. See especially the famous *logion* Matt. 11:25-27 par. Luke 10:21-22.

49. A. E. Harvey, *Jesus and the Constraints of History* (London, 1982), pp. 154-73. See also J. Bieneck, *Sohn Gottes als Christusbezeichnung der Synoptiker,* ATANT 21 (Zürich, 1951); V. Taylor, *The Names of Jesus* (London, 1953), pp. 52-65;

21-22 It was to the synagogues of Damascus that Saul had been sent with the commission from the high priest, and to the synagogues of Damascus he went. But instead of presenting his letters of credence and demanding the extradition of the disciples of Jesus, he appeared as the bearer of a very different commission, issued by a higher authority than the high priest's, and as a disciple and messenger of Jesus he announced his Master's claims. No wonder that his hearers were amazed by the change that had come over him. The news of his mission had not been kept secret: here was the man whose arrival they had expected, but far from arresting the disciples of Jesus he was confounding the Jews of Damascus by his argument that the disciples' witness was true: Jesus was indeed the Messiah, the Son of God.[50] The filling of the Spirit which he had received gave his words a demonstrative power which could not be confuted: as with Stephen at an earlier date, so now with Saul, his hearers "could not resist the wisdom and spirit with which he spoke" (6:10).

7. Saul Escapes from Damascus (9:23-25)

23 *When many days had elapsed, the Jews plotted to kill him;*
24 *but Saul learned of their plot. They actually guarded the gates by day and by night in order to kill him,*
25 *but his disciples took him and let him down through the wall by night, lowering him in a basket.*

23-25 With the adventure thus recorded by Luke must be compared Paul's account in 2 Cor. 11:32-33: "In Damascus the ethnarch of King Aretas was guarding the city of the Damascenes in order to seize me, but I was let down in a basket through a window in the wall, and escaped his hands." Aretas IV (9 B.C.-A.D. 40) was ruler of the Nabataean kingdom in which Saul spent some time after his conversion (Gal. 1:17). It is commonly supposed that Paul's sojourn in Arabia had the nature of a religious retreat: that he sought the solitude of the desert—perhaps even going to Mount Horeb as Moses and Elijah had done—in order to commune with God and think out all the implications of his new life, without disturbance. But the context in which he tells of his going to Arabia, immediately after receiving his commission to proclaim Christ among the Gentiles, suggests that he went there to preach

---

G. Vos, *The Self-Disclosure of Jesus* (Grand Rapids, 1954), pp. 141-226; M. Hengel, *The Son of God,* E.T. (London, 1976).

50. The verb rendered "proved" (Gk. συμβιβάζω) means literally "placing together"—here placing the OT promises alongside their fulfilment and hence "proving" that Jesus was the one to whom they pointed. This was the method of argument regularly employed (according to Luke) by Paul, Apollos, and others in synagogues around the eastern Mediterranean (cf. 17:2-3; 18:28; 26:22-23).

the gospel.[51] The hostile interest which the Nabataean authorities took in him implies that he had done something to annoy them—something more than withdrawal to the desert for solitary contemplation. The ethnarch looked after the interests of the many Nabataean subjects who lived in Damascus, and in general acted as King Aretas's representative in the city.[52] Whatever part the local Jews had in the plot, Paul avoids saying anything to the detriment of his own people, but one possibility is that, knowing of the official Nabataean animosity toward him, they advised the ethnarch of his whereabouts, so that he might arrest him as he left the city and take him back to be dealt with by the Nabataean authorities.[53] However, while Saul's enemies were watching the city gates to catch him, some of his new friends and sympathizers got him safely away.[54] One of them had a house built on to the city wall, and he was lowered in a large basket or net[55] through a window of the house, which was actually cut in the city wall.

Luke says that this incident took place "when many days had elapsed"; Paul, more definitely, says in Gal. 1:18 that it was three years after his conversion (by inclusive reckoning, no doubt) that he went up to Jerusalem—and from the narrative of Acts he seems to have gone to Jerusalem immediately after his escape from Damascus.

8. Saul in Jerusalem; He Is Sent to Tarsus (9:26-30)

26 *When he arrived in Jerusalem, he tried to join the disciples. But they were all afraid of him; they could not believe that he was a disciple.*

27 *But Barnabas took him, and brought him to the apostles, and told them how he had seen the Lord on the road, and what he had said to him, and how he had preached boldly at Damascus in the name of Jesus.*

28 *So he stayed with them in Jerusalem, coming in and going out,*

51. Cf. K. Lake, *The Earlier Epistles of St. Paul* (London, 1914), pp. 320-23.

52. E. Meyer, *Ursprung und Anfänge des Christentums*, III (Stuttgart/Berlin, 1923), p. 346, describes the ethnarch as "head of the Nabataean colony in Damascus"; cf. E. A. Knauf, "Zum Ethnarchen des Aretas 2 Kor 11,32," *ZNW* 74 (1983), pp. 145-47. It was been argued—e.g., by Schürer (II, pp. 129-30)—from the absence of Roman coins at Damascus between A.D. 34 and 62 that Damascus was at this time included in the Nabataean kingdom. For arguments against this view Meyer refers with approval to E. Schwartz, "Die Aeren von Gerasa und Eleutheropolis," *NGG* 1906, pp. 367-68. If Damascus had been under Nabataean control the ethnarch could have arrested Saul openly.

53. Cf. H. Windisch, *Der zweite Korintherbrief*, KEK 6 (Göttingen, ⁹1924), p. 366.

54. The expression "his disciples" (v. 25) suggests that Saul's preaching in Damascus had not been unfruitful.

55. The word rendered "basket" here is σπυρίς (otherwise spelled σφυρίς), the word used in the narrative of the feeding of the 4,000 (Mark 8:8). The word in 2 Cor. 11:33 is σαργάνη, "a large woven or network bag or basket suitable for hay, straw . . . or for bales of wool" (Lake-Cadbury, *Beginnings* I.4, p. 106).

29 *and preached boldly in the Lord's name. He also spoke to the Hellenists[56] and debated with them, but they tried to kill him.*

30 *When the brothers learned of this, they brought him down to
Caesarea and sent him off to Tarsus.*

26 When Saul returned to Jerusalem, he was in a difficult position. His old
associates knew all about his defection, and he could expect no friendly
welcome from them. On the other hand, the disciples of Jesus, with whom
he now wished to associate himself, had not forgotten his campaign of
persecution. One can scarcely feel surprise at their suspicion when he made
overtures to them. The role of the *agent provocateur* was as familiar in
antiquity as in more recent times; what assurance had they that this was not a
scheme of Saul's to gain their confidence for their more effective undoing?

27 It was Barnabas who, true to his name, acted as Saul's sponsor
and encouraged them to receive him. It is possible that Barnabas was already
acquainted with Saul, knew his integrity of character, and was convinced of
the genuineness of his conversion.[57] When Saul desperately needed a true
friend in Damascus, Ananias played that part to him; now, when he stood in
equal need of one in Jerusalem, he found a friend in Barnabas. And Barnabas's prestige with the apostles and other believers in Jerusalem was such
that when he gave them his guarantee that Saul was now a true disciple of
Jesus, they were reassured.

When Luke says that Barnabas brought Saul "to the apostles," the
narrative of Gal. 1:18-20 compels us to interpret this as a generalizing plural.
According to Paul's own solemn affirmation, the only leaders of the Jerusalem church whom he met on that occasion were Peter (Cephas) and James
the Lord's brother (whom Paul calls an apostle, although he would not have
satisfied Luke's conditions for that designation).

28-30 With Luke's account here the whole passage in Gal. 1:18-24
must be compared: "Next, after three years I went up to Jerusalem to get to
know[58] Cephas, and stayed with him for fifteen days. But I saw none of the
other apostles, except James, the Lord's brother. I assure you, in what I am
writing to you, as God is my witness, I am telling no lie. Then I came into the
territories of Syria and Cilicia. I remained unknown by face to the churches
of Judaea which are in Christ; they only kept on hearing, 'Our former
persecutor is now preaching the faith which he once tried to devastate,' and

56. For "Hellenists" (Ἑλληνιστάς) A reads "Greeks" (Ἕλληνας).

57. For an imaginative reconstruction of Barnabas's earlier relations with Saul
see J. A. Robertson, *The Hidden Romance of the New Testament* (London, 1920), pp.
46-61.

58. Perhaps the verb rendered "to get to know" (ἱστορῆσαι) should be pressed to
yield its more precise classical sense: "to make inquiry of Cephas." See F. F. Bruce, *The
Epistle to the Galatians*, NIGTC (Grand Rapids/Exeter, 1982), pp. 98-99; also O. Hofius,
"Gal 1,18: ἱστορῆσαι Κηφᾶν," *ZNW* 75 (1984), pp. 73-85.

they glorified God on my account." The emphasis with which Paul affirms the truth of this account suggests that he knew of another account, which may have come to the ears of his Galatian converts, and which he is anxious to refute. It has indeed been argued that this rival account is the one on which Luke draws here,[59] but this is quite improbable.

Paul's chief concern in this section of Galatians is to show that he received his gospel, and his commission to preach it, without human mediation—in particular, that he was in no way indebted to the Jerusalem authorities. He had started fulfilling his commission (in Arabia) before he had any contact with Jerusalem, and when in due course he went up to Jerusalem, it was for a short private visit. Luke may generalize and say that he saw the apostles, but for Paul it was important to particularize and say which apostles he actually met. But Luke's generalizing report does not suggest at all that "the apostles" to whom Barnabas introduced Saul conferred any authority on him.

It is not so easy to reconcile Luke's description of Saul's public activity at Jerusalem in association with the apostles with the statement in Gal. 1:22 that, until the time of his departure for Syria and Cilicia (and after that), he "remained unknown by face to the churches of Judaea," which knew of him only by hearsay. One commentator removes the phrase "in Jerusalem" from verse 28 (taking it to be a gloss) and regards verses 28 and 29 as a continuation of Barnabas's description of Saul's activity at *Damascus*. Verse 30 would then go on: "And the brothers recognized him[60] (that is, as a disciple) and brought him down to Caesarea and sent him off to Tarsus." Thus, we are assured, "the whole difficulty vanishes."[61] It does not, and even if it did vanish, one must have reservations about an emendation, however ingenious it may be, which is proposed not because it has any textual attestation but because its adoption will help to remove a discrepancy. It is true that there is a marked resemblance between the account of Paul's activity at Damascus (his bold preaching and the consequent plot against his life) and that of his activity in Jerusalem. Luke's sources proba-

---

59. Cf. O. Linton, "The Third Aspect: A Neglected Point of View," *ST* 3 (1949), pp. 79-95.

60. As a parallel to this sense of ἐπιγινώσκω its use in 1 Cor. 16:18 is adduced (RSV "give recognition to").

61. L. E. Browne, *The Acts of the Apostles* (London, 1925), pp. 162-66. Another way of mitigating the discrepancy is to suppose that "the churches of Judaea" in Gal. 1:22 are the churches outside the capital, the church of Jerusalem being excluded. (See A. Ehrhardt, *The Acts of the Apostles* [Manchester, 1969], p. 63.) But that is an unnatural interpretation in the context. There would have been little value in Paul's insisting that he remained unknown to the churches of the Judaean countryside if his readers had been free to infer that he *was* known to the church of Jerusalem; that was the very impression that he was concerned to remove.

bly supplied him with little detail about the Jerusalem visit; hence the generalizing terms in which he reports it.

He describes Saul, during his Jerusalem visit, as taking up the work which Stephen had laid down at his death, by engaging in debates with the Hellenists.[62] Their reaction was swift and violent. Saul was worse than Stephen: he was in their eyes a traitor to the true cause, and by his *volte-face* he had let down those who formerly followed him loyally as their leader in the suppression of the new movement. With the information given here we have somehow to combine Saul's account (reproduced at a later point, in 22:17-21) of Jesus' appearing to him in the temple and telling him to leave Jerusalem because his witness would not be listened to. He protested that he was a specially valuable witness because the people of Jerusalem knew his earlier record as a persecutor and his approval of Stephen's death. But the Lord repeated his command to him to depart from Jerusalem, adding that he would send him to the Gentiles.[63]

Jerusalem was too hot to hold Saul. His friends saved his life by getting him safely away to Caesarea, where they put him on board a ship bound for his native Tarsus. Thus, as he says himself, he "came into the territories of Syria and Cilicia" (Gal. 1:21). Syria and Cilicia at this time formed a united imperial province.[64] Tarsus, the chief city of Cilicia, was now about a thousand years old. It had been subject, from time to time, to the Assyrians, Persians, and Graeco-Macedonians. It passed under Roman control in 64 B.C., but retained its autonomy as a free city. Under Augustus the administration of the city was entrusted to his former teacher, Athenodorus the Stoic, himself a native of Tarsus, who appears to have established a property qualification for its citizens.[65] Tarsus was a leading center of culture, with schools devoted to philosophy, rhetoric, and law, although they did not have the international standing of the schools of Athens and

---

62. "The newly converted Saul was not one to keep silence for a fortnight, and very probably preached in the city. The words 'coming in and going out at Jerusalem' do not mean that he visited places outside the city, but that he moved about freely and fearlessly in and out of houses in the city" (A. H. McNeile and C. S. C. Williams, *Introduction to the New Testament* [Oxford, 1953], p. 113); cf. H. N. Ridderbos, *The Epistle of Paul to the Churches of Galatia*, NICNT (Grand Rapids, 1953), pp. 72-73.

63. W. M. Ramsay (*St. Paul the Traveller* [London, [14]1920], pp. 60-64) holds that the vision described in 22:17-21 must have taken place during Paul's second post-conversion visit to Jerusalem (the famine relief visit of 11:30), because (among other reasons) the cause of his departure from Jerusalem at the end of his first visit (as related here by Luke) was "totally different" from that assigned in his description of the vision. L. E. Browne (*Acts*, p. 166) points out that this is another discrepancy removed by his emendation.

64. See E. M. B. Green, "Syria and Cilicia—A Note," *ExT* 71 (1959-60), pp. 52-53.

65. See on 21:39 (p. 413).

Alexandria.[66] It is unwise, however, to exaggerate the influence which the educational system of Tarsus exercised on its most illustrious son.[67]

There, then, we leave Saul for some time, engaged in unchronicled evangelization; we meet him again in 11:25.

9. The Church Enjoys Peace and Prosperity (9:31)

> 31 So the church[68] throughout all Judaea, Galilee, and Samaria had peace and continued to be built up and to increase, as it conducted itself in the fear of the Lord and the encouragement of the Holy Spirit.

31 Luke uses the singular "church" here where Paul prefers to use the plural and to speak of "the churches of Judaea" (Gal. 1:22; cf. 1 Thess. 2:14). It was, in fact, the original Jerusalem church, now dispersed and decentralized. "The Ecclesia," said F. J. A. Hort, "was still confined to Jewish or semi-Jewish populations and to ancient Jewish soil; but it was no longer the Ecclesia of a single city, and yet it was *one:* probably as corresponding, by these three modern representative districts of Judaea, Galilee and Samaria, to the ancient Ecclesia which had its home in the whole land of Israel."[69]

With this summary of progress Luke's narrative of the conversion of Saul of Tarsus comes to an end. The persecution that broke out after Stephen's death died out with the conversion and departure of the leading persecutor. But such is the importance attached by Luke to this event that, in spite of limitations on the space at his disposal, he records it in some detail on two later occasions, on both of which the story is told by Paul in the first person—once to the hostile crowd from which he had just been rescued in the temple precincts (22:1-21), and once in his *apologia* before the younger Agrippa (26:2-29).[70]

With Luke's estimate of the importance of Saul's conversion neither the historian nor the theologian can quarrel. The spread of Christianity in the Roman Empire cannot be imagined apart from his work. He was indeed a

---

66. Strabo, *Geography* 14.5.13.

67. See on 22:3 (p. 415). W. M. Ramsay tends to overestimate Tarsian influence on Paul in his admirable section on Tarsus in *The Cities of St. Paul* (London, 1907), pp. 83-244. On Tarsus see also D. Magie, *Roman Rule in Asia Minor* (Princeton, 1950), I, p. 272; II, pp. 1146-48.

68. The Western and Byzantine texts read "the churches," with plural verbs.

69. F. J. A. Hort, *The Christian Ecclesia* (London, 1897), pp. 55-56. The possibility that the plural reading is original is reopened by K. N. Giles, "Luke's Use of the term ΕΚΚΛΗΣΙΑ with special reference to Acts 20.28 and 9.31," *NTS* 31 (1985), pp. 135-42.

70. On the three accounts see G. Lüdemann, *Paul, Apostle to the Gentiles: Studies in Chronology*, E.T. (London, 1984), pp. 139, 180 (n. 3).

chosen instrument in the hand of the risen Lord, fitted for his life-work before his conversion—set apart for it indeed, as he acknowledges, before his birth (Gal. 1:15). Born a "Hebrew" son of "Hebrew" parents,[71] and given the best education in his ancestral traditions that contemporary Judaism could provide,[72] he also inherited the rare privilege of Roman citizenship, while his debt to Hellenistic culture is plain to every reader of his letters. When in due course God "revealed his Son" in Saul of Tarsus, he devoted all this wealthy inheritance, together with his rare natural qualities, to the task of Gentile evangelization; and, latecomer though he was among the apostles, he "worked harder than any of them, though [he added] it was not I, but the grace of God which is with me" (1 Cor. 15:10).

III. THE ACTS OF PETER AND BEGINNINGS OF GENTILE CHRISTIANITY (9:32–12:25)

A. PETER IN WESTERN JUDAEA (9:32-43)

1. Peter at Lydda: the Healing of Aeneas (9:32-35)

32 *While Peter was making a general tour[73] he came down to the saints who resided at Lydda.*

33 *There he found a man named Aeneas, who was paralyzed and had been confined to bed for eight years.*

34 *"Aeneas," said Peter to him, "Jesus Christ heals you. Get up and make your bed." He got up at once.*

35 *All the residents of Lydda and the (Plain of) Sharon saw him, and they turned to the Lord.*

32   We left Peter in 8:25 when he returned to Jerusalem with John from their visit to Samaria. Now we find him, taking advantage probably of the collapse of the recent persecution, engaged in an itinerant ministry of visitation among the dispersed Christian communities of Judaea. There was one such community in Lydda (the Greek name of Lod). The nucleus of this community was doubtless formed of fugitives from the persecution in Jerusalem; we should remember also that Philip passed through those parts preaching the gospel on his way from Azotus to Caesarea (8:40). Lydda was at this time the center of a Judaean toparchy or administrative district.

33-34   It is natural to suppose that Aeneas, the man whom Peter cured from his eight-year-old paralysis[74] at Lydda, was a member of the

---

71. Phil. 3:5, Ἑβραῖος ἐξ Ἑβραίων.
72. Gal. 1:14; cf. 22:3 below.
73. Gk. διερχόμενον διὰ πάντων, "going through all (parts)."
74. It is possible to understand ἐξ ἐτῶν ὀκτώ (v. 33) in the sense "since eight years old," but the usual interpretation is the more probable.

local Christian group, though this is not expressly stated. The command, "Jesus Christ heals you," may involve a play on words in the Greek.[75] The following words, "Get up and make your bed," might alternatively be rendered, "Get up and set the table for yourself"—that is, "Get yourself something to eat."[76] This has been thought to accord well with the interest shown by Luke and other New Testament writers in the provision of nourishment for convalescents.[77] But the rendering "Make your bed" is more probable in the context. If Aeneas was already at home, he could not be told to roll up his mattress and go home with it, like the paralytic of Capernaum in Mark 2:9 and parallels (cf. John 5:8); but he could at least be told to roll it up and put it away.

35 The news of Aeneas's cure spread throughout the neighborhood and all over the coastal plain of Sharon. Many of the people in that area came to see him, and the result was a further access of believers. Since much of this territory was semi-Gentile in population, a further widening of the range of the saving message is implied.

2. Peter at Joppa: the Raising of Dorcas (9:36-43)

36 *Meanwhile at Joppa there was a disciple named Tabitha—her name means "Gazelle" (Dorcas in Greek). She spent all her time in the performance of good works and acts of kindness.*

37 *About that time she fell sick and died, so they washed her and laid her in an upper room.*

38 *The disciples at Joppa heard that Peter was at Lydda, so, as Lydda was near Joppa, they sent two men to him with the request: "Please come over to us without delay."*

39 *Peter got up and went with the men. When he arrived, they brought him up to the upper room, and all the widows came up to him and stood weeping, showing the dresses and coats which Dorcas made[78] while she was with them.*

40 *Peter put everyone out, knelt down, and prayed, and then, turning to the body, said, "Tabitha, get up."[79] She opened her eyes and, seeing Peter, she sat up.*

---

75. Gk. ἰᾶταί σε Ἰησοῦς Χριστός. In a Greek ear Ἰησοῦς might well seem to be cognate with ἰάομαι, "heal" (see p. 331, n. 35, on 17:18). The present ἰᾶται is aoristic: "he heals you this moment" (see MHT I, p. 119). But H. J. Cadbury, "A Possible Perfect in Acts 9:34," *JTS* 49 (1948), pp. 57-58, suggests accenting the word as perfect, ἴαται ("has healed").

76. Gk. στρῶσον σεαυτῷ. The object to στρώννυμι has to be supplied: it might be "bed" or "table."

77. Cf. v. 19a above; also Mark 5:43 par. Luke 8:55.

78. Gk. ἐποίει ("used to make"). P45 reads ἐποίησεν αὐταῖς ("had made for them").

79. The Western text adds "in the name of our Lord Jesus Christ" (cf. 3:6).

41 *Then he gave her his hand and raised her up; he called in the saints and the widows and presented her alive.*

42 *This became known throughout the whole of Joppa, and many believed on the Lord.*

43 *Then Peter stayed in Joppa for a considerable time with one Simon, a tanner.*

36-38   Joppa (Jaffa, Heb. *Yafo)* is on the Mediterranean coast, about ten or eleven miles northwest of Lydda. It is mentioned in Egyptian records of the fifteenth century B.C., and several times in the Old Testament. Today it is included in a large conurbation with the modern city of Tel-aviv.

In Joppa, as in Lydda, there was a group of believers in Jesus. While Peter was in Lydda, a member of this group fell sick and died. Her name, Tabitha, is Aramaic, meaning "gazelle";[80] Dorcas is the Greek equivalent. (The corresponding Hebrew form, Zibiah, occurs as a woman's name in 2 Kings 12:1.) Dorcas's works of Christian charity had specially endeared her to her friends and neighbors. The leaders of the believers in Joppa, having heard perhaps of Peter's healing of Aeneas, sent to Lydda and begged him to come on to Joppa.[81] (It is interesting to note how frequently in Acts, as here, a delegation consists of two men.)

39   Peter went to Joppa with the two messengers, and was brought without delay into the room where Dorcas's body had been laid out, after being washed in accordance with the Jewish custom of purification of the dead.[82] There stood the widows who had been the principal beneficiaries of her charity, displaying, as they wore them,[83] the garments that Dorcas had made for them.

40-42   Peter sent them and the other mourners out of the room, as he had seen his Master do before he raised Jairus's daughter from her deathbed; then he uttered a short sentence in Aramaic, differing only in one letter from Jesus' words to Jairus's daughter. Whereas Jesus had said *Talitha qum(i)* (Mark 5:41),[84] Peter now said *Tabitha qum(i)*—"Tabitha, get up." She opened her eyes and sat up, and Peter raised her to her feet and presented her alive to her wondering friends.[85] "The circumstantial details of the

---

80. Aram. *ṭabyeṭāʾ*.

81. Their words in v. 38 (lit., "Do not hesitate to come to us") amount simply to a polite request: "Please come to us."

82. Cf. Mishnah, *Shabbāṭ* 23.5.

83. The middle voice, ἐπιδεικνύμεναι, suggests this. Widows are mentioned here, as in 6:1, because they were natural recipients of charity. They are not members of a special order attached to the church, as in 1 Tim. 5:3-16.

84. The Western text of Mark 5:41, by confusion with this passage of Acts, reads *Tabitha* in place of *Talitha.*

85. "To the saints and widows," says Luke, not meaning that the widows could not be saints. But no doubt Dorcas's charity extended beyond the bounds of the local community of disciples.

gradual recovery of Tabitha," says Hobart, "are quite in the style of medical description."[86] Many other inhabitants of Joppa inevitably joined the followers of a Master by whose power so marvelous an act of healing and restoration had been accomplished.

43 Peter stayed on in Joppa for a considerable time. His host, Simon the tanner, lived by the seaside; no doubt he used sea water in his work.[87] It would not be surprising if he lived a little way outside the town; some degree of uncleanness was reckoned to attach to a tanner's work, because it involved regular contact with the skins of dead animals. Luke shows an interest in the names of hosts and hostesses and in people's occupations.[88]

---

86. W. K. Hobart, *The Medical Language of St. Luke* (Dublin, 1882), p. 41.
87. A. Harnack suggested that Peter's trade of fisherman influenced his choice of a house near the sea (*The Acts of the Apostles*, E.T. [London, 1909], p. 85).
88. See H. J. Cadbury, "Lexical Notes on Luke-Acts, III. Luke's Interest in Lodging," *JBL* 45 (1926), pp. 305-22.

ACTS 10

B. THE STORY OF CORNELIUS (10:1-48)

1. Cornelius the Centurion Sees a Vision (10:1-8)

1 *At Caesarea there lived a man named Cornelius, a centurion of the Italian cohort.*

2 *He was a religious man; he and all his household worshiped God, and he performed many acts of charity to the (Jewish) people and prayed to God regularly.*

3 *One day, about the ninth hour, he saw in a vision, clearly, an angel of God who came in to him and said to him, "Cornelius!"*

4 *Filled with awe, he fixed his eyes on him and said, "What is it, sir?" "Your prayers and your acts of charity," said the angel to him, "have ascended as a memorial into the presence of God.*

5 *Now, dispatch men to Joppa and send for Simon, surnamed Peter.*

6 *He is lodging with one Simon, a tanner, whose house is by the seashore."*

7 *When the angel who spoke to him departed, Cornelius called two of his household servants, and one of the soldiers who were in attendance on him, himself a religious man,*

8 *and when he had told them the whole story, he sent them to Joppa.*

1 The range of the apostolic message has been steadily broadened. Already it has begun to cross the barrier which separated Jews from Gentiles; now the time has come for that barrier to be crossed authoritatively by an apostle.

The apostle who crossed it was Peter, the leader of the Twelve; the place where he crossed it was the largely Gentile city of Caesarea. The Gentiles who first heard the gospel from his lips were the family and friends of Cornelius,[1] a centurion in the Roman army, belonging to one of the auxiliary cohorts stationed in Judaea.[2]

---

1. Cornelius was a specially common name in Rome ever since 82 B.C., when P. Cornelius Sulla emancipated 10,000 slaves who were enrolled in his own *gens Cornelia*.

2. In the regular Roman army a cohort was the tenth part of a legion and had a paper strength of 600 men. But there were no legionary troops in Judaea between A.D. 6

The centurions who make their appearance in the New Testament record make a favorable impression. It is noteworthy that the first Gentile with whom Jesus had dealings during his public ministry (so far as we are informed) was a centurion stationed in Capernaum (possibly seconded from the Roman army to the security forces of Herod Antipas); it was with reference to this man's faith that he is reported to have said, "many will come from east and west and sit at table with Abraham, Isaac, and Jacob in the kingdom of heaven" (Matt. 8:11).[3] These words now began to find their fulfilment in another centurion.

A centurion was nominally in command of a hundred men: although his status was that of a noncommissioned officer, his responsibilities were more like those of a modern army captain. Centurions were the backbone of the Roman army. The historian Polybius sums up their necessary qualifications thus: "Centurions are required not to be bold and adventurous so much as good leaders, of steady and prudent mind, not prone to take the offensive or start fighting wantonly, but able when overwhelmed and hard-pressed to stand fast and die at their post."[4]

Peter and Cornelius were each prepared by a visionary experience for their encounter. The whole narrative, which "bears the stamp both of probability and truth" (in Foakes-Jackson's view),[5] is of great importance not only because it tells how Peter used the keys of the kingdom to open a "door of faith" to Gentiles, but also because it introduces the questions of social intercourse between Jewish believers and Gentiles and of the admission of Gentile believers to the church without circumcision. These questions were later debated at the Council of Jerusalem, and the Cornelius episode was there adduced as a test case (15:7-9). Luke's appreciation of the importance of the Cornelius episode is shown by the space he devotes to Peter's rehear-

---

and 66; the Roman governors of Judaea commanded auxiliary forces. An auxiliary cohort had a paper strength of 1,000 men. The "Italian cohort" was one of these; it was so called presumably because it was originally raised in Italy, but in due course it would have consisted increasingly of provincials. Indeed, the soldiers making up an auxiliary unit were usually provincials; they were, however, awarded Roman citizenship when their term of service had expired. There is inscriptional evidence (*ILS* 9168) for the presence in Syria *c.* A.D. 69 of the auxiliary *cohors II Italica ciuium Romanorum* ("second Italian cohort of Roman citizens"); but we have no direct evidence of the identity of the military units in Judaea between A.D. 6 and 41. See further on 27:1, "the Augustan cohort."

3. The logion occurs also in Luke 13:28-29, but not in the context of the healing of the centurion's servant (which is related in Luke 7:2-10).

4. Polybius, *History* 6.24.

5. F. J. Foakes-Jackson, *The Acts of the Apostles*, MNTC (London, 1931), p. 87. M. Dibelius distinguishes the original story (derived, he thinks, from the tradition of some Hellenistic communities) from Lukan additions; see further on 10:14-16 (p. 206, n. 19); 10:36-37 (p. 212, n. 46); 11:2-3 (p. 220).

sal of his experience in 11:4-17, as well as by the repetition of salient features of the incident within the present narrative.[6]

2 It is further important to observe that Cornelius, though a Gentile, was a worshiper of the God of Israel. Such Gentiles are commonly called "God-fearers"; while this is not a technical term, it is a convenient one to use.[7] Many Gentiles of those days, while not prepared to become full converts to Judaism[8] (the requirement of circumcision being a special stumbling block for men), were attracted by the simple monotheism of Jewish synagogue worship and by the ethical standards of the Jewish way of life. Some of them attended synagogue and became tolerably conversant with the prayers and scripture lessons, which they heard read in the Greek version; some observed with more or less scrupulosity such distinctive Jewish practices as sabbath observance and abstention from certain kinds of food (notably pork). Cornelius's attachment to the Jewish religion appeared particularly in his regular prayer to the God of Israel and acts of charity to the people of Israel. One may say, indeed, that he had every qualification, short of circumcision, which could satisfy Jewish requirements.

The Roman army had its own religious observances, officially prescribed for appointed days and carried out with the same routine punctiliousness as modern church parades, but utterly incapable of feeding men's souls.[9] Roman soldiers who felt the need to satisfy their religious hunger looked elsewhere—many to Mithraism; some, like Cornelius, to Judaism.

That the first Gentiles to hear and accept the gospel (like the Ethio-

---

6. E.g., Cornelius's repetition (vv. 30-32) of the substance of his vision (vv. 3-6).

7. See Schürer III, pp. 150-77; K. G. Kuhn, *TDNT* 6, pp. 743-44 (*s.v.* προσ-ήλυτος, D II); L. H. Feldman, "Jewish 'Sympathizers' in Classical Literature and Inscriptions," *TAPA* 81 (1950), pp. 200-208; F. Siegert, "Gottesfürchtige und Sympathisanten," *JSJ* 4 (1973), pp. 109-64; A. T. Kraabel, "The Diaspora Synagogue: Archaeological and Epigraphic Evidence since Sukenik," *ANRW* 2/19 (Berlin, 1979), pp. 477-510; "The Disappearance of the 'God-fearers,'" *Numen* 28 (1981), pp. 113-26; M. Stern, *Greek and Latin Authors on Jews and Judaism*, II (Jerusalem, 1980), pp. 103-6; M. Wilcox, "The 'God-fearers' in Acts—A Reconsideration," *JSNT*, issue 13 (1981), pp. 102-22; T. M. Finn, "The God-fearers Reconsidered," *CBQ* 47 (1985), pp. 75-84. The "disappearance" of the God-fearers, to which Kraabel refers, amounts to the absence of any mention of them in synagogue inscriptions. There is a similar absence of mention of Jewish freedmen in Jewish catacomb inscriptions in Rome; yet there is ample evidence from other sources of the presence of Jewish freedmen in Rome and elsewhere in the empire; cf. G. Fuks, "Where have all the Freedmen gone? On an Anomaly in the Jewish Grave Inscriptions from Rome," *JJS* 36 (1985), pp. 25-32.

8. See on 2:10 (p. 58 with nn. 44-47).

9. A. Ehrhardt (*The Acts of the Apostles* [Manchester, 1969], p. 54) illustrates this from the *feriale* or table of feast days for the Roman army discovered at Dura Europus on the Euphrates (cf. R. O. Fink, A. S. Hoey, and W. F. Snyder, "The *Feriale Duranum*," *Yale Classical Studies* 7 [1940], pp. 1-222).

pian eunuch and Cornelius) should be worshipers of the God of Israel is the more significant for the record of Acts because, as we shall see, it was such God-fearers who formed the nucleus of the Christian community in one city after another in the course of Paul's missionary activity. Luke's interest in them is such that one may wonder if he himself was not a God-fearing Gentile who believed the gospel when he heard it.

3-6 To Cornelius, then, one afternoon at the regular hour of prayer (cf. 3:1) a heavenly messenger appeared in a vision. His initial alarm at being adressed by such a visitant was overcome when he was assured that his faithfulness in prayer and almsgiving had not been overlooked by God but had been accepted by him as a worthy oblation. The angel's language is full of sacrificial terminology such as we find in the prescriptions for the levitical offerings; Cornelius's acts of piety and charity had ascended into the divine presence like incense or the smoke of a sacrifice.[10] God would honor the "memorial" with a suitable response; the nature of that response would be made clear to Cornelius if he sent to a certain house in Joppa and invited one Simon Peter, who was resident there, to come and visit him.

7-8 Immediately Cornelius carried out the instructions he had received in the vision. He dispatched two of his domestic servants and one of his orderlies, a God-fearing soldier like himself, to Joppa.

2. Peter Sees a Vision (10:9-16)

9 *The next day, while those men were on their way and near the city, Peter went up on the roof to pray. It was about the sixth hour.*

10 *He became hungry and wanted to eat. While something was being prepared for him, he fell into a trance.*

11 *He saw heaven opened and something[11] descending like a great sheet, being let down to earth by its four corners.*

12 *In it were all the quadrupeds and creeping things of the earth[12] and the birds of the sky.*

13 *A voice came to him: "Get up, Peter;[13] kill them and eat them."*

14 *"No, Lord," said Peter; "I have never eaten anything profane or unclean."*

10. "Your prayers and your acts of charity have ascended" (Gk. ἀνέβησαν) like the smoke of a sacrifice (cf. the Hebrew word for a burnt-offering, ʿôlāh, lit. "ascending"). For the sacrificial reference of the word "memorial" (Gk. μνημόσυνον) cf. Lev. 2:2 LXX, where this term is used of the part of the cereal offering which was burnt, i.e., presented to God. For the sacrificial efficacy of such religious acts as those of Cornelius cf. Ps. 141 (LXX 140):2; Tob. 12:12, and in the NT Phil. 4:18; Heb. 13:15-16.

11. Gk. σκεῦος, "instrument" (as in 9:15); here to be rendered by a more indefinite word, such as "thing" or "object." *P*[45] reads "a certain object, tied by the four corners, let down on the earth."

12. The Byzantine text places the phrase "of the earth" after "quadrupeds" and follows on with "and wild beasts" before "and creeping things" (cf. KJV).

13. *P*[45] omits "Peter."

15 *A voice came to him again a second time: "You must not regard as
profane what God has cleansed."*
16 *This happened three times; then the thing was at once[14] taken back
up to heaven.*

9-10 Peter had to be prepared for the encounter as well as Cornelius, and
there were scruples to be overcome on Peter's side as there were not on
Cornelius's. A God-fearing Gentile like Cornelius had no objection to the
society of Jews, but even a moderately orthodox Jew would not willingly
enter the dwelling of a Gentile, God-fearer though he might be. No doubt
some of Peter's inherited scruples were weighing less heavily with him by
this time, but to make him accept an invitation to visit a Gentile a special
revelation was necessary.

Such a revelation came to Peter the day after Cornelius's vision,
when the messengers from Caesarea were approaching Joppa. About noon
Peter went up on the flat roof of the tanner's house for quiet and prayer.
Noon was not one of the appointed times for public prayer, but pious Jews
like Daniel (Dan. 6:10) who prayed three times a day probably prayed then
(cf. Ps. 55:17). While Peter was on the housetop he began to feel hungry[15]
and probably called down for some food. It was while this was being
prepared that the revelation came to him in a vision, and it was no doubt
because of his hunger that the vision centered around food.

11-13 In this ecstatic experience Peter seemed to see a large, sheet-
like object coming down from the sky. Whether it was the awning designed
to give him shade on the housetop, or a sail on the western horizon, that
assumed this form in his vision need not concern us. When it came down
where Peter was, however, the sheet proved to be full of all sorts of quadrupeds, reptiles, and birds,[16] both fit and unfit for food according to Jewish
law and custom.[17] The vision of these was accompanied by a heavenly voice
bidding him slaughter and eat what was thus provided.

14-16 This was all wrong, as Peter's ancestral conscience told
him. Unclean animals could not be used for food at all, and even "clean"
animals had to be slaughtered with ritual propriety before their flesh could be

---

14. The Western and Byzantine texts have "again" in place of "at once" (cf.
KJV).

15. The word translated "hungry" in v. 10 (Gk. πρόσπεινος) occurs elsewhere,
so far as is known, only in a first-century eye doctor named Demosthenes. F. W. Dil-
listone ("πρόσπεινος [Acts x.10]," *ExT* 46 [1934-35], p. 380) suggests that Luke may
have been a pupil of his. "Eat" is literally "taste" (γεύσασθαι); cf. 20:11 (p. 385, n. 30).

16. The animal world is classified under these three divisions in Gen. 6:20
("birds . . . cattle . . . every creeping thing of the ground").

17. The laws distinguishing clean from unclean animals are laid down in Lev.
11:2-47. Those quadrupeds were clean (and therefore fit for food) which both chewed the
cud and had cloven hooves.

eaten. Peter's protest against the divine injunction took verbal shape much as the prophet Ezekiel's protest had once taken when he was commanded to prepare and eat "abominable flesh" (Ezek. 4:14): "No, Lord; I have never eaten anything profane or unclean," said Peter (with the implication: "and I am not going to begin now").[18] Back came the heavenly voice: "You must not regard as profane what God has cleansed." Three times over this interchange took place; then the sheet went up with its contents and the vision dissolved.

The abolition of barriers was pressed home in the vision with special reference to Jewish food restrictions, but Peter soon learned that its range was much wider.[19] Perhaps, as he thought about the vision, he remembered hearing similar words on an earlier occasion, though he had not then grasped their import. No doubt he was present when his Master, in a debate with Pharisees and scribes, insisted that it is not what goes into someone's stomach that conveys defilement, but what comes out of one's heart (Mark 7:14-19a). This was in effect an abrogation of ceremonial food laws and much else of the same character, but it was not until later, as a result of his experience on the roof at Joppa, that Peter appreciated this. It may well be to Peter that we owe the comment appended by the evangelist to Jesus' pronouncement on this subject: "Thus he declared all foods clean" (Mark 7:19b).

The divine cleansing of food in the vision is a parable of the divine cleansing of human beings in the incident to which the vision leads up. It did not take Peter long to understand this: "God has taught me," he says later in the present narrative, "to call *no human being* profane or unclean" (v. 30). Within the framework of the vision it is food that God has cleansed by dominical pronouncement, but in the wider narrative it is men and women, even Gentiles, whose hearts he has cleansed by faith (cf. 15:9). Yet the cleansing of food is not wholly parabolic: there is a connection between the abrogation of the levitical food restrictions and the removal of the barrier between believing Jews and Gentiles, for it was in large measure the Gentiles' eating of food which was "unclean" (not *kosher*) by Jewish law that made association with them a source of "defilement" for Jews (cf. v. 28).

---

18. Peter might no doubt have slaughtered and eaten one of the "clean" animals; but he was scandalized by the unholy mixture of clean animals with unclean. This is specially important in view of the practical way in which he had immediately to apply the lesson of the vision.

19. The fact that Peter's vision had to do with food restrictions, whereas the narrative in which it is set is concerned with the propriety of a Jew's entering a Gentile house, is taken by M. Dibelius as an indication that vv. 9-16 are part of Luke's working over of an original narrative which had nothing of the special significance which it acquires in the scheme of Luke's history (*Studies in the Acts of the Apostles*, E.T. [London, 1956], pp. 111-12).

3. The Messengers from Cornelius Arrive at Joppa (10:17-23a)

17 As Peter was at a loss to understand what might be the meaning of the vision he had seen, the men whom Cornelius had sent, having inquired for Simon's house, stood there and then at the street door.
18 They called out and asked if Simon, surnamed Peter, was lodging there.
19 While Peter was still thinking about the vision, the Spirit said to him, "See, there are three[20] men looking for you.
20 Get up, go down, and accompany them on their way. Do not hesitate; it is I who have sent them."
21 So Peter went down to the men[21] and said, "See, I am the man you are looking for. What is the cause of your being here?"
22 They said, "The centurion Cornelius, a just and God-fearing man, who enjoys a good reputation among the whole Jewish nation, was instructed by a holy angel to send for you to come to his house and to hear what you have to say."
23a Then Peter invited them in and entertained them.

17-20 The trance was over, but Peter remained on the roof, deep in thought, pondering the significance of what he had seen and heard in the vision. Suddenly the Spirit of God, by an inward monition, gave him to know that some men were looking for him, and that he was to go with them without any doubt or hesitation. For at that moment, the messengers from Caesarea, having made inquiry for Simon the tanner's house, were standing at the street door.

It may be asked if there is any distinction between the angelic communication to Cornelius (vv. 3-6) and Peter's prompting by the Spirit, just as a similar question had to be considered in the narrative of Philip and the Ethiopian (8:26-39). Here the distinction is rather obvious: the angelic communication was made "in a vision, clearly" (v. 3), whereas Peter was conscious of a voice within. But the more general question arises of the relation between one's experience of the Holy Spirit and one's experience of the risen Christ—a question all the more difficult to answer because it is through the Holy Spirit that the risen Christ manifests his presence and power.[22] But whom did Peter consider that he was addressing as "Lord" when he declined the invitation to slaughter and eat the meat provided in his vision? On that occasion the voice seemed to come from without, one gathers, and it was probably a voice that Peter well remembered, and instantly recognized.

---

20. Two men, according to B; the Western and Byzantine texts omit the numeral. The reading of B, being the most difficult (because of the discrepancy with v. 7 and 11:11), has claims to be regarded as original; if so, it suggests that the two domestic servants were the actual messengers, the soldier who accompanied them acting as a guard.
21. The Byzantine text adds "who had been sent to him by Cornelius" (cf. KJV).
22. Cf. F. F. Bruce, "Christ and Spirit in Paul," *BJRL* 59 (1976-77), pp. 259-85.

21-23a Peter then went down (by an outside stairway, no doubt) and found Cornelius's messengers at the door asking for him. He told them that he was the man they were looking for, and asked the reason for their visit. So they told him how their master Cornelius had been divinely instructed to invite him to his house, in order to hear an important communication from him. By this time the meal which Peter had called for was ready, so he brought the men in to share it. Not only so, but he provided accommodation for them overnight, as it was too late to set out for Caesarea after he had entertained them. For Peter to entertain these Gentiles in his lodgings was a step in the right direction, although it did not expose him to such a risk of defilement as would a Jew's acceptance of hospitality in a Gentile's house.

4. Peter Enters the House of Cornelius (10:23b-33)

23b *The next day he got up and set out with them. Some of the brothers from Joppa went along with him.*

24 *The following day he entered Caesarea. Cornelius was expecting them;[23] he had called together his relatives and his close friends.*

25 *When Peter arrived, Cornelius met him; he fell at his feet and did him reverence.*

26 *But Peter raised him up: "Stand up," he said, "I too am a human being."*

27 *So, conversing with him, he went in and found many come together.*

28 *Then he said to them, "You know[24] how unlawful it is for a man who is a Jew to associate or make common cause with a foreigner; but God has taught me to call no human being profane or unclean.*

29 *Therefore, when I was sent for, I came without demurring. I should like to know, then, the reason you have sent for me."*

30 *"Four days ago[25] at this time," said Cornelius, "I was praying[26] in my house at the ninth hour. Suddenly a man stood before me in shining clothes.*

31 *'Cornelius,' said he, 'your prayer has been heard and your acts of charity have been remembered in the presence of God.*

32 *Therefore send to Joppa and call for Simon, surnamed Peter; he is lodging in the house of Simon a tanner, by the seashore.'[27]*

23. From here to the end of v. 25 the Western text has the amplified reading: "and having called together his relatives and his close friends was waiting for them. As Peter drew near to Caesarea, one of the slaves ran on ahead and announced that he had arrived. Then Cornelius, leaping up and going to meet him, fell at his feet and did him reverence."

24. D adds "very well" (βέλτιον).

25. D reads "three days ago"; this shortens the time taken for the journey from Joppa to Caesarea.

26. The Western text reads "fasting and praying"; this pietistic amplification is a Western characteristic.

27. The Western and Byzantine texts add "who, having arrived, will speak to you" (cf. KJV).

33 *Immediately therefore I sent to you,*[28] *and you have been so good as to come.*[29] *Now then, we are all here present before God,*[30] *to hear all that the Lord has directed you to say.*"

23b-24   On Day 1 Cornelius saw the angel and sent his messengers to Joppa; on Day 2 they arrived at Joppa about midday, just after Peter's ecstatic experience on the roof of Simon's house. On Day 3 he set out for Caesarea with them. In view of the novelty of his mission, he acted wisely in taking some fellow-believers from Joppa with him—six in number, as he himself reports in 11:12. They spent the night of Day 3 somewhere on the way between Joppa and Caesarea, and reached Caesarea on Day 4.[31] Meanwhile Cornelius had gathered his relatives and close friends in his house, ready for Peter's arrival.

25-26   When Peter arrived, Cornelius hurried out and paid him the respect which he judged fitting for a messenger of God, prostrating himself at the apostle's feet in an attitude of homage and supplication.[32] A messenger of God was supposed to have some godlike quality himself, to be a *theios anēr,* as the technical term has it.[33] It is unlikely that Peter had ever had such reverence paid to him before, and no doubt it embarrassed him considerably: "Please get up," he said, helping his host to rise to his feet; "I am only a mortal myself."

27-29   Then, talking with him in a friendly manner, Peter accompanied him indoors, and there was the whole group of Cornelius's friends, full of eager expectation. Two or three days previously, Peter would not have believed it possible that he could find himself in such company, under a Gentile roof; but much had happened since then. "You know very well," he said to Cornelius and the others, "that to mix in Gentile society is taboo[34] for a pious Jew; but God has taught me not to regard any person as unfit to associate with." Actually, the terms of his vision on the housetop at Joppa

---

28. The Western text adds "requesting you to come to us."

29. The Western text adds "speedily."

30. *P*[45] omits "all" and "before God."

31. But see n. 25 above.

32. As the footnote in ASV points out, Gk. προσκυνέω is used of an act of reverence whether paid to God or (as here) to a creature (of either angelic or human nature).

33. See p. 172, n. 49 (on 8:9-24); p. 499 with n. 14 (on 28:6). Cf. L. Bieler, *Theios Anēr. Das Bild des "göttlichen Menschen" in Spätantike und Frühchristentum* (Darmstadt, 1967); C. R. Holladay, *Theios Anēr in Hellenistic Judaism,* SBLDS 40 (Missoula, MT, 1977).

34. A suitable word to use here as the equivalent of Gk. ἀθέμιτος. The word for "Gentile" or "foreigner" in v. 28 is ἀλλόφυλος, which (significantly enough) is commonly used in LXX to denote an uncircumcised Philistine. Josephus (*BJ* 5.194) uses it (in place of the inscriptional ἀλλογενής) in paraphrasing the warning notice in the temple forbidding Gentiles to trespass into the inner courts (see on 21:28, p. 409, n. 48).

taught him to call no *food* profane or unclean if God pronounced it clean; but he was quick to grasp the analogy between ceremonial food laws and the conventions affecting intercourse with non-Jews. It was largely because of their lack of scruples in food matters that Gentiles were ritually unsafe people for a pious Jew to meet socially. Intercourse with Gentiles was not categorically forbidden; but it was liable to render a Jew ceremonially unclean, as was even the entering of a Gentile building[35] or the handling of articles belonging to Gentiles. The most ordinary kinds of food, such as bread, milk, or olive oil, coming from Gentiles, might not be eaten by strict Jews, not to mention flesh, which might have come from a forbidden animal or from one that had been sacrificed to a pagan divinity, and which in any case contained blood. Hence, of all forms of intercourse with Gentiles, to accept their hospitality and sit at table with them was the most intolerable. However, Peter's lesson had so impressed itself on his mind that he accompanied Cornelius's messengers without scruple or protest. And now that he had arrived, he asked them to state more fully their reason for inviting him.

30-33 Cornelius then described the vision,[36] which he had seen three days before (four days by inclusive reckoning), at the very hour at which he was now speaking, the hour of afternoon prayer. He repeated the words spoken to him by the celestial visitant who stood before him in shining robes.[37] It was in accordance with his directions, he explained, that he had sent for Peter, and he heartily thanked him for coming so promptly. "Now then," he said, "we are all here present before God, to hear all that the Lord has directed you to say." Never had a preacher of the gospel a more promising audience—as promising in its way as Philip's one-man audience on the Gaza road when he was invited to expound the Isaianic prophecy of the suffering Servant (8:30-35).

5. Gentiles Hear the Good News (10:34-43)

34 *Then Peter spoke up. "In truth," he said, "I realize that God has no favorites;*
35 *but in every nation one who fears him and does what is righteous is acceptable to him.*
36 *You know the message that[38] he sent to the people of Israel, preaching good news of peace through Jesus Christ—he is Lord of all—*

35. Thus, on Good Friday, Jesus' accusers stayed out in the courtyard of Pilate's praetorium; to enter the building itself would have necessitated their being ceremonially purified all over again, in order to celebrate the Passover that evening (John 18:28).
36. Cornelius's description of his vision affords an opportunity of repeating part of a narrative very important in Luke's history, as Peter's description of *his* vision in 11:5-10 affords an opportunity of repeating another part.
37. Cf. 1:10 (p. 38) for angelic clothing.
38. The relative pronoun is omitted by A B *et al.* (a haplographic omission of ὅν after λόγον). The Western text recasts the construction of vv. 36-38 thus: "For you know

37 *(you know) what took place³⁹ throughout all Judaea, beginning from Galilee after the baptism⁴⁰ which John proclaimed,*

38 *concerning Jesus of Nazareth, how God anointed him with the Holy Spirit and power. He went about doing good and healing all who were under the devil's domination, because God was with him.*

39 *We indeed are witnesses of all that he did in the country of the Jews and in Jerusalem. The one whom they put to death by hanging him on a gibbet,*

40 *he is the one whom God raised up on the third day⁴¹ and caused to be manifested—*

41 *not to all the people, but to witnesses whom God appointed in advance—to us, in fact, who ate and drank with him after he rose from the dead.⁴²*

42 *He charged us to preach to the people and testify that he is the one ordained by God as judge of living and dead.*

43 *It is to him that all the prophets bear witness, that everyone who believes in him will receive forgiveness of sins through his name."*

34-35 The expression "Then Peter spoke up" (literally, "Peter opened his mouth") is one that is used to introduce some weighty utterance. The first words that Peter spoke were words of the weightiest import, sweeping away the racial and religious prejudices of centuries. The words of Cornelius confirmed the lesson that Peter himself had learned in Joppa: God has no favorites⁴³ as between one nation and another, but anyone, from whatever nation, who fears him and acts rightly⁴⁴ is acceptable to him. This may be

---

the message which he sent to the children of Israel, which was published throughout all Judaea, when he preached good tidings of peace through Jesus Christ (he is Lord of all). For beginning in Galilee, after the baptism which John proclaimed, Jesus of Nazareth, whom God anointed with the Holy Spirit and power, went about doing good. . . ."

39. Gk. τὸ γενόμενον ῥῆμα, lit. "the word which took place" (for ῥῆμα in the sense of "thing," "event," cf. 5:32).

40. B reads κήρυγμα ("proclamation") for βάπτισμα ("baptism").

41. D reads "after the third day" (perhaps an attempted harmonization with Mark 8:31; Matt. 27:63, etc.).

42. The Western text amplifies: "who ate and drank and conversed with him forty days after the resurrection from the dead."

43. Gk. προσωπολήμπτης ("respecter of persons," lit. "lifter of faces") reflects the Hebrew idiom *nāśā' pānîm*, "lift (someone's) face" and hence "show favor" or, in a pejorative sense, "show favoritism." This idiom is rendered in Greek by πρόσωπον λαμβάνω and similar phrases (cf. Luke 20:21; Gal. 2:6); the nouns προσωπολήμπτης (here appearing for the first time in Greek literature and the only time in the NT) and προσωπολημψία ("partiality") are formed on the basis of this phrase (cf. Rom. 2:11; Eph. 6:9; Col. 3:25; Jas. 2:1; 1 Pet. 1:17).

44. Gk. ὁ ἐργαζόμενος δικαιοσύνην (v. 35) no doubt means the practice of righteousness in the widest sense, but it is relevant to recall the more specialized sense of the word (like *ṣᵉdāqāh* in Mishnaic Hebrew) to denote almsgiving (cf. Dan. 4:27; Matt. 6:1), in view of Cornelius's charitable activity.

the veriest truism to us, but it was a revolutionary revelation to Peter. Yet it was implicit in the teaching of the early prophets. They insisted that God's choice of Israel was an act of grace, not of partiality, and that it called for a response of obedient service, not of careless complacency. If God brought Israel out of Egypt into the land of their inheritance, he had also brought the Philistines from Crete and the Syrians from Kir (Amos 9:7). On a coming day God would bless "Egypt my people" and "Assyria the work of my hands" along with "Israel my heritage" (Isa. 19:25). If, as Micah said, the Lord's primary requirements were that men and women should act justly and love mercy and walk humbly with their God (Mic. 6:8), then Gentiles might fulfil these requirements as readily as Israelites. Luke, himself a Gentile by birth, had good reason to emphasize the narrative of the bringing in of the Gentiles, by the cumulative repetitions within the narrative and by other means.

36-37 Peter's address, which Foakes-Jackson pronounced "peculiarly appropriate to the occasion"[45] (although Martin Dibelius regarded it as an interpolation into the original Cornelius story),[46] is devoted almost entirely to a summary of the apostolic preaching. Some acquaintance with the main outline of the story of Jesus is presumed (for Peter's hearers were far from being raw pagans), but more details are given than in the summaries of Peter's earlier speeches.[47] How far this reflects the actual amount of detail given by Peter in his respective addresses, and how far it is due to the way in which Luke summarizes them, cannot easily be decided. C. H. Dodd is no doubt right in suggesting "that the speech before Cornelius represents the form of *kerygma* used by the primitive Church in its earliest approaches to a wider preaching."[48] The scope of the *kerygma,* as attested by this address of Peter's, is almost exactly the scope of Mark's Gospel,[49] beginning with

45. *The Acts of the Apostles,* MNTC, p. 93.

46. "A speech which is so long, relatively speaking, cannot have had any place in a legend told among Christians about the conversion of a centurion" (Dibelius, *Studies,* p. 110). Like the other speeches in Acts, said Dibelius, this speech is a literary composition of the author's; nothing in it is (apart from the introductory remarks of vv. 34-35) relevant to the special question of Gentile evangelization, and Peter's own account of the proceedings leaves no room for such a speech, for he tells how the Holy Spirit fell on Cornelius and his household "as I began to speak" (11:15). But, since Dibelius regarded Peter's defense of his action in 11:4-17 as equally Luke's overworking of the original "legend," there seems to be little force in this last argument.

47. Cf. 2:14-36; 3:12-26; 4:8-12; 5:29-32.

48. C. H. Dodd, *The Apostolic Preaching and its Developments* (London, 1936), p. 56.

49. Cf. C. H. Dodd, "The Framework of the Gospel Narrative," *ExT* 43 (1931-32), pp. 396-400, reprinted in his *New Testament Studies* (Manchester, 1953), pp. 1-11. Against the view propounded by K. L. Schmidt in *Der Rahmen der Geschichte Jesu* (Berlin, 1919), that Mark's record consists mainly of independent *pericopae* strung together by means of short editorial summaries *(Sammelberichte)* which have no historical value of their own, Dodd undertook to show that those summaries, when put together,

John's baptismal ministry, and going on to tell of Jesus' ministry in Galilee, [50] Judaea, [51] and Jerusalem, of his crucifixion and resurrection, followed by the insistence on personal witness and on the coming judgment, with the offer of forgiveness through faith in him here and now. But the reference to Jesus' resurrection appearances corresponds not to Mark's record (in which no such appearances are extant) but to Luke's. This is specially evident in the statement that the apostles "ate and drank" with the risen Lord (v. 41).

In the house of Cornelius Peter may have spoken Greek, but some have thought it more probable that he spoke in Aramaic through an interpreter. [52] This speech, at any rate, is more strongly marked by Aramaisms than Peter's speeches in the earlier chapters of Acts. The presence of Aramaisms suggests that the speech is not Luke's free invention, but a rather literal reproduction of what he found in his source (whether written or oral). The Greek of verses 36-38 in particular reads somewhat awkwardly, as do the fairly literal renderings in the older English versions, but it is claimed that it can be turned back word for word into idiomatic and intelligible Aramaic. [53]

38 The statement that Jesus of Nazareth was "anointed" by God with the Holy Spirit and power is reminiscent of the words of Isa. 61:1-2 which Jesus read in the Nazareth synagogue—"The Spirit of the Lord GOD is upon me, because the LORD has anointed me . . ."—and which he claimed to be fulfilled that day in his ministry (Luke 4:17-21).[54] The prophet who introduces himself in these words may be assuming the role of the Servant of Isa. 42:1–53:12.[55] When the Servant is first presented in Isa. 42:1, he is

---

present a coherent outline of the ministry of Jesus, comparable to outlines of the apostolic preaching found elsewhere in the NT, and in particular to the outline of Peter's address in the house of Cornelius. For a critique of Dodd's argument see D. E. Nineham, "The Order of Events in St. Mark's Gospel—An Examination of Dr. Dodd's Hypothesis," in *Studies in the Gospels: Essays in Memory of R. H. Lightfoot,* ed. D. E. Nineham (Oxford, 1955), pp. 223-39.

50. "This emphasis on the beginning in Galilee seems to have been integral to the pattern of the *kerygma* from the first" (C. H. Dodd, *According to the Scriptures* [London, 1952], pp. 80-81). "Beginning from Galilee" characterizes Jesus' ministry, as "beginning from Jerusalem" (Luke 24:47) characterizes that of the apostles.

51. The expressions "throughout all Judaea" (v. 37) and "in the country of the Jews" (v. 39) probably denote the whole land of Israel and not only the Roman province of Judaea. Cf. 26:20.

52. According to Papias's account of the origin of Mark's Gospel (preserved by Eusebius, *HE* 3.39.15, and probably reflected in the so-called anti-Marcionite prologue to the Gospel), Peter even at a later date used the services of an interpreter.

53. Cf. C. C. Torrey, *Composition and Date of Acts* (Cambridge, Mass., 1916), pp. 27, 35-36.

54. In Jesus' Nazareth exposition of these words the Gentile mission is adumbrated; so here Peter's assertion that Jesus Christ is "Lord of all" implies his lordship over Gentiles as well as Jews (cf. Rom. 10:12). The "good news of peace" preached through him (Isa. 52:7) is intended for those who are "far off" as well as for those who are "near" (Isa. 57:19; see on 2:39 above).

55. The affinities of Isa. 61:1-2 with the Servant Songs can be recognized

described as God's chosen one on whom he had put his Spirit; this brings him into relation with the predicted ruler of David's line in Isa. 11:1-5 on whom "the Spirit of the LORD shall rest." It was at his baptism that Jesus was thus anointed, for then the Holy Spirit descended on him from above, while the voice from heaven acclaimed him as God's Son and chosen one—Messiah and Servant in one. Part of the force of Peter's words will come home to us if for a moment we render "God anointed him" as "God made him Messiah."[56] These words may be understood as "commenting upon the meaning and implication of an already accepted name of Jesus" (i.e., the Christ).[57]

When Jesus had been thus anointed, he "returned in the power of the Spirit into Galilee" (Luke 4:14) and embarked on a ministry which fulfilled the terms of Isa. 61:1-2 and other passages of prophetic scripture—healing the sick and delivering the demon-possessed,[58] proclaiming in word and action the good news of the kingdom of God. When we consider this brief summary of the preaching, we should reflect that in its actual delivery it would be amplified by the inclusion of examples of Jesus' works of mercy and power ("paradigms," to use a technical term of form criticism), such as are recorded in the Gospels.[59]

39 Peter insists that he and his colleagues are eyewitnesses of those things, which took place throughout the whole land of Israel. Yet Jesus' works of healing and release, he goes on, did not prevent him from being put to death—and put to death by that means on which the law of Moses pronounced a curse, for his enemies killed him "by hanging him on a gibbet." We have already considered the significance of this particular expression as a way to describe death by crucifixion (cf. 5:30).[60]

40-41 Again, as so often in the apostolic preaching, comes the

---

without the formal inclusion of that passage as an additional Servant Song (cf. a note on some who have so included it in C. R. North, *The Suffering Servant in Deutero-Isaiah* [Oxford, 1948], pp. 137-38).

56. Cf. 4:27 (p. 99 with n. 46); see also C. H. Dodd, *According to the Scriptures* (London, 1952), pp. 52-53, 94-96.

57. A. E. Harvey, *Jesus and the Constraints of History* (London, 1982), p. 139, n. 95.

58. The participle "doing good" (εὐεργετῶν) is related to the royal designation Euergetes, "benefactor" (cf. Luke 22:25). As for Jesus' "healing all those who were under the devil's domination," the Gospels ascribe not only demon-possession but also certain other ailments to satanic agency (cf. Luke 13:16), not to mention unbelief and falsehood (cf. Matt. 13:19, 39; John 8:44). Gk. διάβολος (translated "devil," as in 13:10) means "slanderer" or "false accuser"; it is the equivalent of Heb. *śāṭān* (see on 5:3, p. 105, n. 14).

59. These examples would not be mere illustrations in the preaching; they were (among other things) proofs of the fulfilment of prophecy, as Jesus himself implied when he sent John the Baptist's messengers back to their master with the command to tell John what they and seen and heard (Luke 7:22). John would recognize from their report that the prophetic program (e.g., of Isa. 35:5-6) was indeed being carried out, and that Jesus was therefore the Coming One to whom the prophets bore witness.

60. See p. 113, n. 40.

pointed contrast between men's treatment of the Christ and God's treatment of him: the very one whom men put to death is the one whom God raised to new life on the third day.[61] There could be no doubt about his resurrection: he appeared to many witnesses—not indeed to the people at large but to those selected by God to see and proclaim the risen Savior, Peter and his fellow-disciples. They could testify with assurance to his resurrection, for they had not only seen him alive again after his passion but had even eaten and drunk with him. Luke, the only one of the four evangelists who records the risen Lord's eating with his disciples (Luke 24:41-43), regarded this as among the most convincing of the many tokens of his bodily resurrection (cf. 1:4 above); so, at a later date, did Ignatius ("he ate and drank with them as a being of flesh, although he was spiritually united to the Father"). The disciples were assured that it was no bodiless phantom that appeared to them.[62]

42 During these appearances, said Peter, Christ commanded him and the other apostles to proclaim "to the people" the message of the kingdom of God, now inaugurated by his death and resurrection, and also to announce him as the one divinely appointed to be judge of all, both living and dead—the "one like a son of man" of Daniel's vision to whom was committed authority to execute judgment (Dan. 7:13-14; John 5:27).[63]

While the apostles' commission was worldwide—"to the end of the earth," according to 1:8—Peter speaks of it as specifically directed to the Jewish people (cf. 13:31); and this is in accord with historical fact. Apart from his present visit to Cornelius, Peter is not recorded as evangelizing Gentiles. A few years after this, at the Jerusalem conference described in Gal. 2:1-10, it was agreed that Peter and his colleagues should concentrate on evangelizing Jews, while Paul and Barnabas should continue to discharge their commission to preach to the Gentiles; and the narrative of Acts reflects this division of labor. As for the commission of 1:8, Peter and the Eleven bore witness in Jerusalem and Judaea and Philip the evangelist (primarily) in

61. The "third day" (v. 40) is mentioned not only for chronological accuracy, but in order to emphasize another fulfilment of prophecy; cf. 1 Cor. 15:4, where Paul quotes the primitive apostolic message as affirming that Christ was "raised on the third day in accordance with the scriptures." The OT testimonies quoted in the apostolic preaching sometimes reflect the recognition that the Messiah's experiences exhibit the same pattern as Israel's experiences; hence such a statement as "After two days he will revive us; on the third day he will raise us up" (Hos. 6:2) could find its fulfilment in the resurrection of Jesus. Paul's reference to the risen Christ as the "firstfruits" in 1 Cor. 15:20, 23 may suggest that he saw in his resurrection a fulfilment of the ordinance of Lev. 23:10-11 that the firstfruits of barley harvest were to be presented to God the day after the paschal sabbath (i.e., on the first day of the week).

62. Luke 24:39; cf. the words ascribed to the risen Christ in a lost work quoted by Ignatius (*Smyrnaeans* 3:2): "I am not a bodiless spirit" (οὐκ εἰμὶ δαιμόνιον ἀσώματον).

63. Cf. 17:31, where Paul's address in Athens finds its climax in the announcement of God's righteous judgment of the world "by the man whom he has ordained."

Samaria, but in Luke's record the spreading of the message to the end of the earth is reserved for Paul.

43 The function of the risen Christ was by no means limited to the execution of judgment; he was also the one through whom, as the prophets agreed, those who believed on him would have their sins forgiven.[64] As Jesus said himself when he cured the paralytic of Capernaum, "the Son of Man has authority on earth to forgive sins" (Mark 2:10). Peter's appeal to "all the prophets" would be supported by relevant quotations from their writings, including most probably the portrayal of the Servant of the Lord who was to "make the many righteous" and "bear their iniquities" (Isa. 53:11).

6. Gentiles Receive the Holy Spirit (10:44-48)

44 *While Peter was still speaking these words, the Holy Spirit fell on all who were listening to the message.*

45 *The believers of the circumcision who had come with Peter were amazed because the gift of the Holy Spirit had been poured out on Gentiles;*

46 *for they heard them speaking with[65] tongues and magnifying God.*

47 *Then Peter said, "Can anyone forbid water? Why should these people not be baptized, since they have received the Holy Spirit as we also did?"*

48 *So he gave orders for them to be baptized in the name of[66] Jesus Christ. Then they asked him to stay on for some days.*

44 Peter had not yet finished his address[67] when the "Pentecost of the Gentile world" took place.[68] The Holy Spirit fell on all his listeners. The event was not so much a second Pentecost, standing alongside the first, as the participation of Gentile believers in the experience of the first Pentecost.[69] What was involved was later summed up by Paul: "in one Spirit we were all baptized into one body, whether Jews or Greeks" (1 Cor. 12:13).

But, so far as the hearers of the apostolic preaching were concerned, the order of events differed markedly from that of the hearers on the day of Pentecost in Jerusalem. The hearers in Jerusalem were exhorted to repent and be baptized in order to receive the remission of sins and the gift of the

---

64. Cf. 13:38; 26:18; Luke 24:47.
65. The Western text inserts "other" (cf. 2:4).
66. The Western text inserts "the Lord" (as it does in 2:38).
67. Cf. 11:15.
68. So this occasion is called by F. H. Chase, *The Credibility of the Acts of the Apostles* (London, 1902), p. 79.
69. Cf. N. B. Stonehouse, "Repentance, Baptism and the Gift of the Holy Spirit," in *Paul Before the Areopagus and Other New Testament Studies* (Grand Rapids, 1957), pp. 76-77.

Spirit. But the experience of the hearers in Caesarea reproduced rather that of the original company of disciples in Jerusalem, on whom the Spirit descended suddenly.[70] This may be recognized in Peter's drawing a parallel (v. 47) between the household of Cornelius and the original disciples rather than between the household of Cornelius and the three thousand who believed on the day of Pentecost (cf. 11:15; 15:8).

45-46 The descent of the Spirit on those Gentiles was outwardly manifested in much the same way as it had been when the original disciples received the Spirit at Pentecost: they spoke with tongues and proclaimed the mighty works of God.[71] Apart from such external manifestations, none of the Jewish believers present, perhaps not even Peter himself, would have been so ready to accept the reality of the Spirit's coming upon them. The Jewish believers who had accompanied Peter from Joppa were astounded by what they saw and heard: *Gentiles*, those "lesser breeds without the law," had actually received the same Holy Spirit as they themselves had received on believing the same message. How right Peter had been in his new insight into the impartiality of God as between people of one race and another! As in Peter's vision the voice of God overruled food restrictions, even those imposed with the authority of divine law, so now the act of God in sending the Spirit overruled the sacred tradition which forbade association with Gentiles.

47-48 On the day of Pentecost (2:37-41) the sequence of initiation into the new community was conviction of sin, repentance and faith, baptism in the name of Jesus Christ for the remission of sins, and the reception of the Spirit. Here the reception of the Spirit comes first. There is no explicit mention of faith in the immediate context, but it is certainly implied; it is suggested more definitely in 11:17, where Peter's words "when *we* believed on the Lord Jesus Christ" clearly mean that the Gentiles received the Spirit when *they* believed,[72] while in 15:7-9 Peter expressly links the Gentiles' reception of the Spirit with their believing and having their hearts cleansed by faith.[73] Only after the manifest descent of the Spirit on these believing Gentiles were they baptized in water. As for the imposition of apostolic hands[74] (whatever inferences may be drawn from the silence on this subject in ch. 2), nothing of the kind took place before the Gentiles received the Spirit, and nothing is said about its taking place subsequently.

Had Peter not been confronted with a divine *fait accompli* in the

---

70. Cf. G. W. H. Lampe, *The Seal of the Spirit* (London, 1951), p. 66.

71. "Magnifying God" (μεγαλυνόντων τὸν θεόν) in v. 46 is synonymous with "declaring the mighty words of God" (λαλούντων . . . τὰ μεγαλεῖα τοῦ θεοῦ) in 2:11.

72. The repentance of these Gentiles is mentioned in 11:18.

73. The "cleansing" of the Gentiles' hearts by faith is closely linked with the words addressed to Peter in his vision: "You must not regard as profane what God has cleansed." The same verb (καθαρίζω) is used in both places.

74. Contrast the experience of the Samaritan believers in 8:17.

outpouring of the Spirit on Cornelius and his friends, he might not have taken the initiative in having them baptized. But, as things were, God had plainly accepted them, and Peter had no option but to accept what God had done. In justifying his action a few days later, he asked, "Who was I to hinder God?" (11:17). Here his question, "Can anyone forbid water?" (like the Ethiopian's question in 8:36, "What prevents me from being baptized?"), has been thought to point to a primitive custom by which, before a convert was baptized, it was inquired if there was any "just cause or impediment" why the baptism should not take place.[75] Whether this was so or not, no impediment was alleged on the present occasion, and Peter gave orders that these new believers should be baptized in the name of Jesus Christ.[76] Their reception of the Spirit was not regarded as a substitute for baptism in water; rather, their baptism in water was the fitting response to the act of God in bestowing his Spirit. But no one appears to have suggested that Cornelius should be circumcised. His case thus served as a specially appropriate precedent when the question of the circumcision of Gentile believers was later raised at the Jerusalem council (ch. 15).

75. The same verb (Gk. κωλύω) is here translated "forbid" as is translated "hinder" in 11:17; it appears also in a baptismal context in 8:36 (see p. 177, n. 71).
76. The same phrase as is used in 2:38 (see p. 70).

218

ACTS 11

C. PETER'S ACTION ENDORSED AT JERUSALEM (11:1-18)

1. Peter Called to Account (11:1-3)

1 *The apostles and the brothers who were in Judaea heard that the Gentiles also had received the word of God.[1]*

2 *So, when Peter went up to Jerusalem, those who were of the circumcision party remonstrated with him.[2]*

3 *"Why," they asked, "did you go in to visit uncircumcised men and actually share a meal with them?"*

1 The news of Peter's revolutionary behavior, in entering a Gentile house at Caesarea, reached Jerusalem before he himself did. The Western text makes him spend a fairly long time at Caesarea, and then engage in a teaching ministry in the region between Caesarea and Jerusalem.[3] There may be some truth in this, although the Western reviser's main concern was probably to avoid giving the impression that the outpouring of the Spirit at Caesarea was followed immmediately by controversy within the Spirit-filled community at Jerusalem. But however long the interval was, Peter's action could not fail to arouse alarm at Jerusalem. Hitherto, even if Stephen and his fellow-Hellenists incurred popular hostility, the apostles had been able to enjoy a measure of general goodwill; but if the news got around that the leader of the apostles himself had begun to fraternize with Gentiles, that goodwill would soon be dissipated. And in fact it may well have turned out

1. Some forms of the Western text add (prematurely) "and they glorified God" (cf. v. 18).

2. The Western text expands v. 2 as follows: "Peter then after a considerable time wished to go to Jerusalem; and calling the brothers to him and establishing them, he took his departure, engaging in much preaching throughout the regions and teaching them. When he met them [at Jerusalem], he reported to them the grace of God, but those who were of the circumcision (part) remonstrated with him."

3. See n. 2 above. Some scholars (e.g., G. Salmon, "Blass's Commentary on the Acts," *Hermathena* 9 [1896], p. 235, quoted with approval by F. Blass, *Philology of the Gospels* [London, 1898], p. 129), accepting the Western reading here, have linked it with the Western reading of 21:16 which makes Mnason the Cypriot live in one of the villages between Caesarea and Jerusalem; but this is improbable. See pp. 402-3, nn. 15, 19.

so. It was not long after this that Herod Agrippa I, appointed ruler of Judaea by the Emperor Claudius in A.D. 41, executed James the son of Zebedee and then, in view of the approval with which this action met, arrested Peter in his turn (12:1-3). About the same time, too, James the brother of Jesus emerges as acknowledged leader of the Jerusalem church, rather than any one of the twelve apostles (cf. 12:17; 15:13).

2-3 When Peter arrived home, then, he was immediately taken to task by "those who were of the circumcision"[4] (as the phrase may be rendered fairly literally). The same phrase is used of the Jewish believers who accompanied Peter from Joppa to Caesarea (10:45), but there it simply denotes people who were of Jewish stock as distinct from Gentiles. Here it refers more particularly to those Jewish believers who were specially zealous for the law and insisted that there should be no social intercourse between circumcised and uncircumcised. Paul uses the phrase in this sense in Gal. 2:12 when he speaks of those visitors from Jerusalem to Antioch who persuaded Peter to abstain from table fellowship with Gentile Christians. "Why," Peter was asked on the present occasion, "did you go to uncircumcised men and eat with them?"

In the original form of the story, Martin Dibelius suggests, Peter had no more need to defend himself for preaching the gospel to Cornelius than Philip had for preaching it to the Ethiopian eunuch.[5] In the original story the issue of eating with Gentiles was not raised; it was introduced later because of the part which it came to play in the discussion of the terms to be laid down for the admission of Gentile believers to church membership. There is, indeed, no express reference to eating with Gentiles in the narrative of chapter 10. But the problem is present in the narrative by implication. It was the thought of eating with Gentiles in particular that made the idea of entering a Gentile house so objectionable, for Gentile food was "profane and unclean"; and it is the thought of eating with Gentiles that supplies the link between Peter's vision in which the levitical food restrictions were abrogated and his practical application of that lesson in ignoring the ceremonial objections to entering a Gentile house.

2. Peter's Defense (11:4-17)

4 *Then Peter began and set the events before them in order.*

5 *"I was at prayer in the city of Joppa," he said, "and in a trance I saw a vision—something like a great sheet descending, let down from heaven by four corners, and it came right to where I was.*

6 *When I had looked at it carefully I was able to make out the four-*

---

4. Gk. οἱ ἐκ περιτομῆς.

5. See his study "The Conversion of Cornelius" in *Studies in the Acts of the Apostles*, E.T. (London, 1956), pp. 109-22.

footed animals of the earth, wild beasts, creeping things, and birds of the sky.

7 *I also heard a voice saying to me, 'Get up, Peter, kill and eat.'*

8 *But I said, 'No, Lord; nothing profane or unclean has ever entered into my mouth.'*

9 *A voice came from heaven a second time and answered,[6] 'You must not regard as profane what God has cleansed.'*

10 *This happened three times; then everything was drawn up again into heaven.*

11 *At that moment, I tell you, three men stood at the house where we were;[7] they had been sent to me from Caesarea.*

12 *The Spirit told me to go with them without making any distinction. And these six brothers went with me, and we entered the man's house.*

13 *He told us how he had seen the angel in his house, standing there and saying, 'Send to Joppa and fetch Simon, surnamed Peter;*

14 *he will speak words to you by which you and your household will be saved.'*

15 *When I had begun to speak, the Holy Spirit fell on them as he did on us at the beginning.*

16 *Then I remembered what the Lord said: 'John baptized with water, but you will be baptized with the Holy Spirit.'*

17 *If, then, God gave them the same gift as he gave to us when we believed on the Lord Jesus Christ, who was I to be capable of hindering God?"[8]*

4-10 Peter's best defense of his conduct was a straightforward narration of his experience. So he told them of his vision on the roof of the tanner's house at Joppa. In this repetition of the story variety of expression is combined with similarity in construction. Although it abridges the fuller account in chapter 10, yet it introduces one or two details which are absent there. In verses 5 and 6 there is a vividness in Peter's description of the great sheet which contrasts with the comparative colorlessness of the third-person account in 10:11-12.[9] Whereas three categories of animal are distinguished in 10:12, 11:6 distinguishes four, adding wild beasts to the domestic quadrupeds, as in the creation narrative of Genesis.[10] The wording of Peter's refusal in verse 8 is closer even than that of 10:14 to Ezekiel's protest when he was directed to eat

6. D reads: "there came a voice from heaven to me."
7. "We were" (ἦμεν) is the reading of P^{74} ℵ A B D pc; "I was" (ἤμην) is the reading of P^{45} E Ψ 33 81 byz (and all the versions).
8. The Western text reads: "who was I that I could hinder God from giving them the Holy Spirit when they believed on him?"
9. Similarly the verb "was drawn up" (v. 10) is more vigorous than "was taken up" (10:16).
10. Gen. 1:24-25; cf. Ps. 148:10 ("beasts and all cattle, creeping things and flying birds").

"unclean" food: "abominable flesh has never entered into my mouth" (Ezek. 4:14).

11-14 Then he told how Cornelius's messengers came to invite him to Caesarea, and how he went with them at the Spirit's prompting, "without making any distinction" (v. 12). The six members of the believing community in Joppa who had accompanied him to Caesarea had come with him also to Jerusalem, and they were present as witnesses to the truth of his account. The reference to "the angel" in verse 13 implies that the story of Cornelius's supernatural visitant is already known—known, that is to say, to Luke's readers rather than to Peter's hearers (although we are probably intended to understand that what we have here is a brief summary of the story as told by Peter). According to this account, the angel informed Cornelius that the words which he would hear from Peter (cf. 10:22) were words which would bring salvation to himself and his household. It has already been made clear that Cornelius was acceptable to God as a man who feared him and practised righteousness (10:35). Throughout the Bible, divine judgment is regularly pronounced in accordance with a person's works;[11] but salvation is not of works but of grace (cf. 15:11), and salvation did not enter Cornelius's house until Peter came there with the gospel. The "household" (v. 14) included not only Cornelius's immediate family in the modern English sense, but all who were under his authority—slaves, attendants, and other dependents.[12]

15-17 Then Peter reached the climax of his narration, telling how he had scarcely begun to address Cornelius and his household when the Holy Spirit descended on them, just as he had descended on Peter and his fellow-disciples at Pentecost.[13] The words of the risen Christ to his disciples, "John indeed baptized with water, but you will be baptized with the Holy Spirit in a few days' time" (1:5), were quickly fulfilled in Jerusalem on the day of Pentecost, but as Peter saw what took place in the house of Cornelius, and heard those Gentiles speak with tongues and magnify God, the words came afresh to his mind, and he recognized that now they were being fulfilled anew. God evidently made no distinction between believing Gentiles and believing Jews; how could Peter maintain a barrier which God plainly ignored? To do so would be to oppose God. There is no express mention here

---

11. Cf. Rom. 2:6 (Cornelius, as portrayed by Luke, is a good example of those persons described by Paul in Rom. 2:7).

12. All, in fact, who came within the scope of the Roman *familia*. Compare the similar language used to the jailer of Philippi in 16:31.

13. M. Dibelius sees a discrepancy between "when I had begun to speak" here and "while Peter was still speaking" in 10:44: "According to 10:44," the Spirit was manifested "at the end of Peter's sermon, according to 11:15, just as he had begun to speak" (*Studies*, p. 110). But the idea of *beginning* need not be pressed unduly (cf. p. 212, n. 46). In several places in the narrative parts of the NT, ἄρχομαι is little more than a semitizing redundant auxiliary; cf. J. H. Moulton in MHT I, pp. 14-15.

(as there is in 10:47-48) of the baptism of the Gentiles, though it is perhaps implied in the language of verse 17.

3. Peter's Defense Accepted (11:18)

18 *When they heard this, they fell silent. Then they glorified God. "So," they said, "to the Gentiles also God has granted repentance to life!"*

18 Nothing could be said to counter Peter's argument. His critics were silenced. God had acted, and had clearly shown his will. That he had bestowed his blessing on Gentiles also—or *even* on Gentiles—giving them through his Spirit a change of mind and heart and the assurance of eternal life, was a matter for wonder and praise. Their objections ceased; their praise began. The practical problems which were to become so acute when large-scale Gentile evangelization began did not arise at this stage. Even so, it may be surmised that the endorsement of Peter's action was more wholehearted on the part of his fellow-apostles than on the part of the zealous rank and file of the Jerusalem church.[14] This may have been one reason for the speed with which James the Just was henceforth acknowledged as the undisputed leader of the mother-church: James at least enjoyed a public reputation which was unspotted by any suspicion of fraternizing with Gentiles.[15] But the apostles had at least admitted the principle of evangelizing Gentiles, and had done so in time to recognize the same principle being worked out farther north on a scale previously unimagined.

D. ANTIOCH BECOMES A CHRISTIAN BASE (11:19-30)

1. Gentile Evangelization in Antioch (11:19-21)

19 *Now those who had been dispersed because of the tribulation that broke out over Stephen made their way as far as Phoenicia, Cyprus, and Antioch, speaking the word to none except Jews only.*
20 *But there were some of them, men of Cyprus and Cyrene, who on coming to Antioch spoke to the Greeks[16] also, telling them the good news of the Lord Jesus.*

14. See 21:20.
15. See on 12:17 (p. 239).
16. Gk. πρὸς τοὺς Ἕλληνας, which is the reading of P^{74} אᶜ A D* 1518, with Eusebius and Chrysostom; πρὸς τοὺς Ἑλληνιστάς is read by B Dᶜ E Ψ byz (and is usually thought to be presupposed by the aberrant εὐαγγελιστάς of א*, which must have been suggested by the following word εὐαγγελιζόμενοι). The versions do not help, as they make no distinction between Ἕλλην and Ἑλληνιστής. But, since Jews in Antioch had already been evangelized, the sense of the passage requires Ἕλληνας, i.e., pagan Greeks (cf. 16:1; Rom. 1:16), not Hellenists (cf. 6:1).

21 *The hand of the Lord was with them, and a great number believed and turned to the Lord.*

19 Luke's narrative now goes back to the same point of departure as we found in 8:4, which opens with the same words. There he related how those who were dispersed by the persecution which followed Stephen's death "went about spreading the good news"; here he tells how some of them made their way north along the Phoenician seaboard, from which some took ship for Cyprus, while others continued farther north until they reached Antioch on the Orontes.

Antioch on the Orontes (modern Antakya in the Hatay province of Turkey), situated some eighteen miles upstream, was founded in 300 B.C. by Seleucus Nicator, first ruler of the Seleucid dynasty, and was named by him after his father Antiochus. He had already given his own name to Seleucia Pieria at the mouth of the Orontes, the port of Antioch (cf. 13:4). As the capital of the Seleucid monarchy Antioch rapidly became a city of great importance. When Pompey reorganized Western Asia in 64 B.C. he made Antioch a free city; it became the seat of administration of the Roman province of Syria. It was at this time the third largest city in the Graeco-Roman world (surpassed in population only by Rome and Alexandria). It was planned from the first on the Hippodamian grid pattern; it was enlarged and adorned by Augustus and Tiberius, while Herod the Great provided colonnades on either side of its main street and paved the street itself with polished stone. The produce of Syria and lands farther east passed through it on its way to the west; it was a commercial center as well as a political capital. Because of its situation between the urbanized Mediterranean world and the eastern desert, it was even more cosmopolitan than most Hellenistic cities. Here Christianity first displayed its cosmopolitan character.

Jewish colonization in Antioch began practically from the city's foundation. By the beginning of the Christian era, proselytes to Judaism are said to have been specially numerous in Antioch;[17] we have already met Nicolaus, a proselyte from Antioch, as a leader among the Hellenists in the primitive Jerusalem church (6:5). Many other nationalities were represented among its residents: it is Antioch that the Roman satirist Juvenal has in mind when he complains that "the sewage of the Syrian Orontes has for long been discharging itself into the Tiber."[18] The city's reputation for moral laxity was enhanced by the cult of Artemis and Apollo at Daphne, five miles distant, where the ancient Syrian worship of Astarte and her consort, with its ritual prostitution, was carried on under Greek nomenclature.[19] But a new

17. Cf. Josephus, *BJ* 7.45.
18. Juvenal, *Satire* 3.62.
19. Hence this Antioch, to distinguish it from other cities of the same name, was sometimes called ἡ ἐπὶ Δάφνῃ, whence Epidaphna (Tacitus, *Annals* 2.83.3). Cf. also

chapter in the history of Antioch was about to be written, for it was to be the metropolis of Gentile Christianity.[20]

20   Thus far, the Hellenistic disciples who had fled from the persecution in Jerusalem had confined their evangelizing activity to the Jewish communities of the various places to which they came. The members of those communities were predominantly Hellenists like themselves. The idea that the gospel could have any relevance for non-Jews was not one that would naturally occur to them. But in Antioch some daring spirits among them, men of Cyprus[21] and Cyrene,[22] took a momentous step forward. If the gospel was so good for Jews, might it not be good for Gentiles also? At any rate, they would make the experiment. So they began to make known to the Greek population of Antioch the claims of Jesus as Lord and Savior. To present him as Messiah to people who knew nothing of the hope of Israel would have been a meaningless exercise, but the Greek terms *kyrios* ("Lord") and *sōtēr* ("Savior") were widely current in the religious world of the eastern Mediterranean.[23] Many were trying to find in various mystery cults a divine lord who could guarantee salvation and immortality to his devotees; now the pagans of Antioch were assured that what they vainly sought in those quarters could be secured through the Son of God who had lately become man, suffered death, and conquered the grave in Palestine.

21   This enterprise met with instant success. The Gentiles took to the Christian message as the very thing they had been waiting for, as something that exactly suited their case, and a large number of them believed the gospel and yielded their allegiance to Jesus as Lord. It may be that some of the Gentiles who believed belonged to the class commonly called God-fearers, who already knew something of the Old Testament revelation by attendance at the Jewish synagogue;[24] it would be in accordance with the

---

1 Macc. 11:41-51; Josephus, *BJ* 3.29; 7.41-62, 106-11; *Ant.* 12.119; 16.148; *Ap.* 2.39; Strabo, *Geography* 16.2.4-7.

20. See G. Downey, *A History of Antioch in Syria from Seleucus to the Arab Conquest* (Princeton, 1961), abridged in *Ancient Antioch* (Princeton, 1963); W. A. Meeks and R. L. Wilken, *Jews and Christians in Antioch in the First Four Centuries of the Common Era* (Missoula, MT, 1978); R. E. Brown and J. P. Meier, *Antioch and Rome: New Testament Cradles of Catholic Christianity* (London, 1983), pp. 11-86 ("Antioch," by J. P. Meier); D. S. Wallace-Hadrill, *Christian Antioch: A Study of Early Christian Thought in the East* (Cambridge, 1982).

21. Like Barnabas (4:36).

22. Cf. 2:10; 6:9; 13:1. The sons of Simon of Cyrene were well known in some areas of the early church (Mark 15:21).

23. Cf. Paul's reference to "many 'lords'" (1 Cor. 8:5). But it does not follow that the proclamation of Jesus as Lord and Savior developed in a Gentile environment by analogy with the terminology and interests of the mystery cults. See J. G. Machen, *The Origin of Paul's Religion* (New York, 1921), pp. 211-317, for a full and conclusive discussion.

24. See p. 203, n. 7.

analogy of other places if such people formed the nucleus of the new church of Antioch. But Luke does not say so, and we cannot be sure. At any rate, the power of God was manifest in the conversion of the Gentiles in this city. An Ethiopian chamberlain might have become a Christian some time previously while traveling home along the Gaza road, and a Roman centurion and his household might have believed the gospel as an apostle unfolded it in their home at Caesarea, but the scale of Gentile evangelization in Antioch was something entirely new.

2. Barnabas and Saul's Ministry at Antioch (11:22-26)

22 *When word of this came to the ears of the church at Jerusalem, they sent off Barnabas all the way to Antioch.*
23 *When he arrived there, and saw the grace of God, he rejoiced, and encouraged them all to adhere to the Lord with resolute hearts;*
24 *for he was a good man, full of the Holy Spirit and faith. A large number were added to the Lord.*[25]
25 *Then Barnabas set out for Tarsus to search for Saul,*
26 *and when he had found him, he brought him to Antioch. So they spent a whole year meeting together in the church and teaching a great multitude. It was in Antioch that the disciples first came to be known as "Christians."*[26]

22-24 The leaders of the Jerusalem church recognized the novelty of the situation at Antioch when news of it reached them. They considered themselves responsible for the direction of the movement in all its extensions. Therefore, as Peter and John had earlier gone to Samaria to investigate Philip's missionary service there, so now Jerusalem sent a delegate to Antioch to look into the strange events that were being enacted in that city. It was a critical moment: much—far more than they could have realized—depended on their choice of a delegate. In the providence of God, they chose the best man for this delicate and important work—Barnabas, the "son of encouragement" (4:36). Barnabas himself was a Cypriot Jew by birth, like some of those who had begun to preach the gospel to the Antiochene Gentiles, and his sympathies would in any case be wider than those of such Jerusalem believers as had never set foot outside Judaea. It may indeed be that he took the initiative in offering his services for this mission, and his offer was eagerly accepted.[27]

25. The first hand in B omits "to the Lord."
26. The Western text recasts vv. 25 and 26 thus: "And hearing that Saul was in Tarsus, he went away looking for him, and when he had met with him, he encouraged him to come to Antioch. And when they arrived they consorted for a whole year with the church and taught much people, and then the disciples first came to be known as Christians at Antioch."
27. Cf. M. Hengel, *Acts and the History of Earliest Christianity*, E.T. (London, 1979), pp. 101-2.

To Antioch, then, Barnabas was sent, as the representative or "apostle"[28] of the mother-church. When he reached Antioch, his generous spirit was filled with joy at what he found. Here was the grace of God in action, bringing blessing not only to the local Jews but also to the Gentile population as they heard and accepted the good news. True to his name, he gave them all the encouragement he could. Missionaries and converts alike had begun well; what they needed was the gift of perseverance, and he urged them to carry on and maintain their loyal service to the Lord in whom they had believed. The presence of a man of such sterling character and faith, a man "full of the Holy Spirit,"[29] gave them the stimulus they needed to prosecute their evangelism still more vigorously; the number of converts increased rapidly.

25-26 Soon the scale of Barnabas's responsibility was such that he could not hope to discharge it single-handedly. He had to find a colleague. But it was no easy matter to find the right man for the situation. Barnabas, however, decided that he knew the man, if only he could locate him. Several years had gone by since Saul of Tarsus had been escorted to Caesarea by his new friends in Jerusalem and put on board a ship bound for his native city. Barnabas could think of no one more eminently suited for the responsibility of sharing his ministry in Antioch. He therefore went to Tarsus in person to seek him out[30]—a task of some difficulty, perhaps, since Saul appears to have been disinherited for his joining the followers of Jesus and could no longer be found at his ancestral home. Barnabas found him, however, and took him to Antioch. There for a whole year the good work proceeded apace under their joint direction. More converts were added to the believing com-

---

28. "'Apostles' of churches" (ἀπόστολοι ἐκκλησιῶν) are mentioned elsewhere in the NT; cf. 2 Cor. 8:23. In such a context the word has a more general significance than when it is used of the specially commissioned apostles of Christ. See p. 271, n. 7 (on 14:4).

29. The same words are used of Stephen in 6:5.

30. The verb ἀναζητέω, over and above its general meaning, "is specially used of searching for human beings, with an implication of difficulty, as in the NT passages" (J. H. Moulton and G. Milligan, *The Vocabulary of the Greek Testament* [Edinburgh, 1930], p. 32). Cf. Luke 2:44. For the likelihood that Paul was disinherited cf. his statement in Phil. 3:8 that for Christ's sake he had "suffered the loss of all things." During those years in Syria and Cilicia (cf. Gal. 1:21) he probably endured some of the sufferings listed in 2 Cor. 11:23-27 and underwent the mysterious experience described in 2 Cor. 12:2-9. Moreover, it may be inferred from a number of allusions in his letters that Paul had begun Gentile evangelization on his own initiative before Barnabas brought him to Antioch (cf. Gal. 1:23). His commission to proclaim the Son of God *among the Gentiles* was evidently received on the Damascus road (Gal. 1:16), and his references in Gal. 2:2, 7 to his evangelization of Gentiles probably point back to a time earlier than his association with Barnabas in the work at Antioch. See also 22:21 (pp. 418-19). Barnabas indeed may have known something of Paul's evangelistic activity in Cilicia and was moved on that account to bring him to Antioch. The present narrative strengthens the impression received from 9:27 that Barnabas had some knowledge of him even before his Damascus-road conversion.

munity, and when they were added, they received systematic instruction in the principles of the new way on which they had entered.

No difficulty seems to have been felt at this stage about the uniting in one believing community of Jewish converts and Gentile converts. The new way was wide enough to accommodate believers of the most diverse backgrounds. Antioch was a cosmopolitan city, where Jew and Gentile, Greek and barbarian rubbed shoulders, where Mediterranean civilization met the Syrian desert; racial and religious differences which loomed so large in Judaea seemed much less important here. The church of Antioch from the outset had an *ethos* quite distinct from that of the Jerusalem church. The pagans of Antioch, too, knew all about these people, for they did not keep quiet about their faith, but proclaimed it wherever they went. Christ— *Christos,* the Greek form of the title Messiah ("the anointed one")—might be the name of an office to Greek-speaking Jews, but to the pagans of Antioch it was simply the name of a man of whom these people were always talking: a curious name, to be sure, unless it was the same as *Chrēstos* ("serviceable"), a name attested for slaves and free persons alike.[31] "Who are these people?" one Antiochene would ask another, as two or three unofficial missionaries gathered a knot of more or less interested hearers and disputants around them in one of the city colonnades. "Oh, these are the people who are always talking about *Christos,* the Christ-people, the Christians." Just as, in Palestine, the adherents of the Herod dynasty were called Herodians, so, says Luke, in Antioch the adherents of Jesus the Christ first came to be popularly known as Christians.[32]

---

31. Suetonius (*Claudius* 25.4) speaks of the riots which broke out in the Jewish community of Rome "at the instigation of Chrestus," i.e., most probably Christ (see p. 347 with n. 10, on 18:2). Chrestus occurs in *CIL* VI.10233 as the cognomen of a Roman citizen. The spelling Χρηστιανός for Χριστιανός is similarly found (e.g., in the first hand of ℵ in all three NT occurrences of the term: 26:28 and 1 Pet. 4:16 as well as here).

32. The verb translated "came to be known as" is χρηματίσαι, literally meaning "to transact business." To transact business under a particular name is in effect to be publicly known by that name. E. J. Bickerman, "The Name of Christians," *HTR* 42 (1949), pp. 71-124, argues that χρηματίζω must mean "assume the name," "style oneself," and that it was therefore the disciples themselves who first adopted the designation "Christians," meaning thereby "servants of Christ," *ministri regis* (cf. οἱ τοῦ Χριστοῦ in 1 Cor. 15:23), just as the *Caesariani* were the emperor's servants (οἱ τοῦ Καίσαρος). This intransitive χρηματίζω must be distinguished from χρηματίζω meaning "give an oracular response" (used in the passive in 10:22). Cf. MHT II, p. 265. The term Χριστιανός is a Latin formation (with suffix -ιανός from Lat. *-ianus*). In the NT it is used only by non-Christians (*pace* Bickerman)—in 26:28 on the lips of the younger Agrippa, and in 1 Pet. 4:16 in the language of the indictment when one is made to suffer "as a Christian." The earliest occurrences of the term in non-Christian literature are in Josephus, *Ant.* 18.64 (where "the tribe of Christians" is said to be called after "the so-called Christ"); Pliny, *Epistles* 10.96-97 (correspondence with Trajan about Christians in Bithynia); Tacitus, *Annals* 15.44.3-4 (where Nero's scapegoats for the fire of A.D. 64 are

3. Famine Relief (11:27-30)

27 *About that time prophets came down from Jerusalem to Antioch.[33]*

28 *One of them, named Agabus, stood up and indicated through the Spirit that there would be a great famine over the whole world. (This took place under Claudius.[34])*

29 *Then each of the disciples decided on a sum of money, according to each one's means, to be sent as a charitable offering to their brothers who lived in Judaea.*

30 *This they did, and sent it to the elders by Barnabas and Saul.*

27 The gift of prophecy in the apostolic church was like the gift of tongues in that it was exercised under the inspiration of God; it differed from it in that it was expressed in the speaker's ordinary language. The place for this spiritual gift in the church is recognized in the Pauline letters: Paul regarded it as of high value and ranked the prophet next after the apostle.[35] Here and there the narrative of Acts illustrates how it was exercised.

28 Among the prophets who came to Antioch from Jerusalem in those days was one called Agabus,[36] who announced by inspiration that there would be a great famine throughout the whole Roman world.[37] It may be that Agabus had in mind the famine conditions which would make their contribution to the expected woes of the end-time (cf. Mark 13:8).[38] Such famine conditions, says Luke, were actually experienced in the principate of Claudius (A.D. 41-54). We know from other sources that Claudius's princi-

---

those "people loathed for their vices, who were commonly styled Christians—a name derived from Christ, who was executed by the procurator Pontius Pilate when Tiberius was emperor"); and Suetonius, *Nero* 16.2 ("punishment was inflicted on the Christians, a class of people addicted to a novel and mischievous superstition").

33. The Western text links vv. 27 and 28 thus: "and there was much rejoicing; and when we were gathered together, one of them, Agabus by name, spoke signifying . . ."

34. The Byzantine text reads "Claudius Caesar" (cf. KJV).

35. Cf. 1 Cor. 12:28; 14:24-25, 29-32; Eph. 4:11. See D. Hill, *New Testament Prophecy* (London, 1979); D. E. Aune, *Prophecy in Early Christianity and the Ancient Mediterranean World* (Grand Rapids, 1983).

36. Agabus reappears in 21:10, in a "we" section of Acts. There is no sound reason for supposing that his introduction here is a reading back into this context of details from Paul's last visit to Jerusalem (when the relief fund organized in his Gentile mission field was handed over to the mother-church); cf. G. W. H. Lampe, *St. Luke and the Church of Jerusalem* (London, 1969), p. 24.

37. The "world" here, as in Luke 2:1, is the οἰκουμένη (Lat. *orbis terrarum*). C. C. Torrey (*CDA*, pp. 20-21) maintained (improbably) that "the whole world" represents a misunderstanding of the Aramaic phrase which here means "the whole land" (of Israel). But this is not one of the sections of Acts for which an Aramaic substratum is at all probable. See M. Wilcox, *The Semitisms of Acts* (Oxford, 1965), pp. 147-48.

38. Cf. M. Hengel, *Acts,* p. 111.

pate was marked by a succession of bad harvests and consequent scarcity in various parts of the empire—in Rome, Greece, and Egypt as well as in Judaea.[39]

If a true tradition is reflected in the Western reading of this passage, according to which Agabus uttered his prophecy "when we were gathered together,"[40] then Luke may have had personal cause to remember the prophecy and the effect which it produced on the church of Antioch. This reading does at least show the influence of the tradition preserved in the so-called anti-Marcionite prologue to the third Gospel, and elsewhere, that Luke was a native of Syrian Antioch.[41] If Luke was one of the Antiochene Gentiles who were evangelized in those days, we can readily appreciate both his interest in Antioch and his enthusiasm for the Gentile mission.

29-30 How the Christians of Antioch inferred from the general terms of Agabus's prophecy that Judaea would be specially hard hit by the predicted famine Luke does not say. We know that Judaea did in fact suffer severely from a famine at some point between A.D. 45 and 48. At that time Helena, queen-mother of Adiabene, a Jewish proselyte, bought grain in Egypt and figs in Cyprus and had them taken to Jerusalem for distribution, while her son King Izates sent a large sum of money to the authorities in Jerusalem to be used for famine relief.[42] The church of Antioch similarly organized a relief fund for the mother-church.[43] The various members of the

---

39. Famine conditions are attested for Rome, at the beginning of Claudius's rule (Dio Cassius, *History* 60.11), for Egypt, in his fifth year (*P.Mich.* 123, 127), for Greece, in his eighth or ninth year (Eusebius, *Chronicle,* Year of Abraham 2065), and again in Rome, between his ninth and eleventh years (Tacitus, *Annals* 12.43; Orosius, *History* 7.6.17). More generally, Suetonius says that his principate was marked by "persistent droughts" (*Claud.* 18.2).

40. See p. 229, n. 33.

41. This prologue (of uncertain date, but possibly as early as the second century) begins with the words "Luke was an Antiochene of Syria." The statement is repeated by Eusebius (*HE* 3.4.6) and Jerome (*On Illustrious Men* 7; *Preface to Commentary on Matthew*). Cf. p. 5, n. 6, and 6:5 with exposition and note (p. 121, n. 11).

42. Josephus, *Ant.* 20.51-53. In *Ant.* 20.101 he dates the famine in the procuratorships of Cuspius Fadus and Tiberius Julius Alexander (i.e., between A.D. 44 and 48) or, according to a variant reading, in that of Alexander (A.D. 45/46-48). K. S. Gapp, "The Universal Famine under Claudius," *HTR* 28 (1935), pp. 258-65, identifies this famine with one mentioned in *Ant.* 3.320-21, and concludes that it extended to the spring of 46 or 47. J. Jeremias, "Sabbathjahr und neutestamentliche Chronologie," *Abba* (Göttingen, 1966), pp. 233-37, points out that, if the harvest failed in 46/47, the incidence of the sabbatical year 47/48 would have intensified the scarcity of food in Judaea: famine conditions would have prevailed until the spring of 49.

43. Such an act of fellowship was calculated to strengthen the bond of a common faith which linked the totally Jewish-Christian church of Jerusalem with the mainly Gentile-Christian church of Antioch. The Jerusalem church in the apostolic age appears to have suffered from chronic poverty; this helps to explain why its members, or an influential group of them, were called "the poor" (Heb. *hā'ebyônîm,* whence the later "Ebionites").

church appear to have allocated a fixed sum out of their income or property as a contribution to this fund, much as Paul was to advise the Corinthian Christians to do when he was organizing a later relief fund for Jerusalem (1 Cor. 16:1-4). When the collected sum was ready to be sent to Judaea, Barnabas and Saul were deputed to take it there. On their arrival, they handed it over to the elders, who from now on play an increasing part in the leadership of the church of Jerusalem.[44]

This is the second occasion in Luke's record on which Paul visited Jerusalem after his conversion (the first being briefly described in 9:26-30). He himself records two visits which he paid to Jerusalem; the possibility arises that the famine-relief visit of Acts 11:30 is identical with that described in Gal. 2:1-10, when he went up to Jerusalem with Barnabas in the fourteenth year after his conversion (which is the most probable interpretation of Gal. 2:1).[45] More common, however, is the identification of the visit of Gal. 2:1-10 with that of Acts 15; this raises problems which will be considered later.[46]

---

44. With the dispersal of the Hellenistic almoners of 6:5 in the persecution that followed Stephen's death, the charge of financial affairs in the church seems to have devolved on the elders. The elders (among whom James the Just emerges as *primus inter pares*) constituted a kind of Nazarene Sanhedrin. In Acts 15 they share the leadership of the church with the apostles; from then on, the apostles disappear from the Jerusalem scene and the elders exercise the whole corporate leadership (cf. 21:18).

45. See F. F. Bruce, *The Epistle to the Galatians*, NIGTC (Grand Rapids/Exeter, 1982), pp. 105-28.

46. See pp. 282-84 below. See also J. Knox, *Chapters in a Life of Paul* (London, 1950), pp. 71-72; C. H. Buck, "The Collection for the Saints," *HTR* 43 (1950), pp. 1-29 (especially pp. 15-21); J. Dupont, "La famine sous Claude, Actes 11,28," *Études sur les Actes des Apôtres* (Paris, 1967), pp. 163-65; R. W. Funk, "The Enigma of the Famine Visit," *JBL* 75 (1956), pp. 130-36; G. Strecker, "Die sogenannte zweite Jerusalemreise des Paulus (Act 11,27-30)," *ZNW* 53 (1962), pp. 67-77; G. Ogg, *The Chronology of the Life of Paul* (London, 1968), pp. 43-57; R. Jewett, *Dating Paul's Life* (London, 1979), p. 34; G. Lüdemann, *Paul, Apostle to the Gentiles: Studies in Chronology*, E.T. (London, 1984), pp. 13-15, 149-52; S. Dockx, *Chronologies néotestamentaires et vie de l'Église primitive* (Leuven, 1984), pp. 62-69, 89-95.

ACTS 12

E. HEROD AGRIPPA I AND THE CHURCH (12:1-24)

1. Martyrdom of James and Imprisonment of Peter (12:1-4)

1 *It was about that time that King Herod laid hostile hands on some members of the church.*
2 *He beheaded[1] James, the brother of John;*
3 *and when he saw that this[2] was acceptable to the Jews, he went on to arrest Peter also. This was at the season of unleavened bread.*
4 *Having arrested Peter, he put him in prison, handing him over to be guarded by four quaternions of soldiers. His intention was to bring him out before the people after Passover.*

1 King Herod, introduced rather abruptly at the beginning of this narrative, is the elder Herod Agrippa, a grandson of Herod the Great and of his Hasmonaean queen Mariamne. When his father Aristobulus was executed in 7 B.C., Agrippa, then four years old, was sent by his mother to be brought up at Rome. There he grew up on terms of close friendship with some members of the imperial family, notably with Claudius, his exact contemporary, and with Gaius, grandnephew of Tiberius. When Gaius succeeded Tiberius as emperor in A.D. 37, he bestowed on Agrippa the former tetrarchies of Philip and Lysanias in southern Syria (cf. Luke 3:1), together with the title "king." Two years later Agrippa's kingdom was enlarged by the addition of Galilee and Peraea, the former tetrarchy of his uncle Antipas, whom Gaius deposed from his rule and sent into exile. When Claudius was made emperor in A.D. 41, after the assassination of Gaius, he further increased Agrippa's realm by the addition of Judaea, which since A.D. 6 had been governed on the emperor's behalf by a prefect.[3] Agrippa was more popular with the Jews than

1. Lit., "killed with the sword" (ἀνεῖλεν . . . μαχαίρῃ).
2. For "this" (unexpressed in Greek) the Western text reads "his attack on the believers" (πιστοί, as in 10:45).
3. See Josephus, *Ant.* 18.126, 131-34, 143-69, 179-204, 228-56, 289-301; 19.236-44, 265, 274-77, 288, 292-354; Philo, *Flaccus* 25-29, 103; *Embassy to Gaius* 179, 261-333; also Schürer I, pp. 442-54; A. H. M. Jones, *The Herods of Judaea* (Oxford, 1938), pp. 184-216.

many members of the Herod family had been: his descent from the Hasmonaean dynasty was a point in his favor. He set himself sedulously to win and retain their goodwill.[4]

2 The "members of the church" whom he singled out for attack were apostles. It is evidence of a change in the attitude of the people of Jerusalem toward the apostles, who had not been molested in the persecution that followed Stephen's death, that Agrippa should now make them his principal targets.[5]

The first of his victims was James, the son of Zebedee, whom he had executed. James was the first of the apostles to meet a martyr's death; thus he experienced the fulfilment of Jesus' promise to him and his brother John that they would both drink from his cup and share his "baptism" (Mark 10:39). Jesus did not say, or even imply, that they would both suffer death together; indeed, John appears to have outlived all the other apostles. The theory propounded by Eduard Schwartz and others, that in the original form of the present narrative both James and John were executed by Herod Agrippa, is quite without warrant.[6]

3 If it is asked why this attack on the apostles should have proved "acceptable to the Jews," the answer may be found in the wider phase of apostolic activity which had recently set in with Peter's visit to the Gentile

4. The Mishnah (*Sôṭāh* 7.8) relates how he read "the law of the kingship" (Deut. 17:14-20) publicly at the Feast of Tabernacles in a sabbatical year (presumbably in A.D. 41), and wept as he read the words, "you may not put a foreigner over you, who is not your brother" (v. 15), for he remembered the Herods' Edomite ancestry. But the people, remembering rather his Hasmonaean descent, called out repeatedly, "Be not dismayed; you are indeed our brother!"

5. The phrase "about that time" (v. 1) refers to the events narrated in 11:27-30. Actually the events of 12:1-23 fell between the prophecy of Agabus (11:28) and the Jerusalem visit of Barnabas and Saul (11:30).

6. E. Schwartz, "Über den Tod der Söhne Zebedaei" (1904), in his *Gesammelte Schriften* V: *Zum Neuen Testament und zum frühen Christentum* (Berlin, 1963), pp. 48-123; "Zur Chronologie des Paulus" (1907), *Gesammelte Schriften* V, pp. 128-31; "Noch einmal der Tod der Söhne Zebedaei," *ZNW* 11 (1910), pp. 89-104. The chief basis for the theory is provided by one manuscript (Codex Coislinianus 305, discovered in 1862) of the ninth-century Georgios Hamartolos, *Chron.* 3.134.1, according to which Papias of Hierapolis, writing as an "eyewitness of John," recorded in the second book (of his *Exegesis of the Dominical Oracles*) that John was "killed by Jews." This peculiar reading may have been interpolated from an epitome of the fifth-century *Chronicle* of Philip of Side: "Papias in his second book says that John the divine and James his brother were killed by Jews" (Bodleianus MS Baroccianus 142, published by C. de Boor, "Neue Fragmente des Papias, Hegesippus und Pierius," *TU* 5.2 [1888], pp. 165-84, especially p. 170). The evidence of early church calendars and martyrologies has also been cited. But the "critical myth" of John the apostle's early death rests on evidence so flimsy that it "would have provided derision if it had been adduced in favour of a conservative conclusion" (A. S. Peake, *Holborn Review* 19 [1928], p. 394). See J. H. Bernard, "The Traditions as to the Death of John, the Son of Zebedee," *Studia Sacra* (London, 1917), pp. 260-84.

Cornelius in Caesarea. Those members of the Jerusalem church who, under the leadership of James the Just and his fellow-elders (cf. v. 17), maintained a more rigorous resistance to the weakening of the bonds of Jewish particularism, continued to enjoy general toleration for some two decades more. It was not by accident that Agrippa, after putting James the Zebedaean to death[7] and testing the popular reaction to this, laid hands next on the leader of the apostles—the one, moreover, who had taken the initiative in fraternizing with Gentiles.

4 The seven days of "unleavened bread"[8] were beginning when Peter was arrested. He was therefore kept in prison for the duration of the festal period. Agrippa's intention was to bring him out for trial and public execution immediately after this period had expired.[9] But, knowing how many sympathizers, secret as well as open, the apostles had in Jerusalem, he took special precautions against any attempt to free the prisoner. Four relays of soldiers took it in turn to guard him:[10] four guards at a time, one on either side of him (to whom he was chained) and two at his cell door.

2. Peter's Escape from Prison (12:5-11)

5 *So Peter was kept in prison,[11] and earnest prayer on his behalf was being offered to God by the church.*

6 *The night before Herod was about to bring him out, Peter was asleep between two soldiers, bound to them with two chains, while sentries were in front of the door, guarding the prison.*

7 *Suddenly an angel of the Lord stood over him and a light shone in the cell. He struck Peter's side and roused him: "Quick!" he said. "Get up!" The chains fell off from his hands.*

8 *Then the angel said, "Fasten your belt and tie on your sandals." Peter did so. "Put on your cloak," said the angel, "and follow me."*

9 *Peter went out and followed him: he did not realize that the angel's action was real, but thought he was seeing a vision.*

---

7. Eusebius (*HE* 2.9.2-3) preserves the tradition from the seventh book of Clement of Alexandria's *Hypotyposes* that the officer who guarded James was so impressed by his witness that he professed himself a Christian and was beheaded along with him.

8. The days of unleavened bread lasted from Nisan 14 (Passover Eve) until Nisan 21 (Ex. 12:18). "Passover" in v. 4 is used in a broad sense of the whole festal period which began with the paschal celebrations. Cf. Luke 22:1, in distinction from Mark 14:1.

9. A public execution would be offensive during the sacred season; cf. Mark 14:2, where Jesus' enemies plan his arrest and execution "not during the feast [of unleavened bread], lest there be a tumult of the people."

10. This may refer particularly to nighttime, one relay being assigned to each of the four watches of the night. "The watches are divided into four, according to the water-clock, so that it is not necessary to keep watch for more than three hours of the night" (Vegetius, *On Military Affairs* 3.8).

11. Some witnesses to the Western text add "by the king's cohort."

234

10 *They passed through the first watch and the second, and came to the iron gate leading into the city. It opened to them of its own accord, so they went out[12] and went along one street. Then immediately the angel left him.*

11 *Peter then, coming to himself, said, "Now I know that the Lord has sent his angel and delivered me from the hand of Herod and from what the Jewish people were expecting."*

5-9 Meanwhile, continuous prayer was being offered for Peter by the church of Jerusalem—the supplication of righteous people which "has great power in its effects" (Jas. 5:16). And while they were persevering in fervent prayer during what, in Agrippa's intention, was to be Peter's last night on earth, their prayer, unknown to themselves, was receiving an effective answer. For Peter was roused from sleep—the calm sleep that springs from a good conscience and quiet confidence in God—by a blow on his side and a voice which bade him get up quickly. The chains by which he was hand-cuffed to the soldiers on either side fell away as he rose. The cell was lit up; an unknown visitor stood by him, and ordered him to fasten his girdle, tie on his sandals, wrap his cloak around him, and follow. It was this narrative, probably, that was in Charles Wesley's mind when he wrote the lines:

> "I woke; the dungeon flamed with light.
> My chains fell off, my heart was free,
> I rose, went forth, and followed thee."

Amazed at it all, and only half-awake, Peter did as he was told, not realizing that it was really happening, but suspecting that it was a dream, and that he would soon wake up to find himself with the soldiers in the cell, compelled to face what the morning might bring. Through one gate and another they passed, both of them guarded. It may be that Peter was "al-lowed to pass the first and the second, being taken presumably as a servant; but no servant would be expected to pass beyond the outermost ward at night, and a different course was needed there."[13] Wonderful to relate, however, the outermost gate opened automatically as Peter and his myste-rious guide approached it, and they found themselves in the open street—after descending "the seven steps," as the Western text informs us. This addition has such a circumstantial character that many regard it as a genuine piece of local color, derived from an informant who knew Jerusalem as it stood before A.D. 70. Luke does not say where Peter's prison was, but it was quite probably in the Antonia fortress, where Paul was later confined (cf.

---

12. The Western text adds "and went down the seven steps."
13. W. M. Ramsay, *St. Paul the Traveller* (London, [14]1920), p. 28.

21:31–23:32). The fortress stood northwest of the temple area, and a flight of steps may have led down from it to street level comparable to flights excavated south and southwest of the temple mount since 1968.[14]

10-11 They traversed one street, and Peter suddenly found himself alone. Thus far he had followed his rescuer like a man in a trance or a sleepwalker; now he woke up to his strange situation and took stock of it. This was the finger of God: it was an angel of the Lord who had come to snatch him from his imminent fate.

What account are we to give of Peter's escape from prison? What kind of messenger was it that released him? Whether human or superhuman, he was no doubt a messenger of God. There are some features of the narrative that would point to a carefully planned and skillfully executed "inside job"; probably that was Agrippa's conclusion. There are other features which are strongly reminiscent of the "form" in which other miraculous escapes from prison are described in ancient literature.[15] But Peter apparently recognized divine intervention of a supernatural kind, and so evidently did Luke: he introduces the incident in septuagintal idiom, and the opening words of verse 7 are very similar to those at the beginning of Luke 2:9, where the angel appears to the shepherds to announce the birth of Christ.

A striking modern parallel has been quoted more than once from the experiences of Sundar Singh. By order of the chief lama of a Tibetan community he was thrown into a dry well, the cover of which was securely locked. Here he was left to die, like many others before him, whose bones and rotting flesh lay at the bottom of the well. On the third night, when he had been calling to God in prayer, he heard someone unlocking the cover of the well and removing it. Then a voice spoke, telling him to take hold of the rope that was being lowered. He did so, and was glad to find a loop at the bottom of the rope in which he could place his foot, for his arm had been injured before he was thrown down. He was then drawn up, the cover was replaced and locked, but when he looked around to thank his rescuer, he could find no trace of him. The fresh air revived him, and his injured arm felt whole again. When morning came, he returned to the place where he had been arrested, and resumed preaching. News was brought to the chief lama that the man who had been thrown into the execution well had been liberated and was preaching again. Sundar Singh was brought before him and questioned, and told the story of his release. The lama declared that someone

---

14. See N. Avigad in *Jerusalem Revealed*, ed. Y. Yadin (New Haven/London, 1976), pp. 25-30.

15. Cf. 5:19-23 (p. 110, n. 29); 16:25-28 (p. 316, n. 67). Josephus tells (*BJ* 6.293) how, shortly before the outbreak of war in A.D. 66, the heavy eastern gate of the inner court of the temple opened by night "of its own accord" (αὐτομάτως, with which cf. αὐτομάτη, v. 10).

must have got hold of the key and let him out, but when search was made for the key, it was found attached to the lama's own girdle.[16]

"Now," says Laurence Browne, "although this story is in our own time, its interpretation is as difficult as the story of St. Peter's escape. It is possible that both events were nonmiraculous, that some well-disposed person acted as rescuer. But the difficulty in the way of a rescue in either case suggests that both were actually miraculous interventions of God. One striking difference between the two accounts is the opinion of the prisoner at the time. St. Peter thought it was all a vision until he found himself safe and sound. The Sadhu thought the rescuer was a man until he disappeared."[17]

In any case, the narrative bears witness to the delivering grace of God and to the power of believing prayer. That James should die while Peter should escape is a mystery of divine providence which has been repeated countless times in the history of the people of God. By faith, says the writer to the Hebrews, some "escaped the edge of the sword"; by faith others "were killed with the sword" (Heb. 11:34, 37).

3. Peter Reports His Escape (12:12-17)

12 *Peter, having taken stock of the situation, came to the house of Mary the mother of John (surnamed Mark), where many were gathered together praying.*

13 *He knocked at the door of the outer gateway, and a servant-girl named Rhoda came to answer his knock.*

14 *When she recognized Peter's voice, she was so overjoyed that she did not open the gate but ran in and reported that Peter was standing at the gate.*

15 *"You are mad," they said to her. But she insisted that it was so. Then they said, "It is his angel."*

16 *Meanwhile Peter kept on knocking, and when they opened the gate they saw him and were astounded.*

17 *But he gestured to them with his hand to keep quiet, and told them how the Lord had brought him out of the prison. Then he said, "Report this to James and the brothers." So saying, he departed and went to another place.*

12 The first thing for Peter to do was to acquaint his fellow-believers in Jerusalem with his escape; the next was to go into hiding, lest Agrippa's police should find him again. So he first made his way to one of the chief Christian meeting places in Jerusalem, the house of Mary. Luke's readers

16. See B. H. Streeter and A. J. Appasamy, *The Sadhu* (London, 1921), pp. 30-32.

17. L. E. Browne, *The Acts of the Apostles* (London, 1925), pp. 204-5.

would be more familiar with Christians of the second generation than with those of the first, especially when a second-generation Christian attained such distinction as Mark eventually did; hence Mary is identified as the mother of Mark (one might compare the identification of Simon the Cyrenaean as the father of Alexander and Rufus in Mark 15:21).

Like several other persons mentioned in Acts, Mary's son had both a Jewish name (John) and a Roman name (Mark). Joseph, surnamed Justus (1:23), was one such person; the most outstanding example is "Saul, who is also called Paul" (13:9). This John Mark is probably identical with the Mark mentioned elsewhere in the New Testament (Col. 4:10; Philem. 24; 2 Tim. 4:11; 1 Pet. 5:13) and with the author of the Second Gospel.[18]

The church of Jerusalem was too large to meet in any one building: its members were evidently divided for fellowship and worship into a number of house churches, one of which—presumably that to which Peter himself was attached—met in Mary's house. Her house was a large one: Martin Hengel calls it a "splendid" one,[19] for it was distinguished by a gatehouse or forecourt[20] leading from the courtyard to the street door. The high priest's palace was similarly equipped: when Peter was leaving its courtyard on the night of Jesus' trial, he "went out into the forecourt" (Matt. 26:71).

13-16 The scene that now unfolds itself at the street door and inside the house is full of quiet humor. Rhoda's excitement at hearing Peter's voice makes her forget to open the door and let him in; those inside cannot believe that their prayers have been answered so quickly: Rhoda must be mad, or else it is Peter's guardian angel, his spirit-counterpart, that she has heard.[21] Meanwhile Peter stands outside, continuing to knock for admission—not too loudly, for the hue and cry may already have been raised, and Mary's house is one of the first to which a search party will come.

17 When at last he was admitted, he told them about his miraculous release, and directed them to pass on the news to "James and the brothers." Then he took his departure, and went underground so successfully that no

18. Later writers tell how he served Peter as his aide-de-camp and interpreter in Rome, and how he afterwards founded the church of Alexandria (this last tradition probably reflects the arrival of the Gospel of Mark in Alexandria). See extracts from Papias, Irenaeus, Clement of Alexandria, and others preserved by Eusebius (*HE* 2.15.1-16.2; 3.39.14-16; 5.8.3; 6.14.6); also M. Hengel, *Studies in the Gospel of Mark*, E.T. (London, 1985), pp. 2-24.

19. M. Hengel, *Between Jesus and Paul*, E.T. (London, 1983), p. 108.

20. Gk. πυλών (vv. 13-14).

21. This "angel" (like the *fravaši* in Zoroastrianism) was regarded as capable of assuming the bodily appearance of the human being whom he protected. The role of the angel Raphael in Tob. 5:4-16 probably reflects this belief. Cf. Matt. 18:10. See J. H. Moulton, "It is his angel," *JTS* 3 (1902), pp. 514-27, especially pp. 516-17; *Early Zoroastrianism* (London, 1913), pp. 254-85.

one to this day has discovered for certain where he went. Luke's informant probably did not know, and Luke had no other means of finding out.[22]

The description of Peter's anxious gesture, as he beckoned to surprised and excited company to make less noise, is the authentic touch of an eyewitness—whether Luke got the story from Mark (whom he later knew in Rome) or from Rhoda, as Ramsay argued, or from someone else.

In addition to the company which met in Mary's house, there was evidently another associated with James the brother of Jesus. They too must be told of Peter's escape. The "brothers" mentioned along with him probably include his fellow-elders (cf. 11:30; 21:18). It appears that by this time James had attained a position of undisputed leadership in the Jerusalem church. When Barnabas and Paul had the conference with the "pillars" of that church described in Gal. 2:1-10, the three "pillars" with whom they conferred were James, Cephas (Peter), and John, named in that order. James on that occasion concurred with his two colleagues in exchanging "the right hand of fellowship" with Barnabas and Paul on the understanding that the latter two should evangelize Gentiles, while the Jerusalem leaders would continue to concentrate on their mission to Jews. James had a statesmanlike breadth of vision, as appears from his policy at the Council of Jerusalem (15:13-21). But he was careful to retain the confidence of the ordinary church members in Jerusalem, many of whom were "zealots for the law" (21:20). In addition, he continued to the end to command the respect of the Jerusalem populace, largely because of his ascetic way of life and his regular participation in the temple services of prayer, where he interceded for the people and their city. Whatever Peter and other members of the Twelve may have done, James was free of any suspicion of fraternizing with Gentiles. When he was stoned to death in A.D. 62, at the instance of the high priest Ananus II, many of the people were gravely shocked; and some years later some ascribed the calamity which overtook the city and its inhabitants to the cessation of James's prayers on their behalf.[23]

4. Peter's Escape Discovered (12:18-19)

18 *When day dawned, there was great commotion among the soldiers:*
what had become of Peter?

22. Antioch (cf. Gal. 2:11) or Rome has been suggested as the "other place" to which he went at this time. Eusebius *(Chron.)* brings him to Rome in A.D. 42, but this date is almost certainly too early, and probably belongs to the traditions underlying the *Acts of Peter* and the Clementine corpus, which recorded his coming to Rome in the time of Claudius to contend with Simon Magus (see pp. 166-67, with nn. 30-35). It is difficult to take seriously suggestions that the "other place" was the heavenly abode of the faithful departed, Acts 12:3-17 being a pictorial account of Peter's martyrdom (cf. D. F. Robinson, "Where and when did Peter die?" *JBL* 64 [1945], pp. 255-67; W. M. Smaltz, "Did Peter die in Jerusalem?" *JBL* 71 [1952], pp. 211-16). See also J. W. Wenham, "Did Peter go to Rome in AD 42?" *TynB* 23 (1972), pp. 94-102.

23. Josephus, *Ant.* 20.200-201. A more legendary account by Hegesippus is

19 *Herod instituted a search for him and, when he could not find him, he interrogated the guards and ordered them to be punished.[24] Then he went down from Judaea and spent some time in Caesarea.*

18-19 Search was made for Peter, but he was nowhere to be found. Agrippa examined the soldiers who were responsible for guarding him, and sent them off to be punished, suspecting perhaps that Peter's escape was the result of a plot, and that the guards had been bribed. By Roman law (which, however, was not binding on Agrippa in the internal administration of his kingdom) a guard who allowed a prisoner to escape became liable to the same penalty as the escaped prisoner would have suffered.[25]

Soon afterward, Agrippa left Jerusalem for Caesarea, the seat of government of Judaea under the Romans. When it is said that he "went down from Judaea," Judaea is used in its narrower sense of the territory of the Jews. Caesarea, although it belonged politically to Judaea, was not in strictly Jewish territory: from its foundation by Herod the Great it was a predominantly Gentile city.

5. Death of Herod Agrippa I (12:20-23)

20 *Now Herod had a furious quarrel with the people of Tyre and Sidon. A united deputation from those cities appeared before him and, having secured the good offices of[26] Blastus, the king's chamberlain, they sought a reconciliation. Their country depended for its food on the king's territory.*

21 *On an appointed day Herod put on royal robes, sat down on his judgment seat, and made a public oration to them.[27]*

22 *The populace called out, "It is a god, not a human being, that is speaking!"*

23 *Immediately the angel of the Lord struck him down, because he did not give God the glory;[28] and he died, consumed by worms.*

20 It was while he was in Caesarea that Agrippa met his death, and Luke relates the circumstances. The cities of the Phoenician seaboard, Tyre and Sidon, depended on Galilee for their food supply, as they had done a thou-

---

preserved by Eusebius (*HE* 2.23). See F. F. Bruce, *Men and Movements in the Primitive Church* (Exeter/Grand Rapids, 1979), pp. 86-119.

24. Lit., "to be led away" (ἀπαχθῆναι). Cod. D (the chief Western witness) says "to be put to death" (ἀποκτανθῆναι); this agrees with the idiomatic Attic use of ἀπάγω in the sense of leading off to execution (cf. Luke 23:26). This meaning is more likely in the present context than the Hellenistic meaning "arrest" or "lead off to prison."

25. *Code of Justinian* 9.4.4.

26. Lit., "having persuaded" (πείσαντες).

27. The Western text adds "having been reconciled to the Tyrians."

28. The Western text amplifies after "glory" as follows: "and, having come down from the tribunal, he was eaten by worms while still alive, and so died."

sand years earlier in the time of Hiram and Solomon (1 Kings 5:9-12). When, therefore, the inhabitants of those cities found that they had given Agrippa grave offense, for some reason which has not been recorded, they realized that it would be wise for them to regain his favor as soon as possible. They made use accordingly of the good offices of his chamberlain Blastus (whatever his services cost them, the price was worthwhile), and an opportunity was found for them to present themselves before the king and make their peace with him publicly.

21-23   We are indebted to Josephus for a parallel account of what followed. At Caesarea, says Josephus, Agrippa "exhibited shows in honor of Caesar, knowing that this was celebrated as a festival for his welfare. There came together for this occasion a large number of provincial officials and others of distinguished position. On the second day of the shows Agrippa put on a robe made of silver throughout, of quite wonderful weaving, and entered the theatre at break of day. Then the silver shone and glittered wonderfully as the sun's first rays fell on it, and its resplendence inspired a sort of fear and trembling in those who gazed at it. Immediately his flatterers called out from various directions, in language which boded him no good, for they invoked him as a god: 'Be gracious to us!' they cried. 'Hitherto we have reverenced you as a human being, but henceforth we confess you to be of more than mortal nature.' He did not rebuke them, nor did he repudiate their impious flattery. But soon afterward he looked up and saw an owl sitting on a rope above his head, and recognized it at once as a messenger of evil as on a former occasion it had been a messenger of good;[29] and a pang of grief pierced his heart. At the same time he was seized with a severe pain in his bowels, which quickly increased in intensity. . . . He was hastily carried into the palace, and . . . when he had suffered continuously for five days from the pain in his belly, he died, in the fifty-fourth year of his life and the seventh year of his kingship."[30]

The accounts of Luke and Josephus are independent, but they agree in all essentials.[31]

The "appointed day" on which the Phoenicians were to be publicly reconciled with Agrippa is commonly held to have been a festival celebrated quinquennially on March 5 in honor of the foundation of Caesarea.[32] (An-

---

29. When Agrippa had been thrown into chains some years before, by order of Tiberius, he leaned against a tree on which an owl sat; a German fellow-prisoner told him that the bird betokened an early release and great good fortune, but that if he ever saw it again he would have but five days longer to live (Josephus *Ant.* 18.195-201). The fact that Josephus calls the bird a "messenger" (Gk. ἄγγελος), while Luke says in v. 23 that "the angel (ἄγγελος) of the Lord smote him," is nothing more than a verbal coincidence.

30. Josephus, *Ant.* 19.343-50.

31. See E. Meyer, *Ursprung und Anfänge des Christentums,* III (Stuttgart/Berlin, 1923), pp. 167-68.

32. The date of the city's *dies natalis* is preserved by Eusebius (*Martyrs of*

other possibility is that it was held to celebrate the emperor's birthday on August 1.)[33] The "royal robes" which Agrippa wore are described in greater detail by Josephus. The way in which the silver weaving reflected the rays of the rising sun has suggested to one or two students that Agrippa presented himself to the assembled crowd as a manifestation of divinity (more precisely of the sun-god), *theos epiphanēs,* as Phoenician rulers had done in earlier days.[34] This is improbable. Both Luke and Josephus agree in saying that he was hailed as a god and not as a mere mortal, and in deprecating his tacit acceptance of such blasphemous adulation. (There is a further reminiscence of this in rabbinical tradition.)[35] The mortal pain which seized him is interpreted by Luke as a stroke of divine judgment. Medical experts have attempted to diagnose the trouble, but the data are too imprecise: suggestions include peritonitis (resulting from a perforated appendix),[36] arsenical poisoning,[37] acute intestinal obstruction,[38] the rupture of a hydatid cyst.[39] Luke's statement that he was "consumed by worms" provides a clue of sorts, but such a term is used by several ancient writers in relating the deaths of people deemed worthy of so unpleasant an end.[40]

On the death of Agrippa, Judaea reverted to administration by Roman governors. Three children of his figure later in the narrative of Acts: Agrippa the younger and Bernice (25:13), and Drusilla (24:24).

6. Continued Progress of the Gospel (12:24)

24 But the word of God[41] increased and multiplied.

Palestine 11.30). The institution of the festival in 9 B.C. is recorded by Josephus (*BJ* 1.415; *Ant.* 16.136-44). The identification of this festival as that which witnessed the onset of Agrippa's mortal illness was propounded by E. Schwartz, "Zur Chronologie des Paulus" (1907), in *Gesammelte Schriften* V (Berlin, 1963), pp. 127-28.

33. The date is known from Suetonius (*Claudius* 2.1).

34. See S. Lösch, *Deitas Jesu und Antike Apotheose* (Rottenburg a/N, 1933), pp. 14-15; J. Morgenstern, "The Chanukkah Festival and the Calendar of Ancient Israel," *HUCA* 20 (1947), pp. 1-136, especially pp. 89-90, n. 167, and "The King-God among the Western Semites and the Meaning of Epiphanes," *VT* 10 (1960), pp. 138-97, especially pp. 156-59.

35. "In that hour the enemies of Israel earned destruction, for they flattered Agrippa" (Tosefta, *Sôṭāh* 7.16; cf. TB *Sôṭāh* 41b).

36. E. M. Merrins, "The Deaths of Antiochus IV, Herod the Great, and Herod Agrippa I," *Bibliotheca Sacra* 61 (1904), pp. 561-62.

37. J. Meyshan, "The Coinage of Agrippa the First," *IEJ* 4 (1954), p. 187, n. 2.

38. A. R. Short, *The Bible and Modern Medicine* (London, 1953), pp. 66-68.

39. The late C. C. Harvey (of the Department of Child Health, University of Sheffield), in a private communication.

40. Cf. 2 Macc. 9:5-12 (of Antiochus Epiphanes); Josephus, *Ant.* 17.168-70 (of Herod the Great); Lucian, *Alexander* 59 (of Alexander the impostor); Eusebius, *HE* 8.16.3-5 (of Galerius); Theodoretus, *HE* 3.9 (of the uncle and namesake of Julian the Apostate).

41. For "God" B lat^vg cop^bo.codd read "the Lord."

24   This is the third of the brief reports of progress with which the narrative of Acts is punctuated (cf. 6:7; 9:31). In the present report the progress and prosperity of the cause of the gospel are emphasized by contrast with the miserable end of the royal persecutor.

IV. CHURCH EXTENSION FROM ANTIOCH AND APOSTOLIC DECREE AT JERUSALEM (12:25-15:35)

A. BARNABAS AND SAUL (12:25-13:3)

1. The Envoys from Antioch Return (12:25)

25 Barnabas and Saul[42] returned, having fulfilled their ministry at Jerusalem;[43] they took along with them John, surnamed Mark.[44]

25   Barnabas and Saul's famine-relief visit from Antioch to Jerusalem was related in 11:30 by way of completing the account of Agabus's prophecy and the Antiochene Christians' response to it. The response took the form of weekly contributions, and some time elapsed before the collection was complete and the need arose in Judaea. By the time Barnabas and Saul went to Jerusalem, Agrippa was dead. Their return, though not their setting out, is related in chronological order.

Both the textual variations and the syntax of this sentence have prompted many questions, to which diverse answers have been proposed.[45] But, as it stands in Luke's narrative, the sentence provides the transition from 11:30, where Barnabas and Saul go to Jerusalem, to 13:1, where they are in Antioch again. As for the reference to Mark, it provides the transition from 12:12, where Mark is by implication in Jerusalem, to 13:5b, where he accompanies Barnabas and Saul as they set out from Antioch to Cyprus. If (as is most probable) this is the Mark mentioned in Col. 4:10, the latter passage informs us that he was Barnabas's cousin.

42. Some Western witnesses (614 lat^p syr^{hcl*}) add "who was surnamed Paul."

43. Gk. εἰς Ἰερουσαλὴμ πληρώσαντες τὴν διακονίαν, the reading of ℵ B 81 byz syr$^{hcl.mg}$ eth. For εἰς P^{74} A 33 945 1739 al read ἐξ, D E Ψ 36 614 1175 al read ἀπό. Some minuscules substitute εἰς Ἀντιόχειαν for εἰς Ἰερουσαλήμ, while E 104 323 945 1175 1739 1898 lat^c ^{p} syr^{pesh} cop^{sa} have the conflate reading ἐξ (or ἀπὸ) Ἰερουσαλὴμ εἰς Ἀντιόχειαν.

44. After "Mark" Ephrem adds "and Luke the Cyrenaean" (see p. 244 with n. 1, on 13:1).

45. See n. 43. The reading "from (out of) Jerusalem" instead of "at (to) Jerusalem" arises from the attempt to construe the phrase with the verb "returned" (since "returned to Jerusalem" makes no sense in the context). The phrase is to be construed with "having fulfilled their ministry." To delete the phrase as a gloss, as L. E. Browne does (cf. his treatment of a similar phrase in 9:28), is a counsel of despair. See J. Dupont, "La mission de Paul 'à Jérusalem' (Actes 12,25)," *Études sur les Actes des Apôtres* (Paris, 1967), pp. 217-41, for an admirably satisfactory account of this sentence.

ACTS 13

2. Barnabas and Saul Sent Out from Antioch (13:1-3)

1 *In Antioch, in the church that was there, there were prophets and teachers—Barnabas, Symeon called Niger, Lucius of Cyrene, Manaen, foster-brother of Herod the tetrarch, and Saul.*

2 *While they were serving the Lord and fasting, the Holy Spirit said,[1] "Come, set Barnabas and Saul apart for the work to which I have called them."*

3 *Then, after[2] fasting and praying, they laid their hands on Barnabas and Saul and released them.*

1 The church of Antioch had among its leaders some very remarkable men. In addition to Barnabas and Saul, three receive special mention as "prophets and teachers." We may wish that we knew more about them. Who was "Symeon called Niger"? Why was he given a *Latin* surname?[3] The reason for the surname, apart from its Latinity, can scarcely be in question; he was presumably of dark complexion. It is tempting to identify him with

---

1. A remarkable reading of vv. 1 and 2 down to this point is found in a Latin work entitled *Prophecies collected from all the books,* originating in the African church early in the fourth century: "Now there were in the church prophets and teachers, Barnabas and Saul, on whom the following prophets laid their hands—Symeon who is called Niger, and Lucius of Cyrene who remains to this day, and Titus his foster-brother; they had received a response from the Holy Spirit, by reason of which they said . . ." As this work is also a witness for the Western reading at 11:27-28, which introduces the narrator at Antioch, it may be that here it identifies Lucius of Cyrene with Luke the evangelist. As for Titus, it is a natural inference from Gal. 2:1-3 that he was an Antiochene; that he was Luke's brother has been suggested, e.g., by W. M. Ramsay, *St. Paul the Traveller,* p. 390; *Luke the Physician* (London, 1908), pp. 17-18; A. Souter, "A Suggested Relationship between Titus and Luke," *ExT* 18 (1906-7), p. 285; "The Relationship between Titus and Luke," pp. 335-36. T. Zahn, in reconstructing the Greek text presumed to underlie this Latin reading, supposes that some words have fallen out and expands "Titus his foster-brother" to "Titus (an Antiochene, and Manaen, Herod the tetrarch's) foster-brother" (*Urausgabe der Apostelgeschichte* [Leipzig, 1916], pp. 280-81; he reproduces the Latin text on p. 80). He takes this reading to be the original Western text of the passage.

2. D expands: "when they had *all* fasted and prayed."

3. Latin was spoken in the Roman province of Africa, but that lay farther west along the North African coast than Cyrene. Do the evangelists use "Cyrenaean" in the general sense of "African"?

Simon of Cyrene, who was made to carry Jesus' cross on the way to the place of execution,[4] but Luke does not suggest the identification, although he mentions Simon in his passion narrative (Luke 23:26); moreover, it is Lucius, not Symeon, who is here called the Cyrenaean.

As for Lucius, there is no evidence to connect him with the Lucius (Paul's kinsman) of Rom. 16:21, and his identification with Luke the physician and evangelist is not only unprovable but improbable, although it was made in early Christian times, as appears from variant readings in the text.[5] Lucius, one of eighteen Latin *praenomina,* was a common name in the Roman world. This Lucius may well have been one of the men of Cyrene who, along with men of Cyprus, first preached the gospel to Gentiles in Antioch (11:20).[6]

Manaen is a Greek form of Hebrew Menahem (meaning "comforter"). The title "foster-brother" was given to boys of the same age as royal princes, who were taken to court to be brought up with them. (The word is found in inscriptions with the looser meaning "courtier" or "intimate friend,"[7] but there is no reason to give it this looser meaning here.) Herod the tetrarch, to whom Manaean was foster-brother, was Herod Antipas, youngest son of Herod the Great, who ruled Galilee and Peraea as tetrarch from 4 b.c. to a.d. 39.[8]

Josephus[9] mentions an earlier Menahem, an Essene, who was honored by Herod the Great for having foretold his rise to royal estate; it has been conjectured that he might have been the grandfather of this Menahem (Manaen). It is natural to suppose that Luke's access to information about the Herod family was derived from Manaen. But what a commentary on the mystery and sovereignty of divine grace that, of these two boys who were brought up together, one should attain honor as a Christian leader, while the other should be best remembered for his inglorious behavior in the killing of John the Baptist and in the trial of Jesus!

2 As these prophets and teachers were carrying out their appointed ministry in the church, the Holy Spirit made known his will to them— doubtless through an inspired utterance from one of their number.[10] There are indications in the New Testament that Christians were specially sensitive

4. Mark 15:21, where this Simon is identified as "the father of Alexander and Rufus." If he is so identified because Alexander and Rufus were known in the Roman church, the question arises if Rufus is the man to whom Paul sends greetings in Rom. 16:13.

5. See p. 243, n. 44; p. 244, n. 1.

6. See H. J. Cadbury, "Lucius of Cyrene," *Beginnings* I.5 (London, 1933), pp. 489-95.

7. See MM, *s.v.* σύντροφος (p. 615); *New Docs.* 3 (1978), § 9.

8. See p. 99, with n. 44 (on 4:27).

9. Josephus, *Ant.* 15.373-78.

10. This is implied by the reading quoted on p. 244, n. 1.

to the Spirit's communications during fasting. On this occasion, the divine message directed the leaders of the church to set Barnabas and Saul apart for a special work to which he had called them. It is perhaps worth noticing that the two men who were to be released for what would nowadays be called missionary service overseas were the two most eminent and gifted leaders in the church.

3 After further fasting and prayer, Barnabas and Saul were commissioned and released for their new service. Their colleagues laid their hands on them, and sent them away with their blessing and goodwill. The laying on of hands in this instance imparted to Barnabas and Saul no spiritual gift or authority that they did not already possess; but by this means the church of Antioch, through its leaders, expressed its fellowship with them and recognized them as its delegates or "apostles."[11] They were sent out by the whole church, and it was to the whole church that they made their report when, in due course, they returned to Antioch (14:26-27).

B. CYPRUS (13:4-12)

1. The Missionaries Arrive in Cyprus (13:4-5)

4 *So Barnabas and Saul, commissioned thus by the Holy Spirit, went down to Seleucia, and from there they set sail for Cyprus.*

5 *Arriving at Salamis, they proclaimed the word of God in the synagogues of the Jews. They had John as their attendant.*

4 Barnabas and Saul, then, having been sped on their way by the Antiochene church, took ship from Seleucia Pieria, the port of Antioch, five miles north of the mouth of the Orontes,[12] and sailed for Cyprus. Cyprus figures in cuneiform texts from the eighteenth century B.C. on under the name Alashiya, the Elishah of Gen. 10:4.[13] Its principal export was copper, to which it gave its name.[14] Its inhabitants in early days were known to the Greeks as Eteocypriots, but in historical times it was extensively colonized by Greeks and Phoenicians. It was annexed by Rome in 57 B.C., and was incorporated in the province of Cilicia two years later. In 27 B.C. it became a separate province, governed on behalf of Augustus by an imperial legate; in 22 B.C. Augustus transferred it to the control of the Roman senate, and from that year, like other senatorial provinces, it was administered by a proconsul,[15] as Luke indicates in verse 7.

11. See on 14:4 (p. 271).

12. On or near the site of modern Samandağ. Seleucia was founded by Seleucus Nicator (founder of the Seleucid dynasty) in 301 B.C.

13. It is usually called Kittim in the Old Testamemt, from the name of its chief Phoenician settlement Kition (modern Larnaka).

14. Lat. *cuprum* = *aes cyprium,* "Cyprian bronze."

15. As Gk. ὕπατος was used as the equivalent of Lat. *consul,* so ἀνθύπατος (ἀντί + ὕπατος) served as the equivalent of *proconsul.*

5 John Mark, the cousin of Barnabas, whom they had taken with them from Jerusalem to Antioch, accompanied them on this mission, and acted as their "attendant"—which some scholars have taken to imply that they availed themselves of his eyewitness knowledge of certain important phases of the gospel story, in particular the passion narrative.[16]

The first place in Cyprus where they preached was Salamis, a Greek city on the east coast of the island and the administrative center of eastern Cyprus. It was a flourishing commercial *entrepôt*, and its Jewish community, dating probably from the time when the island belonged to the Ptolemies, was apparently large enough to require more synagogues than one. The practice of presenting the Christian message first of all in the Jewish synagogue or synagogues of each city they visited was to be a regular feature of Barnabas and Paul's missionary procedure. It was a practical expression of the principle laid down by Paul in Rom. 1:16—that the gospel should be presented "to the Jew first." It has been asked if Barnabas and Paul would have continued this policy after the Jerusalem agreement described in Gal. 2:9, by which they were to concentrate on preaching the gospel to Gentiles, leaving the evangelization of Jews to Peter and the leaders of the Jerusalem church. But even then the synagogue provided a bridgehead for reaching Gentiles: Paul "was always sure of a good opening for his Gentile mission among the 'God-fearing', who formed part of his audience in every synagogue."[17]

2. Confrontation at Paphos (13:6-12)

6 *They traversed the whole island as far as Paphos. There they found a magician, a Jewish false prophet named Barjesus.*[18]

7 *He was in the entourage of the proconsul, Sergius Paullus. The proconsul, a man of intelligence, sent for Barnabas and Saul, and asked to hear the word of God.*

16. The word "attendant" represents Gk. ὑπηρέτης, used also in Luke 1:2, ὑπηρέται . . . τοῦ λόγου, "ministers of the word"—among whom Mark is probably reckoned. A. Wright, *Composition of the Four Gospels* (London, 1890), pp. 15-16, argued that Mark attended Barnabas and Saul as a duly authorized catechist; cf. G. Salmon, *Some Thoughts on the Textual Criticism of the New Testament* (London, 1897), p. 142. "It may be that Mark was taken on Paul's first missionary journey because his eyewitness reminiscences supplied an element in the Gospel-preaching that neither Paul nor Barnabas could supply" (G. J. Paul, *St. John's Gospel: A Commentary* [London, 1965], p. 26, n. 1, quoted by C. F. D. Moule, *Essays in New Testament Interpretation* [Cambridge, 1982], p. 47).

17. W. M. Ramsay, *St. Paul the Traveller*, p. 72. W. Schmithals, *Paul and James*, E.T., SBT 46 (London, 1965), pp. 46-61, agrees that Paul started his mission in each new place by trying to establish a connection with the local "God-fearers," but denies that, after the agreement of Gal. 2:9, he did so by going to the synagogue to find them. But the synagogue was the most convenient place for him to get in touch with them.

18. D reads *Bariēsouan*, a closer approximation to Aram. *Bar-Yēšûaʿ*, supplied with the Greek accusative termination -*n*.

8 *But Elymas[19] the magician (which is what his name means when interpreted) opposed them, and endeavored to divert the proconsul from the faith.*

9 *Then Saul, whose other name was Paul, was filled with the Holy Spirit; he fixed his eyes on him and said,*

10 *"You son of the devil, full of all guile and craftiness, will you not cease perverting the right ways of the Lord?*

11 *See now, the Lord's hand is against you; you will be blind, and for a time you will not see the sunlight." Immediately a misty darkness fell on him, and he went around trying to find people to guide him by the hand.*

12 *When the proconsul saw what had happened, he believed: he was astonished at the teaching of the Lord.*

6-8 From Salamis the two missionaries traversed the island from east to west until they reached Paphos, the seat of the provincial government, on the southwest coast. This was the Greek settlement of New Paphos, so called to distinguish it from the Phoenician settlement of Old Paphos, which lay about seven miles to the southeast. Both cities were noted, among other things, for the cult of the goddess called "the Paphian," a divinity of Syrian origin identified with the Greek Aphrodite. Here the missionaries had an interview with the proconsul; here, too, they met the sorcerer Barjesus, who was somehow attached to the proconsular entourage.

The proconsul at this time was Sergius Paullus,[20] member of a family which rendered distinguished services to the empire in the first and second centuries. This man may be identical with Quintus Sergius Paullus, who is mentioned in an inscription from Kythraia, in the north of the island, as holding office in Cyprus under Claudius (apparently).[21] The proconsul summoned Barnabas and Saul to his presence, questioned them about their message, and showed an interest in it. But the sorcerer did his best to distract the proconsul's attention from the gospel, opposing it for all he was worth; no doubt he suspected that, if the proconsul paid too much attention to the

19. The Western text seems to have read Etymas or Hetoimas, spellings which remind one of Atomos, the name of another Jewish magician who is recorded as living in Cyprus about this time (Josephus, *Ant.* 20.142; cf. pp. 447-48 below). See also p. 249, n. 24.

20. The Latin spelling is Paullus rather than Paulus.

21. *IGRR* 3.935, corrected reading in J. L. Myres, *Handbook of the Cesnola Collection of Antiquities from Cyprus* (New York, 1914), § 1903 (pp. 319, 548). An inscription from Soloi, N. Cyprus, mentions a proconsul named Paullus who held office in some emperor's tenth year (*IGRR* 3.930). The writing is probably too late for the principate of Claudius; in any case, even if the emperor were Claudius, his tenth year (A.D. 50/51) would be too late for the present incident. Others have favored the identification of our proconsul with Lucius Sergius Paullus, a curator of the Tiber under Claudius (*CIL* VI.31545); there is no evidence to connect him with Cyprus.

faith the missionaries were proclaiming, his own place at court was likely to be endangered.

The Greek word translated "magician" or "sorcerer" is *magos*.[22] As Peter confronted Simon Magus in Samaria, so Paul confronts Barjesus in Cyprus.[23] A Jew, even a renegade Jew (as this man evidently was), would not have been a member of the magian priesthood; he was a *magos* in the more popular sense. Luke calls him a false prophet, not (probably) in the sense that he foretold things which did not come to pass, but in the sense that he claimed falsely to be a medium of divine revelation. Elymas, the alternative name which Luke gives him, is probably a Semitic word with a similar meaning to *magos*;[24] it cannot be an interpretation of "Barjesus."

9-11 For his attempt to prejudice the proconsul against the gospel, the sorcerer was severely rebuked by Saul—who here for the first time in Acts is given his Roman *cognomen* Paullus (Paul), by which he is henceforth regularly called.[25] By his opposition to the truth he had shown himself to be a child of the devil,[26] rather than a son or follower of Jesus (as his name Barjesus might imply).[27] Divine judgment had been pronounced against him, and it would take the form of temporary blindness. Paul, says the Venerable Bede, "remembering his own case, knew that by the darkening of the eyes the mind's darkness might be restored to light."[28] As Paul spoke the words, the man was smitten with blindness, and fumbled around for someone to guide his unseeing steps.

12 The proconsul was greatly impressed. What exactly is meant by the statement that he "believed" is a matter of dispute. Ramsay suggests that, for Luke, belief is the first stage in the process of conversion, in which the

22. Cf. p. 166 with n. 29 (on 8:9).

23. See A. D. Nock, "Paul and the Magus," *Essays on Religion and the Ancient World,* ed. Z. Stewart (Oxford, 1972), I, pp. 308-30.

24. Perhaps akin to Arab. ʿ*alīm,* "sage." The attempt has been made (by A. Klostermann and T. Zahn) to associate the Western reading Ἐτοιμᾶς (cf. Gk. ἕτοιμος, "ready") with the Western reading Βαριησοῦα(ν) in v. 6, as though the latter were derived from Heb. *šāwāh* in the sense "be ready" (cf. the name Ishvah in Gen. 46:17; 1 Chron. 7:30). This is too farfetched to be plausible.

25. As a Roman citizen, Paul would have had three names—*praenomen, nomen gentile,* and *cognomen*—of which Paullus was his *cognomen.* It is probably a mere coincidence that Luke should first designate him by his Roman name in a context where another Paullus figures. The apostle's *praenomen* and *nomen gentile* have, unfortunately, not been preserved; the *nomen gentile* would probably have given some indication of the circumstances in which his family acquired Roman citizenship (see on 22:28). See C. J. Hemer, "The Name of Paul," *TynB* 36 (1985), pp. 179-83.

26. Gk. διάβολος, "slanderer," was used as a rendering of Heb. *śāṭān,* "adversary" (cf. 10:38). In his letters Paul prefers to use the Gk. transliteration Σατανᾶς (cf. p. 105, n. 14, on 5:3); διάβολος occurs in Eph. 4:27; 6:11; 1 Tim. 3:6-7; 2 Tim. 2:26.

27. His father's name was probably Jeshua.

28. *Comm. on Acts, ad loc.;* cf. Chrysostom, *Homilies on Acts,* 28.

second is "turning to the Lord" and the third the settled Christian life.[29] Lake and Cadbury, on the other hand, suspect that the missionaries "may have mistaken courtesy for conversion."[30] But if the proconsul had already been impressed by their teaching, that impression could well have been confirmed by the sudden blindness which fell on the magician. At the beginning of our Lord's ministry, the people of Capernaum were impressed by the authority of his teaching, as they not only heard his words but witnessed his healing power (Mark 1:22, 27).

Ramsay thought he had found inscriptional evidence for the presence of Christianity in the family of Sergius Paullus in later generations: his arguments are more ingenious than convincing.[31]

C. PISIDIAN ANTIOCH (13:13-52)

1. Arrival at Pisidian Antioch (13:13-15)

13 *Then Paul and his companions put to sea from Paphos and came to Perga in Pamphylia. There John left them and returned to Jerusalem.*

14 *They for their part crossed (the mountain range) from Perga and arrived at Pisidian Antioch. On the sabbath day they entered the synagogue and sat down.*

15 *After the reading of the law and the prophets, the rulers of the synagogue sent them a message: "Brothers, if one of you has a word of exhortation for the people, let us have it."*

13 Having evangelized part of Cyprus, the missionaries now sailed to the south coast of Asia Minor. Perga stood near the river Cestrus (modern Aksu); one could reach it from the sea, Strabo tells us, by sailing some seven miles up the river.[32] The city (the impressive ruins of which are a tourist attraction today) stands on a flat-topped hill about three miles from the nearest point on the Cestrus, where it presumably had a landing stage and port facilities. Perga, as its name indicates, was a pre-Greek foundation, but it was colonized by Greeks from the late Mycenaean age on, and after the conquests of Alexander the Great it became thoroughly hellenized.

Pamphylia lay between the Taurus range and the Mediterranean; it was bordered on the west by Lycia and on the east by Cilicia. At this time (between A.D. 43 and 68) it formed part of the Roman province Pamphylia-Lycia.

Luke does not say why John Mark left Barnabas and Paul at Perga

29. W. M. Ramsay, *BRD* (London, 1915), p. 165.
30. *Beginnings* I.4 (London, 1933), p. 147.
31. *BRD*, pp. 150-72.
32. Strabo, *Geog.* 14.4.2.

and returned home. He indicates at a later point in his narrative (15:38) that Paul regarded his departure as desertion. Perhaps he was unprepared for the increasing rigors which evangelization in Asia Minor would involve; perhaps he resented the way in which his cousin Barnabas was falling into second place. When the expedition sets out from Syria, Luke speaks of "Barnabas and Saul"; by the time they leave Cyprus, it is "Paul and his company." It is unlikely that this change of expression is due purely to a change of source.

14 Paul and Barnabas now struck up-country. It has been suggested that, on leaving Perga, they crossed the Taurus range by the Klimax pass (modern Çubuk Boğaz) and traveled north to Lake Limnae (modern Eğridir), moving then along the southeastern shore of that lake into the Anthios valley, and so to Pisidian Antioch.[33] W. M. Ramsay inferred from Paul's reference in Gal. 4:13 to the ill health which caused his first visit to Galatia that he had caught malaria in the low-lying territory around Perga, and went to recuperate in the higher altitudes to the north.[34] Certainly Pisidian Antioch was high enough: it lies 3600 feet above sea level. But Ramsay's inference is quite speculative.

Pisidian Antioch, or Antioch of Pisidia, was so called because it was situated near Pisidia, or over against it, as Strabo points out.[35] It actually lay in Phrygia, in that part which had belonged to the kingdom of Galatia and was incorporated in the province of Galatia, established by Augustus in 25 B.C.[36] At that time Augustus made it a Roman colony (with the name Colonia Caesarea); it was the civil and military center of that part of Galatia. Paul seems to have attached importance to the evangelization of such centers, from which the gospel would readily radiate out into the adjoining country. The ruins of Pisidian Antioch are still to be seen near the village of Yalvaç.

15 There was a Jewish colony in Pisidian Antioch, and therefore a synagogue. On the first sabbath after their arrival the two missionaries made

33. Cf. T. R. S. Broughton, "Three Notes on St. Paul's Journeys in Asia Minor," in *Quantulacumque: Studies presented to K. Lake*, ed. R. P. Casey etc. (London, 1937), pp. 131-33.

34. *St. Paul the Traveller*, pp. 94-97.

35. *Geog.* 12.3.31, 6.4, 8.14. See W. M. Ramsay, *The Cities of St. Paul* (London, 1907), pp. 245-314; "Colonia Caesarea (Pisidian Antioch) in the Augustan Age," *JRS* 6 (1916), pp. 83-134; W. M. Calder, "Colonia Caesareia Antiocheia," *JRS* 2 (1912), pp. 78-109; B. Levick, *Roman Colonies in Southern Asia Minor* (Oxford, 1967), pp. 34-35, 58-67, 130-44 *et passim*.

36. The Roman province of Galatia, formed in 25 B.C. after the death of Amyntas, the last king of Galatia, was (like Amyntas's kingdom) more extensive than "ethnic Galatia," the inland territory so called from the Galatians (Gauls) who settled there after their invasion of Asia Minor in the third century B.C. In addition to ethnic Galatia the province of that name included parts of Pontus, Phrygia, Lycaonia, Pisidia, Paphlagonia, and Isauria, with a number of Greek cities and Roman colonies. An enlarged province of

their way to the synagogue and took their places among the congregation. After the call to worship and the recitation of the appropriate prayers the scripture lessons were read—one from the Pentateuch and one from the Prophets.[37] (The Pentateuch was read in sequence according to a triennial lectionary;[38] the lesson from the Prophets was normally selected because of some relation to the Pentateuchal lesson.)[39] Then an address was usually delivered by some suitable member of the congregation. It was part of the duties of the ruler or rulers of the synagogue to appoint someone to deliver the address.[40] In the synagogue of Pisidian Antioch there was more than one such official. They sent an attendant to approach the two visitors and invite them to speak a "word of exhortation"[41] to the gathering.

We are indebted to Luke for accounts of two synagogue services— one in Palestine, in the Nazareth synagogue at the beginning of Jesus' public ministry (Luke 4:16-27),[42] and the other, given here, in a synagogue of the dispersion. These two accounts make a valuable contribution to our knowledge of synagogue procedure in the first century A.D.

2. Paul's Synagogue Address in Pisidian Antioch (13:16-41)

a. Exordium (13:16)

16 Then Paul stood up, made a gesture with his hand, and said, "Fellow Israelites, and those of you who worship God, listen to this.

16 Paul responded to the invitation by going to the *bēma* or pulpit and addressing the congregation. He made a gesture inviting attention, and

---

Pisidia was formed in A.D. 295, with Pisidian Antioch as its principal city; hence, no doubt, the reading "Antioch of Pisidia" (τῆς Πισιδίας, Δ E Ψ 33 81 byz), replacing the earlier "Pisidian Antioch" (τὴν Πισιδίαν, P⁴⁵ ⁷⁴ ℵ A B C *pc*, where Πισιδίαν is an adjective).

37. See Schürer II, pp. 447-54.

38. See A. Büchler, "The Reading of the Law and the Prophets in a Triennial Cycle," *JQR* 5 (1892-93), pp. 420-68; 6 (1893-94), pp. 1-73; J. Mann, *The Bible as Read and Preached in the Old Synagogue* (Cincinnati, 1940); J. Heinemann, "The Triennial Lectionary Cycle," *JJS* 19 (1968), pp. 41-48. For this purpose the text of the Pentateuch was divided into 154 sᵉḏārîm. Beyond the Euphrates an annual lectionary cycle was used, the Pentateuchal text being divided for this purpose into 54 pārāsiyyôṯ; it is essentially this cycle that is followed today in orthodox synagogues throughout the world.

39. See I. Abrahams, "The Freedom of the Synagogue," *Studies in Pharisaism and the Gospels*, I (Cambridge, 1917), pp. 1-17.

40. The ἀρχισυνάγωγοι were chosen from the elders of the congregation to take general charge of the synagogue services. Sometimes the office was hereditary; sometimes the title was bestowed *honoris causa*. See Schürer II, pp. 433-36.

41. For λόγος παρακλήσεως cf. Heb. 13:22; perhaps it was current as an expression denoting a synagogue sermon.

42. See N. B. Stonehouse, *The Witness of Luke to Christ* (Grand Rapids/London, 1951), pp. 68-92.

began to speak. His opening words indicate quite clearly the twofold composition of the audience. There were the "Israelites" (Jews by birth and possibly, in some cases, by conversion) and there were Gentiles who recognized that the true God was worshiped in the synagogue, and desired to join in his worship. They are the people who are commonly, but not technically, known as God-fearers.[43] In this as in many another synagogue where Paul preached, it was the latter group that proved more ready to accept the good news which he proclaimed.

The standing posture seems to have been the normal one for synagogue preachers in the dispersion. Jesus, on the other hand, stood up to read the lesson but sat down to expound it. This may reflect a difference in practice between Palestinian synagogues and those of the dispersion; it has also been suggested that a word of exhortation was delivered by a standing preacher, whereas one sat to expound the scriptures.[44]

b. Preparation for Christ (13:17-22)

17 *"The God of this people Israel chose our forefathers and exalted the people during their sojourn in the land of Egypt, and he brought them out of it with uplifted arm.*

18 *For about forty years he supported them[45] in the wilderness.*

19 *Then, having destroyed seven nations in the land of Canaan, he allotted their land to them after 450 years.[46]*

20 *After that,[47] he gave them judges until Samuel the prophet.*

21 *Then they asked for a king, and God gave them Saul the son of Kish, a man from the tribe of Benjamin, for forty years.*

22 *When he removed him, he raised up David to be their king. Concerning him he bore this testimony: 'I have found David the son of Jesse, a man who is all that my heart could wish; he will do everything that I desire.'*

17 Paul's exhortation takes the form of a historical retrospect,[48] as Stephen's defense did. Paul's retrospect surveys the course of God's dealings with his people Israel from his election of the patriarchs and deliverance of the nation from Egypt on to the accession of David and the establishment of

43. See p. 203 with n. 7 (on 10:2).

44. See I. Abrahams, *Studies in Pharisaism and the Gospels*, I, p. 8.

45. The textual evidence is fairly evenly balanced between ἐτροφοφόρησεν, "he nourished them" ("carried them like a nurse") and ἐτροποφόρησεν, "he endured their ways." The same two variants are found in Deut. 1:31 LXX (to which Paul is here alluding). The Hebrew text reads simply *nāśā'*, "bore."

46. The Western and Byzantine texts read "for about 450 years" immediately before "he gave them judges" (v. 20) instead of in the position indicated above (which is that of the Alexandrian text, the Latin Vulgate, and the Armenian version).

47. The Western text omits "after that."

48. Cf. I. Abrahams, *Studies in Pharisaism and the Gospels*, I, p. 8: the address, he says, "follows Jewish lines in its structure."

his dynasty; it then moves directly from David to Christ, as the one in whom the divine promises given to David for himself and his posterity were fulfilled.

Verses 17-22 correspond to an ancient confessional summary: they narrate "precisely those redemptive acts of God to which the Israelite bore witness in his confessional recital of the works of God."[49] The earlier phases of this recital are embodied in the acknowledgment of Deut. 26:5-10, in which the worshiper, bringing his offering of firstfruits to the altar, remembered with gratitude how God had chosen the patriarchs and redeemed their descendants for himself in the events of the Exodus, and how he had given them the land of Canaan as their inheritance (cf. also Josh. 24:2-13, 17-18). To these acts of God the worshiper of later days added his choice of David as king over Israel (cf. Pss. 78:67-72; 89:3-4). These events, in fact, constitute an Old Testament *kerygma* which is summarized in Paul's address as a prelude to the New Testament *kerygma:* the events proclaimed in the apostolic preaching are shown to have taken place as the inevitable sequel to God's dealings with his people in ancient days.

This address, says J. W. Doeve, was composed by someone who "must have had an excellent command of hermeneutics as practised in rabbinic Judaism."[50] More specifically, J. W. Bowker has recognized in it a particular form of synagogue homily, the "proem homily." This form of homily was related not only to the scripture lessons for the day but also to a relevant text which served as a proem to the homily.[51] The proem text on this occasion may have been 1 Sam. (LXX 1 Kms.) 13:14 (quoted in v. 22 below). It has further been conjectured that the Pentateuchal reading was either Deut. 1 or Deut. 4:25-46, and that the reading from the Prophets was 2 Sam. (LXX 2 Kms.) 7:6-16.[52] These are only tentative inferences from the address itself; we do not know at what time of the year it was delivered.

The language in which the history of Israel is outlined from patriarchal times is strongly reminiscent of the very wording of the Old Testament narration. The "uplifted arm" with which God led his people out of Egypt is an allusion to Ex. 6:1, 6 and Ps. 136 (LXX 135):11-12; the figure of speech emphasizes the mighty power manifested by God at the Exodus.

18 God's supporting them through the wilderness is taken from Deut. 1:31. There are two variant readings: according to our decision for the

49. G. E. Wright, *God Who Acts* (London, 1952), p. 76.

50. J. W. Doeve, *Jewish Hermeneutics in the Synoptic Gospels and Acts* (Assen, 1954), pp. 175-76.

51. J. W. Bowker, "Speeches in Acts: A Study in Proem and Yelammedenu Form," *NTS* 14 (1967-68), pp. 96-111, especially 101-10.

52. That the *seḍer* was Deut. 1 has been suggested by A. Guilding, *The Fourth Gospel and Jewish Worship* (Oxford, 1960), p. 78; the other suggestions are those of J. W. Bowker (see n. 51).

one or the other, he either sustained them or endured them. Both would be true to the record, but the former is more probably what is meant.

19 The seven nations destroyed in the land of Canaan are enumerated in Deut. 7:1, the wording of which is reflected here; they are named there as the Hittites, the Girgashites, the Amorites, the Canaanites, the Perizzites, the Hivites, and the Jebusites, "seven nations greater and mightier than yourselves." The dispossession of these nations and the occupation of their territory were spread over a long term of years; it was not until the seventh year of David's reign that the Jebusites, the last mentioned, were reduced. (The Jebusites were the pre-Israelite inhabitants of Jerusalem.) The 450 years seem to cover the period of sojourning in Egypt (four hundred years, according to Gen. 15:13; cf. Acts 7:6), together with the forty years of wandering in the wilderness and the interval that elapsed between the crossing of the Jordan and the distribution of the land recorded in Josh. 14:1-5.[53] (The wording of Josh. 14:1-2 has also left its mark on the language of verse 19.)

20-21 The age of the judges, terminating with Samuel the prophet,[54] was followed by the reign of Saul[55]—"a man from the tribe of Benjamin," like the Saul who was delivering this address.[56] But King Saul proved not to be all that the heart of God could wish, and his dynasty did not endure; he was removed from his kingship and replaced by another.[57]

22 This other man was David, to whom God confirmed his promise of abiding sovereignty, because of his readiness to do whatever God desired.[58] To him God bore witness in the words reproduced in Ps. 89:19-29:

"I have set the crown upon one who is mighty,
I have exalted one chosen from the people.
I have found[59] David, my servant;

53. The dative ὡς ἔτεσιν τετρακοσίοις καὶ πεντήκοντα expresses point of time, not duration of time; one might have expected the ordinal numerals: "in the 450th year."

54. Samuel, the last of the judges, appears in 3:24 as first in the succession of prophets (after Moses).

55. The figure of 40 years given here for Saul's reign is paralleled in Josephus, *Ant.* 6.378 (Greek text; the Latin version gives 20 years, as also does the Greek text of *Ant.* 10.143). J. A. Bengel (*Gnomon Novi Testamenti*, p. 441) reckoned that the 40 years here covered the administration of Samuel and Saul together.

56. Rom. 11:1; Phil. 3:5.

57. Cf. 1 Sam. 13:13-14; 15:23, 26, 28.

58. The words "a man who is all that my heart could desire" (ἄνδρα κατὰ τὴν καρδίαν μου) are taken from 1 Sam. (LXX 1 Kms.) 13:14 (ἄνθρωπον κατὰ τὴν καρδίαν αὐτοῦ.) ἄνδρα (*om* B) is a more precise equivalent of Heb. 'îš than is LXX ἄνθρωπον. The added clause "he will do everything that I desire" (ὃς ποιήσει πάντα τὰ θελήματά μου) conforms to the paraphrase of Heb. kilᵉbābô ("according to his heart") in the Targum of Jonathan: 'ăbêd rᵉ'ûṭêh (or plural ra'wāṭêh). See M. Wilcox, *The Semitisms of Acts* (Oxford, 1965), pp. 21-24.

59. LXX εὗρον (Ps. 88:21), whence "I have found" in v. 22.

with my holy oil I have anointed him;
so that my hand shall ever abide with him,
my arm also shall strengthen him. . . .

And I will make him the firstborn,
the highest of the kings of the earth.
My steadfast love I will keep for him forever,
and my covenant will stand firm for him.
I will establish his line forever
and his throne as the days of heaven."[60]

These words, recording the promises made by God to David, were written in a day when disaster had overtaken David's house, and the psalmist was distressed by the contrast between the divine promises and the sorry sight that met his eyes—the crown of David profaned and cast to the ground. No wonder that he cried (Ps. 89 [LXX 88]:49):

"Lord, where is thy steadfast love of old,
which by thy faithfulness thou didst swear to David?"

In later days, however, when the sovereignty of the house of David seemed to have passed away forever, so far as human agency was concerned, it came to be recognized that the promises made to David would be fulfilled and indeed surpassed in a ruler of David's line whom God would raise up. The Davidic kingship, according to the word of God through Ezekiel when the Judaean monarchy fell, was to lie in ruins: "there shall not be even a trace of it until he comes whose right it is; and to him I will give it" (Ezek. 21:27).[61] This coming ruler would be a new and greater David; the character of his rule was expressed by his name which, said Jeremiah, would be "The LORD our righteousness" (Jer. 23:5; 33:16).[62] As the postexilic centuries passed, and especially after the Roman extinction of the national independence enjoyed briefly under the Hasmonaeans, the longing for this messianic deliverer became more intense than ever.[63]

c. Fulfilment in Christ (13:23-37)

23 *"From David's offspring God, according to his promise, has brought[64] to Israel a Savior—namely, Jesus.*

60. These verses of Ps. 89 (LXX 88) are based on the narrative of 2 Sam. (LXX 2 Kms.) 7, where Yahweh undertakes to maintain the dynasty of David in perpetuity (cf. 7:46 above, with accompanying exposition, pp. 147-49).

61. Probably an expanded reference to Jacob's blessing of Judah in Gen. 49:10, ". . . until he comes to whom it belongs."

62. Cf. also Jer. 30:9; Ezek. 34:23-24; 37:24.

63. This longing finds eloquent expression in the *Psalms of Solomon*, composed shortly after the Roman conquest of Judaea in 63 B.C., especially in the passage beginning "Behold, O Lord, and raise up for them their king, the son of David . . ." (*Ps. Sol.* 17:23).

64. A number of witnesses (including C D 33 614 syr^{pesh hcl} cop^{sa} arm) read "raised up" (ἤγειρεν) instead of "brought" (ἤγαγεν). This variant reading may have been influenced by such OT passages as Judg. 3:9, "the LORD raised up a deliverer for the children of Israel."

24 *Before his coming, John had already proclaimed a baptism of repentance to all the people of Israel.*

25 *As John was completing his course, he said, 'What[65] do you suppose that I am? I am not he.[66] But see: after me someone is coming whose sandals I am not worthy to untie from his feet.'*

26 *Brothers, sons of Abraham's race, and all of you[67] who worship God, it is to us[68] that this message of salvation has been sent.*

27 *The inhabitants of Jerusalem[69] and their rulers failed to recognize him. Not understanding the utterances of the prophets which are read every sabbath, they fulfilled them by condemning him.[70]*

28 *Although they found no charge deserving death proved against him, yet they asked Pilate that he should be killed.*

29 *Then, when they had fulfilled all that had been written concerning him, they took him down from the gibbet and laid him in a tomb.*

30 *But God raised him from the dead,*

31 *and he appeared over a period of several days to those who had gone up with him from Galilee to Jerusalem: they are now his witnesses to the people.*

32 *So, we bring you good news about the promise made to our forefathers:*

33 *God has fulfilled it to us and to our children[71] by raising up Jesus.[72]*

---

65. The Western and Byzantine texts have "whom" for "what."

66. It is possible to punctuate differently and take these two clauses together as one sentence: "I am not what you suppose I am." But the punctuation above gives better emphasis.

67. A D 81 read "those among us" (οἱ ἐν ἡμῖν) for "those among you" (οἱ ἐν ὑμῖν).

68. P[45] C E byz lat syr cop[bo] read "to you" (ὑμῖν) for "to us" (ἡμῖν).

69. The Western text of vv. 27-29 has been reconstructed by J. H. Ropes (*Beginnings* I.3, p. 261) in a form which may be translated thus: "For the inhabitants and rulers of Jerusalem, not understanding the writings of the prophets which are read publicly every sabbath day, have fulfilled them, and although they found no charge deserving death proved against him, they judged him and handed him over to Pilate to be put to death. And when they were completing all the things that had been written concerning him, they requested Pilate after his crucifixion that he might be taken down from the gibbet, and having obtained their request they took him down and laid him in a tomb."

70. The phrase "by condemning him" (κρίναντες) was transferred by Lachmann to follow immediately after "failed to recognize him" (Moffatt accepts this emendation in his version: "by condemning him in their ignorance"). Blass emended κρίναντες ("condemning") to μὴ ἀνακρίναντες ("not discerning").

71. The weight of the evidence (P[74] ℵ A B C* D *pc* lat) favors "to our children" (τοῖς τέκνοις ἡμῶν). But as the promise was made to the fathers, we should expect to be told that it was fulfilled to *their* children; in fact, "to us [their] children" (τοῖς τέκνοις [αὐτῶν] ἡμῖν) appears as the reading in C[3] E byz syr. "It can hardly be doubted that ἡμῶν is a primitive corruption of ἡμῖν," says Hort. But the wording ἡμῖν καὶ τοῖς τέκνοις ἡμῶν ("to us and to our children"), conjectured by F. H. Chase, *The Credibility of the Acts of the Apostles* (London, 1902), p. 187, n. 1, is very attractive; it would bring the passage into line with 2:39, "to you and to your children" (cf. *Ps. Sol.* 8:39, "to us and to our children is his good pleasure forever").

72. The Western text has the reverential expansion "the Lord Jesus Christ."

Thus it stands written in the second psalm:[73] *'You are my Son; today I have begotten you.'*[74]

34 *And with regard to his raising him from the dead, to return to corruption no more, he has spoken thus: 'I will give you the holy and sure blessings promised to David'* —

35 *for in another psalm he says further, 'You will not let your holy one see corruption.'*

36 *As for David, when he had served the will of God in his own generation, he fell asleep and was gathered to his forefathers, and underwent corruption;*

37 *but he whom God raised up did not undergo corruption.*

23 What Paul announced, then, was that the messianic deliverer had been raised up by God in the family of David, and that his name was Jesus. The significance of Jesus' Davidic descent is emphasized in this address as it was in Peter's address in Jerusalem on the day of Pentecost (2:25-36).[75]

24-25 These verses introduce an outline of the primitive *kerygma* comparable to Peter's preaching in the house of Cornelius, beginning with John the Baptist's ministry (cf. 10:37). John's baptism of repentance paved the way for the public appearance of Jesus, as John himself made clear: when people wondered if John himself might not be the object of widespread expectation, he replied, "I am not he."[76] So far did he reckon himself beneath the coming one whose way he was preparing that he declared himself unfit even to untie his sandal straps.

This summary of John's ministry combines features from the Synoptic record (the baptism of repentance and the impending advent of the one who was greater and stronger than John) with features peculiar to the Fourth Gospel, especially John's denial that he was the Messiah.

26-29 "To us," said Paul, again addressing the two elements in his audience, the Jews and the God-fearing Gentiles, "to us this message of salvation has been sent." Then he went on to tell of the death of their deliverer: the people of Jerusalem, in the person of their rulers, showed their ignorance of the true meaning of prophetic scripture and consequently failed to recognize in Jesus the deliverer to whom it pointed forward. Instead, they

---

73. The Western text reads "in the first psalm" (P[45] reads simply "in the psalms"). Origen (on Ps. 2) says that he has seen two Hebrew manuscripts in which the first two psalms were joined as one. Justin, Tertullian, Cyprian, Eusebius, and Hilary also testify more or less explicitly to the practice of regarding these two psalms as one, and there is rabbinic evidence for the tradition that "Blessed is the man" (Ps. 1) and "Why do the nations conspire?" (Ps. 2) form "one chapter" (TB *Berākôt* 9b).

74. The Western text continues the OT quotation by adding "Ask of me, and I will give the nations as your heritage, and the ends of the earth as your possession."

75. See pp. 64-66.

76. Cf. Luke 3:15-17; John 1:20 ("I am not the Christ"). See on 19:4 (p. 364 with n. 13).

passed adverse judgment on him, and thus unwittingly fulfilled the prophecies which foretold how he must suffer and die. Yet their adverse judgment was totally unjustified: he did no more than claim to be the person he actually was. In spite of his innocence, they asked Pilate to sentence him to death, and the sentence was carried out by crucifixion. As on some earlier occasions (cf. 5:30; 10:39), the cross is called the "gibbet," in order to emphasize the connection with Deut. 21:23. When all was over, and the prophecies of his passion had been fulfilled, his body was taken down and buried.[77] The explicit mention of the tomb in which he was laid may be intended to underscore the reality of his death, and therefore also of his resurrection.[78] Besides, the burial of one who has been hanged on a tree or any erection of wood is specifically enjoined in Deut. 21:23, and there may be an implied insistence that everything was carried out in accordance with scripture.

30-31   But God reversed the judgment of men: here the constant note of triumph which made the apostolic preaching so joyful a message is struck again. God raised Jesus up from death, and over a period of many days—forty in all, Luke has said at the beginning of his second volume (Acts 1:3)—he appeared to his disciples who had accompanied him from Galilee to Jerusalem. They were now personal and public witnesses to his resurrection and messiahship; in Luke's eyes, they are the primary guarantors of the gospel story (cf. 1:21-22). No more than in the Gospel of Luke is any mention made of resurrection appearances in Galilee. More surprising still is the absence, in an address ascribed to Paul, of any mention of the Lord's appearance to him on the Damascus road. We may be sure that, if Paul referred to the appearances witnessed by Peter and others, he added, "Last of all he appeared to me also" (1 Cor. 15:8).

32-33   Here then is great good news. The promise made by God to the patriarchs has now been confirmed to their children—and not only to them, the historical Paul would have said, for believing Gentiles as well as believing Jews are blessed with believing Abraham (Gal. 3:8-9).

After long ages of earnest expectation, God, who had once "raised up David to be their king," had now raised up the Son of David, in accordance with the royal oracle of Ps. 2:7, "You are my Son; today I have begotten you."[79] The day of the king's anointing in Israel "was ideally the

---

77. The plural subject, "they took him down . . . and laid him in a tomb," may be generalizing; in the Gospels Joseph of Arimathaea and Nicodemus (members of the Sanhedrin) are specially mentioned in this connection (Luke 23:50-53; John 19:38-42). The rulers appear in any case to have taken steps to ensure that his body should be removed from the cross before sunset (John 19:31).

78. The mention of the burial of Jesus, immediately before the mention of his resurrection (cf. 1 Cor. 15:4), implies that the tomb was found empty, as the Gospel narratives explicitly affirm.

79. The raising up of Jesus to be his people's Messiah, rather than his being

day in which he, the nation's representative, was born into a new relation of sonship towards Jehovah."[80] Jesus entered into no *new* relation of sonship to his heavenly Father; but on the day when God anointed him with the Holy Spirit and power[81] and called him to his messianic mission, it was in terms of that oracle that he addressed him: "You are my Son" (indeed, the Western text of Luke 3:22 reproduces the full quotation from Ps. 2:7, "You are my Son; today I have begotten you").[82]

34-37 Not only did God raise Jesus up to be his people's Messiah; he raised him up in a further sense when he brought him back from death; and this too was a fulfilment of prophetic scripture. The promises made to David and his posterity could not have been realized apart from the resurrection of the crucified Messiah. Centuries after the promises were made to David himself, God renewed them at the time of restoration after exile by assuring his people that he would yet give them the pledged tokens of his "steadfast, sure love for David" (Isa. 55:3). One of these pledged tokens—indeed, the greatest of them—was the resurrection of the Son of David, in accordance with the assurance of Ps. 16 (LXX 15):10, quoted in this same sense by Peter on the day of Pentecost (cf. 2:27): "You will not let your holy one see corruption." In the Greek version a link between these two texts is provided by a common term, the adjective *hosios*, "holy"—"I will give you the *holy* and sure blessings promised to David" and "You will not let your *holy* one see corruption."[83] The exploitation of such a common term is a well-known feature of rabbinical interpretation: Paul practises it in his letters, even when (as here) the common term is found only in the Greek version, and not in the Hebrew text.

The argument used by Peter at Pentecost is, in essence, repeated here by Paul: the words of Ps. 16 (LXX 15):10 could not refer personally to David, for he died, was buried, and underwent bodily decomposition, after he had accomplished the will of God in his own lifetime. They refer rather to the one who was not permitted to "see corruption"—the one whom God raised from the dead, thus demonstrating him to be the Messiah.

The similarity between Peter's speech in Jerusalem on the day of Pentecost and Paul's speech in the synagogue of Pisidian Antioch has caused

raised from the dead, seems to be the sense in v. 33 (his being raised from the dead is mentioned in v. 34). For this sense of ἀνίστημι cf. 3:22, 26; 7:37; the synonymous ἐγείρω is used in this sense in 5:20; 13:22. On the use of Ps. 2 in the apostolic preaching see 4:25-26 with exposition and notes (pp. 98-99).

80. F. H. Chase, *The Credibility of Acts*, p. 126.

81. Cf. 10:38 with exposition (pp. 213-14).

82. Cf. C. H. Dodd, *According to the Scriptures* (London, 1952), pp. 31-32.

83. In Isa. 55:3 LXX ὅσια renders ḥasdê, "pledged mercies"; in Ps. 16 (LXX 15):10 τὸν ὅσιόν σου renders ḥāsîdᵉkā, "thy holy one." The rabbinical exegetical principle of *gezerah shawah* (in which the sense of two texts is linked to their sharing a common term) is here applied to the Greek text (as in Gal. 3:10, 13).

some readers to question the authenticity of one, if not both, of the two speeches. B. W. Bacon, for example, held that the present speech could not "be more than the historian's attempt to tell what Paul might have said: for as a whole it simply rehearses the speech of Peter at Pentecost, with a few variations, some of which remind us of the speech of Stephen. At all events, it is quite un-Pauline, and contains not one trait of his characteristic gospel."[84] Percy Gardner, on the other hand, thought that Peter's speech at Pentecost "so nearly resembles the speeches given to Paul that we can scarcely be mistaken in regarding it as a free composition," whereas the matter of the present speech "is eminently Pauline; and the manner, apart from the mere choice of words, is also Pauline. . . . We may then fairly consider the speech at [Pisidian] Antioch as an abridgement of the kind of address used by Paul towards his own countrymen."[85]

More common is the view that both the Petrine and Pauline speeches are Lukan compositions, a view based on the twofold ground of their common style and common interdependent exegesis.[86] But we should bear in mind (a) Paul's own insistence that the gospel story which he proclaimed was the same as that proclaimed by the other apostles and early witnesses, (b) the fact that the common outline of the primitive *kerygma* may be traced throughout the New Testament, no matter who the speaker or writer may be, and (c) the evidence for a common stock of *testimonia* or Old Testament selections used by all the early preachers of the gospel, which goes far to account for their common interdependent exegesis.[87]

d. Peroration (13:38-41)

38 *"Therefore, brothers, take knowledge that this is the one through whom forgiveness of sins is proclaimed to you.[88]*

39 *By him, indeed, everyone who believes is justified from all things—a justification which you could not have received by Moses' law.*

40 *See to it, then, that the saying in the prophets does not come upon you:*

41 *'See, you despisers, be amazed and vanish away; in your days I am*

---

84. B. W. Bacon, *The Story of St. Paul* (London, 1905), p. 103.

85. P. Gardner, "The Speeches of St. Paul in Acts," in *Cambridge Biblical Essays*, ed. H. B. Swete (Cambridge, 1909), pp. 397-98.

86. Cf. H. J. Cadbury, "The Speeches in Acts," *Beginnings* I.5, pp. 402-27.

87. Cf. C. H. Dodd, *The Apostolic Preaching and its Developments* (London, [2]1944), p. 30: "If we recall the close general similarity of the *kerygma* as derived from Acts, as well as Paul's emphatic assertion of the identity of his gospel with the general Christian tradition, we shall not find it altogether incredible that the speech at Pisidian Antioch may represent in a general way one form of Paul's preaching, the form, perhaps, which he adopted in synagogues when he had the opportunity of preaching there."

88. The Western text recasts v. 39 thus: ". . . and repentance from all things from which you could not be justified by Moses' law; in him therefore everyone who believes is justified in the sight of God."

doing a work which you will never believe, even if someone tells you of it.' "[89]

38-39 The preaching was regularly rounded off with a direct application to the hearers. Here the application comprises the offer of forgiveness and justification through faith in Christ and a warning against rejecting this offer. Forgiveness of sins has been regularly proclaimed at the end of similar speeches in Acts (cf. 2:38; 3:19; 5:31; 10:43), but now justification is mentioned as well. Knowing Paul's gospel as it is unfolded in the letters to the Galatians and the Romans, we are not surprised to find this reference to justification in the first address attibuted to him in Acts. But we may be warned not to be misled by a purely verbal coincidence. "The language of 13:39," says B. W. Bacon, "is claimed as Pauline because of the single word 'justify'. The doctrine is exactly that which Paul fundamentally repudiates, and which in Gal. 2:15-21 he demonstrates against Peter to be untenable, namely that a man may rest upon the works of the law for his general justification, and rely on the death of Christ to make up the deficiencies."[90]

Even if Bacon were on the right lines in his exegesis of the words, they need not involve so radical a contradiction with the argument of Galatians as he supposes. One could conceivably understand the words in this sense: "Even if you hope to enjoy a right relationship with God on the basis of Moses' law, remember that Moses' law does not provide for the forgiveness of sins committed 'with a high hand.' For such deliberate sins, by contrast with sins of ignorance, no atonement is available: the full penalty is prescribed. Why, then, go on trying to establish a right relationship with God in this way, now that you have presented to you a Savior who assures justification from *all* sins and complete acceptance with God to everyone who believes in him?"

Grammatically, the words could indeed be taken to mean that Christ provides for everyone who believes justification from all those things from which Moses' law provides no justification—namely, most deliberate sins. But quite certainly they mean that believers in Christ are *completely* justified ("justified from all things")—something which Moses' law could never achieve for anyone. In other words, Moses' law does not justify; faith in Christ does.[91] If the agreement of this interpretation with the doctrine of justification in the Pauline letters is dismissed as irrelevant to the exegesis of

89. The Western text (614 syr^hcl*) reads "and he held his peace" (the reading of D, "and they held their peace," is probably a corruption of this).

90. B. W. Bacon, *The Story of St. Paul*, p. 103, n. 1; cf. A. Harnack, *Date of the Acts and of the Synoptic Gospels*, E.T. (London, 1911), p. 58; P. Vielhauer, "On the 'Paulinism' of Acts" (1950/51), E.T. in *Studies in Luke-Acts*, ed. L. E. Keck and J. L. Martyn (Nashville/New York, 1966), pp. 41-42.

91. This is practically what Peter says in 15:7-11. Cf. William Tyndale's marginal note on our present text: "Fayth iustifieth and not the lawe."

the words in their present context, let it be said that the context itself, with the natural emphasis of the argument, requires this interpretation. Paul in this peroration is not making partial but total claims for the efficacy of the gospel over against the law. It is true that, in expounding justification by faith, Paul in his letters does not speak of it as being justified *from* anything. But that does not make the general sense of the present words un-Pauline. It is relevant to recall, too, that in the only other place in the Lukan writings where justification is spoken of as an act of God, the tax-collector who confessed himself to be a sinner and cast himself on the divine mercy went home *justified,* rather than the man who carefully regulated his life by the demands of Moses' law (Luke 18:14).

40-41   The address ends on a note of warning. The prophet Habakkuk, on the eve of the Chaldaean rise to world power, called on the nations, in the name of God, to look with astonishment on the impending invasion:

"Look among the nations, and see;
    wonder and be astounded.
For I am doing a work in your days
    that you would not believe if told" (Hab. 1:5).

As these words of Habakkuk were reminiscent of warnings uttered earlier by Isaiah in the days of the Assyrian peril (Isa. 28:21-22; 29:14), so Paul now takes them up (in the Septuagint version, which makes the application more pointed)[92] and applies them to the new situation in which God is offering deliverance through the greatest of all his mighty works. Great as was the disaster that overtook those who ignored the prophetic warnings, an even greater disaster will befall those who refuse the gospel.[93]

3. Response to Paul's Address (13:42-43)

42 *As they were going out, the people begged that these words might be spoken to them the following sabbath.*
43 *When the synagogue congregation had dispersed, many of the Jews and worshiping proselytes followed Paul and Barnabas. They spoke to them further and urged them to persevere in the grace of God.*

42   Paul's words aroused intense interest in a large part of his congregation. They had heard expositions of Scripture before, and moral exhortations, but

92. MT *baggôyîm* ("among the nations") is replaced in LXX by οἱ καταφρονηταί ("despisers"), which renders the Hebrew variant *habbôgᵉḏîm*, a reading attested in the Qumran commentary on Habakkuk (1QpHab). There is nothing in MT corresponding to LXX καὶ ἀφανίσθητε ("and vanish away").
93. Cf. C. H. Dodd, *According to the Scriptures,* p. 87. In addition to other literature cited in the exposition and notes above, see M. Dumais, *Le langage de l'évangelisation: L'annonce missionnaire en milieu juif (Acts 13,16-41)* (Tournai/Montreal, 1976).

nothing like this. They wanted to learn more of this new message, and asked to hear more on the same subject the next sabbath day. This request had to be addressed to the rulers of the synagogue, for it was their province to invite preachers to address the gathering.

43 The rulers of the synagogue, however, with other persons of authority in the community, had listened to the discourse with misgivings. They dismissed the congregation, perhaps, as Hort suggests, "for prudential reasons."[94] Many of the hearers, however, both Jews by birth and proselytes, followed Paul and Barnabas and showed themselves favorably disposed to the message, with its proclamation of forgiveness and justification through faith in Jesus. Paul and Barnabas encouraged them to continue in this mind, to persevere in their joyful response to the grace which God extended to them in the gospel.

A question arises about the "worshiping proselytes" mentioned here. Some commentators identify them with the Gentile God-fearers of verses 16 and 26, and the participle used here occurs in reference to such people elsewhere in Acts. But it is not a technical term, and the determinant word is "proselytes," which must be taken here as elsewhere to denote full converts to Judaism. Proselytes were members of the synagogue, as Gentile God-fearers were not; it would probably have been regarded as improper for the latter to make suggestions regarding the conduct of the service or the subject of the preaching.[95]

4. Gentile Interest Arouses Jewish Opposition (13:44-52)

44 *The next sabbath day almost the whole city assembled to hear the word of the Lord.[96]*

45 *But when the Jews saw the crowds, they were filled with jealousy and contradicted what Paul was saying, reviling him.[97]*

46 *Then Paul and Barnabas spoke out boldly: "It was necessary," they said, "that the word of God should be spoken to you first. But since you reject it, and judge yourselves unworthy of eternal life, see, we are turning to the Gentiles.*

47 *For this is the command the Lord has given us:*

---

94. "Notes to Select Readings," Westcott and Hort's *The New Testament in the Original Greek*, II (London, 1882), Appendix 1, pp. 95-96.

95. K. Lake properly takes the Greek to mean "many of the Jews and the proselytes who were worshipping" ("Proselytes and God-fearers," *Beginnings* I.5, p. 88). It is not necessary, with E. Haenchen (*Acts*, p. 413, n. 5), to suspect that προσηλύτων is a gloss (similarly K. G. Kuhn, *TDNT* 6, p. 743, § 4, *s.v.* προσήλυτος).

96. For "the Lord" B* C E Ψ byz lat[vg.cl] syr cop[bo] read "God" (cf. similar variation in v. 48).

97. The Western text amplifies to "contradicting and reviling" ("contradicting" is pleonastic after "contradicted" in the main clause).

'I have set you as a light for the Gentiles,
as a means of salvation[98] to the end of the earth.' "

48 *When the Gentiles heard this, they rejoiced and glorified[99] the word*
of the Lord;[100] and all who were enrolled for eternal life believed.
49 *So the word of the Lord was carried throughout the whole region.*
50 *But the Jews incited the God-fearing women of high rank, and the*
principal men of the city, and stirred up persecution[101] against Paul
and Barnabas. The authorities expelled them from the district.
51 *They, however, shook off the dust of their feet against them and came*
to Iconium.
52 *The disciples, meanwhile, were filled with joy and the Holy Spirit.*

44-45 During the following week, the Gentiles who had heard Paul's
address spread the news through the city to such good purpose that on the
next sabbath a great crowd of Gentiles turned up at the synagogue. Knowing
(as we unfortunately do) how regular Christian worshipers can manifest
quite un-Christian indignation when they arrive at church on a Sunday
morning to find their customary seats occupied by rank outsiders who have
come to hear some popular visiting speaker, we can readily appreciate the
annoyance of the Jewish community at finding their synagogue practically
taken over by a Gentile audience on this occasion. But there was a further
reason for their annoyance: these Gentiles were plainly disposed to give a
favorable hearing to a message which they themselves, for the most part,
found unacceptable. Many Jews, according to the narrative, did welcome
the gospel as Paul had proclaimed it the previous sabbath, but the majority,
and especially their leaders, had no use for a salvation which was open to
Gentiles on the same terms as Jews. It was just this, indeed, that aroused
their opposition. So they spoke out in an endeavor to refute Paul's arguments, and cast unworthy aspersions on the missionaries (perhaps including
the name of Jesus in their defamatory remarks).

46 Paul and Barnabas gave a straightforward answer to their disparaging words. It was right and proper, they affirmed, that Jews should
have the first opportunity of hearing and believing the good news.[102] Had
the Jews of Pisidian Antioch accepted the message, theirs would have been
the privilege of evangelizing their Gentile neighbors, in accordance with the
terms of Israel's world mission laid down in the Isaianic servant songs and

98. Literally, "that you should be for salvation" (τοῦ εἶναί σε εἰς σωτηρίαν).
99. Some Western witnesses (D lat^g) read "accepted" (ἐδέξαντο) for "glorified"
(ἐδόξαζον).
100. B D E and some other witnesses read "the word of God."
101. The Western text amplifies to "great tribulation and persecution" (cf. the
similar amplification in 8:1).
102. See p. 247.

their contexts.[103] But if they refused to receive the light themselves, they could not be allowed to pursue a dog-in-the-manger policy. The life of the age to come[104] had been brought near to them here and now as God's free gift in Christ; if they showed themselves unworthy[105] of the gift by declining to accept it, there were others who would appreciate it: it would be offered direct to the Gentiles.

Thus we are introduced to a pattern of events which was to be reproduced in one place after another to which the gospel was brought, right on to the end of Luke's narrative. The local Jews, almost invariably,[106] gave a corporate refusal to the gospel (though in every place there were some among them who did believe it), and it was accordingly proclaimed to Gentiles, who embraced it in large numbers.[107] It was regularly the God-fearing Gentiles who attended the synagogue that formed the nucleus of Paul's "churches of the Gentiles."

This in itself won Paul the disapproval of the Jewish leaders. They regarded him as one who poached on their preserves, a sheep stealer who seduced from the synagogue many well-disposed Gentiles for whose complete conversion to Judaism they had hoped—and seduced them by offering them God's full blessing, with incorporation in his people, on what seemed to be easier terms than those which the synagogue required from would-be proselytes. Paul's reply to this complaint would have been that it was only their own refusal to receive the gospel light that prevented them from being light-bearers to the Gentiles. A synagogue which yielded its allegiance to Jesus as the Messiah would not be in danger of losing its Gentile adherents but, as Paul (and Luke) saw the logic of the situation, would be able forthwith to incorporate them as full members.

47 This is in effect what Paul and Barnabas said on this occasion, quoting the words of Isa. 49:6. It is noteworthy that in the context of this prophecy (the second Servant Song) the nation of Israel is first addressed as the servant of Yahweh (v. 3):

> "You are my servant,
> Israel,[108] in whom I will be glorified."

But Israel as a whole was a disobedient servant, and the prophecy was to find

103. See exposition of v. 47 below.

104. "Eternal life" ($\zeta\omega\grave{\eta}$ $\alpha\grave{\iota}\acute{\omega}\nu\iota o\varsigma$) reflects Heb. $\d{h}ayy\hat{e}$ $h\bar{a}\!\acute{}\,\hat{o}l\bar{a}m$ $habb\bar{a}\!\acute{}$, "the life of the age to come"—i.e., the resurrection age. In Christ this life may be possessed and enjoyed here and now as God's free gift. In Paul's teaching it is Christ's own risen life shared by him with those who are united to him by faith.

105. For the idea of worthiness or unworthiness in this respect cf. Matt. 22:8; Luke 20:35.

106. Those of Beroea are recorded as an exception (17:11).

107. Cf. 28:28 with exposition (pp. 508-9).

108. For arguments against the extrusion of "Israel" from the text here see H. H. Rowley, *The Servant of the Lord* (Oxford, ²1965), pp. 8-9.

its particular fulfilment in one who is in some sense the representative or embodiment of Israel, yet distinguished from the nation, to which indeed his mission is first directed, as well as (thereafter) to the Gentile world:

"It is too light a thing that you should be my servant
to raise up the tribes of Jacob
and to restore the preserved of Israel;
I will give you as a light to the nations,
That my salvation may reach to the end of the earth."

In the New Testament this obedient servant is identified with Jesus (who was probably himself the pioneer in making this identification). Luke has already told how, in Jesus' infancy, Simeon of Jerusalem, seeing the long-expected Lord's Anointed lie at last in his arms, rejoiced that he should have lived to greet that day (Luke 2:29-32):

"Lord, now lettest thou thy servant depart in peace,
according to thy word;
for mine eyes have seen thy salvation
which thou hast prepared in the presence of all peoples,
a light for revelation to the Gentiles,
and for glory to thy people Israel."

But if the faithful Servant, through suffering and consequent triumph, accomplished the saving work single-handedly, his mission was henceforth shared with his followers, as they spread the gospel light in his name throughout the nations. Paul's own account of his call echoes the language of the Servant's call. But he would have said, more clearly than Luke does, that while others shared that aspect of the Servant's ministry which was directed to Israel, his own specific commission was to proclaim the Son of God among the Gentiles[109]—and, according to Paul's account, Barnabas was also recognized as called primarily to Gentile evangelization.[110] Here both of them read their own appointment in the Servant's commission: "this is the command the Lord has given us."

48-49   Distasteful as this announcement was to the synagogue leaders, it was joyful news to the Gentiles who heard it, and many of them believed the gospel—all, in fact, who had been enrolled for eternal life in the records of heaven (for this appears to be the sense of the words here used).[111]

---

109. Cf. Gal. 1:15-16, "God . . . was pleased to reveal his Son in me, that I should preach him among the Gentiles" (ἐν τοῖς ἔθνεσιν), echoing not only Isa. 42:1; 49:6, etc., but also Jer. 1:5.

110. Cf. Gal. 2:9.

111. There is no good reason for weakening the predestinarian note here, as (e.g.) H. Alford does by rendering "as many as were disposed to eternal life." The Greek participle is τεταγμένος from τάσσω, and there is papyrus evidence for the use of this verb in the sense of "inscribe" or "enroll" (cf. ὁρισμὸν ἔταξας, "thou hast signed a decree," in Theodotion's version of Dan. 6:12). The idea of being enrolled in the book of life or the like is found in several biblical contexts (e.g., Ex. 32:32-33; Ps. 69 [LXX

And not only in the city itself, but throughout the surrounding countryside as well, those who believed the good news carried it to others.

50 The Jewish leaders could not prevent the Gentiles from accepting the gospel, but they could make the place too hot to hold the missionaries. This they did by prejudicing the civic authorities of Pisidian Antioch against them. The wives of many of these authorities—like well-to-do women in many other cities of the Roman world—were attracted to the Jewish religion and were found among the God-fearing Gentiles who frequented the synagogue, and it was evidently through them that their husbands were influenced, to the disadvantage of Paul and Barnabas. Luke is at pains to represent the Jewish leaders as foremost in stirring up opposition to Paul in one place after another, rather than civic or provincial authorities acting on their own initiative.[112] This is an element in Luke's apologetic argument. The influential part played by the women, says Ramsay, "is in perfect accord with the manners of the country. In Athens or in an Ionian city, it would have been impossible."[113]

51-52 Thus forced to leave Pisidian Antioch, Paul and Barnabas "shook off the dust of their feet" against those who had expelled them—a gesture which Jesus had commended to his disciples when they left an inhospitable place[114]—and took the eastward road to Iconium. The gesture did not in this instance imply complete breach of relations with Pisidian Antioch: the missionaries had left a body of believers there, and they paid a return visit to them a few months later (14:21).

Iconium (modern Konya), lay about ninety miles east-southeast of Pisidian Antioch. It was the easternmost city of Phrygia.[115] For two and a half centuries it had been ruled by Seleucid, Galatian, and Pontic kings. It passed into the Roman sphere of influence in 65 B.C., and became part of the empire in 25 B.C., when the former kingdom of Galatia was incorporated as the province of Galatia. From Claudius it received the honorific imperial

---

68]:28; Isa. 4:3; Dan. 12:1; Luke 10:20; Phil. 4:3; Rev. 13:8; 17:8; 20:12-15; 21:27), in the pseudepigrapha (e.g., Jub. 30:20; 1 Enoch 47:3; 104:1; 108:3), and in rabbinical literature (e.g., TJ *Rosh ha-Shanah* 1.9.57a; TB *Rosh ha-Shanah* 16b). The Targum of Jonathan on Isa. 4:3 ("written among the living") explains this as being "written for the life of the age to come" (i.e., eternal life).

112. Exceptions are the incidents at Philippi (16:19-24) and at Ephesus (19:23-41).

113. W. M. Ramsay, *St. Paul the Traveller*, p. 102. Cf. 16:14; 17:12.

114. Luke 9:5; 10:11. The original idea behind the gesture was that the community against which it was directed was doomed (possibly self-doomed) to destruction—a destruction so thorough that it extended to its very dust, which must therefore be removed. Cf. 18:6.

115. It had been so since Xenophon's day (*Anabasis* 1.2.19). See further on 14:6 below (p. 272 with nn. 10-15).

prefix and became known for a time as Claudiconium.[116] To this city, then, the two missionaries came. But the converts whom they left behind in Pisidian Antioch, far from being discouraged by the expulsion of the men who had brought them the gospel, were (in spite of that expulsion, and doubtless in spite of some persecution which they themselves had to endure) filled with the joy begotten by the indwelling Spirit of Christ.

116. See W. M. Ramsay, *The Cities of St. Paul*, pp. 317-82.

ACTS 14

D. ICONIUM, LYSTRA, DERBE (14:1-28)

1. Adventures in Iconium (14:1-7)

1 At Iconium, in the same manner,[1] they entered the synagogue of the Jews and spoke in such a way that a great multitude believed, both Jews and Greeks.[2]

2 But the Jews who did not believe[3] agitated the minds of the Gentiles and inflamed them against the brothers.

3 They spent a considerable time, then, speaking boldly in reliance on the Lord, while he bore confirming witness to the message of his grace by enabling them to perform signs and wonders.

4 The city populace was divided: some sided with the Jews and some with the apostles.[4]

5 But when an attack was planned by the Gentiles and Jews, with their rulers, with the aim of maltreating and stoning them,

6 they got wind of it and made their escape to the cities of Lycaonia, Lystra and Derbe, and to the surrounding region,

7 and there they continued to preach the gospel.[5]

1-2 When Paul and Barnabas came to Iconium, they followed the same

---

1. Gk. κατὰ τὸ αὐτό. See E. Nestle, "Acts xiv.1," *ExT* 24 (1912-13), pp. 187-88.

2. Greeks, that is, who attended the synagogue, the so-called God-fearers. "Indeed, the term 'Greeks' found in Acts 11:20 was sometimes used to describe this class of person" (S. Brown, *The Origins of Christianity* [Oxford/New York, 1984], p. 98; he compares also 18:4; 19:10).

3. Gk. οἱ . . . ἀπειθήσαντες, "who disobeyed." The Western text recasts v. 2 as follows: "But the synagogue chiefs and their rulers stirred up persecution against the righteous and inflamed the minds of the Gentiles against the brothers; but the Lord soon gave peace." The last clause tries to explain why Paul and Barnabas spent a considerable time at Iconium (v. 3) in spite of the hostile action of v. 2. Ramsay regarded v. 3 as an early gloss (*St. Paul the Traveller,* pp. 107-9); others, like Moffatt, have transposed vv. 2 and 3. The Western reading implies two separate attacks (a short one in v. 2, at the beginning of the missionaries' visit, and a more violent one in v. 5, at the end); but we may leave the text as it stands, taking v. 2 to indicate the beginning of the opposition and v. 5 the success of the attempt to stir up the magistrates and populace.

4. The Western text adds "adhering to them because of the word of God."

5. The Western text adds "and the whole populace was moved at the teaching. And Paul and Barnabas spent some time in Lystra."

procedure as in Pisidian Antioch, visiting the Jewish synagogue and preaching the gospel there. Here, too, many of their hearers believed the good news, Jews and God-fearing Gentiles alike. But here, too, the Jewish authorities who would not accept the gospel took active steps to expel the two missionaries, and did their best to prejudice the minds of the local magistrates and the citizen body against them.

3 It took a long time, however, for the opposition to become serious, and the missionaries continued to preach the gospel freely and boldly. The preaching was attended by miraculous signs, of a kind which confirmed its truth in the minds of the people. Later, when writing to the converts of Iconium and the other cities evangelized at this time in South Galatia,[6] Paul appealed to the mighty works performed among them by the power of the Spirit, as evidence that the message of faith, and not the preaching of the law, was the gospel approved by God (Gal. 3:5). The gospel is here called "the message of his grace" because divine grace is its subject matter (cf. 20:24, 32).

4-5 The longer this work of evangelization went on, the more decisively did the populace take sides, either with the Jewish leaders or with Paul and Barnabas—who are here, as in verse 14 (exceptionally in Acts), called "the apostles."[7] At last a riot broke out, and the city mob was incited to assault and stone the two men.

6 Fortunately, Paul and Barnabas came to know about the plot against them, and made their escape from Iconium before the mob could gain its objective. But they had made their mark in Iconium; a body of converts was left behind to maintain the witness which they themselves had started. It has been argued that Paul's physical appearance left an impression in Iconium that was not soon forgotten—that it is reflected in the description of him preserved in the mid-second-century *Acts of Paul*. There one Onesiphorus, a resident of Iconium, sets out to meet Paul, who is on his way to the city. "And he saw Paul approaching, a man small of stature, with a bald head and crooked legs, in a good state of body, with eyebrows meeting and nose somewhat hooked, full of friendliness; for now he appeared like a man, and now he had the face of an angel."[8] It has been felt that a description

6. For the view that the churches addressed in the letter to the Galatians were those planted during the present missionary campaign see F. F. Bruce, *The Epistle to the Galatians*, NIGTC (Grand Rapids/Exeter, 1982), pp. 5-18.

7. Only here and in v. 14 does Luke use the term "apostles" of any outside the circle of the Twelve. This wider usage, perhaps referring to the two men as commissioned by the church of Antioch (13:3-4), may have been taken over by Luke from a travel document which provided him with the framework for the narrative of chs. 13 and 14. Luke does not give the designation "apostle" to Paul in the special sense in which Paul claimed it for himself. (Paul apparently places Barnabas on a level with himself in Gal. 2:9; 1 Cor. 9:6.)

8. *Acts of Paul* 3.3; cf. W. M. Ramsay, *The Church in the Roman Empire* (London, 1893), pp. 31-32.

so vigorous and unconventional must rest on a good local tradition of what Paul looked like.[9] This may be so, but it might well be the product of the writer's lively imagination.

From Iconium, then, Paul and Barnabas made their way to "the cities of Lycaonia, Lystra and Derbe." The implication is that Iconium itself was not in Lycaonia. The ancient realm of Lycaonia was at this time divided: its western part (called perhaps Galatic Lycaonia) lay within the province of Galatia, to the east of Galatic Phrygia, while its eastern part (Antiochian Lycaonia) belonged to the domain of Antiochus IV, king of Commagene (a client of the Roman state).

Sir William Ramsay has recorded how it was this geographical note that led to his "first change of judgment" with regard to the historical value of Acts. Xenophon, to be sure, in 401 B.C., refers to Iconium as "the last [i.e., most easterly] city of Phrygia,"[10] but writers such as Cicero[11] and the elder Pliny,[12] who lived much nearer to apostolic times, call it a Lycaonian city. Ramsay at first assumed, as others had done, that the author of Acts, wishing to add verisimilitude to an account of events in an area with which he was not personally acquainted, borrowed from Xenophon the information that Iconium was in Phrygia, not realizing that the regional frontier had shifted since Xenophon's day. But further acquaintance with both literary and epigraphic evidence convinced him that the statement in Acts was entirely correct, that Iconium was as Phrygian a city in the middle of the first century A.D. as it had been 450 years earlier. In the *Acts of Justin* (c. A.D. 165) Hierax, one of Justin Martyr's associates, tells an examining magistrate in Rome that he was "dragged away from Iconium of Phrygia,"[13] and in A.D. 232 a provincial church council was held in "Iconium, a place of Phrygia."[14] Local inscriptions show clearly that Phrygian was spoken in Iconium until the end of the second century.[15] Those writers who refer to Iconium as Lycaonian do so loosely because it lay near the frontier of Lycaonia and commonly shared the fortunes of that region.

Lystra, like Pisidian Antioch, was made a Roman colony by Augustus in 25 B.C. It served as a base for the more effective suppression of marauders from the Taurus mountains who threatened the Roman peace. The two colonies, which were about 100 miles apart, were connected by a military road which did not pass through Iconium. The site of Lystra, about

9. W. M. Ramsay, *BRD*, pp. 35-52.

10. *Anabasis* 1.2.19.

11. *Letters to Friends* 15.4.2.

12. *Natural History* 5.25. But later in the same book (5.41) Pliny mentions Conium (which may be identical with Iconium) as a Phrygian city.

13. *Acts of Justin* 4.

14. Cyprian, *Epistles* 75.7 (from Firmilian to Cyprian).

15. See W. M. Calder, "Corpus Inscriptionum Neophrygiarum," *JHS* 31 (1911), pp. 159-215, especially pp. 188-94; W. M. Ramsay, *BRD*, pp. 39-78.

eighteen miles south-southwest of Iconium, was identified by J. R. S. Sterrett in 1885 at Zostera or Zoldera, near Hatunsaray.[16]

7 The statement that Paul and Barnabas preached the gospel in the cities of Lycaonia anticipates the more detailed account of their doing so in verses 15-17 (at Lystra) and verse 21 (at Derbe).

2. Miraculous Healing at Lystra (14:8-13)

8 *At Lystra there sat a man who had no strength in his feet; he was lame from birth and had never walked.*

9 *He[17] listened to Paul speaking, and Paul, seeing that he had faith to be made well,*

10 *said in a loud voice,[18] "Stand up on your feet—straight up!"[19] He jumped up, and began to walk.*

11 *When the crowds saw what Paul had done, they raised their voices, saying in Lycaonian, "The gods have come down to us in human semblance!"*

12 *They called Barnabas Zeus; as for Paul, they called him Hermes, because he was the leading speaker.*

13 *Then the priest of Zeus, whose temple was in front of the city,[20] brought oxen and wreaths to the gates, intending to offer sacrifice along with the crowds.*

8 The description of the lame man at Lystra, and of his healing through the word of power spoken by Paul, is notably similar to the description of the lame man at the temple gate in Jerusalem, who was healed through his faith in the name of Jesus, invoked by Peter.[21] But the sequel to the present healing is totally different, and is narrated in a form remarkably full of local color. The genuine and apparently incurable nature of the man's disability is emphasized by repetition: he had, we are told, no strength in his feet; he was a cripple from birth; he had never walked.

9-10 Yet, as Paul was preaching, he saw this man listening to him and recognized that he "had faith to be made well." While the expression

---

16. The decisive clue was a Latin inscription (*CIL* III.6786) naming the place *Col(onia) Iul(ia) Felix Gemina Lustra* (see W. M. Ramsay, *Historical Geography of Asia Minor* [London, 1890], p. 332; *The Cities of St. Paul* [London, 1907], pp. 407-19; B. Levick, *Roman Colonies in Southern Asia Minor* [Oxford, 1967], pp. 37, 52, 154, 195-97; A. H. M. Jones, *The Cities of the Eastern Roman Provinces* [Oxford, ²1971], pp. 134-35).

17. The Western text adds "being in fear."

18. The Western text inserts "I tell you, in the name of the Lord Jesus Christ"— an addition calculated to intensify the resemblance to 3:6.

19. The Western text adds "and walk" (cf. 3:6), and continues: "and immediately he jumped up forthwith and began to walk."

20. The Western text reads: "Then the priests of the local Zeus Propolis."

21. See 3:2-10.

here refers to the recovery of bodily health, yet even in a pagan context "there lies latent in it some undefined and hardly conscious thought of the spiritual and the moral, which made it suit Paul's purpose admirably."[22] In Acts, as in the Gospels, faith is regularly emphasized as a condition of receiving both physical and spiritual healing.[23] That this lame man had faith was made plain by his ready obedience to Paul's command to stand up: he jumped to his feet, found that they supported his weight, and began to walk for the first time in his life.

11-12 The miraculous cure struck amazement into the crowd of bystanders. These were not the Roman citizens of the colony, whose language (as appears from funerary inscriptions) was Latin, but the native Anatolian population, who still spoke their Lycaonian vernacular. The fact that they called out in Lycaonian on this occasion is mentioned by Luke for two reasons: first, Paul and Barnabas recognized that this language (though they did not understand it) was different from the Phrygian speech which they had heard on the lips of the indigenous population of Pisidian Antioch and Iconium; second, the crowd's use of Lycaonian explains why Paul and Barnabas did not grasp what was afoot until the preparations to pay them divine honors were well advanced.

For the Lystrans, seeing the instantaneous cure performed on the lame man, concluded that they were being favored with a divine visitation. Local legend told of earlier occasions when the gods came down to them in the likeness of human beings—in particular, the two gods known to the Greeks as Zeus (father of gods and men) and Hermes (his son by Maia, and messenger of the gods).[24] We cannot be sure if the crowds used these two names or (since they were speaking Lycaonian) the names of two Anatolian divinities identified with Zeus and Hermes.

Ovid tells the story of a pious old couple of the region, Philemon and Baucis, who entertained Jupiter and Mercury (the Roman equivalents of Zeus and Hermes) unawares and were rewarded for their hospitality. In the earlier part of the twentieth century the evidence of epigraphy has effectively supplemented that of classical legend. Of two inscriptions from Sedasa, near Lystra, dating from the middle of the third century, and discovered by W. M. Calder, one records the dedication to Zeus of a statue of Hermes by men with Lycaonian names; the other mentions "priests of Zeus."[25] Another

22. W. M. Ramsay, *The Teaching of Paul in Terms of the Present Day* (London, 1914), p. 95; cf. H. C. Kee, *Miracle in the Early Christian World* (New Haven, 1983), p. 101 (for the use of the same word σωθῆναι in this sense in the Asklepios cult). Cf. σωτηρία, 16:17 (pp. 312-13).

23. Cf. Mark 5:34, ἡ πίστις σου σέσωκέν σε.

24. See Ovid, *Metamorphoses* 8.620-724. Cf. W. M. Calder, "New Light on Ovid's Story of Philemon and Baucis," *Discovery* 3 (1922), pp. 207-11.

25. See W. M. Calder, "A Cult of the Homonades," *Classical Review* 24 (1910), pp. 76-81, especially pp. 77-79; "Zeus and Hermes at Lystra," *Exp.* 7, 10 (1910), pp. 1-6.

indication of the joint worship of Zeus and Hermes in those parts is preserved by a stone altar discovered in 1926 near Lystra by W. M. Calder and W. H. Buckler, dedicated to the "Hearer of Prayer" (presumably Zeus) and Hermes.[26]

Barnabas may have been identified with Zeus because of his more dignified bearing; Paul, the more animated of the two, was called Hermes "because he was the leading speaker"—a very similar expression is used of Hermes by the early fourth-century Neoplatonist writer Iamblichus when describing the Egyptian mysteries.[27]

13 If the gods had condescended to pay the people of Lystra a visit, they must be greeted with appropriate honors, so the people, led by the priest of Zeus Propolis (Zeus whose temple stood at the city gates,[28] and who therefore would be regarded as the city's protector),[29] prepared to offer them a sacrifice of oxen, the oxen being duly decked with woolen garlands or fillets as befitted animals about to be sacrificed.

3. Proclamation of the Living God (14:14-18)

14 *When the apostles Barnabas and Paul heard what was going on, they tore their clothes and rushed out[30] among the crowd, calling out,*

15 *"Men, what is this you are doing? We ourselves[31] are human beings with feelings like yours. We bring you the good news that you should turn from these vain things to the living God[32]—the God who made heaven and earth and sea and everything that is in them.*

16 *In past generations he allowed all the nations to go their own ways;*

17 *yet he did not leave himself without witness, for he did you good, sending you rain from heaven and seasons of fruitfulness, satisfying you with food and rejoicing."*

18 *So they spoke, but even so they had difficulty in dissuading the crowds from offering them sacrifice.[33]*

26. *MAMA* 8 (Manchester, 1962), § 1; cf. W. M. Calder, quoted in an editorial note in *Discovery* 7 (1926), p. 262. "Hearer of Prayer" represents Gk. ἐπήκοος.

27. Iamblichus, *On the Egyptian Mysteries* 1 (θεὸς ὁ τῶν λόγων ἡγεμών, with which cf. Luke's expression here: ὁ ἡγούμενος τοῦ λόγου).

28. See W. M. Calder, "The 'Priest' of Zeus at Lystra," *Exp.* 7, 10 (1910), pp. 148-55, for arguments in favor of accepting the Western reading, "the priests of the local Zeus Propolis."

29. For this sense of πρό see Aeschylus, *Seven against Thebes* 164 (σύ τε, μάκαιρ' ἄνασσ' Ὄγκα, πρὸ πόλεως ἑπτάπυλον ἕδος ἐπιρρύου); cf. also B. Reicke, *TDNT* 6, pp. 684-85 (*s.v.* πρό).

30. The Byzantine text reads εἰσεπήδησαν ("sprang in").

31. Gk. καὶ ἡμεῖς (*P*45 omits καί).

32. א^c A B C D² read "a living God"; most other authorities have "the living God," but in a sufficient variety of forms to suggest that the definite article was originally absent (as in 1 Thess. 1:9).

33. The Western text (represented by C 6 33 36 81 431 614 1175 1739 *al* lat^h syr^{hcl.mg} arm) apparently added "but that each of them should go home."

14 It was some time before Paul and Barnabas understood what the people had in mind. When they did so, they rushed out from the place where they were,[34] with every mark of horror[35] at the idolatrous worship of which they were to be the unwitting recipients, and protested against it as vehemently as they could.

Here, as in verse 4, the two men are called "apostles"—a designation given to neither of them anywhere else in Acts. The opinion that its use in these two places is taken over by Luke from the source which he followed for this journey is strengthened by the word order "Barnabas and Paul," in contrast to Luke's customary "Paul and Barnabas."[36]

15-17 They protested that they were no gods, not even "divine men," but ordinary human beings,[37] who had come to them as messengers bringing them news of the one true God. The summary which Luke proceeds to give of their expostulation provides us with one of the two examples in Acts of the preaching of the gospel to purely pagan audiences—to people who, unlike the Gentiles who attended synagogue worship, had no acquaintance with the God of Israel or with the Hebrew prophets.[38] The other, and fuller, example is the speech delivered by Paul to the Athenian Court of the Areopagus (17:22-31).[39] Preachers to such audiences would not be expected to insist on the fulfilment of Old Testament prophecy, as they did in addressing synagogue congregations; instead, an appeal to the natural revelation of God the Creator is put in the forefront. Yet this appeal is couched in language largely drawn from the Old Testament. Martin Dibelius points out that the speech at Lystra shows dependence on the Septuagint—even more so, he thinks, than does the later speech at Athens. "The proclamation about God," he says, ". . . is preached completely in Old Testament style (see Ex. 20:11); the gods are described as 'vain ones' (or 'vanities'), as in 3 King[dom]s 16:2, 13, 26; 4 King[dom]s 17:15; Esth. 4:17 [LXX]; Jer. 2:5; 8:19; 3 Macc. 6:11."[40]

---

34. Ephrem the Syrian thought (perhaps rightly) that the sacrificial ox was brought to the door of the house where Paul and Barnabas were staying.

35. The rending of garments among the Jews was a gesture of horror at blasphemy (cf. Mark 14:63).

36. So long as he calls Paul by his Jewish name, Luke says "Barnabas and Saul," but when he calls him by his Roman cognomen, he prefers the order "Paul and Barnabas" (the order "Barnabas and Paul" in 15:12, 25 is natural in a Jerusalem context).

37. Gk. ὁμοιοπαθεῖς . . . ἄνθρωποι (for the adjective cf. Jas. 5:17). Luke is far from portraying the missionaries as "divine men" (θεῖοι ἄνθρωποι); cf. Peter in 10:26 (p. 209, n. 33).

38. Although Cornelius and his household were Gentiles when Peter visited them in Caesarea, they were not unenlightened pagans but worshipers of the God of Israel, acquainted with the OT scriptures and also, it is implied, with the general outline of the story of Jesus.

39. See pp. 332-42 below.

40. M. Dibelius, "Paul on the Areopagus," *Studies in the Acts of the Apostles,*

If it be asked if Paul and Barnabas would have expressed themselves in these terms, even to a pagan audience, it may be pointed out that the description given by Paul, Silvanus, and Timothy of the Thessalonians' conversion from paganism (1 Thess. 1:9) presupposes preaching very similar to that given here at Lystra. To Jews and God-fearing Gentiles, who already knew that God is one, and that he is the living and true God, the gospel proclaimed that this God had sent his Son as Messiah and Savior; but pagans had first to be taught what Jews already confessed regarding the unity and character of God. "God is one," the pagans of Lystra are told, "and has not left himself without witness. His works of creation and providence show him to be the living God who supplies the needs of men and women; therefore abandon those gods which are no gods but empty figments of the imagination, and turn to the true God." Only then could they be taught, like the Thessalonian converts, "to wait for his Son from heaven, the Son whom he raised from the dead—Jesus, our deliverer from the coming wrath" (1 Thess. 1:10).[41]

That God in former days permitted nations to "go their own ways" is paralleled by the statement in 17:30 that he "overlooked" the times of ignorance which preceded the full revelation of his will. Yet the ignorance should not have been so great as it actually was, for God's ordering of the seasons so as to provide food for all ought to have made people mindful of him and his claims on their worship. In Rom. 1:19-20 Paul similarly insists that, if men and women had paid heed to the works of God in creation, they might even in them have found tokens of his "everlasting power and divinity." There is, indeed, a difference in emphasis between what he writes in this regard to the Roman Christians and what he says to pagan audiences in Lystra and Athens: in these speeches the point is that, until the full revelation of God came to the Gentiles, he overlooked their errors which arose through ignorance of his will, whereas in the letter to the Romans God's giving the pagan world up to its own devices is the penalty for its rejection of even the limited light which was available to it. But his "overlooking" their errors betokened not indifference but patience.

The providence of God in giving human beings rainfall and harvest is an Old Testament theme (cf. Gen. 8:22), and the conjunction of "food and rejoicing" (cf. 2:46) is a feature of Old Testament language (cf. Ps. 4:7; Isa. 25:6; Eccl. 9:7).

18 Thus Paul and Barnabas spoke, and succeeded—not without

E.T. (London, 1956), p. 71, n. 23. An exegetical review of the Lystra and Athens speeches and of Rom. 1:18-23 is provided by M. Lackmann, *Vom Geheimnis der Schöpfung* (Stuttgart, 1952); see also B. Gärtner, "Paulus und Barnabas in Lystra: Zu Apg 14, 8-15," *SEÅ* 27 (1962), pp. 83-88.

41. The point at which a transition could be made from the general argument from natural revelation to distinctively Christian preaching may be seen in 17:30-31.

difficulty—in dissuading the Lystrans from paying divine honors to human beings with feelings like their own.[42]

4. Persecuted at Lystra, the Missionaries Go On to Derbe and Then Retrace Their Steps (14:19-23)

19 Then[43] Jews came from Antioch and Iconium and talked the crowds over to their way of thinking. They pelted Paul with stones and dragged him out of the city, supposing that he was dead.
20 But when the disciples[44] had gathered around him, he rose up[45] and went into the city. The next day he set out for Derbe with Barnabas.
21 When they had preached the gospel in that city and made many disciples, they returned to Lystra, Iconium, and Antioch.
22 They strengthened the souls of the disciples, encouraging them to stand fast in their faith. "It is through many tribulations," they said, "that we must enter the kingdom of God."[46]
23 Then they appointed elders for them in each church, and with prayer and fasting they commended them to the Lord in whom they had believed.

19 Luke does not say if there was a Jewish community and synagogue at Lystra. Probably there was, however; this would more readily explain how Jews from Pisidian Antioch and Iconium were able to incite the Lystrans against Paul and Barnabas. This would not have been so easy had those Jews been complete strangers, lacking any point of contact with the populace of Lystra, but they could achieve their purpose more conveniently through a Jewish community in Lystra. Although more than a hundred miles separated Lystra from Pisidian Antioch, the relation between the two places is evidenced by a statue of Concord which citizens of Lystra set up in Pisidian Antioch.[47]

The Lystrans, moreover, were probably offended by the mission-

42. M. Dibelius, who considers the speech of vv. 15-17 an editorial insertion in an independent and dramatic narrative, thinks that the narrative must originally have ended in a less "insipid" way ("Paul on the Areopagus," p. 72 with n. 24; "The Acts of the Apostles in the Setting of the History of Early Christian Literature," *Studies*, p. 198, n. 11).
43. The Western text expands this verse: "And as they spent some time there and taught, certain Jews came from Iconium and Antioch, and while they [the missionaries] were discoursing with boldness, these persuaded the crowds to revolt against them, saying, 'Nothing that they say is true; it is all lies.' So, having stirred up the crowds and having stoned Paul, they dragged him out of the city . . ."
44. P[45] D E read "his disciples."
45. The Western witness lat[h] and the Alexandrian witness cop[sa] add "at evening," which is implied also by the paraphrase of Ephrem the Syrian.
46. The pronoun "we" indicates that this is direct speech: the ὅτι which introduces the quoted words is therefore an instance of "recitative ὅτι."
47. W. M. Ramsay, *The Church in the Roman Empire*, p. 50.

aries' refusal to accept divine honors from them: they had been made to look foolish, and felt resentful. Paul, so recently acclaimed as the messenger of the immortals, was the chief target for the violent assault that followed. When, some years later, he recalled the hardships he had endured for the gospel's sake, he says, "once I was stoned" (2 Cor. 11:25), referring necessarily to this occasion. And when, writing to Christians in the cities which figure in the present narrative, he says, "I bear on my body the marks of Jesus" (Gal. 6:17), those marks or *stigmata* certainly included the indelible scars left by the stones at Lystra. There is grim irony in the quick reversal of the local attitude to the two visitors![48]

20 Luke's description of Paul's suddenly standing up and going back into the city after being dragged out and left for dead by the roadside has a flavor of miracle about it. The additional statement in the Western text that it was evening when he reentered Lystra is very probably true.

Derbe, for which he set out with Barnabas the following day, lay some sixty miles southeast of Lystra, on the eastern frontier of the province of Galatia, "very near to Cappadocia," says Strabo.[49] Its site has been identified at or near the mound called Kerti Hüyük, about thirteen miles north-northeast of Karaman (the ancient Laranda).[50] Its name is said to have been derived from the Lycaonian word *delbeia,* meaning "juniper."[51] Like Iconium, it received the emperor's name as an honorary prefix, and was known for a time as Claudioderbe.[52]

21 Having preached the gospel and planted a church in Derbe, Paul and Barnabas retraced their steps. It was no part of their present plan to go beyond the provincial frontier. "New magistrates," Ramsay suggests, "had now come into office in all the cities whence they had been driven, and it was therefore possible to go back."[53] Even so, tribute must be paid to the courage of the two men in returning so soon to Lystra, Iconium, and Pisidian Antioch—cities from which they had so lately been expelled with shameful brutality.

48. Contrast the quick reversal of judgment in the opposite direction at Malta (28:4-6). See p. 499 with n. 14.

49. Strabo, *Geography* 12.6.3.

50. See M. Ballance, "The Site of Derbe: A New Inscription," *AS* 7 (1957), pp. 147-51; "Derbe and Faustinopolis," *AS* 14 (1964), pp. 139-40; G. Ogg, "Derbe," *NTS* 9 (1962-63), pp. 367-70; B. Van Elderen, "Some Archaeological Observations on Paul's First Missionary Journey," in *Apostolic History and the Gospel,* ed. W. W. Gasque and R. P. Martin (Grand Rapids/Exeter, 1970), pp. 156-61. The chapter on Derbe in W. M. Ramsay, *The Cities of St. Paul,* pp. 383-404, was written fifty years before the epigraphically attested identification of the site at or near Kerti Hüyük, but still contains material of value.

51. So Stephanus of Byzantium (*c.* A.D. 500).

52. A. D. Momigliano, *Claudius: The Emperor and his Achievement,* E.T. (Cambridge, ²1961), p. 118, suggests that the honorific prefix was granted *c.* A.D. 41, when Derbe "became the Roman frontier post facing the kingdom of Commagene."

53. *St. Paul the Traveller,* p. 120.

22 In those three cities they strengthened and encouraged the young churches so recently planted there. The members of those churches needed to be encouraged: they had seen Paul and Barnabas violently assaulted and driven out, and they themselves had certainly had to endure some measure of persecution. It is almost taken for granted throughout the New Testament that tribulation is the normal lot of Christians in this age: it is those who suffer for and with Christ now who will share his glory. "No cross, no crown."[54]

Luke indeed records the irresistible progress of the gospel, but he does so in no triumphalist spirit. In C. K. Barrett's words, he "does make it clear that the road his heroes were travelling was the way of the cross."[55]

23 One way of strengthening the churches was making provision for leadership in them. In each of them there were some members who had already attained a sufficient degree of spiritual maturity to serve their fellow-believers as guides and give them the further instruction and encouragement they required in face of the hardship and persecution which they must expect as they maintained their Christian witness. It is held by many readers of Acts that the formal appointment of elders reflects the later situation of the Pastoral Epistles rather than this early stage in apostolic history. The language may be Luke's,[56] but it is plain from Paul's letters that he made provision for spiritual guidance in the churches which he founded and encouraged the members to recognize and respect their leaders.[57] What Barnabas's policy in this matter was we have no independent means of knowing. It has more than once been pointed out that more recent missionary policy would have thought it dangerously idealistic to recognize converts of only a few weeks' standing as leaders in their churches; perhaps Paul and Barnabas were more conscious of the presence and power of the Holy Spirit in the believing communities.[58]

With prayer and fasting, then, they commended the young churches, with their leaders, to the Lord, and continued their journey.

5. Return to Antioch on the Orontes (14:24-28)

24 *Then they passed through Pisidia and came into Pamphylia.*

---

54. Cf. Rom. 8:17; 2 Tim. 2:12a.

55. C. K. Barrett, "Theologia Crucis—in Acts," in *Theologia Crucis—Signum Crucis: Festschrift für E. Dinkler*, ed. G. Andresen and G. Klein (Tübingen, 1979), p. 79.

56. In 20:17 Luke designates as πρεσβύτεροι those Ephesian churchmen whom Paul calls ἐπίσκοποι and (by implication) ποιμένες (20:28). See p. 392 with n. 63.

57. Cf. 1 Cor. 16:15-18; Gal. 6:6; Phil. 1:1; 2:29 ("honor such people"); 1 Thess. 5:12-13.

58. See R. Allen, *Missionary Methods: St. Paul's or Ours?* (London, 1927), pp. 107-42; G. Schneider, "Die Entwicklung kirchlicher Dienste in der Sicht der Apostelgeschichte," *Theologisch-praktische Quartalschrift* 132 (1984), pp. 356-63; C. K. Barrett, *Church, Ministry and Sacraments in the New Testament* (Exeter, 1985), p. 52.

25 *When they had spoken the word in Perga, they came down to Attalia.*[59]

26 *From there they sailed away to Antioch, from which they had been commended to the grace of God for the work which they had now completed.*

27 *When they arrived, they gathered the church together and reported all that God had done with them,*[60] *telling how he had opened a door of faith to the Gentiles.*

28 *Then they spent a considerable time with the disciples.*

24-26   Setting out from Pisidian Antioch, they crossed the regional frontier from Phrygia into Pisidia, which was the southernmost territory of the Galatian province. Crossing Pisidia from north to south, they entered the province of Pamphylia. Here they preached in Perga, where they had called when they landed in Asia Minor from Cyprus (13:13); then they went down to Attalia (modern Antalya), the principal seaport of Pamphylia, at the mouth of the Cataractes (modern Düden-su). Attalia derived its name from its founder, Attalus II, king of Pergamum; he built and fortified it about 158 B.C. The Roman general Pompey used it as a base of ope͏ tions in his campaign against the pirates in 67 B.C. Its brief mention here is a further illustration of Luke's interest in ports of embarkation and disembarkation. From Attalia the two missionaries took ship for Syria and went up to Antioch on the Orontes, having completed a very eventful circular tour.

27-28   The church of Antioch was naturally eager to learn how they had fared: it shared in the responsibility and the glory of their service, for it was with its blessing and fellowship that they had set out on their campaign of more extended Gentile evangelization. The missionary tour had occupied the best part of a year, if not more; and now Paul and Barnabas resumed their ministry in Antioch for a period. But their activity in Cyprus and Asia Minor was a matter of interest not only in the Antiochene church but farther afield as well: in particular, the church of Jerusalem was concerned about the implications of a forward movement which so decisively altered the balance of Jews and Gentiles in the whole Christian fellowship.

59. The Western text adds "preaching the gospel to them."

60. For "with them" the Western text has the Semitism "with their souls" (cf. Ps. 66 [LXX 65]:16, τῇ ψυχῇ μου = "for me").

ACTS 15

E. THE COUNCIL OF JERUSALEM (15:1-35)

The Council of Jerusalem[1] is an event to which Luke attaches the highest importance; it is as epoch-making, in his eyes, as the conversion of Paul or the preaching of the gospel to Cornelius and his household. As he reports it, the Council was a meeting of the apostles and elders of the Jerusalem church convened to consider, primarily, the terms on which Gentile believers might be admitted to church membership (with special attention to the question whether they should be circumcised or not); in the second place, the means by which social intercourse, and especially table fellowship, might be promoted between Jewish and Gentile believers. Paul and Barnabas, with some representatives of the church of Antioch on the Orontes, were present at the meeting, where they were given an opportunity to relate their recent experiences in Cyprus and Asia Minor, but they took no part in making the decision; that was the responsibility of the Jerusalem leaders.

Luke's account is straightforward: difficulties arise when the attempt

---

1. See (among much other relevant literature) H. Lietzmann, "Der Sinn des Aposteldekretes und seine Textwandlung," in *Amicitiae Corolla . . . presented to J. R. Harris*, ed. H. G. Wood (London, 1933), pp. 203-11; K. Lake, "The Apostolic Council of Jerusalem," in *Beginnings* I.5 (London, 1933), pp. 195-212; M. Dibelius, "The Apostolic Council" (1947), E. T. in *Studies in the Acts of the Apostles* (London, 1955), pp. 93-111; B. Reicke, "Der geschichtliche Hintergrund des Apostelkonzils und der Antiocheia-Episode," in *Studia Paulina in honorem J. de Zwaan*, ed. J. N. Sevenster and W. C. van Unnik (Haarlem, 1953), pp. 172-87; E. Haenchen, "Quellenanalyse und Kompositionsanalyse in Act 15," in *Judentum, Urchristentum, Kirche: Festschrift für J. Jeremias*, ed. W. Eltester (Berlin, ²1964), pp. 153-64; M. Simon, "The Apostolic Decree and its Setting in the Ancient Church," *BJRL* 52 (1969-70), pp. 437-60; G. Zuntz, "An Analysis of the Report about the 'Apostolic Council,'" in *Opuscula Selecta* (Manchester, 1972), pp. 216-49; T. Holtz, "Die Bedeutung des Apostelkonzils für Paulus," *NovT* 16 (1974), pp. 110-48; D. R. Catchpole, "Paul, James and the Apostolic Decree," *NTS* 23 (1976-77), pp. 428-44; E. Bammel, "Der Text von Apostelgeschichte 15," in *Les Actes des Apôtres* = BETL 48, ed. J. Kremer (Gembloux/Leuven, 1979), pp. 439-46; A. Strobel, "Das Aposteldekret als Folge des antiochenischen Streites," in *Kontinuität und Einheit: Festschrift für F. Mussner*, ed. P.-G. Müller and W. Stenger (Freiburg, 1981), pp. 81-104; C. K. Barrett, "Apostles in Council and in Conflict," in *Freedom and Obligation* (London, 1985), pp. 91-108.

is made to relate it to Paul's account in Gal. 2:1-10 of a conference which he and Barnabas had in Jerusalem with the three "pillars" or leaders of the mother-church: James, Peter, and John. The great majority hold that Luke and Paul report the same occasion; indeed, one scholar declares that the identity of Paul and Barnabas's Jerusalem visit of Gal. 2:1-10 with that of Acts 15:2-30 is "one of the assured results of Acts criticism."[2] But in biblical criticism no result is so "assured" that someone will not be found to question it, and there are sound reasons to question the identity of these two visits.[3] The discussion reported by Paul in Gal. 2:1-10 centered around the demarcation of spheres of missionary activity (it was agreed that Paul and Barnabas should continue their work of Gentile evangelization, while the Jerusalem leaders should concentrate on the witness among Jews); circumcision receives only marginal mention (in terms which do not necessarily mean that it was discussed at the conference at all),[4] and nothing is said about facilitating table fellowship between Jewish and Gentile Christians. Moreover, the conference of Gal. 2:1-10 is expressly said to have been a private one;[5] the meeting of Acts 15 was held publicly, in the presence of the Jerusalem church.[6] It could be argued that the private interview of Gal. 2:1-10 took place during the visit which also witnessed the public meeting;[7] if so, it is difficult to understand why Paul told the Galatian Christians nothing of the decisions reached by the public meeting, since they were relevant to the Galatian controversy. Another suggestion is that in Acts 15 Luke combines into one narrative two originally separate meetings: one (recorded also in Gal. 2:1-10) at which Paul and Barnabas were present, and the other (which

2. G. Strecker, "Die sogenannte zweite Jerusalemreise des Paulus (Act 11,27-30)," *ZNW* 53 (1962), pp. 67-77 (p. 73).

3. See F. F. Bruce, *The Epistle to the Galatians,* NIGTC (Grand Rapids/Exeter, 1982), pp. 19-32, 43-56, 105-34, for the view that the Jerusalem conference of Gal. 2:1-10, the Antioch controversy of Gal. 2:11-14, and even the writing of the letter to the Galatians itself (to the churches whose foundation is recorded in Acts 13:48–14:23) antedated the council of Acts 15.

4. Gal. 2:3-5 should probably be taken as a digression, and vv. 4-5 as a parenthesis within that digression, with reference to an occasion slightly later than Paul and Barnabas's conference with the Jerusalem "pillars": the circumcision issue, Paul means, was not introduced at that conference, but later, when false brothers infiltrated our fellowship. Cf. T. W. Manson, *Studies in the Gospels and Epistles* (Manchester, 1962), pp. 175-76; B. Orchard, "A New Solution of the Galatians Problem," *BJRL* 28 (1944), pp. 154-74; "The Ellipsis between Galatians 2,3 and 2,4," *Bib.* 54 (1973), pp. 469-81.

5. Gal. 2:2, κατ' ἰδίαν.

6. Acts 15:12 (πᾶν τὸ πλῆθος), 22 (σὺν ὅλῃ τῇ ἐκκλησίᾳ).

7. For this view cf. J. B. Lightfoot, *St. Paul's Epistle to the Galatians* (London, 1865), pp. 125-26; H. N. Ridderbos, *The Epistle of Paul to the Churches of Galatia,* NICNT (Grand Rapids, 1953), pp. 78-82. But "we have no reason for supposing that the Church had by this date reached that stage of democracy in which the public meeting registers its assent to a decision reached in advance by its leading members" (W. L. Knox, *The Acts of the Apostles* [Cambridge, 1948], p. 42).

produced the decisions of Acts 15:28-29) at which Paul and Barnabas were not present.[8] It is simpler to conclude that the occasion reported by Paul and that described by Luke were not the same.

On the other hand, part of Paul's autobiographical narrative in Galatians probably provides the background to Acts 15. In Gal. 2:11-14 Paul tells how (presumably sometime after the conference of Gal. 2:1-10)[9] Peter visited Antioch and (in accordance with his convictions and general practice) shared meals freely with Gentile Christians there. But some people[10] came from Jerusalem—"from James," says Paul—and persuaded Peter to withdraw from table fellowship with Gentiles. What they said to Peter must be conjectured: probably they told him that news of his free and easy fraternizing with Gentiles was coming back to Jerusalem and causing embarrassment, and possibly danger, to the church leaders there.[11] Peter was sufficiently impressed to withdraw (temporarily, at least) from common meals with Gentile Christians, and his example was followed by other Jewish Christians in Antioch, including "even Barnabas." Peter and Barnabas might have pleaded that their action was undertaken out of consideration for weaker brothers, but Paul saw their action as a threat to gospel liberty for Gentiles, and he remonstrated publicly with Peter. Peter's action, he said, amounted to forcing Gentiles to adopt the Jewish way of life.

Peter no doubt was distressed by the dismay which his action at Antioch had caused. Since that action had been prompted by a message from James, the problem must be sorted out with James. Accordingly a meeting of the Jerusalem leaders was held under the chairmanship of James. This

8. For this suggestion cf. H. Lietzmann, "Der Sinn des Aposteldekretes . . ."; H. W. Beyer, *Die Apostelgeschichte*, KEK 3 (Göttingen, 1951), pp. 91-97; O. Cullmann, *Peter: Disciple-Apostle-Martyr*, E.T. (London, 1953), p. 49; T. W. Manson, *Studies in the Gospels and Epistles*, p. 186; M. Dibelius, *Studies in the Acts of the Apostles*, pp. 98-99, 106-7; F. Hahn, *Mission in the New Testament*, E.T., SBT 47 (London, 1963), pp. 77-86. The cogency of this suggestion is weakened if in fact the Jerusalem visits of Gal. 2:1-10 and Acts 15 were quite distinct.

9. Other views of the chronological sequence have been put forward. Some have dated the controversy of Gal. 2:11-14 before the conference of Gal. 2:1-10; see, e.g., T. Zahn, *Der Brief des Paulus an die Galater* (Leipzig, ³1922), p. 110; H. M. Feret, *Pierre et Paul à Antioche et à Jérusalem* (Paris, 1955); J. Munck, *Paul and the Salvation of Mankind*, E.T. (London, 1959), pp. 100-103. W. L. Knox (*The Acts of the Apostles*, p. 49) supposes that the Antioch controversy preceded the first missionary expedition of Paul and Barnabas: that it was, in fact, the controversy that made the Antiochene church decide "to launch a vigorous Gentile mission."

10. For the plural τινας (Gal. 2:12) P^{46} and some Latin witnesses have the singular τινα ("a certain person"), while P^{46} and several uncials have the singular ἦλθεν ("came") for the plural ἦλθον in the second half of the verse. If the singular be preferred, the person in question may simply have been the spokesman of a group.

11. See T. W. Manson, *Studies in the Gospels and Epistles*, p. 181; B. Reicke, "Der geschichtliche Hintergrund . . . der Antiocheia-Episode"; R. Jewett, "The Agitators and the Galatian Congregation," *NTS* 17 (1970-71), pp. 198-212.

meeting refused the demand voiced by some members of the Jerusalem
church that Gentile converts should submit to circumcision and other requirements of the Mosaic law, and then turned to consider terms on which
table fellowship between Jewish and Gentile Christians might become acceptable. When what seemed to be a satisfactory decision was reached,
Peter, the bridge-builder among the apostles,[12] must have been well
pleased. The decision, which had to do largely with the avoidance of certain
kinds of food by Gentile Christians, promised to prevent the recurrence of
the awkwardness which had recently arisen at Antioch,[13] and Peter, in the
course of his more extended missionary journeys, probably recommended it
to other churches.[14]

As for Paul, he took a different line. Where true religion and basic
Christian ethics were involved, he was as peremptory as anyone could well
be in directing his converts to avoid idolatry and fornication.[15] But in matters (like food) which were religiously and ethically neutral, he refused to lay
down the law. No food, he maintained, was "common or unclean" per se—
not even if it had been forbidden by the law of Moses, not even if it came
from an animal that had been sacrificed to a pagan divinity. It was human
beings that mattered, not food; if a Christian was considering whether or not
to eat this or that kind of food, the decision should depend on the effect
which the taking or leaving it would have on the conscience of a fellow-
Christian.[16] When Paul was asked for a ruling on eating the flesh of animals
which had been "sacrificed to idols" (cf. 1 Cor. 8:1–11:1), the last thing that
would have occurred to him would be to quote a decision of the Jerusalem
church as binding on Gentile Christians. When faced with such questions he
argues from the order of creation and the ethical implications of a law-free
gospel.

1. Judaizers Visit Antioch (15:1-2)

1 *Some people[17] came down from Judaea and began instructing the
brothers: "Unless you are circumcised[18] according to the custom of
Moses," they said, "you cannot be saved."*

2 *Division resulted, and Paul and Barnabas held considerable debate*

---

12. Cf. J. D. G. Dunn, *Unity and Diversity in the New Testament* (London,
1977), p. 385.

13. See A. Strobel, "Das Aposteldekret als Folge des antiochenischen Streites."

14. See H. Lietzmann, *The Beginnings of the Christian Church*, E.T. (London,
1949), p. 151; C. K. Barrett, "Things Sacrificed to Idols," *NTS* 22 (1964-65), p. 150.

15. E.g., 1 Cor. 6:12-20; 10:7-8, 14-22.

16. Cf. Rom. 14:14-23.

17. The Western text adds "of the party of the Pharisees, who were believers" (cf.
v. 5).

18. The Western text inserts "and walk."

with them.¹⁹ Then Paul and Barnabas were appointed²⁰ to go up to the apostles and elders in Jerusalem about this question.

1 The people who came down from Judaea may have been those who, in Paul's narrative, came to Antioch "from James" (Gal. 2:12). Whether they were so or not, they exceeded the terms of their commission, according to the apostolic letter in verse 24. Another possibility is that they were the "false brothers secretly brought in" of Gal. 2:4, if (as seems likely) Antioch was the place where these latter tried to "spy out" the freedom which Paul and the Gentile Christians enjoyed in their fellowship.²¹

The rapid progress of Gentile evangelization in Antioch and farther afield presented the more conservative Jewish believers with a serious problem. The apostles had acquiesced in Peter's action in the house of Cornelius because it was attended by such evident marks of divine approval; but now a new situation confronted them. Before long there would be more Gentile Christians than Jewish Christians in the world. Many Jewish Christians no doubt feared that the influx of so many converts from paganism would bring about a weakening of the church's moral standards, and the evidence of Paul's letters shows that their misgivings were not unfounded. How was this new situation to be controlled?

Some members of the Jerusalem church had a simple answer. Since so many Jews had failed to acknowledge Jesus as the Messiah, they would have conceded the necessity of admitting Gentiles into the messianic community in order to make up the full complement. But those Gentiles should be admitted on terms similar to those required of proselytes to Judaism: they must be circumcised and assume the obligation to observe the Mosaic law.

But it seems clear that these conditions had not been insisted on. Cornelius and his household do not appear to have had the duty of circumcision pressed on them; and certainly the Gentile converts in the recently evangelized cities of South Galatia, like those in Antioch itself, had been welcomed into church fellowship without being circumcised. There were

19. The Western text adds: "for Paul insisted that they should remain just as they were when they believed (cf. 1 Cor. 7:20, 24). Those who had come from Jerusalem charged Paul and Barnabas and some others to go up to the apostles and elders at Jerusalem to be judged before them concerning this question" (a form of words perhaps borrowed in part from 25:9, but here implying that the judaizers were vested with the authority of the Jerusalem church, and that Paul and Barnabas were under their orders).

20. Lit., "they appointed (ἔταξαν) Paul and Barnabas . . ."; the subject of the verb is not expressed, but the implication is that "they" were the church of Antioch, or its leaders.

21. They are identified with the "false brothers" by J. Weiss, *Earliest Christianity*, E.T., I (New York, 1959), pp. 263-67; H. Lietzmann, *An die Galater*, HNT 10 (Tübingen, ²1923), p. 11; H. Schlier, *Der Brief an die Galater*, KEK 7 (Göttingen, ⁵1971), p. 39; A. Oepke, *Der Brief des Paulus an die Galater*, THKNT 9 (Berlin, ²1957), p. 47; F. Hahn, *Mission in the New Testament*, p. 78.

indeed some Jews in those days who thought that the outward rite of circumcision might be omitted, if only its spiritual significance was realized; but these formed a negligible minority.[22] The vast majority, including such a hellenized Jew as Philo of Alexandria,[23] insisted on circumcision as indispensable for all males in the commonwealth of Israel, whether they entered it by birth or by proselytization. This was probably the attitude of the rank and file in the Jerusalem church—"zealots for the law," as they are called on a later occasion (21:20). For many of them the church was the righteous remnant of Judaism, embodying the ancestral hope which all Israel ought to have welcomed, preparing itself for the impending day of the Lord: to countenance any relaxation in the terms of the covenant with Abraham, sealed in the flesh by circumcision, would be to forfeit all claim to remnant righteousness, all title to salvation on the last day. If Paul and Barnabas neglected to bring the requirements of the law to the attention of Gentile members of the church of Antioch and her daughter-churches, there were those in the Jerusalem church who were ready to repair this omission, and they went to Antioch, the citadel of Gentile Christianity, to repair it there.

2   It was not enough to indulge in dissension and questioning at Antioch: the whole issue had to be debated and decided at the highest level. Otherwise, there was grave danger of a complete cleavage between the churches of Jerusalem and Judaea on the one hand and the church of Antioch and her daughter-churches on the other. The church of Antioch therefore sent Paul, Barnabas, and a number of other responsible members to discuss the question with the leaders of the church of Jerusalem.[24]

2. Paul and Barnabas Go Up to Jerusalem (15:3-5)

> 3 *Being sent off by the church, then, they went through Phoenicia and Samaria, relating the conversion of the Gentiles, and brought great joy to all the brothers.*

22. According to Josephus (*Ant.* 20.38-46), Ananias, the Jewish instructor of Izates, king of Adiabene (*c.* A.D. 40), advised him to worship God according to the Jewish religion without being circumcised; but a stricter Jewish visitor, Eleazar, persuaded him to be circumcised, since otherwise God would be displeased with him. In debates with the school of Shammai, some Hillelites maintained that, for Gentiles to become proselytes of Judaism, the initiatory baptism was sufficient apart from circumcision (TB *Yᵉbāmôṭ* 46a, baraita); but this was more likely to have been a proposition for debate than a matter of practice.

23. Philo (*Migration of Abraham* 89-94) opposes those Jews who neglect the literal observance of ceremonial laws on the ground that it is sufficient to learn and practise the spiritual lessons which those laws teach; "nor, because circumcision signifies the cutting away of pleasure and all passions and the destruction of impious glory, . . . let us abolish the law of circumcision."

24. Luke does not say if they did in fact have an opportunity to discuss the question with the Jerusalem leaders. As for Paul's own account, the discussion which he and Barnabas had with three of those leaders (two apostles and one elder, in Luke's nomenclature) dealt with another question (Gal. 2:6-9).

287

4 *On their arrival in Jerusalem, they were welcomed by the church,
and by the apostles and elders, and reported all that God had done
with them.*[25]

5 *But some members of the party of the Pharisees, who were believers,
stood up and said,*[26] *"They*[27] *must be circumcised, and charged to
keep Moses' law."*

3 Paul, Barnabas, and their companions had to pass through Phoenicia and
Samaria on their way south to Jerusalem.[28] They took the opportunity to
visit the Christian groups in these regions and tell them of the success of the
Gentile mission. As the churches of Samaria and Phoenicia were themselves
the fruit of the Hellenistic mission which followed the death of Stephen
(8:5-25; 11:19), they would naturally rejoice at the news, without being
troubled by the misgivings which were felt by so many of the believers in
Jerusalem.

4 Even in Jerusalem the leaders and other members of the church
listened with great interest to Paul and Barnabas's account of "all that God
had done with them," but this interest by no means involved wholehearted
satisfaction.

5 Dissatisfaction was voiced in particular by those members of the
Jerusalem church who were associated with the Pharisaic party. Pharisees,
as believers in the doctrine of the resurrection, could become Christians
without relinquishing their distinctive beliefs: to what they already believed
they could add the belief that Jesus had been raised from the dead and was
thus divinely proclaimed to be Lord and Messiah. But if their Christianity
did not amount to more than this, they remained legalists at heart—unlike
their illustrious fellow-Pharisee Paul, whose whole outlook was totally re-
oriented by his Damascus-road experience: not only was Jesus revealed to
him as the risen Lord but he was called to preach a law-free gospel in his
name. The believing Pharisees in the Jerusalem church were naturally the
leaders in insisting that Gentile converts should be instructed to submit to

25. Cf. 14:27.
26. The Western text does not repeat the reference to believing Pharisees, already
introduced by it in v. 1, but recasts the beginning of v. 5 thus: "But those who charged
them to go up to the elders stood up and said."
27. Gk. αὐτούς, i.e., the Gentile converts. The antecedent to αὐτούς is not
expressed, except in the Byzantine addition at the end of v. 4: "and that he had opened a
door of faith to the Gentiles" (taken over from 14:27).
28. M. Hengel (*Between Jesus and Paul*, E.T. [London, 1983], p. 123) points
out that this text refutes a current misinterpretation of Luke 17:11, according to which
Luke was ignorant of the geography of Palestine, by showing that he knew that Samaria
lay immediately north of Judaea and that it was possible to move directly between Samaria
and Phoenicia.

circumcision and the general obligation to keep the Mosaic law which circumcision carried with it.[29]

The repetitions in the textual tradition of verses 1-5 suggest that these verses are Luke's composition, forming an editorial transition from the record of the Anatolian mission to that of the apostolic council.

3. The Council Meets (15:6)

6 *So the apostles and elders came together to see about this matter.*[30]

6 How many of the apostles were still resident in Jerusalem is uncertain; probably those who were accessible were brought together for this consultation. Peter probably came back from his ministry among Jews of the dispersion in order to be present.[31] While other members of the church were present at the meeting,[32] the deliberation and decision rested with the responsible leaders. They evidently had no doubt of their competence to rule on matters affecting the Gentile mission as well as matters which were their personal responsibility.

4. Peter's Speech (15:7-11)

7 *After long debate, Peter stood up[33] and addressed them.[34] "Brothers," he said, "you know that a long time ago[35] God chose us[36] in order that from my lips the Gentiles should hear the message of the gospel and come to faith.*

8 *God, who knows the heart, bore witness in their favor by giving[37] them the Holy Spirit just as he did to us:*

9 *he made no difference between us and them, but purified[37] their hearts by faith.*

---

29. Cf. Gal. 5:3.

30. A literal rendering of Gk. ἰδεῖν περὶ τοῦ λόγου τούτου. See J. L. North, "Is ΙΔΕΙΝ ΠΕΡΙ (Acts 15:6; cf. 18:15) a Latinism?" *NTS* 29 (1983), pp. 264-65; he suggests that it is a coinage on the analogy of Latin *uidere de* (he finds two other examples of the Greek phrase: Epictetus, *Dissertations* 1.17.10; 4.8.24).

31. Cf. O. Cullmann, *Peter: Disciple–Apostle–Martyr*, E.T., p. 50.

32. Cf. vv. 12 ("the whole congregation"), 22 ("the whole church").

33. After "stood up" the Western text adds "in Spirit," implying that he spoke by inspiration.

34. For "them" *P*[45] reads "the apostles."

35. Gk. ἀφ' ἡμερῶν ἀρχαίων, "in the early days" (i.e., of the church's history).

36. Gk. ἐν ὑμῖν ἐξελέξατο, a Semitic idiom for "chose you." Cf. Neh. 9:7 (LXX 2 Esdr. 19:7), ἐξελέξω ἐν Ἀβραάμ, "thou didst choose Abraham"; also 1 Sam. (LXX 1 Kms.) 16:9-10; 1 Kings (LXX 3 Kms.) 8:16, 44; 1 Chron. 28:4-5. See G. Zuntz, *Opuscula Selecta*, pp. 250-51. God chose the apostles that through one of them (Peter, as their representative) the Gentiles should hear the gospel.

37. Gk. δοὺς . . . καθαρίσας. Both these participles are examples of the

10 *Now then, why do you try God's patience (with the proposal) to place on those disciples' necks a yoke which neither we nor our forefathers have been able to bear?*

11 *No: it is by faith in the Lord Jesus that we are saved,[38] just as they are."[39]*

7-9 Peter, as leader of the apostles, spoke out unambiguously in the interests of gospel liberty. He had maintained these interests with purpose of heart ever since his visit to Cornelius in Caesarea: he had no thought of putting them at risk when he made his tactical withdrawal from table fellowship with Gentiles at Antioch. "The figure of a Judaizing St. Peter is a figment of the Tübingen critics with no basis in history."[40]

He now reminds the company that the fundamental principle which they were discussing had been settled when, several years before, he had been led by God to the house of Cornelius and Gentiles had heard the gospel from his lips. On that occasion God gave an evident token of his acceptance of Gentiles, for the Holy Spirit came on them as they listened to Peter, just as he had come on Peter and his fellow-apostles at the first Christian Pentecost. Cornelius and his household had not even made an oral confession of faith when the Holy Spirit took possession of them, but God, who reads the human heart, saw the faith within them. And if God accepted those Gentiles and cleansed them in heart and conscience by the impartation of his Spirit as soon as they believed the gospel,[41] why should further conditions now be imposed on them—conditions which God himself plainly did not require?

10-11 Besides, the yoke which some were now proposing to place on the necks of Gentile Christians was one which they themselves and their forefathers had found too heavy. The term "yoke" is particularly appropriate in this context: a proselyte, by undertaking to keep the law of Moses, was said to "take up the yoke of the kingdom of heaven."[42]

"simultaneous" or "coincident" aorist participle ("giving . . . cleansing"): God testified to the genuineness of these people's faith by giving them the Spirit and thus cleansing their hearts in one regenerative moment.

38. Gk. πιστεύομεν σωθῆναι, which might mean either (1) "we believe we shall be saved" (for the aorist infinitive in this future sense cf. 2:30; 3:18), (2) "we believe we have been saved," or (3) "we believe so as to be saved" (epexegetic infinitive), i.e., we are saved by faith (which seems most probable here).

39. Gk. καθ' ὃν τρόπον κἀκεῖνοι. Here the Gentile Christians are the standard of comparison, as the Jewish Christians are at the end of v. 8, καθὼς καὶ ἡμῖν (cf. 10:47, ὡς καὶ ἡμεῖς).

40. K. Lake, *The Earlier Epistles of St. Paul* (London, 1911), p. 116.

41. For the association of inward cleansing with the impartation of the Spirit cf. the variant reading at the end of Luke 11:2, "let thy Holy Spirit come on us and cleanse us" (162 700 Marcion Greg.-Nyss. Max. Conf.), which may have been Marcion's replacement for "thy kingdom come" (although B. H. Streeter, *The Four Gospels* [London, 1924], p. 277, considered it highly probable that this is what Luke wrote).

42. This expression came to denote the reciting of the *Shemaʻ*, the Jewish confes-

Not all Jews thought of the law as an intolerable burden. Some thought that God had honored Israel by giving them so many commandments.[43] The author of Ps. 119 found them his delight; Philo declared that they were "not too numerous or too heavy for the strength of those who are able to make use of them."[44] But Peter spoke as a representative of the rank and file of Galilaean Jews. He knew enough to refuse nonkosher food and not to fraternize with Gentiles (10:14, 28), but he and people like him could not be expected to know or practise all the details of legal tradition. By contrast with those "heavy burdens, hard to bear" (Matt. 23:4), he and his associates had learned to rejoice in their Master's easy yoke (Matt. 11:29-30). They recognized that their own salvation was due to the grace of Christ; were they to acknowledge a different and more burdensome principle of salvation for Gentile believers?

Peter now disappears from the narrative of Acts;[45] so far as Luke is concerned, says Martin Hengel, "the legitimation of the mission to the Gentiles is virtually Peter's last work."[46]

5. Paul and Barnabas Address the Council (15:12)

12 Then[47] the whole congregation fell silent, and listened to Barnabas and Paul as they related all the signs and wonders that God had done through them among the Gentiles.

12 During the silence which followed Peter's appeal, Barnabas and Paul (who are named naturally in this order in a Jerusalem setting) added further evidence which could only support Peter's argument. The mind of God in this matter, decisively shown in the house of Cornelius, had been further displayed in the blessing he had bestowed on Gentile believers in Antioch and in their recent mission in Cyprus and Asia Minor. But Barnabas and Paul spoke as witnesses, not as consultants or as participants in the debate; and in Jerusalem their words could carry nothing like the weight that Peter's did.

---

sion of faith, "Hear, O Israel . . ." (Deut. 6:4-5). It appears in this sense in Mishnah, Berākôt 2.2, along with the expression "to take upon oneself the yoke of the commandments" (by reciting them).

43. On the place of the law in first-century Jewish life see Schürer II, pp. 464-87; E. P. Sanders, *Paul and Palestinian Judaism* (London, 1977), pp. 33-428; W. D. Davies, *Jewish and Pauline Studies* (London, 1984), pp. 3-26, with bibliography on p. 303.

44. *On Rewards and Punishments* 80.

45. He had probably interrupted the missionary activity on which he had already embarked in the dispersion in order to be present at the council. See O. Cullmann, *Peter: Disciple–Apostle–Martyr*, p. 50.

46. M. Hengel, *Acts and the History of Earliest Christianity*, E.T. (London, 1979), p. 125.

47. The Western text inserts "when the elders had consented to the words spoken by Peter."

Even Peter's words were not decisive, however; one voice remained to be heard.

6. James's Summing Up (15:13-21)

13 When they had finished speaking, James replied (to the debate): "Brothers, listen to me.

14 Symeon[48] has related how God first visited the Gentiles to take from them a people for his name.

15 This is in keeping with the words of the prophets, as it is written:

16 'After this I will return
and build up David's fallen tent:
I will build up its ruins and set them upright,

17 that the remainder of humanity may seek the Lord,
even all the Gentiles over whom my name has been invoked,

18 says the Lord who makes these things known from of old.'[49]

19 Therefore my ruling is that we stop troubling those of the Gentiles who turn to God,

20 but send them a letter bidding them abstain from idolatrous pollutions, from fornication, from strangled animals, and from blood.[50]

21 After all, since generations long ago Moses has had his preachers in every city;[51] he is read in the synagogues every sabbath day."

13 The eyes of all now turned to James, the brother of the Lord, a man who enjoyed widespread respect and confidence.[52] If the elders of the Jerusalem church were organized as a kind of Nazarene Sanhedrin, James was their president, *primus inter pares*. The church's readiness to recognize his leadership was due more to his personal character and record than to his blood relationship to the Lord. (There were other brothers, but they were shadowy figures compared with James.) When he said "Listen to me,"[53] they listened.

48. Gk. Συμεών (cf. 2 Pet. 1:1, Συμεὼν Πέτρος), the LXX form of Simeon, approaches the Hebrew or Aramaic pronunciation of the name more closely than the common NT Σίμων.

49. The Western text recasts these words: "says the Lord, who does these things. Known from of old to the Lord is his work" (Byzantine text: ". . . are all his works").

50. Gk. τοῦ ἀπέχεσθαι τῶν ἀλισγημάτων τῶν εἰδώλων καὶ τῆς πορνείας καὶ πνικτοῦ καὶ τοῦ αἵματος. The Western text omits καὶ πνικτοῦ, and after αἵματος adds καὶ ὅσα μὴ θέλουσιν ἑαυτοῖς γίνεσθαι ἑτέροις μὴ ποιεῖν. P[45] omits καὶ τῆς πορνείας (its evidence is not available for the repetitions of the decree in v. 29 and 21:25). See p. 297, n. 70.

51. P[45] omits "in every city."

52. See p. 239 (on 12:17).

53. Cf. Jas. 2:5, "Listen, my dear brothers." J. B. Mayor (*The Epistle of St. James* [London, 1897], pp. iii-iv) has enumerated what he calls "remarkable agreements" between this speech and the letter of James.

14 James began by summarizing Peter's speech (referring to him as Symeon, the Hebrew or Aramaic form of his personal name). No mention is made of the report which Barnabas and Paul had just given. This indeed may have been politic: James wanted to carry a difficult audience with him, and it was the activity of Barnabas and Paul that had created the situation which roused such apprehension in the minds of the Jerusalem rank and file.

The English translation of the words, "God first visited the Gentiles to take from them a people for his name," scarcely bring out the paradoxical force of the Greek. In the Old Testament the "nations" or "Gentiles" (Gk. *ethnē*) stand in contrast to the "people" (Gk. *laos*), that is to say, Israel. When Moses says to the Israelites in Deut. 14:2, "Yahweh has chosen you to be a *people* for his own possession, out of all the *nations* that are on the face of the earth," the Greek version uses *laos* for "people" over against *ethnē* for "nations"; the two terms are opposed the one to the other.[54] But when James uses the same two terms here, he does not speak of God's taking a people *in contrast to* the Gentiles, but of his taking a people *consisting of* Gentiles— an "outstanding paradox," as Bengel says.[55] The *Scofield Reference Bible*, in its note on this text, had a point in calling it "dispensationally, . . . the most important passage in the NT." What James states concisely here is implied throughout the New Testament: one example is 1 Pet. 2:9, where God's description of the returning exiles of Judah, "the people whom I formed for myself, that they might declare my praise" (Isa. 43:21), is applied to Gentile converts to Christianity. Cf. also Tit. 2:14.

15-18 God's initiative in thus "visiting the Gentiles" was shown when he sent his Spirit on Cornelius and his household as they listened to Peter's preaching. But he had foretold his action through the prophets. To demonstrate this James quotes Amos 9:11-12.

This oracle of Amos is quoted in the main from the LXX version. The chief deviations from LXX are the replacement of "In that day" by "After this I will return" (Jer. 12:15) at the beginning of the quotation, and the replacement of "who does this" by "who makes these things known from of old" (cf. Isa. 45:21) at the end. More striking are the deviations of LXX from MT, especially in the rewording of the clause "that they may possess the remnant of Edom." The primary sense of MT is that God will restore the fallen fortunes of the royal house of David, so that it will rule over all the territory which had once been included in David's empire, not only what is left of the Edomites but also "all the nations who are called by my name."

---

54. The usual Hebrew equivalent of ἔθνη is *gôyim* and of λαός *ʿam;* in Deut. 14:2, however, it is MT *ʿammîm,* not *gôyim,* that is rendered ἔθνη in LXX.

55. *Egregium paradoxon* (J. A. Bengel, *Gnomon Novi Testamenti* [London, ³1862], p. 449). See N. A. Dahl, "A People for his Name (Acts xv. 14)," *NTS* 4 (1957-58), pp. 319-27; J. Dupont, "Un Peuple d'entre les Nations," *NTS* 31 (1985), pp. 321-35.

The LXX rewording involves two variant readings,[56] but the result is a complete spiritualization of the passage: "that they may possess the remnant of Edom" becomes "that the remainder of humanity may seek" (the object of "seek" is not expressed in LXX, but the implied object is clearly "me"—that is, "the Lord," as James's quotation makes plain). The LXX spiritualization is in line with Israel's mission to bring the knowledge of the true God to the Gentiles. It thus paved the way for James's application of the prophecy to the church's Gentile mission.

It has already been emphasized in Acts that, by the resurrection and exaltation of Jesus, the Son of David, God has fulfilled his dynastic promises to David (cf. Peter's argument in 2:25-36 and Paul's in 13:23, 32-37). This may be what is understood here as the raising up of David's fallen tent. But the promised extension of the sovereignty of the house of David over the Gentiles is taking place here and now, says James, through the Gentile mission: over a far wider area than David ever ruled, men and women of Gentile stock are making haste to yield willing and glad allegiance to great David's greater Son. "The remainder of humanity" comprises the Gentiles—"all the Gentiles over whom my name has been invoked" (i.e., in baptism). Similar phraseology appears in Jas. 2:7, where the readers are reminded of "that honorable name by which you are called."

The Gentile mission, then, is the work of God: he has made it known in advance "from of old" and now he has brought it to pass.

It may be asked if James is likely to have quoted the LXX version in such a setting. Perhaps not (the choice of LXX is more probably Luke's); but it has been pointed out that "even our Massoretic Hebrew would have served the present purpose admirably, since it predicted that 'the tabernacle of David', i.e. the church of the Messiah, would gain possession of all the nations which are called by the name [of the God of Israel]."[57]

James's speech has been recognized as taking the form known to the rabbis as.a $y^e lamm^e \underline{d}\bar{e}n\hat{u}$ response, in which an appeal is made to scripture as confirming what has been said or done already and what is about to be decided.[58]

---

56. LXX (ἐκζητήσωσιν) presupposes Heb. $yi\underline{d}r^e\check{s}\hat{u}$ ("may seek") instead of MT $y\hat{i}r^e\check{s}\hat{u}$ ("may possess") and the vocalization $\prime\bar{a}\underline{d}\bar{a}m$ ("humanity," "mankind") instead of MT $\prime\check{e}\underline{d}\bar{o}m$ ("Edom"); moreover, it ignores the particle $\prime e\underline{t}$ before $\check{s}^e\prime\bar{e}r\hat{i}\underline{t}$, which marks it out as the object of the verb; its Greek rendering οἱ κατάλοιποι τῶν ἀνθρώπων treats it as the subject.

57. C. C. Torrey, *Composition and Date of Acts* (Cambridge, MA, 1916), pp. 38-39. So also C. Rabin: "MT would actually have supported the exegesis here offered" (*The Zadokite Documents* [Oxford, ²1958], p. 29).

58. A response made to the request $y^e lamm^e \underline{d}\bar{e}n\hat{u} \, rabb\bar{e}n\hat{u}$, "let our teacher instruct us." See J. W. Bowker, "Speeches in Acts: A Study in Proem and Yelammedenu Form," *NTS* 14 (1967-68), pp. 96-111 (especially pp. 107-9).

19 The quotation from Amos did not answer the question about circumcision: it might have been argued that the Gentiles over whom the name of the Lord was invoked should respond to that invocation by being circumcised. But James does not accept that argument. In fact, he does not mention circumcision, but when he rules that Jewish believers should "stop troubling"[59] Gentile converts he repeats in different terms Peter's protest against placing an intolerable yoke on those converts' necks. The demand for their circumcision carried with it the obligation to assume such a yoke: James's "stop troubling" means in effect "stop demanding circumcision."[60]

20 There remained, however, a practical problem. In most cities Gentile believers had to live alongside Jewish believers, who had been brought up to observe the levitical food restrictions and to avoid contact with Gentiles as far as possible. If there was to be free association between these two groups, certain guidelines must be laid down, especially with regard to table fellowship. Members of the church of Jerusalem might have little experience of this social problem at home, but it disturbed them to hear of Jewish Christians elsewhere who associated with Gentile Christians in a totally relaxed manner, as though the time-honored food restrictions were no longer valid. Peter's initial breach with convention in entering the house of Cornelius had been overlooked, since he acted under divine compulsion; but his sitting at table with Gentile Christians in Antioch caused grave scandal in Jerusalem. Readers of the New Testament today are familiar with Paul's totally emancipated attitude in such matters, and may be tempted to suppose that it was generally shared; in fact, Paul was probably quite exceptional in this regard (as in several others) among Jewish believers.

James therefore gave it as his considered judgment that Gentile Christians should be directed to avoid food which had idolatrous associations and the flesh of animals from which the blood had not been completely drained, and that they should conform to the Jewish code of relations between the sexes instead of remaining content with the pagan standards to which they had been accustomed.

It is natural that, when the stumbling block of circumcision had been removed, an effort should have been made to provide a practical *modus vivendi* for two groups of people drawn from such different ways of life. The *modus vivendi* was probably similar to the terms on which Jews of the dispersion found it possible to have a measure of fellowship with God-

---

59. Gk. μὴ παρενοχλεῖν. See G. Zuntz, *Opuscula Selecta*, p. 240 with n. 3.

60. This decision, despite the conditions that were attached to it, must have compromised the church in the eyes of its Jewish neighbors: it called for no little courage and "bears witness to an astounding magnanimity that can hardly be explained on other grounds than the sense of obligation . . . to follow the intent of Jesus' message" (M. Hengel, *Victory over Violence*, E.T. [London, 1975], p. 87).

fearing Gentiles. The prohibition against eating flesh with the blood still in it (including the flesh of strangled animals) was based on the "Noachian decree" of Gen. 9:4.[61] At a later time, when the issue dealt with by the apostolic council was no longer a live one, the provisions moved by James and adopted by the other leaders were modified so as to become purely ethical injunctions; thus the Western text makes James propose that Gentile converts "abstain from idolatry, from fornication and from bloodshed,[62] and from doing to others what they would not like done to themselves."[63]

21 This policy, James urged, would not work to the detriment of Israel's mission in the Gentile world; there was still ample opportunity for Gentiles to learn the law of Moses, for it was read publicly every sabbath in synagogues throughout the civilized world. But with regard to Gentile converts to Christianity, "Moses, so to speak, would suffer no loss, in failing to obtain the allegiance of those who had never been his."[64] This observation was perhaps intended to calm the apprehensions of the believing Pharisees, in whose eyes it was specially important that the whole Torah should be taught among the Gentiles; this, said James, was being attended to already by the synagogues.

7. The Apostolic Letter to Gentile Christians (15:22-29)

22 *Then the apostles and elders, with the whole church, resolved to select men from their ranks and send them to Antioch in the company of Paul and Barnabas—Judas (who was called Barsabbas) and Silas, leading men among the brothers.*

23 *By them they wrote a letter as follows:*
"The apostles and elders, your brothers,[65] to the brothers of Gentile birth at Antioch and in Syria and Cilicia: greetings.

24 *We have heard that some of our people have confused you with their*

---

61. Cf. Lev. 17:10; Deut. 12:16, 23-25.

62. Idolatry, fornication, and murder were the three cardinal sins in Jewish eyes; avoidance of these was held to be binding on the whole human race. During the severe repression that followed the crushing of the Bar-kokhba revolt (A.D. 135), the rabbis of Lydda laid it down that a Jew, if his life were at stake, might break any of the commandments except those which prohibited these three things. But the situation dealt with by the Council of Jerusalem was quite different.

63. The negative form of the Golden Rule appears elsewhere in Jewish and Christian literature; cf. Tobit 4:15; *Didachē* 1.2; TB *Shabbāṭ* 31a; *'Aḇôṭ de-R. Nathan* 2.26. The idea that the positive form of the Golden Rule (cf. Matt. 7:12) is peculiar to Christianity and unknown in Judaism is wrong; it appears, e.g., in Maimonides (*The Code of Maimonides*, E.T. 14 [New Haven, 1949], p. 200).

64. R. B. Rackham, *The Acts of the Apostles* (London, ⁶1912), p. 254. Another interpretation makes James mean that, since Jewish communities are to be found in every city, their scruples must be respected.

65. Gk. οἱ ἀπόστολοι καὶ οἱ πρεσβύτεροι ἀδελφοί.

arguments, upsetting[66] your minds,[67] although we gave them no such directions;

25 *we have resolved therefore, having reached one mind in the matter, to select men and send them to you in the company of our dear friends Barnabas and Paul,*

26 *who have endangered their lives for the name of our Lord Jesus Christ.[68]*

27 *The men whom we are sending are Judas and Silas, and they will give you the same message by word of mouth.*

28 *The Holy Spirit and we ourselves have resolved to impose no further burden on you than this: it is necessary[69]*

29 *to abstain from food that has been sacrificed to idols, from blood, from strangled meat, and from fornication.[70] If you guard yourselves from these things, you will do well.[71] Farewell."*

22 James's proposal commended itself to his colleagues, and appears to have won at least the acquiescence of the Jerusalem church as a whole. The leaders of the church then selected two of their number to go to Antioch and carry the findings of the council to the church of that city. Of these two messengers, Judas—who had the same surname as the Joseph mentioned in 1:23—does not appear outside this context. The other, Silas, continues to figure in the narrative of Acts as a companion of Paul in the evangelization of Philippi, Thessalonica, and Corinth. He is plainly identical with the Silvanus of Paul's letters (2 Cor. 1:19; 1 Thess. 1:1; 2 Thess. 1:1); his relation to the Silvanus of 1 Pet. 5:12 is uncertain. It is preposterous exegesis to

---

66. Gk. ἀνασκευάζοντες, a military metaphor, of plundering a city.

67. Many Western witnesses add "saying that you should be circumcised and keep the law."

68. The Western text adds "in every trial."

69. Translating πλὴν τούτων ἐπάναγκες (ℵ* Δ 33 *pc*). Most witnesses read "these necessary things" (τούτων τῶν ἐπάναγκες ℵ2 B C Ψ 81 614 945 1175 1739 *al* or τῶν ἐπάναγκες τούτων byz).

70. The Western text omits "from strangled meat" and adds the negative Golden Rule, as in v. 20. Tertullian omits "from strangled meat" but does not add the negative Golden Rule; some MSS of the Latin Vulgate omit "and from fornication." It is suggested by some that the highest common factor of the readings in vv. 20 and 29 represents the original text: that the decree was exclusively a food law, prohibiting the eating of meat which had been sacrificed to pagan divinities and meat from which the blood had not been completely drained; and that this twofold prohibition was later expanded in the various ways to which our several textual authorities bear witness. See P. H. Menoud, "The Western Text and the Theology of Acts," *SNTS Bulletin* 2 (1951), pp. 19-32, especially pp. 22-28; C. S. C. Williams, *Alterations to the Text of the Synoptic Gospels and Acts* (Oxford, 1951), pp. 72-75; for the view that it was a threefold prohibition, omitting the reference to fornication, see G. Zuntz, *Opuscula Selecta*, pp. 224-29.

71. The Western text characteristically adds "being carried along by the Holy Spirit" (cf. 2 Pet. 1:21).

identify Judas and Silas with the troublesome emissaries from James mentioned by Paul in Gal. 2:12.[72]

23 Judas and Silas were not only to communicate the council's findings to the church of Antioch by word of mouth, but also to carry a letter from the apostles and elders at Jerusalem. The senders call themselves "the apostles and elders, your brothers" (so NIV; similarly RSV). The rendering "the apostles and elder brothers" might commend itself as more natural, but since "elder brothers" (in a religious sense) is a locution unparalleled in the New Testament, it may be better to take "brothers" here as being in apposition to "apostles and elders."[73] The letter is addressed to the Gentile Christians of Antioch and of the united province of Syria-Cilicia, of which Antioch was the capital. The recently founded churches in South Galatia may have been envisaged as coming within the scope of the letter, but they are not mentioned.

24-27 Since trouble had been caused by the unauthorized activity of previous Jerusalem visitors to Antioch (v. 1), it was necessary to emphasize that the present delegates, whose business it was to undo the damage caused by those earlier visitors, were fully accredited by the Jerusalem church. A conciliatory note was added by the pointedly friendly references to Barnabas and Paul and to the hazards they had undergone in their work of evangelization.

28 The words "it has been resolved by the Holy Spirit and ourselves," with which the terms of the council's decision are introduced, stress the church's role as the vehicle of the Spirit. "There is no parallel," says Wilfred Knox, "for such a phrase to pronounce a corporate decision by a deliberative body."[74] So conscious were the church leaders of being possessed and controlled by the Spirit that he was given prior mention as chief author of their decision.

Significance has been attached to the fact that none of the Greek verbs of commanding is used when the council's directives are conveyed.[75]

---

72. So H. Lietzmann, *The Beginnings of the Christian Church*, p. 108. D. W. B. Robinson, "The Circumcision of Titus, and Paul's Liberty," *Australian Biblical Review* 12 (1964), pp. 40-41, reading τινα rather than τινας in Gal. 2:12 (see n. 10 above), treats the form as neuter plural and takes "certain things" to be the contents of the decree; for the view that the dispute of Gal. 2:11-14 was precipitated by the arrival of the decree at Antioch see also D. R. Catchpole, "Paul, James and the Apostolic Decree" (p. 282 above, n. 1); J. D. G. Dunn, "The Incident at Antioch," *JSNT*, issue 18 (1983), pp. 3-57.

73. W. L. Knox (*The Acts of the Apostles*, p. 50) regards the unusual expression οἱ πρεσβύτεροι ἀδελφοί as one of a number of peculiarities in this letter "which suggest that we are dealing with an original document copied by Luke more or less verbatim." Cf. E. A. Judge, who says with regard to this letter and that of Lysias (23:26-30), "We must ask . . . whether the author of Acts did not mean his readers to take them as the direct citation of transcripts available to him" (*New Docs.* 1 [1976], § 26, p. 78).

74. *The Acts of the Apostles*, p. 50, n. 1.

75. Cf. F. J. A. Hort, *The Christian Ecclesia* (London, 1897), p. 82.

But the form of words that is used, "it has been resolved," is authoritative enough: it was a form widely used in the wording of imperial and other government decrees. Moreover, the four abstentions prescribed are said to be "necessary," not optional. Apart from them, however, no further burden was to be imposed on the Gentiles: that would include circumcision and other legal obligations, part of the "yoke" which Peter said they should not be required to bear.

29 The four abstentions are those indicated by James in his summing up. His more general "idolatrous pollutions" is replaced by the more specific "food that has been sacrificed to idols." Food of various kinds might be offered to idols, but the flesh of animal sacrifices is in view here: "an animal would constitute the only offering of sufficient size that a saleable portion would be left over following the sacrifice."[76] Such flesh (which would be of prime quality) was freely exposed for sale on the butchers' stalls of pagan cities, since the temples received more than they could use; the question of eating it (whether its origin was known or unknown) was a matter of conscience for some Gentile Christians, as Paul's Corinthian correspondence shows.[77] The Jerusalem decree forbids it outright. It also forbids eating the meat of strangled animals, or the eating of blood in any form.

The prohibition of fornication, understood generally, is an ethical prohibition in all forms of the text (Western or otherwise), but the word may be used here in a more specialized sense, of marriage within degrees of blood relationship or affinity forbidden by the legislation of Lev. 18:6-18. It is used in this sense in 1 Cor. 5:1 and also possibly in the "excepting clauses" of Matt. 5:32 and 19:9.[78] Ordinary fornication, like ordinary idol-worship, was ruled out by the most elementary principles of Christian instruction.

The decree is regarded as binding in the letters to the seven churches of proconsular Asia (Rev. 2:14, 20). Toward the end of the second century it was observed by the churches of the Rhone valley (which had close links with those of Asia) and of the province of Africa.[79] Toward the end of the ninth century the terms of the decree, together with the negative Golden

76. *New Docs.* 2 (1977), § 7, p. 37. The term εἰδωλόθυτον was used by Jews and Christians, to whom the pagan divinity was a mere idol; a pagan would call it ἱερόθυτον (cf. 1 Cor. 10:28).

77. See p. 285. C. K. Barrett, "Things Sacrificed to Idols," *NTS* 11 (1964-65), pp. 138-53, suggests that the issue became a live one in the church of Corinth because of an attempt to impose the Jerusalem decree there.

78. See F. Hauck/S. Schulz, *TDNT* 6, p. 593 (*s.v.* πορνεία); W. K. L. Clarke, *New Testament Problems* (London, 1919), pp. 59-65; J. Bonsirven, *Le divorce dans le Nouveau Testament* (Paris, 1948), pp. 46-60; W. A. Heth and G. J. Wenham, *Jesus and Divorce* (London, 1984), pp. 153-68. Heb. *z^enût* is used in a similar specialized sense (CD 4.17). But G. Zuntz dismisses this restricted interpretation of πορνεία in the decree as "wishful thinking" (*Opuscula Selecta*, p. 228).

79. Eusebius, *HE* 5.1.26, reports one of the martyrs of Vienne and Lyon as protesting, "How could Christians eat children, when they are not allowed even to drink

Rule, were included by the English king Alfred in the preamble to his law-code.

8. The Church of Antioch Receives the Apostolic Letter (15:30-35)

30 *They were sent off, then, and came down to Antioch. There they gathered the congregation together and handed over the letter.*
31 *When the Antiochenes read it, they rejoiced at the encouragement.*
32 *Judas and Silas, who were also prophets themselves,[80] gave the brothers much encouragement by word of mouth, and strengthened them.*
33 *When they had spent some time there, the brothers sent them back with a salutation of peace[81] to those who had commissioned them.[82]*
35 *But Paul and Barnabas stayed on in Antioch, teaching and preaching the word of God together with many others.*

30-35 The news from Jerusalem brought great relief to the Gentile Christians of Antioch. Probably the restrictions laid down in the letter did not seem too burdensome; in any case, they were a small price to pay for the prevention of any recurrence of the embarrassing situation occasioned by previous visitors from James. On the terms prescribed, table fellowship between Jewish and Gentile believers could now be resumed. (What Paul thought about it may be inferred from his letters rather than from Luke's record.) Over and above the encouragement contained in the apostolic letter, the church received further encouragement from the prophetic ministry of Judas and Silas,[83] who spent some time in Antioch before returning to Jerusalem. When they set off on their homeward journey, it was with the Antiochenes' farewell "Peace be with you!" sounding in their ears. After their departure, Paul and Barnabas stayed on in Antioch a little longer, serving the Lord in the church together with their colleagues in the ministry. (Verse 35 repeats more fully the statement of 14:28.)

---

the blood of brute beasts?" So also Tertullian: "We abstain from eating strangled animals and those that have died of themselves" (*Apology* 9.13).

80. The Western text adds "full of the Holy Spirit."

81. Lit., "with peace" (μετ' εἰρήνης), i.e., with the greeting "Go in peace" or "Peace be with you."

82. The Western addition, "But Silas resolved to remain there; only Judas went," was designed to pave the way for v. 40 (which does not necessarily imply that Silas was still in Antioch; in any case, there is a change of source between this paragraph and the next). The former of the two clauses was taken over by the Byzantine text, and appears as v. 34 in the *textus receptus* (cf. KJV).

83. The statement that they "were also prophets themselves" may imply that they added their prophetic gifts to those of the local "prophets and teachers" (13:1).

V. PAUL LEAVES ANTIOCH AND MOVES TO THE AEGEAN WORLD (15:36–19:20)

A. RECENTLY PLANTED CHURCHES REVISITED (15:36–16:5)

1. Paul Parts Company with Barnabas and Takes Silas as His Colleague (15:36-41)

36 After some time[84] Paul said to Barnabas, "Let us go back and visit the brothers in all the cities where we preached the word of the Lord, and see how they are getting on."

37 Barnabas wished to take John, surnamed Mark, along with them.

38 But Paul refused to take him along,[85] because he had parted from them in Pamphylia and not gone on with them to the work.

39 The disagreement between them became so sharp that they separated. Barnabas took Mark and set sail for Cyprus,

40 but Paul chose Silas and set out, having been commended by the brothers to the grace of the Lord.

41 He made his way through Syria and Cilicia, strengthening the churches.[86]

36-39 The story of the disagreement between Paul and Barnabas does not make pleasant reading, but Luke's realism in recording it helps us to remember that the two men, as they themselves said to the people of Lystra, were "human beings with feelings like" any other. Luke does not relate the dispute in such a way as to put Paul in the right and Barnabas in the wrong. In view of Luke's restraint, it is idle for the reader to try to apportion the blame.

When Paul proposed to Barnabas that they should revisit the churches planted during their recent tour of Cyprus and central Anatolia, Barnabas agreed, and suggested that they should take Mark along with them as they had done on the former occasion. But Paul, believing that Mark's departure from Perga during their former journey was unjustified,[87] and probably reckoning that it revealed some defect of character which made him unsuitable for such work, refused point-blank to take him again. We can

---

84. A quite indefinite time note (Gk. μετὰ . . . τινας ἡμέρας), here probably marking the transition from one source to another.

85. In v. 37 "to take along with them" renders the Greek aorist infinitive (συμπαραλαβεῖν), in v. 38 "to take along" renders the present infinitive (συμπαραλαμβάνειν). On this "delicate nuance" J. H. Moulton remarks, "Barnabas, with easy forgetfulness of risk, wishes συνπαραλαβεῖν Mark—Paul refuses συνπαραλαμβάνειν, to have with them day by day one who had shown himself unreliable" (MHT I, p. 130). For the verb cf. 12:25.

86. The Western text adds "handing over the commands of the elders" (cf. 16:4).

87. Cf. 13:13b (pp. 250-51).

believe that it would indeed have been unwise for Mark at this stage to join another missionary expedition of which Paul was one of the leaders. On the other hand, Barnabas probably discerned promising qualities in his young cousin which could be developed under his care rather than under Paul's. It did Mark good to spend more time in the company of such a "son of encouragement"; in the event his latent qualities reached full maturity and were appreciated in due course by Paul himself (Col. 4:10; Philem. 23; 2 Tim. 4:11).

It is a pity that the dispute was allowed to generate such bitterness; it might not have done so but for the memory of the incident at Antioch when "even Barnabas," as Paul says, followed Peter's example in withdrawing from the society of Gentile Christians.[88] After that, it is doubtful if Paul and Barnabas could ever be so happy in their association as they had once been. The old mutual confidence had been damaged and could not be restored: "never glad confident morning again." It is not Luke's policy to record such disagreements on points of principle, but the disagreement on a personal matter which he does record here can be read with greater understanding in the light of Paul's account in his letter to the Galatians. Even so, the present disagreement was overruled for good: instead of one missionary and pastoral expedition there were two. Barnabas took Mark and went back to Cyprus to continue the evangelization of his native island; Paul visited the young churches of Anatolia.

40-41 Paul now had to find a new travel companion. He had had opportunity, during the recent visit to Antioch of Judas and Silas, to make an assessment of Silas, and in many ways found him to be a kindred spirit.[89] Luke certainly intends his readers to identify the Silas whom Paul chose as his companion with the Silas who, with Judas Barsabbas, had carried the apostolic letter from Jerusalem to Antioch, and there is no good reason to question the identification. Not only did he commend himself to Paul as a congenial colleague; it would be advantageous to have a leading member of the Jerusalem church as his companion. It appears, moreover, from the story of their adventures in Philippi that Silas, like Paul himself, was a Roman citizen (16:37-38); Paul would thus be spared the embarrassment of claiming for himself civic privileges or exemptions which his colleague could not share. Commended afresh to the divine grace by the Antiochene church, as on the earlier occasion when he set out with Barnabas (13:3),[90] Paul went with Silas through the cities of Syria and Cilicia, encouraging the believers and strengthening the churches.

88. Gal. 2:13.

89. F. C. Burkitt, hazarding a guess, says, "I should say that Silas had heard St. Stephen gladly" (*Christian Beginnings* [London, 1924], p. 133).

90. But Antioch no longer served Paul as a missionary base; his center of operations was for the next few years moved west to the Aegean world.

ACTS 16

2. Paul and Silas in South Galatia; Timothy Joins Them (16:1-4)

1 Then he arrived[1] at Derbe and Lystra. Now at the latter place there was a disciple named[2] Timothy, the son of a Jewish woman who was a believer, although his father was a Greek.
2 Timothy received a good report from the brothers at Lystra and Iconium.
3 Paul wished him to set out as his companion, so he took him and circumcised him because of the Jews in those places. (Everyone knew that his father was a Greek.)
4 As they went through the cities, then, they handed over the decrees which had been decided upon by the apostles and elders at Jerusalem.[3]

1-2 Having passed through Cilicia, Paul and Silas crossed the Taurus range by the pass called the Cilician Gates,[4] and after traversing part of the territory of Antiochus IV, king of Commagene,[5] they entered the southeastern region of the province of Galatia. There they visited the cities which had been evangelized by Paul and Barnabas two or three years previously—Derbe, Lystra, Iconium, and (probably) Pisidian Antioch.

At Lystra[6] (the common term in "Derbe and Lystra" of v. 1 and "Lystra and Iconium" of v. 2) Paul decided to take along as his personal

---

1. The Western text (D lat⁸ syrʰᶜˡ·ᵐᵍ) reads "And passing through these nations he arrived . . ."

2. *P*⁴⁵ omits "named."

3. The Western text reads "and going through the cities they proclaimed the Lord Jesus Christ with all boldness, at the same time also handing over the commandments of the apostles and elders at Jerusalem."

4. See W. M. Ramsay, "St. Paul's Road from Cilicia to Iconium," *Pauline and Other Studies* (London, 1906), pp. 273-98; also J. Murphy-O'Connor, "On the Road and on the Sea with St. Paul," *Bible Review* 1.2 (1985), pp. 38-47 (where it is pointed out that on journeys from east to west Paul preferred to go by land, because of delays caused by contrary winds at sea).

5. See p. 272.

6. The Latin translation of Origen's commentary on Romans (at 16:21) calls Timothy "a citizen of Derbe" (cf. Valckenaer and Blass's emendation at 20:4, mentioned on p. 380, n. 4).

companion a young man named Timothy who with his mother had come to faith in Christ during the previous missionary visit and who had since then made promising progress in the Christian life. That the brothers in Lystra and Iconium should have known him better than those in Lystra and Derbe is quite natural: Lystra was much nearer to Iconium than to Derbe, although Lystra and Derbe were Lycaonian cities and Iconium was in Phrygia.

The statement that Timothy's mother (Eunice by name, according to 2 Tim. 1:5) had married a Gentile suggests that there was less rigid social segregation among the Jews of central Asia Minor than among those of Palestine. In Phrygia, says Ramsay, "there can be little doubt that the Jews married into the dominant families";[7] and the same may well have been true in Lycaonia.

3   It was Timothy's mixed parentage that made Paul decide to circumcise him before taking him along as his junior colleague. By Jewish law Timothy was a Jew, because he was the son of a Jewish mother, but because he was uncircumcised he was technically an apostate Jew. If Paul wished to maintain his links with the synagogue, he could not be seen to countenance apostasy.[8] He set his face implacably against any move to circumcise Gentile believers like Titus (Gal. 2:3-5), but Timothy was in a different situation. For Paul, circumcision in itself was a matter of indifference (Gal. 5:6; 6:15); only when it was regarded as a condition of acceptance with God did it involve a lapse from grace and the obligation to keep the whole law of Moses (Gal. 5:3-4). Timothy's circumcision was a minor surgical operation carried out for a practical purpose—his greater usefulness in the ministry of the gospel. No doubt Paul was charged with inconsistency for his action (as he has been charged in more recent times); but the consistency which some would like to impose on Paul is that "foolish consistency" which R. W. Emerson describes as "the hobgoblin of little minds, adored by little statesmen and philosophers and divines."[9] Those who deplore the absence of this consistency from Paul miss the higher consistency which aimed at bringing all the activities of his life and thought "into captivity to the obedience of Christ" (2 Cor. 10:5) and at subordinating every other interest to the paramount interests of the gospel (1 Cor. 9:23).

There are indications in the Pastoral Epistles that the leaders of

---

7. *BRD*, p. 357.

8. Cf. M. Hengel, *Acts and the History of Earliest Christianity*, E.T. (London, 1979), p. 64; also A. E. Harvey, *The New English Bible: Companion to the New Testament* (Oxford/Cambridge, 1970), p. 459. Since everyone, not least "the Jews in those places," knew that his father was a Greek, it would be taken for granted that he was uncircumcised. The imperfect tense of the last verb of v. 3 (ὑπῆρχεν) may imply that his father was no longer alive; this is made explicit by a handful of witnesses in v. 1 (104 *pc* late *p* vg.codd) which say that his mother was a widow.

9. "Essay on Self-Reliance," *Essays, Lectures and Orations* (London, 1848), p. 30; cf. F. J. Foakes-Jackson, *Life of St. Paul* (London, 1927), p. 15.

Timothy's home church associated themselves with Paul in commissioning him for the gospel ministry.[10]

4 Since 15:40 the successive verbs have been in the singular number, with Paul as subject. Now the plural is used: "they handed over the decrees." This was Silas's duty, not Paul's.[11] The decrees indeed had been addressed expressly to the Gentile believers of Antioch and of Syria and Cilicia, not of South Galatia; since, however, the cities now being visited had been evangelized from Antioch, it might have been argued that they were included by implication. But, if the churches in these cities were those to which Paul's letter to the Galatians had only recently been sent, how would they have reacted to the delivery of directives from Jerusalem by Paul's fellow-traveler? Paul himself, as we have seen, never invokes the Jerusalem "decrees" when he deals with the practices which they forbid.[12] There are reasons for doubting if this verse is part of the original text of Acts.[13]

4. The Churches Grow in Faith and Numbers (16:5)

5 *So the churches were established in their faith and increased in number day by day.*

5 A crucial phase of Luke's narrative is now concluded with the third of six brief reports of progress. The scene of action shifts to the Aegean world.

B. PHILIPPI (16:6-40)

1. The Call from Macedonia (16:6-10)

6 *So they passed through[14] the Phrygian and Galatian region: they had been forbidden by the Holy Spirit to speak the word in Asia.*

7 *When they came opposite Mysia, they tried to make their way into Bithynia, but the Spirit of Jesus[15] did not allow them;*

10. In 1 Tim. 4:14 Timothy is said to have received his spiritual gift "by prophetic utterance" when the elders of his church laid their hands on him (cf. 1 Tim. 1:18); in 2 Tim. 1:6 he is said to have received it when *Paul* laid his hands on him.

11. Cf. 15:22, 27.

12. See p. 285.

13. It is a doublet of the Western reading of 15:41 (except that there it is the churches of Syria and Cilicia that receive the "commandments," whereas here it is the churches of Derbe, Lystra, etc.). See A. S. Geyser, "Paul, the Apostolic Decree and the Liberals in Corinth," in *Studia Paulina in honorem J. de Zwaan* (Haarlem, 1953), p. 137.

14. Gk. διῆλθον. The Byzantine text reads "having passed through" (διελθόντες), which suggests that the prohibition to preach in Asia came after they had traversed the "Phrygian and Galatian region," whereas it actually came before, or at an early point in, their passage through it.

15. The Byzantine text omits "of Jesus."

8 *so they passed by Mysia and came down to the sea at Troas.*[16]

9 *Here a vision appeared to Paul by night: a man of Macedonia was standing and appealing to him, "Come over into Macedonia and help us."*

10 *When he had seen the vision, we immediately sought means to set out for Macedonia, concluding that God had called us to preach the gospel to them.*[17]

6 Paul's missionary journeys display an extraordinary combination of strategic planning and keen sensitiveness to the guidance of the Spirit of God, however that guidance was conveyed—by prophetic utterance, inward prompting, or the overruling of external circumstances. On this occasion his intention had probably been, after visiting the churches planted in South Galatia by Barnabas and himself, to continue along the westward road to Ephesus. But the Spirit forbade him and his associates to take this road. The prohibition was evidently given before they passed through the "Phrygian and Galatian region"[18] (probably the Phrygian territory incorporated in the province of Galatia, in which Iconium and Pisidian Antioch lay);[19] it perhaps took the form of a prophetic utterance in the church at Lystra. The Spirit, we may observe, gave them ample warning to change their plans.

7-8 If the province of Asia was not to be the field of their immediate evangelistic activity, then it was natural for them to cast their eyes farther north, and think of the highly civilized province of Bithynia in northwest Asia Minor, with its Greek cities (of which Nicomedia and Nicaea were the most important) and Jewish settlements.[20] So, instead of continuing west to Ephesus, they turned north (probably from Pisidian Antioch), crossed the Sultan Dağ range, and arrived at Philomelium (modern Akşehir). From there they struck northwest, taking one of two possible routes leading through Asian Phrygia. We could plot the remainder of their journey more certainly if we knew where they received the second divine monition, warning them away from Bithynia. If "over against Mysia" or "opposite Mysia" means, as

16. The Western text reads "and passing through Mysia, they arrived at Troas."

17. The Western text recasts this verse: "Having awaked, then, he related the vision to us, and we recognized that the Lord had called us to evangelize those in Macedonia."

18. It may have been known as Phrygia Galatica (on the analogy of Pontus Galaticus, attested in *CIL* III.6818). The frequently repeated objection that Φρυγία (feminine singular) is not used adjectivally is sufficiently refuted by C. J. Hemer, who adduces thirty-one instances of its being so used ("The Adjective 'Phrygia,'" *JTS* n.s. 27 [1976], pp. 122-26; "Phrygia: A Further Note," *JTS* n.s. 28 [1977], pp. 99-101).

19. See W. M. Calder, "The Boundary of Galatic Phrygia," *MAMA* 7 (Manchester, 1956), pp. ix-xvi.

20. It was united under one governor with the western part of the former kingdom of Pontus. For Jewish settlements in Bithynia cf. Philo, *Embassy to Gaius* 281. Bithynia was evangelized before long; cf. 1 Pet. 1:1 and Pliny, *Epistle* 10.96 (his letter to the Emperor Trajan on the growth of Christianity in the province).

Ramsay put it, "when they had reached such a point that a line drawn across the country at right angles to the general line of their route would touch Mysia,"[21] then they would have arrived at one or the other of the road-junctions Dorylaeum (modern Eskişehir) or (more probably) Cotiaeum (modern Kütahya), and instead of continuing north into Bithynia turned west until they reached the sea at Troas.[22]

In saying that this second prohibition was imposed by "the Spirit of Jesus," does Luke suggest some significance in the change of terminology? It was the same Spirit who forbade them to "speak the word in Asia," but the fact that on this occasion he is called "the Spirit of Jesus" may indicate that his guidance was now given through a prophecy uttered expressly in the name of Jesus. Paul and Silas were both prophets,[23] and available for use by the Spirit or by the exalted Lord for the declaration of his will.

9 Troas—Alexandria Troas (to give it its full name)—was founded at the end of the fourth century B.C. and remained a free city until Augustus gave it the status of a Roman colony. It was a regular port of call for vessels journeying between proconsular Asia and Macedonia (cf. 20:5) and was an important center in the Roman system of communications. Traces of its harbor and other buildings may still be seen at Dalyan.[24]

At Troas, then, the series of divine prohibitions gave way to a positive direction. The direction this time took the form of a night vision seen by Paul. In this vision a man of Macedonia stood appealing to Paul to cross over to Macedonia and help the people there. Macedonia, which became the dominant power in the Greek world and Western Asia under Philip II and Alexander the Great in the fourth century B.C., had been a Roman province since 146 B.C. It is needless to ask how Paul recognized the man to be a Macedonian: his request, "Come over into Macedonia and help us," indicated his nationality clearly enough.

10 At this point the narrator shows unobtrusively that he himself now joined the missionary party as a fourth member, by continuing the story in the first person plural instead of the third. In the prologue to the Third Gospel (which was designed as the prologue to the whole of Luke-Acts), he claims to have kept in touch with the events related "for some time back"; the "some time back" goes back at least to this point.[25] Here, then, the first of

21. *The Church in the Roman Empire* (London, ⁴1895), p. 75n. If so, κατὰ τὴν Μυσίαν might be rendered in modern idiom by "in the latitude of Mysia."

22. See T. R. S. Broughton, "Three Notes on St. Paul's Journeys in Asia Minor," in *Quantulacumque: Studies presented to K. Lake* (London, 1937), pp. 135-38. Paul and his companions had to pass through part of Mysia to get to Troas; they "passed by Mysia" in the sense that they did not stop to preach there.

23. Cf. 13:1; 15:32.

24. See J. M. Cook, *The Troad* (Oxford, 1973), pp. 16-21; C. J. Hemer, "Alexandria Troas," *TynB* 26 (1975), pp. 79-112.

25. See H. J. Cadbury, "Commentary on the Preface of Luke," *Beginnings*

the "we" sections of Acts begins. No other explanation of them is so probable as that the "we" which characterizes them includes the "I" of the prologues to Luke and Acts. A writer incorporating into his narrative the diary of some personal eyewitness other than himself would scarcely have done so in such an artless way.[26] If the narrator was Luke the physician of Col. 4:14, we may wonder if he was practising his profession in Troas at the time, or waiting to be signed on as a ship's doctor; but we have no means of knowing. At any rate, he accompanied Paul, Silas, and Timothy to Macedonia, having taken part in the joint decision to go there in response to Paul's vision.

If Paul's original plan had been to evangelize the eastern shore of the Aegean by planting Christianity in Ephesus, "that great metropolis in which the East looked out upon the West,"[27] then the plan was only postponed, not jettisoned altogether. But first he was directed to the western shore of the Aegean, to plant the faith in Philippi, Thessalonica, Beroea, and Corinth before he settled in Ephesus. Strategic points on the circumference of the circle of which Ephesus was the center were to be evangelized first—in Macedonia and Achaia as well as in South Galatia—and then he was to complete his work in that whole area by nearly three years' ministry at the center. The Spirit's interventions did not frustrate Paul's strategy, but enhanced its effectiveness.

2. Troas to Philippi (16:11-12a)

11 *Setting sail*[28] *from Troas, then, we had a straight run to Samothrace, and the next day (we came) to Neapolis.*

12a *From there we went to Philippi, a city of the first district of Macedonia,*[29] *a Roman colony.*

I.2 (London, 1922), pp. 501-3; J. H. Ropes, "St. Luke's Preface: ἀσφάλεια and παρα-κολουθεῖν," *JTS* 25 (1923-24), pp. 70-71.

26. On the uniformity of the style and language of the "we" sections with those of the rest of Acts see A. Harnack, *Luke the Physician*, E.T. (London, 1907), pp. 26-120; J. C. Hawkins, *Horae Synopticae* (Oxford, ²1909), pp. 182-89. If the narrator incorporated the diary of someone else, he must have worked over it very thoroughly; why then did he leave this abrupt transition from the third person to the first, with no hint of the identity of the diarist? If, on the other hand, the first-person narrative style were a fictitious device to suggest the presence of an eyewitness and thus give an impression of greater authority or immediacy to the record, would it not have been used less sparingly? See p. 7.

27. F. J. A. Hort, *Prolegomena to Romans and Ephesians* (London, 1895), p. 83.

28. The Western text adds "next day."

29. This rendering, which presupposes Gk. ἥτις ἐστὶν πρώτης μερίδος τῆς Μακεδονίας πόλις, is found in no Greek manuscript, but is supported by some codices of the Latin Vulgate and by mediaeval versions in Provençal and German. It was conjectured by F. Field, F. Blass, and C. H. Turner, and has been defended more recently by

11   The wind was favorable for the voyage across the North Aegean, and they finished it in two days. (The reverse journey from Philippi to Troas, recorded in 20:6, took five days.) On the evening of the first day they reached Samothrace, a mountainous island rising to 5,000 feet, which forms a conspicuous landmark. In religious history the chief importance of Samothrace lies in its being the seat of a widely patronized mystery cult, the worship of the Cabiri, which had been practised there from time immemorial. Paul and his friends did not linger there, however; the next day their ship took them to Neapolis, on the mainland. Neapolis, the modern Kavalla, was the port of Philippi, which lay some ten miles inland. At Neapolis the great Egnatian Way, a Roman road linking the Adriatic with the Aegean, reached its eastern terminus.[30] Luke likes to note the ports of arrival and departure, and in the "we" sections he is specially careful to note the daily progress made during voyages.

12a   Disembarking at Neapolis, the missionaries went on to Philippi along the Egnatian Way. This city received its name from Philip II, father of Alexander the Great, who seized the gold mines in the vicinity and fortified what had formerly been the Thasian settlement of Crenides. With the rest of Macedonia, Philippi passed under Roman control at the end of the Third Macedonian War in 168 B.C. At that time Macedonia was divided into four administrative districts or republics. Later, in 146 B.C., it was reduced to provincial status. Near Philippi was fought the battle in 42 B.C. which resulted in the victory of Mark Antony and Octavian (the future Emperor Augustus) over Brutus and Cassius, assassins of Julius Caesar.[31] After the battle, the victors settled a number of their veterans at Philippi and made the city a Roman colony; Octavian settled further colonists there after his victory over Antony and Cleopatra at Actium in 31 B.C.

Luke describes Philippi as a city of the first district of Macedonia[32]—that is, the first of the four districts into which the former king-

---

E. Haenchen and H. Conzelmann (cf. NA[26]). The majority Greek reading is πρώτη, not πρώτης, but it is difficult to make sense of "which is first city of the district of Macedonia." The Western text interprets this to mean that Philippi was "capital of Macedonia" (κεφαλὴ τῆς Μακεδονίας), but that distinction belonged to Thessalonica, not to Philippi. The historical situation is reflected accurately by the reading "which is a city of the first district of Macedonia."

30. Its western termini were at Apollonia and Dyrrhachium (modern Poyani and Durrës in Albania). See N. G. L. Hammond, "The Western Part of the Via Egnatia," *JRS* 64 (1974), pp. 185-94. The Romans built the road across Macedonia after the country became a province in 146 B.C.

31. The battle immortalized in Shakespeare's *Julius Caesar*, especially in the ominous *au revoir*, "thou shalt see me at Philippi" (Act 4, Scene 3).

32. See n. 29 above. For the division into four districts see Livy, *History* 45.29.

dom was divided by the Romans. While he refers to several other cities which are known to have been Roman colonies at the time, Philippi is the only one which he expressly calls a Roman colony.[33] The details of its administration given in the ensuing narrative are those which were specially characteristic of such a colony. A Roman colony used Roman law, and its constitution was modeled on the municipal constitution of Rome.

3. The Faith of Lydia (16:12b-15)

12b *In this city we spent several days.*

13 *On the sabbath day we went outside the gate by the riverside to a place habitually used for prayer,[34] and we sat down and talked to the women who had come together.*

14 *One of the women, Lydia by name, a purple merchant from the city of Thyatira, listened carefully.[35] The Lord opened her heart to pay heed to what Paul was saying.*

15 *When she was baptized, with her household, she begged us, "If you have judged me to be a believer in the Lord, come into my house and stay there." She would take no refusal.[36]*

12b-13 At Philippi, then, they spent several days. When Paul visited a new city, it was his practice, as we have seen, to attend the local Jewish synagogue on the first sabbath after his arrival and seek an opportunity to make his message known there. At Philippi, however, there does not appear to have been a regular synagogue. That can only mean that there were very few resident Jews; had there been ten Jewish men, they would have sufficed to constitute a synagogue.[37] No number of women could compensate for the absence of even one man necessary to make up the quorum of ten. There

33. He transliterates Lat. *colonia* (κολωνία) instead of using Gk. ἀποικία. The original purpose of Roman colonies was military; it was reckoned a good thing to have settlements of Roman citizens planted at strategic points throughout the Roman sphere of influence. Other Roman colonies which figure in Acts are Pisidian Antioch, Lystra, Troas, Corinth, and Ptolemais.

34. The chief authorities for the Alexandrian text are corrupt here (ℵ A B require emendation); the true reading may be preserved in the Byzantine text, οὗ ἐνομίζετο προσευχὴ εἶναι, correctly rendered in KJV: "where prayer was wont to be made" (the Western reading οὗ ἐδόκει προσευχὴ εἶναι is probably due to the misinterpretation of ἐνομίζετο as "it was thought"). Here and in v. 16 προσευχή may mean either "prayer" or "a place of prayer" (almost, if not altogether, synonymous with συναγωγή).

35. Gk. ἤκουεν (imperfect), "kept on listening."

36. Gk. παρεβιάσατο ἡμᾶς, "she compelled us."

37. For ten as the quorum *(minyān)* for a synagogue congregation cf. *Pirqê 'Aḇôṯ* 3.7: "Rabbi Halafta ben Dosa, of the village of Hananya, said, 'When ten people sit

was, however, a place outside the city where a number of women—either of Jewish birth or Gentiles who worshiped the God of Israel—met to go through the appointed Jewish service of prayer for the sabbath day, even if they could not constitute a valid synagogue congregation. Paul and his companions found this place, by the bank of the river Gangites, and sat down with the women and told them the story of Jesus.

14-15 One of these women, a God-fearing Gentile, came from Thyatira in the province of Asia. Her name Lydia, "the Lydian woman," reminds us that Thyatira lay in the territory of the ancient kingdom of Lydia. The people of that area were famed for their skill in the manufacture of purple dye, extracted from the juice of the madder root.[38] This was still in use there for the dyeing of carpets at the end of the nineteenth century, before it was superseded by chemical dyes.[39] Lydia had evidently come to Philippi as a trader in that dye. There is inscriptional evidence for the existence of a guild of purple merchants in Philippi.[40] But she had possibly learned to worship the true God in her native Thyatira; there was probably a Jewish community there.[41]

As Paul and his friends spoke, Lydia believed what they said and acknowledged Jesus as Lord. She thus became Paul's first convert in Europe. When she was baptized, together with her household (which would include her servants and other dependents as well as her family), she gave practical proof of her faith by pressing the four missionaries to become her guests. Women in Macedonia were noted for their independence; moreover, under Roman law (which governed life in the colony) freeborn women with three children and freedwomen with four children were at this time granted a number of privileges, including the right to undertake legal transactions on their own initiative.[42]

---

together and occupy themselves with the Torah, the *shekhinah* abides among them, as it is said, God stands in the congregation of God' (Ps. 82:1)."

38. See C. J. Hemer, "Lydia and the Purple Trade," *New Docs.* 3 (1978), pp. 53-55.

39. See W. M. Ramsay, *Historical Geography of Asia Minor* (London, 1890), p. 123. Lydian women are associated with purple dyeing as early as Homer (*Iliad* 4.141-42).

40. *CIL* III.664 *(purpurarii).*

41. Since Thyatira was founded by Seleucus I, it may be included among "the cities which he founded in Asia" in which, according to Josephus (*Ant.* 12.119), he granted citizenship to Jews. Cf. Schürer II, p. 440, n. 63 (*CIG* 3509, cited there, speaks of a Σαμβαθεῖον in front of the city of Thyatira). Thyatira was later the seat of a church, one of the seven addressed in the Apocalypse (Rev. 2:18-29).

42. Since she had already confessed her faith in baptism, "if you have judged me to be a believer in the Lord" must be equivalent to "*since* you have judged me to be a believer. . . ." See W. D. Thomas, "The Place of Women in the Church at Philippi," *ExT* 83 (1971-72), pp. 117-20; cf. p. 323, n. 5 below.

4. The Pythoness (16:16-18)

> 16 *Now, as we made our way to the place of prayer,[43] we were encountered by a slave girl who was possessed by a pythonic spirit. She brought her owners much profit[44] by her fortune-telling.*
>
> 17 *She kept on following Paul and us, calling out as she did so, "These men are servants[45] of God Most High; they are proclaiming the way of salvation to you!"[46]*
>
> 18 *She did this for many days on end. Paul was annoyed, and turned and said to the spirit, "I command you in the name of Jesus Christ, Come out of her!" It came out there and then.*

16 Three individuals are singled out by Luke among those whose lives were influenced for good by the gospel at Philippi; they differ so much one from another that he might be thought to have selected them deliberately in order to show how the saving power of the name of Jesus was shown in the most diverse types of men and women. The first is Lydia, the independent businesswoman of reputable character and God-fearing mind; as she heard the gospel, "the Lord opened her heart" and she believed it. The second is a person of a very different stamp: an unfortunate demon-possessed slave girl, whose owners exploited her condition for their material gain. She is described by Luke as "having a pythonic spirit" or being a "pythoness"—that is, a person inspired[47] by Apollo, the Greek deity specially associated with the giving of oracles, who was worshiped as the "Pythian" god at the oracular shrine of Delphi in central Greece. His priestess there was the Pythian prophet *par excellence;* the girl of whom Luke speaks was a very pale reflection of her. This girl's involuntary utterances were regarded as the voice of the god, and she was thus much in demand by people who wished to have their fortunes told or to receive information or advice which they believed could be supplied from such a source.

17 The slave girl's deliverance demanded much more spectacular measures than Lydia's quiet turning in heart to the Lord. Day by day, as the missionaries went to the place of prayer, she followed them through the streets of Philippi, advertising them aloud as servants of God Most High, who were bringing the way of salvation to the city. The title "God Most High" provided Jews and Gentiles with a convenient common denominator

---

43. Or "to prayer" (εἰς τὴν προσευχήν); cf. n. 34 above.

44. Gk. ἐργασία, "work," "business."

45. P⁴⁵ omits δοῦλοι, probably by accident.

46. The textual evidence is fairly evenly balanced between "you" (ὑμῖν) and "us" (ἡμῖν), with a slight preponderance in favor of "you."

47. Plutarch (*The Failure of the Oracles* 9.414e) calls such people "ventriloquists" (Gk. ἐγγαστρίμυθοι)—ventriloquists, that is to say, whose utterances were really and not only apparently beyond their conscious control. In LXX the same Greek

for the supreme being,[48] and "salvation" in a religious sense was as eagerly sought by Gentiles as by Jews.[49]

18 The missionaries, however, did not appreciate her unsolicited testimonials, and at last Paul, vexed by her continual clamor, exorcized the spirit that possessed her, commanding it in the name of Jesus Christ to come out of her. The words had scarcely left his lips when she was released from its power. The superior authority which such spirits had recognized when Jesus himself commanded them to leave their victims was equally recognized when his name was invoked by one of his disciples, and proved as potent in exorcism as in other forms of healing (cf. 3:6).

5. Paul and Silas Imprisoned (16:19-24)

19 *When her owners saw that their hope of profit[50] had "come out" of her, they seized Paul and Silas and dragged them into the forum[51] before the magistrates.*

20 *Bringing them before the praetors,[52] they said, "These men are causing disturbance in our city. Jews as they are,*

21 *they are proclaiming customs which we may neither accept nor practise, Roman citizens as we are.*

22 *The crowd joined in attacking them, and the praetors tore off their cloaks and ordered them to be beaten with rods.*

23 *When they had inflicted many strokes on them, they threw them into prison and charged the jailer to guard them securely.*

24 *Receiving such a charge, he threw them into the inner prison and secured their feet in the stocks.*

---

word is used of those who have a familiar spirit (Heb. 'ôḇ), like the witch of Endor (1 Sam. [LXX 1 Kms.] 28:7).

48. In LXX θεὸς ὕψιστος is the rendering of 'ēl 'elyôn, the divine designation found in Gen. 14:18, etc. For its use by Gentiles cf. Num. 24:16; Isa. 14:14; Dan. 3:26 (LXX/Theod. 3:93); 1 Esdr. 2:3. In Mark 5:7 "Legion" address Jesus as υἱὲ τοῦ θεοῦ τοῦ ὑψίστου. Josephus (Ant. 16.163) quotes an edict of Augustus in which Hyrcanus II is called ἀρχιερεὺς θεοῦ ὑψίστου. With the slave girl's use of θεὸς ὕψιστος here compare (and contrast) Stephen's use of ὁ ὕψιστος in 7:48. See A. B. Cook, Zeus II.2 (Cambridge, 1925), p. 889; A. Deissmann, Light from the Ancient East, E.T. (London, ²1927), pp. 413-24; A. D. Nock, C. H. Roberts, and T. C. Skeat, "The Gild of Zeus Hypsistos" (1936), in Nock, Essays, pp. 414-43; also CIJ 2.1433, where a synagogue in Alexandria (second century B.C.) is dedicated θεῷ ὑψίστῳ, and other dedications cited in New Docs. 1 (1976), § 5.

49. See on 14:9 (p. 274 with n. 22).

50. Gk. ἐργασία, as in v. 16 above.

51. Gk. ἀγορά, which, in reference to a Roman city, is a translation of Lat. *forum*. The forum of Philippi, which lies on the south side of the Egnatian Way, is one of the chief features of the site, although the buildings seen today date mostly from the time of Marcus Aurelius (161-80).

52. This clause practically repeats the preceding one, with a less violent verb. The "praetors" (στρατηγοί) here are the "magistrates" (ἄρχοντες) of v. 19.

19 The good deed done to the slave girl was not at all to the liking of her owners; when Paul exorcized the spirit that possessed her, he exorcized their means of income: she could no longer tell fortunes. There is a literary parallel in one of the comedies of Menander in which a girl possessed not by Apollo but by Cybele laments the loss of her cymbals and tambourine and of her gift of prophecy, which depends on them.[53] The righteous indignation of the Philippian slave girl's owners was aroused at the missionaries' wanton attack on the sacred rights of property (as they saw it).[54] Moreover, the men who had infringed these rights were not Roman citizens like themselves (or so they thought); they were not even Greeks, like the population around them, but wandering Jews, engaged in propagating some variety of their own perverse superstition. They therefore dragged Paul and Silas before the magistrates and lodged a complaint against them. Luke and Timothy were apparently unmolested: Paul and Silas were not only the leaders of the party but also most obviously Jews (Luke was a Gentile and Timothy a half-Gentile). Anti-Jewish sentiment lay very near the surface in pagan antiquity.

20-21 As Philippi was a Roman colony, its municipal administration, like that of Rome itself, was in the hands of two collegiate magistrates. The collegiate magistrates of a Roman colony were commonly called duumvirs, but in some places they preferred the more dignified title of praetors, and this is what the chief magistrates of Philippi were apparently called.[55] Before the two praetors, then, Paul and Silas were dragged, and their accusers represented them as vagabond Jews who were causing disturbances in the city and inculcating customs which Roman citizens of all people could neither admit nor practise. Proselytization of Roman citizens by Jews was not positively illegal, so far as the evidence indicates,[56] but it certainly incurred strong disapproval. The magistrates were bound in any case to take cognizance of such religious activity as threatened to provoke a breach of the peace or to encourage unlawful practices or organizations; and Paul and Silas were charged with precisely this kind of activity.

22 There was great indignation that Roman citizens should be molested by strolling peddlers of an outlandish religion. Such people had to be taught to know their proper place and not trouble their betters. There was no

---

53. Menander, *Theophoroumenē* ("The Divinely Inspired Girl"), Act 2, Scene 1; see T. B. L. Webster, *An Introduction to Menander* (Manchester, 1974), p. 191.

54. The only occasions on which Luke reports an attack by Gentiles on Christian missionaries arise from a threat (real or imagined) presented by the gospel to property interests; cf. 19:23-27 (pp. 374-75).

55. Compare the chief magistrates of Capua (a Roman colony in Italy itself), of whom Cicero said, "While they are called duumvirs (*duo uiri*, 'two men') in our other colonies, these men wished to be called praetors" (*On the Agrarian Law* 2.93).

56. See A. N. Sherwin-White, *Roman Society and Roman Law in the New Testament* (Oxford, 1963), p. 81.

serious investigation of the charge: Paul and Silas were summarily stripped[57] and handed over to the lictors—the magistrates' police attendants—to be soundly beaten; the city jailer was then ordered to lock them up.

The lictors[58] were the official attendants on the chief magistrates in Rome and other Roman cities. They carried as symbols of office bundles of rods, with an axe inserted among them in certain circumstances—the *fasces et secures*[59]—denoting the magistrates' right to inflict corporal and, where necessary, capital punishment. It was with the lictors' rods that the two missionaries were beaten on this occasion. It was not the only time that Paul had this treatment meted out to him: five or six years later he claims to have been beaten with rods three times (2 Cor. 11:25), although we have no information about the two other occasions.

23-24   When, after this severe beating, they were handed over to the jailer's custody, he interpreted his instructions strictly and fastened their legs in the stocks, in the inmost part of the prison. These stocks had more than two holes for the legs, which could thus be forced apart in such a way as to cause the utmost discomfort and cramping pain.[60] It was not the jailer's business to take any thought for his prisoners' comfort, but to make sure that they did not escape. He was possibly a retired soldier, and while service in the Roman army developed many fine qualities, these did not include the milk of human kindness. Yet this man is the third person in Philippi whom Luke describes as influenced by the saving power of Christ. He was a totally different character from both Lydia and the fortune-teller, and it took an earthquake and confrontation with death to make him take thought for his salvation; yet the same gospel as had blessed those two women now brought blessing to him.

6. Earthquake at Midnight: the Jailer's Conversion (16:25-34)

25 *At midnight Paul and Silas were praying and singing hymns to God, and the prisoners were listening to them.*

26 *Suddenly there was a great earthquake; the foundations of the prison were shaken, all the doors were opened at once,*[61] *and all the fetters were unfastened.*

27 *The jailer woke up; when he saw the prison doors open, he drew his*

---

57. The idea that it was their own clothes that the praetors tore off (cf. 14:14) is ludicrously misconceived.

58. Gk. ῥαβδοῦχοι, "rod-carriers."

59. It is in part from the adoption of such a bundle of rods as the symbol of an Italian political party after World War I that the political term "fascist" is derived.

60. Eusebius tells how this form of torture was endured by the confessors of Vienne and Lyon in A.D. 177 (*HE* 5.1.27) and by Origen at a later date (*HE* 6.39).

61. B and lat^g omit "at once."

*sword and was on the point of killing himself, for he thought the
prisoners had escaped.*

28 *But Paul called in a loud voice, "Don't harm yourself; we are all
here!"*

29 *The jailer then called for lights, rushed in, and fell down trembling
before Paul and Silas;*

30 *he brought them out[62] and said, "Gentlemen, what must I do to be
saved?"*

31 *"Believe on the Lord Jesus,"[63] they replied, "and you will be saved—
you and your household."*

32 *Then they spoke the word of the Lord[64] to him, and to all those who
were in his house.*

33 *At that very hour of the night he took them and bathed their
wounds;[65] then he was baptized immediately, together with all who
belonged to him.*

34 *Then he brought them up into his house and set food before them.[66]
Having believed in God, he rejoiced with all his household.*

25 This paragraph bears the marks of being an independent narrative,
inserted by Luke into the record of events at Philippi. He probably derived it
from another source than its context: if verse 35 had followed immediately
after verse 24, the reader would have been conscious of no hiatus.[67] But we
may be glad that Luke did add it at this point: it enriches his account of Paul's
Philippian ministry.

The double discomfort of the lictors' rods and the stocks was not
calculated to fill Paul and Silas with joy, but around midnight the other

62. The Western text inserts "having secured the other prisoners."

63. The Western and Byzantine texts add "Christ."

64. Cod. B with the first hand in ℵ and a few other witnesses read "the word of
God."

65. Gk. πληγαί, "blows" (translated "strokes" in v. 23 above).

66. Gk. παρέθηκεν τράπεζαν, "placed a table alongside (each)." The expression is ancient and idiomatic: it occurs in Herodotus (*Hist.* 6.139) and similar phrases are found in Homer (e.g., *Iliad* 24.476; *Odyssey* 5.196; 7.174-75; 17.333-35). Individual tables were brought up beside each guest, and food was placed on them.

67. M. Dibelius, in an essay on the style criticism of Acts, concludes that the account of the earthquake is an independent legend inserted in the itinerary, having no connection with it, although Luke (he considers) has complicated the picture by adding the preaching and the baptism of vv. 32-33 (*Studies in the Acts of the Apostles*, E.T. [London, 1956], pp. 23-24). R. Reitzenstein points out a recurring pattern of escape stories in Greek literature; cf. 5:19; 12:6-10 above (*Die hellenistischen Wundererzählungen* [Leipzig, 1906], pp. 120-22). Origen (*Against Celsus* 2.34) compares this narrative and that of Peter's release in 12:6-10 with Euripides' account of the escape of the Bacchanals and of Dionysus in *Bacchae* 443-50, 586-602 (Celsus had asked why Jesus did not escape from his bonds as Dionysus did from his). As for the singing at midnight, a literary affinity to this had been found in *Testament of Joseph* 8:4-5, 9:4, where, after Joseph is beaten and thrown into prison, he is overheard "giving thanks to the Lord and singing praises in the house of darkness" (W. K. Lowther Clarke, "St. Luke and the Pseudepigrapha: Two Parallels," *JTS* 15 [1913-14], pp. 597-99; also *Beginnings* I.2, pp. 77-78).

prisoners, as they listened, heard sounds coming from the inmost cell—sounds, not of groaning and cursing, but of prayer and hymn-singing. "The legs feel nothing in the stocks when the heart is in heaven," says Tertullian.[68] What sort of men were these?

26 Perhaps it was the awed impression which the two missionaries' behavior produced on the other prisoners that enabled them to dissuade those others from making their escape while the going was good when a sudden earthquake shook the prison foundations, threw open the doors, and loosened the staples that attached the prisoners' fetters to the walls.

27 The earthquake that rocked the prison foundations wakened the jailer out of his midnight sleep. Immediately he went to investigate his charge. The worst had happened: the prison doors were open; the prisoners, of course, had seized their opportunity and escaped. For a man brought up to a Roman soldier's ideals of duty and discipline, only one honorable course was open—suicide.

28 But as he stood there, by the outer door of the prison, about to drive the point of his short sword into his throat or heart, his hand was arrested by a voice from the darkness within: "Don't harm yourself; we are all here!" While he could see nothing as he looked into the darkness, those inside could see his figure silhouetted in the doorway and could see what he was about to do. Not only were Paul and Silas still there, but they had apparently restrained the other prisoners also. There was something uncanny about these two men!

29-30 So, calling for light, he rushed into the prison and brought Paul and Silas out. First, according to the Western reviser (who probably imagined what he himself would have done had he been in the jailer's shoes), he prudently secured the other prisoners again.[69] Then he earnestly asked Paul and Silas, "What must I do to be saved?"

How much he meant by this question it would be difficult to determine. He might have heard (or heard about) the fortune-teller's announcement that these men had come to proclaim a "way of salvation";[70] if so, he might have seen in the earthquake a supernatural vindication of them and their message. What was involved in this salvation would not have been clear to him, but he was thoroughly shaken, in soul as well as in body, and if anyone could show him the way to peace of mind, release from fear, and a sense of security, Paul and Silas (he was convinced) could do so.

---

68. *To the Martyrs* 2. Cf. Epictetus: "Then we shall be emulators of Socrates, when we are able to compose paeans in prison" (*Dissertations* 2.6.26).

69. W. M. Ramsay is inclined to accept the Western addition as authentic, as "suggestive of the orderly well-disciplined character of the jailor" (*St. Paul the Traveller* [London, ¹⁴1920], p. 222); W. L. Knox dismisses it as "an amusing insertion" (*St. Paul and the Church of Jerusalem* [Cambridge, 1925], p. xxiv). So differently do students of Acts react to the peculiar Western readings!

70. See also on 14:9 (pp. 273-74).

31-32 There and then the two missionaries assured him that faith in Jesus, the Lord whom they proclaimed, was the way of salvation for himself and his family. What was meant by faith in Jesus as Lord they proceeded to make plain to the whole household, presenting the gospel to them in terms which they could readily grasp.

33-34 This was the message they had lived for! With joy they embraced it at once. The jailer bathed the wounded backs of the two men, probably at a well in the prison courtyard, and there too he and his household were baptized. "He washed and was washed," says Chrysostom: "he washed them from their stripes, and was himself washed from his sins."[71] If nothing is said explicitly of their receiving the Holy Spirit, this is implied in the emphasis on the rejoicing which filled the house.[72]

There, in the jailer's house, into which Paul and Silas were brought up,[73] they received hospitable treatment: food was set before them, and hosts and guests exulted together, united in Christian faith and love. The jailer was guilty of no dereliction of duty in thus taking two prisoners into his house; his responsibility was to produce them when called upon to do so. He had no reason to fear that they would run away and leave him in the lurch. Luke's third example of the power of the gospel at Philippi is the most wonderful of all. And perhaps Paul and Silas reckoned the rods and the stocks well worth enduring for the joy that they shared in the jailer's house.

7. Paul and Silas Leave Philippi (16:35-40)

35 At daybreak[74] the praetors sent the lictors with a message: "Release those men."

36 The jailer reported their words to Paul: "The praetors have sent word that you two are to be released; now then, depart and be on your way in peace."[75]

37 But Paul said to the lictors, "They have beaten us publicly, without a proper trial,[76] Roman citizens as we are, and threw us into prison. Do they now think they can turn us out secretly? No indeed; let them come in person and escort us out."

71. *Homilies on Acts* 36.2. For the baptism of the jailer's household cf. v. 15; also 10:44-48 with 11:14; 1 Cor. 1:16.

72. Cf. the Ethiopian, who "went his way rejoicing" (8:39).

73. It was on an upper floor, if one may judge from ἀναγαγών.

74. After "at daybreak" the Western text continues: "the praetors came together into the forum and, calling to mind the earthquake that had taken place, they were struck with fear and sent the lictors . . ." An answer was thus supplied to the natural question: What effect did the earthquake have on people outside the prison precincts?

75. Some Western witnesses omit "in peace."

76. Gk. ἀκαταχρίτους, "uncondemned" (the Western text has ἀναιτίους, "not guilty"). Here, as in 22:25, the Greek word may represent Lat. *re incognita*, "without investigating our case" (cf. W. M. Ramsay, *St. Paul the Traveller*, pp. 224-25).

38 *The lictors reported these words to the praetors. The praetors were afraid when they learned that the men were Roman citizens,*

39 *and they came[77] and appealed to them; they brought them out and begged them to leave the city.*

40 *So, leaving the prison, they went to Lydia's house, where they saw the brothers[78] and encouraged them; then they took their departure.*

35 By the next morning the excitement of the previous day had died down. The praetors decided that the two vagabond Jews had been taught the necessary lesson by the lictors' rods and the night in the lock-up. All that was required now was to release them and send them out of town; they would be in no hurry to come back. Imprisonment in itself was not a common penalty for breaches of civil law; by having Paul and Silas locked up overnight after their beating, the praetors had simply exercised their police right of *coercitio*—summary correction or chastisement. They now sent the lictors to the jail with orders to the jailer to set the two prisoners free.

36-37 But when the jailer reported this message to Paul and Silas and told them that they were at liberty to depart, Paul demurred. An injustice had been committed, and it must not be covered up in this way. He and his companion were Roman citizens—as good Roman citizens as the colonists and magistrates of Philippi—and their rights as Roman citizens had been grossly violated. The charges against them ought to have been properly investigated, but they had been beaten and imprisoned without any inquiry. By a series of Valerian and Porcian laws enacted between the beginning of the Roman Republic and the early second century B.C. Roman citizens were exempted from degrading forms of punishment and had certain valued rights established for them in relation to the law.[79] These privileges had been more recently reaffirmed under the empire by a Julian law dealing with public disorder.[80]

Why then did not Paul appeal to his Roman citizenship the day before?[81] The answer sometimes given, that it would have been embarrass-

---

77. The Western text reads: "And having arrived with many friends at the prison, they begged them to depart, saying, 'We did not know the truth about you, that you were righteous men.' And having led them out, they begged them, saying, 'Depart from this city, lest perchance they come to us in a body again, crying out against you.'"

78. The Western text adds "they related all that the Lord had done to them" (cf. 14:27; 15:4).

79. Referring to an enactment of 195 B.C., Cicero says, "The Porcian Law removed the rods from the bodies of all Roman citizens" (*On behalf of Rabirius, charged with treason* 12).

80. The *lex Iulia de ui publica* (see A. H. M. Jones, *Studies in Roman Government and Law* [Oxford, 1960], pp. 97-98).

81. In 22:25 Paul is careful to claim his citizen rights before being beaten, but there he was about to be scourged, with a more murderous instrument than the lictors' rods (see pp. 420-21).

ing for him to have to claim privileges which Silas could not share, seems to be excluded by the plain implication of the present passage, that both Silas and he were Roman citizens. It may be that they did protest at the time, but that no one paid any attention to them in the excitement of the moment. A Roman citizen claimed his legal rights by the affirmation *ciuis Romanus sum,* "I am a Roman citizen."[82] It is uncertain if there was any documentary evidence which could be produced on the spot in confirmation of the claim. Paul was probably registered as a Roman citizen in the public record office at Tarsus, and a certified copy of the registration might be obtained, but did he carry this around with him wherever he went?[83] At any rate, on this occasion Paul's claim neatly turned the tables on the self-important complaint of his accusers, that respectable Roman citizens should not be disturbed by wandering Jews. If the praetors wanted them to leave Philippi, he said, let them come and show the courtesy due to Roman citizens, and not expel them in this hole-and-corner manner.

38-39 The lictors brought Paul's message back to the praetors, who were dismayed to learn what, in yesterday's excitement, they had failed to ascertain—that these two Jews were as good Roman citizens as themselves. If a complaint about their illegal treatment of these Roman citizens reached the ears of the authorities in Rome, they would be in an awkward position. Their self-importance was healthily deflated, as they went to the jail and requested Paul and Silas to leave Philippi. Roman citizens who had been convicted of no crime could not be *expelled* from a Roman city, but the responsibility of protecting two unpopular Roman citizens was more than the praetors felt able to undertake. They therefore apologized to Paul and Silas and escorted them out of the prison precincts, asking them to be good enough not to remain in Philippi any longer.

40 Being released from prison, they went to Lydia's house and spoke words of encouragement to the Christians gathered there. Paul's insistence on an official apology may have served in some degree as a protection to them for the time being. (That the Christians of Philippi had to endure persecution for their faith some years later is evident from Phil. 1:27-30.) Then Paul and Silas, with Timothy, departed from Philippi in the westward direction along the Egnatian Way. Luke perhaps stayed behind; at any rate he reappears in Philippi in 20:5-6, at the beginning of the second

---

82. Cicero (*Verrine Orations* 2.5.161-62) relates, as an outrageously illegal proceeding, how a Roman citizen was publicly beaten in the forum of Messina, Sicily, despite his protest *ciuis Romanus sum.*

83. See F. Schulz, "Roman Registers of Births and Birth Certificates," *JRS* 32 (1942), pp. 78-91; 33 (1943), pp. 55-64; A. N. Sherwin-White, *Roman Society and Roman Law in the New Testament,* pp. 144-50.

"we" section of Acts. He is possibly the "true yokefellow" to whom Paul addresses a special request in Phil. 4:3.[84]

The later history of the Philippian church makes pleasant reading. The same kindness as provided Paul and his friends with hospitality during their first visit to the city was shown in repeated gifts to Paul during his subsequent travels and Roman imprisonment (Phil. 4:10-16).[85]

---

84. This presupposes that the section of Philippians in which the "true yokefellow" is addressed belongs to an earlier date than Paul's Roman imprisonment, to which the bulk of that letter probably belongs. The identification with Luke is at least less improbable than the view that Lydia is so addressed, especially when "yokefellow" (σύζυγος) is taken to mean "wife" (so E. Renan, *St. Paul,* E.T. [London, 1889], p. 76; S. Baring-Gould, *A Study of St. Paul* [London, 1897], pp. 213-16).

85. Cf. F. F. Bruce, *Philippians,* GNC (San Francisco, 1983), pp. 123-29.

ACTS 17

C. THESSALONICA TO ATHENS (17:1-34)

1. Arrival at Thessalonica (17:1-4)

1 *Taking the road through Amphipolis[1] and Apollonia, they came to Thessalonica. There was a Jewish synagogue there,*

2 *and according to Paul's custom he went in among them, and for three sabbath days in succession he discoursed to them from the scriptures.*

3 *He opened them up and, setting them alongside (the events which fulfilled them), showed that it was necessary for the Messiah to suffer and to rise from the dead, adding, "This is the Messiah—this Jesus, whom I proclaim to you."*

4 *Some of them believed[2] and attached themselves to Paul and Silas, including a large company of God-fearing Greeks, and not a few of the leading women.*

1 From Philippi Paul and Silas, with Timothy, took the Egnatian Way westward through Amphipolis on the Strymon (formerly an important strategic point on the Thraco-Macedonian frontier) and then, a second day's journey on, through Apollonia, and arrived at Thessalonica, then as now the principal city of Macedonia. Thessalonica was founded in 315 B.C., on the site of the earlier settlement of Therme, by Cassander, who named it after his wife, a half-sister of Alexander the Great. The three travelers apparently halted only for a night at Amphipolis and again at Apollonia, but at Thessalonica (about 62 miles west of Philippi) they made a longer stay: the importance of this city commended it as a suitable place for intensive evangelization.

2-3 In accordance with his regular practice, Paul visited the local synagogue, and (having probably been invited to address the congregation,

1. After "Amphipolis" the Western text continues: "they came down to Apollonia and from there to Thessalonica."
2. After "believed" (ἐπείσθησαν, "were persuaded") the Western text continues: "and many of the God-fearers adhered to the teaching, and a large number of the Greeks, and not a few of the wives of the leading men." (The Western reviser plays down feminine initiative.)

as previously at Pisidian Antioch) he expounded the Old Testament scriptures on the next three sabbath days. He brought forward as evidence of their fulfilment the historical facts recently accomplished in the ministry, death, and resurrection of Jesus, setting these events alongside[3] the predictions in order that the force of his argument might be readily grasped. According to those predictions, the Messiah was appointed to suffer and then rise again from the dead.[4] Both these experiences had been fulfilled in Jesus, and in nobody else; therefore, said Paul, this Jesus of whom I tell you is the promised Messiah.

4 As had happened in the synagogues of South Galatia, so also in Thessalonica some of Paul's Jewish hearers were convinced by what he said, but the majority of his converts during these three weeks were God-fearing Gentiles. Among these were a considerable number of women of high station. Macedonian women had a well-earned reputation for their independence and enterprising spirit.[5] If some of the women who believed the gospel at this time were the wives of leading citizens, the initiative was theirs, not their husbands'. Jason, who is mentioned as the missionaries' host in verse 5, was presumably one of the Jews who believed (the Greek name Jason was assumed by many Jews who were originally named Joshua); Aristarchus and Secundus, described as Thessalonians in 20:4, were probably also converted to the Christian faith at this time.

2. Trouble in Thessalonica (17:5-9)

5 *The Jews, however, were stirred to envy and, enlisting the aid of some characters who loafed around the* agora, *ready for mischief,[6] they assembled a mob and set the city in an uproar. They attacked Jason's house and searched for the men in order to bring them out before the public assembly.*

6 *When they did not find them, they dragged Jason and some of the brothers before the politarchs. "These men," they shouted, "who have subverted the whole world have arrived here too;*

7 *Jason has harbored them. They all practise things in opposition to Caesar's decrees; they say there is another emperor, Jesus."*

8 *The crowd and the politarchs were agitated when they heard this.*

3. Gk. παρατιθέμενος, "setting side by side" and hence "bringing forward as evidence."

4. "It was necessary" for the Messiah to suffer and to rise from the dead in order that the scriptures might be fulfilled. Cf. Luke 9:22; 24:26, 44. Cf. also 3:18 above; 26:23. Paul (1 Cor. 15:3-4) and Peter (1 Pet. 1:11) emphasize that the death and resurrection of Christ took place in accordance with the scriptures.

5. See W. W. Tarn and G. T. Griffith, *Hellenistic Civilisation* (London, ³1952), pp. 98-99.

6. Gk. τῶν ἀγοραίων ἄνδρας τινὰς πονηρούς, "certain lewd fellows of the baser sort" (it is difficult to improve on this KJV rendering, even if it is not twentieth-century English).

9 *The politarchs took security from Jason and the others, and dismissed them.*

5 It was not only in the synagogue preaching and the making of many converts that the pattern of events in the South Galatian cities was reproduced at Thessalonica. Here too the Jews who did not believe the gospel, incensed at the readiness of so many potential proselytes to embrace the missionaries' message and adhere to them, incited the city rabble against Paul and his companions. By the time that the rabble assaulted the house where the missionaries had been staying, they had succeeded in making their escape; no doubt some of their converts, getting wind of what was afoot, hid them where they were not likely to be found. The mob was thus unable to drag them before the civic assembly,[7] as it had hoped to do.

6-7 But if Paul and his colleagues were not there, Jason himself, the owner of the house, was at home, and he, together with some other new Christians, was dragged before the magistrates. The magistrates of Thessalonica are called "politarchs," a title which is known from many inscriptions to have been given to the chief magistrates of Macedonian cities.[8] A most serious complaint was lodged against the missionaries and their hosts. Jason and his friends were charged with harboring Jewish agitators, political messianists such as had stirred up unrest[9] in other cities of the Roman Empire. Rome[10] and Alexandria[11] had recently experienced such trouble; now, said the accusers, the troublemakers had come to Thessalonica. Their seditious and revolutionary activity was not only illegal in itself; they were

7. Gk. δῆμος. As Thessalonica was a free city, its civic assembly (comprising the citizen body) discharged legislative and juridical functions. The law in many Greek cities, like Roman law, depended largely on private informers to set it in motion.

8. The title πολιτάρχης or πολίταρχος is found in some 32 inscriptions from the second century B.C. to the third century A.D., being used in the majority of these for the magistrates of Macedonian cities. The form πολιτάρχης is otherwise attested in inscriptions only; πολίταρχος occurs in Aeneas Tacticus, *Siege Warfare* 26.12. The similar term πολιάρχης/πολίαρχος was used for the magistrates of Thessalian cities. See E. D. Burton, "The Politarchs," *AJT* 2 (1898), pp. 598-632; C. Schuler, "The Macedonian Politarchs," *Classical Philology* 55 (1960), pp. 90-100; J. H. Oliver, "Civic Constitutions for Macedonian Communities," *Classical Philology* 58 (1963), pp. 164-65; F. Gschnitzer, "Politarchēs," PW Supplement 13 (1973), cols. 483-500; J. M. R. Cormack, "The Gymnasiarchal Law of Beroea," in *Ancient Macedonia*, ed. B. Laourdas and Ch. Makaronas, II (Thessaloniki, 1977), pp. 140-41; B. Helly, "Politarques, Poliarques et Politophylaques," in *Ancient Macedonia*, II, pp. 531-44; cf. *New Docs.* 2 (1977), § 5.

9. This is the sense of the verb ἀναστατόω, which is regularly used pejoratively, as in 21:38 below (cf. Gal. 5:12, οἱ ἀναστατοῦντες ὑμᾶς, "those who unsettle you"). It appears in Dan. 7:23 LXX in the sense of "trample down"; it is found also in vernacular papyri, notably in the letter from the bad boy Theon to his father (*P. Oxy.* 119.10, second/third century A.D.), where he quotes his harassed mother as saying ἀναστατοῖ με, ἆρρον αὐτόν ("he upsets me; away with him!").

10. Suetonius, *Claudius* 25.4 (see on 18:2 below).

11. See Claudius's letter to the Alexandrines (*P. Lond.* 1912).

actually proclaiming one Jesus as a rival emperor to him who ruled in Rome. This was a subtle charge: even an unfounded suspicion of this kind was enough to ruin anyone against whom it was brought. In the present instance there was just enough color of truth in the charge to make it plausible and deadly. The missionaries proclaimed the kingdom of God—a very different kingdom, to be sure, from any secular empire—and they may even have given Jesus the Greek designation *basileus* ("king"), which was accorded to the Roman emperor by many of his Greek-speaking subjects.[12] This Jesus, moreover, had been executed for sedition by the sentence of a Roman judge.

It may be that more than straightforward sedition was implied in the charge that Paul and his colleagues contravened "Caesar's decrees."[13] Sedition *(maiestas)* was an offense against public law[14] and required no special decree of Caesar to make it illegal. But it is plain from the summary of the apostolic message which the Thessalonians accepted (1 Thess. 1:9-10), and from other references in the Thessalonian correspondence, that there was a strong eschatological emphasis in the preaching. Such teaching as that reflected in 2 Thess. 2:5-7, with its veiled allusion to the removal of the imperial power, might well have been construed as infringing one or more of Caesar's decrees.[15] Augustus and Tiberius had been very sensitive about the activities of astrologers and other prognosticators and had issued decrees forbidding predictions or inquiries affecting affairs of state or the emperor's personal well-being.[16]

8-9   On hearing these charges, the politarchs shared the crowd's perturbation. It was their responsibility to make sure that the imperial decrees were respected in the city.[17] The provincial administration, not to speak of the imperial authorities in Rome, would not be pleased if they treated such grave accusations lightly. But, unlike the magistrates at Philippi (who reacted so violently to a much less serious charge), they behaved very sanely. The evidence for the charge was scanty, and the men against whom it was really brought could not be found. Jason and his associates were made responsible for seeing that there was no more trouble; they had to give

---

12. The emperor is called βασιλεύς in John 19:15; 1 Pet. 2:13, 17.

13. See E. A. Judge, "The Decrees of Caesar at Thessalonica," *RTR* 30 (1971), pp. 1-7.

14. See R. A. Bauman, *The* Crimen Maiestatis *in the Roman Republic and Augustan Principate* (Johannesburg, 1967); *Impietas in Principem* (Munich, 1974); C. W. Chilton, "The Roman Law of Treason under the Early Principate," *JRS* 45 (1955), pp. 73-81.

15. "It would not have been hard to interpret such announcements as predictions of a change of ruler" (E. A. Judge, "The Decrees of Caesar. . . ," p. 3).

16. Dio Cassius, *Hist.* 56.15.5-6; 57.15.8; cf. also Tacitus, *Annals* 2.27-32; Paulus, *Sententiae* 5.21.

17. Cf. E. A. Judge, *The Social Pattern of the Christian Groups in the First Century* (London, 1960), pp. 34-35.

security for the missionaries' good conduct, and this meant in practice that the missionaries had to leave the city quietly and not return.

Paul and his friends had no choice in the matter. Paul would have liked to stay and strengthen his converts with further teaching. By this time his converts from outright paganism outnumbered those who had believed the gospel when they heard it in the synagogue: the clear testimony of the Thessalonian correspondence is that those who received it had "turned to God from idols" (1 Thess. 1:9). Would such people's faith survive Paul's sudden departure (leaving them, as it might appear, in the lurch) and the pressure which was bound to be exerted on them to return to their former way of life? It is probably with regard to this situation that Paul told them, some weeks later, that he was eager to go back and see them, "but Satan hindered us" (1 Thess. 2:18).[18] He might well discern satanic machinations behind the politarchs' decision, while they themselves would regard their decision as mild but effective. In the event, the newly planted church of Thessalonica was subjected to open persecution and more subtle forms of discouragement, yet it maintained its faith and witness in a manner that filled the hearts of Paul and his companions with unbounded joy when they learned of it.

3. Beroea (17:10-15)

10 Then the brothers sent off Paul and Silas secretly by night to Beroea. When they arrived there, they made their way to the Jewish synagogue.

11 The Beroean Jews were more open-minded than those of Thessalonica: they accepted the message with all eagerness and examined the scriptures daily to see if these things were so.[19]

12 Many of them believed, then, as well as a considerable number of the. Greek women of better class, and men also.[20]

13 But when the Jews of Thessalonica learned that the word of God had been proclaimed in Beroea also, they came there too, disturbing the[21] crowds and throwing them into agitation.[22]

14 Then the brothers immediately sent off Paul to make his way as far as the sea,[23] while Silas and Timothy stayed behind in Beroea.

15 The men who were conducting Paul took him to Athens.[24] Then they

18. Cf. W. M. Ramsay, *St. Paul the Traveller* (London, [14]1920), p. 231.

19. The Western text adds "as Paul declared."

20. The Western text reads: "some of them therefore believed, but some did not believe [cf. 28:24], and many of the Greeks, both men and women of the better class, believed" (the Western reviser reverses the priority given to women).

21. The Western text expands: "and did not cease disturbing."

22. P^{45} omits "and throwing . . . into agitation."

23. ἕως ἐπὶ τὴν θάλασσαν. The Byzantine text reads ὡς ἐπὶ τὴν θάλασσαν ("as if to the sea"), the Western text reads ἐπὶ τὴν θάλασσαν ("to the sea").

24. After "Athens" the Western text continues: "but he passed by Thessaly, for he was prevented from preaching the word to them [an imitation of 16:6-8?]; and they

took their departure, after receiving orders for Silas and Timothy to come to him there as quickly as possible.

10 Paul and Silas were spirited away from Thessalonica by their friends who had guaranteed their departure, and made their way to Beroea. They had to leave the Egnatian Way and take the road which led south, to Thessaly and the province of Achaia. Paul, it is thought by some, had conceived the plan of traveling along the Egnatian Way to its Adriatic terminus, where it would have been a simple matter to cross the Straits of Otranto and take the road to Rome. He makes it clear that he had planned to visit Rome several times before he actually did so (Rom. 1:13; 15:22).[25] But if he had tried to do so at this time, he might have found his plan frustrated: he would probably have met Jews from Rome traveling eastward along the Egnatian Way, telling how the Emperor Claudius had expelled them from the capital. His turning south may have been contrary to his plan but, as events proved, it was in the plan of God.

Beroea is described by Cicero as an "out-of-the-way town,"[26] but all that he means is that it lay off the Egnatian Way. It is about forty miles west-southwest of Thessalonica, on a tributary of the Haliacmon at the foot of Mount Bermios. It was the first city of Macedonia to surrender to the Romans at the end of the Third Macedonian War (168 B.C.); it was then included in the third of the four districts into which Macedonia was divided. At Beroea Paul and Silas were rejoined by Timothy.

11-12 Here too there was a Jewish synagogue, but when it was visited by Paul and Silas the congregation gave their message a reception far different from that given by the Jews of Thessalonica. With admirable freedom from prejudice,[27] they brought the missionaries' claims to the touchstone of Holy Writ. Their procedure is worthy of imitation by all who have some new form of religious teaching pressed on their acceptance. These Beroean Jews would have been surprised could they have foreseen how many Christian groups of later days would call themselves "Beroeans" after their noble example of Bible study. As might be expected from people who welcomed the gospel so eagerly, many of them believed. As at Thessalonica, the believers included many God-fearing Greeks, both men and

---

departed, having received an order from Paul to Silas and Timothy to come to him quickly."

25. Cf. A. Harnack, *The Mission and Expansion of Christianity,* E.T., I (Edinburgh, 1908), pp. 74-77; H. J. Cadbury, *The Book of Acts in History* (New York, 1955), pp. 60-61; E. A. Judge and G. S. R. Thomas, "The Origin of the Church at Rome," *RTR* 25 (1966), p. 90; G. Bornkamm, *Paul,* E.T. (London, 1971), pp. 51-55; A. Suhl, *Paulus und seine Briefe* (Gütersloh, 1975), pp. 94-96.

26. *Against Piso* 36.89.

27. This seems to be meant here by εὐγενέστεϱοι, "more open-minded," lit. "more noble."

women, and some of these, particularly the women, belonged to leading families in the city. Among the Beroean converts one at least is known to us by name—Sopater son of Pyrrhus, mentioned below in 20:4.[28]

13 But as, on an earlier missionary journey, the Jews of Pisidian Antioch and Iconium followed the missionaries to Lystra and stirred up trouble for them there, so now the Jews of Thessalonica, hearing that Paul and Silas had arrived in Beroea, sent a deputation there to repeat the course of action that had been so effective in Thessalonica.

14-15 Once again Paul, the main target for the opposition, had to be gotten out of the city quickly and quietly. Some of his Beroean friends took him to the coast—to Methone or Dium—and put him on board a ship bound for Piraeus (the port of Athens). There is, however, another reading of the text (represented in KJV)[29] which implies that they made as though they were taking him to the coast, but actually, having thus thrown possible pursuers off their track, escorted him southward by road as far as Athens. One way or the other, he arrived at Athens, and sent his Beroean friends back with instructions to Silas and Timothy to come and rejoin him there as soon as possible, while he waited for them.[30]

4. Athens (17:16-21)

16 *While Paul waited for them in Athens, it irked his spirit within him to see the city so full of idols.*

17 *So he conversed in the synagogue with the Jews and God-fearers and in the* agora *day by day with those who chanced to be around.*

18 *Some of the Epicurean and Stoic philosophers also met with him. Some asked, "What would this charlatan be at?" Others said, "He seems to be advertising foreign divinities" —because he was preaching the gospel of Jesus and the Resurrection.*

19 *So they laid hold on him and brought him to the Areopagus. There they said, "May we know what this new teaching is, of which you speak?*

20 *You are bringing some strange things to our notice; we should like to know what they mean."*

28. Perhaps identical with the Sosipater of Rom. 16:21.

29. The Byzantine reading (cf. p. 326, n. 23).

30. Silas and Timothy's movements between Paul's departure from Beroea and their rejoining him at Corinth (18:5) must be reconstructed with the aid of 1 Thess. 3:1-6. It appears that, as instructed, they rejoined Paul in Athens (1 Thess. 3:1), from which Timothy was sent back to Thessalonica (1 Thess. 3:2). (T. W. Manson suggested that on this occasion Timothy was the bearer of 2 Thessalonians, which he believed to have been written before 1 Thessalonians.) Silas also went back to Macedonia—where exactly is not indicated (18:5). Paul then went on from Athens to Corinth (18:1), where he was rejoined by Silas and Timothy on their return from Macedonia (18:5; 1 Thess. 3:6). See K. Lake, *The Earlier Epistles of St. Paul* (London, 1911), p. 74; T. W. Manson, *Studies in the Gospels and Epistles* (Manchester, 1962), pp. 266-67.

21 *Now all the Athenians and the resident foreigners found time for nothing else than telling or hearing the latest novelty.*

16   Although Athens had long since lost the political eminence which was hers in an earlier day, she continued to represent the highest level of culture attained in classical antiquity. The sculpture, literature, and oratory of Athens in the fifth and fourth centuries B.C. have, indeed, never been surpassed. In philosophy, too, she occupied the leading place, being the native city of Socrates and Plato, and the adopted home of Aristotle, Epicurus, and Zeno. In all these fields Athens retained unchallenged prestige, and her political glory as the cradle of democracy was not completely dimmed. In consideration of her splendid past, the Romans gave Athens the right to maintain her own institutions as a free and allied city within the Roman Empire.[31]

Visitors to Athens today who view the masterpieces of the great architects and sculptors of the age of Pericles are free to admire them as works of art: to no one nowadays are they anything more. But in the first Christian century they were not only admired as works of art: they were temples and images of pagan divinities. Temples and images of pagan divinities were no new thing to a native of Tarsus, but this native of Tarsus had been brought up in the spirit of the first and second commandments of the decalogue. Whatever Paul may have felt in the way of artistic appreciation—and his education had not fostered any capacity for this—the feeling that was uppermost in his mind as he walked here and there through the violet-crowned city was one of indignation: the city was full of idols, dedicated to the worship of gods that were no gods—for "what pagans sacrifice they offer to demons and not to God" (1 Cor. 10:20).

17   Paul was not the man to take a holiday from the main business of his life, so he did not while away the time while he waited for his friends to rejoin him from the north. In any case, the spectacle of a city so entirely dedicated to false worship stirred him to the conviction that here, if anywhere, were men and women who sorely needed the gospel with which he had been entrusted. Athens afforded him ample confirmation of what he had already learned, that, "in the wisdom of God, the world did not know God through wisdom" (1 Cor. 1:21). He visited the synagogue in Athens, therefore, and held discourse there with Jews and God-fearing Gentiles, while in the Agora, the center of Athenian life and activity, he debated day by day with those who happened to be around. It has often been observed how subtly and accurately Luke suggests the local color and atmosphere of each city with which he deals. "In Ephesus Paul taught 'in the school of Tyran-

31. See D. J. Geagan, "Roman Athens: Some Aspects of Life and Culture, I. 86 B.C.-A.D. 267," *ANRW* 2.7.1 (Berlin, 1975), pp. 371-437.

nus'; in the city of Socrates he discussed moral questions in the market-place. How incongruous it would seem if the methods were transposed!"[32] The Agora lay north of the Acropolis. If it was the first place for which Paul made on coming to Athens, he would have seen herms (square pillars surmounted by a head of Hermes) wherever he looked, "a veritable forest of idols."[33]

18 Among those with whom Paul met and conversed in the Agora were philosophers of the rival Stoic and Epicurean schools.

The Stoics, who claimed the Cypriot Zeno (*c*. 340-265 B.C.) as their founder, were so called because they met in the *stoa poikilē*, the "painted colonnade" in the Agora, where he habitually taught in Athens. Their system aimed at living consistently with nature, and in practice they laid great emphasis on the primacy of the rational faculty in humanity, and on individual self-sufficiency. In theology they were essentially pantheistic, God being regarded as the world-soul. Their belief in a *cosmopolis* or world-state, in which all truly free souls had equal citizen rights, helped to break down national and class distinctions. Stoicism at its best was marked by great moral earnestness and a high sense of duty. It commended suicide as an honorable means of escape from a life that could no longer be sustained with dignity. Something of the proud spirit of personal independence which it fostered comes to expression in W. E. Henley's *Invictus:*

> "I thank whatever gods may be
> For my unconquerable soul."

As it happens, another English poet uses the same phrase, "whatever gods may be," in a setting as distinctively Epicurean as Henley's is essentially Stoic. That is A. C. Swinburne in *The Garden of Proserpine:*

> "From too much love of living,
> From hope and fear set free,
> We thank with brief thanksgiving
> Whatever gods may be
> That no life lives for ever;
> That dead men rise up never;
> That even the weariest river
> Winds somewhere safe to sea."

The Epicurean school, founded by Epicurus (340-270 B.C.), member of a family of Athenian settlers on Samos, based its ethical theory on the atomic physics of Democritus and presented pleasure as being the chief end in life, the pleasure most worth enjoying being a life of tranquillity *(ataraxia)*, free

---

32. W. M. Ramsay, *St. Paul the Traveller*, p. 238.
33. R. E. Wycherley, "St. Paul at Athens," *JTS* n.s. 19 (1968), pp. 619-20; cf. S. Halstead, "Paul in the Agora," in *Quantulacumque: Studies presented to K. Lake* (London, 1937), pp. 139-43.

from pain, disturbing passions, and superstitious fears (including in particular the fear of death). It did not deny the existence of gods, but maintained that they took no interest in the life of men and women.

Stoicism and Epicureanism represented alternative attempts in pre-Christian paganism to come to terms with life, especially in times of uncertainty and hardship; post-Christian paganism has never been able to devise anything appreciably better. But Stoics and Epicureans alike, much as they might differ from each other, agreed at least on this: that the new-fangled message brought by this Jew of Tarsus was not one that could appeal to reasonable people. They looked on him as a retailer of secondhand scraps of philosophy, "a picker-up of learning's crumbs" (like Browning's Karshish), a type of itinerant peddler of religion not unknown in the Agora, and they used a term of disparaging Athenian slang to describe him.[34] Others preferred to class him as a propagandist for foreign divinities—he spoke of Jesus and *Anastasis* (the Greek word for "resurrection"), and to some of his hearers these two words sounded as if they denoted the personified and divinized powers of "healing" and "restoration."[35]

19-20 But there was in Athens a venerable institution, the Court of the Areopagus, which exercised jurisdiction in matters of religion and morals. This aristocratic body, of venerable antiquity, received its name from the Areopagus, the "hill of Ares" (the Greek god of war), southwest of the Acropolis, on which it traditionally met. At the time with which we are dealing it held its ordinary meetings in the Royal Colonnade *(stoa basileios)*, in the northwest corner of the Agora.[36] (It continued to meet on the Areopagus to judge cases of homicide.) Its traditional power was curtailed with the growth of Athenian democracy in the fifth century B.C., but in Roman times its authority was enhanced and it commanded great respect.[37] Before this body, then, Paul was brought, not to stand trial in a forensic

---

34. Gk. σπερμολόγος, lit. "seed-picker," "gutter-sparrow"; then someone who picked up scraps in the market, a worthless character (cf. Demosthenes's description of Aeschines as σπερμολόγος, περίτριμμα ἀγορᾶς, "a prater, a market hack," *On the Crown* 127); then of someone who picked up scraps of learning wherever he could, which is the meaning here.

35. F. H. Chase, *The Credibility of Acts* (London, 1902), pp. 205-6) suggests that they may have associated Ἰησοῦς with ἴασις ("healing") or with Ἰασώ (Ionic Ἰησώ), the goddess of health, a daughter of Asklepios. "This interpretation of the words Ἰησοῦς and ἀνάστασις would be confirmed in the minds of the Athenians if they caught the words σωτηρία and σωτήρ in St. Paul's teaching." The view that he was a preacher of foreign divinities recalls the charges brought at an earlier date in Athens against Protagoras, Anaxagoras, and Socrates (cf. Plato, *Euthyphro* 3B, *Apology* 24B-C; Xenophon, *Memorabilia* 1.1.1).

36. See C. J. Hemer, "Paul at Athens: A Topographical Note," *NTS* 20 (1973-74), pp. 341-50.

37. See D. J. Geagan, *The Athenian Constitution after Sulla* (Princeton, 1950), p. 50: "Ordo Areopagitarum Atheniensium," in *Phoros: Tribute to E. D. Meritt,* ed. D. W. Bradeen and M. F. McGregor (New York, 1974), pp. 51-56.

sense, nor yet to be examined with a view to being licensed as a public lecturer,[38] but simply to have an opportunity of expounding his teaching before experts.

21 Then, commenting on the Athenians' interest in the novelty of Paul's teaching, Luke sums up their general attitude in a sentence which Eduard Norden described as "the most cultured thing to be found anywhere in the New Testament."[39] The Athenians themselves admitted that their passion for anything new could be carried to excess; the orator Demosthenes, for example, four centuries earlier, had reproached them for going about asking what was the latest news in a day when Philip of Macedon's aggressive policy called for deeds, not words.[40]

5. Paul's Areopagitica (17:22-31)

22 *So, standing in the midst of the Areopagus (court),[41] Paul said, "Gentlemen of Athens! I see that you are uncommonly religious in everything.*

23 *As I was passing through (your city) and looking at your objects of worship, I found an altar bearing the inscription: 'To the Unknown God.' This God, whom you worship as one unknown, is the God of whom I tell you.*

24 *The God who made the world and everything in it, Lord of heaven and earth as he is, does not reside in temples made with hands.*

25 *It is not because he is in need of anything that he accepts service from the hands of human beings; it is from him that all receive life, breath, and everything.*

26 *From one man[42] he has made every nation of mankind to inhabit the whole of earth's surface. He appointed the allotted seasons and the frontiers of their residence,*

27 *in order that they might seek God,[43] if indeed they might grope for him and find him. Indeed, he is not far from each one of us,*

---

38. This was Ramsay's view (*St. Paul the Traveller*, p. 247); he recalls how "Cicero induced the Areopagus to pass a decree inviting Cratippus, the Peripatetic philosopher, to become a lecturer in Athens," and infers "that some advantage was thereby secured to him" (cf. Plutarch, *Cicero* 24.5).

39. *Agnostos Theos* (Leipzig, 1913), p. 333.

40. Demosthenes, *Philippic* 1.10; cf. Cleon's reproach: "you are the best people at being deceived by something new that is said" (Thucydides, *Hist.* 2.38.5).

41. Gk. ἐν μέσῳ τοῦ Ἀρείου πάγου. The phrase "in the midst" shows that it is the court, not the hill, that is meant here by "the Areopagus" (cf. ἐκ μέσου αὐτῶν, v. 33; ἐν τῷ μέσῳ, 4:7). That the full expression "the court (council) of the Areopagus" was shortened in common parlance to "the Areopagus" is attested by Cicero (*Letters to Atticus* 1.14.5), Seneca (*On Tranquillity* 5), Valerius Maximus (*Memorable Deeds and Words* 2.64), and by an inscription at Epidaurus (*IG* 4.937.2).

42. Gk. ἐξ ἑνός. The Western and Byzantine texts add αἵματος (cf. KJV "of one blood").

43. The Western text reads "especially that they might seek the divine nature" (τὸ θεῖον, as in v. 29).

28 *'for in him we live and move and have our being'*
—as indeed some of your[44] poets[45] have said:
'for we are truly his offspring.'

29 *Since, then, we are God's offspring, we ought not to think that the divine nature is like gold or silver or stone, the engraving of human art and design.*

30 *God has overlooked the times of ignorance, but now his command to all people everywhere is to repent,*

31 *because he has set a day on which he is going to judge[46] the world in righteousness, by a man whom he has appointed; and of this he has provided a pledge to all, by raising him from the dead."*

22 Probably no ten verses in Acts have formed the text for such an abundance of commentary as has gathered around Paul's Areopagus speech.[47]

---

44. P^{74} B and a few other witnesses read "our" (καθ' ἡμᾶς) for "your" (καθ' ὑμᾶς); "our" may have been judged appropriate because Aratus, about to be quoted, was a Cilician like Paul.

45. The Western text omits "poets" (the meaning then is "your own men"); the Peshitta Syriac has "wise men" instead of "poets."

46. The Western text reads "a day for judging" (ἡμέραν κρῖναι).

47. See, in addition to discussions in commentaries, E. Curtius, "St. Paul in Athens" (1893), E.T. in *Exp.* 7, 4 (1907), pp. 436-55; E. Norden, *Agnostos Theos: Untersuchungen zur Formengeschichte religiöser Rede* (Leipzig/Berlin, 1913, ²1929), pp. 1-140; A. von Harnack, *Ist die Rede des Paulus in Athen ein ursprünglicher Bestandteil der Apostelgeschichte?* = *TU* 39.1 (Leipzig, 1913); R. Reitzenstein, "Die Areopagrede des Paulus," *Neue Jahrbücher für das klassische Altertum* 31 (1913), pp. 393-422; E. Meyer, *Ursprung und Anfänge des Christentums*, III (Stuttgart/Berlin, 1923), pp. 89-108; A. Schweitzer, *The Mysticism of Paul the Apostle*, E.T. (London, 1931), pp. 6-9; W. L. Knox, *St. Paul and the Church of the Gentiles* (Cambridge, 1939), pp. 1-26; W. Schmid, "Die Rede des Apostels Paulus vor den Philosophen und Areopagiten in Athen," *Philologus* 95 (1942), pp. 79-120; M. Pohlenz, *Paulus und die Stoa* (1949; Darmstadt, 1964); M. Dibelius, "Paul on the Areopagus" (1939) and "Paul in Athens" (1939), E.T. in *Studies in the Acts of the Apostles* (London, 1956), pp. 26-92; A. D. Nock, "The Book of Acts" (1953), *Essays on Religion and the Ancient World*, II (Oxford, 1972), pp. 829-32; W. Eltester, "Gott und Natur in der Areopagrede," in *Neutestamentliche Studien für Rudolf Bultmann*, ed. W. Eltester, BZNW 21 (1954), pp. 202-27; G. Schrenk, *Studien zu Paulus* (Zürich, 1954), pp. 131-48; B. Gärtner, *The Areopagus Speech and Natural Revelation* (Lund, 1955); H. Hommel, "Neue Forschungen zur Areopagrede Acta 17," *ZNW* 46 (1955), pp. 145-78; W. Nauck, "Die Tradition und Komposition der Areopagrede," *ZTK* 53 (1956), pp. 11-52; N. B. Stonehouse, *Paul Before the Areopagus and Other New Testament Studies* (Grand Rapids, 1957), pp. 1-40; H. Conzelmann, "The Address of Paul on the Areopagus" (1958), E.T. in *Studies in Luke-Acts*, ed. L. E. Keck and J. L. Martyn (Nashville/New York, 1966), pp. 217-30; H. P. Owen, "The Scope of Natural Revelation in Romans 1 and Acts 17," *NTS* 5 (1958-59), pp. 133-43; R. E. Wycherley, "St. Paul at Athens," *JTS* n.s. 19 (1968), pp. 619-21; T. D. Barnes, "An Apostle on Trial," *JTS* n.s. 20 (1969), pp. 407-19; A.-M. Dubarle, "Le discours à l'Aréopage (Actes 17, 22-31) et son arrière-plan biblique," *RSPT* 57 (1973), pp. 576-610; S. G. Wilson, *The Gentiles and the Gentile Mission in Luke-Acts,* SNTSM 23 (Cambridge, 1973), pp. 196-218; C. J. Hemer, "Paul at Athens: A Topographical Note," *NTS* 20 (1973-74), pp. 341-50; C. K. Barrett, "Paul's Speech on the

Diametrically opposing views have been expressed on the question whether Paul did deliver, or indeed could have delivered, such a speech. In the earlier years of the twentieth century B. W. Bacon, a critic not marked by conservatism, concluded that this speech, "in distinction from that attributed to Paul in Acts 13:16-41, is really of Pauline type,"[48] whereas Percy Gardner found the viewpoint expressed in it so different from that of the first chapter of Romans, and indeed so contradictory to it, that he called it "the least authentic of the Pauline discourses in *Acts*."[49] Eduard Norden regarded it as out of the question that Paul could have delivered this speech; the historian Eduard Meyer, however, who confessed himself unable to understand "how this scene could be explained as an invention,"[50] claimed to have persuaded Norden to admit the possibility that Luke correctly reproduced the contents of a genuine speech of Paul.[51] But since then the careful stylistic studies of Martin Dibelius, leading to the conclusion that "Paul would never have written in this way,"[52] have weighed heavily with students of the speech: "what we have before us," he says, "is a *hellenistic* speech about the true knowledge of God."[53]

When the gospel was presented to pagans, even cultured pagans like the members of the Court of the Areopagus, it was necessary to begin with a statement about the living and true God. The knowledge of God, according to Paul in Rom. 1:19-22, was accessible to all in his works of creation, but the capacity or desire to acquire it had been impaired by idolatry. If the author of Romans 1-3 had been invited to address an Athenian audience on the knowledge of God, it is difficult to see how the general purport of his words could have been much different from what Luke here reports Paul as saying. The tone of the *Areopagitica* is different from that of Romans 1-3, but Paul knew the wisdom of adapting his tone and general approach to the particular audience or readership being addressed at the time.

If the address at Pisidian Antioch in 13:16-41 is intended to serve as a sample of Paul's preaching to a synagogue congregation, the present speech

---

Areopagus," in *New Testament Christianity for Africa and the World: Essays in honour of Harry Sawyerr*, ed. M. E. Glasswell and E. W. Fasholé-Luke (London, 1974), pp. 69-77.

48. *The Story of St. Paul* (London, 1905), p. 164.

49. "The Speeches of St. Paul in Acts," in *Cambridge Biblical Essays*, ed. H. B. Swete (Cambridge, 1909), p. 401.

50. *Ursprung und Anfänge des Christentums*, III, p. 105.

51. *Ursprung und Anfänge*, III, p. 92, n. 4. H. J. Cadbury remarks that "the classicists are among the most inclined to plead for the historicity of the scene at Athens" (*Beginnings* I.5, p. 406, n. 1). One outstanding exception to this rule was U. von Wilamowitz-Moellendorff: while second to none in his appreciation of Paul as "a classic of Hellenism," he felt he had no common ground with those who could attribute the *Areopagitica* to the Paul of the genuine epistles (*Die griechische Literatur des Altertums* = *Die Kultur der Gegenwart*, ed. P. Hinneberg, I.8 [Berlin/Leipzig, ³1912], p. 232).

52. M. Dibelius, *Studies*, p. 61.

53. *Studies*, p. 57.

is equally well designed to serve as a sample of his preaching to pagans (cf. the much briefer summary in 14:15-17). Here he does not quote Hebrew scriptures which would have been quite unknown to his hearers; the direct quotations in this speech are quotations from Greek poets. But he does not condescend to his hearers' level by arguing from first principles as one of their own philosophers might do. His argument is firmly based on biblical revelation; it echoes throughout the thought, and at times the very language, of the Old Testament. Like the biblical revelation itself, his argument begins with God the creator of all and ends with God the judge of all.

He starts by mentioning that what he has seen in their city has impressed him with the Athenians' extraordinary religiosity (an impression made on many other people in antiquity, some of whom considered the Athenians to be the most religious of all human beings).[54] This characterization of the Athenians by Paul was not necessarily meant to be complimentary: we are told that it was forbidden to use complimentary exordia in addressing the Areopagus court, with the hope of securing its goodwill.[55] The expression Paul used could also mean "rather superstitious"; it was as vague a term in Greek as "religion" is in English, and what was piety to Greeks was superstition to Jews (and *vice versa*).[56]

23 Paul goes on to tell them that, among their religious installations there was one which particularly attracted his attention: an altar inscribed "to the Unknown God" (or possibly "To an unknown god").[57] Other writers say that altars to "unknown gods" were to be seen at Athens;[58] Didymus of Alexandria[59] and Jerome probably had such statements in mind when they said that Paul changed the plural "gods" into the singular. Jerome[60] indeed says that the altar seen by Paul bore the inscription "To the gods of Asia, Europe and Africa, to unknown and foreign gods" (presumably he knew of such an altar-inscription in Athens, which he translates into Latin). But Paul may have seen an altar dedicated exactly as he says. When a

---

54. Cf. Sophocles, *Oedipus at Colonus* 260 ("they say that Athens is most pious towards the gods"); Josephus, *Ap.* 2.130 ("the most pious of the Greeks"); Pausanias, *Description of Greece* 1.17.1 ("the Athenians venerate the gods more than others"); also Strabo, *Geog.* 9.1.16; Livy, *Hist.* 45.27.

55. Cf. Lucian, *Anacharsis* 19.

56. Gk. δεισιδαιμονεστέρους. Cf. 25:19 for the noun δεισιδαιμονία.

57. Gk. ἀγνώστῳ θεῷ. Paul takes the reference to be to the one true God; the dedicators may have meant something different. The lapidary style would in any case dispense with the definite article.

58. Cf. Pausanias, *Description of Greece* 1.1.4; Philostratus, *Life of Apollonius* 6.3.5.

59. *Commentary on 2 Corinthians* (10:5).

60. *Commentary on Titus* (1:12). E. Norden (*Agnostos Theos*, pp. 118-20) thought this statement might be dependent on Minucius Felix (*Octavius* 6.2), according to whom the Romans venerated the gods of conquered nations, erecting altars to divinities unknown to themselves.

derelict altar was repaired and the original dedication could not be ascertained, the inscription "To the (an) unknown god" would have been quite appropriate. An altar on the Palatine hill in Rome was rebuilt about 100 B.C. and dedicated "whether to a god or to a goddess";[61] the vagueness of the wording reflects ignorance of the divinity in whose honor it had first been erected.[62]

This God whom they venerated, said Paul, while they confessed their ignorance of his identity, was the God whom he now proposed to make known to them. But he did not express himself quite so personally, as if unreservedly identifying the "unknown god" of the inscription with the God whom he proclaimed. He used neuter, not masculine, forms: "what therefore you worship as unknown, this I proclaim to you" (RSV).[63] Since they acknowledged their ignorance of the divine nature, he would tell them the truth about it.

24 He then begins to tell them about the true God. He it is who created the universe and everything in it; he is Lord of heaven and earth. Here is the God of biblical revelation; no distinction is pressed between a supreme being and a demiurge who fashioned the material world. The God who is creator of all and universal Lord is introduced in language strongly reminiscent of the Old Testament scriptures. Equally reminiscent of those scriptures is the language in which Paul describes the true God as not inhabiting sanctuaries built by human hands.[64] If even the shrine at Jerusalem, erected for the worship of the true God, could not contain him, how much less the splendid shrines on the Athenian Acropolis, dedicated as they were to divinities that had no real existence! True, even the higher paganism had acknowledged that no material house could accommodate the divine nature,[65] but the affinities of the terms here used by Paul are biblical rather than classical.

61. *CIL* I.632. Another parallel has been discerned in a Pergamene inscription of the imperial period, θεοῖς ἀγν[ώστοις] Καπίτ[ων] δαδοῦχος, "To un[known] gods: Capit[o], torchbearer" (H. Hepding, *Athenische Mitteilungen* 35 [1910], pp. 454-57; cf. A. Deissmann, *Paul*, E.T. [London, 1926], pp. 287-91, with Plates V and VI); but it is not certain if the second word is really ἀγνώστοις.

62. Mention should also be made of Diogenes Laertius, who tells (*Lives of Philosophers* 1.110) how the Athenians once, during a pestilence, sent for Epimenides, the wise man of Crete (*c.* 600 B.C.), who advised them to release black and white sheep from the Areopagus and then, on the spot where each lay down, to sacrifice it to "the appropriate god" (the god of the locality). Accordingly, says Diogenes, "anonymous altars" (altars to unnamed gods) might be seen throughout Attica. The presence of such altars is attested by other writers.

63. Cf. τὸ θεῖον, "the divine nature," in v. 29, instead of τὸν θεόν, "God." See N. B. Stonehouse, *Paul Before the Areopagus*, p. 19.

64. Cf. 1 Kings 8:27; Isa. 66:1-2; and see the discussion on the similar statement in Stephen's speech (pp. 149-51 above, on 7:47-50).

65. Cf. Euripides, fragment 968: "What house built by craftsmen could enclose the form divine within enfolding walls?"

25 The God who created all could not be envisaged as requiring anything from his creatures. If he is pleased to accept their service, it is not because he lacks something which they can supply. Here again parallels to Paul's argument can be adduced from Greek literature and philosophy.[66] But the great prophets of Israel also had to refute the false notion that God is somehow dependent on his people's worship and service, when they saw how many of their fellow Israelites were devoted to it. How can the Lord of heaven and earth *need* anything that his creatures can give him?

> "I will accept no bull from your house,
>   nor he-goat from your fold.
> For every beast of the forest is mine,
>   the cattle on a thousand hills.
> I know all the birds of the air,
>   and all that moves in the field is mine.
> If I were hungry, I would not tell you;
>   for the world and all that is in it is mine."[67]

Far from their being able to supply any need of his, it is he who supplies every need of theirs: to them all he gives "life, breath, and everything."

26 The creator of all things in general is creator of the human race in particular. The Athenians might pride themselves on being autochthonous—sprung from the soil of their native Attica[68]—but this pride was ill-founded. All mankind was one in origin—all created by God and all descended from a common ancestor. This removed all imagined justification for the belief that Greeks were innately superior to barbarians, as it removes all justification for comparable beliefs today. Neither in nature nor in grace, neither in the old creation nor in the new, is there any room for ideas of racial superiority.

And God, having created the whole race of human beings, has given them the whole earth for their dwelling place, allotting appropriate living space to each nation. Another interpretation, favored by Dibelius, is that God has appointed the habitable zones of the earth for the human family to live in.[69] But the divine allocation of national territories has biblical authority, the *locus classicus* being Deut. 32:8:

---

66. Cf. Euripides, *Heracles* 1345-36 ("God, if he be truly God, has need of nothing"); Plato, *Euthyphro* 14C ("What advantage accrues to the gods from what they get from us?").

67. Ps. 50:9-12. The psalmist's argument is precisely Paul's: God has no need of anything because he is owner of everything. It is strange, then, that M. Dibelius should say that "only twice is it emphasized in the LXX that God needs nothing, but even these two passages are sufficient to prove the Greek origin of the idea" (*Studies*, p. 44); he refers to 2 Macc. 14:35 and 3 Macc. 2:9. Cf. Mic. 6:6-8.

68. This belief reflects the historic fact that the Athenians were the only Greeks on the European mainland who had no tradition of their ancestors' coming into Greece: they belonged to the earliest (Ionic) movement of Greek immigration.

69. Cf. Dibelius, *Studies,* pp. 35-37.

"When the Most High gave to the nations their inheritance,
when he separated the sons of men,
he fixed the bounds of the peoples
according to the number of the sons of God."[70]

According to the Genesis account, the earth was formed and furnished to be a home for humanity before humanity itself was brought into being to occupy it; the tenses of the Greek verbs here similarly suggest that "the determination of man's home *preceded* his creation, in the Divine plan."[71] And part of the forming and furnishing of this home consisted in the regulation of the "allotted seasons," by which, after the analogy of the Lystran speech (14:17), we are probably to understand the seasons of the year by whose sequence annual provision is made for the supply of food. (Another, but less likely, interpretation sees in the "allotted seasons"[72] the divinely determined periods for the rise and fall of empires, as in the visions of the book of Daniel.)

27 What was God's purpose in thus arranging time and place so providentially for men and women's well-being? It was, says Paul, in order that they might seek God and find him.[73] Ever since the creation, he says in Rom. 1:20, the things that God has made have pointed clearly to "his everlasting power and divinity." If human beings, beguiled and confused by false worship, have failed to perceive the nature of God in the works of creation, they are without excuse. The attitude expressed in the letter to the Romans is not so widely different from that of the *Areopagitica*. There is, indeed, a difference of emphasis: in that letter Paul writes to established Christians, while here he is trying to gain a hearing from pagans; but there is no hint in the speech that the Athenians' confessed ignorance of the divine nature was blameless. Even some of their own teachers had realized the folly of trying to represent the divine nature by material images, worship it at material altars, or house it in material temples, and had perceived, however dimly, how near God was to those who truly sought him.[74]

28 At this point Paul illustrated his argument by two quotations from Greek poets in which the relation of humanity to the supreme God was set forth. One of these appears to have been the fourth line of a quatrain preserved from a poem attributed to Epimenides the Cretan (*c*. 600 B.C.), but actually of later date:

70. MT reads ". . . sons of Israel"; but the LXX reading is attested in Hebrew in one Qumran manuscript (4QDt[q]).

71. J. H. Moulton, MHT I (Edinburgh, 1906), p. 133.

72. Gk. προστεταγμένοι καιροί. Cf. Luke 21:24, καιροὶ ἐθνῶν, the period appointed for Gentile domination of Jerusalem (the resemblance is mainly verbal).

73. The verb ψηλαφάω conveys the idea of "groping" after God in the darkness or semi-darkness, when the light of his full revelation is not available.

74. A verbal link has been found in Dio Chrysostom, *Oration* 12.28, where those

"They fashioned a tomb for thee, O holy and high one—
The Cretans, always liars, evil beasts, idle bellies!—
But thou art not dead; thou livest and abidest for ever,
For in thee we live and move and have our being."[75]

The other is part of the fifth line of the *Phainomena* of Paul's fellow-Cilician Aratus (born 310 B.C.), which opens with the words:

"Let us begin with Zeus. Never, O men, let us leave him
unmentioned. All the ways are full of Zeus,
and all the market-places of human beings. The sea is full
of him; so are the harbors. In every way we have all to do with Zeus,
for we are truly his offspring."[76]

In both these poems Zeus is considered not as the ruler of the traditional pantheon of Greek mythology but as the supreme being of Greek, and especially Stoic, philosophy. But did Paul intend to identify the Zeus of Greek philosophy *simpliciter* with the God of biblical revelation, whom in his letters he repeatedly calls "the God and Father of our Lord Jesus Christ"? Quite certainly not. Is he then simply detaching from their original contexts sentiments which, so far as their actual phraseology goes, lend themselves to incorporation into his Judaeo-Christian context? Again, no. Even in their contexts, the words quoted (especially those of Aratus) could be taken as pointing to some recognition of the true nature of God—that recognition which, according to the writer to the Hebrews, is his reward to "those who seek him" (Heb. 11:6); they "could be acknowledged," says N. B. Stonehouse, "as up to a point involving an actual apprehension of revealed truth."[77]

---

of primaeval days are described as "not settled separately by themselves far away (οὐ μακράν, as here) from the divine being or outside of him, but . . . sharing his nature."

75. The quatrain is quoted in a Syriac version by the ninth-century commentator Isho'dad (ed. M. D. Gibson, *Horae Semiticae*, X [Cambridge, 1913], p. 40). Isho'dad was probably dependent here on Theodore of Mopsuestia (350-428); he reproduces Theodore's use of Diogenes Laertius's story (see p. 336, n. 62) to illustrate the inscription "To the unknown God." The Cretans' claim to be able to point out the tomb of Zeus was felt to be an impious falsehood. The second line of the quatrain is quoted in Tit. 1:12; according to Clement of Alexandria (*Miscellanies* 1.14.59.1-2) it comes from a work by Epimenides. A similar sentiment appears in Callimachus's *Hymn to Zeus* (lines 7-8): "Cretans are always liars: for the Cretans, O King, actually fashioned a tomb for thee. But thou hast not died; thou art for ever." The line here quoted by Paul can with little difficulty be given hexameter form; Cod. D spoils the rhythm by adding "day by day" at the end of it.

76. These last words (τοῦ γὰρ καὶ γένος ἐσμέν) may have been imitated by Aratus from the opening words of line 4 of Cleanthes' *Hymn to Zeus* (ἐκ σοῦ γὰρ γένος ἐσμέν). K. Lake (*Beginnings* I.5, p. 247) points out that the immediately following lines of the poem by Aratus have "a strong general resemblance" to v. 26 of Paul's *Areopagitica*.

77. *Paul Before the Areopagus*, p. 30; cf. R. Stob, *Christianity and Classical Civilization* (Grand Rapids, 1950), pp. 58-60.

29 We are, then, the offspring of God, says Paul, not in any pantheistic sense but in the sense of the biblical doctrine of man, as beings created by God in his own image. There is, indeed, a mighty difference between this relation of men and women to God in the old creation and that redemptive relation which members of the new creation enjoy through faith as sons and daughters of God "in Christ Jesus" (Gal. 3:26). But Paul is dealing here with the responsibility of all human beings as creatures of God to give him the honor which is his due. And this honor is certainly not given if they envisage the divine nature in the form of plastic images.[78] Even if pagan philosophers rationalize the images as material symbols of the invisible divinity, the great bulk of the worshipers will pay divine homage to the images themselves.

30 The Athenians had good reason, then, to acknowledge their ignorance of God. But, even if such ignorance was not free from blame, God in mercy had passed it over. There is a parallel here not only to the statement in the Lystran speech that in past generations God "allowed all the nations to go their own ways" (14:16),[79] but also to Paul's teaching in Rom. 3:25 about God's forbearance in passing over sins committed before the coming of Christ. It is implied in all these places that the coming of Christ marks a fresh start in God's dealings with the human race. In the present place God's overlooking people's earlier ignorance of himself is seen to have had in view the full revelation now given in the advent and work of Christ. "But now" in the present context is parallel to "but now" in Rom. 3:21.[80] If ignorance of the divine nature was culpable before, it is inexcusable now. Let all people everywhere (the Athenian hearers included) repent therefore of their false conception of God (and consequent flouting of his will)[81] and embrace the true knowledge of his being now made available in the gospel.

31 For God the creator of all is also God the judge of all. Already in his sovereign counsel he has fixed a day in which he will "judge the world in righteousness"[82]—another biblical expression. Greek thought had no room

78. This is an echo of the OT polemic against image-worship found in such passages as Isa. 44:9-20; Ps. 115 (LXX 114):4-8 par. 135 (LXX 134):15-18; the argument is developed in Wisd. 13:5, 10; 15:4, 15-17; in the *Letter of Aristeas* 134-37; and by the early Christian apologists.

79. This, says W. L. Knox, "is simply another way of saying that God 'handed them over to a reprobate mind'" (*The Acts of the Apostles* [Cambridge, 1948], p. 70, referring to Rom. 1:28).

80. "But now" in Rom. 3:21 is related to the revelation of God's way of righteousness in Christ and his atoning death.

81. For the association of repentance with the passing over of sins cf. Wisd. 11:23, "thou dost overlook men's sins, that they may repent."

82. Cf. Ps. 9:8; 96 (LXX 95):13; 98 (LXX 97):9. For other Pauline references to the appointed day of judgment cf. Rom. 2:5, 16; 1 Cor. 1:8; Phil. 1:6, 10; 1 Thess. 5:2, 4; 2 Thess. 1:10; 2:2.

for such an eschatological judgment as the biblical revelation announces.[83] But not only is the judgment day fixed; the agent of the judgment has also been appointed.[84] Paul does not refer directly to the human figure—the "one like a son of man"—of Dan. 7:13; but this is "the man" whom he has in mind, the one in whom God's eternal purpose finds its fulfilment, the one to whom the Father has given "authority to execute judgment, because he is Son of Man" (John 5:27).[85] Moreover, he assures his audience, God has furnished firm proof that this is the man through whom he is going to judge the world, because this is the man whom he has raised from the dead.

Thus, then, Paul concludes his *Areopagitica*. There is no need to suppose that the speech was seriously curtailed by the ridicule with which some members of the audience received his reference to Jesus' rising from the dead. The speech as it stands admirably summarizes an introductory lesson in Christianity for cultured pagans. The first thing the Athenians, like the Thessalonians, had to learn was to "turn to God from idols, to serve a living and true God" (1 Thess. 1:9). Therefore the greater part of the speech is, as Dibelius observed, concerned with the true knowledge of God. He qualified it as "a *hellenistic* speech about the true knowledge of God";[86] with this too one can only agree. But would the historical Paul, with his policy of being "all things to all" (1 Cor. 9:22), have tried to win the Athenians from paganism with a *Hebraic* speech about the knowledge of God? The man who calls himself "a Hebrew of Hebrews" (Phil. 3:5) was at the same time, from another point of view, a Hellenist of Hellenists. The essential content of the speech is biblical, but the presentation is Hellenistic.

The knowledge of God set forth here is no merely philosophical discipline: it involves moral and religious responsibilities, and for lack of this knowledge, in the measure in which it was accessible to them, the hearers are summoned to repentance. The knowledge of God is viewed in the Old Testament scriptures as belonging to the same moral order as truth,

83. There is no implication about the end of time in the judgment exercised in the realm of the dead by Minos, Rhadamanthys, and Aeacus, three mortals who for piety in this life were appointed as judges over the shades, according to Greek mythology, nor is there any such implication in Plato's reinterpretation of the myth (*Gorgias* 523A-527A).

84. Cf. 10:42.

85. In John 5:25-27 the Son's authority to execute judgment "because he is Son of Man" (ὅτι υἱὸς ἀνθρώπου ἐστίν) seems to be the corollary of his authority, also received from the Father, to have "life in himself" and to impart life to others. W. L. Knox (*Some Hellenistic Elements in Primitive Christianity* [London, 1944], p. 28) considers the christology of the *Areopagitica* to be simply that of Rom. 1:4, where the resurrection of Christ marks him out as Son of God—this in answer to the doubts expressed about the christology of this passage by J. de Zwaan in "Was the Book of Acts a Posthumous Edition?" *HTR* 17 (1924), pp. 95-153, especially pp. 132-41 (an article with which Knox is otherwise in general agreement).

86. See p. 334, n. 53 above.

goodness, and steadfast love (cf. Hos. 4:1; 6:6); the lack of this knowledge brings destruction in its train (Hos. 4:6), while the earth will be filled with this knowledge when God's will is perfectly done and his covenant finally established with his people (Hab. 2:14; Jer. 31:34). It is in these categories that this speech moves, together with the thought behind it, even if the prophets are not formally quoted; the "delicately suited allusions" to Stoic and Epicurean tenets which have been discerned in the speech,[87] and the direct quotations from pagan poets, have their place as points of contact with the hearers, and illustrate the argument in terms familiar to them, but they in no way commit the speaker to acquiescence in their philosophical presuppositions. One may agree with Dibelius in looking at the speaker before the Areopagus as "the precursor of the Apologists,"[88] without denying that Paul could have filled this role and without assuming that such an apology to the Gentiles involves a compromise of biblical principles.

Dibelius characterizes the concluding words as "the *only Christian* sentences in the Areopagus speech."[89] Agreed: they announce the subject of the second lesson. After turning to the living and true God, the Thessalonians had to learn "to wait for his Son from heaven, whom he raised from the dead, Jesus, our deliverer from the coming wrath" (1 Thess. 1:10). The terms in which Jesus is introduced here at Athens are as thoroughly eschatological as those in which he was introduced at Thessalonica. Paul would have told them more, says J. A. Bengel, had they wished to listen.[90] The second lesson would have unpacked the compressed contents of verse 31. Who was this man of God's appointment? And what were the circumstances of his being raised from the dead? It might have been said that, in the report of Paul's synagogue address in 13:16-41, no Christian word is spoken before verse 23. The difference between that address and the present one (apart from the contrast between the "Hebraism" of the former and the "Hellenism" of the latter) is that, in the former, fulfilment is treated as fully as preparation, whereas the latter is devoted almost entirely to preparation, a detailed statement of the fulfilment being presumably left until later.

6. The Athenians' Reaction (17:32-34)

> 32 When they heard of the resurrection of the dead, some of them ridiculed (the idea); the others said, "We will listen to you about this once again."[91]

87. MHT II (Edinburgh, 1929), p. 8, n. 3. Such allusions have been traced in v. 25, where there are parallels both to the Epicurean doctrine that the divine being needs nothing from mortals (not even worship) and to the Stoic doctrine that he is the source of all life.

88. *Studies*, p. 63.

89. *Studies*, p. 56.

90. "Plura erat dicturus audire cupientibus" (*Gnomon Novi Testamenti*, p. 460).

91. Gk. καὶ πάλιν.

33 *So Paul went out from their midst.*

34 *But some men adhered to him and believed; among them was Di-*
onysius the Areopagite.[92] *There was also a woman named Damaris,*
and others with them.

32   The idea of resurrection of dead people was uncongenial to the minds of
most of Paul's Athenian hearers. All of them except the Epicureans would
no doubt have agreed with him had he spoken of the immortality of the
individual soul; but as for resurrection, they would have endorsed the sentiments of the god Apollo, expressed on the occasion when that very court of
the Areopagus was founded by the city's patron goddess Athene: "Once a
man dies and the earth drinks up his blood, there is *no resurrection.*"[93] Some
of them, therefore, ridiculed a statement which seemed so absurd. Others,
more polite if equally skeptical, suggested that there might be an opportunity
later for a further exposition of his teaching.[94]

33-34   Paul then left the meeting of the court, and not long afterward he left Athens. Before he left, he had secured a few adherents, of whom
two are mentioned by name. One of them was a member of the Areopagus
court, Dionysius by name. Eusebius reports, on the authority of a later
Dionysius (bishop of Corinth *c.* A.D. 170), that Dionysius the Areopagite
became the first bishop of Athens;[95] this is the kind of tradition which was
bound to arise. He was later credited with the authorship of a body of
Neoplatonic literature, actually dating from the fifth and sixth centuries.

As for Damaris, Ramsay suggested that she must have been "a
foreign woman, perhaps one of the class of educated Hetairai,"[96] in view of
the unlikelihood of an ordinary Athenian woman being present on such an
occasion. A meeting held in one of the colonnades of the Agora could not be
a private meeting; there was bound to be a crowd of bystanders listening to
whatever they found interesting,[97] and Damaris was probably one of them.
It is less likely that she was a God-fearing Gentile who heard Paul in the

---

92. Cod. D reads "one Dionysius, an Areopagite of honorable station," and omits
all reference to Damaris; this, however, may not represent the original Western text. The
Graeco-Latin codex E/e attaches the description "of honorable station" to Damaris, not to
Dionysius.

93. Aeschylus, *Eumenides* 647-48 ("there is no *anastasis,*" the same word as is
used in v. 32).

94. J. S. Stewart sees something more than a polite dismissal here: "these men at
Athens resolved to hear the apostle again; for wistfully they hoped his message might be
true" (*A Faith to Proclaim* [London, 1953], p. 117).

95. Eusebius, *HE* 3.4.11; 4.23.3.

96. *St. Paul the Traveller,* p. 252; cf. *The Church in the Roman Empire* (London,
1893), p. 161.

97. Formal meetings of the Areopagus court were roped off, but this was scarcely
a formal meeting.

synagogue; the impression given is that she heard his *Areopagitica*. Chrysostom makes her the wife of Dionysius.[98]

There is no mention of any baptisms at Athens, nor is Paul said to have planted a church there. Although Athens was in the Roman province of Achaia, it is a family resident in Corinth that Paul describes as "the firstfruits of Achaia" (1 Cor. 16:15).[99] If the response to his preaching in Athens was scanty, the reason may lie with the Athenians' refusal to take him seriously rather than with the terms of his message. The idea, popular with many preachers, that his determination, when he arrived in Corinth, to "know nothing" there "except Jesus Christ and him crucified" (1 Cor. 2:2), was the result of disillusionment with the line of approach he had attempted in Athens, has little to commend it.[100] The Athenians of today have made up for their ancestors' indifference by engraving the text of Paul's *Areopagitica* on a bronze tablet at the foot of the ascent to the Areopagus, and by naming a neighboring thoroughfare in honor of the apostle.[101]

98. *On the Priesthood* 4.7. The name Damaris is a variant of δάμαλις, "heifer" (lat[h] actually has the spelling *Damalis*). The original form of the Western text perhaps described her as εὐσχήμων ("of honorable estate"), like the God-fearing Greek women of Beroea (v. 12).

99. It is idle to maintain, with Zahn (*INT*, E.T. [Edinburgh, 1909], I, p. 266) and some others, that Stephanas must have been converted in Athens. See W. M. Ramsay, "The Firstfruits of Achaia," *BRD*, pp. 385-411.

100. See the critique of this popular idea in N. B. Stonehouse, *Paul Before the Areopagus*, pp. 31-40.

101. Another street in the vicinity bears the name of Dionysius the Areopagite.

ACTS 18

D. CORINTH (18:1-17)

1. Paul Arrives in Corinth (18:1-4)

1 *After that, Paul left Athens and came to Corinth.*

2 *There he met with a Jew named Aquila, whose family belonged to Pontus; he had recently come from Italy, with his wife Priscilla, because of Claudius's edict that all Jews should leave Rome. So Paul joined them,*

3 *and stayed with them and worked, because he followed the same trade: they were tentmakers by trade.[1]*

4 *He discoursed in the synagogue every sabbath, speaking persuasively to both Jews and Greeks.[2]*

1 From Athens Paul continued his journey in a southwesterly direction, until he reached Corinth.

Corinth, on the Isthmus of Corinth, the land-bridge connecting the Peloponnese with Central and Northern Greece, occupied a most favorable position for commercial enterprise, at the junction of sea routes to the west and east and of land routes to the north and south. It had two ports— Lechaeum, on the Gulf of Corinth (leading to the Ionian Sea and the central and western Mediterranean), and Cenchreae, on the Saronic Gulf (leading to the Aegean Sea and eastern Mediterranean and Black Sea). For long Corinth was a political, commercial, and naval rival of Athens. In 146 B.C., in savage reprisal for an anti-Roman revolt, Corinth was leveled to the ground by the Roman general L. Mummius, and the site lay derelict for a century. Then in 44 B.C., the city was refounded by Julius Caesar and given the status of a Roman colony, with the title *Laus Iulia Corinthus* ("Corinth, the praise of Julius"). In 27 B.C. it became the seat of administration of the Roman

---

1. The Western text of vv. 2 and 3 appears to have run somewhat as follows: "And he found Aquila, a man of Pontus by family, who had lately come from Italy with Priscilla his wife, and he joined them. Now these had departed from Rome because Claudius Caesar had commanded all Jews to leave Rome, and they settled in Achaia. And Paul became known to Aquila because he was of the same race and the same trade, and he stayed with them and worked, for they were tentmakers by trade."

2. The Western text of v. 4 runs: "And entering into the synagogue each sabbath day he held discourse, inserting the name of the Lord Jesus, and spoke persuasively not only to Jews but also to Greeks."

province of Achaia. Corinth was not long in regaining its old commercial prosperity.[3] In earlier days Corinth had acquired a reputation for sexual license remarkable even in classical antiquity,[4] and with the regaining of commercial prosperity Roman Corinth regained something of this old reputation: it is plain to readers of Paul's Corinthian correspondence that the Christian community which he founded in Corinth had difficulty in maintaining the standard of sexual conduct which the gospel required.[5]

2-3 Even so, Corinth was the kind of city which Paul's strategic eye discerned as a promising center for intensive evangelism, and there he settled for a considerable time. Not long after, he met a married couple, recently come to Corinth from Italy, with whom he quickly formed a firm and lifelong friendship. These were Aquila and Priscilla, "tentmakers"—or perhaps, more generally, leatherworkers[6]—by trade. It was this that first apparently brought Paul into contact with them, for he himself had been apprenticed to the same trade. This trade was closely connected with the principal product of Paul's native province, a cloth of goats' hair called *cilicium*, used for cloaks, curtains, and other fabrics designed to give protection against wet. In Judaism it was not considered proper for a scribe or rabbi to receive payment for his teaching, so many of them practised a trade in addition to their study and teaching of the law.[7] Paul, as a matter of policy, earned his living in this way during his missionary career (cf. 20:34; 1 Cor. 9:3-18; 2 Cor. 11:7; 1 Thess. 2:9; 2 Thess. 3:8).[8]

3. See O. Broneer, "Corinth: Center of St. Paul's Missionary Work in Greece," *BA* 14 (1951), pp. 78-96; J. Wiseman, *The Land of the Ancient Corinthians* (Göteborg, 1978), and "Corinth and Rome, I: 228 B.C.-A.D. 267," *ANRW* 2.7.1 (Berlin, 1979), pp. 438-548; J. Murphy-O'Connor, *St. Paul's Corinth: Texts and Archaeology*, GNS 6 (Wilmington, DE, 1983).

4. In classical Greek κορινθιάζομαι (lit., "act the Corinthian") means to practise fornication; Κορίνθιαι ἑταῖραι ("Corinthian companions") or Κορίνθιαι κόραι ("Corinthian girls") were harlots. The temple of Aphrodite on Acrocorinthus (the acropolis of Corinth) gave religious sanction to this kind of activity. In Roman Corinth the temple of Aphrodite was on a much more modest scale than its classical predecessor.

5. Cf. 1 Cor. 5:1-13; 6:12-20; 2 Cor. 12:21.

6. For this extended sense of σκηνοποιός cf. the extended sense of Eng. "saddler," which has come to mean a worker or dealer in leather and not only a maker of saddles.

7. Hillel is credited with the observation: "He who makes a profit from the crown of the Torah shall waste away" (*Pirqê ʾAḇôt* 4.7)—i.e., one should not give religious instruction for money. At a later date, Gamaliel III commended the study of the Torah in combination with some "secular" occupation: "All study of the Torah which is not combined with work will ultimately be futile and lead to sin" (*Pirqê ʾAḇôt* 2.2). Greek culture, on the other hand, tended to despise manual labor; an exception is provided by scientific writers, who speak respectfully of craftsmen. In their attitude L. C. A. Alexander finds a possible background for Luke's totally matter-of-fact reference to Paul's practice here ("Luke's Preface in the Context of Greek Preface-Writing," *NovT* 28 [1986], p. 70).

8. R. F. Hock, who examines Paul's manual work in a Hellenistic social setting (cf. "Paul's Tentmaking and the Problem of his Social Class," *JBL* 97 [1978], pp. 555-64;

Aquila and Priscilla, we are told, had come to Corinth because the Emperor Claudius had ordered all Jews to leave Rome. This was not the only occasion on which the authorities at Rome saw fit to clean up the city by expelling undesirable groups of oriental incomers. Claudius's edict is usually connected with a statement by Suetonius, that he banished the Jews from Rome because they were "indulging in constant riots at the instigation of Chrestus."[9] This Chrestus may have been an otherwise unknown troublemaker who was active in Jewish circles in Rome about the middle of the first century, but in that case Suetonius would probably have called him "a certain Chrestus."[10] Most probably he had the Founder of Christianity in mind but, writing some seventy years after these events, he mistakenly supposed that "Chrestus," who was mentioned in one of his sources of information as the leader of one of the parties involved, was actually in Rome at the time, taking a prominent part in the contention.[11] Suetonius's statement, in fact, points to dissension and disorder within the Jewish community of Rome resulting from the introduction of Christianity into one or more of the synagogues of the city.

It is difficult to say whether Aquila and Priscilla had any part in this dissension or were simply involuntary victims of the emperor's expulsion order. In Paul's references to them he does not suggest that they were converts of his; the greater likelihood is that they were Christians before they left Rome, founder-members, perhaps, of the Roman church.[12] More often

---

"The Workshop as a Social Setting for Paul's Missionary Preaching," *CBQ* 41 [1979], pp. 438-50; *The Social Context of Paul's Ministry: Tentmaking and Apostleship* [Philadelphia, 1980]), discerns a polemic note in Paul's own references to it; there is no such note in Luke's record here.

9. *Life of Claudius* 25.4. The question arises of the relation between this action and that recorded by Dio Cassius (*History* 60.6): "As the Jews had again increased in numbers, but could with difficulty be banished from the capital without a tumult because of their number, he [Claudius] did not actually expel them, but forbade them to meet in accordance with their ancestral customs." The action recorded by Dio is dated at the beginning of Claudius's principate. E. M. Smallwood rightly distinguishes two actions— the earlier one, when Claudius imposed limited restrictions on the Jews of Rome, and the later one, when (the limited restrictions having proved ineffective) he expelled them (*The Jews under Roman Rule* [Leiden, 1976], pp. 210-16). The expulsion order is most probably to be dated in A.D. 49—a date which has the doubtful authority of Orosius (*History* 7.6.15-16) but fits in well with other chronological data.

10. *Chrestus* (Gk. χρηστός, "useful") was a common name in the Graeco-Roman world, especially among slaves, and appears as a variant spelling for the unfamiliar *Christus* (Χριστός). (In Greek the two words were pronounced alike.) For the view that the reference is to some messianic claimant actually present in Rome at the time see R. Eisler, *The Messiah Jesus and John the Baptist* (London, 1931), p. 581; E. A. Judge and G. S. R. Thomas, "The Origin of the Church at Rome," *RTR* 25 (1966), p. 87.

11. For a similar inference in the twentieth century see R. Graves and J. Podro, *Jesus in Rome* (London, 1957), pp. 38-53.

12. See A. Harnack, "Probabilia über die Adresse und den Verfasser des Hebräerbriefs," *ZNW* 1 (1900), pp. 16-41, especially pp. 32ff.

than not, Priscilla is named before her husband by both Luke and Paul;[13] some have inferred from this that she belonged to a higher social class than he—that she was connected, by emancipation if not by birth, with the noble Roman family called *gens Prisca*. It cannot be known if, like Aquila, she was Jewish by birth. When Paul mentions her in his letters, he uses her more formal name Prisca; Luke calls her by her more familiar name Priscilla, following a practice which is evident in the names of other characters in his narrative.[14] Whatever their antecedents were,[15] Priscilla and Aquila came to Corinth to pursue their trade there, and were joined before long by Paul as a fellow-tradesman.

4 A great commercial city like Corinth inevitably had a considerable Jewish colony, and Paul was able immediately to follow his usual procedure and proclaim the Christian message in the local synagogue.[16] Here, sabbath by sabbath, he held discourse with the Jews and God-fearing Gentiles, showing how Jesus had fulfilled the Old Testament prophecies. According to the Western text, he did so by "inserting the name of the Lord Jesus" as an interpretative expansion in those passages which—as the event proved—pointed forward to him. Even if the Western addition is no part of the original text, it does give us a convincing picture of the sort of thing Paul did.[17]

2. Paul Spends Eighteen Months in Corinth (18:5-11)

5 *When Silas and Timothy came back from Macedonia, Paul devoted himself to preaching, testifying to the Jews that the Messiah was Jesus.*[18]

13. Cf. vv. 18, 26; Rom. 16:3; 2 Tim. 4:19.
14. "Luke regularly uses the language of conversation, in which the diminutive forms were usual; and so he speaks of Priscilla, Sopatros and Silas always, though Paul speaks of Prisca, Sosipatros and Silvanus" (Ramsay, *St. Paul the Traveller* [London, [14]1920], p. 268).
15. "There is probably much to discover with regard to this interesting pair" (*St. Paul the Traveller*, p. 269)—these words are as true today as when Ramsay first penned them in 1895. There is no reason to connect this Priscilla with the lady of the same name after whom the Cemetery of Priscilla on the Via Salaria, one of the earliest Christian catacombs in Rome, is named. Nor should the name of Aquila be connected with the Acilii Glabriones, a noble Roman family which owned a crypt in this cemetery.
16. A fragmentary door-inscription in Greek, found at Corinth, and dated variously between 100 B.C. and A.D. 400, evidently read when complete: "Synagogue of the Hebrews" (cf. B. Powell, "Greek Inscriptions from Corinth," *AJA* 2, 7 [1903], pp. 60-61, § 40; A. Deissmann, *Light from the Ancient East*, E.T. [London, [2]1927], p. 16).
17. For such an interpretative insertion cf. Isa. 42:1; 52:13 in the Targum of Jonathan, where "Messiah" is inserted after "my servant," or Isa. 42:1 LXX, where "Jacob" is inserted before "my servant" and "Israel" before "my chosen one."
18. The Western text characteristically amplifies to "the Lord Jesus," and goes on: "And while much discussion was taking place and the scriptures were being interpreted . . ."

6 *When they opposed and reviled him, he shook out his clothes and said to them, "Your blood is on your own heads; I am clear of it. From now on I will go to the Gentiles."*

7 *So, quitting the synagogue,[19] he went into the house of a God-fearer called Titius[20] Justus, whose house was next door to the synagogue.*

8 *Crispus, the ruler of the synagogue, with all his household, became a believer in the Lord, and many of the Corinthians, as they listened, believed and were baptized.*

9 *Then the Lord spoke to Paul in a vision by night: "Do not be afraid," he said; "speak, and do not be silent,*

10 *for I am with you, and no assailant will do you any harm. I have many people[21] in this city."*

11 *So he remained there for a year and six months, teaching the word of God among them.*

5 After a few weeks, Paul was rejoined by his companions Silas and Timothy, who had returned from Macedonia (perhaps by sea). The news that they brought—especially Timothy's news about the steadfastness of the sorely tried converts of Thessalonica—came as a great relief to Paul.[22] At the same time, a gift of money from his friends in Philippi relieved him for the time being of the necessity to support himself by tentmaking;[23] he was able therefore to concentrate on the preaching of the gospel, and he sought to convince his Jewish hearers that the promised Messiah had come, and had come in the person of Jesus.

6-7 At last his witness in the synagogue stirred up such intense opposition there that he had to find some other place in which to prosecute his evangelism. By a spectacular gesture (shaking out his cloak so that not a speck of dust from the synagogue might adhere to it[24]) he expressed his resolve to have done with that building and his abhorrence of the slanderous talk in which his opponents were indulging—not so much against Paul himself as against the one whom Paul proclaimed as Messiah and Lord. He had discharged his responsibility to them, he assured them; if they would not accept the news of salvation which he brought, he was now free of blame.[25]

---

19. Gk. ἐκεῖθεν ("thence"), which the Western text mistakenly interprets as "from Aquila" (but Paul did not move his private lodgings from Aquila's house to that of Titius Justus, but made Titius Justus's house his teaching base instead of the synagogue).

20. Titius is spelled as Titus in ℵ E 36 1175 1739 *al* syr^pesh cop and omitted from A B² D* Ψ and the Byzantine text.

21. Gk. λαός . . . πολύς. As in 15:14, λαός, the designation of Israel as the people of God, now embraces all believers without distinction, Gentiles as well as Jews.

22. Cf. 1 Thess. 3:6-10.

23. Cf. 2 Cor. 11:9; also Phil. 4:16, which probably means, "Both (when I was) in Thessalonica, and more than once (in other places) you sent me something for my need."

24. Cf. 13:51.

25. For the general sense cf. Ezek. 33:5.

As at Pisidian Antioch and elsewhere, so at Corinth too he would take his saving message to people who knew how to appreciate it. And he had not far to go. For adjoining the synagogue was the house of a God-fearing Gentile who had listened to Paul and been persuaded of the truth of his words. This man now placed his house at Paul's disposal, and people who had been accustomed to attend the synagogue did not have to leave their habitual route if they wished to go on hearing Paul: they made their way toward the synagogue, as usual, but turned in next door.

The most probable form of this God-fearer's name, as given by Luke, is Titius Justus—a Roman *nomen* and *cognomen* suggesting that he was a Roman citizen, perhaps a member of one of the families settled in Corinth by Julius Caesar when he made it a Roman colony. But what was his *praenomen*? There is much to be said for the view, favored by W. M. Ramsay and E. J. Goodspeed, that it was Gaius—that this man is the Gaius named by Paul in 1 Cor. 1:14 as one of the few converts in Corinth whom he baptized with his own hands.[26] If so, he is almost certainly to be identified also with "Gaius, who is host to me and to the whole church," as Paul puts it in Rom. 16:23. A man whose house was large enough to accommodate Paul's voluntary congregation and (later) the whole church of Corinth (if the identification is well founded) would have been a fairly well-to-do citizen.

8 In 1 Cor. 1:14 Paul mentions another Corinthian convert who was baptized by him personally, Crispus by name. Luke shows us who this Crispus was—no less than the ruler of the synagogue. He and his family[27] evidently followed Paul on his departure from the synagogue, and joined the new Christian community in Corinth. Many other Corinthians came to hear the good news, and believing it they were baptized and swelled the new community.

9-10 Shortly after Paul's leaving the synagogue, he had an encouraging experience: he received one of the visions which came to him at critical junctures in his life, heartening him for whatever might lie ahead.[28] On this occasion the risen Christ appeared to him by night and assured him that no harm would befall him in Corinth, for all the opposition his witness might stir up. His opponents had made it impossible for him to stay in Thessalonica and Beroea; his opponents in Corinth would not have similar success, however hard they might try to force his departure. He had come to Corinth full of misgivings—"in much fear and trembling," he says himself (1 Cor. 2:3)—but he should abandon all fear and go on proclaiming the

---

26. Cf. W. M. Ramsay, *Pictures of the Apostolic Church* (London, 1910), p. 205, n. 2; E. J. Goodspeed, "Gaius Titius Justus," *JBL* 69 (1950), pp. 382-83.

27. For the conversion of households cf. 16:15, 31-34.

28. Cf. 23:11; 27:23-24.

gospel boldly. He would reap an abundant harvest by so doing, for the Lord had many in Corinth who were marked out by him as his own people.[29]

11 Thus filled with fresh confidence, Paul stayed in Corinth and continued his work of preaching and teaching for a year and a half. The next five years, in fact, were devoted not so much to traveling as to inaugurating and consolidating Christian witness in two important centers west and east of the Aegean—first Corinth and then Ephesus. The time spent in Corinth probably stretched from the fall of A.D. 50 to the spring of A.D. 52; we are able to date this period of Paul's career with considerable accuracy from the following mention of Gallio as proconsul of Achaia.

3. Paul before Gallio (18:12-17)

12 *When Gallio was proconsul of Achaia, the Jews made a concerted attack on Paul. They brought him before the tribunal[30]*

13 *with the charge:[31] "This man incites people to worship God in a manner contrary to the law."*

14 *When Paul was on the point of defending himself, Gallio said to the Jews, "Listen, Jews.[32] If this were a crime, or some act of malicious fraudulence,[33] it would be reasonable for me to take up your case.*

15 *But if these are disputes about words and names and your own law, see to it yourselves. I refuse to be a judge of such things."*

16 *So he drove them from the tribunal.*

17 *Then all[34] (the bystanders) seized Sosthenes, the ruler of the synagogue, and proceeded to beat him up in front of the tribunal. But Gallio paid no heed to this.[35]*

12 Paul received a divine promise that no harm would befall him through any attack in Corinth, but he was not promised that no attack would be made. An attack was indeed made on him, and one which might have had serious consequences. On this occasion his Jewish opponents, instead of stirring up the city rabble against him or accusing him before the civic authorities, approached the Roman administration of the province. Any decision taken by civic magistrates, like the politarchs of Thessalonica, would have effect

29. Cf. p. 349, n. 21.

30. The Western text reads, "the Jews with one accord [ὁμοθυμαδόν, translated "concerted" above], having taken counsel among themselves against Paul, laid hands on him and led him to the proconsul."

31. The Western text reads "shouting against him and saying."

32. Gk. ὦ Ἰουδαῖοι (the Western text has the fuller form ὦ ἄνδρες Ἰουδαῖοι).

33. Gk. ἀδίκημά τι ἢ ῥᾳδιούργημα πονηρόν. Moulton and Milligan, *Vocabulary of the Greek Testament* (London, 1930), p. 563, quote the sense "false pretences" for ῥᾳδιούργημα (cf. 13:10, ῥᾳδιουργία).

34. The Western and Byzantine texts read "all the Greeks" (a correct gloss).

35. The Western text paraphrases, "Gallio pretended not to see."

only within their limited jurisdiction, but the verdict of a Roman governor would not only be effective within his province but could be followed as a precedent by governors of other provinces. Had the proconsul of Achaia[36] pronounced a judgment unfavorable to Paul, the progress of Christianity during the next decade or so could have been attended by much greater difficulties than were actually experienced.

Gallio was a son of the elder Seneca, the rhetorician (c. 50 B.C.-c. A.D. 40), and brother of the younger Seneca, the Stoic philosopher (c. 3 B.C.-A.D. 65). His name was originally Marcus Annaeus Novatus; but after his father brought him to Rome from his native Cordova in the principate of Tiberius, he was adopted by the rhetorician Lucius Junius Gallio, and thereafter bore the same name as his adoptive father. His contemporaries speak of him as a man of great personal charm—"no mortal," said his brother Seneca, "is so pleasant to any one person as Gallio is to everybody."[37] After holding the praetorship in Rome, he was appointed proconsul of Achaia. From an inscription at Delphi in Central Greece, recording a directive from the Emperor Claudius, it can be inferred rather precisely that he entered on his proconsulship in the summer of A.D. 51.[38] He left Achaia because of a fever (perhaps before his year of office had expired) and went on a cruise for his health.[39] At a later date, after his consulship (A.D. 55),[40] he took a cruise

36. Achaia was governed by a proconsul from 27 B.C. to A.D. 15, when it was combined with Macedonia and Moesia to form one imperial province; in A.D. 44 it was handed back to the senate and was once more governed by a proconsul. "It was a province of the second rank"; the proconsul held office "after holding the praetorship, and generally before the consulship" (Ramsay, *St. Paul the Traveller*, p. 258).

37. Seneca, *Natural Questions* 4a, Preface, 11; cf. Statius, *Silvae* 2.7.32; Dio Cassius, *Hist.* 61.35.

38. This inscription, dated in the period of Claudius's twenty-sixth acclamation as *imperator* (i.e., within the first seven months of A.D. 52), refers to "my friend Gallio, proconsul of Achaia," in terms which imply that Gallio has held that office recently but holds it no longer. The summer of A.D. 51 is thus indicated as the latest date for Gallio's taking up the proconsulship. On this inscription (*SIG* 2³, § 801) see A. Brassac, "Une inscription de Delphes et la chronologie de Saint Paul," *RB* 10 (1913), pp. 36-53, 207-17; A. Plassart, "L'inscription de Delphes mentionnant le Proconsul Gallion," *RÉG* 80 (1967), pp. 372-78; B. Schwank, "Der sogenannte Brief an Gallio und die Datierung des 1 Thess.," *BZ* n.s. 15 (1971), pp. 265-66; J. H. Oliver, "The epistle of Claudius which mentions the Proconsul Junius Gallio," *Hesperia* 40 (1971), pp. 239-40; K. Haacker, "Die Gallio-Episode und die paulinische Chronologie," *BZ* n.s. 16 (1972), pp. 252-55; C. J. Hemer, "Observations on Pauline Chronology," in *Pauline Studies*, ed. D. A. Hagner and M. J. Harris (Exeter/Grand Rapids, 1980), pp. 6-9; J. Murphy-O'Connor, *St. Paul's Corinth*, pp. 149-50, where Paul's appearance before Gallio is dated between July and October, A.D. 51. G. Lüdemann (*Paul, Apostle to the Gentiles: Studies in Chronology*, E.T. [London, 1984], pp. 158-75), who dates Paul's evangelization of Corinth ten years earlier than this, assigns the Gallio incident to Paul's last visit to the city (cf. 20:2-3)—a conclusion to be accepted only if the evidence for it were singularly compelling (which it is not).

39. Seneca, *Moral Epistles* 104.1.

40. On the date of his consulship see E. M. Smallwood, "Consules Suffecti of A.D. 55," *Historia* 17 (1968), p. 384.

from Rome to Egypt because of threatened phthisis.[41] In A.D. 65, like other members of his family, he fell victim to Nero's suspicions.[42]

13 The charge which was preferred against Paul before Gallio was that of propagating a religion and on that basis forming a society not countenanced by Roman law. The Jewish community and synagogue of Corinth, like Jewish communities and synagogues elsewhere throughout the empire, had the status of a *collegium licitum*,[43] but Paul's accusers maintained that the gospel which he preached had nothing to do with their ancestral faith: it was no true form of Judaism, and therefore should not share in the protection extended to Judaism by Roman law. Paul should be prohibited from further propagation of the gospel, if not indeed punished for his activity in propagating it thus far.

14-16 An elaborate podium overlooking the lower terrace of the forum of Roman Corinth is commonly pointed out as Gallio's tribunal, where he sat to administer justice.[44] On this occasion, Paul was about to open his mouth in reply to the charge brought against him, when Gallio abruptly brought the proceedings to an end. Listening to the charge, he quickly decided that the dispute was internal to the Jewish community, that it concerned conflicting interpretations of Jewish religious law. Paul was obviously as much a Jew as his accusers were. What Paul was propagating, Gallio reckoned, was simply a variety of Judaism which did not happen to commend itself to the leaders of the local Jewish community; and he had no intention of adjudicating on a matter of this kind. Had Paul been charged with a recognizable crime or misdemeanor, he said, he would naturally have taken the matter up;[45] but as it was plainly a disagreement about Jewish religious terminology, they must settle it themselves. So he bade them begone from his tribunal.

17 As they went away, an incident occurred which reveals how prone the populace of these Gentile cities was to anti-Jewish demonstrations. Taking advantage of the rebuff which the proconsul had dealt to the Jewish leaders, the crowd of bystanders seized one of those leaders, Sosthenes (possibly the successor to Crispus as ruler of the synagogue),[46]

41. Pliny, *Natural History* 31.33.

42. Dio Cassius, *Hist.* 62.25.

43. See S. Applebaum, "The Legal Status of the Jewish Communities in the Diaspora," in *The Jewish People in the First Century,* ed. S. Safrai and M. Stern, I (Assen, 1974), pp. 420-63, especially p. 460; also Schürer III, pp. 107-25.

44. It has been held, however, that this βῆμα was used only for specially formal occasions and not for trivial hearings like that recorded here; cf. E. Dinkler, "Das Bema zu Korinth," in *Signum Crucis: Aufsätze zum Neuen Testament und zur christlichen Archäologie* (Tübingen, 1967), pp. 118-33.

45. Gk. κατὰ λόγον ἂν ἀνεσχόμην ὑμῶν (for this legal sense of ἀνέχομαι, meaning "accept a complaint," cf. BAGD, p. 65).

46. If this is the Sosthenes of 1 Cor. 1:1, then he became a Christian soon after this painful experience. But there is no means of knowing if the same person is intended.

and beat him up in the very presence of the proconsul, who had not yet left the tribunal. But Gallio turned a blind eye to this brutal ventilation of anti-Jewish sentiment.

Gallio's ruling meant in effect that Paul and his associates, so long as they committed no breach of public order, continued to share the protection which Roman law granted to the practice of Judaism. It probably served as a precedent for other Roman judges, especially as it proceeded from a man whose brother (Seneca) occupied a position of influence at the imperial court. It meant that for the next ten or twelve years, until imperial policy toward Christians underwent a complete reversal,[47] the gospel could be proclaimed in the provinces of the empire without fear of coming into conflict with Roman law. The next charges brought against Paul before a Roman judge were personal to himself.[48] Luke's account of Gallio's decision is of high relevance to the apologetic motive of his history. And it may be that, as Ramsay thought, the memory of Gallio's decision was one of the things that encouraged Paul, some years later, to appeal "from the petty outlying court of the procurator of Judaea, who was always much under the influence of the ruling party in Jerusalem, to the supreme tribunal of the Empire."[49]

E. EPHESUS (18:18–19:20)

1. Hasty Visit to Ephesus (18:18-21)

18 *So Paul spent many more days there; then, taking his leave of the brothers, he set sail for Syria, in the company of Priscilla and Aquila. He had his hair cut short in Cenchreae, for he was under a vow.*[50]

19 *They landed at Ephesus, and*[51] *Paul left his companions there. He himself went into the synagogue and held discourse with the Jews.*

20 *They asked him to stay with them longer, but he did not consent;*

21 *he took his leave of them, saying,*[52] *"I will come back to you, God willing," and set sail from Ephesus.*

47. Nero's action against the Christians of Rome in the aftermath of the fire of A.D. 64 was evidently a personal initiative. But with the growth of Gentile Christianity it was no longer possible for the church to profit from the protection extended by Roman law to the synagogue.

48. Cf. 24:5-8.

49. *St. Paul the Traveller*, p. 260.

50. The Western text (represented by lat^h) ascribes the vow and the hair-cutting to Aquila ("Aquila, who since he had made a vow, had shorn his head"); the Latin Vulgate ascribes the action to both Priscilla and Aquila ("who had shorn their heads in Cenchreae, for they had a vow").

51. The Western text inserts "on the following sabbath."

52. The Western and Byzantine texts add: "I must by all means keep the coming festival in Jerusalem, but . . ."

18   Paul was not likely to leave Corinth immediately after Gallio had given his decision. That decision, which (without Gallio's intending it so) proved so favorable for Paul's mission, was probably given in the summer or early fall of A.D. 51; Paul stayed on for the ensuing winter. At last, however, he left Corinth, for he wished to pay a short visit to Syria and Judaea. Along with Priscilla and Aquila, therefore, he sailed across the Aegean from Cenchreae, the eastern port of Corinth. Before setting sail, he had his hair cut: he had allowed it to grow long for the duration of a vow which he had undertaken. This was probably not a formal Nazirite vow, which could not properly be undertaken outside the Holy Land,[53] but a private vow, the fulfilment of which was an act of thanksgiving—possibly for the divine promise of verse 10, which had been confirmed by his preservation from harm throughout his Corinthian ministry.

19   The ship on which they embarked took them to Ephesus. Here Priscilla and Aquila settled down for some years, either transferring their business from Corinth to Ephesus or leaving their Corinthian branch in the care of a manager (as perhaps they had already left their Roman branch) and opening a new branch in Ephesus.

Ephesus was at this time the greatest commercial city of Asia Minor north of the Taurus range, although its harbor required constant dredging because of the alluvium carried down by the Caÿster, at the mouth of which it stood. Standing on the main route from Rome to the east, it enjoyed political importance in addition to its geographical advantages: it was the seat of adminstration of the province of Asia, and at the same time a free Greek city, with its own senate and civic assembly; it was an assize town, and prided itself especially on its title "Temple Warden of Artemis" (cf. 19:35). The great temple of Ephesian Artemis, built to replace an earlier one which was destroyed by fire in 356 B.C., was reckoned one of the seven wonders of the ancient world. Much of the site of Roman Ephesus is unoccupied; it has been excavated over many years by Austrian archaeologists, who have restored some of the buildings. Part of the site is occupied by the town of Selçuk, formerly called Ayasoluk (a name commemorating the Ephesian residence of "John the Divine").[54]

There was a large settlement of Jews at Ephesus. The privileges granted them in 44 B.C. by Dolabella (a partisan of Julius Caesar, and Roman

---

53. If the vow was made in another country, its fulfillment required a residence of at least thirty days in Judaea, and at the end of that time the hair would be shorn and offered in the temple (cf. Num. 6:18). The vow mentioned in 21:23-26 below was a real Nazirite vow (see the Mishnaic tractate *Nāzîr*). It is grammatically possible to make Aquila the subject of the following verbs, but "the natural emphasis marks Paul as the subject here" (Ramsay, *St. Paul the Traveller*, p. 263).

54. Ayasoluk is a corruption of Gk. ἅγιος θεολόγος, "the holy divine." The hill on which Justinian's basilica of St. John stands is still commonly called the hill of Ayasoluk.

consul in that year) were subsequently confirmed by the civic authorities[55] and by the Emperor Augustus and his lieutenants.[56] Paul now paid a brief visit to their synagogue before continuing his journey.

20-21 According to the Western text, Paul was eager to reach Jerusalem in time for one of the Jewish festivals. If the festival was Passover, there was probably a good reason for his haste: the seas were closed to navigation until March 10,[57] and in A.D. 52 Passover fell in early April. He had time to hold some preparatory discourse with the members of the synagogue, but although they were interested in what he had to say and asked him to stay longer, he was unable to do so. A ship was about to leave the Ephesian harbor which might bring him to Judaea in time for his appointment, so he bade them farewell and promised, if it were God's will, to come back and spend more time with them.

2. Brief Visit to Judaea and Syria (18:22-23)

22 *Having landed at Caesarea, he went up and greeted the church, and then went down to Antioch.*

23 *Having spent some time there, he departed and went through the Galatian region and Phrygia, city by city, strengthening all the disciples.*

22 Paul's ship from Ephesus brought him to Caesarea, then the chief Mediterranean port of Palestine. When the wind is east of north, it is easier to put in at Caesarea than at Seleucia. Having landed at Caesarea, he went up to Jerusalem and greeted the mother-church. Jerusalem is not mentioned, but it is certainly implied:[58] a reference in a Judaean setting to "the church" without qualification could only be to the church of Jerusalem, and it is from Jerusalem, not from Caesarea, that one would "go down". (One would not "go down" from a place on the coast, like Caesarea, to an inland city, like

---

55. Cf. Josephus, *Ant.* 14.225-27.

56. Cf. Josephus, *Ant.* 16.162-68, 172-73. On Ephesus see O. Benndorf and others, *Forschungen in Ephesos*, I- (Vienna, 1906-); W. M. Ramsay, *Letters to the Seven Churches of Asia* (London, 1909), pp. 210-50; D. Magie, *Roman Rule in Asia Minor* (Princeton, 1950), I, pp. 74-76; II, pp. 885-88; F. Miltner, *Ephesos: Stadt der Artemis und des Johannes* (Vienna, 1958); J. Keil, *Ephesos: Ein Führer durch die Ruinenstätte und ihre Geschichte* (Vienna, ²1964); also "Asia," *RAC* I, cols. 740-49; C. Foss, *Ephesus After Antiquity* (Cambridge, 1979); D. Knibbe and W. Alzinger, "Ephesos vom Beginn der römischen Herrschaft in Kleinasien bis zum Ende der Prinzipatszeit: Geschichte und Archäologie," *ANRW* 2.7.2 (Berlin, 1980), pp. 748-830; C. J. Hemer, *The Letters to the Seven Churches of Asia in their Local Setting* (Sheffield, 1986), pp. 35-56.

57. Vegetius, *On Military Affairs* 4.39.

58. *Pace* B. H. Streeter, "The Primitive Text of the Acts," *JTS* 34 (1933), p. 237, who maintains that Caesarea is intended and that the Western text of 19:1 (see p. 362, n. 1) should be transferred to this point, as explaining Paul's failure to carry out his original plan to go to Jerusalem, voiced by him in the Western text of v. 21 above (see p. 354, n. 52).

Antioch.) Whether he had any special commission to discharge in Jerusalem in connection with the festival or otherwise, Luke does not say. A few scholars attach considerable importance to this Jerusalem visit, identifying it with the visit described by Paul in Gal. 2:1-10.[59] Apart from chronological problems involved in this identification, there is the major difficulty that Barnabas, who accompanied Paul to Jerusalem on the occasion mentioned in Gal. 2:1, was no longer in his company at this time.

When Paul had completed whatever he had to do in Jerusalem, he "went down" to Antioch (for the expression we may compare 11:27, where a group of prophets "came down" from Jerusalem to Antioch).[60]

23 Antioch (on the Orontes) was the city from which Paul had set out on his missionary journey with Silas (as on his earlier missionary journey with Barnabas), and, although Antioch was no longer his base, he may well have told the church there of God's continued dealings with him and of other Gentiles who had entered by the same "door of faith" as the Gentiles of Cyprus and South Galatia, whose conversion he and Barnabas had reported to that church some years before (14:27).

After spending some time in Antioch, he set out on his travels again. An impression of haste is given by the succession of participles in the Greek text of verses 22 and 23; in fact a journey of about 1500 miles is covered in these two verses and in 19:1. Luke was probably dependent here on a skeleton itinerary—not the same itinerary as that represented by the "we" narrative of Acts, which includes more detail. From Antioch Paul set out for central Asia Minor by the same land route which he and Silas had previously followed, crossing the Taurus range by the Cilician Gates. Although "the Galatian region and Phrygia" here is not the same phrase as is used in 16:6 ("the Phrygian and Galatian region"),[61] there is probably not much material difference between them. W. M. Ramsay and W. M. Calder thought (rightly, it may be) that "the Galatic region" here meant Lycaonia Galatica (i.e., that part of Lycaonia which lay within the province of Galatia, as distinct from eastern Lycaonia, which formed part of the kingdom of Antiochus).[62]

---

59. J. Knox, *Chapters in a Life of Paul* (Nashville, TN, 1950), pp. 68-69; J. van Bruggen, *"Na Veertien Jaren"* (Kampen, 1973), pp. 40-43, 223-25; G. Lüdemann, *Paul, Apostle to the Gentiles: Studies in Chronology,* pp. 152-56. According to Knox and Lüdemann this was Paul's only visit to Jerusalem between those of 9:26 (= Gal. 1:18) and 21:15. J. Wellhausen earlier held this visit to be a doublet of that in 21:15 ("Noten zur Apostelgeschichte," *NGG* [1907], pp. 1-25; "Kritische Analyse der Apostelgeschichte," *AGG* n.s. 15.2 [1914], pp. 37-38), followed by A. Loisy, *Les Actes des Apôtres* (Paris, 1920), pp. 708-9.

60. That different verbs are used—κατῆλθον in 11:27 (cf. 15:1, 30) and κατέβη here—does not affect the force of the common prefix κατά.

61. Φρυγία is used substantivally here, adjectivally in 16:6.

62. See W. M. Ramsay, *HDB* II (Edinburgh, 1899), p. 90 (*s.v.* "Galatia, Region of"); W. M. Calder, "Asia Minor in the New Testament," in *Commentary on the Bible,* ed. A. S. Peake, Supplement (London, 1936), p. 32. K. Lake agrees (*Beginnings* I.5, pp.

In any case, Paul seems to have passed once more through Derbe, Lystra, Iconium, and Pisidian Antioch, not carrying out pioneer evangelism but giving help and encouragement to old friends and converts. On this occasion no hindrance was placed on his westward path, so his way was now open to Ephesus.

3. Apollos (18:24-28)

24 Now a Jew named Apollos,[63] whose family belonged to Alexandria, came to Ephesus. He was a man of learning,[64] well versed in the scriptures.

25 He had been instructed[65] in the way of the Lord and was aglow with the Spirit;[66] as he spoke, he taught the story of Jesus accurately, although the only baptism he knew was John's.

26 He began to express himself freely in the synagogue. When Priscilla and Aquila[67] heard him, they took him home with them and set forth the way of God to him more accurately.

27 When he wished to cross over to Achaia, the brothers encouraged him and wrote to the disciples there, asking them to give him a welcome. When he arrived, he gave great help to the believers through (divine) grace;[68]

28 he argued strenuously and convincingly with the Jews, and that in public, as he showed[69] by the scriptures that the Messiah was Jesus.

24-25 Between Paul's departure from Ephesus (after his hasty visit) and his return to it (after he had been to Judaea and Syria) another extremely interesting Christian arrived in the city. This was Apollos, a Jew from Alexandria—perhaps a traveling merchant of a type not unknown in the first century,[70] who gave welcome help in the synagogues of cities which he visited. It is not expressly stated (except in the Western text) that Apollos

---

239-40) that Ramsay's view, which he himself accepted when he wrote *The Earlier Epistles of St. Paul* (London, 1911), pp. 260-61, "certainly fits the facts."

63. ℵ calls him "Apelles," D "Apollonius" (the full form of his name) and the Latin Vulgate "Apollo."

64. Gk. ἀνὴρ λόγιος (the adjective means "learned" in both classical and Modern Greek; the meaning "eloquent" is secondary).

65. The Western text adds "in his native place" (ἐν τῇ πατρίδι).

66. Or "fervent in spirit" (Gk. ζέων τῷ πνεύματι).

67. The Western text reverses the order to "Aquila and Priscilla" (see p. 326, n. 20, on 17:12).

68. It is difficult to decide whether "through (divine) grace" should be construed with "help" or "believe." In the Western text v. 27 is expanded: "And some Corinthians who were on a visit to Ephesus and had heard him invited him to cross over with them to their native place. When he consented, the Ephesians wrote to the disciples to receive the man; and when he took up residence in Achaia he was of great help in the churches."

69. The Western text reads "discoursed and showed."

70. Like Ananias in Adiabene (Josephus, *Ant.* 20.34-42).

received his accurate instruction in "the way of the Lord" (i.e., the gospel) in his native Alexandria, but he may well have done so. The gospel certainly reached Alexandria at a very early date, although the origins of Alexandrian Christianity are lost in obscurity (only in the second half of the second century does the obscurity begin to be dissipated).[71]

Apollos's understanding of Christianity deviated in at least one important respect from the form of Christianity, based on Jerusalem, which is depicted for us in Acts: the only baptism of which he knew was the baptism administered by John the Baptist; baptism in the name of Jesus, as proclaimed by Peter on the day of Pentecost (cf. 2:38), was evidently unknown to him. It has been suggested that his "accurate" knowledge of the story of Jesus came to him from a primitive gospel writing not unlike our Gospel of Mark;[72] it is doubtful, however, if the word "instructed" would be satisfied by a reading knowledge; it rather implies listening to a teacher. But Apollos combined great knowledge of the scriptures with a masterly skill in expounding their messianic content, and this was coupled with spiritual fervor—an expression which probably denoted not so much an enthusiastic temperament as possession by the Spirit of God (which is what it means when used by Paul in Rom. 12:11).[73] It may seem strange, no doubt, that

---

71. See H. I. Bell, *Jews and Christians in Egypt* (London, 1924); "Evidences of Christianity in Egypt during the Roman Period," *HTR* 37 (1944), pp. 185-208; W. Bauer, *Orthodoxy and Heresy in Earliest Christianity* (1934, ²1964), E.T. (Philadelphia, 1971), pp. 44-60; E. Molland, *The Conception of the Gospel in Alexandrian Theology* (Oslo, 1938); C. H. Roberts, "The Christian Book and the Greek Papyri," *JTS* 50 (1949), pp. 155-68; *Manuscript, Society and Belief in Early Christian Egypt* (London, 1971); S. G. F. Brandon, *The Fall of Jerusalem and the Christian Church* (London, 1951), pp. 217-43; A. Ehrhardt, "Christianity before the Apostles' Creed," *The Framework of the New Testament Stories* (Manchester, 1964), pp. 151-99; L. W. Barnard, "St. Mark and Alexandria," *HTR* 57 (1964), pp. 145-50; "St. Stephen and Early Alexandrian Christianity," *NTS* 7 (1960-61), pp. 31-45; M. Smith, *Clement of Alexandria and a Secret Gospel of Mark* (Cambridge, MA, 1973); E. A. Judge and S. R. Pickering, "Papyrus Documentation of Church and Community in Egypt to the Mid-Fourth Century," *JAC* 20 (1977), pp. 47-71. Those works which are based on papyrus evidence (e.g., those by H. I. Bell, C. H. Roberts, E. A. Judge, and S. R. Pickering) are less speculative than some of the others listed.

72. F. Blass, *Philology of the Gospels* (London, 1898), pp. 29-31.

73. "The use of the expression 'fervent in the Spirit' is unambiguously defined by Rom. 12:11 as a phrase current in the language of Christian edification; and its position between two clauses concerned with Apollos as a Christian establishes its meaning" (E. Käsemann, "The Disciples of John the Baptist in Ephesus," E.T. in *Essays on New Testament Themes* [London, 1964], p. 143). G. W. H. Lampe goes farther (indeed too far): "Possibly a direct commission from the Lord was deemed to have been conferred upon him [by] the Spirit, for he ranked high among the apostles, being regarded by the Corinthians as standing approximately upon the same level as St. Peter or St. Paul" (*The Seal of the Spirit* [London, 1951], p. 66). See also J. H. A. Hart, "Apollos," *JTS* 7 (1905-6), pp. 16-28; B. T. D. Smith, "Apollos and the Twelve Disciples at Ephesus," *JTS* 16 (1914-15), pp. 241-46; H. Preisker, "Apollos und die Johannesjünger in Act 18,24–19,6," *ZNW* 30 (1931), pp. 301-4; E. Schweizer, "Die Bekehrung des Apollos, Ag

someone who was indwelt and empowered by the Spirit should nevertheless know nothing of Christian baptism; but primitive Christianity was made up of many strands, and of some of those strands we have little or no knowledge. Even after his further instruction, Apollos is not said to have received Christian baptism.[74]

26 Priscilla and Aquila, who continued to attend the synagogue in Ephesus after Paul's departure, listened to Apollos when he began to expound the scriptures there, and were greatly impressed by the learning and skill which he devoted to the defense of the gospel. No one else, in their experience, came so near their friend Paul in this ability. As they listened, they became aware of some gaps in his knowledge, accurate as it was, so they took him home and set forth "the way of God" to him more accurately still (they themselves had probably had the same experience when they met Paul and he supplemented the knowledge of the Way which they had acquired in Rome). Arnold Ehrhardt remarks that Paul was a greater asset to the Jerusalem church than it gave him due credit for, for either directly (as in 19:1-7) or indirectly, through his disciples (as here), he brought deviant forms of primitive Christianity into line with the Jerusalem way.[75] That the Jerusalem way is the norm is taken for granted by Luke.[76] But Priscilla and Aquila's procedure was admirable: how much better it is to give such private help to a teacher whose understanding of his subject is deficient than to correct or denounce him publicly!

27-28 After some time, Apollos wished to cross the Aegean and visit Greece: according to the Western text, he was invited to do so by some Corinthians who made his acquaintance in Ephesus. At all events, he went to Corinth, armed with a letter of introduction from his friends in Ephesus to the Corinthian church. He proved himself a tower of strength to the believers in Corinth, both by his teaching in the church and by his preaching to those outside, especially to the Jews of Corinth, as he argued cogently (refuting all

---

18, 24-26," *Beiträge zur Theologie des Neuen Testaments: Neutestamentliche Aufsätze (1955-1970)* (Zürich, 1970), pp. 71-79; C. K. Barrett, "Apollos and the Twelve Disciples of Ephesus," in *The New Testament Age: Essays in Honor of Bo Reicke*, ed. W. C. Weinrich, I (Macon, GA, 1984), pp. 29-39.

74. B. T. D. Smith ("Apollos and the Twelve Disciples at Ephesus," p. 245) thinks it "may safely be inferred from the narrative" that he did now receive Christian baptism. But this is not a safe inference. Apollos, if he had already received the Spirit, was not on the same footing as the disciples of 19:1-7. For him, as evidently for the original apostles, John's baptism *plus* the receiving of the Spirit conveyed all that Christian baptism could have conveyed. (The baptism of the Gentile Cornelius in 10:44-48 after his reception of the Spirit was a sign of his being welcomed into the community of God's believing people.)

75. *The Framework of the New Testament Stories*, p. 94.

76. Cf. G. W. H. Lampe, *St. Luke and the Church of Jerusalem* (London, 1969), p. 26.

counter-arguments) that the Messiah of whom the scriptures spoke must be identified with Jesus of Nazareth.[77] The influence that Apollos exercised in Corinth may be gauged from the references made to him in Paul's Corinthian correspondence. Paul speaks of him as watering the seed which he himself had sown.[78] If some of the Corinthian Christians were disposed to claim Apollos as a party leader to the detriment of Paul[79] (impressed perhaps by his Alexandrian methods of biblical interpretation), there is no hint that Apollos himself encouraged this tendency, and Paul speaks of him in warm terms as an appreciated colleague.[80]

77. The same turn of phrase is used of him here as is used of Paul in v. 5 above.
78. 1 Cor. 3:6.
79. 1 Cor. 1:12; 3:4.
80. Cf. 1 Cor. 16:12. Luther's suggestion that Apollos was the writer to the Hebrews (in a sermon on 1 Cor. 3:4ff. in 1537 [Weimar edition 45, p. 389] and in his *Commentary on Genesis*, 1545 [Weimar edition 44, p. 709]) has been propounded afresh and supported with new arguments by (among others) T. W. Manson, "The Problem of the Epistle to the Hebrews" (1949), *Studies in the Gospels and Epistles* (Manchester, 1962), pp. 242-58; W. F. Howard, "The Epistle to the Hebrews," *Interpretation* 5 (1951), pp. 80-91; C. Spicq, *L'Épître aux Hébreux* (Paris, 1952-53), I, pp. 209-19; H. W. Montefiore, *A Commentary on the Epistle to the Hebrews* (New York/London, 1964), pp. 9-29.

ACTS 19

4. Paul and the Twelve Disciples of Ephesus (19:1-7)

1 *While Apollos was at Corinth, Paul passed through the higher country and came down to Ephesus.[1] There he found some disciples.*
2 *"Did you receive the Holy Spirit when you believed?" he asked them. "No," said they; "we never even heard that the Holy Spirit is available."[2]*
3 *"What baptism did you receive,[3] then?" he asked. "John's baptism," said they.*
4 *Then Paul said, "John baptized with a baptism of repentance, telling the people to believe in the one who was coming after him, that is to say, in Jesus."*
5 *When they heard this, they were baptized into the name of the Lord Jesus.[4]*
6 *Then, when Paul had laid his hands on them, the Holy Spirit came on them, and they proceeded to speak with tongues and to prophesy.*
7 *The men were about twelve in all.*

1 Having visited the churches of South Galatia, Paul continued his westward way to Ephesus, "taking the higher-lying and more direct route, not the regular trade route on the lower level down the Lycus and Maeander valleys."[5] Part of Asian Phrygia, through which he passed, was popularly known as Upper Phrygia. He would approach Ephesus from the north side of Mount Messogis (modern Aydin Daǧlari).

By the time he reached Ephesus, Apollos had crossed the Aegean to Corinth. Shortly after his arrival in Ephesus, Paul met a dozen men whose knowledge of the Way was considerably more defective than Apollos's had

1. The Western text reads: "But when Paul wished, according to his own plan, to go to Jerusalem, the Spirit bade him return to Asia, and having passed through the upper country he came to Ephesus." See p. 354, n. 52; p. 356, n. 58 (on 18:21-22).
2. Lit., "if there is a Holy Spirit" (εἰ πνεῦμα ἅγιόν ἐστιν). The Western text reads "if any are receiving the Holy Spirit."
3. Lit., "into what were you baptized?"
4. The Western text adds "Christ" and continues: "for the remission of sins" (ineptly, because this was the purpose of John's baptism, which these disciples had already received).
5. W. M. Ramsay, *St. Paul the Traveller* (London, [14]1920), p. 265; cf. *The Church in the Roman Empire* (London, [4]1895), pp. 93-96.

been before Priscilla and Aquila gave him the instructions he lacked. When the men are called "disciples" without further qualification, that (in accordance with Luke's usage) seems to mean that they were disciples of Jesus.[6] Had Luke meant to indicate that they were disciples of John the Baptist (as has sometimes been deduced from v. 3), he would have said so explicitly.[7] How they acquired their knowledge of Jesus can only be guessed—it must have been from a source independent of the main Jerusalem-based stream which Luke traces in Acts—but when they heard of him, they believed in him. This at least is implied in Paul's question, "Did you receive the Holy Spirit when you believed?"[8]

2 Paul's question implies something else: when he met them and conversed with them, he not only sensed that their knowledge of the Way was defective; he was able to put his finger on the defect. There was nothing to show that they had ever received the Holy Spirit. Hence his straightforward question. Their answer to it proved that his diagnosis was correct.

Their answer must be understood in its context. Standing by itself, it might mean that the very expression "Holy Spirit" was new to them. If they had any Old Testament background at all, they would have had some idea of the Spirit of God, sometimes called his "Holy Spirit."[9] More particularly, since they had received John's baptism, they would presumably have been told that John's baptism was preparatory, in view of the approach of one who was going to baptize with the Holy Spirit.[10] If so, they did not know that Jesus, in whom they had believed, was the one who would administer this baptism with the Holy Spirit, or that this baptism had now been inaugurated. Certainly they had never received the Holy Spirit. In this they were less advanced than Apollos, who when he came to Ephesus was already "aglow with the Spirit" (18:25).[11]

3 Paul's question about their baptism implies a connection between the receiving of the Spirit and baptism.[12] He assumed that they had been baptized (an unbaptized believer is scarcely contemplated in the New

---

6. Cf. A. Ehrhardt, *The Acts of the Apostles* (Manchester, 1969), pp. 101-2; J. A. T. Robinson, *The Priority of John* (London, 1985), p. 172.

7. The idea that there was a group of disciples of John the Baptist at Ephesus (against whom, incidentally, the fourth Evangelist is alleged to polemicize) has no substantial evidence in its favor, certainly not in the Fourth Gospel.

8. The clause "when you believed" renders the Gk. aorist participle πιστεύσαντες, the "coincident aorist participle" which "is doctrinally important" (J. H. Moulton, MHT I, p. 131n.). Cf. 11:17; Eph. 1:13.

9. Cf. Num. 11:16-17, 24-29; Joel 2:28-32; and, for the expression "Holy Spirit," Isa. 63:10-11.

10. Cf. 1:5; 11:16. With the wording of their reply, "We never even heard if there is a Holy Spirit," cf. John 7:39, "Spirit was not yet," where the Western and Byzantine texts add "given."

11. See p. 359 with n. 73.

12. Cf. 2:38.

Testament), or else they themselves had mentioned their baptism. It was an anomaly in his eyes that a baptized person should not have received the Spirit, so he questioned them more closely, and learned that they had received John's baptism. Where and from whom they had received it is not said: it is conceivable that they had received it at John's own hands in Judaea a quarter of a century before, but there are other possibilities. There is no way of knowing if John's distinctive ministry was continued by some of his disciples after his death.

4 John's baptism was one of preparation rather than one of fulfilment, as Christian baptism now was. Accordingly, Paul explained to them the anticipatory character of John's baptism and its close association with his announcement of the stronger one than himself who was about to come. Paul's summary of John's message combines the Markan account, with its emphasis on repentance, and the Johannine account, in which John points expressly to Jesus as the coming baptizer with the Holy Spirit.[13] Now that Jesus had come and accomplished his mission on earth, now that he had returned to the Father's presence and sent to his followers the promised gift of the Holy Spirit, an anticipatory baptism was no longer appropriate or adequate.

5-7 The twelve men then received baptism "into the name of the Lord Jesus" (the same form of words as is used of the Samaritan believers in 8:16). This is the only account of rebaptism found in the New Testament. The apostles themselves (or many of them) appear to have received John's baptism, but no question of rebaptism was raised for them. Probably their endowment with the Spirit at Pentecost transformed the preparatory significance of the baptism which they had already received into the consummative significance of Christian baptism. Similarly there is no suggestion that Apollos was required to receive Christian baptism over and above the baptism of John, which he already knew; his existing experience of the Spirit would have made such a requirement unnecessary. But the Ephesian disciples had no such experience of the Spirit. They were therefore baptized in a Christian sense, and when Paul laid his hands on them, they received the Spirit in pentecostal fashion, with audible signs of his entering into them. There may be an intentional parallel here between the imposition of Paul's hands on these men and the imposition of Peter's (and John's) hands on the Samaritan converts at an earlier date.[14] G. W. H. Lampe, in pursuance of his

13. With v. 4a cf. Mark 1:4; with v. 4b cf. John 1:26-34. See on 13:24-25 (p. 258 with n. 76).

14. Luke appears deliberately but unobtrusively to trace a number of parallels between Peter's ministry and Paul's; e.g., both, at an early point in their ministry, heal lame men (3:2-8; 14:8-10); both exorcize demons (5:16; 16:18); both have triumphant encounters with sorcerers (8:18-24; 13:6-11); both raise the dead (9:36-41; 20:9-12); both have miraculous escapes from prison (12:7-11; 16:25-26). Cf. the exposition of v. 12 below (pp. 367-68).

thesis, finds that Paul's coming to Ephesus marks "another decisive moment in the missionary history."[15] Ephesus was to be a new center for the Gentile mission—the next in importance after Antioch on the Orontes—and these twelve disciples were probably to be the nucleus of the Ephesian church. By this exceptional procedure, then, they were integrated into the church's missionary program.[16]

5. The Lecture Hall of Tyrannus (19:8-10)

8 *Paul then went into the synagogue and spoke freely[17] for three months; in his discourses he spoke persuasively about the kingdom of God.*

9 *But when some were obstinate and would not believe,[18] but spoke evil of the Way in front of the congregation, Paul withdrew from them and took the disciples away, discoursing day by day in the lecture hall of Tyrannus.[19]*

10 *This went on for two years, so that all those who lived in Asia, both Jews and Greeks, heard the word of the Lord.*

8 Paul had already established relations with the Jews who met in the Ephesian synagogue, when he paid them a flying visit on his way from Corinth to Judaea. Then they had pressed him unsuccessfully to stay longer. Now, however, having completed his business in Judaea and Syria, he had come back to Ephesus and resumed his synagogue discourses in accordance with his promise. But the familiar pattern of events began to reproduce itself. For three months he enjoyed the freedom of the synagogue, debating with its members and setting forth the truth about the kingdom of God—that is to say, all that is implied in the death and exaltation of Jesus.[20]

9 In extending this liberty to Paul for three months, the synagogue authorities in Ephesus showed themselves more enlightened than their counterparts in Thessalonica, who had tolerated him for no more than three weeks. But at last the weight of opposition to his preaching, even in

---

15. *The Seal of the Spirit* (London, 1951), p. 76. See also B. T. D. Smith, "Apollos and the Twelve Disciples at Ephesus," *JTS* 16 (1915), pp. 241-46; N. B. Stonehouse, "Repentance, Baptism and the Gift of the Holy Spirit," in *Paul before the Areopagus and Other New Testament Studies* (Grand Rapids, 1957), pp. 80-82; E. Käsemann, "The Disciples of John the Baptist in Ephesus," E.T. in *Essays on New Testament Themes* (London, 1964), pp. 136-48; J. K. Parratt, "The Rebaptism of the Ephesian Disciples," *ExT* 79 (1967-68), pp. 182-83; C. K. Barrett, "Apollos and the Twelve Disciples of Ephesus," in *The New Testament Age: Essays in Honor of Bo Reicke,* ed. W. C. Weinrich, I (Macon, GA, 1984), pp. 29-39.

16. On the Jerusalem way as the norm see p. 360 with nn. 75 and 76.

17. Gk. ἐπαρρησιάζετο. The Western text adds "with great power."

18. Gk. ἠπείθουν, "were disobedient."

19. The Western text adds "from the fifth to the tenth hour."

20. See on 1:3 (pp. 32, 33 with nn. 17-19).

Ephesus, reached a point where he could no longer make use of the synagogue as his teaching center. He had to find a new center where he would not be interrupted with public slanders directed against the gospel and the Savior whom it proclaimed. This center he found in the lecture hall of Tyrannus. Tyrannus (a name otherwise attested in Ephesus) is usually supposed to have been the lecturer who regularly taught there; it is just possible, however, that he was the owner of the building, who was willing to rent it to Paul at times when it was not required by the regular lecturer (or lecturers). According to the Western text, Paul had the use of the building from 11 a.m. to 4 p.m. Whatever the textual basis of this reading may be, it probably represents what actually happened. Tyrannus (if he was the lecturer) no doubt delivered his lectures in the early morning. At 11 a.m. public activity came to a stop in the cities of Ionia (as in many other parts of the Mediterranean world),[21] and Lake and Cadbury are no doubt right in saying that more people would be asleep at 1 p.m. than at 1 a.m.[22] But Paul, after spending the early hours at his tentmaking (cf. 20:34), devoted the burden and heat of the day to his more important and more exhausting business, and must have conveyed something of his own energy and zeal to his hearers, who had followed him from the synagogue to this lecture hall, for they were prepared to forgo their own siesta in order to listen to Paul.

10 For two full years this work went on.[23] While Paul stayed in Ephesus, a number of his colleagues carried out missionary activity in neighboring cities. During those years his colleague Epaphras appears to have evangelized the cities of the Lycus valley, Colossae, Laodicea, and Hierapolis—cities which Paul evidently did not visit in person (Col. 1:7-8; 2:1; 4:12-13). Perhaps all seven of the churches of Asia addressed in the Revelation of John were also founded about this time. The province was intensively evangelized, and remained one of the leading centers of Christianity for many centuries.

6. Conflict with the Magicians (19:11-19)

11 *God accomplished mighty works of no ordinary character through Paul.*

12 *Sweat-rags and aprons which had been in contact with his body were actually taken from him and applied to those who were sick, so that their diseases left them and evil spirits were expelled.*

13 *Some of the itinerant Jewish exorcists also undertook to pronounce*

---

21. Cf. Martial, *Epigrams* 4.8.3: "Rome prolongs her varied tasks to the fifth hour."

22. *Beginnings* I.4, p. 239.

23. The period indicated in v. 10 may have been rather more than two years; then, if we add the three months of v. 8, we have something approaching the three years of 20:31—probably from the fall of 52 to the summer of 55.

the name of the Lord Jesus over those who were possessed by evil spirits. "I adjure you," one would say, "by that Jesus whom Paul proclaims."

14 *There were seven sons of one Sceva, a Jewish chief priest, who were doing this.*[24]

15 *But the evil spirit answered them, "Jesus I know, and Paul I know, but who are you?"*

16 *Then the man who was possessed by the evil spirit sprang on them and overpowered them; indeed, he so got the better of them all*[25] *that they made their escape from that house naked and wounded.*

17 *This became known to all those who lived in Ephesus, Jews and Greeks alike. Fear fell on them all, and the name of the Lord Jesus was magnified.*

18 *Many of those who believed also came and made confession, divulging their spells.*[26]

19 *A considerable number of those who had practised magic arts*[27] *brought their scrolls together and burned them in the sight of all. They reckoned up their value, and found that it amounted to fifty thousand silver coins.*

11-12   Paul's ministry in Ephesus was marked by manifestations of divine power, especially in healing and exorcism. The use of pieces of material which had been in contact with Paul for the healing of the sick is reminiscent of the healing of those who touched the fringe of Jesus' cloak (Mark 5:27-34; 6:56). One may also detect a parallel here to the healing effect of Peter's shadow in 5:15.[28] The pieces of material were presumably those which Paul used in his tentmaking or leather-working—the sweat-rags for tying around his head and the aprons for tying around his waist.[29] No intrinsic healing

24. V. 14 is expanded as follows in the Western text: "among whom also the sons of Sceva a priest wished to do the same (they were accustomed to exorcize such people), and entering into the demon-possessed man they began to invoke the Name, saying, 'We charge you by Jesus, whom Paul proclaims, to come out.'" While most Western witnesses omit the number of the sons, the Latin codex *gigas* says "two sons" (cf. n. 25 below).

25. Gk. ἀμφοτέρων ("both"); there is good evidence for the use of this word in the sense of "all" in later Greek. Cf. F. G. Kenyon (ed.), *Greek Papyri in the British Museum*, II (London, 1898), p. 221, on *P.Lond.* 336.13 (A.D. 167), where ἀμφότεροι refers to five men: "ἀμφότεροι = πάντες in late Byzantine Greek . . . and it is possible that colloquially the use existed earlier." A similar observation (as pointed out by E. Haenchen, *ad loc.*) was made about the same time by E. Nestle in *Berliner Philologische Wochenschrift* 18 (1898), col. 254. The apparent discrepancy between ἀμφοτέρων here and ἑπτά in v. 14 led the Western revisers to omit the numeral there.

26. Gk. πράξεις, here a technical term for magic practices (the verb πράσσω also has the technical sense of "practise magic" in appropriate contexts).

27. Gk. περίεργα, lit. "superfluous works," another technical term for magic practices (like Lat. *curiosa*). Cf. G. A. Deissmann, *Bible Studies*, E.T. (Edinburgh, ²1909), p. 323, n. 5.

28. See p. 364, n. 14.

29. Both the Greek words used here are of Latin origin: σουδάρια from *sudaria*,

efficacy is ascribed to these things; the healing efficacy lay in the powerful name of Jesus.

13 So potent did this name, as invoked by Paul, prove in the exorcizing of demons from those who were possessed by them that other exorcists began to invoke it too. Among practitioners of magic in ancient times Jews enjoyed high respect,[30] for they were believed to have exceptionally effective spells at their command. In particular, the fact that the name of the God of Israel was not to be pronounced by vulgar lips was generally known among the pagans, and misinterpreted by them according to regular magical principles. Several magical papyri which have survived from those days to ours contain attempts to reproduce the true pronunciation of the ineffable name—*Iaō, Iabe, Iaoue,* and so forth—as well as other Jewish expressions and names such as Sabaoth and Abraham, used as elements in magic spells.[31] The closest parallel to the Ephesian exorcists' misuse of the name of Jesus appears in a magical papyrus belonging to the Bibliothèque Nationale in Paris, which contains the adjuration: "I adjure you by Jesus, the God of the Hebrews."[32]

14-16 Among those Jewish exorcists were the sons of one Sceva,[33] a Jew, described here as a chief priest. It is possible that this Sceva actually belonged to a Jewish chief-priestly family, but more probably "Jewish chief priest" (or even "Jewish high priest") was his self-designation, set out on a placard: Luke might have placed the words between quotation marks had these been invented in his day.[34] The Jewish high priest was the one man who was authorized to pronounce the otherwise ineffable name; this he did once a year, in the course of the service prescribed for the day of atonement.[35] Such a person would therefore enjoy high prestige among magicians. It was not the ineffable name, however, but the name of Jesus that Sceva's sons employed in their attempt to imitate Paul's exorcizing ministry. But when they tried to use it, like an unfamiliar weapon wrongly handled it exploded in their hands. "That Jesus whom Paul proclaims" was a name

---

"sweat-rags" (cf. Luke 19:20; John 11:44; 20:7), and σιμικίνθια from *semicinctia,* "aprons."

30. See M. Simon, *Verus Israel* (Paris, 1948), pp. 394-416.

31. See G. A. Deissmann, *Bible Studies,* pp. 322-36; *New Docs.* 1 (1976), § 8.

32. K. Preisendanz, *Papyri Graecae Magicae,* I (Leipzig, 1928), Pap. Bibl. Nat. Suppl. gr. 574, lines 3018-19. The use by Jews of Jesus' name in healing was sternly denounced by some rabbis; cf. Tos. *Hullin* 2.22-23; TJ *Shabbāt* 14.4.14d and *'Abôdāh Zārāh* 2.2.40d-41a; TB *'Abôdāh Zārāh* 27b.

33. On the name Sceva see B. A. Mastin, "Scaeva the chief priest," *JTS* n.s. 27 (1976), pp. 405-12; "A Note on Acts 19:14," *Biblica* 59 (1978), pp. 97-99.

34. Mastin suggests that his designation ἀρχιερεύς was intended to "authenticate the activity of his sons as *bona fide* exorcists" ("Scaeva the chief priest," p. 405). The Western text calls him ἱερεύς, not ἀρχιερεύς.

35. Mishnah, *Yômā* 5.1; 6.2.

well known to the demon that they were trying to cast out,[36] but what right had they to use it? The man possessed by the demon, energized with abnormal strength, assaulted the would-be exorcists so violently that they ran for their lives from the building in which they were, their clothes torn off and their bodies battered.

17 The news of this incident spread quickly and filled those who heard it with awe; this name, invoked by Paul and his colleagues with such beneficial effects, was plainly no name to be trifled with.

18-19 The whole atmosphere of this passage, in fact, tallies admirably with the reputation which Ephesus had in antiquity as a center of magical practice. Shakespeare sums up that reputation in words which he puts into the mouth of the Syracusan Antipholus in his *Comedy of Errors:*

"They say this town is full of cozenage,
As, nimble jugglers that deceive the eye,
Dark-working sorcerers that change the mind,
Soul-killing witches that deform the body,
Disguised cheaters, prating mountebanks,
And many such-like liberties of sin."[37]

Yet even among the Ephesian practitioners of magic the gospel proved its power. Many of them believed, and came to Paul and his fellow-missionaries, confessing their sorcery and revealing their spells. According to magical theory, the potency of a spell is bound up with its secrecy; if it be divulged, it becomes ineffective. So these converted magicians renounced their imagined power by rendering their spells inoperative. Many of them also gathered their magical papyri together and made a bonfire of them. A number of such magical scrolls have survived to our day; there are specially famous examples in the London, Paris, and Leiden collections.[38] The special connection of Ephesus with magic is reflected in the term "Ephesian letters" for magical scrolls.[39] The spells with which they abound are for the

36. It is doubtful if we should attach great importance to the change of verb: "Jesus I know (γινώσκω) and Paul I know (ἐπίσταμαι)." There was a distinction in fact, in that he knew Jesus by name and Paul by sight, but that is not the normal distinction in meaning between the two Greek verbs.

37. Act 1, scene 2, lines 97-102.

38. The best collection of such documents is Preisendanz's (I, 1928; II, 1931); see n. 32 above. Cf. G. A. Deissmann, *Light from the Ancient East*, E.T. (London, ²1927), pp. 254-64, 302-8, 453-60. A papyrus amulet in the library of Princeton University has been edited with translation and notes by B. M. Metzger in *Papyri in the Princeton University Collections*, III (1942), pp. 78-79; he has given a popular account of it in "St. Paul and the Magicians," *Princeton Seminary Bulletin* 38 (1944), pp. 27-30, where he describes it as "a firsthand specimen of the same sort of magical craft which Paul encountered at Ephesus." See now H. D. Betz (ed.), *The Greek Magical Papyri in Translation*, I- (Chicago, 1986-).

39. Gk. Ἐφέσια γράμματα (Anaxilas, quoted by Athenaeus, *Deipnosophists* 12.548c; Plutarch, *Convivial Questions (Table Talk)* 706e; Clement of Alexandria, *Mis-*

most part the merest gibberish, a rigmarole of words and names considered to be unusually potent, arranged sometimes in patterns which were essential to the efficacy of the spell. They fetched high prices. On the present occasion it was reckoned that documents to the value of 50,000 drachmae went up in smoke. (The public burning of literature as an open repudiation or condemnation of its contents can be paralleled from both ancient and modern times.)

7. Further Progress Report (19:20)

20 *So mightily did the word of the Lord keep on spreading and increasing in strength.*

20 Luke pauses at this point to make a fifth report of progress.[40] One further episode from Paul's Ephesian ministry remains to be related, but the plan of Acts requires a break here.

VI. PAUL PLANS TO VISIT ROME AND GETS THERE BY AN UNFORESEEN ROUTE (19:21–28:31)

A. HE PREPARES TO LEAVE EPHESUS FOR MACEDONIA AND ACHAIA (19:21–20:6)

1. Paul Makes Plans for the Future (19:21-22)

21 *When all this had been done, Paul planned in the Spirit to pass through Macedonia and Achaia and then go to Jerusalem. "After I have been there," he said, "I must also see Rome."*

22 *So, sending two of his helpers, Timothy and Erastus, into Macedonia, he himself stayed on for some time in Ephesus.*

21 The period of Paul's Ephesian ministry drew to an end. It had been a most fruitful and encouraging ministry, even if it was attended by personal dangers of which little is said in Acts, although there are several allusions to them in the letters which Paul sent elsewhere (especially to Corinth) about this time.[41] Now some two and a half years had passed since he made Ephesus his headquarters. Christianity had established a firm foothold on the east shore of the Aegean (as previously on the west shore), and the young

---

cellanies 5.8.45.2; cf. A. Deissmann, "Ephesia Grammata," in *Abhandlungen zur semitischen Religionskunde und Sprachwissenschaft W. W. Graf von Baudissin . . . überreicht* (Giessen, 1918), pp. 121-24; E. Kuhnert, *RE* 5, cols. 2771-73 (*s.v.* "Ephesia Grammata"); K. Preisendanz, *RAC* 5, cols. 515-20 (*s.v.* "Ephesia Grammata").

40. See on 6:7 (p. 123, n. 20).

41. Cf. 1 Cor. 15:32; 2 Cor. 1:8-11. It has been thought also that one or more of the frequent imprisonments to which Paul refers in 2 Cor. 11:23 may have been endured in Ephesus; cf. H. Lisco, *Vincula Sanctorum* (Berlin, 1900); A. Deissmann, "Zur

churches of Asia (as of Macedonia and Achaia) could safely be left to continue their life of fellowship and witness under the direction of the Holy Spirit. Paul's activity could be transferred to other areas, and he looked around for fresh worlds to conquer for Christ. His settled policy not to build on someone else's foundation (Rom. 15:20) forbade him to consider missionary enterprise in Egypt or Cyrene; in Rome, too, there was already a Christian community.[42] He looked forward, however, to visiting Rome, not with the intention of settling down there but of halting there for some time on his way to Spain. For Spain, the most westerly outpost of Roman civilization, was the new Macedonia which called him to come over and plant the faith among its hitherto unevangelized inhabitants.[43] But Rome is the goal of Luke's narrative, and he is more interested in Paul's plan to visit Rome than he is in his Spanish project. Whether or not Paul's Spanish project was ever realized is something which Luke knew by the time he published his work, but something which we do not know. It is probable, too, that Rome played a part in Paul's missionary strategy, which makes Luke's choice of it as the goal of his narrative doubly appropriate.[44] From this point on, then, we follow Paul to Rome until, at the end of Acts, he reaches the imperial city by an unforeseen route and is busily preaching the gospel there when the readers take their leave of him.

Before putting his plans into execution, however, Paul intended to visit his friends in Macedonia and Achaia, and then go to Jerusalem. Luke does not mention the main reason for this visit to Jerusalem,[45] but Paul's

---

ephesinischen Gefangenschaft des Apostels Paulus," in *Anatolian Studies presented to Sir W. M. Ramsay* (Manchester, 1923), pp. 121-27 (in *Light from the Ancient East*, p. 237, n. 1, Deissmann says he introduced this hypothesis while lecturing at Herborn in 1897); W. Michaelis, *Die Gefangenschaft des Paulus in Ephesus* (Gütersloh, 1925); G. S. Duncan, *St. Paul's Ephesian Ministry* (London, 1929). Luke's reticence on Paul's troubles in Ephesus (apart from the riot of vv. 23-41) has been attributed to his apologetic motive: if these troubles were in any way connected with the proconsul Lucius Junius Silanus (see p. 379, n. 82), it would probably have been impolitic to mention any incident in which he was involved (so Duncan, *St. Paul's Ephesian Ministry*, pp. 103-4).

42. It was no doubt greatly diminished by the expulsion edict of A.D. 49 (cf. p. 347 with nn. 9-12); but that would have become a dead letter on the death of Claudius in A.D. 54, and little more than two years after that the Christian community in Rome was large and flourishing, with Gentiles now apparently in the majority (Rom. 1:8; 11:13; 15:14; 16:3-16, 19).

43. Cf. Rom. 15:24, 28. The expression "Paul planned in the Spirit" most probably deno es a consciousness of guidance by the Holy Spirit; it "seems intended to describe a purpose formed with intense earnestness" (J. H. Kennedy, *The Second and Third Epistles of St. Paul to the Corinthians* [London, 1900], p. 20). Cf. 20:22.

44. See H. Chadwick, "The Circle and the Ellipse: Rival Concepts of Authority in the Early Church" (1959), in his *History and Thought of the Early Church* (London, 1982), pp. 3-17; F. F. Bruce, "The Romans Debate—Continued," *BJRL* 64 (1981-82), pp. 334-59.

45. Apart from a vague allusion in Paul's defense before Felix in 24:17 (see p. 445 with nn. 28 and 29).

own writings make it clear that he wished to be there in person, along with delegates from his Gentile churches, east and west of the Aegean, in order to hand over to the leaders of the Jerusalem church the proceeds of the fund which he had organized in those churches for the relief of the poor in Jerusalem.[46]

22 So he sent two of his companions, Timothy and Erastus, over to Macedonia in advance of his own journey thither. Timothy has not been mentioned in the record of Acts since he returned from Macedonia to rejoin Paul in Corinth (18:5). But he was certainly with Paul for part at least of the Ephesian ministry; at some point in the course of that period Paul sent him to Corinth and expected him to return to Ephesus (1 Cor. 4:17; 16:10-11). It is uncertain if that was the trip referred to here.[47] It is unlikely that the Erastus mentioned here is identical with Erastus the city treasurer of Corinth, to whom Paul refers in Rom. 16:23.[48]

2. The Riot at Ephesus (19:23-41)

a. Indignation of the silversmiths (19:23-28)

23 *About that time a serious disturbance broke out in connection with the Way.*

24 *A silversmith named Demetrius, who made silver[49] shrines[50] of Artemis and provided considerable business for his fellow-craftsmen,*

25 *called them together, along with those who were engaged in the same line of business, and addressed them as follows:*

"Gentlemen,[51] you know that our prosperity is based on this business.

26 *Now, as you see and hear, not only in Ephesus[52] but almost through-*

---

46. Cf. 1 Cor. 16:1-4; 2 Cor. 8:1–9:15; Rom. 15:25-28. When 1 Corinthians was written (shortly before Paul's departure from Ephesus, to judge from 1 Cor. 16:8), Paul had not finally decided to visit Jerusalem in person with the bearers of their churches' contributions (1 Cor. 16:4); by the time Romans was written, he had definitely made up his mind to go himself. For the importance which Paul attached to this collection see F. F. Bruce, *Paul: Apostle of the Free Spirit* (Exeter/Grand Rapids, 1977), pp. 319-24.

47. At some point between the writing of 1 Corinthians and the third visit paid by Paul to Corinth (2 Cor. 12:14; 13:1), probably the visit implied in 20:2-3 below, Paul paid his "painful visit" to Corinth (2 Cor. 2:1).

48. The Erastus of Rom. 16:23 is probably the man named on a Latin limestone pavement inscription discovered in Corinth by American archaeologists in 1929: "Erastus, in gratitude for his aedileship, laid this pavement at his own expense" (cf. J. H. Kent, *Corinth* VIII/3: *The Inscriptions 1926-1950* [Princeton, 1966], p. 99).

49. Cod. B omits "silver."

50. A gloss on "shrines" has found its way into the text of Cod. 1739 and a few other witnesses: "perhaps small cups" (ἴσως κιβώρια μικρά).

51. Gk. ἄνδρες, to which the Western text adds συντεχνῖται, "fellow-craftsmen."

52. The Western text reads "as far as Ephesus."

*out the whole province of Asia this fellow Paul[53] has persuaded a
great number of people to go over to his way of thinking: he insists
that gods made by hand are no gods.*

27 *There is a twofold danger here: not only is our line of business[54]
likely to be discredited, but the temple of the great goddess Artemis
will become of no account, and she who is worshiped by all Asia and
indeed by the whole world will be dragged down from her
preeminence."[55]*

28 *Hearing this, they were filled with fury and[56] kept on shouting,
"Great is Artemis of the Ephesians!"[57]*

23   The narrative style of Acts has been compared to "a lecture with lan-
tern-slides; the pictures are shown one after another illustrating the story the
lecturer wants to tell while he makes the transition from one plate to another
by some general remarks."[58] This comparison is specially apt in the account
of Paul's ministry in Ephesus. Three "pictures" have already been shown
(the incident of the twelve disciples, the program of discussions in Tyrannus's lecture hall, and the encounter with the magicians); now comes the
fourth, which is the most vivid of all. It is postponed until Paul's further
travel plans have been announced—partly to give prominence to those
plans, and partly because the disturbance about to be described took place
very shortly before Paul's departure from Ephesus.

The disturbance, which might have led to very ugly consequences,
arose out of the threat which the gospel presented to all pagan worship, and
especially to the cult of the great goddess Artemis, and to those industries
which were largely dependent on the cult.

The cult of Ephesian Artemis was of earlier date than the Greek
settlement at Ephesus; the name Artemis is non-Greek. Artemis was traditionally venerated as the protector of wild creatures.[59] This association with
wild creatures survives, in an altered form, in her worship on the Greek

---

53. The Western text adds "whoever (he may be)" (τίς ποτε).

54. Gk. μέρος. Moulton-Milligan (*Vocabulary*, p. 399) cite a papyrus document
of the third century A.D. for this word used in the sense "branch or line of business."

55. The Western text recasts these three clauses: "but also the temple of the great
goddess Artemis will become of no account and her preeminence is likely to be brought
low."

56. The Western text inserts "running into the open street" (or "square," Gk. εἰς
τὸ ἄμφοδον).

57. The Western text reads this as an invocation (in the vocative), not an acclamation: "Great Artemis of the Ephesians!" (as also in v. 34 below). See p. 376, n. 69.

58. W. C. van Unnik, "The 'Book of Acts' the Confirmation of the Gospel,"
NovT 4 (1964), p. 35.

59. Homer calls her "Artemis of the wilds, mistress of wild beasts" (*Iliad*
21.470-71); Aeschylus pictures her indignant concern for injured wild things (*Agamem-
non* 134-38). See W. K. C. Guthrie, *The Greeks and their Gods* (London, 1950), pp.
99-106.

mainland as the "queen and huntress, chaste and fair" of Ben Jonson's poem;[60] Ephesian Artemis, on the other hand, seems to have acquired some of the features of the great mother-goddess venerated from time immemorial in Asia Minor. Her temple, replacing an earlier one which was destroyed by fire in 356 B.C., was reckoned one of the seven wonders of the ancient world. It covered an area four times as large as that of the Parthenon in Athens; it was supported by 127 pillars, each of them sixty feet high, and was adorned by Praxiteles and other great sculptors of antiquity.[61] It stood about a mile and a half northeast of the city which Paul knew. All knowledge of its whereabouts had been forgotten for centuries, when its foundations were discovered on the last day of 1869.[62] The great altar, west of the main building, was discovered in 1965.

24 The silversmiths of Ephesus regarded their guild as being under the special patronage of Artemis, in whose honor so many of their wares were manufactured. Among these wares were miniature silver niches, containing an image of the goddess, which her votaries bought to dedicate in the temple.[63] The sale of these was a source of considerable profit to the silversmiths, and they were alarmed at the fall in the demand for them which the spread of Christianity was causing. When religious devotion and economic interest were simultaneously offended, a quite exceptionally fervid anger was aroused.[64]

---

60. *Hymn to Diana*, line 1. "That such a goddess [as Ephesian Artemis] should come to be represented in English by the name Diana is almost ridiculous" (A. Souter, *Dictionary of the Apostolic Church*, I [Edinburgh, 1915], p. 295, *s.v.* "Diana").

61. The earlier temple was burned down (on the night when Alexander the Great was born, it was said) by a young man named Herostratus, who said he did it so that his name might be remembered. On the temple of New Testament times see Strabo, *Geog.* 14.1.22-23; Pliny, *Nat. Hist.* 16.213; 36.95-97, 179.

62. By J. T. Wood; see his *Discoveries at Ephesus* (London, 1877); also J. Fergusson, *The Temple of Diana at Ephesus* (London, 1883); R. C. Kukula, "Literarische Zeugnisse über den Artemistempel," *Forschungen in Ephesos*, I (Vienna, 1906), pp. 237-82; D. G. Hogarth, *Excavation at Ephesus: The Archaic Artemisia* (London, 1908); A. Bammer, *Die Architektur des jüngeren Artemision von Ephesos* (Wiesbaden, 1972); "Forschungen im Artemision von Ephesus von 1976 bis 1981," *AS* 32 (1982), pp. 61-87.

63. We know of such miniature shrines of terra-cotta, but no silver ones are known to have survived. A Greek and Latin inscription found in the theater of Ephesus (*BMI* III.481 = *Insch. Eph.* 1.27) records how a Roman official, Gaius Vibius Salutaris, presented a silver image of Artemis and other statues to be set up in the theater during meetings of the civic assembly (see R. Heberdey and others, *Das Theater = Forschungen in Ephesos*, II [Vienna, 1912], pp. 147-49; A. Deissmann, *Light from the Ancient East*, pp. 112-13). See nn. 69, 72 below. E. L. Hicks, "Demetrius the Siversmith: An Ephesian Study," *Exp.* 4,1 (1890), pp. 401-22, pointed out that "shrine-maker" (νεωποιός) was a designation of a member of the temple vestry (comprising probably twelve men).

64. Compare the indignation of the owners of the fortune-telling slave girl in 16:16-21; also the report of the younger Pliny (*Epistles* 10.96.10) that the sale of fodder for sacrificial animals had fallen off in Bithynia about A.D. 112 because of the spread of Christianity in the province.

25-27 Demetrius, a prominent member of the guild of silversmiths, probably their president, called a meeting of those who were involved in this trade, and persuaded them to stage a mass protest against the subversive propaganda spread by Paul and his colleagues. Those preachers, by denying all existence to divinities that were made by human hands,[65] and condemning any attempt to represent the divine likeness in visible form, were threatening the livelihood of those who carried on such a profitable business in the manufacture of images of Artemis. More than that, they were challenging the preeminent majesty of the great goddess herself—a goddess venerated not only at Ephesus and throughout the province of Asia, but over the whole civilized world.[66] It was intolerable that they should stand idly by and allow such an affront to be offered to the goddess and her temple, the most magnificent shrine on earth.

28 Fired by the words of Demetrius, his hearers ran into the open street (as the Western text expressly says), acclaiming their goddess aloud with the cultic cry, "Great is Artemis of the Ephesians!"

b. Demonstration in the theater (19:29-34)

29 *The city was filled with the uproar, and all rushed as one man into the theater. They seized on two of Paul's traveling companions, Gaius and Aristarchus, men of Macedonia,[67] and took them along with them.*

30 *Paul wanted to go in to confront the populace, but the disciples would not allow him.*

31 *Some of the Asiarchs also, who were well disposed to him, sent to urge him not to venture into the theater.*

32 *So some were shouting one thing, some another, for the assembly was in a state of confusion, and most of them had no idea why they had come together.*

33 *Some of the crowd put Alexander up;[68] the Jews had pushed him to the front. Alexander, motioning with his hand, wished to make a speech of defense to the populace.*

---

65. This description is applied to material temples in 7:48; 17:24.

66. K. Wernicke, in Pauly-Wissowa's *Real-enzyklopädie* II, cols. 1385-86 (*s.v.* "Artemis"), enumerates thirty-three places, all over the known world, where Ephesian Artemis was venerated.

67. Some minuscules (36 307 431 453 and a few others) read the singular "a man of Macedonia" (Μακεδόνα) instead of the plural (Μακεδόνας), possibly under the influence of 20:4, where Gaius is said to be a man of Derbe (see p. 380, n. 4). But it may not have been the same Gaius; the name was very common in the Roman world. If the singular be the true reading here, then the plural has arisen through dittography of the initial letter of the following word συνεκδήμους ("traveling companions"); if the plural is original, the singular is due to haplography. Aristarchus was "a Macedonian from Thessalonica" (27:2; cf. 20:4).

68. Gk. συνεβίβασαν. The Western text reads κατεβίβασαν, i.e., the crowd "pulled him down" when the Jews put him up to speak.

34 *But when they recognized that he was a Jew, they shouted continuously for two hours, saying one thing only: "Great is Artemis of the Ephesians!"* [69]

29 The enthusiastic resentment of the silversmiths infected their fellow-citizens. Ramsay may be right in thinking that the silversmiths, on leaving the place where Demetrius addressed them, ran into the street later reconstructed as the Arcadian Way, leading from the harbor up to the left front of the theater.[70] When the excitement spread to the crowd, the theater was the natural place for them to stage a demonstration. The theater of Ephesus, cut out of the western slope of Mount Pion (modern Panayirdağ), could accommodate nearly 25,000 people.[71] It was the regular meeting place of the civic assembly, which was held three times a month; on this occasion the demonstrating populace appears to have constituted itself as a meeting of the assembly, but a highly irregular one.[72] As the people rushed along, they laid hands on two of Paul's companions, Gaius and Aristarchus, and dragged them into the theater with them. It has been conjectured that the vividness of Luke's description of what went on in the theater owes something to the account given by one or the other of these two men.

30-31 The crowd had not been able to lay hands on Paul himself, but as soon as he knew what was afoot, he prepared to go and face the unruly assembly in person. But the Ephesian Christians, in alarm, forcibly prevented him from doing what seemed to them such a mad thing. The Asiarchs also, leading citizens of Ephesus, sent him a message to dissuade him from running such a risk to his life. The title Asiarchs was given to leading citizens of those cities in the province which were linked in a league, more particularly to those who were currently holding high office in the league, or had formerly done so. (It was apparently from their ranks that the annually elected high priest of the imperial cult in the province was drawn.)[73] That

69. The Western text, as in v. 28, makes this an invocation (see n. 57 above). Here the clause is repeated in Cod. B—"picturesquely," say Lake and Cadbury, who reproduce the repetition in their translation (*Beginnings* I.4, p. 249), adding, "It may be a dittography; if so, it is a happy one." In the Salutaris inscription (see n. 63 above) Artemis is repeatedly designated "the greatest goddess."

70. W. M. Ramsay, *The Letters to the Seven Churches* (London, 1909), p. 224.

71. See R. Heberdey and others, *Das Theater = Forschungen in Ephesos*, II (Vienna, 1912).

72. According to Chrysostom (*Homilies on Acts* 42.2), the regular assembly met three times a month. "Even this excited mob still retained some idea of method in conducting business. It was quite in the old Greek style that they should at once constitute themselves into a meeting of the Ephesian People, and proceed to discuss business and pass resolutions. . . . But this meeting was not conducted by persons used to business and possessing authority with the crowd" (Ramsay, *Letters to the Seven Churches*, pp. 224-25). Cf. the inscription mentioned in n. 63 above.

73. In A.D. 155 or 156 Philip of Tralles, an Asiarch, was apparently also "high priest of Asia" (*Martyrdom of Polycarp* 12.2; 21.1). See L. R. Taylor, "The Asiarchs,"

such men were friendly to Paul suggests that imperial policy at this time was not hostile to Christianity, and that the more educated classes did not share the antipathy to Paul felt by the more superstitious rank and file.

32 In the theater, however, the popular indignation was enjoying uninhibited expression. There was total disorder, for the majority of the crowd had no clear idea of why they were there—a remark which reveals Luke's Greek sense of humor.[74]

33-34 One group of residents in Ephesus had special cause for anxiety at this turn of events. This was the Jewish community. True, the prime occasion of the riot was Paul's mission, but Paul was a Jew, and Jews were known to be disbelievers in Artemis and all other pagan divinities. Those members of the populace who were insufficiently informed about the cause of the demonstration were likely to indulge in general anti-Jewish agitation when they learned that the honor of the great goddess was in peril.

The Jews of Ephesus judged it necessary to dissociate themselves openly from Paul and the other missionaries, so they put forward Alexander,[75] one of their number, to make it plain to the crowd that they had nothing to do with the present trouble—that they were as much opposed to Paul, indeed, as the demonstrators were. But when Alexander got up to speak, the people were in no mood to listen to him. All that they cared about was that he was a Jew, and therefore no worshiper of Artemis; some of them may even have thought that he was the cause of the trouble, seeing that he appeared so eager to make a speech for the defense. When he beckoned for silence and attention, therefore, they howled him down, and for the next two hours they kept up the cry: "Great is Artemis of the Ephesians!"

c. The town clerk calms the agitation (19:35-41)

35 *At last the town clerk quieted the crowd. "Gentlemen of Ephesus,"
he said, "no one in the world is unaware that the city of the Ephesians is temple warden of Great Artemis and of the image that fell
down from the sky.*

36 *This is indisputable; therefore you must calm down, stay quiet, and
do nothing rash.*

37 *You have brought these men here, although they are guilty neither of
sacrilege nor of blasphemy against our goddess.*

Beginnings I.5, pp. 256-62; D. Magie, *Roman Rule in Asia Minor* (Princeton, 1950), I, pp. 449-50; II, pp. 1298-1301; M. Rossner, *Studii Clasice* 16 (1974), pp. 101-42, summarized in *SEG* 26 (1976-77), § 1864; *New Docs.* 1 (1976), § 32.

74. On Luke's sense of humor see H. McLachlan, *St. Luke: The Man and his Work* (Manchester, 1920), pp. 144-60.

75. Alexander is introduced as though readers might be expected to recognize his name, but nothing more is known of him. His identity with Paul's enemy "Alexander the coppersmith" of 2 Tim. 4:14 is a matter of conjecture. Cf. also 1 Tim. 1:20 for another Alexander, evidently an errant Christian.

38 *If Demetrius and his associated craftsmen have a case to bring
against anyone, assizes are in session and there are such persons as
proconsuls; let them state their charges against one another.*

39 *If you want any further action taken, the matter will be settled in the
lawful assembly.*

40 *Indeed, we are in danger of being charged with riotous assembly for
this day's action: we can show no cause to plead in justification of
this commotion."*

41 *So saying, he dismissed the assembly.*

35 There was one citizen of Ephesus who was particularly alarmed by the
people's riotous conduct. This was the town clerk,[76] the executive officer of
the civic assembly, who took part in drafting the decrees to be laid before it,
and had them engraved when they were passed. He acted also as liaison
officer between the civic government and the Roman provincial administration, which had its headquarters in Ephesus. The Roman authorities would
hold him responsible for the riotous assembly, and might impose severe
penalties on the city. He therefore did his best to calm the assembly, and
when at last he succeeded, he addressed them.

They need not be alarmed for the honor of the great goddess, he said,
for her fame and majesty were universally acknowledged. Everyone knew
that her image was of no mortal workmanship but had fallen from the sky[77]
to be guarded by the people of Ephesus; everyone knew that in consequence
the city bore the proud title, "Temple Warden of Artemis."[78] (There were
several images in antiquity which were reputed to have fallen from the sky.
Originally the term was used of meteorites, but was later extended to include
sacred objects of other origin or material.)[79]

36-37 Therefore, the town clerk went on, the divine power of the
goddess was undeniable and unassailable. The citizens ought to keep calm

76. Gk. γραμματεύς, "secretary." See W. M. Ramsay, *HDB* I, p. 723 (*s.v.*
"Ephesus"); A. W. Gomme, *Oxford Classical Dictionary*, p. 476 (*s.v.* "Grammateis").

77. Gk. διοπετές (cf. KJV "the image which fell down from Jupiter").

78. Gk. νεωκόρος, a word which literally means "temple-sweeper"; it acquired
a more honorable status, being given as a title of dignity both to individuals and to cities.
There is inscriptional evidence for the designation of Ephesus as "temple warden of
Artemis" (*CIG* 2972). See W. M. Ramsay, *Cities and Bishoprics of Phrygia*, I (Oxford,
1895), pp. 58-60; D. Magie, *Roman Rule in Asia Minor*, I, p. 637; II, pp. 1497-98; A. N.
Sherwin-White, *Roman Society and Roman Law in the New Testament* (Oxford, 1963),
pp. 88-89; L. Robert, "Sur des inscriptions d'Éphèse," *Revue de Philologie* 41 (1967), pp.
7-84, especially p. 48.

79. Replicas of the "many-breasted" image of Ephesian Artemis have survived
from antiquity. Other images or cult objects of supernatural workmanship were the
Palladium of Troy, and the images of the Tauric Artemis (Euripides, *Iphigenia in Tauris*
87-88, 1384-85), of the *Magna Mater* brought from Pessinus to Rome in 204 B.C. (Livy,
Hist. 29.11, 14), of Ceres at Enna (Cicero, *Verrines* 2.5.187), and of El Gabal of Emesa
(Herodian, *Hist.* 5.3, 5). On the cult of meteorites see A. B. Cook, *Zeus*, III (Cambridge,
1940), pp. xii, 881-942.

and not be led by excitement into some course of behavior which they would later regret. The men whom they had dragged into the theater were guilty of no crime: they had committed no act of temple robbery or other form of sacrilege; they had spoken no evil of Artemis.[80]

38-41 If Demetrius and his fellow-craftsmen had a serious complaint to make, said the town clerk, let them make it in the appropriate manner. There were regular assize days[81]—the days when the convention of citizens met under the presidency of the provincial governor (perhaps it is implied that the assizes were being held right then). The provincial administration was functioning, even if at the moment there was an interregnum between two proconsulates.[82] The aggrieved parties should avail themselves of these legal means of redress. If the matters which caused them concern were such as might more suitably be dealt with by the citizen body of Ephesus, they should wait for one of the regular meetings of the civic assembly, instead of convening an irregular and riotous assembly like this.[83] The Roman authorities would not tolerate such disorderly proceedings; as it was, they might very well arraign the city on a charge of riot in consequence of what had happened, and the city could plead no justification for it. By this time the people were considerably subdued, as they listened to the town clerk's sobering arguments, and when he spoke the words of dismissal (as he would have done at the end of a regular assembly), they went quietly home. The town clerk's reasoned rebuttal of vulgar charges brought against Christians, not only in Ephesus but in other places too, is an important element in the apologetic motive of Acts.

80. Jewish interpretative tradition read Ex. 22:28a (cf. p. 426) as a prohibition of scurrilous attacks on pagan divinities (cf. Josephus, *Ant.* 4.207; *Ap.* 2.237; Philo, *Life of Moses* 2.205; *Special Laws* 1.53).

81. Gk. ἀγοραῖοι, originally "market days"; these were convenient days for the *conventus* of citizens of an assize city to meet under the presidency of the proconsul. The assizes were held in about nine of the cities of Asia in turn.

82. Hence the generalizing plural "proconsuls." The proconsul of Asia, Marcus Junius Silanus (who was, like Nero, a great-grandson of Augustus), was poisoned at the instigation of Agrippina, Nero's mother, soon after Nero's accession to the imperial power in October, A.D. 54 (Tacitus, *Annals* 13.1-3; cf. Dio Cassius, *Hist.* 61.6.4-5). The interregnum between his death and the arrival of his successor was perhaps a specially dangerous period for Paul; see G. S. Duncan, *St. Paul's Ephesian Ministry* (London, 1929), pp. 102-7. But Duncan's suggestion that the plural "proconsuls" here refers to Helius and Celer, the officials in charge of Nero's personal affairs in Asia, as though they carried out the proconsular responsibilities in the interregnum—a suggestion anticipated in H. M. Luckock, *Footprints of the Apostles as traced by St. Luke in the Acts* (London, 1897), II, p. 189—is improbable; see W. M. Ramsay, "Some Recent Editions of the Acts of the Apostles," *Exp.* 6,2 (1900), pp. 334-35.

83. Gk. ἐκκλησία is used both of the regular assembly and of the present disorderly assembly. The expression "lawful assembly" (ἔννομος ἐκκλησία) was "the correct technical term . . . to distinguish the regularly appointed meetings of the people from the present concourse" (A. N. Sherwin-White, *Roman Society and Roman Law in the New Testament*, p. 87).

ACTS 20

3. Paul Visits Macedonia and Greece (20:1-6)

1 *When the uproar was ended, Paul sent for the disciples and encouraged them; then he took his leave of them and set out on his journey into Macedonia.*
2 *Having passed through that territory and spoken many words of encouragement to the people there, he came into Greece.*
3 *There he spent three months. Then, when he was about to set sail for Syria, a plot was hatched against him by the Jews and he decided to return through Macedonia.[1]*
4 *He was accompanied[2] by Sopater, son of Pyrrhus,[3] a Beroean, by Aristarchus and Secundus from Thessalonica, by Gaius from Derbe[4] and Timothy, and by Tychicus[5] and Trophimus from Asia.[6]*
5 *These went on ahead[7] and were waiting for us at Troas,*
6 *but we set sail from Philippi after the days of unleavened bread, and came to them at Troas in five days. We stayed there seven days.*

1 The riot in the Ephesian theater was one of the last—if also one of the

---

1. The Western text reads: "a plot was hatched against him by the Jews, so he decided to set sail for Syria, but the Spirit told him to return through Macedonia." His decision to set sail for Syria was not due to the plot; for the introduction of the Spirit as dictating a change of plan cf. 16:6-8; also the Western text of 19:1.
2. A D and the majority of Byzantine witnesses insert "as far as Asia" (pointlessly, since two of the men mentioned had come from Asia to join him).
3. The Byzantine text omits "son of Pyrrhus."
4. The Western text calls Gaius a "Doberian" (instead of "Derbaean"), i.e., a native of Doberus in Macedonia, twenty-six miles northwest of Philippi. This would ease his identification with the Gaius of 19:29, who was evidently a Macedonian (see p. 375, n. 67). But there is no compelling reason to identify them. L. C. Valckenaer, followed by F. Blass, emends the text here to make it read "of the Thessalonians, Aristarchus and Secundus and Gaius; and the Derbaean Timothy." There is no necessity for such an emendation; and in any case Timothy was probably a Lystran (see 16:1-2 with exposition, and cf. p. 303, n. 6).
5. D calls him Eutychus, by confusion with the young man of v. 9.
6. The Western text, more explicitly, calls them "Ephesians" and not simply Asians (cf. 21:29).
7. Gk. προελθόντες, for which the Alexandrian text (א B* etc.) reads προσελθόντες, "having come to (us)."

most spectacular—of the incidents attending Paul's ministry at Ephesus. According to 1 Cor. 16:8, written a few months before, he planned to leave Ephesus after Pentecost (probably in A.D. 55); it has been conjectured that the riot took place about the time of the Ephesian festival of the Artemisia, held annually in March/April.[8] In the year 55 Pentecost fell on May 25. Paul may, of course, have had to change his plans because of the riot and other troubles which he experienced in the province of Asia.

In the light of 2 Cor. 2:12-13, W. M. Ramsay supposes that Paul took a coasting ship from Ephesus to Troas.[9] At Troas he hoped to meet Titus, whom he had sent to Corinth to deal with a disquieting situation in the church there. Although there was ample opportunity for gospel witness in and around Troas, he could not settle down to take full advantage of it because of his anxiety about Corinth. When Titus did not arrive, Paul bade farewell to his friends at Troas, and continued his journey into Macedonia. He may have waited at Troas until he knew that Titus could no longer be expected to arrive by sea across the Aegean and would have to travel overland.[10] So he set out in hope of meeting him at some point on the road, and did in fact meet him in Macedonia. The reassuring news which Titus brought from Corinth brought Paul great relief and joy—feelings which find eloquent expression in 2 Cor. 1–9.

2 How long Paul spent in Macedonia we are not told; it seems to have been a rather prolonged period. It was probably at this time that he went as far as Illyricum (Rom. 15:19); his earlier Macedonian journey through Philippi, Thessalonica, and Beroea (16:12–17:10) did not bring him anywhere near the Illyrian frontier. On this occasion we must understand that he traveled west along the Egnatian Way, perhaps as far as its termination at Dyrrhachium (modern Durrës) on the Adriatic, and then turned north in the direction of Illyricum. The period between his departure from Ephesus and his leaving Macedonia for "Greece" (i.e., the province of Achaia), including his stay at Troas and his missionary and pastoral activity in Macedonia, may well have covered about a year and a half—say, from the summer of A.D. 55 to the late part of 56.[11]

3 The three months that he spent in Greece were the winter months of A.D. 56-57. Most of this time was probably spent in Corinth, where he enjoyed the hospitality of his friend Gaius (plausibly identified with the

---

8. Cf. G. S. Duncan, *St. Paul's Ephesian Ministry* (London, 1929), p. 34.

9. *St. Paul the Traveller* (London, [14]1920), p. 283.

10. Cf. W. L. Knox, *St. Paul and the Church of the Gentiles* (Cambridge, 1939), p. 144, n. 2.

11. G. S. Duncan thought that after Paul reached Dyrrhachium "there was a period of evangelistic work, which need not have been extensive or prolonged, in Illyricum; from there, as winter approached, he sailed south to Nicopolis (cf. Tit. 3:12), and in course of time he came to Corinth" (*St. Paul's Ephesian Ministry*, p. 221). He linked Titus's visit to Dalmatia (2 Tim. 4:10) with this Illyrian ministry.

Titius Justus of 18:7),[12] and sent his letter to the Christians of Rome, preparing them for the visit which he hoped to pay them quite soon, on his way to Spain.[13] Among his concerns in Macedonia and Achaia at this time must be included the completion of arrangements for delivering the collected gifts from the churches of those provinces to Jerusalem.[14] Toward the end of winter the delegates from the contributing churches gathered at Corinth to be ready to sail with Paul to Judaea when navigation started again. It may have been their first intention to take a pilgrim ship from Cenchreae (cf. 18:18), which picked up at the principal ports those who wished to be in Jerusalem for the forthcoming festival. But Paul got wind of a plot to kill him, when once he was on board this ship, so he changed his plan, and decided to go back to Macedonia and sail from there.[15] The delegates set sail as arranged, disembarked at Troas, and waited there until Paul should catch up with them.

4-5 Luke mentions Paul's fellow-travelers by name, but does not say why they were accompanying him on this voyage. He is strangely reticent about the Jerusalem fund. But when Paul, shortly before leaving Corinth, sent the Roman Christians greetings from "all the churches of Christ" (Rom. 16:16), he had good reason to do so, because representatives from those churches were joining him at the time. The churches of Macedonia were represented by Sopater,[16] Aristarchus,[17] and Secundus; those of Asia by Tychicus[18] and Trophimus;[19] those of Galatia by Gaius the Derbaean.[20] (Timothy also belonged originally to one of the churches of Galatia, namely Lystra, but he was in the party probably not as a church delegate but as Paul's junior colleague and *fidus Achates*.)

No mention is made of a delegate from the Corinthian church. The absence of any such reference may have something to do with the strained relations between Paul and that church. But Paul had recently told the Christians of Rome that contributions were coming from Achaia (Rom. 15:26). One possibility is that the church of Corinth had entrusted its contribution to Titus (cf. 2 Cor. 8:6-23; 12:18); if so, the failure to mention Titus here is part of the problem of his absence from the whole record of Acts.

12. See Rom. 16:23 (cf. p. 350 with n. 26).
13. Cf. Rom. 1:9-15; 15:22-29.
14. See pp. 371-72 with nn. 45 and 46 (on 19:21).
15. Ramsay (*St. Paul the Traveller*, p. 287) supposed that the original plan was to be in Jerusalem for *Passover*, but when the delay caused by the plot and consequent change of itinerary made that impossible, Paul determined to arrive at the latest in time for Pentecost (cf. v. 16).
16. Probably the Sosipater of Rom. 16:21 (see p. 348, n. 14).
17. Cf. 19:29; 27:2; Col. 4:10.
18. Cf. Eph. 6:21-22; Col. 4:7-8; 2 Tim. 4:12; Tit. 3:12.
19. Cf. 21:29; 2 Tim. 4:20.
20. Possibly a convert of Barnabas and Paul during their first visit there (14:20-21); see also p. 380, n. 4.

Another possibility is bound up with the tradition that Luke is "the brother whose praise in the gospel is among all the churches"[21] and who was appointed by the churches to travel with Paul and the others "in this gracious work which we are carrying on" (2 Cor. 8:18-19). He went to Corinth along with Titus, and may have been commissioned by the church there to convey its contribution. If that "brother" is to be identified with Luke, and Luke is the narrator here, that would explain the lack of any allusion to a delegate from Corinth. But all this lies in the realm of speculation.

6 As for Paul, he waited at Philippi until the week of the unleavened bread was completed (in A.D. 57 it lasted from April 7 to 14). Then he set sail with Luke, presumably from Neapolis (cf. 16:11). Their five days' journey to Troas was over twice as long as the journey from Troas to Neapolis had been a few years before; the prevalent wind, which had helped them on the earlier occasion, was contrary this time. At Troas they rejoined their companions who had sailed from Cenchreae, and spent a week there with them and the local Christians.

B. THE JOURNEY TO JERUSALEM (20:7–21:16)

1. Paul at Troas (20:7-12)

7 *On the first day of the week, when we were gathered together to break bread, Paul discoursed with them. He intended to set out the next day, and kept on talking until midnight.*

8 *There were many torches[22] in the upper room where we were gathered together.*

9 *One young man, named Eutychus, who was sitting on the window ledge, dropped into a deep sleep as Paul continued his discourse; being quite overcome by sleep he fell down from the third floor and was picked up dead.*

21. The identification of this "brother" with Luke is made in a passage from Origen quoted by Eusebius (*HE* 6.25.6), where Luke's Gospel is described as "the gospel praised (ἐπαινούμενον) by Paul" (with ἐπαινούμενον cf. 2 Cor. 8:18, where Paul speaks of the "brother's" ἔπαινος ἐν τῷ εὐαγγελίῳ). (Possibly, however, to Eusebius at least, ἐπαινούμενον simply meant "quoted," and Eusebius may have had in mind the mistaken notion which he expresses in *HE* 3.4.7, that Paul's phrase "according to my gospel" [Rom. 2:16, etc.] refers to Luke's Gospel.) Compare the echo of 2 Cor. 8:18 ("whose praise is in the Gospel") in the Collect for St. Luke's Day (October 13) in the Anglican *Book of Common Prayer*. If Luke is indeed the person referred to in 2 Cor. 8:18, that rules out a conjecture of more recent days—that Titus is unmentioned in Acts because he was Luke's brother (W. M. Ramsay, *St. Paul the Traveller*, pp. xxxviii, 390; A. Souter, "A Suggested Relationship between Titus and Luke," *ExT* 18 [1906-7], p. 285; "The Relationship between Titus and Luke," *ibid.*, pp. 335-36). Nothing could have been more counterproductive than for Paul to send Titus's blood-brother with him on the delicate financial mission to Corinth.

22. Gk. λαμπάδες. D reads ὑπολαμπάδες ("windows"), but the Latin text of the same codex (d) has *faculae* ("little torches").

10 *But Paul went down, threw himself on him,[23] and put his arms around him. "Do not be alarmed," he said; "his life is (still) in him."*

11 *Then he came up and broke the bread. After eating, he engaged in much further conversation until dawn. Then he took his departure.*

12 *They[24] brought the young man alive, to their very great comfort.[25]*

7 The description of this critical journey to Jerusalem is given in considerable detail. Some have compared the detailed description given in the Gospel of Luke of Jesus' critical journey to Jerusalem. But the kind of detail is different; the exactitude of this second "we" narrative in matters of time and place is due to the fact that the diarist was one of the party and kept a logbook. We may contrast the cursory treatment of Paul's travels in Macedonia (vv. 1-2), on which he was not accompanied by Luke.

The reference to the meeting for the breaking of the bread on "the first day of the week" is the earliest text we have from which it may be inferred with reasonable certainty that Christians regularly came together for worship on that day.[26] The breaking of the bread was probably a fellowship meal in the course of which the Eucharist was celebrated (cf. 2:42). It is plain from the narrative that members of the church at Troas ("they") were present as well as the travelers of Paul's company ("we"); the occasion was probably the church's weekly meeting for worship. Paul's ministry in Troas a year or two previously had evidently been more fruitful than he realized at the time (2 Cor. 2:12-13). This Sunday (perhaps April 24, A.D. 57) was the travelers' last full day at Troas; they were to continue their journey the next day. The meeting was held in the evening[27]—a convenient time for many members of the Gentile churches, who were not their own masters and were not free in the daytime—and Paul conversed with them. Church meetings were not regulated by the clock in those days, and the opportunity of listening to Paul

23. Lit., "fell on him" (ἐπέπεσεν αὐτῷ).

24. The Western text reads "And as they were saying farewell, he [Paul] brought the young man alive . . ."

25. Lit., "and were comforted not moderately (οὐ μετρίως), i.e., "very greatly" (a typical instance of Luke's litotes).

26. See O. Cullmann, *Early Christian Worship,* E.T. (London, 1955), pp. 10-14, 88-93; C. F. D. Moule, *Worship in the New Testament* (London, 1961), pp. 16, 28-29; R. P. Martin, *Worship in the Early Church* (London, 1964), pp. 78-80; W. Rordorf, *Sunday,* E.T. (London, 1968), pp. 196-205; S. Bacchiocchi, *From Sabbath to Sunday* (Rome, 1977), pp. 101-11; R. T. Beckwith and W. Stott, *This is the Day* (London, 1978), pp. 28, 31-32, 36-38, 89-90. In the still earlier reference to the "first day of the week" in 1 Cor. 16:2 there is no explicit mention of a meeting for worship, though it may be implied. Compare also the implication of John 20:19, 26.

27. On Sunday evening, not Saturday evening. Luke is not using the Jewish reckoning from sunset to sunset but the reckoning from midnight to midnight: although it was apparently after sunset when they met, their departure in the morning was "the next day."

was not one to be cut short; what did it matter if his conversation went on until midnight?

8-10   But the air in that crowded upper room began to grow heavy with the smoke of torches which had been lit to dispel the evening darkness, and a young man named Eutychus, even though he sat at the window (where the air was freshest), found it impossible to keep awake. Perhaps he had put in a hard day's work from dawn to sunset, and now in the stuffy atmosphere not even the words of an apostle could keep him from falling asleep. Suddenly he overbalanced, and fell through the window (a mere opening in the wall) to the ground beneath—and the room was three floors up.[28] No wonder then that he was "picked up dead," as Luke says, "implying apparently that, as a physician, he had satisfied himself on the point."[29] It is impossible to be sure whether Eutychus was clinically dead or not; Luke's statement that he was "picked up dead" has to be weighed against Paul's reassuring words: "his life is in him." Luke may intend his readers to understand that the young man's life returned to him when Paul embraced him. Paul's treatment, similar to that given in other circumstances by Elijah and Elisha (1 Kings 17:21; 2 Kings 4:34-35), suggests artificial respiration. It may have been a few hours before Eutychus regained consciousness.

11-12   After this untoward interruption, Paul resumed his discourse. It was probably past midnight (and therefore strictly Monday morning) when at last Paul "broke the bread" and shared their fellowship meal;[30] then he continued to talk to them until daybreak. At daybreak the ship on which they were to sail was due to leave, and the party went on board—all except Paul, who stayed till the last possible moment, probably to be assured of Eutychus's complete restoration to consciousness and health, and then took a shortcut by land to join the ship at Assos.

2. From Troas to Miletus (20:13-16)

13   We[31] went on ahead[32] to the ship and set sail for Assos. We intended

---

28. The building was evidently a tenement block like the one in Rome where Martial lived: "I live up three flights of stairs, high ones at that" (*Epigrams* 1.118.7).

29. Ramsay, *St. Paul the Traveller*, pp. 290-91.

30. Perhaps κλάσας τὸν ἄρτον (v. 11), where the article points back to κλάσαι ἄρτον (v. 7), refers to the eucharistic breaking of the bread, while γευσάμενος (translated "after eating" above, lit. "having tasted"; for γεύομαι = "eat" cf. 10:10) refers to the fellowship meal.

31. Ephrem the Syrian's commentary on Acts (preserved in an Armenian translation) presupposes an Old Syriac text which read here: "But I Luke, and those who were with me, went on board." The usual "we" was deemed inappropriate because Paul was not with them from Troas to Assos. See F. C. Conybeare's translation of Ephrem in *Beginnings* I.3, p. 442.

32. Gk. προελθόντες. As in v. 5, there is a variant reading προσελθόντες (A B* etc.); the Western text reads κατελθόντες, "having gone down (to the shore)."

> *to take Paul on board there, for so he had decided: he was to do that*
> *part of the journey by land.[33]*
>
> 14 *So, when he met up with us at Assos, we took him on board, and came*
> *to Mitylene.*
> 15 *Setting sail from there, we arrived the next day opposite Chios, the*
> *following day[34] we crossed over to Samos, and[35] the day after that*
> *we came to Miletus.*
> 16 *Paul had decided to sail past Ephesus, so as not to spend time in*
> *Asia. He was making haste, if he could make it, to be in Jerusalem*
> *for the day of Pentecost.*

13   The ship which they boarded at Troas was due to put in at some of the main ports along the coast of Asia Minor, but it was a faster vessel than some which they might have taken; for example, it sailed across the mouth of the Ephesian Gulf, instead of calling at Ephesus. In one of the harbors of southwest Asia Minor, they expected to find another ship which would take them to Syria and Judaea; and so it turned out (21:1-2).

When it left Troas, the ship had to round Cape Lectum (modern Baba-burun) to get to Assos. Paul waited a little longer, and then, taking the direct road by land to Assos (a distance of twenty miles), got there in time to join his companions on board their ship.

Assos (modern Behram-kale) was a well-fortified city standing on a volcanic cone about 750 feet high. Its harbor, on the shore below, was protected by a mole, which is still to be seen.[36]

14-15   From Assos, the ship brought them to Mitylene, the chief city of the island of Lesbos (at an earlier date the home of the lyric poets Alcaeus and Sappho); then, calling at a point on the mainland opposite the island of Chios (somewhere near Cape Argennum, modern Beyaz-burun) and, a day later, at the island of Samos, they put in at Miletus three days after leaving Troas. The Western text says that they spent the night before arriving at Miletus off Trogyllium. Trogyllium is a promontory jutting out from the mainland toward the southeast of Samos, forming a strait less than a mile wide. An overnight stay off Trogyllium could have been dictated by the difficulty of navigating the strait in the dark.

Miletus stood on the south shore of the Latmian Gulf. Even then the gulf was being constantly silted up by the river Maeander, which entered it

---

33. Gk. πεζεύειν, normally to go on foot as opposed to riding, but here to go by land as opposed to sailing.

34. B and some minuscules add "in the evening."

35. The Western and Byzantine texts add "having stayed at Trogyllium (Trogyllia)."

36. See Strabo, *Geography* 13.1.57-58, 66; also J. M. Cook, *The Troad* (Oxford, 1973), pp. 240-50. Assos was the birthplace of Cleanthes the Stoic (see p. 339, n. 76).

from the north. Today the Latmian Gulf survives as an inland lake (Lake Bafa), which is connected with the Maeander by an outlet on the north. The island of Lade, which then stood off the coast to the west of Miletus, has for long been part of the mainland. Miletus was a city of high antiquity; it is mentioned in Hittite and Mycenaean texts. Homer knew it as a Carian city,[37] before the Ionians settled there; it was in fact the most southerly of the Ionian settlements in Asia Minor. The presence of a Jewish community in the city in Roman times is attested by an inscription found in the theater, allocating a block of seats to "Jews who are also called God-fearers."[38]

16 In spite of his natural desire to see Ephesus again, Paul had decided that this was out of the question if he was to be sure of reaching Jerusalem in time for Pentecost (which in A.D. 57 fell on May 29); he therefore chose a ship which was to make the straight run from Chios to Samos. But the ship was due to spend several days in harbor at Miletus; this gave him an opportunity to see some of his Ephesian friends.

3. Paul Sends for the Elders of the Ephesian Church (20:17)

17 *From Miletus he sent to Ephesus, and summoned the elders of the church.*

17 While the ship remained in harbor at Miletus, Paul sent a message to Ephesus, which lay some thirty miles to the north, asking the elders of the church in that city to come and see him. (Probably some able-bodied member of the church of Miletus acted as messenger.) Ramsay reckons that the messenger could have shortened his journey by taking a boat across to the north side of the Latmian Gulf and continuing by land from Priene.

Paul wished to give the Ephesian leaders such encouragement as they needed. The speech which follows is not only his farewell speech to them (and to the church which they represented) but (so far as the perspective of Acts is concerned) his last will and testament to the churches which he had planted both east and west of the Aegean.

This speech is quite distinctive among all the speeches reported in Acts. It is the only Pauline speech delivered to Christians which Luke has recorded, and it is not surprising to discover how rich it is in parallels to the Pauline letters (especially, in fact, to the later ones). To explain these parallels along literary-critical lines, by supposing that Luke drew some suitable material for the composition of this speech from Paul's letters,

37. *Iliad* 2.868-69.
38. See A. Deissmann, *Light from the Ancient East*, E.T. (London, ²1927), pp. 451-52. On Miletus see also T. Wiegand and others, *Milet: die Ergebnisse der Ausgrabungen und Untersuchungen* (Berlin, 1906); A. G. Dunham, *The History of Miletus* (London, 1915); G. Kleiner, *Alt-Milet* (Wiesbaden, 1966); *Die Ruinen von Milet* (Berlin, 1968); *Das römische Milet* (Wiesbaden, 1970).

appears to be ruled out by the consideration that, elsewhere throughout Acts, Luke betrays no knowledge of them, even in places where they would have served him as firsthand sources had they been accessible to him. Besides, even on grounds of literary criticism, the report could not be described as a mere cento of passages from Paul's letters. "The speech is altogether in the style of the writer of *Acts*," wrote Percy Gardner, "and yet offers phenomena which seem to imply that he was guided by memory in the composition."[39] As the synagogue sermon at Pisidian Antioch (13:16-41) is intended to be a sample of Paul's approach to Jewish audiences, and the speeches at Lystra (14:15-17) and Athens (17:22-31) samples of his approach to pagan audiences, so it might be said that this Milesian speech is a sample of his ministry to Christian audiences. But it is more than the sort of thing that Paul was accustomed to say to Christian audiences: it is a farewell speech, suited to the special occasion on which it was delivered. Since it comes in the context of a "we" section of Luke's narrative, Luke may well have heard it; if so, he could be reproducing its gist from memory.[40]

The speech is mainly hortatory, but also in part apologetic. It seems to be implied here and there that Paul's opponents in the province of Asia had tried to prejudice his converts' minds against him in his absence; he therefore defends his teaching and general behavior by appealing to his hearers' personal knowledge of him.[41] He perceives that the opposition to his teaching which has already begun to manifest itself in the Ephesian church will increase, and that the church will be invaded by false teachers from outside. Its leaders must therefore fulfil their responsibility as shepherds, appointed by God to guard his flock.

Luke calls those men "elders," but Paul speaks of them as "guardi-

---

39. "The speeches of St. Paul in Acts," in *Cambridge Biblical Essays*, ed. H. B. Swete (Cambridge, 1909), p. 403. Gardner considered further that among the Pauline discourses in Acts "that at Miletus has the best claim of all to be historic" (*ibid.*, p. 401). See also M. Dibelius, "The Speeches in Acts and Ancient Historiography" (1949), E.T. in *Studies in the Acts of the Apostles* (London, 1956), pp. 155-58; C. L. Mitton, *The Epistle to the Ephesians* (Oxford, 1951), pp. 210-13, 217-20, 266-67; J. Munck, "Discours d'adieu dans le Nouveau Testament et dans la littérature biblique," in *Aux sources de la tradition chrétienne: Mélanges offerts a M. Goguel* (Neuchâtel/Paris, 1950), pp. 155-70; J. Dupont, *Le discours de Milet: Testament pastoral de saint Paul (Ac 20,18-36)* (Paris, 1962); "La construction du discours de Milet," *Nouvelles études sur les Actes des Apôtres* (Paris, 1984), pp. 424-45; H.-J. Michel, *Die Abschiedsrede des Paulus an die Kirche Apg 20, 17-38: Motivgeschichtliche und theologische Bedeutung* (Munich, 1973); C. K. Barrett, "Paul's Address to the Ephesian Elders," in *God's Christ and His People: Studies in Honour of N. A. Dahl*, ed. J. Jervell and W. A. Meeks (Oslo, 1978), pp. 107-21; J. Lambrecht, "Paul's Farewell-Address at Miletus (Acts 20,17-38)," in *Les Actes des Apôtres*, ed. J. Kremer, BETL (Leuven, 1979), pp. 307-37.

40. Cf. F. H. Chase, *The Credibility of the Acts of the Apostles* (London, 1902), pp. 234-88; A. Harnack, *The Acts of the Apostles*, E.T. (London, 1909), p. 129.

41. For similar appeals to personal knowledge cf. 1 Cor. 6:11, etc.; Gal. 3:2-5; 4:13; Phil. 4:15; 1 Thess. 2:1-2, 5, 10-11; 3:3-4; 4:2; 2 Thess. 2:5; 3:7.

ans" and "shepherds." There is little or nothing of institutionalism in the part which they are seen to play here.

4. Paul Bids Farewell to the Ephesian Church (20:18-35)

a. Retrospect on his Ephesian ministry (20:18-21)

18 When they arrived, he said to them, "You know how I conducted myself all the time[42] I was with you from the first day I set foot in Asia,

19 serving the Lord in all humility and with tears amid the trials that befell me through the plots of the Jews.

20 I kept back nothing that was to your advantage: I preached and taught you publicly and in your homes,

21 proclaiming earnestly[43] to Jews and Greeks alike repentance before God and faith in our Lord Jesus.[44]

18-21   In the introductory part of his address Paul reminds his hearers of his manner of life all the time he spent in their midst—his humble and faithful service, his sorrows, the dangers to which he was exposed by reason of Jewish hostility and conspiracy, his unceasing proclamation of the gospel to both Jews and Gentiles,[45] the profitable and all-embracing Christian instruction which he gave his converts, both publicly (first in the synagogue and then in the lecture hall of Tyrannus) and in private homes. His words contain a hint of trying experiences in Ephesus of which little is said elsewhere in Acts, although further hints are given of them in Paul's own correspondence.[46] Insofar as those trying experiences arose out of the opposition of Jews in the province in Asia, they brought him face to face once again, and perhaps in a specially intensified form, with a problem with which he had recently grappled in Rom. 9–11.

---

42. For "all the time" D reads "three years or even more."

43. Gk. διαμαρτυρόμενος, "a favorite Lukan word" (E. Plümacher, *Lukas als hellenistischer Schriftsteller* [Göttingen, 1972], p. 48); of its fifteen NT occurrences, ten are in Luke's writings. Like the simple μαρτύρομαι, it usually has in Acts the sense of preaching in the Spirit's power (cf. 5:32).

44. "Christ" is added by P74 ℵ A C E and very many minuscules, with lat^vg syr^pesh. D reads "through our Lord Jesus Christ."

45. The gospel is here said to evoke "repentance before God (or turning back to God) and faith in our Lord Jesus." In Paul's letters repentance does not figure soteriologically as faith so emphatically does. But "true repentance," says C. F. D. Moule, ". . . means responding in kind to the creative efforts of reconciliation." If so, then this "is precisely what Paul is all the time expressing" in different language. "Justification *by faith* involves such a response to that finished work [of Christ] as identifies the believer most intimately with the costly work of Christ, involving him inescapably in the cost and pain of repentance" ("Obligation in the Ethic of Paul," *Essays in New Testament Interpretation* [Cambridge, 1982], pp. 271-72).

46. See p. 370, n. 41.

b. Paul's prospects (20:22-24)

22 *"And now, as you see, I am on my way to Jerusalem, under the constraint of the Spirit.*[47] *I do not know what will happen to me there:*
23 *I know only this, that in one city after another the Holy Spirit assures me that imprisonment and tribulation lie in store for me.*
24 *But I do not reckon my life of any account, as though it were precious to myself,*[48] *if only I may complete my course*[49] *and the ministry I have received from the Lord Jesus—to proclaim*[50] *the good news of God's grace.*

22-24 Paul then goes on to tell them of his present enterprise and of his misgivings about its outcome. That these were real misgivings is plain from his sharing them with the Roman Christians as matters concerning which he desires their prayers (Rom. 15:30-31). They found increasing confirmation as he went from port to port on his voyage to Judaea: in city after city the Holy Spirit, speaking presumably through the lips of prophets, as later at Tyre and Caesarea (21:4, 11), showed him that imprisonment and other hardships would be his lot when he reached Jerusalem. That the misgivings were well founded is evident from Luke's narrative of events following Paul's arrival in Jerusalem.

But Paul was ready to surrender his liberty and, if need be, his life itself for the sake of Christ and his service.[51] Self-preservation was not a motive which he esteemed highly: his main concern was to fulfil the course which Christ had marked for him to run,[52] preaching in the Spirit's power the good news of God's free grace in Christ. Life or death was not the issue that mattered: what mattered most was, as he told another church, that Christ should be magnified in his body, "whether by life or by death" (Phil. 1:20).

c. His charge to the elders (20:25-31)

25 *"And now, I tell you, I know that you will never see my face again—*

47. Gk. δεδεμένος . . . τῷ πνεύματι, where (especially in view of what he says in v. 23) it is best to understand a reference to the Spirit of God, and not simply to Paul's own sense of spiritual compulsion. Cf. 19:21 (p. 371 with n. 43).
48. The Western text expands: "But I make no reckoning of any thing for myself, nor do I value my own life as precious to me." The Byzantine text reads "But I make no reckoning of anything nor do I hold my life precious to myself."
49. The Byzantine text adds "with joy."
50. Gk. διαμαρτύρασθαι (cf. p. 389, n. 43). D and some other witnesses add "to Jews and Greeks."
51. For Paul's ready surrender of himself for the gospel's sake cf. also 2 Cor. 4:7-12; 6:4-10; 12:9-10; Phil. 2:17; 3:8; Col. 1:24.
52. For the comparison of Christian service to a race (δρόμος) to be run cf. 1 Cor. 9:24-27; Gal. 2:2; Phil. 2:16; 2 Tim. 4:7; also the words about John the Baptist in 13:25 above.

none of you among whom I have gone about[53] *proclaiming the kingdom.*[54]

26 *Therefore, I testify before you that I am free of responsibility for anyone's blood.*

27 *I have not refrained from setting before you the whole will and purpose of God.*

28 *Keep watch over yourselves and over the whole flock in which the Holy Spirit has set you as guardians: feed the church of God,*[55] *the church which he purchased with the blood of his own Son.*[56]

29 *I know that after my departure*[57] *harmful wolves will come in among you and will not spare the flock;*

30 *and not only so, but from your own number some will rise up and pervert the truth by their words, so as to entice the disciples to follow them.*

31 *Be watchful, therefore; remember that for three years, night and day, I never ceased to counsel each one of you, weeping as I did so.*

25-27   And now he was addressing the leaders of the church of Ephesus as one who spoke to them for the last time. He was bidding farewell to the Aegean world, the area in which for seven or eight years now he had "gone about proclaiming the kingdom."[58] Henceforth, if he got safely away from Jerusalem, the western Mediterranean was to be his field of action.[59]

53. Lit., "that you all among whom I have gone about . . . will no longer see my face."

54. The Western text adds "of Jesus"; the Byzantine text adds "of God."

55. *P*[74] A D and the Western text read "of the Lord" (which would go smoothly with the phrase "with his own blood," if that were the proper rendering of διὰ τοῦ αἵματος τοῦ ἰδίου). The Byzantine text exhibits the conflate reading "of the Lord and God."

56. Gk. διὰ τοῦ αἵματος τοῦ ἰδίου, for which the Byzantine text reads διὰ τοῦ ἰδίου αἵματος. The Byzantine reading could mean only "with his own blood," but the reading here adopted is best rendered "with the blood of his own one." This sense of ὁ ἴδιος is well attested in the vernacular papyri, where it is "used thus as a term of endearment to near relations, e.g. ὁ δεῖνα τῷ ἰδίῳ χαίρειν ['So-and-so to his own (friend), greeting']" (J. H. Moulton, MHT I, p. 90). As used here, ἴδιος is the equivalent of Heb. *yāḥîḏ* ("only"), elsewhere represented by Gk. ἀγαπητός ("beloved"), ἐκλεκτός ("choice"), and μονογενής ("only-begotten"). In view of this, it is unnecessary to conjecture, with F. J. A. Hort, that υἱοῦ ("son") may have dropped out of the text after ἰδίου (it may be supplied for the purpose of translation).

57. Gk. ἄφιξις, related to ἀφικνέομαι ("arrive"); the sense "arrival" is well attested for the noun in classical Greek. But in Hellenistic Greek the sense "departure" is equally well attested, and that is the only sense which suits the context here.

58. It is a fruitless task to try to make a distinction between "proclaiming the kingdom" and "proclaiming the good news of God's grace." Such a distinction is made by W. Kelly, who deplores the "confusion which, mingling both characters, never enjoys the simple and full truth of either" (*The Acts of the Apostles* [London, ³1952], p. 306). For the subject matter of the kingdom see on 1:3 (pp. 31-33).

59. See Rom. 15:23-29.

(Whether or not the Ephesians ever did see him again is not of primary relevance to the exegesis of these words, but Luke would not have reported and repeated them so emphatically if he had known that, in the event, they were falsified.) Paul had lived in Ephesus (as in other cities) and gone in and out among the people as a herald of the kingdom of God; he had planted the gospel seed and now it was the business of others to water it. His hearers could bear witness to his faithfulness in the proclamation of the divine message: he had made God's saving plan clear to them, the whole of his will for their lives.[60] Like Ezekiel's trustworthy watchman,[61] he had sounded the trumpet so that all the province of Asia had heard. If there were any who paid no heed, their blood would be on their own heads: Paul was free of responsibility for their doom.

28 On those elders, then, lay a weighty responsibility. The Holy Spirit had entrusted them with the charge of the people of God in Ephesus; they had to care for them as shepherds cared for their flock. It may be implied that their commission to take pastoral responsibility for the church had been conveyed through prophetic utterances, in which the direction of the Spirit was recognized.[62] The word translated "guardians" is the word from which "bishop" is derived,[63] but to use that word here might give it an official flavor which would be an anachronism. If their commission was received through prophetic utterances, they received it no doubt because they were known to be those on whom the requisite qualifications for this work had been bestowed—and bestowed by the same Spirit whose will was declared by the prophetic utterances.[64] Their responsibility was the greater in that the flock which they were commissioned to tend was no other than the church of God which he had purchased for himself (an echo here of Old Testament

60. In Gk. βουλή here the ideas both of God's will and of his plan or purpose seem to be combined; see the translation above.

61. Ezek. 3:16-21; 33:1-9.

62. Cf. 1 Tim. 4:14; also 13:2, 4 above.

63. Gk. ἐπίσκοπος (cf. Phil. 1:1; 1 Tim. 3:2; Tit. 1:7). Other designations for those exercising this kind of ministry in the churches appear in 1 Thess. 5:12; Rom. 12:8; Heb. 13:17. The present wording is far from the stereotyped terminology of "incipient catholicism," as frequently conceived, especially in the sense given to *Frühkatholizismus* by German Protestant scholars. See J. B. Lightfoot, "The Christian Ministry," dissertation in *Saint Paul's Epistle to the Philippians* (London, 1868), pp. 181-269 (also pp. 95-99, excursus on "The synonyms 'bishop' and 'presbyter'"); T. M. Lindsay, *The Church and the Ministry in the Early Centuries* (London, 1902); H. B. Swete (ed.), *Essays on the Early History of the Church and Ministry* (London, 1918); B. H. Streeter, *The Primitive Church* (London, 1929), pp. 27-83; T. W. Manson, *The Church's Ministry* (London, 1948), pp. 53-77; *Ministry and Priesthood: Christ's and Ours* (London, 1958); R. P. C. Hanson, *Christian Priesthood Examined* (London, 1979), pp. 7-32; G. Schneider, "Die Entwicklung kirchlicher Dienste in der Sicht der Apostelgeschichte," *Theologisch-Praktische Quartalschrift* 132 (1984), pp. 356-63.

64. Cf. 1 Cor. 12:7-11.

language)[65]—and the purchase price was nothing less than the life-blood of his beloved Son.[66]

29-31   Paul now looks forward to the future, and the prospects for the Ephesian church are not wholly promising. The sheep will have to be guarded with unceasing vigilance, for ferocious wolves will try to force their way among them and ravage them. As in our Lord's parable of the good shepherd, so here the true pastors of the flock are contrasted with false teachers, described as wolves because of the havoc they cause.[67] But it is not only from intruders from outside that false teaching will proceed: from their own ranks some will arise to seduce their followers into heretical by-paths. That this development did in fact take place at Ephesus is evident from the Pastoral Epistles[68] and from the letter to the Ephesian church in Revelation. In 2 Tim. 1:15 mention is made of a general revolt against Paul and his teaching throughout the province of Asia; and in the apocalyptic letter the church of Ephesus is reproached for having abandoned the love it had at first.[69] (Happily, Ignatius's letter to the same church a decade or two later shows that it paid heed to the admonition and recovered its love in full measure.[70]) Foreseeing these trends, then, Paul urges the elders to be vigilant[71] and to follow his own example. Let them remember how he himself had shown such careful and compassionate concern for his converts, during

---

65. Cf. in particular Ps. 74 (LXX 73):2, "Remember thy congregation (LXX συναγωγή, rendering Heb. ʿēḏāh), which thou hast gotten of old"; Isa. 43:21, "the people whom I formed (LXX περιεποιησάμην, "acquired," "purchased," the same verb as is used here) for myself." For "church" (Gk. ἐκκλησία) see on 5:11 (pp. 107-8).

66. Redemption by the blood of Christ is Pauline, not Lukan, doctrine, although Paul prefers the verb ἀγοράζω (ἐξαγοράζω) or the noun ἀπολύτρωσις to express redemption rather than περιποιέομαι, which is used here (both περιποιέομαι and the related noun περιποίησις are used in LXX for God's acquisition of his people Israel; cf. Eph. 1:14; 1 Pet. 2:9 for περιποίησις used with regard to the church as God's possession). The Pauline language here cannot be dismissed as a "turn of phrase" introduced "to give the speech a Pauline stamp" (H. Conzelmann, *The Theology of St. Luke*, E.T. [London, 1960], p. 201). Rather, "this is Paul, not some other speaker; and he is not evangelizing but recalling an already evangelized community to its deepest insights. In other words, the situation, like the theology, is precisely that of a Pauline epistle, not of preliminary evangelism" (C. F. D. Moule, "The Christology of Acts," in *Studies in Luke-Acts: Essays in Honor of Paul Schubert*, ed. L. E. Keck and J. L. Martyn [Nashville/New York, 1966], p. 171).

67. John 10:12. False prophets are described as wolves in sheep's clothing in Matt. 7:15; cf. also 4 Ezra 5:18; 1 Enoch 89:13-27.

68. Cf. 1 Tim. 1:19-20; 4:1-3; 2 Tim. 2:17-18; 3:1-9.

69. Rev. 2:4.

70. Ignatius, *To the Ephesians* 1:1–2:1.

71. "Be watchful," Gk. γρηγορεῖτε (v. 31), is a "pastoral word," as Bengel calls it. Cf. 1 Cor. 16:13; Col. 4:2; 1 Thess. 5:6, 10; also the synonymous ἀγρυπνέω in a similar context in Heb. 13:17 (the leaders "keep watch" over the souls of those entrusted to their care).

the three years[72] of his residence among them, pointing out unceasingly, night and day, the right path for them to pursue.[73]

d. Final admonition (20:32-35)

32 *"Now then, I commend you to God and to his gracious word,[74] for that is able to build you up and give you an inheritance among those who are sanctified.[75]*

33 *I have coveted no one's gold or silver or clothes.*

34 *You yourselves know that these hands of mine made provision for my own needs and for the needs of my companions.*

35 *In all this I showed you how we ought to work hard to help those who are less able, and to recall the words of the Lord Jesus: 'It is a more blessed thing to give than to receive.'"*

32 Now he was leaving them: they could no longer count on his personal presence for pastoral guidance and wise instruction. But, though Paul might go, God was with them still, and so was God's word which they had received—the word that communicated his redeeming and sanctifying grace.[76] (There is no appreciable difference between the "gracious word" here and the "good news of God's grace" in verse 24.) To God, then, and to his word (with the grace which it proclaimed) Paul committed them. By that word, as they accepted and obeyed it, they would be built up in faith and love together with their fellow-Christians; by that word, too, they were assured of their inheritance among all the people of God, all whom he had set apart for himself.[77] In due course Paul, with all the apostles, passed from earthly life; but the teaching which they left behind to be guarded by their successors as a sacred deposit, preserved not only in their memory but eventually in the New Testament scriptures, remains to this day as the word of God's grace. And those are most truly in the apostolic succession who receive this teaching, along with the rest of Holy Writ, as their rule of faith and life.

72. For the duration of Paul's stay at Ephesus see p. 366, n. 23 (on 19:10).

73. For "counsel" (Gk. νουθετέω, "admonish") cf. 1 Cor. 4:14; Col. 1:28.

74. Gk. τῷ λόγῳ τῆς χάριτος αὐτοῦ, a phrase used already in 14:3. If τῆς χάριτος is genitive of quality (i.e., the "word" is characterized by God's own grace), then "gracious word" is a suitable rendering (cf. Luke 4:22); if it expresses the subject matter of the word, then "the word of his grace" (cf. v. 24) is the proper rendering.

75. The Western text added: "To him be the glory for ever and ever. Amen" (a doxology evidently derived from a lectionary, in which a prescribed lesson came to an end at this point).

76. "This message of the free bounty of God is the word which has the greatest effect on the heart of man, and so it is able to build up the church" (R. B. Rackham, *The Acts of the Apostles*, WC [London, 1902], p. 395).

77. For their inheritance among the saints cf. 26:18b; Col. 1:12. The language recalls Deut. 33:3-4, "all those consecrated to him were in his hand; . . . an inheritance for the assembly of Jacob."

33-35 Returning once more to the example which he had set them, Paul reminds them finally that those who take care of the people of God must do so without thought of material reward. As Samuel called all Israel to witness when he was about to lay down his judicial office (1 Sam. 12:3), so Paul calls the elders of Ephesus to witness that all the time he spent among them he coveted nothing that was not his. On the contrary, he did not even avail himself of his right to be maintained in temporal matters by those for whose spiritual welfare he cared; instead, he earned his livelihood, and that of his colleagues, by his own work (tentmaking): "these hands," he said (inevitably with the attendant gesture), "made provision for my own needs and for those of my companions."[78] Let those to whom he was speaking likewise work hard and support not only themselves but others as well—the weak and sick in particular.[79] To much the same effect is the admonition to elders in 1 Pet. 5:2-3, to "tend the flock of God . . . , not as compelled to do so but willingly, not for sordid gain but eagerly, not as domineering . . . but being examples to the flock." Thus they would fulfil the saying of the Lord Jesus, which they ought ever to bear in mind: "It is a more blessed thing to give than to receive." This dominical *logion* does not appear in any of the canonical Gospels, but its spirit is expressed in many other sayings of Jesus which they record.[80]

On this appropriate note Paul concludes his exhortation to the Ephesian elders.

5. An Affectionate Parting (20:36-38)

36 *So saying, he knelt down and prayed with them all.*
37 *They all broke into loud weeping, and, embracing Paul, they covered him with kisses.*
38 *What grieved them most was his saying that they would never see his face again. So they escorted him to the ship.*

---

78. For this insistence on Paul's part cf. 1 Cor. 4:12; 9:3-15; 2 Cor. 4:5; 11:7-11; 12:13; 1 Thess. 2:3-12; 2 Thess. 3:7-10.

79. Cf. the admonitions in Rom. 15:1; Gal. 6:2; Eph. 4:28; 1 Thess. 4:11-12; 2 Thess. 3:10-13.

80. Cf. Luke 6:38; 11:9-13; John 13:34; also Matt. 10:8, "You received without pay; give without pay." When Paul wishes to affirm the right of those who preach the gospel to live by the gospel, he can refer to another saying of Jesus (1 Cor. 9:14). He also refers to sayings of Jesus in Rom. 14:14; 1 Cor. 7:10; 11:24-25; 1 Thess. 4:15; 1 Tim. 5:18. H. Windisch argued that the occurrence of this *logion* here shows that Luke the physician could not have been the author of Luke-Acts because, if he were, he would certainly have incorporated "so fine a saying" in his Gospel (*Beginnings* I.2, p. 331). This argument, as W. L. Knox rightly pointed out, "betrays a complete failure to understand his methods" (*Some Hellenistic Elements in Primitive Christianity* [London, 1944], p. 29).

36-38 When Paul had finished speaking to them, and had knelt in prayer with them, they bade him an affectionate but sorrowful farewell. It was in particular his saying that they would never see him again that filled their hearts with grief and their eyes with tears. But the ship was now on the point of setting out from Miletus after its stay of several days, and they escorted Paul to the quay before returning home to Ephesus.

ACTS 21

6. Miletus to Tyre (21:1-6)

1 When we tore ourselves away from them and put out to sea, we followed a straight course and arrived at Cos. The next day we came to Rhodes and from there to Patara.[1]
2 There we found a ship that was crossing over to Phoenicia, so we went on board and put out to sea.
3 Sighting Cyprus, and leaving it on the port side, we sailed to Syria and put in at Tyre; it was there that the ship was to unload its cargo.
4 We located the disciples and stayed there for seven days. Those disciples told Paul through the Spirit not to go on to Jerusalem.[2]
5 When we had completed our week's stay, we departed and continued on our journey. They all escorted us out of the city, with their wives and children. Then we kneeled down on the beach and prayed,
6 and said good-bye to one another. We embarked on board the ship, while they returned home.

1-2 The Ephesian elders escorted Paul and his friends to the ship, and at last, as Luke says, "we tore ourselves away from them" (if we give the verb its full force).[3] From Miletus they sailed to Cos, one of the islands of the Dodecanese, famed as the home of the medical school founded by Hippocrates in the fifth century B.C. The following day they put in at the harbor of Rhodes. "Rhodes" is here the city rather than the island of the same name (the largest island of the Dodecanese). The city of Rhodes, lying at the island's northeastern extremity, was founded in 408 B.C. by the amalgamation of three earlier settlements. As the prevailing wind was from the northeast, they were able to accomplish this part of the voyage with a straight course. From Rhodes they turned east and sailed along the south coast of Lycia, putting in at Patara (formerly the port of Xanthus, capital of the kingdom of Lycia, and now the headquarters of the Roman governor of the

---

1. The Western text adds "and Myra" (see n. 4 below).
2. Or "set foot (ἐπιβαίνειν) in Jerusalem" (ASV).
3. The Greek verb here is the passive of ἀποσπάω (the verb is used in the active voice in 20:30 in the pejorative sense of enticing people to follow false teaching).

province). There (or, according to the Western text, at Myra)[4] they found, as they had hoped, a ship bound for the Phoenician ports, which would take them quite close to their destination.

3 The first port at which this new ship was due to put in was Tyre, in Phoenicia. This meant a cross-sea voyage instead of a coasting voyage; the journey was thus considerably shortened. (The ship was probably a large merchant vessel; smaller craft hugged the coast.) According to Chrysostom, the voyage from Patara to Tyre took five days. On the way Luke reports that they sighted Cyprus on the port side. So they arrived at Tyre, and there it was necessary to spend a week, as the ship's cargo had to be discharged; but the time saved on the voyage meant that the party could afford to wait at Tyre until the ship was ready to sail on again. Paul knew that there was now every prospect of achieving his intention of being in Jerusalem in time for Pentecost (cf. 20:16).

4 They knew that there was a Christian church in Tyre; it had been founded, in all probability, as a result of the dispersal of Jerusalem Hellenists after Stephen's death (cf. 11:19). Paul and his friends sought out the Tyrian Christians and spent the week with them. Among those Christians were some who had the gift of prophecy; as they foresaw by its means that grave danger awaited Paul in Jerusalem, they warned him to abandon his plan of going on there. But Paul's mind was already made up, and he was not to be diverted from his purpose by such predictions. Tyre was not the first place in which indications of this kind had been given him of what lay in store for him at Jerusalem (cf. 20:23). It should not be concluded that his determination to go on was disobedience to the guidance of the Spirit of God; it was under the constraint of that Spirit that he was bound for Jerusalem with such determination (19:21; 20:22). It was natural that his friends who by the prophetic spirit were able to foresee his tribulation and imprisonment should try to dissuade him from going on, but with a complete lack of concern for his own safety, so long as he could fulfil his sacred stewardship, Paul like his Master "set his face to go to Jerusalem" (Luke 9:51).

5-6 The disciples at Tyre were not old friends of Paul, as the Ephesian elders were, but the love of Christ is the strongest of bonds, and at the end of a week he and they were as firm friends as if they had known each other all their lives. When the ship was due to sail, all the Christians of Tyre, with their families, accompanied Paul and his companions to the shore.[5]

---

4. Myra was the great port for transshipment for cross-sea traffic to Syria and Egypt; the Western reviser (see n. 1 above), knowing this, may have thought it must have been so used on this occasion (if indeed he was not simply influenced by its mention in 27:5). But Myra lies fifty miles east of Patara in a straight line, too long a distance to be accommodated within the day's voyage, which is all that the itinerary implies here.

5. In the Roman period Tyre was a prosperous commercial city, noted for its purple dye-works. The mole which Alexander the Great constructed to facilitate his siege

There they knelt and prayed, before taking an affectionate farewell of each other. Then the Tyrian disciples went back home, while the ship continued its journey.

7. Tyre to Caesarea (21:7-9)

7 *Then we continued the voyage[6] from Tyre and arrived at Ptolemais. We greeted the brothers there and spent a day with them.*

8 *The next day we set out and came to Caesarea. There we went into the house of Philip the evangelist, one of the seven, and stayed with him.*

9 *He had four unmarried daughters, who had the gift of prophecy.*

7 From Tyre they continued their voyage, and put in next at Ptolemais, the most southerly of the Phoenician ports. It appears in the Old Testament under the name Acco (Judg. 1:31), by which it is known today. Although it was known in Graeco-Roman times by the name Ptolemais (which it received apparently in honor of Ptolemy II, 285-246 B.C.), it later resumed its Semitic name, Gallicized in the age of the Crusaders to Acre.[7] At this time it was a Roman colony. It had been evangelized probably about the same time as Tyre, and Paul and his friends spent the day in the company of the Christians of the city.

8 Ptolemais was perhaps the last port at which their ship was due to put in; it is not clear whether they took another ship to Caesarea or went there by road. At Caesarea they were entertained by Philip. Philip was one of the seven Hellenistic officers appointed in the early days of the Jerusalem church to supervise the distribution of largesse from the common fund to those who were in need (cf. 6:3-6). Later he engaged in missionary activity in Samaria and in the coastal plain of Judaea,[8] and we last heard of him when

---

of the island of Tyre in 332 B.C. was continuously widened by accumulations of sand, which formed two smooth beaches.

6. Gk. τὸν πλοῦν διανύσαντες, otherwise "having completed the voyage," but F. Field notes that the expression is repeatedly attested with the meaning "continue a voyage" in Xenophon Ephesius (second century A.D.); see his *Notes on Translation of the New Testament* (Cambridge, 1899), pp. 134-35.

7. More fully St. Jean D'Acre, after the Knights of St. John. The tendency for the old Semitic names to reassert themselves after the Graeco-Roman period can be copiously paralleled in Syria and Palestine.

8. It is from this missionary activity that he is called "Philip the evangelist," perhaps to distinguish him from Philip the apostle. Even so, they are confused by later writers. Polycrates, bishop of Ephesus, writing to Victor of Rome *c.* A.D. 190, includes among the "great luminaries" whose tombs could be pointed out in the province of Asia "Philip, one of the twelve apostles, who sleeps at Hierapolis, with his two daughters who grew old as virgins, and another daughter who lived in the Holy Spirit and now rests in Ephesus." But Eusebius, to whom we are indebted for this quotation (*HE* 3.31.3), plainly understood the reference to be to Philip the evangelist, for immediately afterward he

he arrived at Caesarea (8:40). Now, after a lapse of some twenty years, we find him at Caesarea still. It is noteworthy that we left him there in the regular third-person narrative of Acts, whereas we find him now in the same city in the course of a "we" section. This is an incidental confirmation of the integrity of the "we" sections with the main narrative of Acts, as is also the reference to "the seven."

9 By this time, Philip had a flourishing family of four daughters, a credit to their father, for they all had the gift of prophecy. Several years later Philip and his daughters, with other Palestinian Christians, migrated to the province of Asia, and spent their remaining days there. The tombs of Philip and of two at least of his daughters were pointed out at Hierapolis in the Lycus valley toward the end of the second century. The daughters, or at least some of them, lived to a great age, and were highly esteemed as informants on persons and events belonging to the early years of Judaean Christianity.[9] It has been surmised that even at the time with which we are dealing information such as Philip and his daughters could supply was highly prized by Luke, who made use of it in the composition of his twofold history[10]—not only during the few days which he spent at Caesarea now, but also during the two years of Paul's imprisonment there (cf. 24:27). But nothing is said of any prophecies which they uttered during the present visit: a romancer could hardly have let slip the opportunity of putting some appropriate words into their mouths.

8. Agabus Reappears (21:10-14)

10 *As we spent several days there, a prophet named Agabus came down from Judaea.*

---

reproduces from Proclus the Montanist's *Dialogue* with the Roman presbyter Gaius (*c.* A.D. 200) the claim that "the four daughters of Philip, who were prophetesses, were in Hierapolis in Asia; their tomb is there, and their father's also"—and quotes Acts 21:8 as the biblical reference to this family. That it was Philip the evangelist who migrated to Asia with his daughters was maintained by T. Zahn, *Apostel und Apostelschüler in der Provinz Asien*, FGNTK 6 (Leipzig, 1900), pp. 158-75; A. Harnack, *Luke the Physician*, E.T. (London, 1907), p. 153; that it was Philip the apostle was maintained by J. B. Lightfoot, *St. Paul's Epistles to the Colossians and to Philemon* (London, 1879), pp. 45-47; J. Chapman, *John the Presbyter and the Fourth Gospel* (London, 1911), pp. 64-71. But others have urged us not to overlook the possibility that the same person is meant, that "Philip was originally one of the 'Twelve' and . . . went over to the 'Seven'" (so, most recently, M. Hengel, *Between Jesus and Paul*, E.T. [London, 1983], p. 14; he refers further to E. Meyer, *Ursprung und Anfänge des Christentums*, I [Stuttgart/Berlin, 1924], pp. 296, 338; J. Weiss, *Earliest Christianity*, E.T. [New York, 1959], p. 167, n. 4).

9. This last piece of information we owe to Papias, Bishop of Hierapolis, quoted by Eusebius (*HE* 3.39.9). For the story which they told about Joseph Barsabbas see on 1:23 (p. 46). See also P. Corssen, "Die Töchter des Philippus," *ZNW* 2 (1901), pp. 289-99.

10. Cf. A. Harnack, *Luke the Physician*, pp. 153-60; J. V. Bartlet, *The Acts of*

11 *Coming to us, he took up Paul's girdle, bound his own feet and hands with it, and said, "Thus says the Holy Spirit: this is how the Jews at Jerusalem will bind the man to whom this girdle belongs, and they will hand him over into the power of the Gentiles."*

12 *When we heard this, we begged him—both we ourselves and the people of the place—not to go up to Jerusalem.*

13 *Then Paul replied, "What are you about, weeping like this and trying to break my will? I am ready not only to be bound but even to die at Jerusalem for the name of the Lord Jesus."*

14 *When he would not be persuaded, we gave up pressing him: "The Lord's will be done," we said.*

10-11 If no report is given of any prophecy uttered by Philip's daughters, another prophet appears with a word for the occasion. The appearance of Agabus provides a further link between the "we" narrative and the general narrative of Acts. In 11:27-28 it was told that Agabus came down from Jerusalem to Antioch with some other prophets and foretold the famine of Claudius's day. Now, in this "we" section, he comes down to Caesarea[11] and foretells Paul's arrest and imprisonment at Jerusalem. But, unlike the Tyrian Christians who spoke "through the Spirit" (v. 4), Agabus does not draw the corollary that Paul ought not to continue his journey. The mode of his prophecy is reminiscent of much Old Testament prophecy: it is conveyed in action as well as in word. As Ahijah the Shilonite tore his new cloak to show how Solomon's kingdom would be disrupted (1 Kings 11:29-39), as Isaiah went about naked and barefoot to show how the Egyptians would be led into captivity by the Assyrians (Isa. 20:2-4), as Ezekiel mimicked the Babylonian siege of Jerusalem by laying siege himself to a replica of the city (Ezek. 4:1-3), so Agabus foretold the binding of Paul by tying himself up with Paul's girdle. The action was as much part of the prophecy as the spoken word: both together communicated the effective and self-fulfilling word of God (cf. Isa. 55:11). The terms of Agabus's prediction resemble our Lord's words about his own arrest by the Jerusalem authorities and delivery to the Gentiles (cf. Mark 10:33); in the event, however, Paul was rescued *by* the Gentiles *from* the Jews, who were compelled against their will to give him up.

12-14 If Agabus did not interpret his prophecy to mean that Paul should not go on to Jerusalem, Paul's companions and the Caesarean Christians drew that conclusion, and entreated him with tears not to proceed. But

---

the Apostles, CentB (London, 1902), p. 23; J. A. Findlay, *The Acts of the Apostles* (London, 1934), pp. 49-50.

11. When it is said that he came down "from Judaea," "Judaea" is plainly used in the narrower sense of the Jewish territory proper, and not in the official sense of the Roman province; the Roman province cf Judaea included Caesarea (cf. 12:19).

all their entreaties failed to weaken his resolve. He could not turn aside from the path of obedience and sacrifice, and he was prepared, if necessary, to suffer death as well as imprisonment for his Master's sake. He was not unmoved by his friends' tearful pleas, and begged them to desist from attempting to soften his determination.[12] When they saw that his mind was made up, they desisted from their entreaties, praying only that the Lord's will might be done. Luke no doubt intends his readers to discern in this prayer an echo of the Lord's own prayer in Gethsemane (Luke 22:42).[13]

9. Arrival at Jerusalem (21:15-16)

15 At the end of those days we got ready for the road[14] and went up to Jerusalem.

16 Some of the disciples from Caesarea came along with us, and brought us[15] to Mnason, a Cypriot, a disciple of long standing, with whom we were to find hospitality.

15 So, after spending several days at Caesarea, they set out on the last stage of their journey. Getting ready for the road, they began the sixty-four miles' journey to Jerusalem. It has been inferred from Luke's language that animals were provided for them so that they might ride rather than go on foot.[16]

16 They were accompanied by some Christian friends from Caesarea, who knew a place in Jerusalem where they could be conveniently entertained.[17] This was the house of Mnason, a Cypriot by family and a foundation member of the Jerusalem church.[18] Not every member of the church of Jerusalem would be prepared to have a party of Gentile Christians in his home; but they might be sure of a hospitable reception from Mnason,

12. Gk. συνθρύπτοντές μου τὴν καρδίαν, "pounding" my heart (i.e., my resolution) "like a washerwoman" (J. A. Findlay). Luke does not explain why Paul regarded his visit to Jerusalem as so solemnly imperative; his determination can be better understood in the light of Rom. 15:25-32, where Paul sets forth the importance of his going there with the evidence of ministry among the Gentiles thus far.

13. Compare Polycarp's reply in a similar situation: "Let God's will be done" (*Martyrdom of Polycarp* 7.1).

14. The Western text reads "we bade them farewell."

15. The Western text expands: "and these brought us to those with whom we were to find hospitality. And when we arrived at a certain village, we put up with one Mnason of Cyprus, a disciple of long standing." See n. 19 below.

16. Chrysostom (*Homily* 45) supplies Luke's ἐπισκευασάμενοι ("having made ready") with an object, τὰ πρὸς τὴν ὁδοιπορίαν ("the things for the journey"). This might refer to necessary supplies, but W. M. Ramsay took it to mean pack animals (*St. Paul the Traveller* [London, [14]1920], p. 302).

17. Perhaps some Caesarean Christians had gone to Jerusalem to arrange hospitality for the party during the "several days" they spent in Caesarea.

18. The expression ἀρχαίῳ μαθητῇ ("a disciple of long standing") probably means that he had been a disciple from the beginning (ἀρχή).

one of the small minority of Hellenists still remaining in the mother-church. There is little probability in the Western reading, according to which Mnason was their host not in Jerusalem but at some village between Caesarea and Jerusalem where they spent a night on the way.[19] Luke's special mention of Mnason's being a disciple of long standing has suggested to some readers that he acquired some valuable information from him about the early days; Ramsay, for example, thought that Mnason was Luke's authority for the episodes of Aeneas and Dorcas (9:32-42).[20]

C. PAUL AT JERUSALEM (21:17–23:30)

1. Meeting with James and the Elders (21:17-26)

17 *When we came to Jerusalem,[21] the brothers received us gladly.*

18 *The next day Paul went in with us to James, and all the elders were present.*

19 *He greeted them, and related to them one by one the things that God had done among the Gentiles through his ministry.*

20 *When they heard him, they gave glory to God. Then they said to him, "You see, brother, how many thousands of believers there are among the Jews,[22] and they are all zealots for the law.*

21 *Now they have heard reports about you, how you teach all[23] the Jews who live among the Gentiles to commit apostasy against Moses, telling them to stop circumcising their children and not to follow the ancestral customs.*

22 *What is to be done, then?[24] They will hear, of course, that you have arrived.*

23 *Therefore do as we tell you. We have four men who have taken a vow on themselves.*

24 *Take them with you and be purified along with them, and pay their expenses so that they may have their heads shaved. Then all the people will know that there is no substance in the reports they have*

---

19. See n. 15 above. The Western reading here has, however, been read in the light of the Western text of 11:2 (see p. 219, nn. 2 and 3). G. Salmon, reviewing F. Blass's *Acta Apostolorum* (Göttingen, 1895) in *Hermathena* 9 (1896), p. 239, finds here a further point of contact between the earlier part of Acts and the "we" narrative, and says it is "a natural combination" that Mnason was one of Peter's converts on his way home from Caesarea to Jerusalem.

20. *BRD*, p. 309, n. 2.

21. The Western text reads: "And when we departed thence [i.e., from the halfway village], we came to Jerusalem."

22. Cod. ℵ omits "among the Jews"; the Western text reads "in Judaea"; the Byzantine text reads "of Jews."

23. A few authorities (including the Greek codices P^{74} A D E 33, the Latin Vulgate, and the Coptic Bohairic version) omit "all."

24. P^{74} ℵ A C² D E, the Byzantine text, and the Latin Vulgate add "a crowd is bound to come together" and continue: "for they will hear. . . ."

received about you; they will see that you yourself live as an observer of the law.

25 *As regards the Gentiles who have believed, we have sent a letter conveying our decision that they should abstain from idol sacrifices, from blood, from strangled meat, and from fornication."* 25

26 *Then Paul took the men and the next day, having been purified along with them, he went into the temple, giving notice of the days of purification which had to be fulfilled until the offering was presented for each one of them.*

17 The "brothers" who "received us gladly" may have been Mnason and his associates, perhaps the Hellenistic remnant in the church. Alternatively, they may have been James and the elders, if verse 17 is an anticipatory summary of the verses that follow. This interpretation involves some awkwardness with "the next day" coming where it does at the beginning of verse 18; this cannot easily be explained by change of source, since the "we" narrative comes to an end with the report of the visit to James in the course of verse 18.

18 Since "all the elders were present" when Paul and his companions went to see James, it may be inferred that notice had been given of their visit. James's house must have been a building of some size, if it could accommodate the whole elderhood as well as the present visitors.26

Nothing is said about the gift which Paul and his companions brought, but it helps to understand Luke's account if the gift is borne in mind. Both Paul and James could remember the injunction to "remember the poor" which, on a previous visit to Jerusalem, Paul had received from the "pillars" of the church (Gal. 2:10). Of those "pillars" only one was now resident in Jerusalem. Peter and John had undertaken more extended missionary responsibilities. But James the Lord's brother remained, exercising wise and judicious leadership over the mother-church, greatly respected not only by its members but by the ordinary Jews of Jerusalem also.27 In his administrative duties he was helped by a band of colleagues—the elders of the Jerusalem church. How many they were is not said, but in view of the large number of believers in Jerusalem28 they may well have numbered

25. The Western text, as in 15:20, 29, reads "we sent a letter conveying our decision that they should observe nothing of the sort save to guard themselves from idol sacrifices and blood and fornication" (but the addition of the negative golden rule is not repeated here). See p. 296, n. 62; p. 297, n. 70.

26. Cf. M. Hengel, *Between Jesus and Paul,* p. 108.

27. It was by the populace at large that he was called "the Just" (possibly "the *ṣaddîq*"), according to Hegesippus (*ap.* Euseb. *HE* 2.23.4, 7).

28. The element of hyperbole in πόσαι μυριάδες ("how many myriads") can be appreciated when it is remembered that, according to the calculations of Joachim Jeremias ("Die Einwohnerzahl Jerusalems zur Zeit Jesu" [1943], in *Abba* [Göttingen, 1966], pp. 335-41; *Jerusalem in the Time of Jesus,* E.T. [London, 1969], pp. 77-84), the normal

seventy—the traditional figure for elders in Israel. However many they were, all of them were present to receive Paul and his associates the day after their arrival in the city.

19-21 Paul's narrative of all that God had accomplished through his ministry on both sides of the Aegean gave his hearers cause for joy. The representatives of many of the Gentile churches which he had planted were there with him as living witnesses to the truth of his report, and the gifts which they brought (though Luke says nothing about them) showed that the divine grace which they had received found a response in action as well as in word. So James and his colleagues praised God for his astounding grace manifested to Gentiles.[29]

But there was something that caused them serious anxiety, and now they had an opportunity of unburdening their minds to Paul about it. It was freely rumored in Jerusalem that Paul not only refused to impose the requirements of the Jewish law on his Gentile converts (and, despite the Jerusalem decree, this was probably still resented by some of the "zealots for the law"[30] in the church); he actually dissuaded *Jewish* believers, it was said, from continuing to practise their ancestral customs, handed down from Moses: he even encouraged them to give up circumcising their sons. James and the elders evidently regarded these rumors as false; but it would take more than a merely verbal assurance to persuade those who paid heed to such rumors that they had been misinformed.

Paul's position in such matters is fairly clear from his letters. The circumcising of Gentile converts as a kind of insurance policy, lest faith in Christ should be insufficient in itself, he denounced as a departure from the purity of the gospel (Gal. 5:2-4). But in itself circumcision was a matter of indifference; it made no difference to one's status in God's sight (Gal. 5:6; 6:15). If a Jewish father, after he became a follower of Jesus, wished to have his son circumcised in accordance with ancestral custom, Paul had no objec-

---

population of Jerusalem at this time was probably between 25,000 and 55,000. Several scholars, with no basis in the textual tradition, have argued for the deletion of τῶν πεπιστευκότων ("of those who have believed") from v. 20, so that the "myriads" would be the Jerusalem Jews in general; so, among others, F. C. Baur, *Paul*, E.T., I (London, ²1876), pp. 201-4; J. Munck, *Paul and the Salvation of Mankind*, E.T. (London, 1959), pp. 240-42; cf. A. D. Nock: "We may well be somewhat sceptical about this reference to the multitude (literally, 'myriads') of Jewish Christians: the danger was from ordinary Jews" (*St. Paul* [London, 1938], p. 136).

29. Cf. 15:3-4.

30. When James and the elders describe the rank and file of the Jerusalem church as "zealots for the law," the term "zealot" is not used in its party sense (for which see on 1:13) but in the sense in which Paul applies it to himself in Gal. 1:14, where he claims to have been "a zealot for the ancestral traditions." Even so, it is unlikely that the church membership remained completely unaffected by the insurgent spirit which was abroad in the land during Felix's governorship.

tion.[31] He adopted the same flexible attitude to such customs as observance of special days or abstention from certain kinds of food: "let everyone be fully convinced in his own mind" (Rom. 14:2-6). He himself was happy to conform to Jewish customs when he found himself in Jewish society. Such conformity came easily to him, in view of his upbringing, but he had learned to be equally happy to conform to Gentile ways in Gentile company. If it is asked what his practice was when he found himself in mixed Jewish and Gentile society, the answer probably is that he acted as he thought each situation required: any Jews who were content to participate in such mixed society had doubtless learned some measure of adaptation already. For anyone who stayed by the letter and spirit of the law, Paul's regarding some of its requirements as matters of indifference, his treating as optional things that the law laid down as obligatory, must in itself have constituted "apostasy against Moses"; but in practice he avoided giving offense to those in whose company he was from time to time.

22-24 There was, however, a way in which Paul himself could give the lie effectively to those disturbing reports. If he were seen to take part publicly in one of the ancestral customs, it would be realized that he was, after all, an observant and practising Jew. Therefore, in their *naïveté,* they put a proposal to him. Four of their number had undertaken a Nazirite vow: if no time limit was specified, their vow would last for thirty days.[32] During that period they would abstain from wine and strong drink, would avoid any defiling contact (e.g., with a corpse), and would leave their hair uncut. At the end of the period they would present an offering in the temple, and their hair, which they had now cut, would be consumed in the sacrificial fire.[33] Another Israelite might associate himself with Nazirites by defraying the cost of their offering; this was regarded as a pious and charitable action.[34] The elders' proposal, then, was that Paul should associate himself with the four Nazirites when they discharged their vow in the temple and pay their expenses.

To do this Paul himself would have to be purified: he had just returned from a long residence in Gentile lands, and the ritual defilement which inevitably attached to him on that account had to be removed before he could take part in such a solemn ceremony. But his purification should be distinguished from the Nazirites' purification. In the LXX the same Greek

31. Compare his circumcision of Timothy, his own "son in the faith" (see on 16:3).

32. Mishnah, *Nāzîr* 6.3.

33. The offering comprised one he-lamb, one ewe-lamb, one ram, and accompanying food and drink offerings (Num. 6:14-15). Together with the "hair of consecration" the whole was called a "hair offering" (Mishnah, *Nāzîr* 6.5-6).

34. Josephus probably implies that Herod Agrippa I performed a meritorious action of this kind when, on his entering Jerusalem as king, he directed many Nazirites to have their hair cut (*Ant.* 19.294).

term[35] does duty both for general purification from ritual defilement (as in Num. 19:12) and for the various forms of abstention which Nazirites had to practise throughout the period of their vow (as in Num. 6:3); and Luke here uses that term in both senses. If the two kinds of purification be distinguished, it will not be necessary to suppose either that Paul had a Nazirite vow of his own to discharge on this occasion[36] or that the four Nazirites had inadvertently contracted some defilement during the period of their vow and had now to be purified from it.[37]

25 The elders added the assurance that they had no thought of going back on the terms of the apostolic decree, and imposing legal requirements on Gentile believers. So far as *they* were concerned, said the elders, all that was required of them was that they should abstain from eating flesh that had been sacrificed to idols or killed in such a way that the blood was not completely drained away, and from the practice of fornication.

There is no good reason for the view sometimes expressed, that this was the first time that Paul was told of the terms of the apostolic decree.[38] The repetition of those terms, as a sort of afterthought or footnote, is perfectly natural in the context.[39] The elders wish to assure Paul that their misgivings are confined to his teaching reportedly given to Jewish believers. We are glad to know, they say in effect, that you do not teach Jewish believers to abandon the ancestral customs, and we should like you to make this clear to everybody here. As for Gentile believers, of course, we have already agreed that nothing is to be imposed on them apart from the abstentions detailed in the apostolic letter.

26 Paul fell in with their suggestion, and accompanied the four Nazirites into the temple. Notice was given simultaneously of the intended date of the discharge of their vow, and of the termination of Paul's purificatory process. The phrase "having been purified along with them"[40] must refer to the initiation of his purificatory process; the process would not be completed until the seventh day.

The wisdom of Paul's complying with the elders' plan may well be doubted. Probably he himself was not too sanguine about its outcome; but if

---

35. The verb ἁγνίζω ("purify") with the derivative noun ἁγνισμός ("purification").

36. Cf. the vow which he discharged at Cenchreae (see on 18:18).

37. Seven days had to elapse before a Nazirite who had contracted such defilement could be purified; the head was shaved on the seventh day and the offering brought on the eighth day (Num. 6:14-15; Mishnah, *Nāzîr* 6.6-9).

38. Thus H. Lietzmann, *The Beginnings of the Christian Church*, E.T. (London, 1949), p. 109, held that the apostolic decree was drawn up after the Council of Jerusalem, behind Paul's back, and that "only towards the end of his life, when he again visited Jerusalem, was he given any direct official information."

39. Cf. H. Conzelmann, *Die Apostelgeschichte*, HNT (Tübingen, 1963), p. 123; E. Haenchen, *The Acts of the Apostles*, E.T. (Oxford, 1971), p. 610.

40. Gk. σὺν αὐτοῖς ἁγνισθείς—is the aorist ingressive?

his falling in with their proposal would relieve them of embarrassment, he was prepared to bend over backward in applying his stated policy: "to those under the law, I became as one under the law—though not being myself under the law—that I might win those under the law" (1 Cor. 9:20). Certainly he cannot fairly be charged with compromising his own gospel principles.

As for the elders themselves, the impression made by Luke's account is that they were well-meaning but deeply worried men. They knew that, if they appeared to countenance Paul by accepting the Gentile churches' gifts, it could prejudice their mission to Israel and their influence with their own flock. But if Paul took some public action which would give the lie to the disturbing rumors that circulated about him, this would ease the situation for them. But attempts have been made to read between the lines of Luke's account. It has been suggested that the course of action which the elders pressed on Paul was a condition for their acceptance of the gifts.[41] It has even been suggested that they knowingly drew Paul "into an ambush by luring him into the Temple"—that this suspicion dawned on Luke himself when Paul was riotously assaulted while carrying out their directions.[42] If any such suspicion did dawn on Luke, he has concealed it very skillfully.

2. Riot in the Temple (21:27-30)

27 When the seven days were about to be completed, the Jews from Asia saw him in the temple. They stirred up the whole crowd and laid hands on him.

28 "Men of Israel," they shouted, "come and help us! This is the man who spreads his teaching everywhere, indoctrinating everyone to the detriment of the people, the law, and this place. Not content with that, he has brought Greeks into the temple and polluted this holy place."

29 They had already seen Trophimus the Ephesian in the city with him, and they supposed that Paul had brought him into the temple.

30 The whole city was set in turmoil, and the people came running together from every quarter. They seized Paul and dragged him out of the temple, and immediately the doors were shut.

27-29 Paul's purificatory process lasted for seven days; there was a special ceremony of purification on the third day and the seventh day.[43] He had

41. Cf. J. D. G. Dunn, *Unity and Diversity in the New Testament* (London, 1977), p. 257.

42. A. J. Mattill, "The Purpose of Acts: Schneckenburger Reconsidered," in *Apostolic History and the Gospel*, ed. W. W. Gasque and R. P. Martin (Exeter/Grand Rapids, 1970), pp. 115-16.

43. Cf. Num. 19:12.

practically completed all that was required of him[44] when a riot broke out in the temple courts. Among the Jews of the dispersion those of the province of Asia were particularly hostile to Paul; he had incurred their enmity during his years of ministry in Ephesus.[45] Some of these Asian Jews had come to Jerusalem for the festival of Pentecost, and finding Paul there, they determined to take more effective action against him now than they had found possible in Ephesus. Among the Gentile friends who had come with Paul to Jerusalem was the Ephesian Trophimus, whom these Asian Jews recognized when they saw him in Paul's company. When they later came on Paul in the temple, in the Court of Israel,[46] discharging the ritual obligations which he had undertaken, they took it into their heads that Trophimus was still with him. But this was a capital offense: Gentiles might visit the outer court of the temple (which for this reason was sometimes called the Court of the Gentiles), but they were forbidden to penetrate any of the inner courts on pain of death. The Roman authorities were so conciliatory of Jewish religious scruples in this regard that they authorized the death sentence for this trespass even when the offenders were Roman citizens.[47] That no Gentile might unwittingly enter into the forbidden areas, notices in Greek and Latin were fixed to the barrier separating them from the outer court, warn. ng Gentiles that death was the penalty for further ingress.[48] Two of these notices (both in Greek) have been discovered—one in 1871 and one in 1935—the text of which runs: "No foreigner may enter within the barricade which surrounds the temple and enclosure. Any one who is caught trespassing will bear personal responsibility for his ensuing death."[49]

If the Asian Jews' charge against Paul had been justified, he would certainly have been guilty of aiding and abetting, and indeed participating in, a most serious crime against Jewish law, and one which was bound immediately to inflame all the Jews of Jerusalem against him. The Asian Jews were well aware of this when they raised a hue and cry against him: this man, they shouted, not content with the attacks on the Jewish people, law, and sanctuary which he made in his teaching all over the world—an accusa-

44. Every requirement for the purificatory process had been met, according to the natural sense of the perfect participle "purified" (ἡγνισμένον) in 24:18.

45. Cf. 20:19.

46. The Court of Israel was the area of the inner precincts to which Jewish men who were not priests or Levites were admitted (see on 3:1-3, p. 77 with n. 7).

47. Titus, the Roman commander-in-chief, reminds the defenders of the temple of this concession in a speech attributed to him by Josephus (*BJ* 6.126).

48. Cf. Josephus, *BJ* 5.194; 6.124-25; *Ant.* 15.417; *Ap.* 2.103-4; Philo, *Embassy to Gaius* 212.

49. Cf. C. S. Clermont-Ganneau, "Discovery of a Tablet from Herod's Temple," *PEQ* 3 (1871), pp. 132-33; J. H. Iliffe, "The ΘΑΝΑΤΟΣ Inscription from Herod's Temple," *QDAP* 6 (1936), pp. 1-3.

tion strongly reminiscent of the charge against Stephen[50]—had actually profaned the holy place by bringing Greeks into it.

30 A tumult broke out at once; the crowd that was present in the Court of Israel set on Paul, and dragged him out of the inner precincts down the steps into the outer court. The news spread quickly from the temple area to the city, and many others hastened to the scene of action. The "gates of the sanctuary" leading from the inner courts into the outer court were closed by the temple police, who were anxious to preserve the sanctity of the sacred precincts proper from being outraged by the violence of the crowd and by its possibly fatal outcome.

Some commentators have seen symbolic significance in the brief statement that "immediately the doors were shut"; and such a significance may well have been intended by Luke. T. D. Bernard, for example, in his Bampton Lectures for 1864, says of this incident: "'Believing all things which are written in the Law and in the Prophets' and 'having committed nothing against the people or customs of [his] fathers', he [Paul] and his creed are forced from their proper home. On it as well as him the Temple doors are shut."[51] For Luke himself, this may have been the moment when the Jerusalem temple ceased to fill the honorable role hitherto ascribed to it in his twofold history. The exclusion of God's message and messenger from the house once called by his name sealed its doom: it was now ripe for the destruction which Jesus had predicted for it many years before (Luke 21:6).

3. Paul Rescued by the Romans (21:31-36)

31 *As they were trying to kill him, a report went up to the military tribune that all Jerusalem was in a tumult.*

32 *Immediately he took soldiers and centurions and ran down among them. When they saw the tribune and the soldiers, they stopped beating Paul.*

33 *Then the tribune came up and arrested him, ordered him to be bound with a chain on either hand, and asked who he might be and what he had done.*

34 *Some of the crowd shouted one thing, some another; so, when he could not learn the certain truth because of the uproar, he ordered him to be taken into the fortress.*

35 *When he came to the steps, Paul had to be carried by the soldiers because of the violence of the crowd,*

36 *for the multitude of people followed him, shouting, "Away with him!"*

50. Cf. 6:13; see pp. 126-27.
51. T. D. Bernard, *The Progress of Doctrine in the New Testament* (London, [5]1900), p. 121.

31-32 Meanwhile, in the outer court, Paul was being fiercely attacked and beaten by the mob, and his life would not have been worth more than a few minutes' purchase had it not been for the timely intervention of the Roman garrison. Northwest of the temple area stood the Antonia fortress (at one time called Baris but rebuilt by Herod the Great and renamed by him in honor of Mark Antony). It was garrisoned at this time by an auxiliary cohort of Roman troops under the command of a military tribune.[52] The fortress was connected with the outer court of the temple by two flights of steps, so that the garrison might intervene as quickly as possible in the event of a riot. On this occasion, then, as soon as the tribune received a report of the tumult, he summoned a detachment of soldiers with their centurions[53] and they, running down the steps into the court, forced Paul's assailants to stop manhandling him.

33-34 The tribune then formally arrested Paul, and ordered him to be handcuffed to two soldiers. No doubt (he thought) the man was a criminal, but whatever he had done to infuriate the mob in this way, he had to be dealt with legally and not by riotous violence. But when he tried to find out what the man had done, or who he was, he could get no clear answer: so great was the din and so confused and conflicting were the accusations which were being hurled at Paul. He must find out the truth of the matter by other means, so he ordered the soldiers to take Paul into the fortress.

35-36 The disappointed crowd, thus peremptorily robbed of their victim, pressed hard on the soldiers who had Paul in their custody; and when they reached the steps leading up to the fortress, Paul had to be carried by the soldiers lest the crowd should pull him away from them. This was no more glorious an escape from danger than his being let down in a basket over the wall of Damascus: Paul could add it to his store of memories of situations which kept him humble in moments when he was tempted to be "exalted above measure" (2 Cor. 12:7). The shout "Away with him!"[54] which pursued him as he was carried up the steps was the shout with which Jesus' death had been demanded not far from that spot some twenty-seven years before (Luke 23:18; John 19:15).

---

52. Gk. χιλίαρχος, lit. "commander of a thousand"; the auxiliary cohort (σπεῖρα) which he commanded had a paper strength of 1,000 men (760 foot-soldiers and 240 cavalry). Cf. p. 433, n. 44 (on 23:23). Details of the Antonia fortress are given by Josephus, *BJ* 5.238-45. See also P. Benoit, "The Archaeological Reconstruction of the Antonia Fortress," in *Jerusalem Revealed*, ed. Y. Yadin (New Haven/London/Jerusalem, 1975), pp. 87-89.

53. Since centurions are mentioned in the plural, there were at least two of them, each in charge of a "century" of 100 men (on paper).

54. Gk. αἶρε αὐτόν (cf. *P.Oxy.* 119.10, quoted p. 324, n. 9).

4. Paul Obtains Leave to Address the Crowd (21:37-40)

37 When he was about to enter the fortress, Paul said to the tribune, "May I have permission to say something to you?" "What?" said he; "do you know Greek?

38 Then you are not that Egyptian who some time ago stirred up a revolt and led the four thousand 'assassins' out into the wilderness?"

39 "No," said Paul; "I am a Jew, a native of Tarsus in Cilicia, a citizen of no mean city. Please give me leave to speak to the people."

40 He gave him leave, so Paul stood on the steps and with his hand motioned to the people to be quiet. When a great silence fell on them, he addressed them in the "Hebrew" speech.

37-38 By the time he reached the top of the steps, Paul must have presented a sorry figure—bruised, battered, begrimed, and disheveled. But, as so frequently in Acts, he is quickly in command of the situation.

The tribune, trying hard to grasp the cause of the trouble, had jumped to a conclusion. Some three years previously, an Egyptian adventurer appeared in Jerusalem, claiming to be a prophet, and led a large band of followers out to the Mount of Olives.[55] There he told them to wait until, at his word of command, the walls of the city would fall flat; then they would march in, overthrow the Roman garrison, and take possession of the place. But Felix, procurator of Judaea, sent a body of troops against them; they killed several and took others prisoner.[56] The Egyptian himself discreetly disappeared. Those whom he had duped would cherish no friendly feelings toward him. Now, thought the tribune, the impostor had reappeared and the people were venting their rage on him.

He was therefore surprised when Paul, having been carried to the top of the steps and set down, addressed him in an educated Greek voice and asked permission to speak to the throng below. He must have been wrong in his identification of Paul, he concluded, and Paul, on being questioned, confirmed that he was indeed no Egyptian.

39-40 On the contrary, said Paul, he was a citizen of the illustrious

55. The story is told by Josephus, *BJ* 2.261-63; *Ant.* 20.169-72. He does not suggest that the man's followers were "assassins" *(sicarii)*, as the tribune says. The *sicarii*, or dagger men (from Lat. *sica*, "dagger"), began to be active about this time and, after murdering the former high priest Jonathan, made pro-Roman Jews their special target; they mingled with crowds at festivals and stabbed their victims by stealth (cf. Josephus, *BJ* 2.254-57; *Ant.* 20.162-65, 185-87). In saying that the Egyptian led them into the wilderness, the tribune may be grouping him with other impostors who at this time did lead their dupes out to the wilderness of Judaea, promising to perform miracles there (cf. Matt. 24:26), according to Josephus (*BJ* 2.259; *Ant.* 20.167-68); see P. W. Barnett, "The Jewish Sign Prophets, A.D. 40-70—Their Intentions and Origin," *NTS* 27 (1980-81), pp. 679-97.

56. Josephus gives the number of his followers as 30,000; the number of 4,000 mentioned here is much more probable.

Cilician city of Tarsus,[57] born of Jewish stock; and he repeated his request for permission to address the angry crowd in the outer court. His request was granted, so, standing at the top of the steps (which would be strongly guarded by soldiers), he began to speak to the crowd of Jerusalemites below, addressing them in their Aramaic vernacular.[58] His securing their silence with a characteristic gesture of his hand[59] is probably intended by Luke to bear witness to the power of his personality.

His choosing to speak to them in Aramaic rather than Greek was a not wholly unsuccessful bid for their tolerance while he spoke. If an audience of Welsh or Irish nationalists, about to be addressed by someone suspected of being a traitor to the national cause, suddenly became aware that he was speaking to them not in the Saxon tongue but in the Celtic vernacular, the gesture would no doubt call forth at least a temporary measure of goodwill. Aramaic was not only the vernacular of most Palestinian Jews; it was also the common speech of all non-Greek speakers in Western Asia, as far east as (and including) the Parthian empire beyond the Euphrates.

57. The tribune was much more impressed by Paul's later revelation that he was a Roman citizen (22:25-29) than by his present claim to be a citizen of Tarsus: what was Tarsus to him?

58. Aramaic appears to be meant wherever reference is made to the "Hebrew" language in the NT, except in Rev. 9:11; 16:16. See F. Rosenthal, *Die aramaistische Forschung* (Leiden, 1939).

59. Cf. 13:16.

ACTS 22

5. Paul's Defense to the People of Jerusalem (22:1-21)

a. His early days (22:1-5)

1 *"Brothers and fathers, listen to me as I now speak in my defense."*
2 *When they heard him addressing them in the Hebrew speech, they listened to him even more quietly.*
3 *"I am a Jew," he went on, "born in Tarsus of Cilicia, but brought up in this city, educated at the feet of Gamaliel according to the strict interpretation of our ancestral law. I was a zealot for God,[1] as you all are today.*
4 *I persecuted this Way to the death; I bound both men and women with chains and handed them over for imprisonment.*
5 *Indeed, the high priest[2] can bear me witness in this, together with the whole body of elders. From them I received letters for our brothers in Damascus and was making my way there in order to bring those who had fled there[3] to Jerusalem as prisoners, for punishment.*

1-2 Speaking Aramaic, then, Paul asked the crowd to listen to what he had to say for himself, beginning with the same words as Stephen had used many years before at the outset of *his* defense.[4] When they realized that the man whom they execrated as a renegade was addressing them in their vernacular, the silence which they had reluctantly accorded to his beckoning hand became deeper still, and they allowed him to go on.

3-4 His defense takes an autobiographical form, as he tells his hearers of his heritage and upbringing as a strictly orthodox Jew, of his call and commission by the risen Jesus on the Damascus road, and of his being sent to evangelize the Gentile world. This is the second account in Acts of

---

1. For "God" the Latin Vulgate reads "the law" and the Harclean Syriac has the asterisked reading "my ancestral traditions" (borrowed from Gal. 1:14).
2. A few Western witnesses add "Ananias" (cf. 23:2). But Ananias was not high priest at the time of Paul's mission to Damascus.
3. Gk. τοὺς ἐκεῖσε ὄντας (this translation is designed to bring out the force of ἐκεῖσε, "thither").
4. Cf. 7:2.

414

Paul's conversion; the first is related in the third person in 9:1-22, and the third (like this) is in the first person, on Paul's own lips, as he makes a further defense—this time before the younger Agrippa (26:2-23). Along with the virtual identity of the subject matter in the three accounts, there are subtle divergences of style and presentation, especially between the two delivered in the first person, each of which is specially adapted to its audience.

Here Paul emphasizes that, while he was born in Tarsus, he was brought up in Jerusalem, exposed only to Jewish influences. Some writers have given rein to free imagination as they have described the Tarsian influences which would have made their mark on Paul in his formative years; according to this account, however, his formative years were spent in Jerusalem.[5] When the time came for him to receive his higher education, it was to none of the academies of his native city that he was sent, but to the school of Gamaliel. We have met Gamaliel already as a leader of the Pharisees in Jerusalem and an illustrious teacher of the law.[6] The "strict interpretation of our ancestral law" which Paul learned in his school accorded with Pharisaic tradition. What is said here may be compared with Paul's account in Gal. 1:14 of his advancing in Judaism beyond many of his contemporaries and his zeal for the ancestral traditions. As in his letters, so here he emphasizes his persecution of the Way[7] as the supreme manifestation of his zeal for God.[8]

5 He goes on to tell how, in pursuance of his campaign of repression against the disciples of Jesus, he went to Damascus, armed with letters accrediting him as an emissary from the high priest and Sanhedrin at Jerusalem. These authorized him to procure the arrest and extradition of those disciples who had sought refuge in that ancient Syrian city.

b. The Damascus road (22:6-11)

6   *"So, as I was on my way to Damascus, I was approaching the city when suddenly, about noon, a great light from heaven flashed round about me.*

5. See W. C. van Unnik, *Tarsus or Jerusalem: The City of Paul's Youth*, E.T. (London, 1962).

6. On Gamaliel see 5:34, with exposition and notes. The pupil's persecuting zeal forms a sharp contrast to the moderation and tolerance of his teacher's policy; but the pupil probably saw more clearly than the teacher how grave a threat the new way presented to the old. The unnamed pupil of Gamaliel who, according to the Babylonian Talmud, manifested "impudence in matters of learning" (*Shabbāṯ* 30b), is identified with Paul by J. Klausner (*From Jesus to Paul*, E.T. [London, 1944], pp. 310-11), but with doubtful cogency.

7. For "the Way" see on 9:2.

8. Cf. 8:3; 9:1; 26:9-11; Gal. 1:13; Phil. 3:6 ("as to zeal, a persecutor of the church"). For the comparison of his former zeal to their present zeal cf. Rom. 10:2 ("they have a zeal for God, but it is not enlightened").

7 *I fell to the ground, and heard a voice saying to me,[9] 'Saul, Saul, why are you persecuting me?'[10]*

8 *'Who are you, Lord?' I answered. 'I am Jesus', said he, '—Jesus the Nazarene, whom you are persecuting.'*

9 *The men who were with me saw the light but did not hear the voice of the one who was speaking to me.*

10 *'What shall I do, Lord?' said I. 'Get up,' said the Lord to me, 'and go into Damascus; there you will be told about all that has been appointed for you to do.'[11]*

11 *As[12] I could not see[13] because of the glory of that light, my companions led me by the hand and I came into Damascus.*

6-9 Paul now describes the blinding light that flashed around him and his fellow-travelers about midday as they approached the walls of Damascus, and the voice that challenged him as he lay prostrate on the ground: "Saul, Saul, why are you persecuting me?" "Who are you, Lord?" was Paul's surprised question, and more astounding still was the swift reply: "I am Jesus of Nazareth,[14] the one you are persecuting." While this interchange was taking place between Paul and the glorified Lord, his companions stood by amazed. They too had seen the lightning flash and were momentarily stunned by it; now they heard Paul speaking, but neither heard nor saw the person to whom his words were addressed.[15]

10-11 That convicting word, "I am Jesus of Nazareth," imposed on Paul a lifelong allegiance to the one whom in ignorance and unbelief he had hitherto withstood. Now he awaited the commands of one whom he henceforth acknowledged as Lord, and was told to go into Damascus, where further instructions would be given him. So in his blindness he was led by hand into Damascus.

c. Ananias of Damascus (22:12-16)

12 *"There was one Ananias, a devout man by the standards of the law, who enjoyed a good reputation among all the Jews who were resident there.*

9. Two Western witnesses (the Latin codex *gigas* and the margin of the Harclean Syriac) add "in the Hebrew speech" (borrowed from 26:14).

10. A number of witnesses, many Western in character, add "it is hard for you to kick against the goads" (borrowed from 26:14).

11. For "about all that has been appointed for you to do" some Byzantine authorities read "what you must do" (from 9:6).

12. The Western text reads: "And rising up I could not see. And as I could not see. . . ."

13. Cod. B reads "I saw nothing."

14. This is the only one of the three narratives of Paul's conversion where Jesus calls himself "Jesus the Nazarene" (see on 2:22, p. 63, n. 72); in 9:5 and 26:15 he says, "I am Jesus." G. H. Dalman reconstructed the Aramaic wording as *'ănā Yēšûa' Nāṣerāyā deʾatt rāḏepinnēh* (*Jesus-Jeshua*, E.T. [London, 1929], p. 18).

15. See on 9:7.

13 *He came to me, stood over me, and said, 'Saul, my brother, look up.' [16] That very moment I looked up and saw him. [17]*

14 *Then he said, 'The God of our fathers has chosen you to learn his will and see the Righteous One and hear words from his mouth,*

15 *because you are to be his witness to all about the things which you have seen and heard.*

16 *And now, why delay? Rise up and get yourself baptized and have your sins washed away, calling on his name.'*

12 As Paul has emphasized his orthodox upbringing and his devotion to the law and the ancestral traditions, so now he emphasizes the part played in his conversion experience by Ananias of Damascus, portrayed as a devout and law-abiding Jew, enjoying the respect of all his fellow-Jews in the city.

13-16 The first thing Ananias did when he came into the house where Paul was staying was to announce the restoration of his eyesight in the name of the risen Christ. The command "Look up" might be otherwise rendered: "Receive the power of sight again." Ananias's first words to Paul, as reported here, summarize the fuller statement of 9:17. But his following words in verses 14-16 are fuller than anything ascribed to him there. [18] It was important to stress on the present occasion that the commission which Paul received from the risen Christ was to a large extent communicated through the lips of this pious and believing Jew. [19] In the later speech before Agrippa there was no need for this particular emphasis, and so the substance of what Ananias says to Paul here in the name of the Lord is there addressed to him directly by the Lord on the Damascus road. It must be said that in this regard the speech before Agrippa is more in line with the testimony of Paul's letters, with their insistence on the unmediated character of Paul's call and commission (Gal. 1:12).

The Jewish style of Ananias's announcement contributes to the general presentation of his role in this narrative: the initiative in Paul's call is taken by "the God of our fathers" (contrast "the Lord—that is, Jesus" in 9:17), and Jesus himself is identified as "the Righteous One." [20]

Thus Paul received his commission. He had seen the risen Christ, [21]

---

16. Gk. ἀνάβλεψον, which may mean either "look up" (ἀνά = "up") or "see again," i.e., "recover your sight" (ἀνά = "again").

17. Gk. ἀνέβλεψα εἰς αὐτόν.

18. See, however, the instruction given to Ananias by the Lord in 9:15-16.

19. On the relation of Ananias's role here to Paul's claim in Gal. 1:1, 11-12, see the exposition of 9:17 (pp. 187-89).

20. For this designation cf. 3:14; 7:52 (see p. 81, n. 29).

21. That Paul actually saw the risen and exalted Lord in addition to hearing his voice is emphasized more explicitly in his letters than in Acts. It is mentioned indeed in Acts (both here and in 26:16); but whereas the narratives in Acts lay chief stress on what the Lord said, Paul himself makes it plain that to him the vision of Christ was the central and all-important feature of his conversion experience (Gal. 1:12, 16; 1 Cor. 9:1; 15:8).

he had heard his voice, and from now on he was to fulfil the ministry of a true witness, telling forth with confidence what he had seen and heard, with all that it implied—that Jesus of Nazareth, crucified by men, exalted by God, was Lord of all. But first he must get himself baptized, as the outward and visible sign of his inward and spiritual cleansing from sin.[22] And in the act of being baptized his invocation of Jesus as Lord would declare the dominant power in his life henceforth.[23]

d. Paul's vision in the temple (22:17-21)

17 *"When I came back to Jerusalem and was praying in the temple, I fell into a trance*

18 *and saw him saying to me, 'Make haste; get out of Jerusalem quickly: they will not accept your testimony about me.'*

19 *'Lord,' said I, 'they know that I used to imprison and flog in synagogue after synagogue those who believed on you.*

20 *And when the blood of your witness Stephen was being shed, I myself was standing by with approval, and guarding the clothes of those who were killing him.'*

21 *'Be on your way,' he said to me; 'I will send you far off to the Gentiles.'"*

17-21 The vision in the Jerusalem temple which Paul now describes was probably experienced during his visit recorded in 9:26-30. The account of it may be influenced by that of Isaiah's inaugural vision in Isa. 6:1-13.[24] But this was no inaugural vision for Paul. His commission to preach Christ to the Gentiles had been received when the risen Lord appeared to him on the Damascus road.[25] His testimony to this effect in Gal. 1:16 is confirmed by the account in 26:16-18. But it is entirely credible that, when he visited Jerusalem for the first time after his conversion, his "heart's desire and prayer to God" for Israel's salvation (of which he speaks in Rom. 10:1) should have made him eager to bear witness to his fellow-Jews. According

22. For the view that Paul was bidden to baptize himself see B. S. Easton, "Self-Baptism," *AJT* 24 (1920), pp. 513-18. In its favor there is the analogy of proselyte baptism, which was self-administered; on the other hand, the passive voice ἐβαπτίσθη, "he was baptized," is used in 9:18. The middle voice here (βάπτισαι) probably means "get yourself baptized"; similarly ἀπόλουσαι (also middle) may be rendered "have (your sins) washed away." Cf. ἀπελούσασθε, 1 Cor. 6:11; ἐβαπτίσαντο, 1 Cor. 10:2.

23. His invocation of the name of Jesus meant that he was baptized "in the name" (or "with the name") of Jesus in the sense of 2:38; 10:48. Such an invocation might be the "word" (ῥῆμα) referred to in Eph. 5:26.

24. See O. Betz, "Die Vision des Paulus im Tempel von Jerusalem," in *Verborum Veritas: Festschrift für G. Stählin*, ed. O. Böcher and K. Haacker (Wuppertal, 1970), pp. 113-23. Both Isaiah and Paul were told that their testimony would be unacceptable, but Isaiah was told to persist, whereas Paul was told to leave.

25. And he began immediately to fulfil it by going to Arabia, i.e., the Nabataean kingdom (Gal. 1:17).

to Luke, he began during that visit to engage in vigorous debate with the Hellenists of Jerusalem, and immediately aroused keen hostility, the more so because they remembered his former zealous opposition to the Jesus movement, and looked on him now as a traitor and turncoat (9:29).

The appearance of Christ which came to him in this moment of ecstasy[26] reaffirmed what he had already learned on the Damascus road— that his call was to be Christ's witness among the Gentiles. Jerusalem would not listen to his testimony. Paul tried to remonstrate: his former anti-Christian activity in that very city, he argued, was fresh in people's minds, and many could remember the responsible part he had played in the martyrdom of Stephen.[27] His point seems to have been that people who knew his former record would be the more readily convinced that his change of attitude must be based on the most compelling grounds. But as a matter of fact their knowledge of his former record made them the more unwilling to listen to him at all. The Lord therefore commanded him peremptorily to leave Jerusalem; his mission field was to be the Gentile world.

According to Luke's account (9:29-30), the leaders of the Jerusalem church, getting wind of a plot against Paul's life during that visit, escorted him to Caesarea and put him on board a ship bound for Tarsus. This is not the only place in our narrative where divine direction and human action coincide.

6. Paul Reveals His Roman Citizenship (22:22-29)

22 *They listened to him until he said this; then they started to shout, "Away with him! A scoundrel like that should not be allowed to live!"* [28]

23 *They were yelling, waving their garments about, and flinging dust into the air,*

24 *so the tribune ordered Paul to be brought into the fortress, and gave directions that he should be interrogated under the lash, so that he might find out why they were shouting against him like that.*

25 *As they were stretching him out for flogging,* [29] *Paul said to the centurion who was standing by, "Is it lawful for you to flog a Roman citizen who has received no proper trial?"* [30]

26 *Hearing that, the centurion went to the tribune and reported it to him: "What are you proposing to do?" he said. "This man is a Roman."*

26. Gk. ἐν ἐκστάσει (v. 17); the phrase is used also of Peter's experience on the roof at Joppa (10:10; 11:5).

27. Cf. 7:58, 8:1a, with exposition and notes. In Paul's words "your witness Stephen" we see the beginning of the Christian semantic development of Gk. μάρτυς from "witness" to "martyr" (cf. Rev. 2:13; 17:6).

28. Gk. αἶρε ἀπὸ τῆς γῆς τὸν τοιοῦτον, οὐ γὰρ καθῆκεν αὐτὸν ζῆν.

29. Or "with the thongs" (τοῖς ἱμᾶσιν).

30. Or "uncondemned" (ἀκατάκριτος), as in 16:37.

27 *The tribune came up and said to him, "Tell me: are you a Roman?"*
"Yes," said he.[31]
28 *The tribune replied, "It cost me a great sum of money to acquire this*
citizenship."[32] *"But I," said Paul, "am a citizen by birth."*
29 *Then the men who were about to interrogate him withdrew from him*
immediately, and the tribune was afraid when he learned that the
man whom he had put in chains was a Roman.

22-23 The crowd below in the outer court listened patiently enough to
Paul, as he spoke from the top of the steps, until he mentioned his mission to
the Gentiles. This word made all their resentment blaze up with redoubled
fury. They screamed and gesticulated in a riot of abandoned rage. The
tribune had not understood what Paul said, since he spoke to them in Aramaic (he might not have understood him much better had Paul used a
language the tribune knew); but while it was impossible for him to discover
the exact nature of their grievance against Paul, it was evident that they were
bitterly hostile to him and were out for his blood. In a few well-chosen words
Luke paints the scene; we can see them waving their clothes in the air[33] and
throwing dust about in their excitement. "In England," as Lake and Cadbury
remark, "mud is more frequently available."[34]

24 Despairing, then, of getting any coherent explanation of all this
sound and fury from the rioters themselves, the tribune decided to find out
the truth from Paul himself, by interrogating him under torture. He therefore
ordered him to be flogged. If the instrument used was the scourge (Lat.
flagellum),[35] that was a fearful instrument of torture, consisting of leather
thongs, weighted with rough pieces of metal or bone, and attached to a stout
wooden handle. If a man did not actually die under the scourge, he might
well be crippled for life. Paul had been beaten with rods on three occasions
(once at least at the hands of Roman lictors), and he had been sentenced five
times to the disciplinary lash inflicted by Jewish synagogue authorities,[36]
but neither of these penalties had the murderous quality of the *flagellum*.

25 Fortunately for Paul, it was a form of treatment from which

---

31. Gk. ἔφη Ναί, for which the Western reading is the synonymous εἶπεν Εἰμί.

32. The Western text reads "I know for how large a sum I acquired this citizenship" (cf. n. 39 below).

33. "Waving" or "shaking" seems to be the sense of ῥιπτούντων here; the verb
ῥιπτέω is a variant form of ῥίπτω ("throw," "cast"). For the action cf. the Latin phrase
iactatio togarum. Chrysostom (*Homilies on Acts* 48.2), describing the scene, explains
ῥιπτέω by ἐκτινάσσω ("shake out"); cf. F. Field, *Notes on the Translation of the New
Testament* (Cambridge, 1899), p. 136.

34. It may be that horror at Paul's imagined sacrilege was also expressed by these
actions. See H. J. Cadbury, "Dust and Garments," *Beginnings* I.5, pp. 269-77.

35. As is suggested by the use of μάστιξ (μάστιξιν ἀνετάζεσθαι) in v. 24.

36. 2 Cor. 11:24-25. One of the beatings with rods had been received at Philippi
(see on 16:22 above).

420

Roman citizens were legally exempt.[37] In earlier days the exemption was total, and although under the empire it was sometimes inflicted on citizens as a penalty after conviction, they were all exempt from it as a third degree method of inquiry before trial. So, as some soldiers were tying Paul up in readiness for the flogging,[38] he asked the centurion in charge of them if it was legal to treat a Roman citizen so, before he had received a fair trial.

26-28   Knowing very well that it was not legal, the centurion went at once and told the tribune what Paul had said. The tribune, alarmed at the news, came quickly to the place and asked Paul if it was true that he was a Roman citizen. "Yes," said Paul. Perhaps he did not look like a Roman citizen at that moment: after being set upon by the crowd and dragged down into the outer court of the temple, along with other rough usage he had received, he must have presented a battered and undignified spectacle. Something of this sort may have been in the tribune's mind as he said, "It cost *me* a very large sum of money to obtain Roman citizenship"—the implication being that the privilege must have become cheap of late if such a sorry-looking figure as Paul could claim it.[39]

He was the more astonished by the calm dignity of Paul's reply. The tribune had virtually bought his citizenship; presumably, since his Gentile name was Claudius (23:26), he had done so in the principate of Claudius. Technically, the great price which he paid was "the bribe given to the intermediaries in the imperial secretariat or the provincial administration who put his name on the list of candidates for enfranchisement."[40] This form of bribery reached scandalous proportions under Claudius.[41] But Paul, the man whom the tribune was interrogating rather contemptuously, was *born* a Roman citizen. This means that his father was a Roman citizen before him. How the citizenship was acquired by Paul's father or grandfather we have no means of knowing, but analogy would suggest that it was for valuable services rendered to a Roman general or administrator in the southeastern

37. By the Valerian and Porcian Laws (see on 16:37).

38. The victim is commonly depicted as tied to a pillar or post of convenient height for scourging. F. Field (*Notes on the Translation of the New Testament,* pp. 136-37) adduces some evidence in support of the view that here the victim was strung up some little distance above the ground.

39. Bede of Jarrow, in his exposition of Acts, says here, "Another edition indicates more clearly what he meant: 'The tribune said, Do you claim so easily to be a Roman citizen? For I know at how great a price I acquired this citizenship.'" Cf. the Western reading (n. 32 above).

40. A. N. Sherwin-White, *Roman Society and Roman Law in the New Testament* (Oxford, 1963), pp. 154-55.

41. Claudius's wife Messalina and her court favorites used the procedure as a means of enriching themselves. Cf. Dio Cassius, *History* 60.17.5-6. The tribune's personal name Lysias indicates that he was of Greek birth. Wealth or influence (probably both) had enabled him to become not only a Roman citizen but also a superior officer in the Roman army.

area of Asia Minor, such as Pompey in 66-64 B.C. or Antony a generation later.[42]

29 The revelation of Paul's Roman citizenship gave the whole business a different aspect. Rough-and-ready methods which might be all right for ordinary mortals must be avoided when the person affected was a Roman citizen. The tribune shuddered as he realized how near he had come to perpetrating a serious illegality; indeed, he had already begun to perpetrate it by giving the order for Paul to be flogged; but at least the flogging itself had been arrested.[43] He was now responsible to his own superiors for the protection of this Roman citizen; he must therefore set up a formal inquiry in order to ascertain the true cause of the disturbance.

7. Paul Brought before the Sanhedrin (22:30)

30 The next day, wishing to learn with certainty the reason for his being accused by the Jews, he released him[44] and ordered the chief priests and all the Sanhedrin to hold a meeting; then he brought Paul down and made him stand among them.

30 If the agitated Jewish crowd could give no coherent account of its grievance against Paul, the supreme Sanhedrin would surely be able to throw light on the situation. Whatever Paul was being charged with, it involved an offense of some kind against Jewish religious custom or sentiment, and the Sanhedrin was the appropriate body to deal with that. So the next day the tribune directed the Sanhedrin to hold a meeting. The Roman administration of Judaea was a military administration, and in the absence of the procurator

---

42. "Had not his father (or possibly grandfather) been made a citizen by Antony or Pompey? Were they not a firm of σκηνοποιοί, able to be very useful to a fighting proconsul?" (W. M. Calder, personal letter, February 18, 1953). Jerome's statement that Paul's family came from Gischala (Gush Ḥalab) in Galilee and emigrated to Tarsus at the time of the Roman conquest of Judaea (*On Illustrious Men* 5) has been treated seriously by a number of scholars (including M. Dibelius, *Paul*, E.T. [London, 1953], p. 16, who links it with Paul's claim in Phil. 3:5 to be a "Hebrew from Hebrews"). W. M. Ramsay's dismissal of Jerome's story as "in itself an impossible one" (*The Cities of St. Paul* [London, 1907], p. 185) seems to have no solid basis.

43. The tribune was afraid also "because he had put him in chains" (v. 29, ὅτι αὐτὸν ἦν δεδεκώς). This probably refers to his action in 21:33, rather than to Paul's being tied up for scourging—the verb used for his being so tied up is not the ordinary verb for binding (δέω) but one which denotes stretching out (προτείνω). It may be that the two ἁλύσεις with which Paul was bound in 21:33 were heavier than the ἅλυσις which he continued to wear during his custody in Judaea (e.g., before Agrippa, 26:29) and later in Rome (28:20). When in v. 30 the tribune is said to have "released him" (ἔλυσεν αὐτόν) before bringing him before the Sanhedrin, the meaning may be that he released him (temporarily) from imprisonment in the fortress (cf. Byzantine reading, n. 44).

44. The Byzantine text adds ἀπὸ τῶν δεσμῶν, "from his bonds," i.e., from custody, making explicit what is in any case implied.

the officer commanding the Antonia garrison was the chief representative of Roman authority in Jerusalem. If he ordered the Sanhedrin to meet, the Sanhedrin met. When the court was in session, he brought Paul down from the fortress to the council chamber on the western slope of the temple hill.[45] It must be determined first of all that there was a *prima facie* case for trial by the Sanhedrin, and at least until that was determined Paul remained under military protection.

45. See p. 91, n. 13.

ACTS 23

8. Paul before the Sanhedrin (23:1-10)

a. Interchange with the high priest (23:1-5)

1 *Fixing his eyes on the Sanhedrin, Paul said, "Brothers, I have conducted myself in all good conscience before God until this day."*
2 *Then the high priest Ananias ordered those who stood by to strike him across the mouth.*
3 *"God will strike you, you whitewashed wall," said Paul to him. "Do you actually sit to judge me according to the law, and order me to be struck in breach of the law?"*
4 *The bystanders said, "Do you insult God's high priest?"*
5 *To which Paul said, "I did not know he was the high priest, brothers; had I known, I should have respected the scripture which says, 'You shall not revile a ruler of your people.'"*

1 Brought thus before the Sanhedrin, Paul addressed that body in his own defense. His claim to have led his life until that day in all good conscience in God's sight was a bold claim, but not an unparalleled claim from Paul. Not long afterward he assured the procurator Felix that it was his constant care to maintain a clear conscience in relation to God and human beings alike (24:16); we may compare his review of his earlier life in Phil. 3:6, where he claims that he was, "as to righteousness under the law, blameless."[1] Conscience is spoken of as an independent witness to one's behavior. Paul might well appeal to the testimony of conscience as he stood before the supreme court of Israel; it was on no righteousness of his own, however, that he relied for justification in the heavenly court (Phil. 3:9). The purest conscience was an insecure basis of confidence under the scrutiny of God: "I am not aware of anything against myself," he told the Corinthian Christians, "but I am not thereby justified; it is the Lord who judges me" (1 Cor. 4:4).[2]

---

1. Even his persecution of the church had been carried out with good conscience; it was, as he thought, his bounden duty (cf. 26:9). The verb πεπολίτευμαι ("I have conducted myself") refers particularly to his life in public.

2. See H. Osborne, "Συνείδησις," *JTS* 32 (1931), pp. 167-79; C. A. Pierce, *Conscience in the New Testament* (London, 1955); J. Stelzenberger, *Syneidesis im Neuen Testament* (Paderborn, 1961); M. E. Thrall, "The Pauline Use of Συνείδησις," *NTS*

2 He was not allowed to proceed far with this line of defense. The high priest, president of the supreme court, was so incensed by his claim that he told those who stood beside him to strike him across the mouth.

The high priest at this time was Ananias, son of Nedebaeus, who received the office from Herod of Chalcis (younger brother of Herod Agrippa I) in A.D. 47 and held it for eleven or twelve years. He brought no credit to the sacred office. Josephus tells how his servants went to the threshing floors to seize the tithes that ought to have gone to the common priests,[3] while the Talmud preserves a parody of Ps. 24:7 in which his greed was lampooned:

> "Lift up your heads, O ye gates;
> that Yoḥanan[4] ben Narbai,[5] the disciple of Pinqai,[6] may go in
> and fill his belly with the divine sacrifices!"[7]

Some five years before this time he had been sent to Rome by the legate of Syria on suspicion of complicity in a sanguinary conflict between Judaeans and Samaritans, but was cleared and restored to the high priesthood by the Emperor Claudius, thanks to the advocacy of the younger Agrippa.[8] His great wealth made him a man to be reckoned with even after his deposition from office; and he did not scruple to use violence and assassination to further his interests. His pro-Roman policy, however, made him an object of intense hostility to the militant nationalists in Judaea, and when the war against Rome broke out in A.D. 66 he was dragged by insurgents from an aqueduct in which he had tried to hide, and put to death along with his brother Hezekiah. His son Eleazar, captain of the temple, took fierce reprisals on his assassins.[9]

3 Such improper behavior from a member of the supreme court stung Paul into an indignant retort. The rights of defendants were carefully safeguarded by Jewish law, and they were presumed innocent until proved guilty. Paul had not yet been properly charged, let alone tried and convicted. The high priest, who was there to administer the law, had broken the law by ordering Paul to be struck.

Paul's reaction has been contrasted with that of Jesus, "who, when

---

14 (1967-68), pp. 118-25; R. Jewett, *Paul's Anthropological Terms* (Leiden, 1971), pp. 402-46.

3. *Ant.* 20.206.

4. Yoḥanan presents the same elements as are found in Ananias = Hananiah (*ḥănanyāhû*, "Yahweh has graciously given"), but in the reverse order.

5. Narbai may be a corruption of Nadbai (= Nedebaeus) arising from the similarity of the letters *r* and *d* in the Hebrew script.

6. There is a satirical word-play here on the personal name Pinqai, itself perhaps a variation of Phinehas *(pinḥās)*, and the noun *pinkā*, "meat-dish" (in allusion to Ananias's proverbial greed).

7. TB P^esāḥîm 57a.

8. Josephus, *Ant.* 20.131-36.

9. Josephus, *BJ* 2.441-42, 448.

he was reviled, did not revile in return" (1 Pet. 1:23).[10] But when Jesus himself was struck during his interrogation before Annas, he too protested against the illegality of the action.[11] There is no need to join the chorus of disapproval voiced by older commentators, who felt free to condemn Paul for his righteous protest in a situation which they themselves were unlikely to face. The warm impetuousness of a man of like passions with ourselves is vividly portrayed in this trial scene, and there is no doubt who presents the more dignified bearing—Paul or the high priest. The metaphor of the "whitewashed wall" suggests a tottering wall whose precarious condition has been disguised by a generous coat of whitewash:[12] in spite of appearances, a man who behaved as Ananias did was bound to come to grief. His was the "haughty spirit" of Prov. 16:18, which "goes before a fall." Paul's words were more prophetic than he realized; had he known the man intimately, he could not have spoken more aptly.

4-5 But the bystanders were shocked: that was no way to speak to the high priest.[13] They do not appear to have been so shocked by Ananias's outburst, although that was no way for the high priest to speak. As soon, however, as they pointed out to Paul that the man to whom he spoke so freely was God's high priest, he apologized to the official, if not to the man. And in the act of apology, he displayed his ready submission to the law which he was accused of flouting. "I did not know he was the high priest," he said, meaning that, had he known, he would not have called him a whitewashed wall, since the law of Moses forbade an Israelite to revile a ruler of his people (Ex. 22:28b).[14]

But what did Paul mean by saying that he did not know the speaker was the high priest? At a regular meeting of the Sanhedrin the high priest presided, and would surely have been identifiable for that reason. Or was Paul not looking in the direction from which the words came, so that he could not be sure who actually uttered them? Or was he speaking ironically, as if to say, "I did not think a man who spoke like that could possibly be the high priest"? R. B. Rackham takes his words to mean that he had not sufficiently reflected that the man who uttered the objectionable words was the high priest, and that therefore he should not have made such a vigorous

10. W. Kelly thinks that "the apostle throughout scarcely seems to be breathing his ordinary spiritual atmosphere" (*An Exposition of the Acts of the Apostles* [London, ³1952], p. 344).

11. John 18:21-23.

12. Cf. the wall of Ezek. 13:10-16, daubed with untempered mortar. The Greek word here translated "whitewashed" is the same as that used in Jesus' reference to "whitewashed tombs" in Matt. 23:27, but the point of the comparison is different.

13. Cf. the remonstrance addressed to Jesus in John 18:22, "Is that how you answer the high priest?"—words which were actually accompanied by a blow.

14. Compare the interpretation of the preceding part of this commandment (Ex. 22:28a) mentioned in the note on 19:37 (p. 379, n. 80).

retort;[15] but this does less than justice to the natural sense of Paul's apology. Paul's visits to Jerusalem since his conversion had been infrequent and short, and he would not probably have known Ananias by sight. One suggestion that can be ruled out of court is Ramsay's; he argued that the meeting was convened by the Roman tribune, who would have conducted proceedings himself as in a Roman assembly, with Paul on one side of him and the Sanhedrin on the other, while Luke and others formed the "circle of bystanders."[16]

b. The resurrection hope (23:6-10)

6 *But Paul, taking cognizance of the fact that one part of them belonged to the Sadducees and the other part to the Pharisees, called aloud in the council, "Brothers, I am a Pharisee, a son of Pharisees. It is concerning the hope of the resurrection[17] of the dead that I am being judged."*

7 *When he said this, a dispute broke out between the Pharisees and Sadducees; the company was divided.*

8 *The Sadducees deny the resurrection, and the existence of angels and spirits, but the Pharisees acknowledge both.*

9 *So a great clamor arose: some scribes of the party of the Pharisees got up and contended, "We find nothing wrong in this man. What if some spirit or angel has spoken to him?"*

10 *The dispute was becoming fierce, and the tribune was afraid that Paul might be torn apart by them, so he ordered the soldiers to go down and snatch him from their midst and bring him into the fortress.*

6 The high priest's interruption had the effect of changing Paul's tactics. Instead of resuming the defense which he had scarcely begun, he took stock of the fact that the Sanhedrin consisted in the main of the Sadducean majority and the strong Pharisaic minority. As he addressed the tribune as a Roman citizen, so now he addresses the Sanhedrin as a Pharisee. "I am a Pharisee," he said; "my forebears were Pharisees, and the charge on which I am now being examined concerns the national hope, which depends for its fulfilment on the resurrection of the dead."

Here again Paul has been criticized by older commentators. (Modern commentators are less disposed to pass moral judgments.) "If we think him very little to blame for his stern rebuke of the High Priest," said F. W. Farrar; "if, referring his conduct to that final court of appeal, which consists in

15. R. B. Rackham, *The Acts of the Apostles* (London, 61912), p. 433.

16. W. M. Ramsay, *BRD,* pp. 90-94. He argued further that, after Paul's appeal to the resurrection hope (v. 6), the Pharisaic members of the court crossed the floor and took their places alongside Paul.

17. Lit., "hope and resurrection"—an instance of hendiadys.

comparing it with the precepts and example of his Lord, we can quite conceive that He who called Herod 'a fox' would also have called Ananias 'a whited wall'; on the other hand, we cannot but think that this creating of a division among common enemies on the grounds of a very partial and limited agreement with certain other tenets held by some of them, was hardly worthy of St. Paul; and knowing, as we do know, what the Pharisees were, we cannot imagine his Divine Master ever saying, under any circumstances, 'I am a Pharisee'."[18] No indeed; Paul's divine Master would not have said, "I am a Pharisee," because he was not a Pharisee; Paul was—indeed, his claim may imply that he was the most consistent Pharisee of them all. Moreover, Paul knew what the Pharisees were much better than Dean Farrar and his contemporaries thought they knew. And the belief in the resurrection, which Paul shared with the Pharisaic members of the Sanhedrin, far from being "a very partial and limited agreement," was fundamental.[19] Paul and they agreed that the ancestral hope of Israel was bound up with the resurrection of the dead. Paul, and other Pharisees who believed in Jesus, went farther, and maintained that the hope of Israel was fulfilled in one who, less than thirty years previously, had been raised from the dead; but the belief in the particular resurrection of Christ was, in Paul's mind, all of a piece with the general resurrection of the dead. "If the dead are not raised, then Christ has not been raised; if Christ has not been raised, your faith is futile" (1 Cor. 15:16-17). A Sadducee could not become a Christian without abandoning a distinctive theological tenet of his party; a Pharisee could become a Christian and remain a Pharisee—in the apostolic age, at least.[20] For believing Pharisees the Christian faith did not necessarily imply the law-free gospel to which Paul was committed.

7-8 Paul's announcement threw the apple of discord into the ranks of the Sanhedrin. The Pharisees were immediately inclined to concede that a man who was so sound on a central Pharisaic doctrine could not be so bad at

18. F. W. Farrar, *The Life and Work of St. Paul* (London, 1879), pp. 327-28.

19. W. Kelly, who agrees with Farrar in finding Paul's behavior here to fall below his usual standard (see n. 10 above)—he suggests that the spiritual atmosphere of Jerusalem had an adverse effect on him!—is far from ascribing a "very partial and limited" significance to this common belief in resurrection: "Nevertheless there was truth and important truth before all here" (*Exposition of Acts*, p. 344).

20. The common view is that it was not until the final decade of the first century that the conclusive breach between Jewish Christians and other Jews took place, when the addition of the *birkat hammînîm*, the prayer that "the Nazarenes and the heretics might perish as in a moment and be blotted out of the book of life," effectively debarred Jewish Christians from participation in synagogue worship. See K. L. Carroll, "The Fourth Gospel and the Exclusion of Christians from the Synagogue," *BJRL* 40 (1957-58), pp. 19-32; R. Kimelman, "*Birkat Ha-Minim* and the Lack of Evidence for an anti-Christian Jewish Prayer in Late Antiquity," in *Jewish and Christian Self-Definition*, ed. E. P. Sanders, II (London, 1981), pp. 226-44; W. Horbury, "The Benediction of the *Minim* and Early Jewish-Christian Controversy," *JTS* n.s. 33 (1982), pp. 19-61.

heart after all; the Sadducees were more enraged than ever, at this public invocation of what was in their eyes a lately invented heresy. For, as Luke explains to his readers (who would not be conversant with the theological differences between the two main Jewish parties), the Sadducees denied the doctrine of bodily resurrection,[21] and rejected the belief in a spirit world of angels and demons,[22] whereas the Pharisees accepted both[23] as essential elements of their creed. The Sadducees claimed in this respect to represent the old orthodoxy of Israel; it has even been thought that they interpreted the term "Pharisees" ("separated ones") to mean "Persianizers," on the ground that the Pharisees imported features of Zoroastrianism into the religion of Israel.[24] But the messianic hope in postexilic times came to be closely interwoven with the belief in resurrection, which in due course became a fundamental principle of "normative" Judaism.[25] In the Mishnah those who say that there is no resurrection of the dead are included among those who have "no share in the age to come."[26]

9-10   The dispute which broke out at once between the two parties in the council chamber excluded all possibility of securing a careful examination of Paul or a clarification of the charges against him. Some of the Pharisaic scholars[27] present contended that he had done no wrong; if he spoke of receiving a divine revelation in a vision, it might well be that some spirit or angel had communicated with him. This concession, admitting the possibility that Paul's Damascus-road experience had some substance to it, is surprising. But Luke never disparages the Pharisees: to him they represent what is best in Judaism, and some of them on this occasion show themselves to be not far from the kingdom of God.[28] According to Ernst Haenchen,

21. Luke has already mentioned this in Luke 20:27 (see also the note on 4:2 above, pp. 89-90, n. 5). Josephus, who tries to portray the Jewish religious parties in the guise of Greek philosophical schools, says it was the immortality of the soul that the Sadducees denied (*BJ* 2.165; *Ant.* 18.16).

22. "What they rejected was the developed doctrine of the two kingdoms with their hierarchies of good and evil spirits" (T. W. Manson, *The Servant-Messiah* [Cambridge, 1953], p. 17, n. 3).

23. The word "both" in v. 8 probably embraces *(a)* the belief in resurrection and *(b)* the belief in angels and spirits. It is less likely that there is here another instance of the loose use of ἀμφότεροι = πάντες as in 19:16 (see p. 367, n. 25), in which case the reference would be to the belief in *(a)* resurrection, *(b)* angels, *(c)* spirits.

24. Cf. T. W. Manson, "Sadducee and Pharisee," *BJRL* 22 (1938), pp. 144-59, especially pp. 153-58.

25. Cf. Dan. 12:2.

26. *Sanhedrin* 10.1.

27. The "scribes" (γραμματεῖς) or experts in the law belonged mostly to the Pharisaic party, so far as can be gathered from our records (cf. Mark 2:16). We may compare the delight with which "some of the scribes" heard Jesus' confutation of the Sadducees' argument against resurrection: "Teacher, you have spoken well" (Luke 20:39). But the Sadducees also had their legal experts.

28. Like the scribe who received encouragement from Jesus in Mark 12:34.

THE BOOK OF THE ACTS

Luke is concerned to show "that the bridges between Jews and Christians have not been broken. It is Luke's honest conviction that fellowship between Pharisaism and Christianity is in the end possible: the Pharisees also hope for the Messiah, await the resurrection of the dead"[29]—what is lacking is their recognition that Jesus, already raised from the dead, has thereby been made "both Lord and Messiah" (2:36).

The Sadducees, for their part, repudiated the idea that a spirit or angel communication was possible. In this atmosphere of theological disputation any hope of a judicial inquiry disappeared. The tribune, seeing that his attempt to have the charge against Paul investigated by the Sanhedrin had proved unsuccessful, ordered soldiers to seize Paul from the midst of the contestants and take him back to the safety of the fortress.

9. The Lord Appears to Paul by Night (23:11)

11 *The following night the Lord came and stood over Paul. "Take courage,"[30] he said; "as you have borne your testimony to me in Jerusalem, so you must bear testimony also in Rome."*

11 Paul's worst apprehensions of what might happen to him in Jerusalem bade fair to be fulfilled.[31] Where now were his plans for carrying the gospel to the far west, and visiting Rome on the way? After the events of these two days, he might well have felt dejected and despondent. No help or encouragement could be expected from the leaders of the Jerusalem church; there was in any case little that they could do, but they probably judged it best to stay clear of the trouble arising from the ill-advised action which they had urged on Paul.

But the night following his abortive appearance before the Sanhedrin, the risen Lord appeared to Paul[32] as he had done at critical moments before,[33] and bade him cheer up: Paul had borne witness to him in Jerusalem (a reference this, no doubt, to his speech at the top of the steps to the crowd in the temple court), and he would live to bear similar witness in Rome. This assurance meant much to Paul during the delays and anxieties of the next two years, and goes far to account for the calm and dignified bearing which from now on marks him out as a master of events rather than their victim. His plan to see Rome, he now knows, is certain of fulfilment; with that he is content.

29. E. Haenchen, *The Acts of the Apostles*, E.T. (Oxford, 1971), p. 643.

30. The Western and Byzantine texts add the vocative "Paul" (cf. 27:24, "Do not be afraid, Paul").

31. Cf. 20:22-23; Rom. 15:31.

32. Gk. ἐπιστάς, translated "came and stood over" above so as to bring out the force of the aorist.

33. Cf. 18:9; 22:17.

10. Plot against Paul's life (23:12-15)

12 *When day broke, the Jews[34] hatched a plot, binding themselves by an oath to eat and drink nothing until they had killed Paul.*

13 *There were more than forty who entered into this conspiracy.*

14 *They approached the chief priests and the elders, and said, "We have invoked a solemn curse on ourselves, that we will taste nothing until we have killed Paul.*

15 *Now then, do you and the Sanhedrin send word to the tribune to bring him down to you,[35] on the pretext that you want to make a more detailed investigation of his case. Then, before he comes near you, we are prepared to kill him."[36]*

12-15   Disappointed at having let Paul slip through their fingers, one group of zealots determined that they would engineer a second opportunity of killing him, and they would not fail this time. They covenanted together, in a band of forty or more, swearing a solemn oath which probably took a form familiar from the Old Testament: "So may God do to us, and more also, if we eat or drink anything until we have killed Paul."[37] Then they went to the chief priests and leaders of the Sanhedrin, telling them of the oath they had sworn, and suggesting that they should request the tribune to bring Paul down to the council chamber for a further inquiry: they would be ready to attack and kill him before ever he reached the council chamber. It may be supposed that the "elders" to whom they divulged their plan did not include any of Paul's Pharisaic sympathizers. But their plan bespeaks their fanatical devotion, for Paul would be guarded by Roman soldiers, and an attempt to assassinate him, whether it succeeded or not, would inevitably involve the assassins in heavy loss of life.

11. The Plot Revealed (23:16-22)

16 *Paul's sister's son heard of the planned ambush, so he went to the fortress, gained entry to it, and reported the matter to Paul.*

17 *Paul summoned one of the centurions and said, "Take this young man to the tribune; he has something to report to him."*

18 *So he took him and brought him to the tribune, and said, "The prisoner Paul summoned me and asked me to bring this young man to you; he has something to tell you."*

---

34. For "the Jews" the Western and Byzantine texts read "some of the Jews," which is of course more accurate—some forty of them, in fact (v. 13).

35. The Western text expands: "Now then, we ask you to grant us this (favor). Gather the Sanhedrin together and give notice to the tribune to bring him down to you."

36. The Western text adds "even if we must die for it."

37. The Mishnah makes provision for relief from such vows as could not be fulfilled "by reason of constraint" (*Nᵉdārîm* 3.1, 3).

19 *The tribune took him by the hand, drew him aside privately, and asked, "What is it you have to report to me?"*

20 *Then he told him, "The Jews have agreed to ask you to bring Paul down to the Sanhedrin tomorrow, on the ground that they intend[38] to make a more detailed inquiry about him.*

21 *But please do not be persuaded by them, for more than forty of them are laying an ambush for him. They have bound themselves by an oath not to eat or drink anything until they have killed him, and right now they are ready, expecting your agreement."*

22 *Then the tribune dismissed the young man. "Tell no one," he said, "that you have brought me this information."*

16 Now comes one of the most tantalizing incidents in Acts, for all who are interested in Paul's private life and family relationships. Who was Paul's nephew, who received such prompt news of the plot? How did he get to know of it so promptly? It is unlikely that he was present when it was hatched, although it would be possible to construe the Greek text in this sense[39] (this would imply that the conspirators assumed that Paul's relatives were his bitterest opponents). When Paul says in Phil. 3:8 that for Christ's sake he has "suffered the loss of all things," it is usually inferred (and very reasonably so) that he was disinherited for his acceptance and proclamation of Jesus as Messiah. His father, a citizen of Tarsus and a Roman citizen also, would certainly be a wealthy man.[40] But it may be that the mother of this young man retained some sisterly affection for Paul, and something of that affection had been passed on to her son. We do not know if she lived in Jerusalem; perhaps she did, but perhaps she lived in Tarsus, and her son had come to Jerusalem for his education, as his uncle Paul had done in years gone by. We may wish we knew more, but we do not.

17-22 Paul, as an unconvicted Roman citizen, was kept in honorable custody in the Antonia fortress: he was allowed to receive visitors, and centurions promptly saw to it that his commissions were carried out. So, when his nephew came to the fortress and reported the plot to Paul, Paul immediately told a centurion to take the young man to the tribune, so that he might hear for himself what was afoot. The tribune received the young man

38. Gk. ὡς μέλλον (א* 33 1891 pc), in agreement with συνέδριον ("Sanhedrin"). Five other forms of the same participle, singular and plural, are represented among the variant readings (ASV, "as though thou wouldest . . ." renders ὡς μέλλων).

39. By taking παραγενόμενος, "having arrived (at the fortress)," to mean "having been present (at the making of the conspiracy)." But this is rendered improbable by the order and position of the verbs in v. 16.

40. A property qualification of 500 drachmae was fixed for admission to the roll of citizens, perhaps by Athenodorus sometime after 30 B.C. (Dio Chrysostom, *Oration* 34.23).

kindly. "Never was a tribune more amiable," comments Alfred Loisy, perhaps in irony[41]—but Luke presents all his Roman officers in an "amiable" light. Having listened to what the young man had to say, the tribune treated his report seriously,[42] made up his mind at once what ought to be done, and dismissed his informant with a warning to tell nobody that he had reported this plot to him.

12. The Tribune Prepares to Send Paul to Caesarea (23:23-24)

23 *Then he summoned two of his centurions, and said, "Get ready[43] two hundred soldiers, with seventy cavalry, and two hundred light-armed troops,[44] to go to Caesarea at the third hour of the night.*
24 *Provide mounts for Paul to ride, and bring him safely[45] to Felix the governor."*

23-24 Paul's life was plainly not safe in Jerusalem. The tribune could not afford to incur responsibility for the assassination of a Roman citizen whom he had taken into custody, or to expose himself to any of the other risks that he must inevitably run so long as Paul was in his charge. Paul must be sent at once to Caesarea, under a strong guard. He would be safer there, and the procurator himself would be responsible for him. So he summoned two centurions and commanded them to get ready a strong escort of heavy infantry, cavalry, and light-armed troops and to set out by night for Caesarea with Paul. Horses or mules were to be provided for Paul: the sixty miles from Jerusalem to Caesarea had to be covered as quickly as possible. The tribune felt that he could not rest until he knew that Paul was safe in the procurator's custody.

41. A. Loisy, *Les Actes des Apôtres* (Paris, 1920), p. 840.
42. Unlike J. Klausner at a later date, who regards this plot as a "probably groundless" suspicion on Paul's part (*From Jesus to Paul*, E.T. [London, 1944], p. 403).
43. The Western text reads: "'Make ready soldiers under arms to go to Caesarea, a hundred horsemen and two hundred light-armed troops.' And they said, 'They are ready.' And he ordered the centurions also to provide mounts that they might set Paul on them and bring him safely by night to Caesarea, to Felix the governor. For he was afraid that the Jews might seize and kill him, and that he himself should be blamed meanwhile for having taken bribes."
44. The meaning of δεξιολάβους (lit., "holding in the right hand") is uncertain. It appears here for the first time, and is not found again until the sixth century. There is a weakly attested variant δεξιοβόλους (A 33, lit. "throwing with the right hand"), which might mean "slingers" or "javelin throwers"; it is adopted by the Syriac Peshiṭta. Whatever be the precise sense of δεξιολάβοι, light-armed troops of some kind are meant. The main part of the escort as far as Antipatris consisted of two hundred heavy infantry, commanded by two centurions. This did not excessively weaken the garrison in the Antonia fortress, for it was an auxiliary cohort, and such a cohort regularly comprised a thousand men.
45. The Western text inserts "to Caesarea."

13. Letter from the Tribune to Felix (23:25-30)

25 He wrote a letter in these terms:[46]

26 "Claudius Lysias to the most excellent governor Felix: greetings.

27 This man had been seized by the Jews and was on the point of being killed by them, when I came upon them with the soldiers and rescued him, having learned that he was a Roman citizen.

28 When I wished to learn the ground of their charges against him, I brought him down to their Sanhedrin,[47]

29 and found that he was being charged in relation to questions of their law,[48] but no charge was brought against him meriting death or imprisonment.[49]

30 Since information has been brought to me that a plot is about to be laid against the man, I am sending him to you forthwith,[50] ordering his accusers to state the facts concerning him[51] before you."[52]

25 Luke, it may well be supposed, was not in a position to see the tribune's letter to Felix, so as to reproduce its contents *verbatim,* although the phrase "in these terms" suggests a claim to give more than the general purport.[53] But even if he presents only its general purport, his version of the letter is very true to life, especially in the emphasis laid on the tribune's timely initiative and in the slight manipulation of the order of events at the end of verse 27.

26 The tribune's name is now mentioned for the first time in the narrative. He was evidently of Greek birth, and his Greek name Lysias became his *cognomen* when he acquired Roman citizenship; at that time he probably assumed the *nomen gentile* Claudius because it was that of the emperor.[54] The title "most excellent" by which he addresses Felix belonged properly to the equestrian order in Roman society[55] (of which Felix was not a member) and was given also to the governors of subordinate provinces like Judaea, who were normally drawn from that order.

27-30 The letter then summarizes the events from the riot in the

46. Gk. ἔχουσαν τὸν τύπον τοῦτον. The Western text reads περιέχουσαν τάδε, "containing these things" (so 15:23, Western text).

47. The clause "I brought him down to their Sanhedrin" is absent from B* and 81, but has been supplied in the margin of B.

48. The Western text adds "concerning Moses and a certain Jesus" (cf. 25:19).

49. The Western text adds "I brought him out with difficulty, by force."

50. For "forthwith" (ἐξαυτῆς) some Alexandrian authorities read "from among them" (ἐξ αὐτῶν).

51. Gk. τὰ πρὸς αὐτόν. B 1175 omit τά, the sense then being "against him."

52. ℵ Ψ 81 and the Byzantine text add "Farewell" (ἔρρωσο).

53. E. A. Judge argues that τύπος in such a context (cf. 3 Macc. 3:30) implies a verbatim copy (*New Docs.* 1 [1976], § 26; cf. 2 [1977], § 27).

54. Cf. 22:28 (p. 421 with n. 41).

55. The equestrian order or order of "knights" *(equites)* ranked next after the senatorial order. For the title κράτιστος see p. 29, n. 3.

temple precincts which endangered Paul's life to Lysias's discovery of the plot against him. Lysias learned that Paul was a Roman citizen not, as his letter says, before he rescued him from the rioters but after he had ordered him to be flogged—this last episode is discreetly omitted. An account is then given of the fruitless appearance of Paul before the Sanhedrin, from which Lysias gathered only that the dispute was not one of which Roman law took cognizance, but one of Jewish theological interpretation.[56] When he says that "no charge was brought against him meriting death," he implies that at the hearing before the Sanhedrin nothing was said of Paul's alleged violation of the sanctity of the temple—that was indeed a capital offense.[57] Lastly, Lysias tells of the plot against Paul's life and of his consequent decision to send him to Caesarea, that his case might be dealt with in the procurator's court.

D. PAUL AT CAESAREA (23:31–26:32)

1. Paul Taken to Caesarea (23:31-35)

31 *So the soldiers, in accordance with their instructions, took Paul and escorted him by night to Antipatris.*

32 *The next day they left the cavalry to go on with him while they themselves returned to the fortress.*

33 *When the others had come to Caesarea and delivered the letter to the governor, they also presented Paul to him.*

34 *He read the letter and inquired from what province Paul came.[58] When he ascertained that he was a Cilician,*

35 *"I will give you a hearing," he said, "when your accusers come here too." He gave orders for him to be kept in Herod's praetorium.*

31-32 The military escort set off three hours after sunset,[59] and reached Antipatris the following morning. It must have been a forced march for the infantry, for Antipatris was some thirty-five miles distant from Jerusalem. Antipatris, at the foot of the Judaean hills, probably on the site of today's Rosh ha'Ayin, was built by Herod the Great in the well-watered and well-

---

56. Compare Gallio's pronouncement in 18:15. Lysias thus makes his contribution to the testimonies to Christians' law-abiding conduct unobtrusively presented by Luke.

57. In Luke's account of the abortive hearing before the Sanhedrin (vv. 1-10) this charge is not mentioned. It was raised at Paul's hearing before Felix (24:6).

58. The Western text exhibits a more vivid reading: "And when he had read the letter, he asked Paul, 'From what province are you?' He said, 'A Cilician.' And when he understood this, he said . . ."

59. "The third hour of the night," according to v. 23. The Romans divided the period between sunset and sunrise into twelve hours, on the analogy of the twelve hours of daylight.

wooded plain of Kaphar-Saba and named after his father Antipater.[60] The conspirators had now been left far behind, so it was no longer necessary for Paul to have such a strong escort. The infantry therefore turned back at Antipatris and left the cavalry to accompany Paul the remaining twenty-seven miles or so to Caesarea. This part of the journey was through open country where the population was largely Gentile. Luke could picture the road as he wrote: he had probably come the same way from Caesarea to Jerusalem with Paul and other companions less than two weeks before Paul's night journey.[61]

33-35 The cavalry, then, went on to Caesarea, and Paul was handed over to Felix. When Felix had read the tribune's letter, he asked which province Paul came from. Had Paul come from one of the client kingdoms in the Syrian or Anatolian area, it would have been diplomatically desirable to consult the ruler of the state in question.[62] But in fact he came from a Roman province—a province, moreover, which was united with the province of Syria, whose governor was Felix's superior—so it was competent for a Roman governor to go ahead and deal with his case without any external consultation. Felix accordingly told Paul that he would hold a full hearing of his case when his accusers arrived; for the present, he ordered him to be detained in the place built by Herod the Great for himself at Caesarea, which now served as the procurator's headquarters or *praetorium*.[63]

Marcus Antonius Felix (as his full name is usually taken to have been)[64] was a man of servile birth, who owed his unprecedented advancement to a post of honor usually reserved for the equestrian order to the influence which his brother Pallas exercised at the imperial court under

---

60. Cf. Josephus, *BJ* 1.99, 417; *Ant.* 13.390; 16.142.

61. Cf. M. Hengel, *Between Jesus and Paul*, E.T. (London, 1983), pp. 119-20.

62. Thus Pontius Pilate, governor of Judaea, hearing that Jesus came from Galilee, remitted his case to Herod Antipas, to whose tetrarchy Galilee belonged. Antipas appreciated the courtesy, but was too wise to take advantage of it (Luke 23:6-12). See p. 99 with n. 44.

63. For Herod's "most costly palace" see Josephus, *Ant.* 15.331. It now provided the procurator's headquarters. Lat. *praetorium* (whence the loanword πραιτώριον) denoted the official residence of the Roman governor of an imperial province. In Mark 15:16 and John 18:28 it is used for Pilate's headquarters in Jerusalem (probably Herod's palace on the western wall). In Phil. 1:13 it probably refers to the praetorian guard in Rome.

64. Tacitus (*History* 5.9) gives Felix's *nomen gentile* as Antonius, implying that, like his brother Pallas, he was manumitted by Antonia, mother of the Emperor Claudius. But the MSS of Josephus (*Ant.* 20.137) give his *nomen gentile* as Claudius, which would imply that he was manumitted by Claudius, who inherited his mother's household after her death. An inscription found in 1956 at Bir el-Malik, near Athlit, Israel, mentions a procurator named Tiberius Claudius, whose *cognomen* is tantalizingly missing. See M. Avi-Yonah, "The Epitaph of T. Mucius Clemens," *IEJ* 16 (1966), pp. 258-64, with plate 28; F. F. Bruce, "The Full Name of the Procurator Felix," *JSNT* 1 (1978), pp. 33-36; C. J. Hemer, "The Name of Felix Again," *JSNT* 31 (1987), pp. 45-59.

Claudius. Pallas was a freedman of Claudius's mother Antonia, and was for a number of years head of the imperial civil service. Felix succeeded Ventidius Cumanus as procurator of Judaea in A.D. 52,[65] but before that he may have occupied a subordinate post in Samaria under Cumanus.[66] His term of office as procurator was marked by increasing insurgency throughout the province, and by the emergence of the *sicarii*. The ruthlessness with which he put down these risings alienated many of the more moderate Jews, and led to further risings. Tacitus sums up his character and career in one of his biting epigrams: "he exercised the power of a king with the mind of a slave."[67] Despite his lowly origins, he was remarkably successful in marriage (from a social point of view, that is); his three successive wives were all of royal birth, according to Suetonius.[68] The first of the three was a granddaughter of Antony and Cleopatra;[69] the third was Drusilla, youngest daughter of Herod Agrippa I, who figures in the following narrative.[70]

65. Josephus, *BJ* 2.247; *Ant.* 20.137-38.
66. This may be inferred from Tacitus, *Annals* 12.137-38.
67. Tacitus, *History* 5.9.
68. Suetonius, *Life of Claudius* 28.
69. Tacitus, *History* 5.9.
70. See 24:24 (p. 447 with n. 36).

ACTS 24

2. Paul Accused before Felix (24:1-9)

1 *Five days later the high priest Ananias came down with some of the elders and an orator named Tertullus. They laid information against Paul before the governor.*
2 *When Paul had been summoned, Tertullus began to accuse him as follows: "Your Excellency![1] Since through you we enjoy great peace, and since through your providence improvements continue to be made for this nation,*
3 *we accept this with all gratitude, at all times and in all ways.*
4 *Not to weary[2] you further, I beg you, of your clemency, to accord us a brief hearing.*
5 *We have found this man to be a pest, a fomenter of strife among Jews throughout the world, and a ringleader of the party of the Nazarenes.*
6 *He even tried to profane the temple, but we arrested him [and intended to judge him according to our law,*
7 *when Lysias, the military tribune, came on the scene and took him away out of our hands with great violence,*
8 *ordering his accusers to come to you.][3] By questioning him you can learn for yourself about all the things of which we accuse him."*
9 *The Jews also joined in the attack, affirming that this was so.*

1 Five days after Paul's arrival, a deputation from the Sanhedrin, led by the high priest, came down to Caesarea to state their case against Paul. They enlisted the services of an advocate named Tertullus to state it in the conventional terms of forensic rhetoric. The advocate was probably a Hellenistic Jew; his name was a common one throughout the Roman world.

2-4 No doubt what is given here is a bare summary of the speech

1. Gk. κράτιστε Φῆλιξ (cf. 23:26). See p. 29, n. 3 (on 1:1).
2. Gk. ἐγκόπτω, "hinder"; here perhaps in one of the senses of κόπτω, "weary," "bore."
3. The words within square brackets are added in the Western text, and were taken over into TR. They are not found in the Byzantine witnesses, and are therefore not included in *The Greek New Testament according to the Majority Text*, ed. Z. C. Hodges and A. L. Farstad (Nashville, TN, 1982).

which Tertullus made for the prosecution, but it may be true to life in devoting so large a proportion of what was said to the lavish flattery of the exordium. This was part of the rhetorical fashion of the time. Tertullus might speak of the "great peace" enjoyed by the people of Judaea as a result of Felix's administration, but there were many Judaeans who, if they had known it in time, would have applied to this "peace" the epigram about the Romans which Tacitus puts into the mouth of the Caledonian hero Calgacus: "they make a desert and call it peace."[4]

The reference to the governor's "providence"[5] is reminiscent of what is said of the high priest Onias III in 2 Macc. 4:6, "he saw that without the king's providence public affairs could not again reach a peaceful settlement." This kind of language was regarded as appropriate in addressing rulers, especially in the Near East. It was customary also to promise brevity, as Tertullus does here (v. 4); the promise was sometimes kept, sometimes not, but it was calculated to secure goodwill for the speaker at the outset of his speech. So was such flattery as the reference to Felix's clemency or moderation[6]—a reference singularly unsuited to a ruler whose ferocity is attested by both Josephus and Tacitus.

5-6   After the excessive courtesy of his proem, Tertullus proceeds to the charges against Paul. After a general characterization of him as a perfect pest—a term with sinister implications, not excluding a hint of treason—he becomes more specific, moving from the less particular to the more particular: Paul is *(a)* a fomenter of risings among Jews all over the empire, *(b)* a ringleader of the Nazarene sect, *(c)* a man who had attempted to violate the sanctity of the temple.[7]

In calling Paul a pest,[8] Tertullus suggested that he habitually stirred up subversion of public law and order. The charge is similar to that brought against Paul and his companions at Thessalonica (17:6-7).[9] The charge of treason against the emperor was explicit there, and is probably implicit here: if Paul does not rebut it directly on this occasion before Felix, he rebuts it directly on a later occasion before Festus (25:8).[10] One of Luke's prime

---

4. Tacitus, *Agricola* 30.
5. Gk. πρόνοια. It was a favorite term among the Stoics; cf. the title of a treatise by Chrysippus, *Concerning Providence* (Περὶ Προνοίας). Its only other NT occurrence is in the nontechnical sense of "provision" (Rom. 13:14).
6. Gk. ἐπιείκεια, a term which was used at this time almost as an honorific title: "Your Clemency."
7. Compare the threefold structure of the charge brought against our Lord before Pilate (Luke 23:2).
8. Gk. λοιμός. Cf. Claudius's letter to the Alexandrines (November 10, A.D. 41) in which he warns the Jews of that city that, if they persist in activities which arouse his suspicion, he "will proceed against them with the utmost severity for fomenting a general plague (νόσος) which infests the whole world" (*P.Lond.* 1912, line 99).
9. Cf. p. 325, n. 14.
10. F. J. Kramer notes that it was not uncommon to "throw in for good measure a

motives in writing his twofold history is to demonstrate that there is no substance in this charge of subversion brought not only against Paul but against Christians in general—that competent and impartial judges had repeatedly confirmed the innocence of the Christian movement and the Christian missionaries in respect of Roman law.

As for the charge of fomenting unrest among Jews throughout the empire, it was well known that recent years had seen such unrest in some of the largest Jewish communities—those in Alexandria and Rome, for example[11]—where Paul had not been involved. But it was also undeniable that Paul's presence in a city had been accompanied time after time by disturbances within the Jewish communities. It had been so in the cities of South Galatia, in Thessalonica, Corinth, and Ephesus.[12] Paul indeed had nothing to do with the political "messianism" which operated like a ferment at that time in many parts of the dispersion as well as in the land of Israel,[13] but it called for more discrimination than many Roman magistrates were able to exercise to distinguish his teaching from the propaganda of messianic agitators.

The next count in the indictment against Paul was that he was a ringleader of the Nazarenes.[14] Was Felix expected to have some idea of what this meant? If so, what sort of impression was this information intended to make on his mind? Perhaps Felix, with his "rather accurate knowledge of the Way" (v. 22), had a clearer idea of the Nazarenes than most Roman officials would have had. This is the only place in the New Testament where the term "Nazarene"—or "Nazoraean," as the particular Greek word here used may be more exactly rendered—is used of the followers of Jesus; elsewhere it is used only of Jesus himself. The most probable view is that it was first applied to Jesus because his hometown was Nazareth, and that from him it came to be used of his followers also. It was apparently used of Jewish Christians from very early days, and remained their designation in Semitic speech: to this day Christians in general are known in Hebrew and Arabic as "Nazarenes."[15] But the word, or one very much like it, may have been

---

maiestas charge along with other less deadly accusations" (*Astrology in Roman Law and Politics* [Philadelphia, 1954], p. 252).

11. For Alexandria cf. Claudius's letter to the Alexandrines (n. 8 above); for Rome cf. Suetonius, *Claudius* 25.4 (see p. 347, n. 9).

12. Cf. 13:45, 50; 14:2-5; 17:5-9, 13; 18:6, 12-17; 19:9; 20:19.

13. Political messianism is a loose term for movements which sought the establishment of Judaean independence by the use of armed force, but it did not necessarily involve belief in an individual Messiah. Thus the anti-Roman revolt of A.D. 66 was not in the strict sense messianic, whereas that of A.D. 132 was.

14. The Nazarenes are here called a party or sect (Gk. αἵρεσις), like the Sadducees in 5:17 and the Pharisees in 15:5. In Judaea they were still reckoned as a Jewish party, albeit a subversive and heretical party from the chief-priestly point of view.

15. See p. 63, n. 72 (on 2:22). Heb. *noṣrîm*, Arab. *Naṣārā*, Aram./Syr. *Nāṣᵉrāyē* (the name by which the Mandaeans are called in their sacred writings). Jesus and his

current among first-century Jews to denote a group or a tendency on which Felix might be expected to look with disfavor;[16] the evidence is inadequate for anything like a positive statement.

The final charge was more concrete and more serious: Paul, it was alleged, had attempted to profane the temple in Jerusalem. It was not so concrete as the rumor which had led to the attack on Paul, which was that he had actually taken a Gentile within the forbidden precincts. If a *prima facie* case had been established in support of this rumor, then Paul could have been handed over to the Sanhedrin's jurisdiction. But his accusers evidently knew that such a *prima facie* case could not be established, as eyewitnesses were not forthcoming. A charge of *attempted* profanation was more difficult to prove or disprove; Tertullus's case was that, by arresting him, the temple authorities had prevented his attempt from being carried out. To represent the riotous attack by the mob as an orderly arrest carried out by the temple police was to twist the facts even more violently than Lysias had done in his letter to Felix; but by this account Tertullus tried to score a point against Lysias, who would have had no right to interfere with those who were maintaining law and order within the temple courts in accordance with their appointed duty.

7-9   The complaint against Lysias is made explicit in the expanded Western text, which has found its way into the Received Text and so into the KJV (as the last clause of v. 6 plus the whole of v. 7 and the beginning of v. 8). The reader who recollects the narrative of 21:27-36 must be amused by this complaint of the "great violence" with which Lysias snatched Paul from those who were trying to lynch him rather than proposing to take him into custody so that he might have a fair trial according to Jewish law! The tone of the Western addition is so thoroughly in accord with the rest of Tertullus's speech that one is inclined to accept it as genuine. It makes one minor difference to the sense: if the addition is accepted, then "by questioning him"

---

followers are regularly called *noṣrîm* in the Talmud; the earliest recorded use of the Hebrew word to denote followers of Jesus is in the *birkat hammînîm* (see p. 428, n. 20). Possibly the Jews associated the word with the "branch (Heb. *nōṣer*) of violence" which, according to the Hebrew text of Sir. 40:15, "has no tender twig" (i.e., no lasting posterity), just as Christians associated it with the messianic Branch (Heb. *nēṣer*) of Isa. 11:1 (probably the scripture alluded to in Matt. 2:23).

16. The Nazarenes may have been confused with people called the *nôṣᵉrim* or "observants." Epiphanius makes a distinction between Nasaraeans (Ναοαραῖοι) and Nazoraeans (Ναζωραῖοι) in his collection of heresies, the former coming fifth in his list of Jewish heresies (*Panarion* 1.18), the latter coming ninth in his list of Christian heresies (*Pan.* 1.29). By the Nazoraeans he means those Jewish Christians who were not in communion with the catholic church, but the Nasaraeans he represents as an ascetic Jewish group, similar to but not identical with the Essenes, living east of the Jordan and dating back to pre-Christian times. But Epiphanius may be as far astray in distinguishing the Nasaraeans and Nazoraeans as he is in distinguishing the Essenes (*Pan.* 1.10) and Ossenes (*Pan.* 1.19).

(v. 8) probably means "by questioning Lysias"; otherwise it means "by questioning Paul." It might be regarded as a point in favor of the shorter reading that it is in fact Paul whom the governor invites to speak after Tertullus; but of course Lysias was not present to give his version: after Paul's reply the governor postpones further inquiry until Lysias himself comes down to Caesarea (v. 22).

Tertullus's speech seems to tail away in a lame and impotent conclusion that forms a striking contrast to the rhetorical flourish with which it starts. But J. H. Moulton is probably too hard on him when he says that he "arrives at the goal by way of anacoluthon—Luke cruelly reports the orator *verbatim*."[17] This is only a summary of his speech, and even so Tertullus is not the only speaker on this occasion who falls into anacoluthon.[18] The deputation from the Sanhedrin appears at any rate to have been satisfied with his presentation of the case, for they affirmed their agreement with his statement of affairs.

3. Paul's Defense before Felix (24:10-21)

10 *The governor then beckoned to Paul to speak,[19] and he replied: "Knowing that you have been a judge of this nation for many years, I gladly speak in my own defense.*

11 *You can ascertain that it is not more than twelve days since I came up to Jerusalem to worship.*

12 *Neither in the temple did they find me disputing with anyone or collecting a crowd, nor in the synagogues, nor anywhere in the city;*

13 *neither can they provide proof of any of the charges which they now bring against me.*

14 *But this I confess to you: I worship the God of our fathers according to the Way,[20] which they call a 'party,' believing all that is laid down by the law or written in the prophets.*

15 *I have the same hope in God as they themselves accept—that there is to be a resurrection both of the righteous and of the unrighteous.*

16 *For this reason I train myself to maintain a blameless conscience continuously in the sight of God and humanity.*

17 *After a lapse of several years I came to brings alms to my nation and offerings.*

17. MHT I, pp. 224-25.
18. Paul himself does it in vv. 18-19, as frequently in his letters (see n. 21 below).
19. The Western text (represented by the marginal reading of the Harclean Syriac) expands: "The governor then beckoned to Paul to make his defense, and he took up a godlike attitude and said . . ." A godlike attitude was thought fitting in an orator (which Paul did not pretend to be).
20. The Western text seems to have omitted "the Way," reading: "according to the party (αἵρεσις), as they call it."

18 *While I was thus engaged, they found me purified in the temple, gathering no crowd and causing no disturbance.*

19 *But there were some Jews from Asia²¹—they ought to have been here in your presence to state any charge they might have to bring against me.*

20 *Or let these men themselves say what crime they found in me when I was made to stand before the Sanhedrin,*

21 *apart from this one declaration which I made aloud as I stood among them: 'It is concerning the resurrection of the dead that I am on trial before you today!'"*

10   When Felix motioned to Paul to reply to Tertullus's speech for the prosecution, he opened likewise with a complimentary exordium, but one which was briefer and less fulsome than his accuser's. He professed himself the readier to make his defense before Felix because Felix was no newcomer to the administration of Judaea: he had governed the province for several years, and the experience of Jews and Judaism which he had gained in that time would enable him to assess the charges against Paul more accurately.

11-13   He went on to explain that he had been absent from Jerusalem for several years until his recent arrival in the city as a worshiper at the festival of Pentecost. Five years in fact had elapsed since his last visit to Jerusalem—the very brief visit which receives a bare mention in 18:22. The twelve days which he mentions were the days during which he was present in Jerusalem since his recent arrival in the city: they are reckoned up to his being taken by night to Caesarea.²² During those twelve days he had little opportunity to cause trouble—for the last three of them, indeed, he had been a prisoner in the Antonia fortress. And during the time that he was a free agent he had done nothing to which exception could be taken: he had engaged in no public disputation, nor had he gathered a crowd or provoked a riotous assembly, whether in the temple courts, the synagogues, or anywhere in the city. He would have been within his rights had he engaged in public debate, but on this occasion he did not wish to draw unnecessary attention to himself or do anything to embarrass the leaders of the Jerusalem

---

21. There is nothing in the Greek text corresponding to "there were": "some Jews from Asia" (τινὲς δὲ ἀπὸ τῆς 'Ασίας 'Ιουδαῖοι) is a subject without a verb.

22. So A. Schlatter, *Die Apostelgeschichte* (Stuttgart, 1948), p. 285, and E. Haenchen, *The Acts of the Apostles*, E.T. (Oxford, 1971), p. 654. The five days which he had now spent in Caesarea are not included. The notes of time since his arrival in Jerusalem are detailed and precise: Day 1, Paul arrives in Jerusalem (21:17); Day 2, Paul and his companions received by James and the elders (21:18); Day 3, Paul initiates the purification ceremony (21:26); Days 3-9, the seven days of purification (21:27); Day 9, Paul attacked in the temple and rescued by Roman soldiers (21:27–22:29); Day 10, Paul brought before the Sanhedrin (22:30–23:10); Day 11, Plot against Paul; Paul sent away from Jerusalem (23:12-30); Day 12, Paul arrives in Caesarea (23:31-33).

church (who were no doubt sufficiently embarrassed by the mere presence of Paul in the city). His accusers, he said, might bring a variety of charges against him, but there was not one which they could substantiate.

14-16 While he had done none of the things that his opponents alleged, Paul had no hesitation in declaring what he actually did: he worshiped the ancestral God of Israel (as he had every freedom to do under Roman law) according to the true Way—that Way which his accusers described as a party or sect, although in fact it embraced and fulfilled most faithfully Israel's national hope. Far from deviating in any particular from the basis of Israel's ancient faith, he believed wholeheartedly all that the sacred scriptures contained—"all that is laid down by the law or written in the prophets"—and cherished the hope of resurrection, as most Jews did.[23] He seems to imply that his accusers themselves shared this hope; the high priest and other members of the Sadducean party, of course, did not share it, claiming in this regard (as in a number of others) to be old-fashioned conservatives.[24] There may, however, have been some Pharisees among the "elders" (members of the Sanhedrin) who had come down to Caesarea with the high priest.

It is interesting to note that this is the only place in the New Testament where Paul is unambiguously credited with believing in a resurrection for the unrighteous as well as for the righteous dead.[25] There is no need to doubt that, like other Pharisees, he had inherited the belief in such a twofold resurrection, but when he develops the doctrine in his letters, he concentrates on the hope set before "those who belong to Christ," for whom resurrection (at the advent of Christ) will be participation in his resurrection, the harvest of which his resurrection was the firstfruits (1 Cor. 15:20-23; cf. Phil. 3:20-21). As it is, with this firm belief in a coming resurrection, with its corollary of an appearance before the divine tribunal, he constantly set himself[26] (he tells Felix, as he had already told the Sanhedrin) to maintain a clear conscience before God and human beings alike.[27]

23. Again he emphasizes the centrality of the resurrection hope in his preaching (cf. 23:6; 26:8); that he related the resurrection hope explicitly to Jesus' resurrection is made evident by 25:19. Cf. L. De Lorenzi (ed.), *Résurrection du Christ et des chrétiens (1 Co 15)*, SMT:SBO 8 (Rome, 1985).

24. See p. 429 with nn. 21 and 22 (on 23:8).

25. For the resurrection of the righteous cf. Luke 14:14; 20:35-36. For the resurrection of the unrighteous in addition to the righteous cf. John 5:28-29 and Rev. 20:12-15. It is usually taken to be the sense of Dan. 12:2 (another interpretation, favored by Saʿadya Gaʾon and others, regards those who are destined "to shame and everlasting contempt" as being left unraised in "the dust of the earth"). It is unlikely that Paul has the resurrection of the unrighteous in view when he says that "in Christ shall all be made alive" (1 Cor. 15:22).

26. Gk. ἀσκῶ, "I exercise myself" (the only NT instance of the word). There is a note of moral strictness in the word, without the later sense of asceticism (which in Pauline Greek is expressed by ἀφειδία σώματος, "severity to the body," as in Col. 2:23).

27. See p. 424 with n. 2 (on 23:1).

17 The reason for his coming to Jerusalem after a lapse of several years, he averred, was to bring alms and offerings to his fellow-Jews there. This is the clearest reference in Acts—indeed, one might say it is the only reference—to the collection which Paul had organized in the churches of his Gentile mission field for the relief of the Jewish Christians of Jerusalem.[28] Since, in response to the Jerusalem church leaders' request to him and Barnabas to "remember the poor" (Gal. 2:10), this gift was designed more particularly "for the poor among the saints at Jerusalem" (Rom. 15:26), it could properly be described as "alms." As for the accompanying term "offerings," Paul makes it very plain (especially in 2 Cor. 8:1–9:15) that the gift was a tribute of thanksgiving to God as well as a donation for the relief of his people. Paul obviously attached great importance to the collection: in his eyes it was a proper acknowledgment on the part of the Gentile Christians of the debt which they owed to Jerusalem, from which the gospel had set out on its progress to them, and he also hoped that it might arouse in the Jerusalem church (many of whose members looked with suspicion on the Gentile mission) a sense of gratitude to the Gentile believers which would help to weld both groups into a spiritual unity. In this last respect the collection achieved at best only partial success, if indeed it was not an outright failure.

Luke evidently knew about the collection but, equally evidently, he is very reticent about it. This may have been because the enterprise ended in disaster; another possible reason is that at Paul's trial it was misrepresented as an improper diversion of money that ought to have swelled the Jerusalem temple tax, and Luke judged it wise to refer to it only in the most general terms.[29]

18-19 Shortly after his coming to Jerusalem, Paul continued, he was set upon in the temple precincts, when he had just completed a purificatory ceremony in an orderly manner. He had done nothing to occasion the public tumult that broke out: those responsible for it were some Jews from the province of Asia. Those Asian Jews ought to have appeared before Felix as Paul's accusers, or as witnesses for the prosecution, if they had any

28. G. W. H. Lampe, *St. Luke and the Church of Jerusalem* (London, 1969), p. 24, suggests that the reference may be "only to his acts of Jewish piety in the Temple concerned with the vows and sacrifices that he undertook" (cf. 21:23-26).

29. For the collection see pp. 371-72 with nn. 45 and 46 (on 19:21), pp. 381-82 (on 20:3 and 4). See also K. Holl, "Der Kirchenbegriff des Paulus in seinem Verhältnis zu dem der Urgemeinde" (1921), in *Gesammelte Aufsätze zur Kirchengeschichte, 2: Der Osten* (Tübingen, 1928), pp. 44-67; C. H. Buck, "The Collection for the Saints," *HTR* 43 (1950), pp. 1-29; J. Knox, *Chapters in a Life of Paul* (London, 1954), pp. 51-58, 60, 69-72; D. Georgi, *Die Geschichte der Kollekte des Paulus für Jerusalem* (Hamburg, 1965); K. F. Nickle, *The Collection: A Study in Paul's Strategy* (London, 1966); K. Berger, "Almosen für Israel: Zum historischen Kontext der paulinischen Kollekte," *NTS* 23 (1976-77), pp. 180-204; S. Garofalo, "Un chef d'oeuvre pastoral de Paul: la collecte," in *Paul de Tarse: Apôtre du notre temps*, ed. L. De Lorenzi, SMT:SBO 1 (Rome, 1979), pp. 575-93.

serious charge to bring against him. This was a strong point in his defense: the people who had raised the hue and cry in the first instance, claiming to be eyewitnesses of his alleged sacrilege, had not troubled to be present. It may be that the Sanhedrin thought it best that the Asian Jews should not come before the court, as cross-examination would soon have revealed the hollowness of their charges, and a Roman judge would not look lightly on people who wasted his time with unfounded accusations.

20-21 But, since the Asian Jews had not seen fit to put in an appearance, said Paul, let the members of the Sanhedrin who were present state more explicitly than Tertullus had done what crime he was discovered to have committed when the tribune brought him before their court for examination in Jerusalem. The only crime with which they could charge him as a result of that examination was the crime of having declared that the real point at issue in his case was the question of the resurrection of the dead—in other words, no crime at all.[30]

4. Felix Adjourns Proceedings (24:22-23)

> 22 *Felix then deferred further hearing: he had a rather accurate knowledge of the Way. "When the tribune Lysias comes down," he said, "I will give my decision in your case."*
>
> 23 *He gave orders to the centurion that Paul should be kept in charge under open arrest, and that none of his friends should be prevented from looking after him.*

22 Felix appears to have summed up the situation fairly accurately. How he came by his special knowledge of the Christian movement is not said; it has been thought that it was through his wife Drusilla, a member of the Herod family—but what opportunities had she of knowing about it? At any rate he probably saw where the truth of the matter lay, but for the present he adjourned proceedings, perhaps with the formula *Amplius* ("judgment reserved").[31] The evidence of Lysias would plainly be of first-rate value; he had given a brief summary of events in his letter (23:25-30), but in view of the conflicting statements made by Tertullus and Paul, it would be necessary to ascertain further details from Lysias.[32]

23 Meanwhile he gave orders that Paul was to be kept in custody

---

30. F. W. Farrar read a confession of wrong into the words of v. 21: "In the remark of St. Paul before the tribunal of Felix I seem to see—though none have noticed it—a certain sense of compunction for the method in which he had extricated himself from a pressing danger" (*The Life and Work of St. Paul*, II [London, 1879], p. 328).

31. The proceedings now adjourned by Felix are identified by J. A. T. Robinson as Paul's "first defense," to which reference is made in 2 Tim. 4:16 (*Redating the New Testament* [London, 1976], p. 74; cf. his *Can We Trust the New Testament?* [London, 1977], pp. 65-66).

32. As Tertullus had suggested, according to the Western text of vv. 7-8.

but to be allowed a reasonable degree of consideration, as befitted a Roman citizen against whom no crime was proved. In particular, he was free to receive visits and any other kind of attention from his friends—possibly members of the church of Caesarea or some Gentile Christians who had accompanied him to Jerusalem and had now come to Caesarea to see if they could do anything for him.

Luke does not say if Lysias did come down to Caesarea or if Felix resumed the hearing. Probably Lysias came and supplied further information, but no decision was reached. Felix saw, no doubt, that the case against Paul could not stand, but he did not wish to offend the Sanhedrin by discharging him. He had given enough offense during his administration of Judaea, and he did not care to give more, especially as he could no longer count on the unchallenged influence of his brother Pallas at the imperial court as he had been able to do under the principate of Claudius.[33]

5. Paul's Interviews with Felix (24:24-26)

24 *After some days Felix came with Drusilla his wife, who was a Jewess.[34] He listened to him speaking about faith in Christ Jesus.*

25 *As Paul conversed about righteousness, self-control, and the future judgment, Felix became afraid. "You may go for the present," he said; "when I have a spare moment I will summon you."*

26 *At the same time he was hopeful that Paul would give him money, so he sent for him quite often and talked with him.*

24 Having this eminent Christian in custody in Caesarea, Felix availed himself of the opportunity to improve his already "rather accurate" knowledge of the Way. According to the Western text, it was Drusilla who was specially anxious to meet Paul. Drusilla was the youngest daughter of Herod Agrippa I, and at this time was not yet twenty years old. As a small girl she had been betrothed to the crown prince of Commagene, in eastern Asia Minor, but the marriage did not take place because the prospective bridegroom refused to become a proselyte to Judaism. Then her brother Agrippa II[35] gave her in marriage to the king of Emesa (modern Homs), a petty state in Syria. But when she was still only sixteen, Felix, with the help (it is said) of a Cypriot magician called Atomos,[36] persuaded her to leave her husband and come to be his wife, promising her (with a play on his name) every

33. According to Tacitus (*Annals* 13.14.1) Pallas was deposed by Nero in A.D. 55 from his very influential post as head of the imperial treasury. See n. 43 below.

34. The Western text (preserved in the margin of the Harclean Syriac) adds: "who asked to see Paul and hear him speak, so wishing to satisfy her he summoned Paul."

35. See pp. 456-57 with n. 23 (on 25:13).

36. It would be farfetched to connect Atomos with Etymas (Hetoimas), the Western reading of the name of Elymas, the Cypriot magician of 13:8. Some manuscripts of *Ant.* 20.142 have "Simon" in place of "Atomos."

"felicity" if she did so. Accordingly, she joined Felix as his third wife, and bore him a son named Agrippa, who met his death in the eruption of Vesuvius in A.D. 79.[37]

25 Felix and Drusilla, then, sent for Paul and listened as he expounded the Christian faith. But he made it clear that the gospel had ethical implications and, as he talked about these, Felix and Drusilla felt that the interview had taken an uncomfortably personal turn. It was certainly not such an "abstract discussion" as Joseph Klausner supposed;[38] on the contrary, Paul's distinguished hearers had probably never listened to such pointed and practical teaching in their lives as when he talked to them about "righteousness and self-control and the future judgment"—three subjects about which that couple specially needed to be informed. No wonder that Felix trembled and decided that he had heard enough for the time being.

26 But he was sufficiently interested to call Paul to his presence fairly frequently and engage him in conversation, although (as Luke suggests) there was a further motive for these repeated interviews. In spite of stern and reiterated edicts against bribery, the wheels of Roman justice, especially in some of the provinces, ran more smoothly and rapidly if they were judiciously oiled; and a number of provincial governors were deplorably venal. Felix had the impression that Paul was in a position to pay a handsome bribe for his release. How he got that impression is uncertain; the fact that Paul had lately come to Jerusalem with substantial "alms and offerings" perhaps gave him the idea that Paul had access to further funds.[39] But Felix's expectations in this matter were disappointed.

6. Felix Replaced by Festus; Paul Left in Custody (24:27)

27 *But after two years Felix was replaced by Porcius Festus, and, wishing to ingratiate himself with the Jews, he left Paul a prisoner.*

27 The two years are most naturally taken to indicate the time that elapsed between Felix's judicial hearing of Paul and his recall from office.[40] It is much less likely that they indicate the duration of Felix's procuratorship of Judaea. The occasion of Felix's recall from his office was an outbreak of

---

37. See Josephus, *Ant.* 19.354; 20.139-44.

38. J. Klausner, *From Jesus to Paul*, E.T. (London, 1944), p. 406.

39. W. M. Ramsay supposed that Paul had command of considerable personal resources around this time, that the expenses of his trial and of his periods of custody in Caesarea and Rome were met from his hereditary property, which may have "come to him as legal heir (whose right could not be interfered with by any will)" (*St. Paul the Traveller*, pp. 310-12). But the whole matter belongs to the realm of speculation—as money matters often do!

40. Paul may have found these two years tedious, but for Luke, says J. H. Moulton, they "were doubtless the opportunity of collecting material for his Gospel and the earlier parts of Acts" (MHT II, p. 19).

civil strife between the Jewish and Gentile inhabitants of Caesarea, in which Felix intervened with troops in such a way as to cause much bloodshed among the leaders of the Jewish faction.[41] On his return to Rome he would have faced a severe penalty, Josephus informs us, had it not been for the advocacy of his brother Pallas.[42] Pallas had been removed from his post as head of the imperial civil service in A.D. 55, but (largely on account of his colossal wealth) he retained great influence for several years after that.[43]

Felix was succeeded as procurator of Judaea by Porcius Festus, whose brief administration, though troubled by outbreaks of insurgency, was not marked by such excesses as those of his predecessor and successors.[44] But the change of administration brought no advantage to Paul. Felix left him in custody, hoping that this at least would be accepted by the Jewish authorities as a gesture of goodwill; and the arrival of a new and inexperienced governor meant the reopening of the case in circumstances less favorable to Paul.

---

41. Josephus, *BJ* 2.266-70; *Ant.* 20.173-78, 182-84.

42. Josephus, *Ant.* 20.182.

43. Even when he was dismissed from office, Pallas could stipulate successfully that there should be no scrutiny of his conduct in office and that his accounts with the state should be treated as balanced (Tacitus, *Annals* 13.14.2). His influence lasted until A.D. 62, when he fell victim to Nero's desire to lay hands on his wealth (Tacitus, *Annals* 14.65.1). There is nothing in the circumstances of Pallas's career to rule out his effective intervention on behalf of Felix in (say) A.D. 59.

44. Cf. Josephus, *BJ* 2.271; *Ant.* 20.182-97. Festus appears to have governed Judaea from A.D. 59 to his death in 62. Eusebius gives A.D. 55 as the year of Felix's replacement by Festus (*Chronicon,* year of Abraham 2072), and in this he has been followed not only by Jerome but by some scholars of more recent date (see K. Lake in *Beginnings* I.5, pp. 464-67, 470-73; H. Conzelmann, *Die Apostelgeschichte* [Tübingen, ²1972], pp. 129-30). But this gives Felix too short a rule and compresses Paul's career since Gallio's proconsulship of Achaia (see p. 352 with n. 38, on 18:12) into too narrow a space. A more reliable pointer to the date of Felix's replacement has been found in a change in the Judaean provincial coinage attested for Nero's fifth year (A.D. 58-59); this coin issue "is more likely to be the work of a new procurator than of an outgoing one who had already minted a large issue" (E. M. Smallwood, *The Jews under Roman Rule,* SJLA 20 [Leiden, 1976], p. 269, n. 40). See F. W. Madden, *History of Jewish Coinage* (London, 1864), p. 153; A. Reifenberg, *Ancient Jewish Coins* (Jerusalem, 1947), p. 27; cf. also H. J. Cadbury, *The Book of Acts in History* (New York, 1955), p. 10; Schürer I, p. 255, n. 42.

ACTS 25

7. Festus Visits Jerusalem (25:1-5)

1 *When Festus arrived in his province, he went up after three days from Caesarea to Jerusalem.*

2 *There the chief priests and principal men of the Jews laid information before him against Paul and appealed to him,*

3 *seeking a favor to Paul's disadvantage, to send for him to come to Jerusalem. They planned[1] to ambush and kill him on the way.*

4 *Festus replied that Paul was being kept in custody at Caesarea, for which he himself was shortly about to set out.*

5 *"So," he said, "let your leading men come down with me and state their accusation against this man, if they have any fault to find with him."[2]*

1-3 It was desirable that a new procurator should make the acquaintance as soon as possible of the leading national authorities of his province. Accordingly, three days after his taking up office in Caesarea, Festus went up to Jerusalem to meet the chief priests and other leaders of the Sanhedrin. After the preliminary salutations, they lost no time in exploiting the favor which Felix had done them by leaving Paul a prisoner in Caesarea. Counting perhaps on the new governor's inexperience, they raised the question of Paul with him, and asked him to send orders to Caesarea to have Paul brought up to Jerusalem. The zealous forty who had been frustrated in an earlier plot against Paul, or others who emulated their zeal, might find a better opportunity to do away with him on the road from Caesarea to Jerusalem.

4-5 Festus, however, saw no need to accede to this particular request. He did not intend to make a long stay in Jerusalem; he was shortly to go back to Caesarea, and if a responsible deputation from the Jewish rulers went along with him, they could state their case against Paul before him there.

---

1. The Western text is probably represented by the fuller reading of the Syriac Harclean margin: "those who had made a vow to get him into their hands planned . . ." (ascribing this plot to the plotters of 23:12-15).

2. Lit., "if there is anything improper (ἄτοπον, with which cf. Luke 23:41) in the man."

8. Paul Appeals to Caesar (25:6-12)

6 When he had spent some days among them, not more than eight or
ten, he went down to Caesarea. Next day he took his seat on the
tribunal and ordered Paul to be brought.

7 When he arrived, the Jews who had come down from Jerusalem
stood round him, urging against him many serious charges which
they were not able to prove.

8 Paul for his part replied in defense, "Neither against the law of the
Jews nor against the temple nor against Caesar have I done anything
wrong."

9 Then Festus, wishing to do the Jews a favor, answered Paul, "Are
you willing to go up to Jerusalem and be judged there before me with
regard to these charges?"

10 Paul said, "It is before Caesar's tribunal that I stand; it is there that I
ought to be judged.[3] I have committed no crime against the Jews, as
you know very well.

11 If I am guilty, if I have done anything deserving the death penalty, I
do not ask to escape death. But if there is no substance in these men's
accusations against me, no one can hand me over to them. I appeal
to Caesar."

12 Festus then conferred with his council and answered, "You have
appealed to Caesar, have you? You shall go to Caesar."

6-8 The whole case against Paul was now opened afresh, thanks to Felix's
neglect to pronounce his acquittal and discharge him. Festus spent a little
over a week in Jerusalem and returned to Caesarea, and a deputation from
the Sanhedrin accompanied him. The day after their arrival in Caesarea,
Festus took his seat as judge,[4] ordered Paul to be brought into court, and
gave his accusers an opportunity to restate their charges against him. This
they proceeded to do, but although the many charges which they brought
were serious in character and deadly in intention (being probably a repetition
of those detailed by Tertullus before Felix), they could produce no evidence
in their support. No witnesses were forthcoming to supply proof of them,
and all that Paul needed to do when replying in his defense was to deny them
categorically one by one.

The nature of the charges can be inferred from Paul's threefold
denial. He was charged in general with breaking the Jewish law and in

---

3. Cod. B repeats the participle "standing" (ἑστώς): "standing before Caesar's
tribunal, I am standing where I ought to be judged" (an attractive reading, which Lake and
Cadbury adopt).

4. This formality was necessary for his decision to have legal validity. For a
Roman magistrate's "tribunal" (βῆμα) cf. 18:12, 16; Matt. 27:19; John 19:13; Josephus,
BJ 2.172, 301; 3.532 (according to Josephus, Ant. 18.207, Philip the tetrarch took his
official seat of office, his θρόνος, around with him when he toured his tetrarchy in order
to judge cases without delay).

particular with violating the sanctity of the temple. As for the general charge, Luke represents him as observing the Jewish law punctiliously, and Paul himself agrees that he observes it when living among law-abiding Jews (1 Cor. 9:20)—especially in Judaea, where the Sanhedrin's writ ran. (What he did in the Gentile lands was outside their jurisdiction.) As for the particular charge of temple profanation, those who first raised a clamor against him on this ground did not come forward as witnesses when the alleged crime was recent; no evidence in its support could be produced now. If a *prima facie* case could have been made out against him on this score, he could have been handed over to the Sanhedrin for trial; but unsubstantiated charges did not constitute a *prima facie* case.[5]

The charge of acting against the emperor's interests was a very serious one, of which Caesar's representative was bound to take special notice. It was probably a repetition of the charge brought against Paul and his friends at Thessalonica (17:6-7) and an expansion of Tertullus's characterization of him as a "pest" (24:5).[6] But by charging him with fomenting disorder in the provinces Paul's accusers overreached themselves, for this was a matter which fell decidedly within the imperial jurisdiction, not the Sanhedrin's, and one on which Paul might very properly appeal to the emperor himself.

9 Between the Sanhedrin's charges and Paul's denials Festus was at a loss, the more so since he could not make out what their real grievance against him was. But he had newly entered on his period of office as governor of Judaea, the Sanhedrin was the supreme court of the nation he had come to govern, and it would be politic to begin his administration by doing something to gain their goodwill, if this could be done without infringing Roman justice. Roman justice must by all means be maintained when the accused man was a Roman citizen. But it was a matter of indifference so far as Roman justice was concerned whether the reopened case was heard in Caesarea or in Jerusalem. The Sanhedrin plainly desired it to be heard in Jerusalem: he would at least concede this to them. So he proposed to Paul that he should go up to Jerusalem and have the matter dealt with there; Festus himself would be the judge. It seemed a reasonable enough proposal, the more so since the one specific crime with which Paul was charged, the violation of the sanctity of the temple, was allegedly committed at Jerusalem.

10-11 But Paul did not regard the proposal as reasonable at all. To go back to Jerusalem meant placing himself in jeopardy all over again. If Festus began by making one concession to the Sanhedrin, he might be persuaded to make further concessions even more prejudicial to Paul's

5. Cf. 21:27-29 (p. 409 with nn. 47-49).
6. See p. 325 with nn. 13-16, pp. 439-40 with nn. 8-13.

safety. Felix had been an experienced administrator of Judaea when Paul's case was submitted to him, but Festus was a novice, and his inexperience might well be exploited to Paul's detriment. There was one way open to Paul as a Roman citizen to escape from this precarious situation, even if it was a way attended by special risks of its own. It was not, he assured Festus, that he wished to circumvent the law of Rome or escape the due penalty for anything he might have done. If he had in fact committed a capital crime, as his accusers maintained, he was prepared to suffer the supreme penalty for it; but if there was no substance in their charges, he must not be placed in their power. Let Roman justice decide. As Festus was Caesar's representative, the tribunal before which Paul stood was Caesar's; but since he had not sufficient confidence in the impartiality of that subordinate tribunal, he appealed to the supreme tribunal. "I appeal to Caesar," he declared.

The right of appeal *(prouocatio)* to the emperor arose out of the earlier right of appeal to the sovereign people (the *populus Romanus*), one of the most ancient rights of a Roman citizen, traditionally going back to the foundation of the republic in 509 B.C. It was usually exercised by appealing against a magistrate's verdict, but might be exercised at any earlier stage of proceedings, claiming "that the investigation be carried out in Rome and judgment passed by the emperor himself."[7] At an early stage in his principate, Augustus was granted the right to judge on appeal;[8] not many years later, the Julian law on public disorder safeguarded Roman citizens not only against degrading forms of coercion or punishment but also against being sentenced after an appeal had been voiced or being prevented from going to Rome to have the appeal heard there within a reasonable time.[9]

Paul did not appeal while Felix was in office: Felix had virtually decided that there was no case against him and was simply postponing the formal acquittal and discharge. One day (Paul might have hoped) Felix's procrastination would come to an end and Paul would be released. But with Felix's recall a new and potentially dangerous situation was developing for Paul; hence his momentous decision. Paul had not lost confidence in Roman justice, of which he had happy experience in a number of places, notably in Corinth before Gallio's tribunal.[10] But he feared that in Jerusalem Roman justice might be overborne by powerful local influences. There was no reason (so far as he knew) for such fear in Rome. There (it might well seem to a Roman citizen who had never actually visited Rome) Roman justice would be administered most impartially.

7. Schürer I, p. 369.

8. Dio Cassius, *History* 51.19; in Dio's Greek phrase ἔϰϰλητον διϰάζειν A. H. M. Jones recognized the equivalent of Lat. *ex prouocatione cognoscere* (*Studies in Roman Government and Law* [Oxford, 1960], p. 96).

9. *Digest* 48.6-7; Paulus, *Sententiae* 5.26.1.

10. Cf. 18:12-17 (pp. 351-54).

Ordinary provincial subjects of the empire had no such privilege as citizens enjoyed. The distinction between the two categories continued to be observed for a long time to come. For example, when the younger Pliny was confronted by the alarming spread of Christianity in Bithynia in A.D. 112, he took summary action against ordinary provincials convicted as Christians, but those who were Roman citizens he sent to Rome for appropriate examination and judgment by the emperor, not being quite sure himself of the correct legal procedure.[11]

To us who know Nero's record in relation to Roman Christianity, it may seem strange that Paul should have appealed to him with such confidence. But whatever Nero's personal character might be, the first five years of his principate (A.D. 54-59), when the imperial administration was carried on under the influence of his tutor Seneca, the Stoic philosopher, and Afranius Burrus, prefect of the praetorian guard, were looked back to as a miniature golden age. There was little in A.D. 59 that gave warning of the events of A.D. 64 and 65.

12 Festus heard Paul's words with much relief. By appealing to Caesar, Paul enabled him to escape from a responsibility with which he felt unable to cope. He conferred with his council[12]—a body consisting of the higher officials of his administration and younger men who accompanied him in order to gain some experience of provincial government—and willingly agreed that Paul's case should be referred to Rome (in fact, once Paul had made his appeal, Festus had no option in the matter).

Paul probably made his appeal not only in the interests of his personal safety but also from a desire to win recognition for the Gentile churches as authorized associations[13] in their own right. And he may have been moved more than anything else by the incomparable opportunity which the hearing of his appeal would provide of preaching the gospel at the seat of imperial power.[14]

---

11. Pliny, *Epistles* 10.96.4. There was a gradual erosion of the privileges of citizens as the second century advanced (this is evident from the *Letter of the Churches of Lyon and Vienne,* reproduced in Eusebius, *HE* 5.1, describing the persecution of Christians in the Rhone valley in A.D. 177, under Marcus Aurelius), until in A.D. 212 the citizenship was extended to all freeborn subjects of the empire. Luke's account of Paul's appeal is consistent with all that is known of relevant conditions in the late fifties of the first century. See A. H. M. Jones, *Studies in Roman Government and Law,* pp. 51-98; A. N. Sherwin-White, *Roman Society and Roman Law in the New Testament* (Oxford, 1963), pp. 57-70; P. Garnsey, "The *Lex Iulia* and Appeal under the Empire," *JRS* 58 (1966), pp. 167-89.

12. Gk. συμβούλιον, comprising his σύνεδροι or *comites.*

13. The legal status desired is expressed by *collegium licitum* (*Digest* 47.22) rather than by Tertullian's *religio licita* (*Apology* 21.1), which is not a technical term of Roman law.

14. Cf. Eph. 6:19-20; Phil. 1:19-20, and possibly 2 Tim. 4:17.

9. Agrippa II and Bernice Visit Festus (25:13-22)

13 When some days had elapsed, King Agrippa and Bernice came to Caesarea to greet Festus.

14 As they were spending several days there, Festus acquainted the king with Paul's case: "There is a man," he said, "who has been left behind by Felix as a prisoner.

15 When I was in Jerusalem, the chief priests and elders of the Jews laid information before me, asking for an adverse verdict against him.

16 I told them in reply that it is not the custom for the Romans to hand over anyone for punishment before the accused person meets his accusers face to face and has an opportunity to defend himself against the charge.

17 So, when they had come together here, I made no delay but took my seat on the tribunal the next day and ordered the man to be brought.

18 They took their stand around him but charged him with none of the offenses[15] that I supposed they would allege.

19 Instead, the charges concerned some disputes which they had with him about their own religion,[16] and in particular about one Jesus, who was dead, but whom Paul claimed to be alive.

20 Since I was at a loss how to handle an investigation of these things, I asked if he would go up to Jerusalem and stand his trial about them there.

21 But Paul appealed to be kept in custody for His Imperial Majesty's examination and decision,[17] so I gave orders for him to be kept until I could send him up[18] to Caesar."

22 Agrippa said to Festus, "I should like to hear the man myself." "You shall hear him tomorrow," said Festus.

13 Only one problem now remained for Festus. When he sent Paul to Rome, to have his case heard before the emperor, it would be necessary for him to send a report of the case as it had developed up to the moment of Paul's appeal. No doubt records of the hearings before Felix could be consulted, and perhaps Lysias's letter (23:26-30) and further evidence were

---

15. Lit., "brought no charge of evil things" (οὐδεμίαν αἰτίαν . . . πονηρῶν); P[74] A C Ψ and other witnesses read "no evil charge" (αἰτίαν . . . πονηράν); ℵ* C² read the accusative πονηρά, "evil things," in apposition with αἰτίαν, while the Byzantine text omits "evil" altogether.

16. Gk. δεισιδαιμονία, which may be mildly disparaging ("superstition") or not according to the context. The disparaging sense is inappropriate here, since Festus was addressing a distinguished Jew. Cf. the adjective δεισιδαιμονεστέρους in 17:22 (p. 335 with n. 56).

17. Gk. εἰς τὴν τοῦ Σεβαστοῦ διάγνωσιν. Here and in v. 25 Festus refers to the emperor by the Greek title Σεβαστός, the equivalent of Lat. Augustus (cf. KJV).

18. That is, "send him up" (ἀναπέμπω, "remand," "refer") to the higher court to which he had appealed.

accessible, but Festus himself would be responsible for the wording of the report, and if it was to be coherent and intelligible he would require a better grasp of the matters at issue than he possessed at present. Listening to the speeches for the prosecution and the defense had only increased his perplexity.

Fortunately for Festus, a way out of this difficulty presented itself. Herod Agrippa II, ruler of a client kingdom to the northeast of Festus's province, arrived in Caesarea on a complimentary visit, to congratulate the new procurator on his appointment. This man was reputed to be an expert in Jewish religious questions, and Festus hoped he might give him some unofficial help in drafting his report.

Marcus Julius Agrippa, as he calls himself on his coins (using his name as a Roman citizen), was the son of Herod Agrippa I.[19] He was in Rome when his father died in A.D. 44, and the Emperor Claudius was disposed to make him king of the Jews in succession to his father; but because of the younger Agrippa's youth (he was seventeen years old at the time) he was dissuaded from this plan, and Judaea was once more administered by Roman governors. In A.D. 50, however, Claudius gave him the kingdom of Chalcis (in Lebanon), in succession to his father's brother Herod, together with the right of appointing the Jewish high priests.[20] In 53 he gave up this kingdom in exchange for a larger one consisting of the former tetrarchies of Philip and Lysanias.[21] This territory was augmented three years later by Nero, who added to it the regions of Tiberias and Tarichaea, west of the lake of Galilee, together with Julias in Peraea and fourteen neighboring villages. In token of gratitude to Nero, Agrippa changed the name of his capital, Caesarea Philippi (modern Banyas),[22] to Neronias.[23]

19. See 12:1-23.

20. Between A.D. 6 and 37 the high priests were appointed by Roman governors. The right of appointment was granted to Herod Agrippa I in A.D. 41. When he died three years later, a Jewish deputation visited Rome and protested to Claudius against the attempt made by Cuspius Fadus, newly appointed procurator of Judaea, to secure the right of appointment (which carried with it the custody of the high-priestly vestments) for himself. Their protest was supported by the younger Agrippa, and Claudius conciliated them by giving the right to Herod of Chalcis (brother of the elder Agrippa). See Josephus, *Ant.* 20.6-16.

21. This was the territory which the Emperor Gaius had given to Herod Agrippa I in A.D. 37. For the two tetrarchies cf. Luke 3:1, where Philip's tetrarchy is described as "the region of Ituraea and Trachonitis" and that of Lysanias as "Abilene." See Schürer I, pp. 561-73.

22. Caesarea Philippi—"Philip's Caesarea"—was so called to distinguish it from Caesarea Maritima, on the Mediterranean seaboard of Judaea. It was the capital of Philip's tetrarchy from 4 B.C. to his death in A.D. 34. Banyas is the Arabic pronunciation of the earlier Greek name Paneas.

23. Agrippa did his best to prevent the revolt of A.D. 66 (see the dissuasive speech attributed to him by Josephus, *BJ* 2.345-401). When his efforts failed, he remained loyal to Rome and was rewarded after the war with a further increase of territory and (in 75) with

On this visit Agrippa was accompanied by his sister, Julia Bernice.[24] She was the eldest daughter of Herod Agrippa I, born in A.D. 28. She was given by her father in marriage to his brother Herod, king of Chalcis.[25] When Herod died in 48, she lived in the house of her brother Agrippa. Later she married Polemon, king of Cilicia, but soon left him and returned to Agrippa.[26] On inscriptions she is entitled "queen" and even "great queen."[27]

14-19 At a suitable opportunity during Agrippa's stay in Caesarea, Festus broached the subject of Paul. He told the king how Paul had been left a prisoner by Felix, how the Sanhedrin had asked him to pronounce a verdict of "guilty" against him, and how he had given them an answer in strict accordance with the principles of Roman justice: the accused party must have an opportunity in open court of hearing the charges against him and replying to them.[28] When such a court was held at Caesarea, the accusers said their say, but to Festus's surprise and perplexity, the accusations

---

promotion to praetorian rank. He corresponded with Josephus about the latter's *Jewish War*, confirming its accuracy (Josephus, *Life* 362-66; *Ap.* 1.51). He died about A.D. 100, leaving no children, and has thus been called "the last of the Herods." See Josephus, *BJ* 2.233, 245, 247, 309, 337-407; 3.56-57; 7.97; *Ant.* 19.354, 360-62; 20.104, 135, 138-40, 159, 179, 189-93, 203, 211-13; *Life* 34, 38-39, 46, 48, 52, 61, 74, 112, 114, 126, 131, 149, 154-55, 162, 180-82, 185, 220, 340-56, 359, 362-67, 381-84, 388-91, 397-98, 407-8, 410; also A. H. M. Jones, *The Herods of Judaea* (Oxford, 1938), pp. 207-31; Schürer I, pp. 471-83.

24. "Bernice" was the popular Hellenistic pronunciation of the Macedonian name Berenice (the form by which Josephus always refers to her).

25. To him she bore two sons, Berenicianus and Hyrcanus (Josephus, *Ant.* 20.104). A remarkable number of marriages between uncles and nieces took place within the Herod family. Thus Herodias, daughter of Aristobulus, was married successively to two of her father's half-brothers—Herod (Philip) and Herod Antipas; her daughter Salome was married to her father's half-brother, Philip the tetrarch.

26. Like her brother, she tried hard to avert the war which broke out in A.D. 66. In spring of that year she performed a Nazirite vow in Jerusalem, and attempted, but in vain (and not without considerable personal risk), to prevent a massacre of Jews by the procurator Gessius Florus. Later, however, when her house (together with Agrippa's) was burned down by insurgent extremists, she became an ardent pro-Flavian. She attracted the attention of Titus during the war, and lived with him on the Palatine when she came to Rome with her brother in 75. Titus would have married her, had it not been for strong expressions of disapproval among the citizens of Rome, which made him sever his connection with her. See Josephus, *BJ* 2.217, 220-21, 310-14, 333-34, 405, 426, 595; *Ant.* 19.276-77, 354; 20.104, 143, 145-46; *Life* 48, 119, 180-81, 343, 355; Juvenal, *Satire* 6.156-60; Tacitus, *Histories* 2.2; Suetonius, *Titus* 7.1; Dio Cassius, *History* 65.15; 66.18; also G. H. Macurdy, "Julia Berenice," *AJP* 56 (1933), pp. 246-53.

27. On a Latin inscription from Beirut she is called "Queen Berenice, daughter of the great king Agrippa" (*Comptes rendus de l'Académie des Inscriptions* [1927], pp. 243-44); on a Greek inscription she is called "Julia Berenice, the great queen" (*IG* III.556 = *CIG* 361).

28. F. Field quotes from Appian, *Civil War* 3.54: "The law requires, members of the council, that a man who is on trial should hear the accusation and speak in his own defense before judgment is passed on him" (*Notes on the Translation of the New Testament* [Cambridge, 1899], p. 140).

seemed to center around disputed points of Jewish religion, with particular reference to "one Jesus, who was dead, but whom Paul claimed to be alive." Paul had already insisted, before the Sanhedrin and before Felix, that his case rested on the resurrection hope. Now it appears, more explicitly than before, that he linked his insistence on the resurrection hope closely with the fact that Jesus had already been raised from the dead. That Jesus' resurrection was the real point at issue had evidently been made clear enough in the hearing before Festus, although Festus did not realize its import. Agrippa probably knew enough about the Christian movement to have his interest whetted by what Festus told him.

20-22 Festus went on to tell him of his suggestion that Paul should go up to Jerusalem and have the trial conducted there, and of Paul's appeal to Caesar. Paul was now being kept in custody at Caesarea until an opportunity arrived of sending him to Rome to have his appeal heard. "Well," said Agrippa, "I should like to hear the man for myself." Festus accordingly undertook to arrange an audience for the following day.

10. Paul Appears before Agrippa (25:23-27)

23 *So the next day, when King Agrippa and Bernice came with great ceremony and entered the audience chamber, with military tribunes and the most distinguished men of the city,[29] Festus gave the order and Paul was brought in.*

24 *Then Festus said, "King Agrippa, and all gentlemen[30] who are present with us, you see this man. The whole community of the Jews made request of me, both at Jerusalem and here,[31] clamoring that he ought to remain alive no longer.*

25 *But I gathered that he had done nothing deserving the death penalty, and when he himself appealed to His Imperial Majesty, I decided to send him (to Rome).*

26 *But I am unable to write anything definite[32] about him to my sovereign lord. Therefore I have brought him before all of you, and especially before you, King Agrippa, in order that, when we have held an inquiry, I may have something to write.*

29. A Western addition is preserved in the Syriac Harclean margin: "who had come down from the province."

30. Gk. ἄνδρες. The masculine is formal, and Bernice would not feel herself to be expressly ignored.

31. After "and here" the Western text reads (to the end of v. 25): "that I should hand him over to them for punishment without any defense. But I could not hand him over, on account of the commands which we have from His Imperial Majesty. But if any one was going to accuse him, I said that he should follow me to Caesarea, where he was in custody; and when they came, they clamored that he should be put to death. But when I heard one side and the other, I found that he was in no way worthy of death. But when I said, 'Are you willing to be judged before them in Jerusalem?' he appealed to Caesar."

32. Gk. ἀσφαλές, "secure."

27 *It seems absurd to me, in remanding a prisoner, not to indicate the charges brought against him."*

23 The next day, then, an audience was held. It was attended not only by Agrippa and his sister, but by members of the procurator's staff[33] and leading citizens of Caesarea (who would be mainly, if not altogether, Gentiles). Festus himself, as was proper, was in charge of the proceedings. There is quiet humor in Luke's account of the "great ceremony"[34] with which they assembled: Luke had a true sense of values, and knew that in Paul there was a native greatness which had no need to be decked with the trappings of grandeur that surrounded his distinguished hearers. History has vindicated Luke's perspective. It has been suggested that, by bringing Paul into contact with so many notabilities, Luke aimed at enhancing his status in the eyes of readers;[35] but even then some people who read this account would reckon that it was a privilege for those notabilities to have this brief contact with Paul. And most people nowadays who know anything about Agrippa and Bernice and Festus know of them as persons who for a brief period of time crossed Paul's path and heard him speak words which might have brought much blessing to them had they been disposed to pay serious heed to what he said. All these very important people would have been greatly surprised, and not a little scandalized, could they have foreseen the relative estimates that later generations would form of them and of the prisoner who now stood before them to state his case.

24-27 Paul was then conducted into the audience chamber, and Festus introduced him to Agrippa and the others, telling how he could find no substance in the capital charges which his Jewish accusers urged against him, and how Paul had appealed to Caesar. It is plain from these words that Festus was quite at a loss about the terms in which he should draw up his report on Paul's case—"I am unable to write anything definite about him to my sovereign lord,"[36] he said—and that he would be very glad for Agrippa's help in this matter. He therefore handed over the conduct of the inquiry to his royal visitor.

---

33. The military tribunes included on his staff were five in number, as there were five auxiliary cohorts stationed at Caesarea (Josephus, *Ant.* 19.365).

34. Gk. μετὰ πολλῆς φαντασίας. The Greek word survives as a loanword in Palestinian Arabic *(fantasya)*, in the sense of a festal procession.

35. See the discussion in E. Haenchen, *The Acts of the Apostles*, E.T. (Oxford, 1971), pp. 673-75, 678-79.

36. "To my κύριος": the title κύριος with a divine connotation was given to Roman emperors by their subjects in the eastern provinces as it had been given to the Ptolemies and other dynasts; Deissmann notes that there is a remarkable rise in the frequency of such inscriptions under Nero and his successors (*Light from the Ancient East*, E.T. [London, ²1927], pp. 353-62; cf. *New Docs.* 2 [1977], § 6).

It was a purely unofficial inquiry;[37] it was in no sense a trial. Agrippa had no authority to conduct a trial in Judaea, and in any case, since Paul had now appealed to Caesar, he could be subjected to no further trial until his appeal was heard in Rome. The inquiry was held in order that Agrippa might understand enough of Paul's case to help Festus frame his report. Festus alone was responsible for framing it, though he was free to receive help from whatever source he chose. He was bound to send a report: in saying that it would be absurd to remand a prisoner to the supreme court and not indicate the charges laid against him he did not imply that it was open to him to send Paul to Rome without any account of the charges and of the conduct of proceedings thus far.[38]

37. The word ἀνάκρισις in v. 26 means "preliminary investigation" when it is used technically; here it is used nontechnically of an informal inquiry.
38. Such a report was called *litterae dimissoriae* or *litterae apostoli* (*Digest* 49.6.1).

ACTS 26

11. Paul Accepts Agrippa's Invitation to Speak (26:1)

1 *Agrippa said to Paul, "You may speak for yourself."[1] Paul[2] then raised his hand and proceeded to make his defense.*

1 Since the proceedings were neither judicial nor in any other way official, Festus left it to Agrippa to conduct them as he thought fit. Agrippa then, turning to Paul, invited him to state his case. Paul was only too willing to accept the king's invitation, so he raised his hand in salutation to him[3] and proceeded to speak. If his speech is called his "defense," it is so called in no forensic sense; it is rather a defense of the gospel which he preached and of his way of life in conformity with it.

To some extent this speech covers the same ground as that which Paul delivered from the top of the steps leading to the Antonia fortress to the riotous crowd in the temple court below.[4] But the general tone and atmosphere of the two speeches are different, each being adapted to its very distinctive audience. Here, in the calm and dignified setting of the governor's audience chamber at Caesarea, Paul delivered the speech which, above all his other speeches in Acts, may worthily claim to be called his *Apologia pro vita sua*. In it he undertakes to show that neither his manner of life nor his teaching should arouse hostility, especially on the part of Jews. The construction of the speech is more careful than usual, the grammar more classical, and the style more literary, as befitted the distinguished audience.[5] The argument is designed to appeal particularly to the mind of Agrippa, who was reputed to be interested in Jewish theology, even if Festus found himself completely out of his depth after the first few sentences.

---

1. Or rather "about yourself" (the reading περὶ σεαυτοῦ is better attested than ὑπὲρ σεαυτοῦ).
2. There is a Western insertion, preserved in the margin of the Harclean Syriac: "confident, and encouraged by the Holy Spirit."
3. This gesture (ἐκτείνω τὴν χεῖρα) is not that with which a speaker beckons for a quiet hearing (κατασείω τῇ χειρί, 13:16; 21:40).
4. Cf. 22:3-21.
5. Cf. F. Blass, *The Philology of the Gospels* (London, 1898), p. 9; J. H. Moulton, MHT I, p. 78, n. 1; H. Conzelmann, *Die Apostelgeschichte* (Tübingen, 1963), p. 137.

12. Paul's "Apologia pro vita sua" (26:2-23)

a. Exordium (26:2-3)

2 *"I congratulate myself, King Agrippa, that it is before you that I am to make my defense today, regarding all the charges brought against me by the Jews,*

3 *especially because[6] you are an expert in all the Jewish customs and disputed questions. Therefore, I beg of you, give me a patient hearing.*

2-3 Paul congratulates himself first of all on the opportunity to state his case and expound his teaching before a man of Agrippa's eminence, particularly one so expert in the details of Jewish religious belief and practice. He, at least, might appreciate the strength of Paul's argument that the message which he proclaimed was the proper consummation of Israel's ancestral faith. For such a hearer and examiner no perfunctory statement, but a reasoned narration and exposition of his whole case, was appropriate. Unlike Tertullus before Felix,[7] Paul did not promise to be brief, but he did ask for a patient hearing; probably he hoped that Agrippa would be interested enough to hear him out at length.

b. The resurrection hope (26:4-8)

4 *"My course of life from my earliest youth[8] among my nation, and (particularly) in Jerusalem,[9] is known to all the Jews.*

5 *They have known me for a long time back,[10] and can testify, if they wish, that I lived as a Pharisee, according to the strictest party of our religion.*

6 *And now it is on the ground of hope based on the promise made by God to our fathers that I stand here on trial.*

7 *It is to the fulfilment of this promise that our twelve tribes, earnestly occupied in the worship of God night and day, hope to attain; and it is with regard to this hope, Your Majesty, that I am accused—accused by Jews![11]*

8 *Why is it judged incredible among you[12] that God should raise the dead?*

---

6. Some authorities (P^{74} ℵ^c A C 33 *al* syr^{pesh}) add ἐπιστάμενος, "knowing" ("especially because I know that you are . . .").

7. Cf. 24:4.

8. Gk. ἐκ νεότητος . . . ἀπ᾽ ἀρχῆς, "from my youth, from the beginning" (for the latter phrase cf. Lk. 1:2).

9. It is unlikely that "among my nation and in Jerusalem" means "among the people of Tarsus and (later) in Jerusalem," as Lake and Cadbury think.

10. Gk. ἄνωθεν (cf. Lk. 1:3), not necessarily going as far back as ἀπ᾽ ἀρχῆς (v. 4).

11. The position of ὑπὸ ᾽Ιουδαίων may denote emphasis.

12. One Western authority (P^{29}) seems to omit "Why is it judged incredible among you?" See also p. 469, n. 36.

4-8   Paul went on, then, to describe his early upbringing. His contemporaries knew all about this, and could bear witness, if called upon, that he had been brought up a Pharisee and lived according to the strictest rules of that party. It went without saying that a faithful Pharisee believed in the resurrection of the dead, and saw no fulfilment of Israel's ancestral hope apart from the resurrection. But the amazing and indeed absurd feature of the present dispute was that he was being prosecuted for his proclamation of this very hope—and prosecuted by Jews, of all people. This hope was the hope that God would keep the promise which he made to the fathers of the nation long ago; it was the hope which gave life and meaning and purpose to the ordinances of divine worship, faithfully maintained by the twelve tribes of Israel[13] generation after generation, especially to the unceasing services of morning and evening sacrifice and prayer. It was the hope that God would one day come down to deliver his people as he had done when they were slaves in Egypt, that he would raise up for them "a horn of salvation . . . in the house of his servant David, as he spoke by the mouth of his holy prophets from of old" (Luke 1:69-70). Why should they think it incredible that God should honor their hope and fulfil his promise by raising the dead?[14]

The Pharisees among them would answer that they did not think it incredible; they ardently believed in God as the raiser of the dead. But Paul's point was that this belief had now been validated by God in his raising one man from the dead, demonstrating by this very fact that this one man was Israel's long-expected deliverer, the one in whom the ancient hope was to be realized. Before Agrippa, as previously before the Sanhedrin and before Felix, Paul insisted that his case hinged entirely on the resurrection hope; but by the resurrection hope he meant that hope as realized in "one Jesus, who was dead, but whom Paul claimed to be alive" (25:19). Even Festus had grasped something of the message, despite his total lack of background. Why should those who believed in the resurrection of the dead find it difficult to believe that God had in fact raised up Jesus, thus designating him "Son of God in power" (Rom. 1:4)? If God did not raise up Jesus, why believe that he raises the dead at all? So Paul now reasoned, but once upon a time he had reasoned quite differently.

13. For the twelve tribes (emphasizing the nation in its totality) cf. Matt. 19:28 par. Luke 22:30; Jas. 1:1 (with F. J. A. Hort's note *ad loc.*); Rev. 7:4-8; 21:12. The myth of the ten lost tribes plays no part in the biblical record.
14. There is no definite article in the Greek text here; the clause may be rendered: "that God raises dead people." The plural is generalizing, but Paul has one particular instance in his mind—the resurrection of Jesus. Cf. Rom. 1:4, where Jesus is "designated Son of God in power . . . by his resurrection from the dead"—lit., "by resurrection of dead people" (here also the generalizing plural points to the resurrection of Jesus in particular). It was useless, Paul implied, to acknowledge the resurrection of the dead in principle and refuse to believe in the one authenticated instance of such resurrection.

c. Paul's persecuting zeal (26:9-11)

9 *"To be sure, I myself once imagined that I ought to do many things against the name of Jesus of Nazareth.*

10 *I opposed his name in Jerusalem: I shut up many of his saints in prison, having received authority to do so from the chief priests, and when they were put to death I cast my vote against them.*

11 *In all the synagogues I took penal action against them repeatedly and tried to make them blaspheme. In the excess of my fury against them I pursued them even to foreign cities.*

9-11 But Paul understood his opponents' frame of mind very well; he had once shared it himself. He himself, for all his belief in the resurrection of the dead at the last day, thought it incredible that God should have raised the crucified Jesus; and when the disciples insisted that he had indeed raised him, Paul treated them as charlatans and blasphemers. He could not take seriously their claim that they seen him alive again. Their movement, as he saw it, was a cancer attacking the vitals of Israel's life; it must be uprooted, and Paul himself eagerly took the lead in uprooting it.

Armed with authority from the chief priests, he said, he went from house to house and dragged the followers of Jesus off to jail; he went from synagogue to synagogue and enforced judicial proceedings against them, and when they were put on trial, he cast his vote for their condemnation and demanded the death-sentence against them. The ruling body of each synagogue constituted a minor law court or *beth din,* but certainly under the Roman administration such a court had no competence to carry out the death-sentence. This competence belonged in principle to the supreme Sanhedrin, but under the Romans it was only where the sanctity of the temple was violated that the Sanhedrin had the authority to inflict capital punishment without reference to the governor. This probably explains Stephen's summary execution, but such restricted authority could not extend to the rank and file of Jesus' followers. In Paul's eyes they might be sharers in Stephen's offense, but his opinion need not have been given legal effect. One possibility is that in the reference to their being put to death the plural is generalizing, and that it is Paul's consent to Stephen's death that is really in view.[15]

In any case, Paul did not want to make martyrs of them if he could help it; if he could make them forswear their faith in Jesus, that was much more satisfactory. He did his best[16] in synagogue after synagogue to force

---

15. For his acquiescence in the execution of Stephen, who was tried and condemned by the supreme Sanhedrin in Jerusalem, see 8:1a (p. 161 with n. 3).

16. Gk. ἠνάγκαζον. The imperfect means "I tried to compel" (not, as in KJV, "compelled").

them to blaspheme, to call Jesus accursed,[17] and thus repudiate his claims. But such attempts met with little success: the disciples preferred death or exile to apostasy.[18] Nor did Paul confine his activities to Jerusalem and Judaea: when his victims took refuge beyond the provincial frontiers he pursued them into the synagogues of Gentile cities as well, where the writ of the Sanhedrin was honored. At the time in question, the new movement was developing exclusively within the community of Israel: the believers were members of the synagogue and amenable to its discipline.

d. The heavenly vision (26:12-18)

12   *"While I was thus engaged, I was on my way to Damascus with the authority and commission of the chief priests.*

13   *It was about midday, Your Majesty, when I saw on the road a light from heaven, brighter than the sun. It shone around me and my fellow travelers.*

14   *We all fell to the ground,[19] and I[20] heard a voice in the Hebrew speech saying to me, 'Saul, Saul, why are you persecuting me? It is hard for you to kick out against the goads.'*

15   *'Who are you, Lord?' I asked. The Lord said to me, 'I am Jesus,[21] the one whom you are persecuting.*

16   *But get up and stand[22] on your feet. This is why I have appeared to you: to appoint you as my servant, a witness to what you have seen of me and to what you will yet see of me.[23]*

17   *I will deliver you from the people and from the Gentiles: it is to them that I am now sending you,*

18   *to open their eyes, to turn them from darkness to light, from the dominion of Satan to God, so that they may receive forgiveness of sins and an inheritance among those who, by faith in me, have been made my holy people.'*

12-15   It was while Paul was thus engaged in the harrying of Jesus' followers that the revolution in his life took place. Again he tells of his journey to Damascus, of the lightning flash that blinded him, of the challenge from the risen Christ. In this version not only Paul himself but all his companions

17. Cf. 1 Cor. 12:3.

18. So, in Pliny the Younger's report to Trajan, if people suspected of being Christians obeyed his order to curse Christ *(male dicerent Christo)*, he discharged them, as he was informed that this was something which "people who are really Christians cannot possibly be made to do" *(Epistles* 10.96.5).

19. The Western text adds "for fear."

20. The Western text reads "I myself alone."

21. The Western text adds "the Nazarene" (from 22:8).

22. Cod. B omits "and stand" (καὶ στῆθι) by accident after "get up" (ἀνάστηθι).

23. Lit., "a witness to the things wherein you have seen me and those in which I will appear to you."

fall to the ground. This is, moreover, the only one of the three accounts of the event to report the Lord's words to Paul, "it is hard for you to kick out against the goads."[24] This homely proverb from agricultural life[25] has been thought to suggest that Paul had already begun to suffer from the prickings of an uneasy conscience, from a half-conscious conviction that there was more in the disciples' case than he was willing to admit. It is even suggested that, at one level of his mind, there was a realization that Stephen's argument was unanswerable and his demeanor strangely disquieting. But there is no hint, either in Acts or in Paul's letters, that before his conversion he was subject to any such inward conflict. His repeated claim in his apologetic speeches to have maintained a clear conscience all his life (23:1; 24:16) is confirmed by the evidence of his letters. Paul enjoyed a robust conscience: up to the moment of his confrontation with the Lord on the Damascus road he regarded his persecuting campaign as a service acceptable to God, and at the height of his apostolic career he could say that (subject to the judgment of the Lord, with whom the last word lay) he was not aware of anything against himself (1 Cor. 4:4). When Augustine and Luther discovered that Paul spoke so directly to their condition, it may have been natural for them to assume that, before his conversion, he endured the same kind of spiritual disturbance as they had known in their own lives; and this has led to the traditional ascription to Paul of what Krister Stendahl has called "the introspective conscience of the West."[26] But if Paul's conversion was preceded by a period of subconscious incubation, it has left no trace in our surviving records (no light is shed on such a period by Rom. 7:7-25). The "goads" against which he was now told it was fruitless for him to kick were not the prickings of a disturbed conscience but the new forces which were now impelling him in the opposite direction to that which he had hitherto pursued, the new "necessity" which was henceforth laid upon him (1 Cor. 9:16).

16-18 There was no need on this occasion to enlarge on the part played by the pious and law-abiding Ananias, as Paul had done when he addressed the crowd of Jerusalemites in the temple court. Here the Lord's message through Ananias is merged with his words spoken directly to Paul on the Damascus road and with those spoken to him in the temple when he returned to Jerusalem (22:14-21). Paul relates the terms in which the Lord

24. This is also the only one of the three accounts where the Lord is said to have addressed him in Aramaic ("in the Hebrew speech"; cf. p. 182, n. 14; p. 413, n. 58); but we should have inferred this in any case from the vocative form Σαοὺλ Σαούλ (9:4; 22:7), not Σαῦλε Σαῦλε.

25. Several parallels to this proverbial saying are adduced from Greek and Latin literature; none seems to be quoted from a Semitic source, but it is the sort of saying that would be current in any community where the ox was used for transport.

26. Cf. K. Stendahl, "The Apostle Paul and the Introspective Conscience of the West" (1963), in *Paul among Jews and Gentiles* (London, 1977), pp. 78-96.

commissioned him to be his witness and messenger—terms which recall those in which Jeremiah[27] and Ezekiel[28] received their prophetic commissions in earlier days. The commission itself echoes the commission of the Servant of the Lord in Isa. 42:1-7, and very properly so, for the commission of Paul and of all Christian witnesses is the perpetuation of the Servant's commission, as has been made very plain already in Acts (cf. 13:47). As the Servant was to open the eyes of the blind and turn their darkness into light, so Paul was summoned to continue this healing ministry.[29] The terms of his commission remained in his mind ever after; they are echoed in the words in which he reminds the Christians of Colossae how God the Father "has qualified us to share in the inheritance of the saints in light, . . . has delivered us from the domination of darkness and transferred us to the kingdom of his beloved Son, in whom we have redemption, the forgiveness of sins" (Col. 1:12-14). For these words sum up the blessing which, in the heavenly vision, he was charged to communicate to all who placed their faith in Christ, not only Jews, but Gentiles as well. That believing Gentiles were to have an equal and rightful share in the heritage of God's holy people was a feature of the gospel which it was Paul's peculiar mission to proclaim and put into effect through his ministry (cf. Gal. 1:16; Eph. 2:19; 3:1-10). We may well wonder if Agrippa, expert as he was in Jewish religious questions, even began to grasp the purport of all this.

e. Paul's obedience to the vision (26:19-20)

19 "Thereupon, King Agrippa, I was not disobedient to the heavenly vision;

20 on the contrary, first to those in Damascus and then in Jerusalem and in every country, to Jews and Gentiles,[30] I proceeded to declare[31] that they should repent and turn to God, and do the works that matched their repentance.

19-20   From the moment when he heard the words, "I am Jesus," Paul

---

27. Cf. Jer. 1:7-8: "to all to whom I send you you shall go, and whatever I command you you shall speak . . . for I am with you to deliver you" (observe also that Jeremiah is appointed "a prophet to the nations," Jer. 1:5; cf. Gal. 1:16).

28. Cf. Ezek. 2:1, 3: "stand upon your feet . . . I send you to the people of Israel."

29. The "dominion (ἐξουσία) of Satan" is the "dominion (ἐξουσία) of darkness" (Col. 1:13); he is chief over the "world rulers of this darkness" (Eph. 6:12). With the terms of Paul's call cf. especially Isa. 42:6-7, where the Servant is commissioned to be "a light to the nations, to open the eyes that are blind, to bring out the prisoners from the dungeon, from the prison those who sit in darkness." On Isa. 42:5-9 see C. R. North, *The Suffering Servant in Deutero-Isaiah* (Oxford, 1948), pp. 131-35.

30. The words "in every country, to Jews and Gentiles" render F. Blass's emendation (εἰς πᾶσάν τε χώραν Ἰουδαίοις καὶ τοῖς ἔθνεσιν) for (εἰς) πᾶσαν τε τὴν χώραν τῆς Ἰουδαίας καὶ τοῖς ἔθνεσιν (see n. 32 below).

31. ἀπήγγελλον, imperfect.

knew but one Master. Henceforth for him to receive a command from that one Master was to set about obeying it. So, after his conversion, he immediately proclaimed Jesus as the Son of God in Damascus (9:20), then in Jerusalem, during a short visit, to the Hellenistic Jews (9:29), and after that in many lands to Jews[32] and especially to Gentiles. In Acts, in distinction from his letters, Paul is a missionary to Jews and Gentiles alike, a "world apostle."[33] With his proclamation went the call to repent and turn to God,[34] and to perform deeds which were the natural fruit of true repentance. John the Baptist had called for such deeds on the part of his hearers, who declared their repentance by receiving baptism at his hands; it was incumbent on them to show the genuineness of this repentance by their subsequent way of life (Matt. 3:8 par. Luke 3:8). While Paul insists that it is "not because of works" but through faith that men and women receive the saving grace of God, he equally insists that those who have received this saving grace are God's "workmanship, created in Christ Jesus for good works, which God prepared beforehand, that we should walk in them" (Eph. 2:8-10).

f. Paul's arrest (26:21)

21 *"Because of this the Jews seized me while I was in the temple, and tried to kill me.*

21 Was it indeed "because of this," because of his unceasing missionary activity, that he was attacked in the temple? It was: the charge that he had profaned the temple by bringing a Gentile within forbidden bounds was only a pretext. The hostility of the Jews of proconsular Asia, who raised the hue and cry against him on that occasion, went back to the years of his ministry in Ephesus. What they objected to was not his announcing the fulfilment of what Moses and the prophets foretold; but the terms in which he announced it—his preaching a law-free gospel which in effect obliterated the religious barrier between Jews and Gentiles—were quite unacceptable. This unacceptable feature in his preaching is not mentioned in the present speech (although it may be implied): the reader of Acts is familiar with it (even more so the reader of Paul's letters), but it is unlikely that Agrippa would learn anything of it from what is said here.

---

32. Blass's emendation (quoted in n. 30 above) is attractive both because of the grammatical awkwardness of the traditional text, even with the (Byzantine?) addition of εἰς before πᾶσαν and especially without it, and because the statement that Paul evangelized "all the country of Judaea" is plainly at variance with the evidence of Luke's narrative (not to speak of the evidence of Paul's account in Gal. 1:17-24). The emendation was approved by Ramsay (*St. Paul the Traveller* [London, 141920], p. 382).

33. Cf. J. Jervell, "Paulus in der Apostelgeschichte und die Geschichte des Urchristentums," *NTS* 32 (1986), p. 380.

34. On repentance cf. 2:38; 3:19; 20:21; on turning to God cf. 3:19; 9:35; 11:21; 14:15; 15:19.

Festus had found it extremely difficult to determine why Paul had been arrested in the first place, and why his Jewish opponents were out for his blood; yet it was important that he should ascertain the reason, in order to include it in his report to Rome. He counted on Agrippa's help in this matter, and even if Agrippa did not grasp the fundamental point in dispute, he no doubt gathered enough to enable him to give Festus the desired help. Paul had at any rate made it clear that he preached the same message to Jews and Gentiles, and Agrippa, knowing the current climate of Jewish religion as he did, could draw his own conclusions.

g. Peroration (26:22-23)

22 "Having received help from God, then, I have continued to this day, bearing witness to both great and small, saying nothing except what Moses and the prophets said would happen—
23 that the Messiah must suffer, and that by being the first to rise from the dead[35] he would announce light both to our people and to the Gentiles."

22-23 In conclusion, Paul emphasized that the teaching which, by God's help, he had consistently given to all to whom he witnessed was thoroughly loyal to Israel's ancestral faith and in complete harmony with the divine revelation imparted through Moses and the prophets. Here we are probably to understand that he adduced one text after another from the Old Testament scriptures which found their fulfilment in the life, death, and triumph of Jesus. At an early stage in the course of Christian preaching these texts appear to have been grouped together under appropriate headings, which sometimes took the form of questions. Here Luke does not reproduce Paul's citations of such messianic "testimonies" *in extenso*, but indicates them briefly by quoting the interrogative captions under which they were grouped: "Must the Messiah suffer? Must he rise from the dead? Must he bring the light of salvation to the people of Israel and to the Gentile nations?"[36] (The "must" of these questions is the "must" of God's predetermined plan, made known before its fulfilment through his servants the prophets.)[37]

---

35. Gk. πρῶτος ἐξ ἀναστάσεως νεκρῶν (cf. Rom. 1:4, where ἐξ ἀναστάσεως νεκρῶν is used in reference to the resurrection of Christ; see n. 14 above). Cf. 1 Cor. 15:20, 23 ("Christ . . . the firstfruits").

36. The captions are here introduced by the interrogative εἰ ("if" as used in indirect questions). E. Nestle, mistakenly taking εἰ as conditional, looked for an apodosis, and found it in v. 8, "Why is it judged incredible among you?" This clause already has one "if" clause attached to it (εἰ ὁ θεὸς νεκροὺς ἐγείρει); Nestle provided it with two more (the "if" clauses of v. 23) by proposing the transposition of v. 8 to follow v. 22. Following him, James Moffatt renders the rearranged words: "Why should you consider it incredible that God raises the dead, that the Christ is capable of suffering, and that he should be the first to rise from the dead and bring the message of light to the People and to the Gentiles?"

37. Cf. J. R. Harris, *Testimonies*, I (Cambridge, 1916), pp. 19-20; *Testimonies*,

The announcing of light to the Jewish people and to the Gentiles is part of the ministry of the Isaianic Servant: "It is too light a thing," says God, "that you should be my servant to raise up the tribes of Jacob and to restore the preserved of Israel; I will give you as a light to the nations, that my salvation may reach to the end of the earth" (Isa. 49:6).[38] Paul and Barnabas at Pisidian Antioch claimed these words as setting out their own commission (13:47), as Simeon of Jerusalem had earlier echoed them when he greeted the infant Messiah (Luke 2:32).[39]

13. Interchange between Festus, Paul, and Agrippa (26:24-29)

24 *While Paul was making his defense in these terms, Festus spoke up loudly: "You are mad, Paul![40] It is all this learning that is turning you mad."*

25 *But Paul[41] replied, "I am not mad, Your Excellency; the words I speak declare the sober truth.[42]*

26 *The king knows all about this: indeed,[43] I speak to him freely. He is not unaware, I am convinced, of any of these things. This business did not take place in a corner.*

27 *Do you believe the prophets, King Agrippa? I know you do."*

28 *"In short," said Agrippa to Paul, "you are trying to make me act the Christian."[44]*

29 *"In short or at length," Paul replied, "I could pray that not only you but all who are listening to me today would become as I am, apart from these chains."*

24 Festus could endure it no longer. Paul was obviously a man of tremen-

---

II (Cambridge, 1920), p. 77; C. H. Dodd, *According to the Scriptures* (London, 1952), pp. 16-17; B. Lindars, *New Testament Apologetic* (London, 1961), p. 80; A. T. Hanson, *The Living Utterances of God* (London, 1983), p. 81. Justin (*Dialogue* 39.7) represents Trypho as saying "It has been sufficiently demonstrated that the necessity of Christ's suffering is proclaimed through the scriptures" (similarly 89.2).

38. See n. 29 above; cf. Isa. 60:1-3. It is because Isa. 60:3 ("nations shall come to your light") was recognized as fulfilled in the visit of the Magi (Matt. 2:1-12) that that incident has been traditionally called "the Epiphany of Christ to the Gentiles."

39. See pp. 266-67 with footnotes.

40. The Western text, preserved in lat[h], has the fuller reading: "You are mad, Paul, you are mad."

41. The Western and Byzantine texts omit "Paul" ("But he replied").

42. Lit., "I utter words of truth and soberness."

43. Cod. B omits "indeed" (καί).

44. Gk. ἐν ὀλίγῳ με πείθεις χριστιανὸν ποιῆσαι, lit., "In short, you are persuading me [με πείθεις, i.e., 'trying to persuade me,' present tense] to act the Christian." For this construction with ποιέω cf. 3 Kingdoms 20:7 LXX (MT 1 Kings 21:7), σὺ νῦν οὕτως ποιεῖς βασιλέα ἐπὶ Ἰσραήλ: "Is it thus that you act the king over Israel?" Failure to recognize this construction has led to several variant readings; thus Cod. A has πείθῃ for πείθεις ("you trust that you can make me a Christian"; cf. Hort's emendation πέποιθας for με πείθεις); the Byzantine text has γενέσθαι for ποιῆσαι (whence KJV "Almost thou persuadest me to be a Christian"). See also p. 228, n. 31·(on 11:26).

dous learning, but equally obviously his learning was driving him mad. Otherwise he could never talk so earnestly and at such length about things to which a sensible Roman could attach no meaning; and no man who retained his senses would have antagonized his whole nation for such insubstantial philosophizing. "You are mad, Paul," he exclaimed; "all this study is turning you crazy."

25-27 But what was sheer madness to the governor's way of thinking was the merest truth and sober good sense for Paul. So he assured Festus, and appealed for confirmation to Agrippa. The events which fulfilled the ancient promises were well known and public: this was no hole-and-corner esoteric mystery, whose initiates were pledged to secrecy. The ministry and death of Jesus were matters of common knowledge; his resurrection was amply attested; the gospel had been openly proclaimed in his name. Anyone who believed the prophets and compared their predictions with the historical facts concerning Jesus of Nazareth must acknowledge the truth of Christianity. Agrippa, who might be expected to believe the prophets, could supply corroborating testimony and tell Festus that Paul's arguments were sane and well founded, that the gospel which he preached contained "nothing except what Moses and the prophets said would happen."

28 The king was embarrassed by Paul's appeal. He may have listened to him with interest enough, but Paul obviously hoped that his apparent interest would grow into something more. The logic of the argument was so plain to Paul that he could scarcely imagine that such an expert in the Jewish religion would fail to accept the obvious conclusion. But Agrippa was not disposed even to appear to lend support to Paul's case. What would Festus think if he expressed—or even seemed to express—agreement with a man whose head had been turned by his learning? Therefore he could not admit that he did believe the prophets; on the other hand, he could not say that he did not believe them, for then his influence with the Jews and his standing with their religious leaders would be gone. So he turned Paul's appeal aside with a smile: "In short," he said, "you are trying to make me play the Christian"—for that seems to be the meaning of his words. He was not going to be maneuvered into anything like that!

29 "In short or at length," said Paul, "I could pray that not only Your Majesty, but all who are here today listening to me, were Christians like myself—apart from these chains" (indicating his shackled wrist with a gesture).

14. Agreement on Paul's Innocence (26:30-32)

30 *Then[45] the king, the governor, Bernice, and their assessors rose up.*
31 *When they had withdrawn, they discussed him one with another.*

45. The Western text adds "when he had said this."

> *"This man,"* they said, *"does nothing that deserves either death or imprisonment."*
> 32 *"No,"* said Agrippa to Festus; *"he might have been set at liberty if he had not appealed to Caesar."* [46]

30-32 However, enough had been heard for the immediate purpose. The audience was over, and the governor, Agrippa, and Bernice, with their adjutants and entourages, discussed what Paul had said. One thing at least was clear: even if Paul was as mad as Festus thought, he had done nothing to incur a major legal penalty. In the eyes of Roman law, indeed, he was completely innocent and, as the king said, he might have been discharged there and then if he had not appealed to Caesar. His appeal, however, had taken the decision out of the governor's hands, and he had to be sent to Rome. Agrippa presumably had no difficulty in suggesting to Festus the lines along which he should frame his report.

The present unanimous agreement on Paul's innocence is a further contribution to Luke's general apologetic motive. But it has been argued that the first readers of Acts would detect a sinister note in Agrippa's last words: "if he had not appealed to Caesar." They would understand, the argument goes, that by appealing to Caesar Paul had forfeited any prospect of ever being set free, for they would be familiar with the record of that particular Caesar to whom he had appealed—Nero.[47] This is reading too much into the text. Nero is not mentioned by name, and after a few decades the average reader might not immediately realize that Nero was emperor when Paul lodged his appeal. At the time, of course, Agrippa's words could have had no sinister implication: the *quinquennium Neronis* (the first five years of Nero's principate which, as has been said above, were later remembered as a miniature golden age) had not yet run its course.[48] What Agrippa meant was

---

46. A few witnesses (97 *pc* lat[h w] syr[pesh hcl.mg]), possibly representing the Western text, add "and so the governor decided to send him to Caesar" (ineptly, because it was no longer within the governor's discretion to make such a decision; he was bound to send him as soon as Paul uttered his appeal).

47. See J. V. Bartlet, "Two New Testament Problems: 1. St. Paul's Fate at Rome," *Exp.* 8,5 (1913), pp. 465-66.

48. The imperial policy toward Christians apparently began to be hostile about A.D. 62. This year marked a turning point in Nero's career; it was the year of Burrus's death and his replacement as prefect of the praetorian guard by Tigellinus and Faenius Rufus (Tigellinus being the more powerful of the two), the year of Seneca's retirement, and of Nero's divorce of Octavia and marriage with Poppaea. Poppaea was a warm friend of the Jews; indeed, Josephus (*Ant.* 20.195) calls her a "God-fearer" (θεοσεβής), whatever he may mean by that. Her influence may well have been inimical to Christianity. About this time, too, it must have become increasingly clear to the Roman authorities that Christianity was not simply a movement within Judaism, entitled to share the recognition which Jewish congregations enjoyed as *collegia licita*. It might therefore at any time become the object of suppression by the imperial police, and an opportunity for such measures arose at Rome in the aftermath of the great fire of A.D. 64. But the situation at the

that, by making his appeal, Paul had put himself into a new position in relation to Roman law,[49] and the course prescribed by the law for citizens in that position—appellants to the emperor—must now be followed. Paul must be sent to Rome, to have his appeal heard in the supreme court.[50]

---

time of Paul's appeal was still largely what it had been when Gallio gave his favorable verdict at Corinth (18:12-17) seven or eight years before.

49. The pluperfect tense (ἐπεκέκλητο, "had appealed," v. 32) points not merely to Paul's action in appealing some days before but to his present legal status as a result of that appeal.

50. See C. J. A. Hickling, "The Portrait of Paul in Acts 26," in *Les Actes des Apôtres*, ed. J. Kremer, BETL 48 (Leuven, 1979), pp. 499-503.

ACTS 27

E. PAUL'S VOYAGE AND SHIPWRECK (27:1-44)

Luke's narrative of the voyage and shipwreck of Paul on his way to Italy is a small classic in its own right, as graphic a piece of descriptive writing as anything in the Bible. It has long been acknowledged as "one of the most instructive documents for the knowledge of ancient seamanship."[1] It bears clear evidence of being the account of an eyewitness, who viewed the sea through Greek eyes and, while not himself a seaman versed in the technical vocabulary of sailing, described his experiences in his own vigorous language. For the description of a storm and wreck at sea he could draw on a well-established literary tradition—not that this in any way depreciates the factual worth of his narrative. From Homer's *Odyssey* onward, ancient accounts of a Mediterranean voyage frequently included a storm or shipwreck. Homer, in fact, set the fashion in which such accounts continue to be related for many centuries. This chapter itself presents one or two unmistakable Homeric reminiscences.[2] Again, the Old Testament contains one famous narrative of the same kind, the story of Jonah's Mediterranean voyage and the storm into which he and his shipmates ran; Luke appears to have drawn on this narrative also.[3]

Human life has often been compared to a voyage across a stormy sea. It is not surprising, therefore, that many readers and expositors have found an allegory of the soul's experience in Acts 27. Some have even detected in it a figurative prediction of the course of church history. This particular form of allegorization becomes specially interesting at the end of the story, when the ship is broken up and the passengers and crew have to make their way ashore as best they can. (The allegorist's own ecclesiastical bias usually appears when he comes to identify those who swam ashore and those who made do with planks or fragments of the ship.) Those who care for this sort

---

1. H. J. Holtzmann, *Handcommentar zum Neuen Testament* (Freiburg im Breisgau, 1889), p. 421.

2. Especially in v. 41; see n. 90 below.

3. Compare vv. 18-19 with Jonah 1:5. See E. S. Krantz, *Des Schiffes Weg mitten im Meer: Beiträge zur Erforschung der nautischen Terminologie des Alten Testaments* (Lund, 1982).

of exposition may work the correspondences out for themselves, but let them beware of supposing that Luke had any such interpretation in mind when he penned his narrative.

That does not mean that the narrative is devoid of moral and spiritual lessons. They are here in abundance for those who have eyes to see. In particular, much may be learned from Luke's portrayal of Paul's character and behavior in circumstances in which the real man is most likely to be revealed. He portrays Paul in many roles throughout Acts, but here he shows him standing out as the practical man in a critical emergency—keeping his head when all about him are losing theirs. Not once or twice the world has had to thank the great saints and mystics for providing timely help in moments of crisis when realistic, practical men of affairs were unable to supply it.

Luke's devoting so much of his narrative to the details of those few weeks at sea is best explained by his desire to emphasize the divine determination that Paul's purpose of seeing Rome must be fulfilled, despite all the factors that rendered his ever getting there unlikely in the extreme.[4] On the open sea Paul shares the peril of his companions, who gave up all hope of ever reaching safety; toward the end of the voyage he is in danger from the soldiers, who plan to kill the prisoners in case any of them should escape; when they land on Malta, his life seems to be threatened by a venomous snake. But it is the will of God that Paul shall preach the gospel at the heart of the empire, and his will is not to be frustrated. The description of the storm and shipwreck is integral to the story of Paul's missionary career. It betrays a failure to grasp Luke's intention when Acts 27 is taken to be basically a popular account of a shipwreck, introduced to add the spice of adventure to the record, and connected with the rest of Acts by the insertion of detachable episodes in which Paul figures.[5] (As for their being "detachable," it has been wisely observed that Paul was but a passenger on board, "and passengers are by definition detachable."[6])

An indispensable aid to the study of this chapter is *The Voyage and Shipwreck of St. Paul*, by James Smith.[7] Smith, an experienced yachtsman and a man of no mean classical scholarship, made a careful study of Luke's narrative in relation to the route which it maps out—a part of the Mediterra-

4. See H. Chadwick, "The Circle and the Ellipse: Rival Concepts of Authority in the Early Church," *History and Thought of the Early Church* (London, 1982), pp. 3-17, especially p. 16.

5. See M. Dibelius, *Studies in the Acts of the Apostles*, E.T. (London, 1956), p. 107; H. Conzelmann, *Die Apostelgeschichte* (Tübingen, 1963), pp. 140-47; E. Haenchen, "Acta 27," in *Zeit und Geschichte: Dankesgabe an R. Bultmann*, ed. E. Dinkler (Tübingen, 1964), pp. 235-54.

6. R. P. C. Hanson, "The Journey of Paul and the Journey of Nikias: An Experiment in Comparative Historiography," *Studies in Christian Antiquity* (Edinburgh, 1985), pp. 22-26.

7. J. Smith, *The Voyage and Shipwreck of St. Paul* (London, 1848, ⁴1880).

nean with which he himself was acquainted—and formed the most favorable estimate of the accuracy of Luke's account of each stage of the voyage. For the seafaring technicalities of this chapter we shall lean heavily on Smith's work: although it is more than a century since Smith produced the last edition of it, it remains unsurpassed, and indeed unequalled for its purpose.[8]

1. Caesarea to Myra (27:1-5)

1 *Since it had been decided that we were to set sail for Italy, they delivered Paul and some other prisoners into the custody of a centurion named Julius,[9] who belonged to the Augustan Cohort.*

2 *We embarked on a ship of Adramyttium, which was about to sail to the places along the coast of (proconsular) Asia, and so we put out to sea. We were accompanied by Aristarchus,[10] a Macedonian from Thessalonica.*

3 *The next day we put in at Sidon. Julius treated Paul kindly, and gave him leave to go to his friends there and be cared for.*

4 *From there we put out to sea and sailed under the lee of Cyprus, because the winds were contrary;*

5 *then we sailed across the open sea off Cilicia and Pamphylia[11] and put in at Myra[12] in Lycia.*

1 The "we" narrative is now resumed, after being broken off at 21:18. We have no information about Luke's movements during the two intervening years, but it would be safe to think of him as spending much of the time in or around Caesarea (where Paul was kept in custody) and making good use of his opportunities of gathering information about the early days of the Christian movement.

Once Paul had appealed to Caesar, the governor was bound to send him to Rome; the first opportunity was therefore seized to have him taken

8. See also A. Breusing, *Die Nautik der Alten* (Bremen, 1886); H. Balmer, *Die Romfahrt des Apostels Paulus* (Bern/Münchenbuchsee, 1905); A. Köster, *Das antike Seewesen* (Berlin, 1923); W. Stammler, *Apostelgeschichte 27 in nautischer Beleuchtung* (Berlin, 1931); L. Casson, *The Ancient Mariners* (London, 1959); *Ships and Seamanship in the Ancient World* (Princeton, NJ, 1971); V. K. Robbins, "By Land and by Sea: The We-Passages and Ancient Sea Voyages," in *Perspectives on Luke-Acts*, ed. C. H. Talbert (Edinburgh, 1978), with critique by C. J. Hemer, "First Person Narrative in Acts 27-28," *TynB* 36 (1985), pp. 79-109; C. K. Barrett, "Paul Shipwrecked," in *Scripture: Meaning and Method*, ed. B. P. Thompson (Hull, 1987), pp. 51-64.

9. The Western text goes on from "and so the governor decided to send him up to Caesar" (26:32b) with the paraphrase: "And the next day he called a certain centurion named Julius and handed Paul over to him, with other prisoners also."

10. The Western text adds "and Secundus" (from 20:4).

11. The Western text adds "in fifteen days."

12. Cod. B gives this place-name a new etymology by spelling it Μύρρα ("myrrh") instead of Μύρα. Cod. 69 replaces this with "Smyrna" (σμύρνη is a dialectal variant of μύρρα). The still more aberrant reading "Lystra" is found in P[74] ℵ with the Latin and Bohairic (Coptic) versions.

there under escort. The centurion Julius,[13] into whose custody he was delivered, belonged (we are told) to the Augustan Cohort. (The term "Augustan," i.e., "His Imperial Majesty's," was a title of honor bestowed on several cohorts of auxiliary troops.)[14] The precise status of Julius is difficult to determine: from the authority which he assumed when once (from Myra onward) he found himself on board a ship of the Alexandrian grain fleet, it might be inferred that he was a *frumentarius,* an officer charged with supervising the transport of grain *(frumentum)* to Rome. At any rate, Paul was entrusted to him because he was bound for Rome, with a body of soldiers under his command. It is not said who the other prisoners were whom they had in charge; in any case, a Roman citizen who had appealed to the emperor would receive special consideration.

2   The port of embarkation is not specified; probably it was Caesarea. Had it been any other (such as Ptolemais), Luke would doubtless have mentioned it, in accordance with his usual practice. The ship in which they embarked belonged to Adramyttium (modern Edremit), a seaport of Mysia in northwest Asia Minor, opposite the island of Lesbos. It was a coasting vessel, which was to call at various ports of the province of Asia; at one of these Julius knew he would find a ship, preferably a grain ship,[15] bound for Italy.[16] Aristarchus[17] is not expressly named later in this narrative; it is possible, therefore, that he was traveling home to Thessalonica and did not join the second ship which took the party in the direction of Italy. On the other hand, if Colossians and Philemon are to be dated in the course of Paul's Roman captivity, he was in Paul's company when those letters were written (Col. 4:10; Philem. 24), so he may have gone all the way with Paul on this occasion; in that case he is no doubt included in Luke's "we" throughout the narrative. It is impossible to be sure. Ramsay argued that Luke and Aristarchus "must have gone" as Paul's slaves, "not merely performing the duties of slaves . . . but actually passing as slaves. In this way not merely had Paul faithful friends always beside him; his importance in the eyes of the centurion was much enhanced, and that was of great importance. The narrative clearly implies that Paul enjoyed much respect during this voyage, such as a penniless traveller without a servant to attend on him would never

13. His *nomen gentile* suggests that he or rather his ancestor acquired the citizenship under Julius Caesar or Augustus.

14. We find inscriptional references to the *Cohors Augusta I* in Syria under Augustus (*ILS* 2683), to the σπεῖρα Αὐγούστη in the same area some decades later (*OGIS* 421); cf. also the *Cohors III Augusta* at Rome (*CIL* VI.3508).

15. In the event, the "ship of Alexandria" which he found at Myra was indeed a grain ship (see p. 479, on v. 6), and if he was a *frumentarius,* this would account for the authority which he exercised on board (cf. v. 11).

16. But if they arrived late and found that the period of sailing was over for the winter, they would no doubt take the land route to Rome along the Egnatian Way from the Aegean to the Adriatic (see p. 309, on 16:11).

17. See 19:29.

receive either in the first century or the nineteenth."[18] While Ramsay's argument merits the respect due to his great knowledge of social history in the Roman Empire of the first century A.D., it is not the *prima facie* inference which one would draw from the narrative, and is really improbable. Aristarchus may have gone as a fare-paying passenger; Luke (if a reader's imagination may be indulged) perhaps signed on as ship's doctor.

3 The day after they set sail, they put in at Sidon, the ancient Phoenician metropolis, which was about 69 miles north of Caesarea. It had a double harbor.[19]

Here Paul received the first of several recorded kindnesses at the hand of Julius. (It is remarkable how uniformly centurions receive a favorable portrayal in the New Testament.)[20] In Sidon there was a Christian community, founded probably during the persecution and dispersion that followed the death of Stephen (11:19). Paul received permission to go ashore and visit members of this community (for so we should certainly understand "his friends"[21]) and enjoy all the attention that their Christian love could suggest while the ship was in harbor. It may be assumed that a soldier was detailed to accompany him.

4 Putting out to sea again for Sidon, they sailed east and north of Cyprus, that is to say, on the lee side of the island, as the prevailing winds in the Levant are westerly throughout the summer months.[22] A ship doing the reverse journey, from southwest Asia Minor to Syria, fared directly over the sea, passing west of Cyprus. Luke no doubt remembered doing this when he sailed with Paul and his companions from Patara to Tyre two years previously (21:1-3), and noticed the different course now taken.

5 A stretch of open sea remained to be crossed—the sea between Cyprus and the south coast of Asia Minor. They reached the coast of Asia Minor at a point well to the east, and then the ship worked slowly toward the west, helped by local land breezes and by a steady westward current which runs along the coast. "The Adramyttian ship crept on from point to point up the coast, taking advantage of every opportunity to make a few miles, and lying at anchor in the shelter of the winding coast, when the westerly wind made progress impossible."[23] In this way they reached Myra, or rather its

18. W. M. Ramsay, *St. Paul the Traveller* (London, [14]1920), p. 316.
19. Cf. Achilles Tatius, *Leucippe and Cleitophon* 1.1. Lucian tells how a ship which set out from Alexandria for Italy was forced by a storm to put in at Sidon (*Ship* 7).
20. Cf. p. 202 with n. 4 (on 10:1).
21. A. von Harnack suggested that πρὸς τοὺς φίλους should be translated "to the Friends"; he regarded this as possibly one of the current designations by which Christians referred to one another (*The Mission and Expansion of Christianity*, E.T., I [London, [2]1908], pp. 419-21). Cf. 3 John 15.
22. J. Smith, *Voyage*, p. 68.
23. W. M. Ramsay, *St. Paul the Traveller*, p. 317.

port Andriakē (about 3¹/₂ miles west by southwest of Myra itself).²⁴ Andriakē was one of the chief ports of the imperial grain service.²⁵ The site of ancient Myra, a city of Lycia, is now known as Kocademre or Old Demre (marked by remains of a theater, aqueduct, and rock tombs); modern Demre stands a mile to the south.²⁶

2. They Transship at Myra and Sail to Crete (27:6-8)

6 *There the centurion found a ship of Alexandria which was sailing to Italy, so he put us on board it.*

7 *We sailed slowly for many days and arrived with difficulty off Cnidus; then, because the wind prevented us (from putting in there), we sailed under the lee of Crete off Salmone.*

8 *Coasting along Crete with difficulty, we came to a place called Fair Havens, near which was the city of Lasaea.*

6 At Myra the first part of the journey came to an end. When the ship of Adramyttium put in at the port of Andriakē, there was a vessel there belonging to the grain fleet that plied between Egypt and Rome; it had set out from Alexandria and was on its way to Italy. Egypt was the chief granary of Rome, and the regular trade in grain between Alexandria and Puteoli or Ostia was of the highest importance; the political stability of Rome depended on it. The service of ships devoted to this trade was organized as a department of state.²⁷ The corporation of owners of these ships received special recognition from the Roman state, for they were in practice its agents and concessionaires. That the "ship of Alexandria" which was in harbor at Myra when the centurion and his party arrived there belonged to this fleet is confirmed later in the narrative, when the ship's cargo of wheat had to be jettisoned (v. 38)—something to be done only in the last extremity. "With the westerly winds which prevail in those seas," says James Smith, "ships, particularly those of the ancients, unprovided with a compass and ill calculated to work to windward, would naturally stand to the north till they made the land of Asia Minor, which is peculiarly favourable for navigation by such vessels, because the coast is bold and safe, and the elevation of the mountains makes it visible at a great distance; it abounds in harbours, and the sinuosities of its shores and the westerly current would enable them, if the

24. Cf. 21:1, where the Western text makes Myra the port of transshipment on Paul's last voyage to Judaea.

25. See C. J. Hemer, "First Person Narrative," pp. 94-95, for evidence of facilities for the storage of grain at Andriakē.

26. See Strabo, *Geography* 13.3.7; also G. E. Bean, *Lycian Turkey: An Archaeological Guide* (London, 1978), pp. 120-30.

27. See M. Rostovtzeff, *The Social and Economic History of the Roman Empire*, II (Oxford, ²1957), p. 708.

wind was at all off the land, to work to windward, at least as far as Cnidus, where these advantages ceased. Myra lies due north from Alexandria, and its bay is well calculated to shelter a windbound ship."[28] Here the centurion no doubt knew he would find a vessel of the grain fleet, on which he had official duties to perform.

7　Having embarked on this vessel, then, they found the going from Myra slow and difficult, because of the strong northwest wind that was blowing.[29] After several days they reached Cnidus, a port on the Carian promontory of Triopium, which was frequented by merchant ships from Egypt.[30] Here they had a choice of two alternatives. If they could put into port at Cnidus, they could wait there for a fair wind; there was ample accommodation at Cnidus, for it had two harbors, the eastern one being particularly large. When a fair wind came, they might then sail due west for the island of Cythera. But if they preferred to continue the voyage (which would probably be the shipowner's choice), their only course was to run for the eastern extremity of Crete (Cape Salmone) and, after rounding it, sail under the lee of that island (along its south coast). This is what they did; in fact, the wording here suggests that their ship was unable to get into port at Cnidus. From the fact that they succeeded in fetching Cape Salmone, Smith deduces that the wind must have been a northwester, which in any case is "precisely the wind which might have been expected in those seas towards the end of summer."[31]

8　Even coasting along the south of Crete was difficult, with the wind blowing from the northwest, but at last they came to the small bay still marked on maps of Crete as Fair Havens (*Kaloi Limenes,* which may be a revival of the ancient name rather than a survival of it). Fair Havens was their first convenient shelter after they rounded Cape Salmone, so they put in here and waited for the wind to change. Two leagues farther west lies Cape Matala, and beyond Cape Matala the south coast of Crete trends suddenly to the north, and would no longer provide effective protection against a northwest wind. In the neighborhood of Fair Havens, Luke points out, lay the city of Lasaea; if they had decided not to proceed beyond Fair Havens, they could have found adequate winter quarters in that city.[32]

---

28. Smith, *Voyage,* pp. 72-73.
29. Smith, *Voyage,* pp. 75-76.
30. Thucydides, *History* 8.35.
31. Smith, *Voyage,* p. 76.
32. Lasaea is variously spelled in our textual witnesses and in other literature. C. J. Hemer ("First Person Narrative," p. 95) quotes from A. Plassart, "Les inscriptions de Delphes. La liste des théorodoques," *BCH* 45 (1921), p. 61, n. 3 (col. 4, line 9), ἐν Λασσοίᾳ (from a list of Cretan cities arranged clockwise in the angle southwest from Gortyna). Lasaea has been (provisionally) identified with Pliny's Lasos or Alos (*Nat. Hist.* 4.59) and also with ruins a little way east of Fair Havens.

3. Paul's Advice Rejected (27:9-12)

9 *It had taken them a long time to get thus far, and sailing was now dangerous—even the Fast was now past. So Paul offered them his advice.*

10 *"Gentlemen," he said, "I see that this voyage is going to be attended by damage and great loss, not only to the cargo and the ship but also to our lives."*

11 *But the centurion paid more heed to the steersman and the shipowner than to what Paul said.*

12 *Since the harbor was unsuitable for spending the winter in, the majority advised that we should put out to sea from there in hope of making Phoenix and wintering there. Phoenix is a harbor of Crete looking southwest and northwest.*

9 The delay that had been occasioned already by the adverse wind began to make them anxious. As they waited for a change of wind at Fair Havens, it soon became clear that they could not complete the voyage to Italy before the onset of winter. The dangerous season for sailing began about September 14 and lasted until November 11; after the latter date all navigation on the open sea came to an end until winter was over.[33] They were now well into the dangerous season; as Luke notes, even the Fast had now gone by. The Fast is the day of atonement *(Yôm Kippûr),* which falls on Tishri 10. Luke's remark has point only if it fell rather late in the solar calendar that year. In A.D. 59 it fell on October 5, but in all the neighboring years from 57 to 62 it fell earlier.[34] A late date for the day of atonement is required also by the time notes of the subsequent journey to Italy. When they set sail from Fair Havens, fifty or sixty miles brought them under the lee of Cauda (v. 16); on the fourteenth night from Cauda they drew near the coast of Malta (v. 27), and the next day (v. 39) they landed on that island, where they spent three months (28:11). The seas were closed to sailing until the beginning of February at the earliest;[35] the three months spent in Malta must therefore have corresponded roughly to November, December, and January, so they must have left Fair Havens not much before mid-October.[36] The solar date of the day of atonement in A.D. 59 thus accords well with Luke's implication that the Fast took place while they waited at Fair Havens.

33. Vegetius, *On Military Affairs* 4.39.
34. Cf. W. P. Workman, "A New Date-Indication in Acts," *ExT* 11 (1899-1900), pp. 316-19.
35. Vegetius, *loc. cit.*
36. "We might be disposed to infer that the Feast of Tabernacles, Oct. 10, fell after they left Fair Havens, otherwise Luke would have mentioned it rather than the Fast, as making the danger more apparent" (Ramsay, *St. Paul the Traveller*, p. 322).

10   Paul, who was no stranger to storm at sea and shipwreck,[37] saw
that any plan to sail on from Fair Havens was attended by grave risk, so he
gave the authorities his advice—it was given in the first instance, probably,
to the centurion, with whom he had established a good relationship. No
doubt, as is implied by verses 11 and 12, a ship's council was held, but it is
unnecessary to suppose, with Ramsay, that Paul, as an experienced traveler,
was invited to attend it.[38] Paul's advice, of which he reminds the others in
verse 21, was that they should stay at Fair Havens for the winter. His
warning that any other course would involve damage to life and limb as well
as the loss of cargo and ship, is contradicted by his own later assurance to
them that not a life would be lost, though cargo and ship would perish
(v. 22). But on that later occasion he was to speak on the strength of a
supernatural revelation; here he expresses his personal, well-founded,
opinion.

11   The helmsman[39] and shipowner,[40] however, thought that there
was a chance of reaching a more commodious port farther west along the
south coast of Crete, and the centurion, not unnaturally, accepted their view
rather than Paul's. (The narrator seems to find the centurion's preference
surprising, not to say reprehensible; this is one of the touches in which A. D.
Nock and others have recognized "an authentic transcript of the recollections
of an eyewitness, with the confusion and coloring which so easily attach
themselves to recollections.")[41] A merchant-shipowner normally acted as
captain of his own ship. The owner of this particular ship would be a
contractor for the state transport of grain. But the final decision was left to
the centurion, who (especially if he belonged to the corps of *frumentarii*)
represented the Roman state. He ruled that the advice of the experts should
be followed. Smith observes "that Fair Havens is so well protected by
islands, that though not equal to Lutro [Loutron, a port some 40 miles farther
west along the coast], it must be a very fair winter harbour; and that considering the suddenness, the frequency, and the violence with which gales of
northerly wind spring up, and the certainty that, if such a gale sprang up in
the passage from Fair Havens to Lutro, the ship must be driven off to sea, the

37. Cf. 2 Cor. 11:25b.
38. Ramsay, *St. Paul the Traveller*, pp. 322-25.
39. Gk. κυβερνήτης. According to Plutarch (*Precepts of Statecraft* 807B), "the
helmsman (κυβερνήτης) chooses the sailors and the shipowner (ναύκληρος) chooses
the helmsman."
40. Gk. ναύκληρος (Latinized as *nauicularius*). Ramsay (*St. Paul the Traveller*, p. 324, n. 2) quotes from *IG* XIV.918 οἱ ναύκληροι τοῦ πορευτικοῦ Ἀλεξαν-
δρείνου στόλου ("the shipowners of the Alexandrian fleet"). Cf. M. Rostovtzeff, *Social
and Economic History*, II, p. 607.
41. A. D. Nock, *Essays on Religion and the Ancient World*, II (Oxford, 1972),
p. 823.

prudence of the advice given by St. Paul may probably be supported even on nautical grounds."[42]

12 The view of the steersman and shipowner, and of the majority of the crew, was that Fair Havens was not a convenient harbor to spend the winter in. It is, as Smith says, protected by small islands, but it labors under the disadvantage of standing open to nearly half the compass. It was therefore decided to set sail from there as soon as the wind changed in their favor, in the hope of reaching the more commodious harbor of Phoenix.

Phoenix is described as a Cretan port facing southwest and northwest. The name is preserved to this day in Phineka Bay, on the west side of Cape Mouros, 34 miles west of Cape Matala and 33 miles east of the western end of the south coast of Crete. Before a seismic upheaval of the sixth century A.D., which raised the coast level here by tilting the island from west to east, this bay had two inlets, one facing southwest and one northwest, exactly as Luke says.[43]

On the east side of Cape Mouros is the harbor of Loutron, which Smith (using the local pronunciation Lutro) preferred to identify with Luke's Phoenix; he was authoritatively informed that this is "the only secure harbour in all winds on the south coast of Crete."[44] But this was not necessarily so in the first century. Besides, Loutron faces the easterly winds, not the southwest and northwest. Smith, however, argues that the Greek text means that the harbor looks in the direction toward which the southwest and northwest winds blow—that is, toward the northeast and southeast (and this thinking underlies the ARV rendering, "looking north-east and south-east").[45] But this argument cannot be sustained. The only sense that the Greek words can bear is that the harbor in question faced southwest and northwest, and Phineka Bay fits the description admirably. Its two sheltered inlets (as they then were) are still marked by raised beaches and the absence of traces of ancient occupation.[46]

---

42. Smith, *Voyage*, p. 85, n. 2.

43. See R. M. Ogilvie, "Phoenix," *JTS* n.s. 9 (1958), pp. 308-14.

44. Smith, *Voyage*, p. 91, n. 1.

45. ARV margin gives as the literal rendering "down the south-west wind and down the north-west wind," but this is a mistranslation in such a context of the preposition κατά in κατὰ λίβα καὶ κατὰ χῶρον. C. J. Hemer ("First Person Narrative," pp. 95-96) quotes, from *IGRR* I.177, the wind directions on a twelve-point scheme, with the names in Greek and Latin: Ἰάπυξ/*Chorus* (30 degrees north of west) and Λίψ/*Africus* (30 degrees south of west). In this inscription Lat. *Chorus*, normally spelled *Caurus*, is aspirated just as it is here in its Greek transliteration χῶρος. The term λίψ is explained (at least by a popular etymology) as meaning "Libyan."

46. Ogilvie, *art. cit.* For Loutron and Phoenix today see Xan Fielding, *The Stronghold* (London, 1955), pp. 215-24, 262-65.

4. They Are Caught by the Wind Euraquilo (27:13-20)

13 *When a gentle south wind sprang up, they thought they had attained their purpose, so they weighed anchor and continued to coast along the shore of Crete, keeping close in to the land.*

14 *But not long after, a violent wind called Euraquilo[47] beat down from the land.*

15 *The ship was caught by it and could not head up to it, so we gave way to it and drifted along.[48]*

16 *When we ran under the lee of a small island called Cauda,[49] we succeeded, with difficulty, in securing the dinghy.*

17 *Taking it on board, they used cables[50] to undergird the ship; then, fearing that they might be cast up on the (greater) Syrtis, they dropped a floating anchor[51] and continued to drift.*

18 *As we were making very heavy weather, they began the next day to jettison the cargo,*

19 *and on the third day they threw the spare gear overboard with their own hands.[52]*

20 *When neither sun nor stars could be seen for many days, and the storm which raged upon us was no ordinary one, we began to lose all hope of ever coming safely through it.[53]*

13 Soon after it was decided to try to make Phoenix, there came the change of wind for which they had been waiting. A gentle south wind sprang up, which promised to bring them to Phoenix with little difficulty. So they set out from Fair Havens and coasted along toward the west, hugging the shore. When once they rounded Cape Matala, a few hours would take them to their desired haven, with this favoring wind to waft them across the mouth of the wide Gulf of Messara.

14 Without warning, however, the wind changed again: "the sudden change from a south wind to a violent northerly wind is a common occurrence in these seas."[54] A furious northeaster sprang up and rushed down on them from Mount Ida, in the center of the island—a typhonic

---

47. The Byzantine text has the variant "Euroclydon."

48. There is an expanded Western reading: "We gave way to the wind that was blowing and shortened sail (συστείλαντες τὰ ἱστία) and, as happens in such cases, scudded before it."

49. Many manuscripts and versions have the spelling Clauda (found also in several ancient authors).

50. Gk. βοηθεῖαι, "helps." See p. 485 with n. 59 below.

51. Gk. χαλάσαντες τὸ σκεῦος (σκεῦος being a word of indeterminate meaning—"instrument," "object," "thing"—as in 10:11).

52. The Byzantine text reads "we threw . . . with our own hands"; the Western text adds "into the sea."

53. Lit., "all hope of our coming safely through was henceforth being taken away" (λοιπὸν περιῃρεῖτο ἐλπὶς πᾶσα τοῦ σῴζεσθαι ἡμᾶς).

54. Smith, *Voyage*, p. 102.

wind,[55] says Luke, referring to the whirling motion of the clouds and sea caused by the meeting of contrary currents of air. The sailors recognized this wind as an old enemy, and had a name for it—Euraquilo.[56] (Today in Mediterranean lands it is known as the *grigal* or *gregale*.)

15-16   The ship was caught up in the gale and, being unable to head up to it, scudded before it. Any chance of making Phoenix was now out of the question. Twenty-three miles or so to leeward lies the small island of Cauda or Clauda (modern Gavdhos, Italian Gozzo),[57] under the lee of which they soon ran. They made speedy and timely use of the brief opportunity of shelter which it afforded. First of all they hauled the dinghy on board. The dinghy was normally towed astern, but was taken aboard in bad weather. On this occasion there had been no time to do so, so suddenly did Euraquilo burst upon them. By this time it must have been full of water, and this made it all the more difficult to secure it. "We succeeded, with difficulty, in securing the dinghy," says Luke, using the first person plural; there were certain jobs which only trained members of the crew could carry out, but any landlubber could haul on a rope, and able-bodied passengers were pressed into service. "With difficulty," says Luke, probably remembering his blisters![58]

17   The next thing to do was to undergird the ship, passing cables around it transversely underneath in order to hold the timbers together. The word which Luke uses for these cables means literally "helps"; it appears in other Greek authors in a nautical context such as this.[59] The typhoon is described by Pliny the elder as "the chief plague of sailors, breaking up not

---

55. Gk. ἄνεμος τυφωνικός. It may have had the effect of a whirlwind or cyclone when it first struck them, but thereafter it blew steadily in one direction. See also p. 486 with n. 60.

56. Euraquilo is a hybrid, from Gk. Εὖρος ("east wind") and Lat. *Aquilo* ("north wind"). It appears (with the spelling *Euroaquilo*) in Latin on a twelve-point wind-rose incised on a pavement at Thugga in the province of Africa, where (beginning from the north and reading clockwise) we find *septentrio aquilo euroaquilo [uo]lturnus eurus* . . . (*CIL* VIII.26652). See C. J. Hemer, "Euraquilo and Melita," *JTS* n.s. 26 (1975), pp. 100-111 (especially p. 103). In this article Hemer answers A. Acworth, "Where was St. Paul Shipwrecked? A Re-examination of the Evidence," *JTS* n.s. 24 (1973), pp. 190-93, where the reading "Euroclydon" is preferred and taken to mean a southeast wind. But a southeast wind would not have driven the ship under the lee of Cauda.

57. In the vicinity of this island the naval engagement usually called the Battle of Cape Matapan was fought on March 28, 1941. There is, according to Smith, an anchorage at Cauda, but it lies on the side of the island open to Euraquilo, and therefore could have given no protection to the ship (*Voyage*, p. 113, n. 1).

58. Lake and Cadbury (*Beginnings* I.4, p. 332) suggest that the foremast, which sloped forward, may have been used as a derrick.

59. Cf. Aristotle, *Rhetoric* 2.5.18; Philo, *On Joseph* 33. In view of such attestation, it is unnecessary to emend βοηθείαις to βοείαις ("with ropes of ox-hide"), with S. A. Naber, "Nautica," *Mnemosyne* n.s. 23 (1895), pp. 267-69. A more technical Greek word for these cables is ὑποζώματα, used in this sense ("undergirders") in Plato (*Republic* 10.616C; *Laws* 12.945C), Callixenus, Herodotus Medicus, and inscriptions.

only the spars but the hull itself."[60] As a safety measure, ancient vessels were provided with cables ready fitted for bracing the hulls to enable them to resist the destructive force of such winds. The undergirding operation is best illustrated by an Egyptian drawing of an expedition of Queen Hatshepsut to the land of Punt (Somalia?) in the late sixteenth century B.C., reproduced on a special series of Egyptian postage stamps issued to mark the International Congress of Navigation at Cairo in 1926.[61]

There was just time for a third precautionary measure to be taken while they enjoyed the shelter of Cauda. The crew were afraid that the ship would be driven on to the Greater Syrtis, quicksands off the African coast, west of Cyrene. (The Lesser Syrtis lay still farther west.) The Greater Syrtis was still a great distance away, but the wind might continue to blow for many days, and that was the direction in which it was blowing them. So, says Luke, they "lowered the instrument," not being more specific perhaps because he did not know, or did not remember, the technical name for whatever it was that was lowered. The most probable account is that they dropped a floating anchor or drift anchor, which was dragged astern at the end of a rope of suitable length so as to offer the maximum resistance every time the ship plunged down from the crest of a wave.[62] Then, when everything had been done that could be done in those circumstances, the ship was laid to on the starboard tack (with her right side to the wind), with storm sails set, and so she drifted slowly, at a mean rate of one and a half miles an hour, in a direction about eight degrees north of west.[63]

18-19 The next day, as there was no abatement of the gale, they began to jettison some of the cargo.[64] True, the narrator does not say that it was some of the cargo that was jettisoned, but it cannot well have been anything else. Since the transport of grain was the purpose of the ship's voyage, on which the shipowner's livelihood depended, the sacrifice of even part of it stressed the desperateness of the situation. The following day, a more drastic measure was necessary: the spare gear had to go if the ship was to have any chance of surviving. Smith suggests that "the mainyard is meant; an immense spar, probably as long as the ship, which would require the united efforts of passengers and crews to launch overboard."[65] The KJV

---

60. *Nat. Hist.* 2.132.

61. See H. J. Cadbury, "'Υποζώματα," *Beginnings* I.5 (London, 1933), pp. 345-54; *The Book of Acts in History* (New York, 1955), p. 10.

62. Cf. J. Renié, "Summisso Vase," *RSR* 35 (1948), pp. 272-75. This interpretation is presupposed by the Old Latin text of codex *gigas:* "they let out a certain instrument to drag" *(uas quoddam dimiserunt quod traheret).* Smith suggests that what was lowered was "the 'top-hamper', or gear connected with the fair-weather sails, such as the *suppara,* or top-sails," which "every ship situated as this one was, when preparing for a storm, sends down upon deck" (*Voyage,* p. 111).

63. Smith, *Voyage,* p. 114.

64. Cf. Jonah 1:5.

65. *Voyage,* p. 116. The Greek word is σκευή (here only in the NT).

uses the first person plural here—"we threw it out with our own hands"—
and while this reading is not nearly so well supported as the third person,
there is no doubt that, as Ramsay says, it "greatly increases the effect."[66]

20 Eleven dreary nights and days followed. The storm blotted out
the sun by day and the stars by night, and thus they had no means of keeping
a reckoning or calculating their whereabouts. The ship was no doubt leaking
badly, and they "could not tell which way to make for the nearest land, in
order to run their ship ashore, the only recourse for a sinking ship; but unless
they did make the land, they must founder at sea."[67] No wonder, then, that
all hope of their ever gaining safety drained away as day succeeded day.

5. Paul's Encouragement (27:21-26)

21 *By this time many were suffering from lack of food,[68] so Paul stood
up among them and said, "Gentlemen, you should have been ruled
by me and not set out from Crete and gained this damage and loss.*

22 *But now, take my advice: cheer up! There will be no loss of anyone's
life; only the ship will perish.*

23 *Last night there stood beside me a messenger of the God to whom I
belong, the God whom I worship.*

24 *He said to me, 'Do not be afraid, Paul; you must stand in the
presence of Caesar, and see, God has granted you (the lives of) all
who are sailing with you.'*

25 *So, gentlemen, cheer up. I have faith in God that it will turn out just
as I have been told.*

26 *But we must be cast up on some island."*

21 Things being as they were, they had little heart to take food; besides, it
would have been difficult to prepare food, and a good part of their supplies
must have been spoiled by the sea water. Among several parallels to their
experience quoted by Smith is a passage from John Newton, the celebrated
English clergyman and hymn writer, relating to his earlier seafaring days:
"We found that the water having floated all our movables in the hold, all the
casks of provisions had been beaten in pieces by the violent motion of the
ship. On the other hand, our live stock, such as pigs, sheep and poultry, had
been washed overboard in the storm; in effect, all the provisions we saved
. . . would have subsisted us but a week, at a scanty allowance."[69] And
anyone who has suffered from seasickness on board a well-appointed
passenger liner of the present day can imagine something of its horrors on

---

66. *St. Paul the Traveller*, p. 332. See n. 52 above.

67. Smith, *Voyage*, p. 117.

68. Gk. πολλῆς . . . ἀσιτίας ὑπαρχούσης, "there being much abstinence from
food."

69. J. Newton, *Omicron's Letters* (London, 1774), Letter 7, quoted by Smith,
Voyage, p. 118.

that storm-tossed vessel, and can realize how little appetite for eating its victims must have had.

In the midst of this general dejection and despair, Paul stood up one morning and spoke cheering words to his companions in distress. It warms our hearts to see, first of all, that in some very human respects he was quite like ourselves: he could not resist the temptation to say "I told you so!" to those who had rejected his advice at Fair Havens.

22-24 But what he went on to tell them was exactly what the situation most needed, a message of encouragement and hope. Nor was this message the product of wishful thinking: he spoke as one who had received divine reassurance. Earlier, at Fair Havens, he had warned them that loss of life, as well as of cargo and ship, would be the result of their setting sail from that port. But on that occasion he spoke simply as an experienced traveler of sound judgment. This was not the first time he had known the destructive power of a storm at sea. He remembered another ship in which he had once sailed: it had come to grief, and he had spent twenty-four hours in the open sea, probably supported by a spar from the wreck, until he was picked up or washed ashore (2 Cor. 11:25). There had been considerable loss of life on that occasion, we may suppose, and he feared that the same thing might happen again. But now he is confident that, while the ship is doomed, no life will be lost. No amount of experience or shrewd calculation could have given him this assurance; he ascribes his new confidence to a supernatural revelation made to him during the night by a messenger (probably an angel)[70] of God. In a vision when his life was endangered at Jerusalem two years previously he had received the assurance that he would survive to bear witness at Rome (23:11); this assurance was now repeated and amplified. Not only so: the lives of his shipmates also were to be spared for his sake. Human society has no idea how much it owes, in the mercy of God, to the presence in it of righteous men and women.[71]

25-26 Having received this communication from heaven, Paul was completely persuaded (such was his faith in God) that things would turn out exactly as he had been told. The ship would go down, but the people on board would be saved: they would be cast up or washed ashore on some island or other. The island, in the event, proved to be Malta. Since there was no chance of a landfall on Sicily (in view of the direction of the drift), Malta was the next best hope. But Paul could scarcely have known this: his reference to "some island" was an expression of faith. If they missed Malta, there would have been nothing for it but to hold on for 200 miles until they struck the Tunisian coast, and no one could have expected the ship to survive that long.

70. Gk. ἄγγελος ("messenger"), usually of a supernatural being in the Greek Bible.

71. See Gen. 18:26-32.

488

6. They Approach Land (27:27-29)

27 *During the fourteenth night, as we were drifting through the sea of Adria, the sailors suspected about midnight that some land was approaching them.*

28 *They took soundings, and found a depth of twenty fathoms; after a short interval they took soundings again and found it was fifteen fathoms.*

29 *Then, fearing that we might perhaps be driven on to the rocks, they dropped four anchors from the stern and waited longingly for day to dawn.*

27 Smith relates how he made careful inquiries of experienced Mediterranean navigators in order to ascertain the mean rate of drift of a ship of this kind laid to in such a gale. The conclusion which he reached was a mean drift of about thirty-six miles in twenty-four hours. The soundings recorded in verse 28 indicate that the ship was passing Koura, a point on the east coast of Malta, on her way into St. Paul's Bay. "But the distance from Clauda to the point of Koura . . . is 476.6 miles, which, at the rate as deduced from the information. . . , would take exactly thirteen days, one hour, and twenty-one minutes." Not only so: "The coincidence of the actual bearing of St. Paul's Bay from Clauda, and the direction in which a ship must have driven in order to avoid the Syrtis, is if possible still more striking than that of the time actually consumed, and the calculated time." Then, after carefully reckoning the direction of the ship's course from the direction of the wind, from the angle of the ship's head with the wind, and from the leeway, he goes on:

"Hence according to these calculations, a ship starting late in the evening from Clauda would, by midnight on the 14th, be less than three miles from the entrance of St. Paul's Bay. I admit that a coincidence so very close as this, is to a certain extent accidental, but it is an accident which could not have happened had there been any inaccuracy on the part of the author of the narrative with regard to the numerous incidents upon which the calculations are founded, or had the ship been wrecked anywhere but at Malta, for there is no other place agreeing, either in name or description, within the limits to which we are tied down by calculations founded upon the narrative."[72]

The "sea of Adria" mentioned in verse 27 is the central Mediterranean; it is so called in several places in ancient literature.[73] Ptolemy, the second-century mathematician and geographer, distinguishes the "sea of Adria" or "Hadria" (the central Mediterranean) from the "gulf of Adria" (the

---

72. *Voyage,* pp. 126-28.

73. E.g., Strabo (*c.* A.D. 19) says that "the Ionian Sea is part of what is now called the Sea of Adria" (*Geography* 2.5.20).

Adriatic Sea).[74] Josephus tells how the ship on which he set sail for Italy in A.D. 63 went down in the midst of the sea of Adria; he was picked up by a ship of Cyrene and carried by it to his destination.[75] In former days, and even in more recent times, some perverse interpretations of our narrative have been suggested by expositors who thought that the Adriatic Sea was intended—as though a northeaster could possibly have blown them in that direction from the south coast of Crete.[76]

The sailors' surmise that some land was approaching them reflects the language of those accustomed to a life on board ship. Luke would normally have said "we were approaching some land." But there is an attractive variant reading according to which "some land was resounding in their ears"[77]—that is, the breakers could be heard. Had it been daylight, they would have seen the breakers as well as heard them. For, as Smith tells us, no ship can enter St. Paul's Bay from the east without passing within a mile of the point of Koura; when she comes within that distance (and only then), the breakers cannot fail to be seen, for they are specially violent there in a northeast wind.[78]

28 The tradition which has given St. Paul's Bay its name as the place of the shipwreck is confirmed by the soundings which Luke records: these agree with the direction of a ship passing Koura on her way into the bay. The twenty fathoms' depth is close to the spot where they would first have had indications that land was approaching, bearing east by south from the fifteen fathoms' depth, at a distance which would allow preparations for anchoring in the way mentioned in verse 29. Smith estimates the "short interval" between the two soundings as about half an hour.[79]

29 It was dangerous to go any farther in the dark; the breakers warned them of rocks ahead, so they dropped four anchors to serve as a brake until daylight showed them where they were.[80] The anchors were dropped from the stern—an unusual procedure, but advantageous in certain circumstances, as naval commanders have known in ancient and modern times[81] (it

74. Ptolemy, *Geography* 3.4.1; 15.1.

75. *Life* 15.

76. See on 28:1 (p. 496 with n. 4).

77. For προσάγειν B* reads προσαχεῖν (a Doric form equivalent to Attic προσηχεῖν), whence probably *resonare* in the Old Latin codices *gigas* and *Bobiensis* (s).

78. *Voyage*, p. 121.

79. *Voyage*, pp. 130-31.

80. "In St. Paul's Bay the anchorage is thus described in the sailing directions: 'The harbour of St. Paul is open to easterly and north-east winds. It is, notwithstanding, safe for small ships, the ground, generally, being very good; and while the cables hold there is no danger, *as the anchors will never start*'" (Smith, *Voyage*, p. 132).

81. In 147 B.C. the Romans under Scipio Aemilianus won a naval victory off Carthage through anchoring by the stern and thus obviating the necessity of exposing the ships' weak points to the Cathaginians in turning round (Appian, *Punic War* 18.213). For the same reason Nelson anchored by the stern at the Battle of the Nile in 1798.

obviates the necessity of exposing the weak points of ships to the enemy in turning around, when the enemy fleet is drawn up along the shore). On this occasion the prow kept pointing to the shore whereas, had they anchored by the bow, the ship would have swung around from the wind. The ship was thus in readiness to be beached when day broke and the anchor cables were cut.[82]

7. The Sailors' Attempt to Escape Frustrated (27:30-32)

30 *When the sailors tried to abandon the ship and lowered the dinghy into the sea on the pretext that they were going to let out anchors from the bow,*
31 *Paul said to the centurion and the soldiers, "Unless these men stay on board, you will not be able to reach safety."*
32 *Then the soldiers cut away the falls of the dinghy and let it drop away.*

30 The sailors now attempted to make sure of their own safety at the expense of the others on board. They lowered the dinghy into the sea, pretending that they were going to lay out anchors from the bow as well as from the stern, but actually with the intention of making for the shore.

31 Paul detected their aim, and prevented it. Perhaps his own nautical experience told him that there could be no possible advantage in anchoring the ship by the bow in the present circumstances. Why the sailors' presence aboard was necessary for the safety of all is not expressly said; but plainly it would have been disastrous had the ship been left as it was with no skilled hands to work it.

32 By this time the centurion had learned that it was unwise to disregard Paul's advice, although his advice was probably misinterpreted when the soldiers cut the hawsers and let the dinghy go adrift. The dinghy could have been very useful in getting the ship's company ashore had it proved impossible to beach the ship, or when the ship stuck fast as it later did (v. 41). However, the centurion may have decided that the soldiers' action was the most effective way of keeping the sailors on board.

8. The Meal on Board (27:33-38)

33 *As day was about to dawn, Paul encouraged them all to take food. "This is now the fourteenth day," he said, "that you have been waiting and remaining without food; you have not taken anything.*
34 *Therefore, accept my advice: take some food. This is something on*

82. Smith reproduces, from a picture at Herculaneum, the figure of a ship fitted with hawse-holes aft, through which anchor-cables could be passed if necessary. "We see, therefore, that ships of the ancients were fitted to anchor by the stern; and in the present instance that mode of anchoring was attended with most important advantages" (*Voyage*, p. 135).

*which your safety depends. Not a hair will be lost from anyone's
head."*

35 *So saying, he took bread, gave thanks to God in the presence of all,
broke it, and began to eat.*[83]

36 *They all cheered up and themselves took some food.*

37 *We were in all two hundred and seventy-six*[84] *persons on board.*

38 *When they had satisfied themselves with food, they proceeded to
lighten the ship by throwing the wheat out into the sea.*

33-34 Paul now imparted further encouragement to his shipmates. As
dawn was breaking he advised them to take some food, after the enforced
abstinence[85] of fourteen long days. The situation was now easier, and food
could be more conveniently prepared: hard work lay ahead if they were all to
come safe to land, and it would do them all good and give them fresh energy
and enthusiasm for what had yet to be done if they had something to eat.
Again he assured them that no harm would befall any of them.

35-36 Then he encouraged them by example as well as by what he
said; he took some bread himself, gave thanks to God in words which all
could hear, broke it, and began to eat it. The rest followed his example; there
was no further need to stint themselves, and they took a full meal.

There is a cluster of words and phrases here—"took bread," "gave
thanks," "broke it"[86]—which are familiar in a eucharistic setting. This
supports the view of many commentators that the meal here described was a
eucharistic meal. Probably it was so in a limited sense: all shared the food,
but to the majority it was an ordinary meal, while for those who ate with
eucharistic intention (Paul and his fellow-Christians) it was a valid eucharist:
"the bread which we break, is it not our participation in the body of Christ?"

83. The Western text adds "giving also to us" (using the same Greek verb,
ἐπιδίδωμι, as in Luke 24:30; cf. also Mark 14:23 and parallels).

84. A few witnesses, including B and the Sahidic (Coptic) read "about seventy-
six" instead of "two hundred and seventy-six."

85. Abstinence from food, not absence of food, is implied by the adjective
ἄσιτος (cf. the noun ἀσιτία in v. 21).

86. Gk. λαβὼν ἄρτον εὐχαρίστησεν . . . κλάσας. These words play a part in
other meals provided or shared by Jesus, e.g., the feeding of the multitudes and the supper
at Emmaus (Mark 6:41; 8:6 and parallels; Luke 24:30), and indeed they belong to the
general vocabulary of Jewish social meals, but there was evidently something distinctive
about Jesus' words and actions on such occasions. The feeding of the multitudes can be
interpreted as an anticipation of the Eucharist, and Jesus' action at Emmaus as a deliberate
reminder of it. See B. Reicke, "Die Mahlzeit mit Paulus auf den Wellen des Mittelmeers,
Act 27,33-38," *TZ* 4 (1948), pp. 401-10. W. Kelly, *Exposition of Acts* (London, ³1952),
p. 387, denies all eucharistic significance to the present meal: "It is the object of the
Eucharist which gives it its character, and this was quite out of place here. But the most
ordinary food should be sanctified by the word of God and prayer, and the apostle here acts
on his own instructions to Timothy (1 Tim. 4:5, 6)." But in Paul's eyes the object of the
Eucharist may have been very much in place here. See Barrett, "Paul Shipwrecked," pp.
59-63.

(1 Cor. 10:16). They did not, however, withdraw into a corner to communicate: Paul gave thanks "in the presence of all," and the communicant Christians broke the bread and ate it with the ship's company. No mention is made of wine; the terms "wine" and "cup" are absent from the whole of Acts.

37 It is at this point that Luke tells us how many were on board. There is some ancient evidence for a smaller figure—"seventy-six" instead of "two hundred and seventy-six"—but there is nothing improbable in the larger and better-attested number: the ill-fated ship on which Josephus set sail for Italy some four years later had about six hundred on board.[87] The mention of the number in the context of the meal suggests that it was necessary to count them in order to divide the available bread among them fairly.

38 When they had eaten their fill, they used their new strength to jettison the remainder of the wheat cargo.[88] Part of it had been thrown overboard at the beginning of the storm (v. 18), but sufficient must have been kept as ballast and possibly also for food. Now, however, it was essential that the ship should draw as little water as possible, and run ashore well up the beach. The abandonment of the wheat was an extreme measure, but there was nothing else for it in the present situation.

9. The Shipwreck (27:39-41)

39 *When day had broken, they did not recognize the land, but noticed a creek with a sandy beach and planned, if possible, to run the ship aground[89] on it.*

40 *So, slipping the anchors, they let them go into the sea. At the same time they unleashed the lashings of the steering paddles and, hoisting the foresail to the wind, they held for the beach.*

41 *But they found themselves in a place between two seas, and ran the ship aground:[90] the bow stuck fast and remained immovable, while the stern was broken up by the violence of the waves.*

---

87. Josephus, *Life* 15. No significance need be seen in the fact that 276 is a triangular number (the sum of all whole numbers from 1 through 23), like 120 in 1:15; 153 in John 21:11; 666 in Rev. 13:18.

88. For the lightening of the ship cf. Jonah 1:5. S. A. Naber, on the ground that the wheat had been jettisoned already (v. 18), emended σῖτον ("wheat") here to ἱστόν ("mainmast"), quite unnecessarily ("Τρίτον τοῦτο ἔρχομαι/Ad Novum Testamentum," *Mnemosyne* n.s. 9 [1881], p. 293; cf. "Nautica," *Mnemosyne* n.s. 23 [1895], p. 269).

89. Gk. ἐξῶσαι (from ἐξωθέω), for which B* C and a number of other witnesses read the homophone ἐκσῶσαι (from ἐκσῴζω), "to bring it out safely," which is a less natural expression here.

90. Gk. ἐπέκειλαν τὴν ναῦν (there is a Western addition, "on a place where there was a quicksand," in the Harclean Syriac). This is the only NT occurrence of the classical word for "ship" (ναῦς), which, in conjunction with the verb ἐπικέλλω ("run aground"), has been put down to a Homeric reminiscence (cf. *Odyssey* 9.148, νῆας . . . ἐπικέλσαι).

39 By this time it was light, but the sailors did not recognize the land which they had approached. St. Paul's Bay is some distance away from the grand harbor of Valletta, with which some of them would have been familiar. But they noticed a creek with a sandy beach, and decided to try to run the ship aground there. The combination of this creek with the rocks (v. 29) and the place between two seas (v. 41) confirms the tradition which locates this incident in St. Paul's Bay. Smith shows in detail "how perfectly these features still distinguish the coast."[91] The west side of the bay, to which the ship must have been driven, is rocky, but has two creeks, one of which still has a sandy beach. (Smith, however, thinks that the other creek was the one mentioned by Luke, since it was nearer to the place "between two seas," considering that its sandy beach has now been "worn away by the wasting action of the sea.")[92]

40 They had no further use for the four anchors, so they slipped them and left them in the sea. At the same time they unleashed the lashings of the steering paddles[93] (which in ancient ships served the purpose of rudders) and hoisted a small sail[94] on the foremast, setting it to the wind; thus they had the ship under control to run her aground on the beach which they had noticed.

41 But there was something which they had not noticed, because it could not be seen until they had entered the bay. "From the entrance of the bay, where the ship must have been anchored, they could not possibly have suspected that at the bottom of it there should be a communication with the sea outside."[95] St. Paul's Bay is sheltered on the northwest by the island of Salmonetta, which is separated from the Maltese mainland by a narrow channel about a hundred yards wide. This channel is the place "between two seas." Here the ship, in Smith's words, "would strike a bottom of mud graduating into tenacious clay, into which the fore part would fix itself and be held fast, whilst the stern was exposed to the force of the waves."[96] After the long battering which the ship had endured for the past two weeks, its exposed part could not take this further punishment, and it quickly disintegrated.

"Thus," says Ramsay, "the foreship was held together, until every

---

91. *Voyage*, p. 141.
92. *Voyage*, p. 142.
93. Gk. πηδάλια.
94. Gk. ἀρτέμων, the earliest occurrence of the word in Greek literature. Its absence earlier is accidental, for it certainly existed; it appears as a loanword in Latin in Vitruvius, who wrote under Augustus, meaning the main block of a tackle (*On Architecture* 10.2.9). In a nautical context it was used of "a smaller sail in the forepart of a ship, by which the speed is not increased but the course is directed" (S. A. Naber, "Nautica," p. 269).
95. Smith, *Voyage*, p. 143.
96. *Voyage*, p. 144.

passenger got safe to dry land. Only the rarest conjunction of favorable circumstances could have brought about such a fortunate ending to their apparently hopeless situation; and one of the completest services that has ever been rendered to New Testament scholarship is James Smith's proof that all these circumstances are united in St. Paul's Bay."[97]

10. Safe Ashore! (27:42-44)

42 *The soldiers planned to kill the prisoners, in case any of them should swim off and make his escape.*

43 *But the centurion[98] wished to save Paul's life, so he prevented them from carrying out their plan. Instead, he ordered those who could swim to jump out first and get away to land.*

44 *The others he ordered to make their way on planks, or on pieces of things from the ship. Thus it turned out that all reached land in safety.*

42-44   In accordance with traditional Roman discipline, the soldiers were responsible for the safekeeping of the prisoners in their charge. But now it would be easy for some of the prisoners to escape in the general confusion of abandoning ship. The soldiers, therefore, decided to forestall any such attempt by slaughtering them. The centurion, however, forbade them to do any such thing: he felt too grateful to Paul to expose him to this fate. Let the prisoners get safe to land along with the others, he said (it should not be too difficult to round them up afterward and keep them under guard). Those of the ship's company who could swim should dive overboard and swim ashore. The rest could float ashore on planks and spars; some nonswimmers might even be carried ashore by swimmers.[99] At any rate, one way or another, they all reached land safely. The angelic assurance given to Paul in their darkest hour had been fulfilled to the letter: the ship and cargo were lost, but every life on board was saved.

97. *St. Paul the Traveller*, p. 341. "The only difficulty," he adds, to which Smith "has applied a rather violent solution," is the fact that at the traditional place where the ship ran ashore there is now no sandy beach. But the evidence is satisfied if the creek with a sandy beach which the sailors noticed is identified with the creek where there is still such a beach (see p. 494 with n. 92). W. Burridge, *Seeking the Site of St. Paul's Shipwreck* (Valletta, 1952), argued on the basis of local observation that the wreck took place not in St. Paul's Bay but in Mellieha Bay farther north.

98. The Old Latin text of *gigas*, perhaps preserving the original Western reading, runs as follows: "But the centurion forbade this to be done, principally on Paul's account, in order to save him. And he commanded those who could swim to get to land first, and some of the rest to make their way to safety on planks; and thus all the souls escaped safe to the land."

99. The words "on pieces of things from the ship"—literally, "on some of the (things) from the ship" (Gk. ἐπί τινων τῶν ἀπὸ τοῦ πλοίου—might conceivably mean "on some of the (persons) from the ship," i.e., on the backs of members of the crew.

ACTS 28

F. WINTER IN MALTA (28:1-10)

1. Welcome to Malta! (28:1-6)

1 *When we got safely ashore, we learned that the island was called Malta.[1]*
2 *The natives showed us extraordinary kindness: they welcomed[2] us all with a fire which they had lit because of the rain which had set in, and the cold.*
3 *When Paul had twisted a bundle of brushwood together and put it on the fire, a viper emerged from the heat and fastened on his hand.*
4 *When the natives saw the creature[3] hanging from his hand, they said one to another, "This man is certainly a murderer: he has escaped from the sea, but Justice has not allowed him to stay alive."*
5 *But Paul shook the creature off into the fire and suffered no harm.*
6 *They expected that he would swell up or fall down dead suddenly, but when they watched a long time and saw that nothing untoward was happening to him, they changed their minds and began to say that he was a god.*

1 It was not until they came ashore that they found out which island it was they had landed on. No doubt many of the crew knew Malta, but they were accustomed to put in at Valletta, in the grand harbor, and did not recognize this part of the coast. The idea that the island on which they landed was Mljet (Meleda) off the Dalmatian coast[4] is bound up with the misinterpretation of the "sea of Adria" (27:27) as the Adriatic Sea; both are impossible identifica-

1. The first hand in B and a few other authorities have "Melitene" (Gk. Μελιτήνη) instead of "Melita" (Gk. Μελίτη); the Latin Vulgate has Militene. The longer forms have arisen through dittography of some of the letters in Μελίτη ἡ νῆσος.
2. Gk. προσελάβοντο, "they brought us (to the fire)." If, with ℵ* Ψ and a number of minuscules, we read προσανελάμβανον (cf. Latin Vulgate *reficiebant*), we have the more satisfactory sense "they refreshed us (all)."
3. Gk. θηρίον (lit., "wild beast"). In later Greek the word came to be specialized in the sense of "snake"; from the word in this sense is derived θηριακή (whence our "treacle"), originally a medicine prepared from snake-flesh to cure snakebite.
4. This identification seems to have been made first by the tenth-century Byzantine emperor Constantine VII Porphyrogenitus (*On Administering the Empire* 36). It has been defended recently by A. Acworth, "Where was St. Paul Shipwrecked? A Re-

tions if Euraquilo be read as the name of the wind which drove them away from the south coast of Crete (27:14). The name Melita was first given to the island by Phoenician seafarers: it is the Canaanite word for "refuge," and they must have found it a true refuge on more than one occasion. It has even been suggested that when Luke wrote "we learned that the island was called Malta (Melita)," he really meant, "we recognized that it was well named."[5] Paul, at any rate, would realize the meaning of the name from his knowledge of Hebrew.

2 The native Maltese were largely of Phoenician extraction, and their language was a Phoenician dialect.[6] They were thus regarded by both Greeks and Romans as "barbarians"—people who spoke a foreign tongue.[7] But on this occasion, if they were barbarians in speech, they showed themselves truly civilized in behavior; they received the 276 shipwrecked people with warm hospitality. It was a cold, rainy morning, and the men from the wrecked ship were wet and shivering as they came ashore; how good it was to see the fire which the Maltese had kindled for them to warm and dry themselves!

3 Paul, who had shown himself such a practical and helpful person on board ship, continued to make himself useful on land. A wood fire out of doors is an excellent thing, but it will soon burn out if it is not fed with fresh fuel. Paul therefore started to gather brushwood to help to keep the fire going. But when he had gathered one bundle and put it on the fire, a poisonous snake crept from the fire and bit his hand or at least fastened on it. He had probably mistaken it for a small twig as it lay on the ground stiff with cold, but the heat quickly brought it back to life. A parallel has been quoted from T. E. Lawrence (of Arabia): "When the fire grew hot a long black snake wound slowly out into our group; we must have gathered it, torpid, with the twigs."[8]

What kind of snake was it? The Greek word means "viper."[9] But we are told that there are no vipers, or indeed poisonous snakes of any kind, in Malta today. That, however, is not a conclusive argument. "The objections which have been advanced, that there are now no vipers in the island, and only one place where any wood grows, are too trivial to deserve notice. Such changes are natural and probable in a small island, populous and long

examination of the Evidence," *JTS* n.s. 24 (1973), pp. 190-92, and O. F. A. Meinardus, "Melita Illyrica or Africana? An Examination of the Site of St. Paul's Shipwreck," *Ostkirchliche Studien* 23 (1974), pp. 21-36 (cf. his *St. Paul's Last Journey* [New Rochelle, NY, 1979], pp. 79-85); they have been conclusively answered by C. J. Hemer, "Euraquilo and Melita," *JTS* n.s. 26 (1975), pp. 100-111.

5. Cf. J. R. Harris, "Clauda or Cauda?" *ExT* 21 (1909-10), p. 18.

6. Modern Maltese is a form of Arabic.

7. Gk. βάρβαρος, as in 1 Cor. 14:11 (cf. also Rom. 1:14; Col. 3:11).

8. *Revolt in the Desert* (London, 1927), p. 107.

9. Gk. ἔχιδνα (v. 3).

civilised."[10] One might compare Ireland, which has been free from snakes for long centuries, although tradition asserts that they were once plentiful there until they were banished—by St. Patrick (according to the Christian account) or by Fionn MacCumhail (according to the earlier pagan legend). When we read that this snake "fastened on"[11] Paul's hand, we must understand that it bit him, if it was indeed a viper, since vipers do not coil.

4-6 The Maltese bystanders looked at the reptile hanging on to Paul's hand by its fangs,[12] and drew their own conclusions. It was plainly the will of heaven that this man should lose his life—no doubt he was a murderer, and Nemesis was on his trail. He had escaped drowning at sea, indeed, but divine Justice was not so easily baffled: she had devised this alternative way of punishing him.[13] For some time, then, they stood watching him, after he shook the snake off into the fire, but nothing happened: he did not begin to swell up or suffer any obvious discomfort. Clearly their original conclusion had been wrong: he was no murderer pursued by divine Justice, but a divine person, immune to mischances that would prove fatal to ordinary mortals. It is not difficult to detect Luke's quiet humor in his account of their sudden change of mind. We may compare and contrast his description of the change of mind among the native populace of Lystra, who first greeted Paul and Barnabas as gods, and then stoned Paul nearly to death (14:11-19). Luke probably implies that only uncultured people like the

---

10. W. M. Ramsay, *St. Paul the Traveller* (London, [14]1920), p. 343.

11. Gk. καθῆψεν. F. Blass insists on the meaning "bit," as also do Lake and Cadbury. "But it is a well-assured fact that the viper, a poisonous snake, only strikes, fixes the poison-fangs in the flesh for a moment, and withdraws its head instantly. Its action could never be what is attributed by Luke the eye-witness to this Maltese viper: that it hung from Paul's hand, and was shaken off into the fire by him." So says W. M. Ramsay, who goes on to suggest that it may have been *Coronella leopardinus*, a snake found in Malta and "so closely resembling a viper as to be taken for one by a good naturalist until he had caught and examined a specimen. It clings, and yet it also bites without doing harm. That the Maltese rustics should mistake this harmless snake for a venomous one is not strange. . . . Every detail as related by Luke is natural, and in accordance with the facts of the country" (*Luke the Physician* [London, 1908], pp. 63-65).

12. *Coronella austriaca*, a species of the same family as *leopardinus* (see previous note), "is known to be rather irritable, and to fix its small teeth so firmly into the human skin as to hang on and need a little force to pull it off, though the teeth are too short to do any real injury to the skin" (Ramsay, *Luke the Physician*, p. 64). The accurate identification of this reptile must evidently be left to the few who combine expert knowledge of this branch of natural history with expert knowledge of Luke's Greek terms (cf. also C. J. Hemer, "Euraquilo and Melita," pp. 109-10). But note Ramsay's additional remark: "A trained medical man in ancient times was usually a good authority about serpents, to which great respect was paid in ancient medicine and custom" (*Luke the Physician*, pp. 63-64).

13. Cf. Wisd. 1:8. A poem in the Greek *Palatine Anthology* (7.290) tells of a man who escaped from a storm at sea and was shipwrecked on the Libyan coast, only to be killed by a viper. See also G. Miles and G. Trompf, "Luke and Antiphon: The Theology of Acts 27-28 in the Light of Pagan Beliefs about Divine Retribution, Pollution and Shipwreck," *HTR* 69 (1967), pp. 256-67.

Lystrans and the Maltese—"barbarians," as he calls them—would think of Paul as a divine being.[14]

2. Works of Healing in Malta (28:7-10)

7 *In the district around that place there was an estate belonging to the chief man of the island, Publius by name. He took us in for three days and entertained us generously.*

8 *Publius's father lay ill from fever and dysentery, but Paul went in where he was and prayed, laid his hands on him, and healed him.*

9 *When this happened, the other people in the island who were sick came to us and were treated.*

10 *They bestowed many honors on us, and when we put out to sea they put on board the things we needed.*

7-8   The expression "the chief man of the island"—literally, "the first man of the island"—is probably an official designation: it appears on a Maltese inscription.[15] The "first man" at this time, named Publius, had an estate near the place where the shipwrecked party came ashore, and he treated them as his guests for three days. Publius was a common *praenomen:* Ramsay suggested that the local peasantry used this name when they spoke of him familiarly, "and Luke (who has no sympathy for Roman nomenclature) took the name that he heard in common use."[16] Publius's father was suffering from intermittent attacks of gastric fever[17] and dysentery, of which Paul cured him by laying his hands on him and praying for him.

9-10   The news of this cure spread rapidly; in consequence, people who were suffering from a variety of ailments came from all over the island

---

14. He is not even a "divine man" (θεῖος ἄνθρωπος or θεῖος ἀνήρ), as supposed (e.g.) by H. Conzelmann, *Die Apostelgeschichte* (Tübingen, ²1972), p. 147; E. Haenchen, *The Acts of the Apostles* (Oxford, 1971), E.T., p. 716. The anecdote, says M. Dibelius, "is told in a completely secular fashion. . . . it does not sound like Christian tradition concerning Paul" (*Studies in the Acts of the Apostles*, E.T. [London, 1956], p. 204, n. 27). It is best taken as the reminiscence of an eyewitness. There may be a reflection of the incident in the longer Markan appendix (Mark 16:18, "they will pick up serpents").

15. In *IG* XIV.601 one L. Castricius, a member of the equestrian order, is called (among other designations) πρῶτος Μελιταίων, "first of the Maltese." A Latin parallel has often been recognized in *CIL* X.7495, where the words *Mel(itensium) primus omni[um]* appear in juxtaposition; the meaning may indeed be "first of all the Maltese," but much of the context is mutilated, and the reference may be to someone who was "first" to bestow architectural and statuary benefactions on the community (see C. J. Hemer, "First Person Narrative in Acts 27-28," *TynB* 36 [1985], p. 100).

16. *St. Paul the Traveller*, p. 343. Polybius, the Greek historian, regularly refers to the Roman general P. Cornelius Scipio Aemilianus by his bare *praenomen* Publius (Gk. Πόπλιος, as here).

17. What is traditionally called Malta fever (now no longer the menace that it once was) is caused by a microbe in goats' milk.

to receive suitable treatment. Perhaps Luke was able to add his medical skill to Paul's gift of healing. At any rate, says Luke, they "honored us with many honors," which in this context might well include honoraria or material gifts.[18] Harnack, pointing out that the whole of the preceding section (vv. 3-6) "is tinged with medical colouring," adds: "and seeing that in verses 7-10 both subject-matter and phraseology are medical, therefore the whole story of the abode of the narrator in Malta is displayed in a medical light."[19]

When at last the time came for the party to leave Malta, the Maltese showed their appreciation of Paul and his friends by putting on board for them things that would supply their need and minister to their comfort for the remainder of the voyage.

G. ROME AT LAST! (28:11-31)

1. The Last Lap: "And So We Came to Rome" (28:11-15)

11 *After three months we put to sea in a ship that had wintered in the island—a ship of Alexandria which had the Heavenly Twins[20] as its figurehead.*

12 *We put in at Syracuse, and stayed there for three days.*

13 *From there we weighed anchor[21] and arrived at Rhegium. After one day a south wind sprang up and on the second day we came to Puteoli.*

14 *We found brothers there, and they invited us to spend[22] seven days with them. And so we came to Rome.*

15 *From Rome the brothers, hearing the news about us, came to meet us as far as Appii Forum and Tres Tabernae. When Paul saw them, he gave thanks to God and took courage.*

11 The three months which they spent in Malta were the three months of winter; they could not continue their journey to Italy until early spring, when the seas began to be opened again for navigation. The elder Pliny[23] says that

18. Gk. τιμή ("honor") may also mean honorarium; cf. Sir. 38:1, "Honor the physician with the honor due to him, according to your need of him" (or ". . . according to his needs," which brings the wording into closer affinity with our present text); Cicero, *Letters to his Family* 16.9.3, "that 'honor' be paid to the physician." For the ambiguity cf. 1 Tim. 5:17, "Let the elders who rule well be considered worthy of double honor."

19. A. Harnack, *Luke the Physician*, E.T. (London, 1907), p. 179.

20. Gk. Διόσκουροι (lit., "sons of Zeus").

21. Gk. περιελόντες (the translation takes it as a shortened form of τὰς ἀγκύρας περιελόντες, "casting loose"; cf. 27:40). A variant reading is περιελθόντες (P74 אc A with a few minuscules and the Byzantine text), "sailing around" or "tacking," as if referring to the sharp angle to be turned in getting through the Straits of Messina.

22. Gk. ἐπιμεῖναι, "to remain." A variant reading is ἐπιμείναντες (H Ψ and several minuscules), "having remained" (which makes difficult sense).

23. Pliny, *Nat. Hist.* 2.122. Vegetius (*On Military Affairs* 4.39) says the seas are closed till March 10; this might be for voyages farther from the shore. In actual practice,

navigation begins to be resumed when the west winds start to blow on February 8; it was probably about this date that the party set sail from Malta. The ship in which they embarked was another Alexandrian ship, probably also belonging to the grain fleet; it had spent the winter in Malta, presumably in harbor at Valletta. Ships, like inns, took their names from their figureheads.[24] The "Heavenly Twins" who formed the figurehead of this ship were Castor and Pollux, patrons of navigation and favorite objects of sailors' devotion. Their constellation, Gemini, was considered a sign of good fortune in a storm:

> "Then through the wild Aegean roar
> The breezes and the Brethren Twain
> Shall waft my little boat ashore."[25]

Ramsay suggests that Luke refers to this ship by name, as he does not refer to any other, because the name was the first thing he knew about it: he heard the news about this vessel before he saw it, whereas he became acquainted with the others by seeing them.[26]

12 In this ship, then, they set sail from Malta, and (probably after a day's sailing) reached the great port of Syracuse, on the east coast of Sicily. Here they spent three days—possibly, as Ramsay suggests, because the southerly wind, which brought them from Malta, fell.[27] Syracuse, with its two harbors, was the most important city of Sicily. It was founded as a Corinthian colony in 734 B.C., and passed under the control of Rome during the Second Punic War, in 212 B.C.

13 From Syracuse they made their way (perhaps by tacking in a northwesterly wind) to Rhegium (Reggio di Calabria), in the toe of Italy. Rhegium was an important harbor on the Italian side of the Straits of Messina, some six or seven miles across from Messina, in the northeast corner of Sicily. They had to wait at Rhegium for a suitable wind to take them through the straits, but they had not to wait long, for a south wind arose after one day, and the following day brought them to Puteoli (Pozzuoli) in the Bay of Naples, "having accomplished a distance of about 180 nautical miles in less than two days."[28]

"Puteoli was then, as it is now," Smith continues, "the most sheltered part of the Bay of Naples. It was the principal port of southern Italy, and, in particular, it was the great emporium for the Alexandrian wheat-

---

the state of the weather would determine the resumption of navigation in any particular year.

24. Gk. παράσημος.
25. Horace, *Odes* 3.29.62-64.
26. *St. Paul the Traveller*, p. 346.
27. *St. Paul the Traveller*, p. 345.
28. J. Smith, *Voyage* (London, 41880), pp. 156-57.

ships. Seneca, in one of his epistles, gives an interesting and graphic account of the arrival of the Alexandrian fleet.[29] All ships entering the bay were obliged to strike their topsails *(suppara)*, except wheat-ships, which were allowed to carry theirs. They could therefore be distinguished whenever they hove in sight. It was the practice to send forward fast-sailing vessels *(tabellariae)* to announce the speedy arrival of the fleet; and the circumstance of their carrying topsails made them distinguishable in a crowd of vessels. The supparum, therefore, was the distinguishable signal of the Alexandrian ships."[30]

To this it should be added that, after the construction of the great harbor installations at Portus, near Ostia, in the principate of Claudius,[31] ships of the grain fleet usually took their cargo on to be unloaded there, but passengers were put ashore at Puteoli (as Paul and his company were).[32]

14 It is not surprising that Christians were to be found in such an important seaport as Puteoli. There was an important Jewish colony there too—apparently the oldest in Italy after that in Rome.[33] We have to conclude from the text that the centurion's official business involved a week's halt at Puteoli, and that during that week Paul was allowed to enjoy the hospitality offered him by the local church. He had received similar permission at Sidon quite early in the voyage.[34] After the week's stay at Puteoli they continued their journey by road; "and so we came to Rome," says Luke, but then he goes back and relates one particularly encouraging feature of the last stage of the journey.

15 A few miles' journey from Puteoli brought them on to the Appian Way, one of the great Roman roads of south Italy, named after Appius Claudius, in whose censorship it was planned (312 B.C.). Along this road they made for Rome. But news of their approach had reached the Christians of the capital already (conveyed, probably, by their brothers in Puteoli); and a number of them set out southward along the Appian Way to meet Paul and escort him for the remainder of his journey to Rome.[35] Some of them got as far as Tres Tabernae ("the Three Taverns"), a halting place on

---

29. Seneca, *Epistle* 77.1.

30. *Voyage,* p. 157.

31. Cf. *CIL* XIV.85 (inscription of Claudius, A.D. 46); Suetonius, *Claudius* 18.3; Dio, *History* 60.11.4, 5.

32. Josephus disembarked at Puteoli (which he calls by its Greek name *Dikaiarcheia*) in A.D. 63 (*Life* 16). See C. J. Hemer, "First Person Narrative. . . ," p. 93.

33. It was there in 4 B.C.; see Josephus, *BJ* 2.104; *Ant.* 17.328.

34. See 27:3; cf. Ramsay, *St. Paul the Traveller,* p. 344, n. 1.

35. This is the sense of Gk. ἦλθαν εἰς ἀπάντησιν ἡμῖν ("they came to meet us"); ἀπάντησις was almost a technical term for the official welcome of a visiting dignitary by a deputation which went out from the city to greet him and escort him for the last part of his journey; cf. the same use in Matt. 25:6; 1 Thess. 4:17 (also Cicero, *Letters to Atticus* 8.16.2; 16.11.6).

the Appian Way about thirty-three miles from Rome; others walked ten miles farther and met him at Appii Forum ("the marketplace of Appius"):

> "Next Appii Forum, filled, e'en nigh to choke,
> With knavish publicans and boatmen folk."[36]

Luke is far from giving the impression that Paul was the first person to bring the gospel to Rome.[37] His coming to Rome certainly led to a great advance in gospel witness in the city,[38] but the presence of those Christians—"the brothers," as Luke calls them—provides evidence enough that the gospel had reached Rome already.

Paul might well thank God and take fresh courage at the sight of these friends. He had long had a desire to visit Rome; it was three years since he had sent his letter to the Christians there to prepare them for his projected visit.[39] Now his prayer was granted and, in circumstances which he had not foreseen when he dictated his letter, he saw Roman Christians face to face. He probably wondered from time to time what kind of reception he would have from them. Now any misgivings he might have had were removed by the heart-warming action of those members of the Roman church who tramped out so far to bid him welcome to their midst.

2. Paul Handed Over to Be Kept under Guard (28:16)

16 *When we entered Rome, Paul was allowed to stay by himself with the soldier who guarded him.*[40]

16 At last, then, they came to Rome, entering the city by the Porta Capena. Here the "we" narrative comes to an end. If the letters to Philemon and Colossians were sent from Rome during Paul's confinement there, then they supply evidence that Luke stayed on in Rome for some time: greetings are sent from him to Philemon and to the church of Colossae.[41]

The Western text, followed in part by the Byzantine text, provides

36. Horace, *Satires* 1.5.3-4. Cicero mentions Appii Forum and Tres Tabernae together in *Letters to Atticus* 2.10.

37. Contrast Haenchen, who even in this context says that Luke "wants Paul to proclaim in Rome the gospel up to that point unknown" (*Acts*, p. 720). The intelligent reader might even infer from the introduction of Priscilla and Aquila in 18:2 that the gospel had reached Rome before they left it: Luke knows that they were believers, but does not imply that they were Paul's converts.

38. Cf. Phil. 1:12-18.

39. Cf. Rom. 1:9-13; 15:22-32.

40. The Western text (followed by the Byzantine) gives a fuller reading of this verse: "When we entered Rome, the centurion handed his prisoners over to the stratopedarch, but Paul was allowed to stay by himself outside the barracks with the soldier who guarded him."

41. Cf. Philem. 24; Col. 4:14.

fuller information at this point: "the centurion handed his prisoners over to the stratopedarch, but Paul was allowed to stay by himself outside the camp with the soldier who guarded him." The "stratopedarch" ("commander of the army" or "commander of the camp") is most probably to be identified with the commandant of the camp or barracks where the emperor's praetorian guard was housed, near the Viminal Gate.[42] We may compare Phil. 1:13, where Paul uses the term *praetorium* either of the praetorian guard or of its headquarters.[43]

Whether the phrase "outside the camp"[44] is part of the original text or not, it expresses the fact that Paul was not kept in the barracks but received leave to stay in lodgings of his own—the place where he received representatives of the local Jewish community in verse 23 and many other visitors according to verse 30. He thus enjoyed a measure of personal liberty while he was under restraint: he was permitted to live as a private resident, and a soldier (presumably one of the praetorian guard) was detailed to guard him. To this soldier he would be lightly chained by the wrist, with the chain to which he draws his visitors' attention in verse 20. The soldier would be relieved every four hours or so, but for Paul there was no comparable relief. The result, however, was that he became a talking point among members of the praetorian guard.[45]

3. Paul and the Roman Jews (28:17-28)

a. First interview (28:17-22)

17 *After three days Paul invited the local leaders of the Jewish community to meet with him. When they had come together, he proceeded to say to them, "Brothers, I am here as a prisoner from Jerusalem.*

---

42. It is hardly likely that such an important officer of state as the prefect of the praetorian guard (at this time Afranius Burrus) is meant. Trajan indeed directs the younger Pliny to send a prisoner in chains "to the prefects of my praetorium" (Pliny, *Epistles* 10.57.2), and fifty-five years earlier Claudius sends the praetorian prefect in person to Baiae to arrest Valerius Asiaticus and bring him to Rome in chains (Tacitus, *Annals* 11.1), but Valerius was a powerful ex-consul. Another interpretation of the stratopedarch, favored by T. Mommsen (*Historische Schriften*, III [Berlin, 1910], pp. 552-53) and W. M. Ramsay (*St. Paul the Traveller*, pp. 315, 348), identifies him with the commandant of the *castra peregrinorum*, the headquarters (on the Caelian hill) of legionary liaison officers (all of centurial rank) on furlough in Rome. (This commandant was called the *princeps peregrinorum*, a form actually given in the Old Latin codex *gigas* as the rendering of Gk. στρατοπέδαρχος.) But this interpretation is less likely than that proposed above.

43. See F. F. Bruce, *Philippians*, GNC (San Francisco, 1983), pp. xxii-xxiv, 17.

44. Gk. ἔξω τῆς παρεμβολῆς, a phrase occurring in an allegorical sense in Heb. 13:11 (reflecting Ex. 33:7; Lev. 16:27, with reference to the camp of Israel in the wilderness). Luke has used Gk. παρεμβολή already (21:34, etc.) of the Antonia fortress in Jerusalem.

45. Cf. Phil. 1:13.

Although I had done nothing against our people or the ancestral customs, I was delivered into the hands of the Romans.

18 *When the latter had examined me,*[46] *they were minded to release me, because no ground for putting me to death was found in me.*

19 *But the Jews objected,*[47] *so I was forced to appeal to Caesar, although I had no charge to lay against my nation.*[48]

20 *For this reason I have invited you, to see you and talk to you, for it is because of the hope of Israel that I am bound with this chain."*

21 *They said to him, "Neither have we received letters about you from Judaea, nor has any of our brothers, coming from there, reported or spoken*[49] *anything bad about you.*

22 *But we desire to hear from you what your views are; as regards this party, it is known to us that people speak against it everywhere."*

17-20 True to his fixed procedure, Paul took steps as soon as was practicable to get in touch with the Jewish community in this new city to which he had come. It was not convenient here to go to one of the synagogues to find them; he had to stay where he was. Had he been able to move around freely, there were several synagogues in Rome which he might have visited; the names of some of them have been preserved on inscriptions.[50] Instead of going to any of these, Paul invited the leaders of the Jewish community in Rome to come and see him. He briefly introduced himself and summarized the course of events that had brought him as a prisoner to Rome, taking care to say as little as possible about the responsibility of the national authorities in Jerusalem. To say that he "was delivered into the hands of the Romans" is a very mild way of describing how he was rescued by Roman soldiers from a mob that was trying to beat him to death—although it conforms well enough with the prophecy of Agabus (21:11) and, more significantly, with language used repeatedly about the passion of Jesus (Luke 9:44; 18:32).

Paul insists that he is speaking strictly in his own defense; that he has no complaint to make against his own nation or its Judaean leaders. His appeal to Caesar has been made purely in order to have his innocence established. As it was, it was his devotion to Israel's ancestral hope that had cost him his freedom and brought him under guard to Rome. In Rome, as in Judaea, he emphasizes that the resurrection message which he proclaims, far from undermining the religion of Israel, is its divinely appointed fulfilment.[51]

21-22 The Jewish leaders' answer to Paul is a model of diplomacy.

46. The Western text adds "much."
47. The Western text adds "and cried out, 'Away with our enemy!'"
48. The Western text adds "but that I might deliver my soul from death."
49. "Reported" (ἀνήγγειλεν) officially or "spoken" (ἐλάλησεν) unofficially.
50. The names of eleven synagogues in Rome have been so preserved; see H. J. Leon, *The Jews of Ancient Rome* (Philadelphia, 1960), pp. 135-66; Schürer III, pp. 95-98.
51. For the general argument, and especially for the emphasis on Jesus' resurrection as vindicating Israel's national hope, see 23:6; 24:14-15; 26:6-8, 23.

It may be thought surprising that the Jewish authorities in Judaea had sent no communication about Paul to the Roman Jews, since "the Jerusalem-Rome axis was strong."[52] Perhaps a letter had been sent, but had not arrived yet because of the difficulties of winter travel. If, on the other hand, a personal representative had been sent, he for his part could equally well have been delayed. Without any message from Jerusalem, the Jewish leaders in Rome were unwilling to commit themselves—"an implicit indication from Luke that Roman Jewry looked to Jerusalem for guidance."[53] They would certainly take no initiative in the prosecution of a Roman citizen who had appealed to Caesar.

As for the Christianity which Paul professed and proclaimed, they had some hearsay information about it, they agreed, and it was not favorable: all that they knew about this "party of the Nazarenes"[54] was that it was the subject of universal ill repute. But we may be sure that they were not entirely ignorant of the Christian presence in Rome itself. When the Christian community in Rome came into being is uncertain, but when Paul sent his letter to the Roman church early in A.D. 57 it was already a well-established church, renowned for its faith and loyalty throughout all the churches.[55] It may well have been one of the earliest churches to be founded outside Judaea and Syria, and ten or eleven years before Paul's arrival in Rome the introduction of the gospel into the Jewish community there, as we have seen, appears to have led to riots which brought down the imperial displeasure on the community.[56] But on this occasion the leaders of the community judged it politic not to commit themselves on the subject—at least not until they heard Paul's account of himself and his beliefs and received instructions from Jerusalem about him.

b. Second interview (28:23-28)

23 *So they fixed a day for him, and many came to him to receive his hospitality.[57] He expounded the matter to them, bearing witness to the kingdom of God and speaking to them persuasively about Jesus from both Moses' law and the prophets, from morning to evening.*

24 *Some of them paid serious heed[58] to what he said; the others would not believe.*

25 *When they failed to agree with one another, they dispersed, after*

---

52. R. E. Brown, *Antioch and Rome* (London, 1983), p. 104.
53. R. E. Brown, *Antioch and Rome*, p. 97.
54. See on 24:5 (p. 440).
55. Cf. Rom. 1:8; 15:14.
56. See on 18:2 (p. 347).
57. Gk. εἰς τὴν ξενίαν (ξενία is primarily "hospitality," but it may be extended to mean the place where hospitality is dispensed; cf. Philem. 22, where it is translated "guest room").
58. Gk. ἐπείθοντο, "were on the way to being persuaded."

Paul had said this one thing:
"Well did the Holy Spirit speak through Isaiah the prophet to your
fathers:

26 *'Go to this people and say,*
You shall hear indeed[59] but by no means understand;
You shall look indeed but by no means see.

27 *For this people's heart has been made dull;*
They have become hard of hearing with their ears;
They have closed their eyes,
Lest they should see with their eyes,
hear with their ears,
understand with the heart,
and turn to me and I should heal them.'

28 *Take knowledge therefore that this saving message of God has been*
sent to the Gentiles: they *will listen to it."[60]*

23 A day was fixed for a thoroughgoing discussion, and on the day appointed many of them came to the place where Paul stayed and heard what he had to say. No considerable summary of what he said is recorded, but from accounts of his regular line of argument with Jews in earlier parts of Acts,[61] as well as from relevant material supplied by some of his letters, the general outline of his exposition may be inferred, as he spoke authoritatively about the kingdom of God and told the story of Jesus persuasively, showing how it marked the fulfilment of the law and the prophets. Throughout that day he labored to prove to them that the gospel of Christ was the fine flowering of Israel's religion, that the whole course of Hebrew history and prophecy led up to it and was consummated by it. His text was the whole volume of what we now call the Old Testament, interpreted by the events of the advent, passion, and triumph of Jesus of Nazareth, "designated Son of God in power according to the Spirit of holiness by his resurrection from the dead" (Rom. 1:4). Most of the messianic "testimonies" which have already been cited in Acts[62] were adduced, no doubt, and more as well. It can readily be conceived how Paul on this occasion must have exerted all his powerful qualities of mind and heart as he endeavored to persuade the leading Jews of Rome of the truth of the gospel. Nor did his exposition take the form of a monologue. The debate must have been keen and impassioned.

59. The construction (lit., "by hearing you shall hear . . . looking you shall look"), taken over here from LXX, represents the Hebrew use of the absolute infinitive before the finite verb to express emphasis.
60. The Western and Byzantine texts add the sentence: "And when he had said these things, the Jews departed, having much debate among themselves" (v. 29 in TR and KJV).
61. Cf. 13:17-41; 17:2-3; 26:22-23.
62. Cf. 2:16-21, 25-28, 34-35; 3:22-23; 4:25-26; 8:32-33; 13:33-35.

Nor, perhaps, was the truth of the gospel the only subject of debate. If some of those present knew anything of Paul, they could have questioned his claim to have "done nothing against our people or the ancestral customs" (v. 17). On his own testimony he did live as a law-abiding Jew when he was among Jews, but did not adhere to the "ancestral customs" when he found himself in Gentile company.[63] A truly loyal Jew, they might have argued, would have been specially scrupulous about observing those customs in a Gentile environment, like some other Jewish prisoners in Rome around this time, who (according to Josephus) restricted their diet to figs and nuts, so as to avoid eating suspect food.[64] But if such matters were raised, Luke says nothing of them.

24-28 Some of Paul's visitors were impressed by what he said, but the majority remained unconvinced. The bulk of the Jewish community in Rome, leaders and led alike, declined to acknowledge Jesus as Messiah. This fulfilled the pattern that had been set in one city after another to which Paul brought the gospel. Since the Jewish people, who had the prescriptive right to hear it first, would not accept it, it had to be offered direct to Gentiles. In Acts as in the Pauline letters, while the order of preaching the gospel is "to the Jew first and also to the Greek" (Rom. 1:16), the order of its reception is "by the Gentile first."[65] It is not clear that Luke would follow Paul in adding to these last words, "and also (if later) by the Jew" (cf. Rom. 11:11-32). Luke records the expansion of Christianity among the Gentiles, but at the same time he records its rejection by one Jewish community after another (the community in Beroea forming a notable exception).[66] In Rome the definitive rejection takes place, and this instance is brought to a fitting conclusion by the quotation of an early Christian "testimony"[67]—the passage from Isa. 6:9-10 in which Isaiah, on his call to the prophetic ministry, is warned not to expect a favorable response from the people to whom he is sent. The effect of his ministry, divinely ordained though it is, will be but to make the deaf still more deaf (there are none so deaf as those who will not hear), to make the blind still more blind (there are none so blind as those who will not see). The early Christian use of this text as a prophetic adumbration of the general Jewish resistance to the gospel had supreme authority: both Mark, followed by the two other Synoptists (Mark 4:12 par. Matt. 13:13 and Luke 8:10), and John (John 12:39-40) tell how our Lord himself applied it to

---

63. See 1 Cor. 9:19-23.

64. Josephus, *Life* 14.

65. See J. Munck, *Paul and the Salvation of Mankind*, E.T. (London, 1959), pp. 42-48 *et passim*.

66. See 17:11-12 (p. 327).

67. "Paul always gets the last word—generally with devastating effect" (Lake and Cadbury, *Beginnings* I.4, p. 347).

his unresponsive hearers.[68] Its position here at the end of Acts is comparable to its position in John 12:39-40, where it appears at the end of John's record of Jesus' revelation to "the world" (cf. John 1:11, "he came to his own home, and his own people received him not").[69] We may also compare Paul's probable allusion to the same Isaianic text (among others) in Rom. 11:8 and, more generally, his wrestling with the sore problem of Israel's unbelief in Rom. 9–11. As before in Pisidian Antioch (13:46), Corinth (18:6), and Ephesus (19:8-10), so here again in Rome he announces—and this time with a note of solemn finality—that henceforth the Gentiles will have priority in hearing the word of life and that, unlike the Jews as a whole, they will accept it. "The narrative reaches a solemn climax—rejection on the one side, unchecked success and hope on the other."[70]

4. The Gospel Advances without Hindrance in Rome (28:30-31)

30 *So Paul stayed there for two full years, living at his own expense. He welcomed all who came in to see him,*

31 *preaching the kingdom of God and teaching the truth about the Lord Jesus Christ. He enjoyed complete freedom of speech, and no one hindered him.[71]*

30 For two years, then, Paul stayed in Rome. The conditions of his custody did not permit him to go anywhere he wished, but anyone who wished might come and see him, as the leaders of the Jewish community had done.[72] He lived, says Luke, "on his own earnings" or "at his own expense";[73] this means that the place were he stayed would indeed have been "his own hired house" (as KJV has it) or at least his own hired apartment (possibly three floors up in a tenement building).[74] Perhaps he was able to

---

68. The full LXX text, as here in Acts, is quoted in Matt. 13:14-15.

69. See J. R. Harris, *Testimonies*, II (Cambridge, 1920), pp. 65, 74, 137; C. H. Dodd, *According to the Scriptures* (London, 1952), pp. 36-39; B. Lindars, *New Testament Apologetic* (London, 1961), pp. 159-67; A. T. Hanson, *The Living Utterances of God* (London, 1983), pp. 34, 67, 114-15; F. Bovon, "Schön hat der heilige Geist durch den Propheten Jesaja zu euren Vätern gesprochen (Act 28,25)," *ZNW* 75 (1984), pp. 226-32.

70. F. H. Chase, *The Credibility of the Acts of the Apostles* (London, 1902), p. 52.

71. There is a Western addition: "saying that this is the Christ, Jesus the Son of God, by whom the whole world is to be judged." This weakens the very effective ending of the true text.

72. See Ramsay, *St. Paul the Traveller*, p. 349.

73. Gk. ἐν ἰδίῳ μισθώματι. The sense "rented lodgings" is not otherwise attested for μίσθωμα. See H. J. Cadbury, "Lexical Notes on Luke-Acts, III. Luke's Interest in Lodging," *JBL* 45 (1926), pp. 321-22.

74. Like the poet Martial (see p. 385, n. 28).

carry on his "tent-making," although this would have been awkward if he was continually chained by the wrist to a soldier.

The significance of the "two full years" has been much debated. There are a few literary parallels, but none of them is of direct relevance.[75] A popular view has been that the two years comprised a statutory period of eighteen months within which the prosecutors might come and state their case against Paul, together with some further months required for the formalities attending his discharge, when the prosecutors failed to appear.

This account of the matter, favored at one time by Ramsay[76] and others,[77] is now known to have arisen from a misinterpretation of a third-century imperial edict dealing with a different kind of case from that in which Paul was involved.[78] Besides, it is wrong to suppose that a case would simply lapse by default if the prosecutors did not appear to press it; the appearance of prosecutors and defendants was compulsory. Defaulting prosecutors would incur penalties, but their default did not mean that the defendant would be discharged automatically.[79]

The two years' prolongation of Paul's stay in Rome could be accounted for adequately by congestion of court business. It took that time for his case to come up for hearing. It was always possible for such congestion to be eased by the discharge of defendants whose cases did not seem to be serious, through the exercise of imperial "clemency";[80] but it is a safe inference from the report of Paul's vision aboard ship (27:24) that his case did come up for hearing, that he did "stand before Caesar," and that Luke, when he wrote, knew this to be so. It may seem the stranger that, if Luke did know this, he said nothing about the outcome of the case. Perhaps the outcome of the case was so well known that Luke's readers did not need to be informed about it; in any case, Luke has attained his object in writing when he depicts Paul preaching the gospel without hindrance in Rome over an extended period of time.

---

75. E.g., Philo (*Flaccus* 128-29) says that Lampon was kept in prison during his trial for two years, described as "a very long time" (πρὸς μήκιστον χρόνον); the younger Pliny (*Epistles* 10.56-57) speaks of a *biennium* fixed as a term within which those unjustly sentenced by Julius Bassus (whose acts had been annulled) might claim the right to a new trial.

76. "The Imprisonment and Supposed Trial of St. Paul in Rome," *Exp.* 8, 5 (1913), pp. 264-84, reprinted in *The Teaching of Paul in Terms of the Present Day* (London, 1913), pp. 346-71.

77. Cf. K. Lake, "What was the End of St. Paul's Trial?" *Interpretation* 5 (1908-9), pp. 147-56; H. J. Cadbury, "Roman Law and the Trial of Paul," *Beginnings* I.5, pp. 325-36.

78. *BGU* II.628 recto, reproduced by Cadbury in *Beginnings* I.5, pp. 333-34, and by H. Conzelmann, *Die Apostelgeschichte,* pp. 157-58.

79. See A. N. Sherwin-White, *Roman Society and Roman Law in the New Testament* (Oxford, 1963), p. 117.

80. Sherwin-White, *Roman Society. . . ,* p. 119.

In 1913 J. V. Bartlet argued that Paul's prosecutors, having given due notice of their intention to proceed with their case against Paul, arrived in Rome early in 62 and successfully prosecuted him as a disturber of the peace of the provinces (cf. 24:5). He argued further that Luke's readers knew from Nero's subsequent record as a persecutor what the result of such a prosecution before him would be (the more so in view of the pro-Jewish sentiments of Poppaea, whom he married in 62).[81] Fifty years later J. N. D. Kelly, attaching considerable weight to the evidence for seeing Paul's execution as an incident in the wider persecution of Christians which broke out as a sequel to the great fire of Rome (dated in July, A.D. 64), has concluded that the view that Paul was released and, after a few years of liberty, was rearrested, imprisoned, condemned, and executed, "seems firmly grounded."[82] It must be confessed that we cannot be sure.

31   During these two years, however—and this is what was important in Luke's eyes—the gospel was proclaimed freely in Rome through the lips of its chief messenger. The apologetic value of this fact was great. It is unlikely, Luke implies, that if the gospel were illegal and subversive propaganda, it could have been proclaimed for two years at the heart of the empire by a Roman citizen who had appealed to Caesar and was waiting under guard for his case to be heard. The authorities must have known what he was doing all that time, yet no obstacle was put in his way. The program mapped out by the risen Lord in 1:8 has been carried out with Paul's residence in Rome, where he bears his witness "unhindered." Luke's final word is a legal expression; with it the record of Acts closes on a triumphant note.[83] "Victory of the word of God," says J. A. Bengel: "Paul at Rome, the apex of the gospel, the end of Acts. . . . It began at Jerusalem; it finishes at Rome. Here, O church, thou hast thy pattern; it is for thee to preserve it and to guard the deposit."[84]

---

81. "Two New Testament Problems. 1. St. Paul's Fate at Rome," *Exp.* 8, 5 (1913), pp. 464-67 (a reply to Ramsay's article, "The Imprisonment and Supposed Trial of Paul," cited in n. 76 above). J. Moffatt was even more positive than Bartlet; with unwarranted assurance he bluntly asserted that "as a matter of fact, Paul was not released" (*Introduction to the Literature of the New Testament* [Edinburgh, ³1918], p. 313).

82. J. N. D. Kelly, *A Commentary on the Pastoral Epistles*, BNTC (London/New York, 1963), pp. 9-10. The tradition of a further period of ministry between Paul's first and second Roman imprisonment is found in Eusebius (*HE* 2.22.2). For reconstructions of the events of this intervening period see L. P. Pherigo, "Paul's Life after the Close of Acts," *JBL* 70 (1951), pp. 277-84; S. Dockx, "Chronologie de la vie de saint Paul depuis sa libération de la première captivité romaine à son martyre à Rome," *Chronologies néotestamentaires et Vie de l'Église primitive* (Leuven, 1984), pp. 151-60.

83. The last word in the book is ἀκωλύτως, "unhindered"; according to J. H. Moulton and G. Milligan, *The Vocabulary of the Greek Testament* (London, 1930), p. 20, "the word is legal to the last" (so that such a legal tag as "without let or hindrance" would be an apt rendering).

84. J. A. Bengel, *Gnomon Novi Testamenti* ([Tübingen, 1742] London, ³1862), p. 489.

GENERAL INDEX

Abraham, 87-88, 130, 132-37, 140-41

Achaia: churches in, 16, 371, 382; evangelization, 308, 327, 344; Roman province, 346, 351-52, 381

Acts of the Apostles: authorship, 5-7, 30; canonicity, 3-6; date, 6, 10-12; dedication, 29-30; purpose, 8-14, 29, 85, 123, 127, 167, 170, 268, 354, 440, 472, 475, 511; sources, 6-13, 194, 239, 245, 251, 261, 283, 308, 316, 363, 376, 387-88, 400, 403; title, 5, 31

Adramyttium (Edremit), 477-79

Adria (Mediterranean), 489-90, 496

Aeneas, 197-99, 403

Agabus, 229-30, 243, 401, 505

Agora, 329-31, 343

Agrippa. *See* Herod Agrippa

Alexander (Ephesian Jew), 377

Alexander the Great, 57, 250, 307, 309, 322

Alexander Jannaeus, 174

Alexandria: biblical interpretation in, 361; church in, 238n.18, 358; Jews in, 57, 124, 324, 358, 440; trade, 479-80, 501-2

Alphaeus, 40

Amphipolis, 322

Ananias of Damascus, 183, 186-89, 193, 416-17, 466

Ananias, high priest, 425-28

Ananias and Sapphira, 100, 102-7, 109

Ananus II, high priest, 239

Angels: messengers, 174, 204, 209, 222, 430, 495; ministry, 110, 178, 236, 238; in Old Testament, 140, 142, 153n.99; in spiritual world, 429

Annas, high priest, 91, 426

Anti-Marcionite Prologue, 5, 7, 230

Antioch, Pisidian (in Phrygia): Gentile converts, 265-69, 303, 305; history, 251, 272, 306; Jews of, 251, 264-66, 268, 278, 328; Paul in, 250-69, 279, 281, 323, 334, 358, 388, 470, 509; synagogue, 252, 264, 266

Antioch, Syrian, on the Orontes (Antakya): church in, 7, 226, 228-30, 244-46, 281-82, 287; and Gentile evangelization, 223-30, 286-87, 357, 365; history, 224, 228; and Jerusalem church, 220, 226, 229-31, 284, 300; and Luke, 121; and Paul, 17, 227, 300

Antiochus III, 57

Antiochus IV of Commagene, 272, 303, 357

Antipater, 436

Antipatris (Rosh ha'Ayin), 435-36

Antonia fortress, Jerusalem, 188, 235-36, 411, 423, 430, 432, 433n.44, 443, 461

Antony, 309, 422, 437

Aphrodite, 248

Apollo, 224, 312, 314, 343

Apollonia, 322

Apollos, 358-62, 364

Apostles: commission, 36-37, 162-63, 167, 169, 215, 246; preaching theme, 32-33, 35-36, 63, 67-68, 81-89, 92, 214; qualifications, 46, 48; term, 5, 14, 30-31, 40, 44, 188, 193, 227, 271, 276; witness, 66-67, 73, 97, 99, 113, 117

Appian Way, 502-3

Appii Forum, 503

Appius Claudius, 502-3

Aquila, 346-48, 355, 360, 363

Arabia, Nabataean, 17, 190-92, 194

Aramaic, 45, 54-55, 120, 182, 188, 199, 213, 229n.37, 413-14, 420

Archelaus, 116

Areopagus, 13, 33, 276, 331, 333-35, 342-44

Aretas IV, 58, 191-92

Aristarchus, 323, 376, 382, 477-78

Aristobulus, 232

Artaxerxes III of Persia, 56

Artemis, 224, 355, 373-79, 381

Ascension, 37-39

Asia: churches of, 16, 299, 366, 371, 382, 400; evangelization, 251, 281-82, 291, 306-7, 392-93; geography, 478-79; Jews of, 56-57, 124, 304, 388-89, 409, 445-46, 468; religion, 374-75; Roman province, 355, 378-79, 477

Asiarchs, 9, 376

Assos (Behram-kale), 385-86

Hellenists (*cont.*)
225, 398, 403-4, 419; and Saul, 195; the
Seven, 121, 139, 219, 224, 399
Hermes (Mercury), 274-75
Herod Agrippa I: biography, 232-33, 425,
437, 447, 456-57; death, 240-42; ex-
ecutes James, 220, 233; imprisons Peter,
110, 234-36
Herod Agrippa II: biography, 456; in
Caesarea, 456-73; family, 242, 447, 457;
influence, 425; and Paul 9, 13, 180, 188,
196, 415, 417, 458-73
Herod Antipas, 8, 59, 99, 202, 232, 245
Herod of Chalcis, 425, 456-57
Herod the Great: building, 66, 165,
179n.82, 224, 240, 411, 435-36; death,
116; family, 232, 245; and Jesus, 428
Herodians, 228
Herodias, 59
Hierapolis, 366, 400
Hillel, 114
Holy Spirit: baptism, 69-70, 222, 363-64;
descent, 49-53, 214, 216-17, 222; filling
by, 100, 121, 124, 128, 169, 188, 191,
227; gift, 61, 66, 69-71, 73, 168-70, 364;
gifts, 71, 169, 359, 392, 398; guide, 175,
178, 207, 298, 306-8, 371, 392, 398, 419;
and last days, 61; and obedience, 113; and
Old Testament prophecies, 45, 61; and
prayer, 42n.57; promised, 34-36; and
signs, 50-51, 171; witness, 52-53, 67,
113, 124, 390
Hospitality, 321

Iconium (Konya), 268-74, 278-79, 303-6,
328, 358
Idolatry: in Athens, 329-30, 340-41; and
converts, 285, 295-96, 299; of Israel,
143-47
Illyricum, 381
Isaac, 135, 141

Jacob, 135-37, 141
James the Just: and Council of Jerusalem,
292-97; death, 159; leader of Jerusalem
church, 42, 220, 223, 231n.44, 234,
238-39, 283-84, 286, 404-5; the Lord's
brother, 42
James, son of Alphaeus, 40
James, son of Zebedee, 41, 47, 168, 220,
233-34, 237
Jason, 323-25
Jerusalem: apostles in, 40, 162, 168, 193,
215, 233 (*see also* Jerusalem, Council of);
and apostolic testimony, 36, 44, 63-66,
71, 85; Christian refugees from, 15,
180-81, 186; disciples in, 43, 193,

216-17, 237, 404; famine-relief fund,
230-31, 243, 371-72, 382, 404-5, 408,
445, 448; Jews in, 53, 124-25, 404, 409;
and Paul, 192-95, 231, 356-57, 403-35,
443
Jerusalem church: dispersed, 15, 180-81,
186, 196-97; to evangelize Jews, 247;
leaders, 231, 239, 283, 404 (*see also*
James the Just); membership, 120, 223,
228, 238, 288, 405; needy, 101, 230-31
(*see also* Jerusalem: famine-relief fund);
Paul visits, 356-57, 402, 418, 445; sends
delegation to Antioch, 226; welcomes Samaritan believers, 170
Jerusalem, Council of, 202, 215, 239,
282-300, 407
John the Baptist: baptism by, 46, 69-70,
258, 359, 363-64; disciples of, 363-64;
ministry, 35, 50-51
John Hyrcanus I, 66, 164
John, son of Zebedee: apostle, 41, 77; arrest,
90, 92; and Jerusalem church, 233, 239,
283; preaches in temple, 89; in Samaria,
168-72, 226; before Sanhedrin, 94-98,
110
Joppa (Jaffa), 198-200, 204-5, 209, 211,
217, 220-22
Joseph (Old Testament), 130, 136-37, 140,
142
Joseph Barsabbas (Justus), 46-47, 238
Joses, brother of Jesus, 42
Joshua, 147, 323
Judas Barsabbas, 296-98, 300, 302
Judas, brother of Jesus, 42
Judas of Damascus, 186-87
Judas the Galilean, 41, 116-17
Judas Iscariot, 5, 28, 30, 40, 44-47
Judas, son of James, 40-41
Julius Caesar, 180, 309, 345, 350, 355
Julius, centurion, 477-78, 491
Justification, 262-63
Justus, 46

Kandakē, 175
Kingdom of God, 32-33, 35-36, 63, 74,
167, 215, 325, 392, 429
Koura, 489-90

Laodicea, 366
Lasaea, 480
Law of Moses, 262-63, 285, 289-91, 296,
304
Laying on of hands, 71, 122, 170, 178, 188,
217, 246
Lesbos, 386, 477
Libya, Jews in, 57
Lictors, 315-16, 319-20, 420

INDEX OF AUTHORS

INDEX OF SCRIPTURE REFERENCES